The History of the

Hudson River Valley

From the Civil War to Modern Times

VERNON BENJAMIN

THE OVERLOOK PRESS
NEW YORK, NY

This edition first published in the United States in 2016 by
The Overlook Press, Peter Mayer Publishers, Inc.

141 Wooster Street
New York, NY 10012
www.overlookpress.com

For bulk and special sales, please contact sales@overlookny.com,
or write us at the address above.

Cataloging-in-Publication Data is available from the Library of Congress

Book design and type formatting by Bernard Schleifer
Manufactured in the United States of America
ISBN: 978-1-4683-1124-2

FIRST EDITION
1 3 5 7 9 10 8 6 4 2

As the moon rose higher the inessential houses began to melt away until gradually I became aware of the old island here that flowered once for Dutch sailors' eyes—a fresh, green breast of the new world. . . . [F]or a transitory enchanted moment man must have held his breath in the presence of this continent, compelled into an aesthetic contemplation he neither understood nor desired, face to face for the last time in history with something commensurate to his capacity for wonder.

—F. SCOTT FITZGERALD, *The Great Gatsby* (1925)

We must welcome the future, remembering that soon it will be the past; and we must respect the past, remembering that it was once all that was humanly possible.

—GEORGE SANTAYANA

Contents

Preface and Acknowledgments

This is the concluding volume of the history that began with *The History of the Hudson River Valley: From Wilderness to the Civil War*. The new book—*From the Civil War to Modern Times*—takes the history forward in the same detailed fashion in which it unfolded, filled with the stories and actions of Valley residents and visitors over the past 150 years—"warts and all" as I say early on in the work. I cannot bring myself to call it "volume two," because for me history is that "seamless web" that cannot be bisected without changing it: the two volumes are best read as a whole.

That said, the same cautions for the reader and personal admonishments at my "cheek" in taking on this task need to be restated. The literature on Hudson Valley history is so voluminous as to render it impossible for an individual to comprehend it in its entirety; I put twenty-three years in the attempt. The primary documents alone are astounding in number, and to those must be added a vast body of secondary literature by historians greater versed at the task than I. Some things must be lost in translation in understanding and conceptualizing the history being written. Mine is a work of synthesis for the most part; some original research was necessary, yet overall I relied on better experts than myself in telling this tale.

Some parts of this account derived from my personal experience, which I need to acknowledge because I am, after all, a part of this history as well. I was born in the village of Saugerties and probably include more of that community's history than other historians might have found worthy—but I do so while asserting that its part in the grand parade of Valley history was poorly told by others in the past. I hope I have done justice to some other communities in the same way. I was also an aide to Assemblyman Maurice Hinchey in the New York State Legislature from 1983 to 1992, a time when his chairmanship of the Assembly Environmental Conservation Committee figured prominently in the evolution of Hudson Valley history; again, I present that part of the history without hesitation or apology. My newspaper, political and government service work over a span of forty years also contributed a bias to this story that I must acknowledge even as I attempt to temper my personal enthusiasms along the way. I accept as my own any errors of inclusion, exclusion, interpretation, or facts as I present them, and hope that the one or two laughable gaffs as appeared in my first volume—I killed Richard Montgomery in Montreal, not Quebec City, and had Lincoln watching a play of the wrong title on the night he was assassinated—are limited, as they were, to settings outside the Hudson Valley.

Most historical accounts these days are thematically based, the historian fixing on an aspect of history that, when fleshed out in context and its proper time and setting, illuminates American history as a whole. A fine example was Russell Shorto's *The Island in the Center of the World: The Epic Story of Dutch Manhattan and the Forgotten Colony that Shaped America* (2004), which retold the story of America's founding—all too long attributed to New England's role in early history—from New York's perspective. We may owe our conservative nature and love of liberty to the New England sense of history, but we owe to New York a piece of that liberty as well, literally in the battles and strategies of the war that was fought here—and the traditional American embrace of cultures and religions. I wrote about that myself in the previous volume, and I admired historical works like Shorto's and other revisionist works of merit. This book is one of them in many ways. Yet rather than follow a single, confined theme, I took an older, or shall I say more traditional, view in composing this work, intent upon establishing a baseline of facts and anecdotes for a region whose full story had not been told before. More than twenty-five fine books have been published about the Hudson River, but *The History of the Hudson River Valley* is the only one that treats the entire Valley's history in a single, comprehensive, narrative and critical fashion. Why impose a fashionable theme on it when the greatest of historical themes—the parade of mankind—lies at its core?

The overriding approach to this work concerns the special sense of place that is the Hudson River Valley, a feeling that the illumination of a moment in time in a particular setting serves, when drawn together with all of the moments in all of the settings—or at least all that fit—as the illumination of the whole. The intricacy of the relationships, activities and connections of those moments in time give form and structure to the work. Anecdotes and small little gems of stories proliferate almost like a color commentary to the text because that is the nature of this history—more than in other regions, I contend. This is a book for all kinds of readers, and hopefully for historians of the future to utilize as well.

I could not have done this work without an immense support understructure. Once again I thank and commend Marist College and Dr. Thomas Wermuth for accepting me into their community as an adjunct lecturer and providing access to the amazing tools of the James Cannavino Library. Library archivist John Ainsley and Dr. James Johnson, Christopher Pryslopski and Andrew Villani of the Hudson River Valley Institute were always enthusiastically supportive of this project as well. Librarians elsewhere, and research specialists in numerous fields have given generously of their time and expertise in helping to further my efforts. I commend my readers to the sources section at the back of the book where many of them are recognized by name and affiliation. And I cannot express strongly enough my thanks to the legions of local historians, historical societies, genealogists, and avocational enthusiasts whose energy and great goodwill so enriched my interactions with them.

The staff at Overlook Press have also been hugely supportive, including for this volume in particular, Emma Venter, Ross Gerstenblatt, Paul Sugarman, Abigail Novak, Tracy Carnes, and of course the publisher, Peter Mayer. Once again, the editorial tinkerings and emendations of Dan Crissman have helped to improve my text and temper my enthusiasms such that this book would have been a much less worthy product without him. I have commented upon Peter's immense patience in the past; I would be remiss in not alluding to his own passionate delight in this history and the region as well. This book is dedicated to the memory of his father, Alfred Mayer, whose love of the regional history around Woodstock made Overlook Press both possible and successful.

I say with Chaucer "go, litel bok" to this task, and unabashedly see it as grandly as a Thomas Cole allegory—the memories of its birth, its teeming adolescence filled with thousands of disparate facts, and its slow maturity into a final product as a process illuminated, as Cole's paintings were, by a bright light from elsewhere, in my case by the sense of self given me by my parents in their hopes and expectations for all their sons over the years. I hope I have done well by them after all.

—VERNON BENJAMIN
Saugerties, NY
April 2016

I. THE AGE OF SHEEN

We have become a nation of climbers. There are no bounds among us to the restless desire to be higher up. It is naturally so. It is the flower of our free institutions. Yes, it is part of the fruit of liberty itself. For here in America artificial barriers have been overthrown.

—SEYMOUR VAN SANTVOORD (Troy, 1897)

1. The Valley That Is A Door

Laughter without a tinge of philosophy is but
a sneeze of humor. Genuine humor is replete
with wisdom.

—MARK TWAIN

How does a valley grow? Outward along the spokes that bind the geography together, its sinews connected in myriad ways to the backbone that holds the frame, the artery of its strength and power flowing through. A valley grows around its river, along its breadths and widths, rife with expectation and promise, vigorous in its amenities, and harsh when in decline. The Hudson River Valley had the most beneficial hallway into the continent's vast interior at its portal, and an unrivalled harbor and island setting through which the river also flowed. The navigable river arose deeper in the continent than anywhere else in the east. In the eighteenth century, the manors of the Valley became large-scale commercial operations where the lords were more than farmers; they were merchants of agriculture to the world markets and the river was at their door. Commerce expanded in the trade and services that visited the docks, hamlets, villages and towns, and the industries that followed. Many communities became urban in character in the proliferation, and all of it was tied together by the lifeblood of the river.

How is the Hudson River Valley bounded? The river enters the Valley from the Adirondacks region above a turn near a small hill that divides this region from another wonderland, Lake George. The river flows south, drawing the waters of the hanging valleys as it flows, loudly and wildly at first over sprightly falls, silting an erosion of centuries in the narrow stretches of calm waters before the breathtaking estuary appears. The Valley lays to the east and west all along the spine, from the Adirondack foothills to the Green Mountains, the Helderbergs to Greylock, the Catskills to the Berkshires, the Ramapos to Connecticut, and down through the Narrows.

Through the river, doors into opportunity opened all through the Valley, often in the old Dutch *keekuten* spirit as "peepholes" into vistas. Even the interior farmer who did not need the river's commerce—he bartered with his neighbors for all that he required—was tied to the river in the amenities. Fishing and ice-gathering, the trading of excess goods and services, the access to the sloops and small packets of the river neighborhoods, and ease of travel to family or friends drew all to the river in time. The river opened the door to romanticism in America and became the Rhine of America for thousands of European travelers.

Opportunity knocked at the door of the former Dobbs Ferry after the death of the local manor lord, Van Brugh Livingston (1792-1868), who forty years earlier had renamed the place Livingston's Landing to the great dissatisfaction of most of the locals. This was the place of Jeremiah Dobbs' ferry in the past, and indeed the dugout canoe that Dobbs began using at Willow Point in the eighteenth century continued in successively reinvented forms. A meeting was convened to come up with a better choice of names for this historic place, but resuming the old name was frowned upon because Dobbs had been a Tory in the Revolutionary War. The fame of the town, as with the region, had grown as a result of the Benedict Arnold scandal over the treason at West Point, and the ship waiting for his co-conspirator had been forced to retreat to the waters off Dobbs Ferry while awaiting his return. Perhaps, the locals reasoned, the name could reflect those patriotic times and even remove the taint of loyalism in the ferryman's name by referencing one of the heroes who captured Arnold's co-conspirator very near to here.

But which one? Three men out on patrol on militia duty had captured the British spy. The crowd discussed the idea of renaming the community Paulding-on-Hudson in honor of one of them, but an old man rose and made a speech against it, perhaps recalling that John Paulding (1758-1818) was born in Peekskill. He had a grandfather or something who had known Paulding personally and "couldn't brook him." No one was interested in another Williamstown—after David Williams (1754-1831), another one of the captors—so the man suggested that the third member of the famous threesome might make a good choice. He was Isaac Van Wart (1762-1828), and if the Van were dropped, the old fellow suggested, the town might comfortably be called "Wart-on-Hudson."

The amusement that the suggestion evoked for his neighbors may have been amplified by the changing times, but it also showed that the community could appreciate the humor in a historic name. Wart's in a word, after all. The meeting, and the idea, broke up in guffaws. The town dropped the Livingston manorial name and resumed using the old moniker of the Tory ferryman. Bygones would be bygones after all.

The story in itself harkens in a way to the pattern of American identity that emerged in the decades following the Civil War. Just as Dobbs Ferry stayed intimately tied to its American Revolution past, the Hudson River Valley remained the landscape that defined America—and in each case the history came warts and all.

2. A New World

> We have neglected the truth that a good farmer is a craftsman of the highest order, a kind of artist.
>
> —WENDELL BERRY, *The Gift of Good Land* (1981)

In 1865, as the Civil War ended and a new world ushered in, fueled by protective tariffs, a homestead law opening the West, laws protecting banking and the new railroad industry—and a new invention, the independent corporation—great changes were in the air. The war ended abruptly the round of benevolent revolutions in transportation, politics, art, culture, science and religion that characterized America's shift from entrepreneurial to corporate capitalism, which the Protestant worldview affirmed as therapeutic to the "manifest destiny" of the people. In reality, the myth was demystified into a peculiar focus on wealth alone and "a contagion of fraudulence," as Frederick Lewis Allen termed it, that settled in over the post-Civil War decades. The horizon opened to a breed of exploiters whose cultural and social standards were distant from the temperate worlds of Emerson, Downing, Irving and Cole. The spoils of the war made politics persistently Republican on the national level and fostered unprecedented growth in government. The Hudson River Valley accepted these changes by welcoming the new wealth in cultural and recreational patterns that crudely adumbrated the old, and participated in the exploitation of its extractive resources that came with the changes.

In 1867, with New York City pugnaciously foisting Democracy's banner amidst the foul stench of an increasingly obnoxious political machine, the

Tweed Ring was just beginning its stranglehold on state affairs. *The Nation* called the state legislators of New York "meat in the market" of commercial opportunism. State Senator William M. "Boss" Tweed (1823–78) introduced the first bill to expand the boundaries of New York City, in 1869, for himself and a corrupt banker, Cornelius Corson, who opened the Eastchester National Bank and bought up cheap land near Mount Vernon. The bill died in committee, yet annexation progressed in the years ahead, and thanks to a Republican boss instead of a Democratic one.

After Andrew H. Green (1820–1903) proposed moving the city's boundary beyond the island, a spurt of new growth and interest in annexation among southern Westchester County towns encouraged Judge William H. Robertson (1823–98), the county's powerful Republican chairman, to embrace the political wisdom of divesting the part of Westchester County that contained the heaviest Democratic Party vote. Robertson already had some experience in this regard; a former congressman, he moved to the state senate in 1871 and immediately helped to incorporate Yonkers into a city, thereby turning Democratic Kingsbridge into a shadow community that Westchester no longer needed. Robertson then aided a group of Morrisania businessmen who wanted city ties to support the financing of new streets, water supplies, and other infrastructure. The chairman secured the support of Governor John A. Dix (1798–1879) when a binding referendum led to the annexation of Morrisania, West Farms, and Kingsbridge and its 35,000 inhabitants into the City of New York in 1873. Only White Plains of all the Westchester towns disapproved, by a vote of 250-222. Three Democratic town supervisors were eliminated in the annexation, and the control of judicial and sheriff elections went to the Republicans. As Neil S. Martin reported, the machine that Robertson subsequently developed "became the political engine in creating New York's first great suburbs." Robertson became the first president pro tempore of the New York State Senate when that office was created by constitutional amendment in 1874.

New horizons in commerce opened throughout the Valley. The Delaware and Hudson Canal, which drew to the Hudson River the coal of Pennsylvania and the agricultural and industrial products of several inland valleys, made Rondout one of the busiest riverfront communities. The Pennsylvania Coal Company had come over in 1851 and carved up three farms for a coal depot a few miles south along the Hudson, creating the community of Port Ewen, named for John Ewen, for twenty years the company president. In 1871, when the D&H shipped 1,287,000 tons of coal to the Hudson River, the company transferred most of its business to Newburgh and began using the New York & Erie Railroad instead of the canal for shipments. That was the end of the boom in Port Ewen, but the name stuck.

The early success of the canal spawned busy little hamlets all along the route—among them Alligerville, a population of five hundred served by two churches, three general stores, wagon shops and smitheries, a grist mill, and flagging and mill stone yards; Port Jackson, three hundred strong, with two hotels and a lumber and coal yard; Mill Hook two miles away and sporting a paper mill, two grist mills, a saw mill, and a hundred inhabitants. By 1871, Kerhonkson in Wawarsing township had sixty-five homes, three hotels, four dry goods stores, and dozens of other businesses, all of them in one way or another reliant on the canal business.

Agriculture was New York's principal industry, but the state did not have an agriculture department until 1893 when product inspections, the regulation of dairy matters, suppressing contagious diseases, and promoting a healthy industry became commissioner-level responsibilities. The department was immediately commended for its product entries in the World's Fair competitions in Chicago, where Goshen butter and cheese won gold ribbons as usual. The dairy industry provided a $60 million business for New York, "as big as all the silver product of the United States," Governor Roswell P. Flower crowed before eight thousand Dutchess County fairgoers on September 28, 1893. A few years later, at century's end, Roswell had to acknowledge that with the older wheat and corn crops stabilized at low rates the "painful fact" of a farming depression was upon the people. He recommended moving into local markets and growing fruit. The new direction provided access to new technology that yielded more varied and better crops. Farmers went into producing specialty crops that carried more bang-for-the-buck per acre, like sweet corn for canning, asparagus, beets, and celery. John Burroughs became the region's largest celery grower after discovering a three-acre muckfield a mile from Riverby. In time he built a cabin retreat there, which he called Slabsides, to escape into his writing and tend a large celery patch. His farm, like the others, diversified to make ends meet. Burroughs and his neighbor William Van Benschoten carried on a friendly competition in "the grape racket," as John called it, marketing table grapes for New York and Boston. While townsfolk came down from

Rondout on the "little boat" to pick and pack the crop, Burroughs sat on his porch nailing together the crates that carried the grapes to market; in one day he could prepare enough for 6,700 pounds of shipment.

Forestry, although not an agricultural industry, was a revenue option when farm prices and interest fell. Horse breeding was also a healthy industry in the Valley. Farm ponds were turned into fish hatcheries, and the state experimented with expanding the range of species available. Atlantic salmon, which had never been indigenous to the Hudson River, were introduced and caught between Glens Falls and Albany for a few years in a state effort to establish the fish for harvesting. A total of 2,091,723 *Salmo saler* fry were stocked between 1882 and 1888, but only a thousand of these were taken as adults on their return to the river from the Atlantic, and none appeared in later years.

Dairying remained an established industry, having saved many a Hudson Valley farm after the Erie Canal came in 1826, the advent of the railroads providing swift and sure access to New York City's markets for fresh milk, eggs and cheese. Walter William Law's Briarcliff Farms in Westchester County, one of the largest dairy farms in the country, operated over ten square miles, with a thousand Jersey cattle milked twice a day, the product available on the shelves of New York City by evening. The farm relocated to Pine Plains in 1907 and was purchased by Oakleigh Thorne in 1918, who turned it into an Angus farm.

Greene County had more than three thousand farms in 1880. Corn, buckwheat, rye, wheat, and barley were all grown in greater numbers than before the Civil War; the production of oats increased threefold since 1855, to 370,615 bushels. The potato crop yielded 186,101 bushels. Greene also produced huge amounts of hay (84,335 tons) and a respectable crop (12,907 pounds) of hops, a product that was virtually unknown in the county twenty-five years earlier. The county dairies churned more than 1.7 million pounds of butter, compared with only 32,940 in 1855. Orchard production yielded 315,078 bushels of apples and 155,447 pounds of grapes.

In 1885, Westchester County contained 2,991 farms, totaling 255,774 acres in all. The large majority of them were cultivated by their owners, almost 1,800 containing between fifty and five hundred acres each. Bartholomew Gedney (b. 1802) of White Plains was considered "one of the most accomplished agriculturists in the county": just one acre of his farm was known to have produced 112 bushels of corn, 47 bushels of wheat, and five tons of hay. The staunch Republican also had the best Short Horn cattle in Westchester.

The Valley celebrated its agricultural largesse with annual gatherings in all of the counties. The fifth annual fair of the Catskill Agricultural and Horticultural Association in 1871 featured "a grand cavalcade" of seventeen decorated farm industry wagons led by a cornet band—brickmaking machines, a steam-carpenter shop, a bakery, blacksmith, sewing machines, harness making, horseshoeing—followed by a hundred more wagons full of people. County farmers raised 216,000 sheep and harvested nearly two million bushels of grain in those years. A permanent home for the Dutchess County Fair was established in Washington Hollow in 1852, a half-mile trotting race track added ten years later, and the grandstand and the rest of the fair relocated to Rhinebeck by 1871. Most of the sheep were gone by then—less than 30,000 remaining in the county—and the grain industry had shifted into dairying, fruit orchards, and poultry.

Traditional husbandry like flax gathering and linen making was already historic, but still produced enough to be shown at the World's Fair in 1896. When in his eighties, Francis Wolven of Highwoods, who grew up in the 1910s, recalled that his father had him plant, harvest and process a flax field using the family's old tools, just so that he would remember a tradition that was once so pervasive in the Valley. He still had the tools and his old yellow tow.

The products of the farm reached the markets at New York as they had for more than two centuries, by water, and the greatest of the markets remained in the west, where the Erie Canal pointed the way. Albany, Troy and other upriver ports boomed with a steady stream of traffic after dredging and dike-building by the federal government finally managed to carve a single well-marked channel through the shallows of the Hudson River's Middle Grounds. Dykes improved tributary ports like Saugerties and Catskill, opening better channels into the business docks and, in the next century, creating natural recreation areas in the spoils that accumulated behind the dykes. Each of the local harbors drew boats for the industrial and commercial products as well as the farm goods, and each had regular customers in the small sloops and packet boats that plied among the towns on the river, carrying coal to this market in return for corn or dairy products for the next town the captain was visiting. Navigation improved with the dyke and channel clearing, and the seven lighthouses that served the river traffic by century's end—Jeffrey's Hook (1889), Tarrytown (1882–83), Stony Point (1826), Esopus Meadows (1838), Rondout (1837, 1867), Saugerties (1838, 1869), and Hudson-Athens (1873–74).

With immigrant populations came large-scale commercial fish harvesting particularly of American shad (*Alosa sapidissima*) and Atlantic (*Acipenser oxyrinchus*) and shortnose (*A. brevirostrum*) sturgeon. The sturgeon—called "Albany beef" as an inexpensive staple for the lower classes—were caught up and down the river, most productively along Hyde Park and Low Point below Newburgh. In one month, May 1869, the Albany market yielded 2,500 of these fish in sizes that averaged one hundred kilograms each. In addition to the food, sturgeon provided a hundred barrels of oil that year that was sold for lamps and machine needs. Sturgeon harvesting and its oil industry was protected in 1894 under state legislation that created a closed season between September 1 and June 1.

The finer commercial product, striped bass (*Morone saxitilis*), were selling in New York for forty-to-sixty-five cents a kilogram between 1879 and 1882; it was not uncommon for a local fisherman to haul in a hundred-pound striper in those days. More than 1.2 million kg of shad were hauled in commercial nets and sold in New York City by 1880. Carp (*Cyprinus carpio*), a non-native species introduced in Newburgh in the 1850s, were also commercially harvested by the 1880s, taken in large, rolled nets and for federal hatcheries that served forty other states; in 1908, 1.425 metric tons—much of it taken in the Hudson River—were sold at the Fulton Fish Market. Barges and ships were outfitted with freshwater tanks to carry the fish live. Local fishermen netted carp in seines in the bays and shallows of the Hudson and held them in family ponds until the dealers arrived at the local docks. These fish were also taken by local dealers by wagon—and later by truck—to the mountain houses, the conveyances fitted with barrels of water to keep them alive.

Fish were not the only profitable commodity to come from the water. Harvesting winter ice was common on the river and many of the tributary streams and ponds, for local or domestic as well as commercial purposes. The industry provoked the same kind of awe and wonder as the other great industries of the Valley, as John Burroughs demonstrated in 1886:

> There is the broad, straight, blue-black canal emerging into view. This is the highway that lays open the farm. On either side lie the fields or ice-meadows, each marked out by cedar or hemlock boughs. . . . Sometimes nearly two hundred men and boys, with numerous horses, are at work at once, marking, plowing, planing,

scraping, sawing, hauling, chiseling; some floating down the pond on great square islands towed by a horse, or their fellow-workmen; others distributed along the canal, bending to their ice hooks; others upon the bridges, separating the blocks with their chisel-bars; others feeding the elevators.

The men were employed day and night in the two icehouses below his home on the river at Black Creek, "dark figures moving about in the moonlight" in his granddaughter Elizabeth Burroughs' childhood memories. Burroughs described the cutting and harvesting in *Signs and Seasons*, comparing the beauty of an ice harvest with the harvesting of grain from a meadow in summertime.

The practice was surprisingly late in arriving at any commercial level, beginning in 1826 at Rockland Lake when Moses G. Leonard and C. Wortendyke cut two boatloads of clear ice worthy of any butcher shop or hotel in New York City. Ice gathering took on stupendous proportions as the century progressed; in a good year, as many as 25,000 jobs were created. By the 1890s, 145 commercial facilities between Troy and Poughkeepsie, large and small, produced more than three million tons a year, most of it for New York City consumption. Eight large houses were in the Smiths Landing–Alsen area alone, probably because the region's sparse population did not contribute as much sewage as elsewhere to the river. In Greene County in 1884, forty large houses produced over a million tons annually, half again lost (melted) in the handling. Coxsackie icehouses reached 400,000-ton capacity. Eventually, the river's three largest companies combined into the Knickerbocker Ice Company, with a workforce of 1,000 and a storage capacity of 3.5 million tons. The company was worth $40 million when it became the American Ice Company in 1901, but had only $2,000 in capital left when it finally closed thirty years later.

Harry Arnold's father was superintendent in charge of the icehouses in Staatsburg, Barrytown, and (under John Burroughs' home) at West Park, and also worked at Glasco, Turkey Point, and other places. Arnold supervised the ice gathering at the Highland Lake house north of Iona Island near the Bear Mountain Day Line dock, where runs were used to slide the ice a half-mile down the steep hillside to a spiral entryway into the house. The ice reached the river barges via an overhead bridge across the West Shore Railroad. Tugs came in during the marketing period with "tows" of barges to be filled, ranging in capacity from 250 to 900 tons each. Sometimes an enterprising fellow would come out to the tows in a "bum boat" with homemade beer, tying to one while a lively trade ensued, thence to another, and another until all the river workers were served. As Regina Burroughs Kelley later related, one of them visited a traveling tow in 1873:

> As she nears the foremost boat in the line he sounds a dinner-horn, which brings all the men and women to their decks with baskets and pails in their hands. A rope is thrown out, and the market man hauled in. He has strawberries, potatoes, lettuce, radishes, ice, milk, peanuts, and figs. . . . Loud petitions are made to him for an honest five cents' worth of ice, two cents' worth of peanuts, a quart of milk with no water in it, and a basket of berries with no false bottom. He is distracted, irritated, and jocular by turns. In half an hour he has passed down the length of the tow, his stock is depleted, and he drops astern into the stream.

One of these dealers, Billy Barton, rewarded his boys with hatsful of peanuts at the end of the day.

Harper's Weekly depicted the operation of a Rondout icehouse in five panels called "The Ice Crop on the Hudson, 1874." Raymond Beecher identified the harvest of 1900–01 as the largest and finest in the industry's history along the river, involving the collection of 2.75 million tons between Catskill and Troy alone.

Such rich trade up and down the river encouraged the shipping industry. Nearly twenty vessels called Newburgh home port in the two decades after the Civil War. A schooner or a sloop took fifteen or sixteen hours ("two ebbs and one flood," as the boatmen reckoned) to travel the sixty miles to New York. Nyack, Piermont, Ossining, Peekskill, Poughkeepsie, and Rondout provided berths to dozens more, and all the river towns hosted one or a few of the sails in the heyday. Second and third generation Hudson River sloop and schooner owners, all significant Hudson Valley businessmen, often diversified (like the farmers) with a mix of sloops and schooners, barges, propeller-driven ships, steamboats, and yachts. Boatmen turned to shad fishing in the spring, stone quarrying all summer, working the harvest in the fall, and ice making as part-time pursuits to make ends meet.

The career of Thomas Collyer of Sing Sing, the principal shipbuilder of all six river-going Collyer brothers, spanned most of the century, from his first sloop the *First Effort* out of Mount Pleasant (1830), to a total of thirty-eight steamers, some huge and fancy like the *Daniel Drew* and, of course, the *Thomas Collyer*. He built his first sloop at aged eighteen in Sing Sing, and his first steamboat in West Troy. His brother John L. Collyer's son, Moses Collyer, wrote eloquently about the North River sloops in his later years, having served variously as cabin boy, cook, hand before the mast, mate, captain (his first the schooner *Henry B. Fidderman*), and sloop owner in his day.

For all the romantic allure of the North River sloops and schooners, life was hard and fraught with danger for the men who ran these sail. The Worragut reach between Storm King and Danskammer passed through a stretch of gale winds that could catch an unwary pilot off-guard. An abiding danger in crosswinds was the Hudson River jibe, especially when the main sheet fell slack. The sloop *James Coats*, under Captain James Lawson, which once made the Kingston-to-Brooklyn trip in forty-eight hours, was rounding West Point in the summer of 1866 when the main sail slackened and looped around the neck of the pilot, Benjamin Hunt, decapitating him in an instant when the sail went taut. The severed head was tossed like a pumpkin into the depths of World's End.

The sails could not survive the competition from the steam-driven barges. White Plains native Thomas C. Cornell (1814–90), who came to work with his uncle, Thomas W. Cornell, in his general store in Rondout when just eight years old, obtained the barge-hauling charter in 1850, and after a distinguished career as a major in the Civil War created a virtual monopoly on barge towing on the Hudson. Cornell also had interests in railroads in Ulster and Dutchess counties, and served two terms as a Republican congressman for Ulster County. He was succeeded by his able and highly competitive son-in-law, Samuel D. Coykendall, who eventually joined water with rail by extending the train (and adding a city trolley line) to his highly popular new Kingston Point Park on the Hudson. The park became "an instant success," according to Cornell historian Stuart Murray, overcoming competition from Rhinecliff and surviving until 1960, when the last of the day lines ended. In time, Coykendall owned, in addition to the steamboat company, the O&D and the trolley, the Wallkill Valley Railroad, the Hudson River Day Line, a couple of banks, and was a trustee of Vassar College. He also tried to consolidate the Rosendale cement industry but abandoned the effort in the Portland cement ascendancy, leaving five thousand people out of work in Rosendale.

By the early twentieth century, gone was the "picturesque sight" of twenty-five or thirty sloops in full sail, caught in the "witch tide" at the south end of the Highlands while waiting for the flood tide to be whisked past Anthony's Nose through the Horse Race into Newburgh Bay. One by one the sailing ships were retired and reduced to their salvageable parts in the scrap yards, or left to rot like the once noble sloop *Congress*, "put on the beach in Rondout Creek, near the West Shore R. R. Bridge." The Hudson River had become a canal, William Verplanck wrote in 1908, again (yet sadly this time) echoing the Rhine in industrial squalor with double-track railways on both banks and twenty factory chimneys to every castle. The romance, the allure, the beauty was tainted by the darkening brushstrokes of smokestacks and waste.

Yet in all these myriad manifestations, the life of the Hudson River Valley persisted as if the gateway to promise and progress had not changed, the doorway into an American largesse made manifest by the great artists and pioneers of an earlier time was still open, and the pursuit of a fuller destiny for a rising population of a "go-ahead" people still achievable. The natural world might totter under the abuse of man's weight, yet the spirit of the people still seemed to ensure that the fulfillment of the promise would be accommodated in time, albeit fitfully, warts and all, and the changes needed to make things right would come.

3. Romancing the Valley

Truly, man made the city, and after he became sufficiently civilized, not afraid of solitude, and knew on what terms to live with nature, God promoted him to life in the country.
—JOHN BURROUGHS, "Phases of Farm Life" (1886)

Once America's violently apoplectic argument with itself concluded, the image of the Hudson Valley and the Catskill Mountains as beauty's American fountain revived in a renewed interest in Washington Irving and James Fenimore Cooper's tales, Thomas Cole, Frederic Church and Asher Durand's paintings, William Curtis and Charles Lanman's peregrinations, N. P. Willis's "letters" to the *Home Journal*, and the fabulous reports of European travelers. The generations of romantics who followed retained a sense of awe and wonder even as the wilderness itself grew smaller, and the Hudson River Valley continued to embody the sublime and the picturesque elements of the American landscape.

Starting in the decade before the Civil War, *Harper's Weekly* routinely sent artists and correspondents to the region, publishing more than a hundred scenes along the Hudson from 1859 to 1903. The second wave of the Industrial Revolution darkened its waters, but the river had not lost its attractiveness, nor the region its importance to the metropolis. *Harper's* celebrated the bright promise of the age—the new Vassar Female College plans received a multipanel treatment on March 30, 1861, that included benefactor Matthew Vassar's dramatic "presentation of funds" to his board; its despair—the destruction of the steamer *Isaac Newton* (December 12, 1863) and the burning of the *Berkshire* near Poughkeepsie on June 8, 1864, the latter with a graphic description of some of the forty lives lost; and its charm—the swirling "Cadet Hop at West Point" drawing by Winslow Homer (1836–1910) in January 1859, before he became a famous *Harper's* illustrator during the Civil War.

The generations of painters who followed Cole expanded the geography of the Hudson River School (as Cole himself had done), and returned with exotic settings that restated the picturesque and the sublime in that tradition, as if affirming the region's importance. Cole's student and protégé Frederic Edwin Church traveled to South America, the West Indies, Labrador and Newfoundland. In later years, when he stopped painting because of arthritis, he turned to Olana and the artistry of his own living space in the painterly land of Cole, making the setting his canvas. In her analysis of the regional landscape, Linda S. Ferber extended the setting-as-canvas strophe to the "ultimate cosmopolitan," Henry James, asserting that his description of the "blinding radiance" of the scene around West Point accorded almost perfectly with the sublime tonalities in the *View from Cozzens' Hotel, near West Point, N.Y.,* painted by John Frederick Kensett in 1863. James indeed ached at the sight of the Valley on his return trip from the West in April 1905, passing through "ancient Albany" in "all but filial tears" at the sight of the old Dutch gabled windows of his childhood neighborhood, lamenting the "ugly presence" of the railroad's intrusion on the Hudson River scenery, and finding in West Point the very "geography of the ideal" that Ferber affirmed. Beauty would not be denied from generation to generation.

Tourism expanded with the growth of the metropolis, adding the health-bearing breezes to the art settings and lore of the region as inducements to upstate travel. The Valley was the outlet for escaping the "miasmic" poisons of the city during typhoid and other epidemics. Nathaniel Parker Willis—described by Oliver Wendell Holmes (1809–94) as "something between a remembrance of Count D'Orsay and an anticipation of Oscar Wilde"—came upriver for a cure for tuberculosis, found it, and ("it was noticed") lived another fourteen years touting the virtues of clean air in his popular *Home Journal* column. He considered the Cornwall area and what he called Highland Terrace on the north side of the Hudson Highlands as the beginning of the Valley—that is, the part that was wholly unconnected to the ocean's influences.

Tarrytown rose as a popular summer resort after 1870, with the Cliff House overlooking the river and the Mott House attracting the most visitors. Carriage rides down Broadway to the afternoon trains—like the pleasure excursions in Saratoga Springs approaching the other end of the Hudson River Valley—attracted the finest sort, as Mrs. Malcolm Murray reported:

> . . . carriages such as you have seldom seem, flawless, drawn by matched pairs with coats like satin, their silver mounted harness[es] gleaming, the coachmen and footmen dressed in white moleskin breeches and boots and gaily colored coats, hunter green, navy blue, and plum. It was a thrilling sight.

Street attractions included buskers with peacock feathers in their hats playing violins and accordions, organ grinders with pet monkeys, German oomph-pah bands, bagpipers, and scissor and knife grinders with their grindstones and bells clanging to attract customers. Mountain women came down from the hills with baskets of huckleberries, farmers went from house to house selling fresh vegetables, and a wagon might pass by filled only with strawberries. The village ladies especially liked the wooden spoons the mountain folk fashioned and sold.

Other communities welcomed acrobats, fire-eaters, fast- and tight-wire walkers, or whatever the local traffic could provide as weekend attractions. In the cold Saugerties winters, villagers repaired to the "upper creek," a long lake-like impoundment of the Esopus Creek where families promenaded in carriages fitted with sleds and young couples in two-seaters slipped into "the cove" for an opportunity to spoon. The drinking stalls served whiskey or gin with dollops of hot sauce to fend off the cold; one of them collapsed into the ice on one rowdy occasion, all hands being saved to enjoy again. Among the attractions was a race featuring a horse with ice cleats against a man on skates. In another event, in which the prize was a kiss on the cheek of the prettiest girl, an African American won the ribbon. As the other young men watched, he approached the girl and presented it to her, courteously declining to claim the remainder of his prize. Applause and approbation followed amid assurances by the girl that she would not have minded.

Not all towns embraced the weekend visitors, however. The *Crystal Stream* excursion boat was banned from the Mount Pleasant Picnic Grove in Westchester County by a Supreme Court injunction in 1883 because Hastings and Dobbs Ferry residents deplored how the Sabbath had become "a day of terror and excitement" for their communities.

Beck's Rye Beach House resolved the problem of rowdyism by simply banning alcohol use among its visitors. Temperance was popular in Westchester (the birthplace of the cocktail), where some saloons closed for want of patronage, even as others flourished. Mt. Kisco denied licenses to establishments after a temperance faction was elected, so the revelers simply repaired to a separate jurisdiction across the road.

As many as 607,542 day-trippers enjoyed the amusements former congressman John Starin (1825–1909) provided on his five-island Glen Island Park off New Rochelle in the summer of 1883, particularly a beer garden and island castle called "Little Germany." The island hosted a dozen steamers a day and a chain ferry from the mainland, its popularity precipitating a boom in housing in the New Rochelle resort area. At the end of the year Starin resolved to add a salt-water aquarium to the amenities, but his venture was short-lived. The burning of the excursion steamer *General Slocum* in the East River in 1905 resulted in more than a thousand lives lost, "broke Starin's spirit," and ended the life of Glen Island as a private recreational reserve; it would be revived as a public park in the 1920s.

Some projects were stillborn. A grand scheme to create a "pleasure resort" out of Dunderberg Mountain resulted in a thirteen-mile-long switchback carved out of the mountain rock for a cable railway to a large hotel at the summit. After a several year effort the million-dollar road failed for lack of funding in 1892; a few years later the Wright Steam Engine Company of Newburgh was commissioned to create an engine to operate the cables, but that scheme also "became discouraged" for lack of funds.

Middletown in this era was bursting its pastoral cocoon into a crossroads for major rail lines along the main route from New York City to the southern Catskills and the Southern Tier. A major brewery, several foundries, hat and bottling plants, and the popular hotels were doing so well that the Orange County village became an incorporated city in 1888. Its largest and most important institution was the State Homeopathic Asylum for the Insane, the largest of its kind in the country. Under the enlightened tenure of its superintendent, Dr. Selden Haines Talcott, who served from 1877 to 1902, America's emerging national pastime was enhanced by the addition of a baseball club as a therapeutic model for patients, who were eager spectators every week. Talcott used a number of schemes to promote his team, charging 25 cents admission, getting the trustees to provide natty uniforms, and offering $5 for any member of the home team who hit a home run. "Go the fiver" became a chant among the patients and spectators as favored batters came to the plate. The manager was hospital supervisor Walter Cook, who had a facility for drawing talented players to the game. Visiting teams included several from Orange County as well as teams from New York City, Brooklyn and New Jersey. A team known as "The 5As" (Actors Amateur Athletic Association of America) included 6'5", 230-pound matinee idol DeWolf Hopper (1858–1935), the first man to recite Ernest Lawrence Thayer's "Casey at the Bat" (August 14, 1888, and about 10,000 times thereafter). DeWolf was also dubbed "The Husband of His Country" for his six wives, including future Hollywood gossip columnist Hedda Hopper (1885–1966).

John Thorn (b. 1947), Major League Baseball's official historian (and coincidentally a Catskill resident), reported that the insane asylum team's best year was 1892, a 22–2 record, the two losses narrow ones to the New York Giants, which had five future Baseball Hall of Fame baseball players on its team. Hall of Famer "Happy Jack" Chesbro was an asylum team pitcher who joined the Pittsburgh Pirates in 1899.

A menu of local community culture developed in lectures, concerts, teas, church dinners and festivals from spring to fall, and each place had their specialty. An annual favorite was the oyster supper the Peekskill Methodist

Episcopal Church held in the great hall at Boscobel at the home's original location in Montrose. Religious revivals continued with as much fervor if not frequency as in the Second Great Awakening times—the fifty-second annual Methodist camp meeting at Sing Sing in 1883 lasted for several days. The era of the local "opera house" was born and flourished, small, popular centers of culture springing up in many towns that drew speakers, singers (including some divas), and theatrical and dance performers who thrilled villagers and farmers in from the country. The opera houses were often sponsored by the newly wealthy captains of local industries that came with the second industrial wave.

The year 1883 was celebrated in Westchester as the centennial of Washington Irving's birth, the Treaty of Paris and evacuation of New York City by the last of the British troops, and the bicentennial of the county's formation. The county had changed significantly since the antebellum years, its population exploding as the concentrations shifted from the northern farming region to the southern suburbia, although there were still nearly three thousand farms (mostly dairy) in the county in 1880.

Great strides were made that benefited society throughout the Valley. Successful local businessmen and ladies' organizations spearheaded the start of numerous community libraries in the 1890s. Henry Crandall (1821–1913), an uneducated yet wealthy lumberman, established a reading room and later a trust that led to the Crandall Public Library in Glens Falls; its local history collections are among the finest in New York State. The Fort Edward library was one of the first projects of a new Civic League created by forty-three local women in 1914. The Women's Civic League of Hudson Falls raised most of the funds for that library, which opened in 1916. Greenwich, which had a small paid library since the 1830s, established its free library in 1902, and in 1916 created an endowment fund that enabled the purchase of a local home fifteen years later. The modern Greenwich Free Library includes the Gill Room and its fine local history collection, and hosts the Willard Mountain Chapter of the Daughters of the American Revolution.

Banker-benefactor Benjamin H. Bancroft established the Bancroft Library in Salem in 1891, a time when the community went "epidemic" in its interest in ornithology. John J. Audubon's granddaughter, Marie R. Audubon, lived in Salem over 1890–1925 and published her grandfather's journals from here in 1897. The library's Starling Collection includes more than 400 natural history works, mostly about birds; almost the entire collection survived a devastating fire in 1976.

Explosions in turnpike, water, and rail transportation opened lateral corridors of movement into the Valley. An Erie Railroad branch that connected the coalfields of Pennsylvania with New England via Beacon–Newburgh boat transports contributed to Asher Durand's flight from the Highlands, even as he (uncritically like Cole) depicted the advance of manifest destiny in all its trappings; *Progress* (c. 1853) was considered Durand's "greatest" painting by Newington–Cropsey Foundation art historian Kenneth W. Maddox. The Erie was seen by Durand's neighbor on Highland Terrace, Nathaniel Parker Willis, as a shining accompaniment to the new technologies (rail, steam and telegraph) that were turning the river banks into "a suburban avenue—a long street of villas" that constituted "but a fifty-mile extension of Broadway." Willis named his estate for its location at the "nearest point of complete inland climate" accessible from the water, the northern side of the Hudson Highlands where salt water yielded to fresh.

Burhan VanSteenburgh ran an electric railroad across an old New Paltz Turnpike Company right-of-way to the ferry at Highland on the Hudson River in 1897, bringing as many as 3,000 visitors to the Wallkill River and the mountain houses on summer Sundays. Boarding houses proliferated wherever a favorable situation could be found; the idyllic retreats were often in picturesque glens and dales tucked within mountain shadows. Further north on the edge of the Hudson Valley against the dramatic outcrop of Round Top mountain and Polly's Rock—where Thomas Cole likely sat and made sketches for "Sunny Morning on the Hudson" in 1827—Catskill gentlemen established a small hunting and fishing camp called Heart's Content on Lampman's Creek. Amy White, a locally famous hunter and woman taxidermist who always dressed in buckskin, lived a couple of miles down near the Kaaterskill Clove at Palenville.

The old Waghgonk Trail used by Native Americans to travel between the Schoharie Valley and the river at Kingston became the boulevard into Woodstock in the boarding house years. George Mead (d. 1905), who had a business in Kingston plating harnesses with silver, began building a hotel on a prominence over Woodstock hamlet in 1865, the year a switchback road up the mountain was constructed. He rented rooms to hikers, artists and other romantics. Mead added a large addition in 1880 and, in 1891 when the

Meads' daughter was married, a small chapel below the mountain house that survived as the Church of the Holy Transfiguration of Christ, a state historical landmark. Mead drove his carriage to the Rondout ferry to meet guests from the Rhinecliff train, a whole day's journey there and back. The business continued under his son William (d. 1913) and his daughter and her husband after William died. Among the famous visitors were General Grant and General Sharpe, over from Staatsburg via a large reception at Kingston, and, on August 26, 1869, Robert E. Lee and his wife. Mead's Mountain House was known for its long-necked chickens, the offspring of George's East Indian naked-neck rooster, which wore tufts of feathers here and there.

Cairo in Greene County (pronounced "care-oh"), had numerous hotels and boarding houses by 1895, and was twelve miles west of the river on the Catskill Mountain Railway; the charge was ten cents a mile. Palenville, several miles south of Cairo at the base of the Kaaterskill Clove, expanded rapidly as a destination, as well as a staging area for the great excursions into the mountains. Palenville had attracted artists, including Thomas Cole, before the Civil War, and in the years after, before the resorts proliferated, the sleepy hamlet offered one of the "less expensive alternatives" to the great mountain houses.

Historians Alf Evers and Ronald Van Zandt considered Palenville America's earliest art colony. Asher Durand brought students to the hardscrabble community on the edge of the wilderness in the 1840s, beginning a tradition that continued into the next century. Benjamin Bellows Grant Stone (1829–1906) became the resident artist most associated with the Kaaterskill Clove in the post-Civil War years. George H. Hall (1825–1913), a still life and landscape painter of international renown, created an attractive entryway into the clove after purchasing Elijah Trumpbour's dry goods and grocery store in 1871 and transforming it into "a visual delight" framed in fencing, flowers and willow trees. He filled the house with his own canvases and Oriental and Spanish collections. Hall was friends with Frederic Church, Sanford Gifford, and other Hudson River School artists, and hosted them and others at his nook near La Belle Falls. His protégé and companion for summers in Palenville from 1908 until his death was Jennie Augusta Brownscombe (1850–1936), a founder of the Art Students League of New York whom he had met in Rome in 1885. Hall influenced her "sense of style, color and craftsmanship" and left his Palenville estate and lands to her. Brownscombe, the last of the nineteenth century Palenville artist community, was a multifaceted commercial artist and noted genre and portrait painter; she has been called "the Norman Rockwell of her era."

Palenville was thriving by the 1880s because of a four-and-a-half hour railroad ride from New York; by 1896, five coaches were needed to accommodate the train crowds on a busy weekend. One of the early and largest of the Palenville resorts (one hundred guest capacity) was Maple Grove House, built by Philo Peck in 1866. Pine Grove House was set in a grove of two hundred trees and offered hay rides, "peanut walks, and progressive euchre parties." In 1878, Theodore C. Teale came up from New York and built the Winchelsea with a popular "Swiss Gothic" cottage addition. Teale had worked under Chester A. Arthur at the New York Customhouse and soon became an influential player in Palenville. President Arthur marked a key change in the growth of tourism, on August 3, 1884, when he came to the new Hotel Kaaterskill on the clove behind Palenville. He went first to Staatsburg to enjoy the thousand-acre Dinsmore estate with its collection of 2,000 roses.

Other Palenville resorts included the Chestnut Lawn House, Central House, the Drummond Falls Hotel, and the Arlington. Pleasant View and Mountain View sponsored "fashionable dances" on summer evenings. Boart's (Barton's) House had a popular bowling alley. The popularity of the place and its proximity to Kaaterskill Falls and the Catskill Mountain House turned the Palenville road into the clove into a commercial nightmare. E. T. Mason, "a gentleman of fortune and a warm admirer of the scenery," came up from Poughkeepsie and began to transform that clove into its former glory by purchasing the old 600-acre Brockett family farm, which included Fawn's Leap, which was near Jonathan Kiersted's old tannery remains. Mason removed the "shanties and catchpenny contrivances" that tourism purveyors had inflicted on the landscape and made the clove attractive for artists again. Winslow Homer, Thomas Nast, John Casilaer, Sanford Gifford and a host of other known and unknown artists sketched and painted in these hills.

The advent of the bicycle took Palenville by storm when a six-foot-wide cycling path to Catskill ("uneven and rough" on the Palenville end) was built by Cornelius DuBois and George Dykeman in the spring of 1899. Dykeman put out a local summer weekly for the trade, *The Palenville Zephyr*. Palenville, like Kerhonkson and some other local areas, also developed a large trout hatchery, producing 100,000 fingerlings in 1880 alone. The Kaaterskill Falls, Haines Falls, and the Catskill Mountain House were just three or four miles away. A peculiar local resort, at least for a brief time, was Dodd House, perched high over the Palenville Hotel on the Palenville Overlook (called Grand View Rocks) as a rival to Beach's Mountain House. The house was owned by Mrs. Elizabeth Adkins of Savannah, but attracted few visitors and by 1896 had become simply William Dodd's home.

The Palenville Hotel and Annex, owned by Peter J. Schroeder in 1894, was built on a steep slope at the entrance to Kaaterskill Clove. The place was destroyed by fire (under Fred Apkes' ownership) in 1896, rebuilt in 1900 with a new "Dewey acetelene gas lighting machine" installed, and became the only year-round hotel in town until destroyed again (the third time by fire) in 1933.

The growth of recreational interest in the central and southern Catskills resulted in at least forty hotels and boarding houses tucked into the Rondout Valley hills between Napanoch and Cragsmoor by the early twentieth century. Ellenville opened the era with the arrival of the railroad in 1871. Cragsmoor, the only community perched atop the Shawangunk ridge, was called Evansville until changed by a petition to the post office in 1893. Frederick Samuel Dellenbaugh (1853–1935), who came in the 1870s, led a group of artists who gravitated to the place, including Edward Lamson Henry (1841–1919), Eliza Pratt Greatorex (1819–97), John George Brown (1831–1913), and William Holbrook Beard (1825–1900). George Inness and Charles Courtney Curran were also associated with Cragsmoor.

Dellenbaugh was the artist on the 1899 Harriman Expedition to Alaska, which John Burroughs and John Muir also joined. Popular for his paintings about travels to exotic places, Dellenbaugh designed many of the homes in Cragsmoor, as well as the 1895–97 Episcopal Chapel of the Holy Name, for Eliza G. Hartshorn (b. 1853) as a memorial to her husband. At their summer home at Cragsmoor, he and his wife Harriet Rogers Otis (an Ellenville girl; they were married by Henry Ward Beecher in 1885) were involved with the local theater group, called the Barnstormers.

E. L. Henry, popular for his depictions of rural nostalgia and his war paintings, courted the historic in *The First Railroad Train on the Mohawk and Hudson Road* (1892–93). He and his wife, Frances Livingston Wells, came to Cragsmoor in 1884, starting the trend of artist interest. Eliza Greatorex, the first woman admitted to the National Academy of Design (1869), was a featured artist at the Philadelphia Exposition of 1876. Her two daughters also painted and exhibited during their years at Cragsmoor. John George Brown, commended by Henry Tuckerman for his "juvenile and sportive kind" of paintings, also was highly popular, as were William Beard's dancing bear paintings. Charles Courtney Curran (1861–1942), came first to Cragsmoor by invitation in 1903, and built a large shingle-style house that he called Winahdin. An American impressionist, Curran was a popularizer, with Henry, of the rural nostalgic genre that so delighted late Victorian generations. Around Cragsmoor, Curran often painted beautiful women perched in dramatic settings. George Inness (1825–94), born in Newburgh, was a transitional Hudson River School painter who became America's most influential tonalist, the principal landscape artist of the late nineteenth century, and a precursor of abstract expressionism in America.

But the crown jewel of the region's tourism boom was the Mohonk Mountain House. Vassar College girls started making annual trips to Mohonk Mountain House in 1872, two years after its opening, taking the ferry over from Poughkeepsie and a carriage ride to the Shawangunk Ridge; the ridge (pronounced "Shon-gum") bore a Native American name for a hard white conglomerate that lay in nonconformity over shale. The annual forays continued until the 1920s, heralded one year by the cry:

> Mohonk! Mohonk!
> Kazoo! Kazoo!
> There's lots of fun in '92.

Many visitors came in by train from New York or Philadelphia, the New York trip shortened to just over three hours when the Wallkill Valley Railroad completed an extension to New Paltz six months after Mohonk's opening. Mohonk provided surreys at New Paltz and a stagecoach for the West Shore Depot in Highland when that railroad was completed in 1883. Each driver was responsible for his vehicle and passengers, and provided with a kit that included lap robes, a kerosene lantern, and a sponge to wipe down the conveyance. By 1898, when the trolley was in full operation from the river to New Paltz, seven different stage lines ran from there to the mountain house daily.

The origin of the Mountain House involved John F. Stokes (1801–73), a farmer in nearby Yeapletown who opened a rustic ten-room inn and tavern at Mohonk Lake on July 4, 1859. The lake lay tucked between Paltz Point (later named Sky Top) and Pine Bluff, a picturesque setting that Daniel Huntington had been painting in the Hudson River School tradition. Stokes was a practical farmer who thought the ridge's most prolific flora, mountain laurel (*kalmia latifolia*), useless because it was not large enough to be burned and unsuitable as feed for cows. He continued to use the land for hemlock bark that he stripped and sold to the tanning trade. The tavern's numerous activities (shooting matches, outdoor dances, ice skating parties) were popular with the young people from New Paltz, Tillson, Rosendale, and the Rondout Valley towns. Stokes returned to his hillside farm upon selling Mohonk to a new owner in 1869; the farm also became part of the Mohonk holdings in later years.

The new owner was Albert K. Smiley (1828–1912), in partnership with his brother Alfred H. Smiley (1828–1903). They were twins, so identical it was said they could only be distinguished by their watch fobs. Alfred wrote to Albert about the property and counseled haste because of others interested in the purchase. They met in Poughkeepsie in September 1869 and rode to Mohonk in a carriage "over a wretched road now abandoned," Albert recalled in 1907. "The mountain was covered with dead trees, the result of a severe fire six years before." The "dreary surroundings" did not deter the brothers, who saw "the making of a fine estate," Albert wrote: "I fell in love with the scenery and felt sure of its development."

The dark green leaves of the laurel and prospect of yellow and white blossoms in the spring drew the brothers into the setting. They spent the day walking the property, from Paltz Point to Eagle Cliff and down to the lake, marveling at how the heavier white rock fell in pieces from the shale, creating a virtual "labyrinth" in a pile that accumulated at the base of the cliffs. The nonconformity was responsible for the scenery, the hard rock offering fine views in all directions at the crests. The lake was one of five "pristine sky lakes," sixty feet deep, not of volcanic origin yet unusually high on the mountain ridge, formed by glacial shifting and erosion.

Alfred managed the hotel for the first ten years, while Albert remained in Rhode Island as principal of the Friends Boarding School. The Stokes building was renovated and a four-story addition added in time for a grand opening of Mohonk Mountain House on June 1, 1870. More changes followed over the next year, three additions and a six-sided observatory on top of the house that took in the Rondout Valley and southern Catskills views. Albert moved to Mohonk in 1879 when Alfred purchased Minnewaska. The accommodations grew from ten bedrooms under John Stokes, to forty in Albert Smiley's first remodeling in 1870, to three hundred bedrooms in 1902, when a stone tower was completed in the middle of the long hotel. The expansive and eminently comfortable Mohonk Parlor—known for its tradition of tea and cookies every afternoon at four—was dedicated with great fanfare in 1899. Large parlors and public rooms, porches, library amenities, a small theater and dining for 450 guests, all done in a tasteful Victorian motif, gave the setting a personal, "homey" atmosphere that has continued to characterize Mohonk. The estate expanded through careful purchases, mainly for conservation purposes, accumulating more than 7,500 acres by the mid-twentieth century.

The Smileys and Daniel Huntington became friends; he painted the Albert and Eliza Smiley portraits at Mohonk. The land was a canvas for Albert, who worked with his half-brother, Daniel, in building roads to the various views and escarpments. "Some people want to see half a mile or a mile," Albert told guests in 1905, "but we like roads that curve all the while so that you are getting surprises." A hundred miles of scenic carriage roads, all handmade from nearby stone and shale resources, were added to the ridge top, but not for the newfangled cars. The automobile was not allowed "to approach the house" until 1930, and then only when driven by Mohonk "pilots," A. Keith Smiley (b. 1910) noted.

Picturesque "summerhouses" inspired by the gazebos of Andrew Jackson Downing and the Arts and Crafts tradition were dappled around the lake and at overlooks along the carriage trails, 172 of them in 1905; a rustic "Swiss Village" grouping, connected by bridges, sat on stilts over the water. A large summerhouse adorned Guyot's Hill in 1880 to honor Albert's friend, Arnold H. Guyot of Princeton (1807–84), the geologist/geographer and measurer of mountain heights. The Cope's Lookout summerhouse, named for Edward Drinker Cope (1840–97), paleontologist and publisher of *American Naturalist*, was built in 1885. In 1912, Smiley dedicated a summerhouse built for General Frederick Dent Grant, the former president's son, after Grant led a temperance parade in uniform. Only one of the 155 remaining summerhouses recorded in 1917 was built of stone, in 1897, and, stone-like, survived the decades.

A wooden tower that had been added to Sky Top toppled over in a windstorm in 1872; two more were added, but each burned, the last in 1909. A stone tower was constructed in the ensuing decades, a cupola completed in 1923 and the tower set into service as a lookout post for state conservation officers until 1971. Another tower, at Eagle Cliff a short walk from Mohonk, survived from 1880 to 1973.

A bowling alley was built in 1876 and lasted for eighty years. Tennis came on the scene in 1883. A modern innovation, a golf course completed in 1903, ran through the pasture and orchards of the Mountain Rest dairy farm; women duffers were allowed. A putting green near the mountain house became popular for summer competitions. Annual events included fireworks on July 4 and a regatta on the lake.

Albert was an accomplished horticulturalist, his first planting at Mohonk a bed of geraniums near the mountain laurel along the lake. The difficulty of setting the early flower beds became a part of Mohonk lore. Only rugged fern and lichens clung to the rocky surfaces, to such an extent that soil had to be brought in for the flowers, yet under Albert's hand they became central to the beauty around the old hotel. Large beds of raspberries, gooseberries, and blackberries, grown for the enjoyment of the guests, were removed in the 1970s and replaced by formal garden beds.

Albert's continuing interest in education led to the effort to replace the New Paltz Academy with a training school for public school teachers. As president of the board (1885–1912), Albert presided over the groundbreaking in 1907.

Mohonk also established the Lake Mohonk Cooperative Weather Station in 1896, which provided daily readings on temperature, rainfall and other vital data to the National Weather Service, never missing a day since. The NWS had only begun the program in 1890, when a thermometer was introduced that recorded minimum and maximum daily temperatures, and Mohonk's station became legendary among the officials who received the reports over the years. Albert Smiley handled the readings until 1906, Daniel took up the task until his death in 1930, whereupon Daniel's grandson, Daniel Smiley Jr. (d. 1989), continued the practice. The thermometer was replaced from time to time (by a duplicate), but the brass rain gauge was never replaced.

Mohonk assumed national and international importance with a series of conferences, begun in 1883, on Native American Indian issues; the meetings continued to 1916 and resulted in thirty-four reports on the proceedings.

Albert Smiley was appointed to the national Board of Indian Commissioners by President Rutherford B. Hayes, who came for four of the conferences. The tradition of interest in international arbitration began with a similar series of meetings in 1895 and continued until the outbreak of the Great War. Conferences for foreign mission activities were conducted in the early 1930s, and Mohonk became the setting for seminars for United Nations and Washington diplomats in the mid-twentieth century.

In 1875, Alfred Smiley came upon a large lake south of Mohonk called Coxen Pond, which he subsequently purchased from Trapps farmer George Davis and renamed Minnewaska. More than 7,000 acres of wilderness, rising to 2,000 feet above sea level, became available to the metropolitan visitor; Alfred added a total of 10,000 acres in time. The land was covered with hemlocks and spotted with lakes, falls, cascades, secluded glens, cliffs, crags, crevices and fissures that all added to the picturesque charm.

Two large houses rose over the bowl-like setting of Lake Minnewaska. Cliff House, which was built in 1879 and enlarged two years later, had a capacity of 225 guests; the view from the veranda encompassed six states on a clear day. Wildmere, on the north end of the lake, opened in 1887 and was enlarged in 1911 for 350 guests. The most modern conveniences were included: large tanks supplying fresh water; "specially-installed" engines to run water pumps for fires; gas lighting; the halls heated by furnaces and the public rooms by large fireplaces, and fireplaces in nearly all the private rooms. Wildmere's 150-foot addition was heated by steam (as were many private baths), and the entire complex connected by telephone. The lake had four bathing cottages, several St. Lawrence skiffs for rent, and a full-time lifeguard on duty. Three-and-a-half miles away, on the south side of Awosting Lake were two 13-room furnished cottages and stables; Jerome F. Kidder ran a boys' camp on the north side of the lake.

Temperance prevailed at Minnewaska, as at Mohonk, in the Quaker tradition. Tuberculosis sufferers, dogs, and automobiles were banned. The six-mile stage ride to the railroad at Kerhonkson took an hour-and-a-half on a good day. The hills that spilled down from the Shawangunk ridge, particularly on the west side from Minnewaska, became rich harvesting grounds for huckleberry picking. As many as 350 pickers arrived each season and lived in tents and makeshift shanties within the hillsides. The harvesting was similar elsewhere in the Valley—three hundred passengers disembarked from the *Mary*

Powell at Cornwall-on-Hudson one Saturday in late July 1892 for huckleberrying on the Schunemunks. The Catskills front drew harvesters from both Valley and mountains; at Huckleberry Hill overlooking Platte Clove—in a custom that continued into the Great Depression years—wives with baskets and cheese sandwiches for the day would walk up from West Saugerties and gather the fruit for pies and breads for the season.

The Minnewaska-Kerhonkson carriage ride took in views of the Catskills rising across the Rondout Valley, where boarding houses and some fine hotels were proliferating. Among the most unusual of the Rondout Valley hotels was Yama-no-uchi ("Home in the Mountains," also called Yama Farms Inn), a 1,300-acre idyllic spread near Honk Lake in Napanoch that was created over 1902–13 by Frank Seaman (1858–1939) and his companion Olive Sarre (1873?–1954). Seaman was a wealthy advertising executive who undertook this ambitious project as a resort for his wealthy clients. He was attracted to the once thriving little canal town (abandoned by the Delaware and Hudson in 1902) through an ostentatious stocks and bonds wizard named William Woodend, who often traveled in the village in a white coach-and-four, the driver and coachman in matching livery showering children with handfuls of pennies. Seaman joined a 15-acre acquisition from Woodend with a 60-room Swiss cottage he purchased in 1912. He retained the cottage's former owner's family at the gatehouse; the daughter, Anita Foraste (1906–2004), hunted butterflies with John Burroughs in Seaman's fields.

Guests were invited to Yama-no-uchi; "Your name is the key," the membership card announced. No one paid, and tipping was not allowed. The guests worked out their bills beforehand or paid later, and the costs were extravagant. Some guests were collected from their yachts or personal train cars; many were picked up in New York City by Seaman and his staff.

The inn was similar to the ones at Cragsmoor (1904), Minnewaska (1887), Sam's Point (1871), and Mohonk (1870) in the beauty of the surroundings and atmosphere of traditional charm, and unique in its Japanese architectural styling and its setting on the west side of the Rondout Valley, looking toward the Shawangunk Ridge. Seaman and Sarre's immersion in Japanese culture and architecture on a visit there in 1906 (fifteen years before Frank Lloyd Wright), coupled with their interest in the Arts and Crafts movement, resulted in a stunning retreat for the elite of America. The buildings, the designs of which were credited to Sarre, were considered "the best adaptation of Japanese architectural principles in America," according to Carlyle Ellis in the July 1910 issue of *American Homes and Gardens.*

Among those who came were John Burroughs (1837–1921) and his friends Henry Ford (1863–1947), Thomas Alva Edison (1847–1931), and Harvey Firestone (1868–1938), called the Famous Four (or the Four Cronies) because they often traveled together. John D. Rockefeller stayed at Yama Farms, and the grandson born on his birthday, Nelson Rockefeller, honeymooned there with his first wife. George Eastman, General Douglas MacArthur, Rabindranath Tagore, Edgar Lee Masters, Alexander C. Flick, Hamlin Garland, Vice President Alton Parker (over from Esopus), Treasury Secretary Ogden Mills (of the Staatsburgh Mills), Edward Everett Hale, the Earl of Sandwich, Leopold Stowkowski, Frederick Remington, Rudolph Wurlitzer, Count Felix Von Luckner, Prince Louis Ferdinand and the Vincent Astors all had their own "keys" to Yama Farms, and their own wooden pegs with brass name plates to hang their hats and coats.

Poultney Bigelow (1855-1954) was an eccentric friend of the Famous Four who was given to walking barefoot on the trails and hooting like an owl. He was said to have been "uncommonly proud" of his two-inch long toenails, yet even Bigelow suffered one-upmanship at times. One evening at Yama Farms, to show off his pedigree, Bigelow announced that he was "one of the few men still alive" who had seen John Wilkes Booth perform. "Sir," said one of his companions, stepping forward: "I was his manager." The speaker was John Burnham, president of the American Protective Association, and he had managed Sarah Bernhardt and John Drew as well.

Buffalo Bill Cody (1846–1917) came one season and drove an old stagecoach through a village of "Indian" teepees in the annual Farms pageant. One of the employees remarked in later life that one evening in 1913 he overheard a group of bankers politicians and industrialists planning America's entry into World War I. The Vitaphone or "talking moving picture machine" was first shown to Bell Telephone Company nabobs at Yama Farms. On another occasion, a convention of American Telephone and Telegraph Company executives was preceded by sixteen engineers who installed an experimental plant that could send photographs by wire—the first fax machine.

Yama-no-uchi excelled in more than architecture, scenery, and style. Seaman's flock of Black Minorcas was considered "the aristocrats of the poultry world." The Yama Farms purebred Jersey herd won blue ribbons across the state. Their collection of Japanese iris was the best in America. The library consisted of more than 4,000 volumes. Olive Sarre also maintained a world-class English ceramics collection. The Jenny Brook Trout Hatchery became "the best private hatchery in this country," of which John Burroughs once confessed: "I lost my heart to Jenny Brook, I think she took it with a hook."

A John Burroughs Night was a standard Yama Farms feature in which stories were told by the rich and famous around a campfire. Burroughs had contributed to the region's themes in a succession of essays that established him as one of America's premier naturalists. He became an attraction himself after achieving fame because of his congenial personality, long white beard, and eagerness to share his knowledge of the minutiae of the natural world.

Burroughs did not seem to be troubled by the anti-Semitism that both Ford and Edison evinced (and their mutual friend Poultney Bigelow was worse), nor by how they or other industrialist friends made their fortunes. Burroughs preached Social Darwinism, but was not blind to progress's deleterious impacts. As a young man, he deplored the movement of people from the country to the cities as a "spiritual catastrophe." The steam locomotive was the metaphor for industry's impact on man in general, Burroughs felt (as Cole had, but in a different way). "A man may live now and travel without hardly coming in contact with the earth or air," he wrote in January of 1866. "He can go around the world in a parlor. Life is intensely artificial."

Burroughs was the most popular of a number of distinguished naturalists who frequented Yama Farms. Others included Roy Chapman Andrews (1884–1960), Raymond Ditmars (1876–1942), Carl Akeley (1864–1926), and Carl Lumholtz (1851–1922). Andrews, an expert on China's Gobi desert, and Akeley, a taxidermist whose advocacy for gorillas led to Africa's first national park, were with the American Museum of Natural History. Ditmars, a herpetologist and zoologist, helped make the Bronx Zoo a world-class institution. Lumholtz was a Norwegian naturalist and ethnographer.

The exclusiveness of Mohonk and Yama Farms was atypical for the Hudson River Valley in the "Gilded Age," as the wealthy and lower classes often mingled in the mountain haunts and houses just as they had at Saratoga Springs since the 1820s. The continuing popularity of steamboat travel and expansion of the railroads and trollies into the nooks and crannies of the Valley made longer trips economically possible, opening new Valley horizons, yet it was still a time when romanticism flourished and appearances meant as much as money. In that regard, the era that followed the Civil War lacked the essential innocence of the antebellum period and presaged an abstracted modernism to come.

4. Great and Greater Estates

Almost all imitations of castles must, as private dwellings, be petty in this country. There is one lately erected, of gray stone, on the lower part of the Hudson. We had the pleasure of welcoming to the Hudson that accomplished daughter of Sweden, Fredrika Bremer, and as we were sailing past the spot, some one near her remarked—"Do you see—a castle!" "Ah," she replied, "but it is a very young castle!"

—ANDREW JACKSON DOWNING,
Architecture of Country Houses (1850)

Rhinebeck's florescence as a Dutchess County river community for the very wealthy was tied to the arrival of the railroad in 1851; until then, men of means like William Backhouse Astor (1792–1875) felt the sloop or steamboat ride from New York just too taxing for the bother. Astor had come into the ownership of Rokeby (in modern Red Hook) after his marriage to Margaret Rebecca Armstrong (1800–72), the only daughter of General John Armstrong and Alida Livingston. Armstrong had built Rokeby in 1815 and was the resident aristocrat of northeast Dutchess County for a while. Astor's father, John Jacob Astor (1763–1848), purchased the estate from Armstrong in 1836 (since Margaret by law could not own property) and deeded it to his son.

Astor had also purchased 400 acres a few miles north behind North Bay in 1790 and constructed a mansion called The Meadows that he conveyed to his brother-in-law, Chancellor Robert Livingston (1746–1813). Livingston in time sold the property to a dealer in contraband, Colonel Andrew DeVeaux. Robert's brother, Henry G. Livingston (1754–1817), once had an estate just to the north of "DeVeaux Park" that belonged to Jeannette James Barker after 1835. She was the aunt of Henry and William James, who visited in the summers and who later owned Linwood, an estate further south near Ferncliff.

South Bay served as a private yacht basin in the 1820s for John Cox Stevens (1785–1857), nephew of Chancellor Livingston's wife Mary and a famous yachtsman and explorer. Stevens was friends with John Church Cruger (1807–79), a wealthy New Yorker who married into the Van Rensselaer family, visited often, and eventually had a home near the river. In 1835, Cruger bought property along North Bay that included an island that had served as the DeVeaux Park dock, and settled into the life of a country gentleman. He stood for the Whig Party for Congress in 1852, was defeated, and soon became an ardent Republican. Cruger sponsored John Lloyd Stephens (1805–52) and his partner, British artist Frederick Catherwood (1799–1854) on Stephens' noted expedition into the Yucatan peninsula in 1839–40. The artifacts and sculptures they took from that region astonished the city when displayed in Catherwood's gallery. A fire wiped out the collection (including many of Catherwood's meticulous drawings of the Mayan civilization), but one ship was still en route from Mexico, so Stephens presented the surviving friezes, statues and other artifacts to Cruger for having funded the failed adventure. Cruger brought the sculptures to his upriver island and framed them in faux-ruins of fieldstone.

William Astor brought his three sons and three daughters up from the city to Rokeby each summer, and they all eventually lived in the neighborhood, except Emily Astor (1819–41), wife of Sam Ward (1814–84), who died when their daughter was two years old. That child was Margaret Astor "Maddie" Ward (1838–75). She was raised by her Astor grandparents (the father having been written out of the family because of his rakish ways), thus commencing a tradition of Astor orphans at Rokeby; Maddie eventually became the estate owner.

William B. Astor began a major remodeling of Rokeby in 1858. The grounds were designed by Louis Augustus Ehlers in the Downing picturesque tradition. The Astors were the wealthiest family in America, and their summer home comparable only to the estate his father had given his brother-in-law and sister, Walter and Dorothea Langdon, just down the river at Hyde Park—which their son's executors sold to Frederick W. Vanderbilt.

A spectacular estate called Ferncliff developed over Vandenburgh Cove south of Rhinecliff after William Astor purchased fifteen farms in the 1850s. Colonel John Jacob ("Jack") Astor IV (1864–1912), called the "Golden Caliban" because of his disagreeable personality and extreme wealth, was born there. His mother, Caroline Webster "Lena" Schermerhorn Astor (1830–1908), was the acknowledged *grand dame* of New York's Social Register "Four Hundred" in the 1890s. Ferncliff had a tennis court house or "casino" styled in 1903 after the Grand Trianon at Versailles by Stanford White (1853–1906). A large dairy barn with a seventy-foot steeple sat amidst a cluster of attractive farm barns and houses north of the mansion, along with stables for up to fifty horses and a small covered racetrack. After Jack Astor's noble death on the *Titanic*, his son (William) Vincent Astor (1891–1959) took ownership of Ferncliff, razed the grandparents' home in 1941, and moved into the tennis court house. He proposed to his third wife and widow, Brooke Astor (1902–2007), during a carriage ride around the grounds, an offer she was flabbergasted to hear (he was still married to his second wife, who suggested Brooke as her successor) but accepted several months later. The casino was spectacularly restored as Astor Courts in modern times, and the barns restored by photographer Annie Leibovitz (b. 1949).

William B.'s youngest son, Henry Astor (1830–1918), spent his youth at Rokeby, despised by his brothers and living in a gardener's cottage. He had no use for the family's society and affairs and was an "irresponsible" drinker; everyone knew Henry in the countryside taverns. He loved to race his trotter around the estate in the mornings, enthused over wrestling and boxing, and sported with the farmhands in water fights and other recreations. His black sheep status was reflected in his choice of homesteads, a 200-acre farm in West Copake that he bought in 1874. He built a most peculiar house; one of the floors was inlaid with silver dollars. Henry's marriage, at age 39, to teenaged Malvina Dinehart, a farmer's daughter from across the river—done without purchasing her dower rights!—caused his father to virtually disown him. His inheritance was reduced to a mere $30,000 after that *faux pas*—but that hardly reflected his income, which also derived from his grandfather's estate. On his death in 1918 (two months before Malvina), his estate included sixty brownstones in New York City, thirty-eight tenements, seven factories, forty-five other parcels, and the sites of the Morosco, Bijou, and Astor theaters. A twelve-hour auction of the properties yielded $5 million for his grandnephews and nieces. Everyone loved Henry after all.

In 1844, Henry's sister, Laura Eugenia Astor (1824–1902), married Franklin Hughes Delano (1813–93), a shipping magnate who had made a fortune in whale oil. In 1851, they added *Steen Valetje* ("little stone valley"), a villa-style mansion designed by Frank Wills, to the Rokeby estate. Franklin was the uncle whom FDR was named after. Eleanor Roosevelt came of age here after her parents' death in the 1890s, although her memory of her grandmother's home was not a happy one.

Clermont was the most important remaining Livingston mansion, home to seven generations of the family. The house was made over in the Colonial Revival fad of the 1920s, yet still retained its old wealth allure. Montgomery Place, built by Janet Livingston in 1803 and then magnificently remodeled by Alexander Jackson Davis in 1843–44 and 1868, was a jewel of American architecture. Other Livingston estates that survived—there were forty of them still extent in 2014 in the forty miles between Hudson and Poughkeepsie—included the many columned Callendar House (Sunning Hill), erected by Henry G. Livingston on Sycamore Point in 1794, and Edgewater, a temple-form villa built in 1821–24 by Robert's brother, John R. Livingston (1755–1851), as a wedding present for his daughter. Edgewater, perhaps the most beautiful of them all, was so noticeable from the river it became a navigational landmark.

Blithewood, a wedding cake of a palace erected in a Federal style by Robert Donaldson, was redesigned by A. J. Davis in 1836 and 1845. The gatehouse along Annandale Road was considered "the first Gothic Revival cottage in America." The grounds were the product of Davis and Downing's first collaboration together, and many elements of the Downing touch were restored by Bard College. The home had a "picture room" for Donaldson's art collection that included a special three-by-four foot oval "landscape window" depicting "a work of the Creator"—a peephole into the Hudson River Valley itself.

Davis's Gothic style also survived a few miles south in the Delamater House in the village of Rhinebeck, which is now a guest house for the Beekman Arms. Hoyt House south of Staatsburgh, also called The Point, was another Calvert Vaux product, designed for Lydia Monson Hoyt and built from 1852 to 1858. Wyndcliffe was a turreted Victorian villa built in 1853 for Elizabeth Schermerhorn Jones (d. 1876), an eccentric cousin of the Astors. One of the most expensive houses ever built in America (and now a long-abandoned ruin), its construction coined the phrase "keeping up with the Joneses." Edith Wharton, Elizabeth's niece, remembered it as "an expensive but dour specimen of Hudson River gothic."

Andrew Jackson Downing designed Woodeneth in Fishkill for his friend and editor, Henry Winthrop Sargent (1810–82), one of the country's finest horticulturalists. The estate represented the epitome of landscape gardening in America. Sargent, in turn, did the grounds for Joseph and Eliza Howland's picturesque Gothic style house at Beacon, designed by Frederick Clarke Withers (1828–1901) using a colorful pattern of brick and stone together. Withers was a Downing scion in the sense that he came to Newburgh in 1853 and entered into partnership with Calvert Vaux, just as Vaux had with Downing three years earlier. Withers' important local works included St. Paul's Church at Matteawan (Beacon), the First Presbyterian in Newburgh, and the Hudson River Insane Asylum at Poughkeepsie.

Warren Delano (1809–98), Franklin's brother, was another friend and client of Downing's. He had made a fortune in trading opium, tea, and silk in China. In 1851, he purchased a sixty-acre fruit farm on the bluffs at Danskammer Point a few miles north of Newburgh. He called the estate Algonac and had Downing enlarge the farmhouse to forty rooms in the Hudson River Bracketed style. His wife Catherine (1825–96) added an international touch with Chinese porcelain and art and two huge Buddhist temple bells in the interior decorations. The Delano's sixth child, Sara, was born here on September 21, 1854.

These grand older estates notwithstanding, the rise of the corporation brought new wealth into the pastoral old world that congenially adopted the elaborate frontispieces and medieval aesthetic models for the newly aristocratic class. Two decades after Downing admonished America against building great mansions, his warning unraveled in a gothic swirl of turrets, spires, rambling porticos, classical columns, gargoyles, hidden passageways; interiors with vaulted ceilings, elaborate stained glass windows, spacious ballrooms, huge libraries; and grounds sculpturally landscaped in the most tasteful picturesque tradition.

Wilderstein, the home of Daisy Suckley in the twentieth century, was built on a sheep field next door to Wyndcliffe in an Italianate style in 1853 and expanded into a pretty Queen Anne style in 1888–89 by Thomas Holy Suckley, a realtor and exports trader as well as a Beekman-Livingston descendant. He named the estate after a nearby Indian petroglyph. The mauve, green and tan paint applied during the remodeling became celebrated for its tastefulness. A five-story tower and third floor with attractive gables were added; the first floor interior was designed by Joseph Burr Tiffany (1856–1917). At one time the home represented the height of late-Victorian technology and fashion. Calvert Vaux designed the network of trails and roads connecting buildings on the estate, and framed the extraordinary river views in planting schemes. Levi Morton (1824–1920) had a 900-acre estate, called Ellersie, built next door to Wilderstein on grounds that dated to a 1686 Thomas Dongan patent. Morton, who married into the Livingston family, added a Queen Anne style mansion and moved in just after being elected Vice President of the United States.

Some estates came from old wealth and were transformed by new wealth. Springwood was a farmhouse that James Roosevelt (1828–1900) purchased and renovated after his own estate, Mount Hope, burned on a hilltop just downriver in 1866. In that year, the state legislature authorized a state hospital for the insane and in effect put its location out to bid among Hudson Valley counties. Dutchess County outdistanced its rival, Orange County, and offered this 200-acre hilltop after purchasing it from Roosevelt. The first part of the Hudson River State Hospital for the Insane was opened in 1871.

Springwood, albeit modest compared to some neighbors, was in the midst of a rising class of well-to-do river mansions whose owners enjoyed common recreational pursuits. John A. Roosevelt (James's brother) was among the charter organizers of the Poughkeepsie Ice Yacht Club in 1861, the first organization of its kind. Ice yachting was not particularly expensive (not yet), and was not altogether new, but by 1866, as other ice craft clubs arose and the technology matured, more than a hundred of these sail were on the river. New Hamburg was another favored ice yachting locale. The principal competition developed between John Roosevelt's *Icicle* and Aaron Innis's *Haze*. *Icicle*, at 68'10" in length, was built for Roosevelt from butternut trees harvested on the Roosevelt estate by Jacob Buckhout, who worked with his son George in a shop under the Poughkeepsie Railroad Bridge into the 1920s. (George Buckhout built FDR's *Hawk*.)

Jacob also worked on "the finest" ice yacht on the Hudson (according to an 1876 estimate), the *Whiff*, commissioned by Irving Grinnell of New Hamburg and displayed at the Philadelphia Centennial that year. The frame was of white pine, the sides stripped in black walnut "relieved by gold bead," the deck made of spruce and red cedar, the bulkhead of black walnut, and the mast a bench of two arched ash pieces. The skates were held in oak chocks. The *Whiff* sported a figurehead of, in Brian Reid's description, "a very handsome flying dragon with open wings, a long tail, a stretched-out neck, and covered with heavy scales, slightly gilded," all carved of black walnut. Grinnell introduced the "Ice Challenge Pennant in America" in 1881. A thirty-foot silk banner became the annual prize, won the first year by *Phantom* of the New Hamburg Ice Yacht Club and on five other occasions by the *Jack Frost*, built for Roosevelt's neighbor, Archibald Rogers. The pennant never left the Hudson Valley and was retired to the Roosevelt Memorial Library museum.

Some of these boats carried a thousand feet of sail, and in their day, the ice boats were the fastest vehicles ever made by man. *Icicle* could easily exceed eighty miles per hour. In his childhood at Black Creek, Julian Burroughs skated over toward Hyde Park to watch the craft come out and draw a line across the river, twenty boats or more, for races to Esopus Island and back. The river had significant traffic in this area in the days before the Coast Guard began to keep the channel open for shipping, mostly walkers to and from the railroad station on the east side but horse and wagon as well, and cars when they appeared on the scene; an auto taxi service used the ferry slips between Highland and Poughkeepsie in the late 1910s. Peddlers were also on the ice, selling food and small wares; Julian delighted in one with a trained bear when young.

The Rogers family estate, Crumwold, just north of Springwood, was designed by Richard Morris Hunt (1827–95) over 1886–89. Built of granite and sandstone in a French Renaissance style, the mansion featured eight stone chimneys, a central parapet, and three towers. Archibald Rogers (the son) was a playmate of his neighbor, Franklin D. Roosevelt, who made frequent visits there. Crumwold was added to the National Register of Historic Places in 1993.

Mills Mansion (also called Staatsburgh) was the home of Ruth Livingston (d. 1920) when she married Ogden Mills (1857–1929), whose father had made a fortune in the California gold rush. The 1,600-acre farm had a twenty-five-room Greek Revival mansion that Ruth (Morgan Lewis's great-granddaughter) and Ogden commissioned Stanford White to remodel into a sixty-five-room home. The new mansion required a staff of twenty-four servants and had fourteen bathrooms. The house was the likely model for Bellomont, the estate in Edith Wharton's 1905 breakthrough novel, *The*

House of Mirth.

Locust Grove, the Poughkeepsie home of Samuel F. B. Morse during the last twenty-five years of his life, was a Tuscan-style villa redesigned by A. J. Davis around a Federal-period farmhouse. The land was originally owned by Henry Livingston (1714–99), a grandson of the first lord. Morse married into the family and lived here from 1847 to 1872, cultivating his interest in landscape architecture.

Although part of the new era, many of these estates arose in old money; forty extant Livingston family estates remained active between Hudson to Poughkeepsie well into the twenty-first century. The new wealth of the corporate era particularly impacted the downriver areas closer to New York. Other river estates included Nevis in Irvington, the home of Colonel James A. Hamilton III, a son of Alexander Hamilton (who had married into Albany's old wealth), done in a dramatic Greek Revival style and then drastically remodeled in Colonial Revival by James's son, Alexander, over 1884–85. Nevis eventually went to Columbia University, whose president, Dwight D. Eisenhower, established an experimental nuclear physics research center with a synchrocyclotron useful in medical physics proton therapy on the site in 1950. Estherwood in Dobbs Ferry was built by James Jennings McComb to encase an octagonal library built, according to Frank E. Sanchez (writing for the Westchester County Bicentennial) "specifically for an octagonal desk he had acquired." The estate was sold in 1910 as the new home for the Master School for girls, which began nearby in 1877.

Woodlea was a seventy-four room Scarborough Renaissance Revival home designed by Stanford White for Colonel Elliott Shepard and his wife, Margaret Louisa Vanderbilt. Margaret, the Commodore's sister and owner herself of the Fifth Avenue Stage Line, was the first of the Vanderbilts to locate in the Hudson Valley. In 1915, she sold the property to Sleepy Hollow Country Club, which carefully preserved it along with the original stables, golf courses, pool, courts, and skeet and trap shooting complexes.

Grand estates east of the Hudson were not restricted to the river settings alone. Thornedale was the first of the "hill-topper" estates of the Millbrook area, where William Thorne, a Quaker merchant, established a store in 1795. The family fortunes expanded in the quality beef breeding business in the 1850s. The village of Millbrook became incorporated in 1895 after the four surviving children of Jonathan and Lydia Thorne donated a fully endowed and furnished school, now on the National Register of Historic Places, complete with a fieldstone home for older boys to study carpentry and the useful arts.

Edwin Thorne established a reputation as a breeder of trotting horses in the next generation, which led naturally to the life and times of Oakleigh Thorne (1866–1948), "Master of Foxhounds," Angus cattle breeder, philanthropist and quintessential country squire. Oakleigh made the Millbrook fox hunts famous after the first Millbrook Hunt was organized in 1907 by Charles C. Marshall. The nucleus of wealthy local landowners grew in numbers thanks to the chase and the excellent hunting terrain.

Tioranda was the Howland family estate on the Fishkill Creek in Matteawan, established in 1859 by Joseph Howland (1834–86), a Pilgrim descendant and nephew of Philip Hone. Howland was the elected Republican treasurer of New York State in 1866 and later helped draft the trust for Cornell University. His brother-in-law was Richard Morris Hunt, the architect who designed the elegant library that became the Howland Cultural Center of Beacon. Tioranda was eventually transformed into Craig House, a wealthy mental health sanitarium.

The Rev. Robert Bolton came to Westchester in 1830, established a farm in Bronxville, and induced the railroad to come through that town after filling a swampland to accommodate them. His initiative led to a profusion of new roads built by Alexander Masterton. Bolton and his sons built a mansion he called the Priory overlooking Long Island Sound in Pelham that included two towers, one an octagon in stone and the other a brick square. The 1838 date over the door was in yellow bricks from Sunnyside that his friend Washington Irving came and installed for him. The Boltons also built a nearby church. This was perhaps the most famous nineteenth-century Westchester family, each of the five sons becoming Episcopal ministers and all sons and daughters distinguishing themselves. Robert wrote the county's first history; his brother Cornelius published the history's well-regarded second edition; architect brother John, an author and draftsman of note, designed the Bartow-Pell mansion, and William Jay Bolton created stained glass windows for several churches. The sisters, Nanette and Adele, managed a school for girls at the Priory.

The mile-square village of Bronxville arose around an 89-acre estate park created by William Van Duzer Lawrence (1842–1927) in 1889. Lawrence, who grew up in Yonkers, was a millionaire real estate and pharmaceuticals magnate and cultured progressive who strongly supported the arts. He used the rural beauty and meandering roads of his estate to plan a twenty-acre affluent housing community that became one of the most significant domestic architectural settings and, in time, the twentieth wealthiest community in the United States. Architect William Augustus Bates, designer of several of the Tuxedo Park cottages, created the first four houses for Lawrence on speculation—all of which were sold and occupied by June of 1891. Colonial Revival, Classical, Shingle, and Tudor Revival were among the styles Bates employed. He also modernized the old Manor House and added a casino as a common community hall.

Subsequent architects of note worked with Lawrence in positioning others in close proximity yet serenely isolated by their orientation within the complicated and attractive landscape. Oak Ridge Cottage, also called Owl House, was designed by William Winthrop Kent (b. 1860) for the well-known portraitist, William T. Smedley, and later occupied by critic Brendan Gill (1914–97). George Armstrong Custer's widow, Elizabeth Clift Bacon (1842–1933), resided in Lawrence Park for twenty years before joining her daughter in France. Joseph P. Kennedy, Don DeLillo, Timothy Geithner, Roger Goodell, Ed McMahan, Jack Paar, Eddie Rickenbacker, and the great imposter, Frank Abagnale, Jr. (b. 1948), also lived in Bronxville, along with numerous other notable personages.

Railroad tycoon William Henry Osborn (1821–94) and his wife Virginia Sturgis Osborn (1831–1902) came upriver after the Civil War and established the first of the family's grand houses on the side of Cat Rock hilltop behind Garrison. Osborn was a childhood friend of Frederic Church and a brother-in-law of Pierpont Morgan. He brought in a neighbor, Stuyvesant Fish (b. 1851), another wealthy New Yorker and son of a New York governor, who also established a Garrison estate. William and Virginia's grandson's wife, Margaret Schiefflin Osborn (1893–1982), created an elaborate garden on Cat Rock in 1924 and provided for the routing of the Appalachian Trail through the family's forest. She was a founder of the Garrison Art Center, active in the Garden Club of America, and one of the early advocates in the fight to save Storm King Mountain.

Lyndhurst, adjacent to Irving's Sunnyside south of Tarrytown (and connected by the Croton Aqueduct walking trail), was designed by A. J. Davis in the Gothic style as The Knoll (1838) for William and Philip Paulding, and enlarged for George Merritt in 1867. Davis became exacerbated by Merritt's call for elaborate new appendages—a large tower, a porte-cochere, new dining rooms—and called a halt when Merritt wanted a moat around the mansion, convincing him that such an addition would invariably draw unwanted vectors. Louis Comfort Tiffany was a neighbor, and he designed the stained-glass windows in the second-floor gallery. Jay Gould (1836–92), the "Skunk of Wall Street" and "the most hated man in America" (his own words)—obnoxious even to fellow robber barons—purchased the rundown estate in 1880. He commuted to Wall Street on his spectacular yacht, the *Atalanta*, which required a crew of 55. Amidst Lyndhurst's spacious grounds he created one of the best privately-owned plant collections in the United States, a grounds designed in a "gardenesque" style by Ferdinand Mangold (1826–1905) with orchids, palms, calemias, roses, ferns, and other flora separated in climate-controlled houses. The main conservatory, called the Palm House for its 320 varieties of that species, stood 376 feet long by 36 feet tall, yet had a light and airy appearance because this was the first greenhouse built with a metal frame. Gould was already growing prematurely old when he moved into Lyndhurst, and would soon be consumed by tuberculosis. His death at age 56 prompted a jump, like a sigh of relief, in the stock values of his various corporations.

Gould became involved with a neighbor in a stock market scandal over New York's elevated rail lines; he forced the neighbor out and into financial ruin. The neighbor was Cyrus W. Field (1819–92), who had succeeded in laying the Atlantic wire cable in 1863. He was a good-hearted man who created a property in Dobbs Ferry he called Ardsley. Field wanted to repay the public for their losses from Gould's chicanery, but the Skunk outwitted him. Field's wife died, his daughter was committed, and a son went to jail, but a friend, J. P. Morgan himself, loaned Field the money to keep Ardsley even though he knew he would never be compensated.

Glenview was an 1876 estate built by John Bond Trevor (d. 1890) for America's centennial. The stone mansion included an eighty-four foot tower, a spacious porch on the Hudson, and a porte-cochere facing Broadway in Yonkers. The home included Eastlake furniture, a stained-glass skylight, stables for Trevor's numerous trotters, grounds filled with specimen trees, and prized chrysanthemums. The estate is now home to the Hudson River Museum. At Scarsdale, a Medieval Revival approach in private residence designs echoed the look of some public buildings—the Schaeffer family estate, for example, designed by Jackson Gourard in 1904, which later became the Larchmont

Shore Club house. The College of New Rochelle, founded by Ursuline sisters in 1904, uses Castleview, Simon Leland's New Rochelle Gothic estate, as its reception center and gallery. Leland was a hotel man whose interest in the Renaissance and Rococo styles defined the interior rooms and created a setting for his elaborate parties in the 1880s. After his death, the property became a boys school, an inn and a girls school before being purchased by the Ursuline order.

Beechwood, a sprawling manor in Tarrytown in the 1840s, in time became the home of Frank A. Vanderlip (1864–1937), an assistant to the treasury under President McKinley and Rockefeller confidante. The estate was distinguished by a double set of white pillars and a lurid tale about Mad Mathias, found dead in a walled-up Dutch oven in 1909. Mathias, who had a coachman drive him in a golden chariot pulled by five white steeds over the White Plains road, was the axe victim of a footman in love with one of five virgins whom Mathias had murdered and buried in the kitchen floor. His trial was underway in White Plains at the time he disappeared. His remains, discovered behind an unused oven by chance years later, were quietly buried on the grounds near a gazebo. Frank Vanderlip, Jr., who witnessed the Mathias discovery as a boy, recalled in 1982 why they decided to look behind one of the ovens:

"There were more chimneys than fireplaces."
"What about the police?" his interviewer asked.
"Why make a fuss?" the aging gentleman replied.

Although eclipsed by the Joneses, the Rockefellers, and a number of other mansion-builders along the Hudson River in terms of elegance and expense, Frederic E. Church's Olana survived as the most famous estate in the Valley. Franklin Kelly in modern times called Olana "the single most important artistic residence in the United States." The canvas-like setting in which Church placed his Moorish-style home was a three-dimensional representation of a Hudson River School painting—the panorama facing downriver, the face of the northeastern Catskills rimming the picture in harmony with the high perspective from Olana's hill—that by itself might have derailed a late 1970s attempt to place a nuclear power plant at the centerpiece of that view.

The story of Olana's genesis has become a staple of art lore. In 1860, on a break from painting *Twilight in the Wilderness*, Church came upriver and purchased Wynson Breezy's farm on the side of *Sienghenburgh* ("Long Hill") over-looking the Hudson River across from Thomas Cole's Catskill estate. Curators of the estate have suggested that, although Church was interested in purchasing property at an earlier date (and likely this property in particular because of his youthful training at Cole's estate just across the river), the impetus to buy and build at this time arose because of Church's recent engagement to Isabel Carnes (1836–99). The property included Red Hill, which he had sketched while studying with Cole in 1845. Architect Richard Morris Hunt (1827–95) was brought in to design a small house, called Cosy Cottage, with gardens and fruit trees beyond. Seven years after the Breezy purchase, Church bought an adjacent eighteen-acre woodlot that covered the top of Long Hill "at a high price but I don't regret it" (he wrote to E. D. Palmer), but before commencing the ambi-tious landscaping that would eventually define the grounds, he and his family traveled to the Middle East. There—and with visits to Italy and the Parthenon in Greece—the artist acquired the transforming vision that would define his house on the hill. His correspondence was unclear regarding his reasons for seeking enlightenment in the East, yet an emerging preoccupation with archi-tecture, design, and a domestic ideal based on Persian styles soon dominated Church's interests. Calvert Vaux offered the advice and support of a trained ar-chitect, but Olana was all Church's design.

Isabel probably suggested the name of the home, from "Olane," an estate on the Araxes River with a view of Mount Ararat. In his posthumously pub-lished account, *Frederic Church's Olana: Architecture and Landscape as Art* (2001), James Anthony Ryan (1942–99) demonstrated why this unusual home became Church's greatest work of art. Church shared Ralph Waldo Emerson's transcendental sense of the aesthetic as employing a combination of "the vast and the intricate" in the making of art. It was a lesson in perspective that Church had learned from Cole as well. Just as the vastness of his magnificent Hudson River School paintings were strengthened and defined by the landscape details they contained, the transformation of the landscape through the addition of roads, pastures and orchards created access to dramatic perspectives that en-abled the artist to "make more and better landscapes in this way than by tam-pering with canvas and paint in the studio." And the castle on the hill was humanized by the details of its creation. The artist, for example, made elaborate stencils on the borders of the doorways, window frames, baseboards, and friezes using copper, zinc, and tin as part of the paint. Ryan wrote that this metallic quality "added reflective light," an understatement to be sure since these rooms practically shimmered with the sunlight in the morning. In time the sheen was dulled by oxidation, but the brilliance of Olana's intimacy was never lost.

Grand estates and both new and old wealth were not limited to the east side of the Hudson River. One of William B. Astor's sons, John Jacob Astor III (1823–90), created a seat on the west side of the river near Black Creek in Ulster County in 1851. He added a twenty-three room French Revival mansion, and called it Waldorf, after the family's ancestral home. Oliver Hazard Payne (1839–1917), a childhood classmate of John D. Rockefeller who became the Standard Oil treasurer and one of the wealthiest men in America, purchased Astor's estate in 1905 and replaced the French Revival mansion with a Beaux Arts palazzo designed by Thomas Hastings of Carrère and Hastings, architects of the New York Public Library and the Frick Collection. The Hastings design was ill-conceived and executed, built of the wrong limestone (which discolored in the Valley climate) and containing an open courtyard where the accumulated snow each winter had to be removed by wheelbarrow through the marble entry hall.

The proliferation of properties owned by religious orders was already occurring by this time. The Episcopal Order of the Holy Cross established a monastery nearby in 1899, ten years after Frances Xavier Cabrini (1850-1917), the first naturalized American to be canonized a Roman Catholic saint, created the Cabrini Home orphanage West Park, the first of sixty-seven orphanages for Italian immigrants she created in America.

Payne also purchased the Colonel George Pratt estate from his widow, which became the home of his estate manager, Julian Burroughs (1878-1954), who proved to be a better architect than Hastings. Julian's contributions included a large stone barn on the west side of Route 9W and a boathouse with a wrought iron peacock gate for Colonel Payne's yacht, the *Aphrodite*, the largest steam yacht on the river at the time. Payne was particularly solicitous toward Julian's children, often having them visit on his veranda or in his library. Elizabeth Burroughs Kelley (b. 1903) considered the Payne home "the most luxurious" of all the Hudson River estates, particularly in the colonel's 'art holdings, which included several Turners and Rubens' *Venus and Adonis*, which went to the Metropolitan Museum of Art.

Payne was a world-famous yachtsman and a noted philanthropist. He never married and left his estate to his nephew, Harry Payne Bingham, who donated the property to the Episcopal diocese in 1933. Part of the property was sold to Marist College and used as a preparatory school and retreat for Marist Brothers. The mansion, valued at $65 million, was bequeathed to the college in 2009 by Raymond A. Rich (b. 1912), along with a $10 million endowment to establish a Leadership Institute.

The West Park stretch of the Hudson River in this vicinity included several *nouveau riche* estates by the end of the century, including those of a malt industry captain, Adam Neidlinger; Frank Seely, the acknowledged "Soda Water King" (until he sold to Canada Dry); William Van Benschoten, who came in 1883 and often removed to Europe in the winter months; spinster sisters Aline and Fanny Gordon, whose home, Aberdeen, was an elegant Greek Revival edifice built in the 1830s; and two of the most well-known New Yorkers in their time, John Burroughs and Alden Parker.

Burroughs' watershed year came in 1873 when he received a long-desired career change within the US Treasury Department that allowed him to pursue his dream of becoming a Hudson Valley farmer. As Special National Bank Examiner for the Hudson River districts, his territory included the mid-Hudson Valley, and his first assignment was the receivership of an insolvent bank in Middletown. He bought a nine-acre West Park fruit farm draped across a mildly terraced upgrade above an ice works on the river. Burroughs boarded in Middletown during the week, leaving early on Monday or Tuesday in one of two Riverby carriages, dressed in a dark three-piece banker's suit with fine overcoat, a gold watch tucked in the vest pocket, and carrying a satchel full of ledger sheets. He disliked the job and the dress, but saw it as necessary to enable him to fulfill his real dream, which began when he returned to Riverby at week's end, changed his clothes, and took off on a tramp in the forest.

Burroughs was often invited to visit the Vanderbilts across the river; Frederick Vanderbilt gave John a terrier that Burroughs greatly enjoyed. Burroughs' home was in an odd situation off a steep, short grade just below the highway. He designed most of it himself, using some of his friend Walt Whitman's suggestions, but probably not enough. (He later admitted that he was not a good house maker.) His farm, like those of his wealthy neighbors, stretched across the highway and was diversified with different crops, all harvested for markets in New York or Boston.

The Burroughs' lives, like those of all their wealthy neighbors, were intimately tied to the river and its commerce. Julian's children often walked with their grandparents, John and Ursula, across on the ice in winter to catch the train at Hyde Park for New York. In summer, a "little boat" ferry plied between Kingston, Esopus, Rondout, Hyde Park and Poughkeepsie, carrying farm workers, fishermen, and families to their river jobs. By the early 1910s, when the lines of chestnut trees along the main (dirt) road through West Park were removed to make way for a new macadam surface, the river traffic changed as well. The snorts and whistles and toots of the sidewheelers, schooners, and bumboats gave way to a metallic hum of commerce of a new era. Julian Burroughs acquired a motorboat with cabin in 1906 and enjoyed summers on the river with his family. On a trip to Lake Champlain in 1907, children along one of the upriver locks saw the white-bearded grandfather and shouted, "There's Santa Claus!"—prompting John to grumble that he might just cut off his beard.

Alton B. Parker (1852–1926), a Kingston lawyer who had been active in the Democratic Party since Grover Cleveland's time, was elected chief justice of the New York State Court of Appeals in 1897 and served until he defeated William Randolph Hearst for the Democratic Party nomination for President in 1904. He accepted the nomination from the porch of his West Park home, Rosemount, and practically never left there during the campaign, preferring to accept visitors to his home as McKinley had done. Unfortunately, very few came. He was no match for Theodore Roosevelt and lost badly in the election, yet retained the Solid South for the Democrats. He remained involved, helping John A. Dix get elected governor in 1910, giving the keynote speech for Woodrow Wilson's 1912 nomination, and then leading the prosecution in the successful impeachment and removal from office of Governor William Sulzer in 1913. Irving Stone, in his 1943 book *They Also Ran*, considered 1904 one of the few campaigns in American history in which two very good candidates were running.

Fifty miles south of Olana, the Hudson Highlands became known as "millionaire's row" during these times. A fair sampling of the century's wealth congregated on its terraces and hills because of the proximity to New York, the beauty and drama of the river corridor, and the healthy living that the country promised. The huge Hudson Highlands Multiple Resource Area—a precursor of the Valley's National Heritage Area—was designated a National Historic District in 1982 based on the work of Rhinebeck preservationist Elise Barry.

Wave Hill, the Greek Revival Riverdale mansion built by William Lewis Morris (d. 1852) in 1843, was a summer residence for William Henry Appleton and his family after 1866, who leased the home to Theodore Roosevelt, Sr. for the summers of 1870–71. Young Teddy spent his summers strengthening and enriching his feelings about nature and the beauty of the natural world. Mark Twain leased the estate over 1901–03, using a chestnut tree on the lawn to create a tree house "parlor" for entertaining famous guests; he loved the roar of the winters along the river. One of Appleton's guests was Thomas Henry Huxley (1825–95), a biologist, zoologist, and naturalist known as "Darwin's Bulldog" for his staunch and early advocacy of the theory of evolution. Huxley was stunned by the Palisades across the way and considered the dramatic cliffs one of the wonders of the geological world.

Insurance executive, Morgan partner, TR-style progressive, and first president of the Palisades Interstate Park Commission, George W. Perkins (1862–1920) purchased Wave Hill in 1903, adding it to his estate (Glyndor House) next door. Perkins and his family greatly expanded the greenhouses and gardens that Appleton had created. Perkins added a casino with a sod roof terrace and underground tunnel connecting the buildings to the billiards room, bowling alley, and squash court. The house was demolished by Perkins' widow following a lightning strike in 1926.

The most notable estate created in the Highlands in these years was Cragston, the seat of J. Pierpont Morgan (1837–1913), "the Jupiter of Wall Street." Morgan turned a 675-acre rock pile near the village of Highland Falls—his wife was a daughter of the village's prominent settler—into one of the most extensive estates in America. He frequently brought friends and associates to Cragston on his 300-foot yacht, the *Corsair*, including Presidents Cleveland and McKinley, Andrew Carnegie, Thomas A. Edison, and Nikola Tesla. The celebrated Morgan yachts (there were four of them by that name) were so huge that Morgan's only indispensable requirement for the site of his mansion was that the river be broad enough for the *Corsair* to turn.

Around Morgan congregated fellow businessmen, friends, and relatives. Charles Tracy, a railroad lawyer who marred Morgan's daughter in 1865, had a Carpenter Gothic home nearby. John Bigelow, whose daughter married into the Morgan family, already had one of the nicest river estates, called the Squirrels, near Cragston at Highland (formerly Buttermilk) Falls. He and his wife Jane had purchased the property in 1856, at the height of his success as co-editor of the *New York Evening Post*, and hired Calvert Vaux to expand the farmhouse. Bigelow enjoyed the two-hour sail on the steamboat *Mary*

Powell to Manhattan each day—the "Queen of the Hudson" (1861–1917), she was captained by owner Absalom Anderson out of Rondout—eventually arranging for a desk in the ship's baggage room to work on a book review or editorial for the day's paper.

Edward Henry ("Ned") Harriman (1848–1909), a friend of Fish's and successful bond merchant, retired from Wall Street in 1885 and bought an estate near Morgan's at Highland Falls. He also picked up a large tract of farmland near Tuxedo that had been owned by a childhood friend, James Parrott. Harriman had not intended to purchase the tract, but became incensed when lumber interests attempted to dominate the auction so as to strip bare the hills of all the timber. Harriman began with a large castle on Mount Orama at the top of the Ramapos (the better to look down on snobbish Tuxedo Park ten miles to the south, or perhaps see over the hills to Cragston), and eventually transformed an initial 8,000 acres into thirty square miles of Highlands hills, dales, lakes and trails. Their mansion, called Arden House, was so large one of his daughters-in-law, after years of living there, confessed she had no idea where the kitchen was.

The girls had their own guesthouse to entertain friends. The boys, W. Averell (1891–1986) and E. Roland (1895–1978), had miles of horseback trails and a lake with an island where they often camped. In 1908, the father took them to the spring crew races at Poughkeepsie on his yacht, the *Sultana*. Rowing competitions here dated at least to the 1830s when a team called the Washingtons competed against crews from Newburgh and elsewhere, and were formalized in the Shatemuc Boat Club, organized in June 1867, the nation's first amateur rowing association. The Harriman boys became so interested in crew that the father hired a famed Syracuse coach, Jim Ten Eyck (1851–1938) of nearby Tompkins Cove, to teach them rowing at Forest Lake. Averell became so proficient that when he returned to Groton, where he had had no sports aspirations in the past, he became a champion rower.

Mary Williamson Averell Harriman (1852–1932) was considered "the world's richest woman" after her husband died. She continued many of his pet projects—the Goshen racetrack, the Bear Mountain land gifts—and added Harriman State Park and the construction of the Bear Mountain Bridge on her own. Her son Averell often went to the Goshen track (he raced here and at Tuxedo), which his father had developed so well that trotting became a national sport in the years that followed. Mary was the track's greatest benefactor.

Averell and his wife Kitty Lanier Lawrence, a Lenox, Massachusetts, debutante and friend and riding companion of his sister Carol, lived in Arden House after their marriage. The mansion had its own electric plant, its own railroad station, huge greenhouses, an unusual air venting system that created the effect of air conditioning all summer, and the "largest privately owned pipe organ in the country." After Pearl Harbor, the house was turned over to the navy for a convalescent hospital while Averell went off as US ambassador to Moscow. Averell ultimately gave Arden House and a thousand acres to Columbia University, which established an American Assembly forum there in 1951. A few years later, when Averell was governor of New York, Roland Harriman's estate, called Homestead, and another five hundred acres were added to the Columbia bequest.

A similar pattern of great, and often quite elaborate estates developed for the wealthiest residents of Westchester along Long Island Sound in the nineteenth and early in the twentieth century. These included the William E. Ward house, Larchmont manor, the Jay Mansion, Lounsberry, Castleview, and Whitby. Their designs—except for Ward's—followed the Renaissance Revival, French Empire, Chateauesque, and Colonial Revival then in vogue, as well as Scots and English tradition castles. Ward's home, on the state line between Rye Brook and Greenwich, was the first built using iron rods to reinforce concrete. His son William L. Ward became an influential congressman from Westchester and leader of the Republican Party for thirty years. The home later became the Museum of Cartoon Art.

The largest of the elaborate Valley "castles" was Ben Holladay's Ophir Farm at Harrison. Holladay (1814–82), who made his fortune running the mail on the Overland Express across the West, created a garish estate that included a narrow gauge railroad to traipse along while admiring the buffalo, elk and other western animals he brought to the site. He lost it all in the Panic of 1873. The property was purchased in 1888 by Whitelaw Reid (1837–1912), the *Herald Tribune* owner and Minister to France at the time. Reid had McKim, Mead and White redesign the mansion (now Reid Hall) and Frederick Law Olmsted the grounds. The house burned a month before completion, so Reid—never in want of funds—had a second built on the site by 1892. A five-story tower with numerous crenelated parapets and a veranda across the whole of the front facade distinguished the exterior; the interior included a reception area laid in pink Georgian and yellow African marble; two of the side rooms were taken intact from a French chateau. This was the first house in Westchester County wired for electricity and telephones. Benjamin Harrison visited while president; Reid was his vice presidential candidate. Later visitors included Admiral Richard Byrd, Amelia Earhart, Gene Tunney, Henry James, the king and queen of Siam, and Presidents Coolidge and Hoover.

Elizabeth Farrington Stevenson brought in New York architect Perry Griffen to create her Croton-on-Hudson mansion, Wyndhurst (1902), and a grouping of stone houses to accommodate artist friends in a landscaped environment featuring gazebos and loggias. She used Italian stonemasons working on the New Croton Reservoir and did most of the design herself. Her son, Harry Stevenson (1895–1984), who was also involved in the project, became an architect and created a notable "avant-garde" home nearby in 1935. As vice-president of the Hudson River Conservation Society, Stevenson led the Boscobel estate restoration. Elizabeth created another beautiful home on North Post Road, where Alexander ("Sandy") Calder (1898–1976) resided in later years. Calder had lived in Croton-on-Hudson and Spuyten Duyvil in his teenaged years, casually creating wistful works of art, and attended Yonkers High School.

One of the grandest of the river estates, at least in its setting, was the mansion that Frederick W. Vanderbilt (1856–1938) constructed on the bluff over the Hudson that he purchased from the Langdon estate at Hyde Park. The "social eruption" of his arrival as a Hudson Valley squire began with a reception for the home's grand opening, a male-only affair that Poultney Bigelow of Highland Falls attended after plucking the engraved invitation from his father John Bigelow's wastebasket. The mansion was small by Vanderbilt standards, the smallest of all the family's homes, yet large enough that Bigelow only learned later that the host himself was there.

The Commodore's grandson's special interests were agriculture and landscape horticulture. Frederick employed a staff of sixty in the busy season, forty-four for the grounds and the farming operation, including thirteen lawn and garden keepers. Between 1897 and 1934, Vanderbilt employed one or another well-regarded landscape architects to redesign the estate's formal gardens, creating thousands of new plantings and indulging his passions for botany and trees, yet Frederick had the good sense not to redesign the grounds that A. J. Downing himself had proclaimed "the finest seat in America" in its day.

John D. Rockefeller (1839–1937) began buying up parcels in Westchester County in 1893 after a visit to his brother William's spectacular estate, Rockwood

Hall, which fronted on the river above Tarrytown. William Avery Rockefeller, Jr. (1841–1922) joined his brother in business in 1866 and became president of Standard Oil in 1882. Rockefeller created an exceptional 200-room mansion on a thousand-acre estate, and William added numerous improvements in the form of carriage trails and ornamental plantings designed by landscape architect Frederick Law Olmsted. Impressed by the beauty of the region, brother John D. in the 1890s accumulated 3,500 breathtaking acres (with a 249-acre "manicured" core), four times the size of Central Park, between the Hudson River and the Saw Mill River Parkway. The holdings included most of the village of Pocantico Hills, which was soon transformed from a busy commercial community to a quiet one that fit the expanding needs of Rockefeller philanthropy. A convent, Christian Brothers college, railroad station, and the adjoining hamlet of Eastview were acquired and demolished, and some houses moved to create a more attractive hamlet setting. A new Union Church of Pocantico Hills was dedicated in 1922 and a public school ten years later, all with Rockefeller money.

A house on the main estate used for weekend and summer visits burned in 1902, so John D. allowed his son, "Junior," to undertake the construction of a new mansion. Eventually (after another fire) a Georgian style forty-room house rose on a panorama overlooking the river, the property appropriately called Kykuit (pronounced "cake-oot") after the original Dutch term *keekute*, meaning "overlook" or "peephole." Additions included a mansard roof, underground grottoes, and a bevy of formal gardens cascading from the hilltop. An "Orangerie" like that at Versailles was added for citrus and other special vegetation, and a playhouse in a French Norman style and brick coach barn built a half mile away. John D. had a twelve-hole golf course added in 1899 after becoming infatuated with the sport. He rode a bicycle around the course to save his energy for each swing.

The second Pierre Lorillard (1764–1843)—his father was said to have made his fortune "by giving [people] to chew that which they could not swallow"—foreclosed on a mortgage in the Ramapo hills in 1814, acquiring a large yet intimate tract of the Highlands barely forty miles from Manhattan. The purchase served to protect a vast forest within fifty miles of the city from logging and other extractive industries. Nothing happened on the property until the germ of Tuxedo Park was born in the heart of Pierre's great-grandson seventy years after the initial purchase. Pierre Lorillard IV (1833–1901) created "the Tuxedo Club" by bringing in 1,800 Italian workers, fencing off 7,000 acres with eight-foot-high barbed wire, and transforming the entire landscape within eight months start to finish. The gatehouse was so elaborate the architect who created it said it looked "like a frontispiece to an English novel." Around the grounds, done by the Italian crews in russet-and-grey stains to blend with the scenery, were twenty-two "casement-dormered English-turreted" cottages complete with lawns. Amenities included twenty stables, four tennis courts, a bowling alley, a swim tank, boat house, ice house, dam, trout pond and hatchery, two rows of stores, including a post office—all for $1.5 million.

The clubhouse was stuffed with English servants and one hundred bedrooms, yet only one private bath. The fireplace could accommodate a five-foot log. There was a stage even though actors were excluded from the park. The eighty-foot circular ballroom had a parquet floor that was soon deemed "the best dance floor of the time" by those in the know. In October of 1886, at the first of the famous Tuxedo balls, Number IV's son Griswald stopped the show by appearing in a dress coat without tails, a suave look to which the colony soon gave its name.

Golf was revived in America on November 14, 1888, when John Reid and some of his friends formed the St. Andrews Golf Club in Yonkers. Tuxedo Park hosted the third course in America, built in 1894, and the Tuxedo colonists claimed the country's love of the sport began with the first inter-club match involving Tuxedo, St. Andrew's, and clubs from Boston and Southampton. Court tennis was another luxury sport identified with Tuxedo Park. This rare, complicated, indoor game led to the Gold Raquet Championships, begun in 1903 when won by Hudson Valley "socialite" Charles E. Sands. Jay Gould, the notorious robber baron, came over from Lyndhurst in 1906 and won the championship for three straight years, whereupon the tournament was "promptly abandoned," until 1926 when Gould's reign as king of the court ended. Ogden Phipps won the first organized national court tennis championship here in 1938 and remained undefeated until 1949.

Undoubtedly in all the years the "Titan of Tuxedo," as he was known, was George F. Baker (1840–1931), a golfing companion of John D. Rockefeller who was still making $50 million in his 90th year—the first year of the Great Depression! A Troy native, Baker was called the Sphinx of Wall Street because of his personal motto, "Silence is golden." He was said to have given only two speeches in his life, the second and longest consisting of the words: "God bless you and thank you." Baker bought Pierre Lorillard IV's original cottage, Imlagh, when Pierre died in 1901. He gave the golf house to the club. The Erie railroad (he was its largest stockholder in 1927) often stopped at the first tee coming up from New York if George wanted to get off and play. At Baker's funeral, the most important in the park's history, only three hundred guests were allowed. A special train was sent up from New York just for the flowers.

Tuxedo Park was founded as a hunting and fishing resort for the very wealthy and became a spectacular trendsetter in its early years, yet over time the park turned into "a social ghost town" and became known as "the Graveyard of the Aristocracy" by the early 1950s. Tuxedo's decline began subtly, some said as early as 1892, when Julia Ward Howe responded with puckered lips to her daughter's inquiry about how the Park compared with Newport that season. "White of an egg," Julia replied. Emily Post (1872-1960), its most perceptive former resident, understood the anachronism that Tuxedo had become, but did not venture a reason for its decline. Who was to say, really? Perhaps it was the telephone that started the decline, perhaps the auto, or the income tax (as the exasperated claimed), or maybe it was just the passing of the hat-wearing era or the lapse in chaperoning—hard to tell, the vicissitudes of wealth. Ultimately it was an era that died, a time that America passed by, and although great homes and great wealth would continue to pour into the Hudson River Valley and its future might indeed resonate with ostentation and decorum, the old guard and the age of sheen that came with it was gone.

5. The Astor Orphans

> Bob Chanler, a latter-day Livingston patroon, declared that once a man had lived in the shadow of the Catskills he'd never be sane again; and Uncle Bob knew whereof he spoke.
>
> —Quoted in CLAIRE BRANDT,
> *An American Aristocracy* (1986)

The Astor saga continued in the Hudson River Valley when Maddie Ward (Sam and Emily's daughter) married John Winthrop Chanler (1826–77), a lawyer and Episcopal clergyman who became a congressman from New York in 1862. They had ten children. In 1875, when 38 years old, Maddie inherited Rokeby upon her grandfather William B. Astor's death, but she contracted pneumonia during the funeral and passed away shortly after. Two years later, her husband, 49, also caught pneumonia and died—he was playing croquet in inclement weather—leaving all ten children orphaned. The oldest was 15. The family's guardians included the formidable aunt, Caroline "Lena" Astor, the wife of William B. Astor, Jr. (1829–92) and acknowledged grand dame of New York's elite. They fretted over the children's future until finally acceding to their wishes to remain together at Rokeby. Two of them died within twenty-six months, leaving eight whose histories helped define the continuing aristocratic history of the Valley.

The eight Astor orphans included John Armstrong Chanler (1862–1935), called Archie (he later changed his surname to the old French form of the family name, Chaloner); Winthrop Astor Chanler ("Wintie," 1863–1926), Elizabeth Winthrop Chanler ("Queen Bess," 1866–1937), William Astor Chanler ("Willie," 1867–1934), Lewis Stuyvesant Chanler (1869–1942), Margaret Livingston Chanler ("Muggins" or "Meg," 1870–1963), Robert Winthrop Chanler ("Sheriff Bob," 1872–1930), and Alida Beekman Chanler (1873–1969). This was a spirited, intelligent, rowdy and often uninhibited clan of kids who "inclined to the opinion," as Margaret once put it, "that rich people had saved the world." They eschewed ostentation with a passion, however, and happily shared the one bathroom that the entire estate provided.

John Armstrong "Archie" Chanler hunted Geronimo with an American army troop in the Southwest. He moved among the best of Europe's circles and married Amélie Rives (1863–1945), a rare beauty of old Virginia who became an international sensation with her scandalous novel, *The Quick or the Dead?* (1888). The novel featured a hero named Brog, who strongly resembled Archie Chanler. "A most sensual bit of rot," his brother Wintie called the book, but considered the Archie character "very well drawn." Amélie so dominated European social circles—among her admirers were Thomas Hardy, George Meredith, Henry James, and Oscar Wilde—that Archie became forever known, forever to his chagrin, as "the husband of Amélie Rives." By 1895, "the former husband of Amélie Rives" had an estate in Virginia and a Napoleon complex that led Stanford White, who held power of attorney over him, to induce him to come to New York. In a brief period of time Archie was bundled off to the Bloomingdale Lunatic Asylum in White Plains and signed in by his brothers Wintie and Lewis. He spent three years in White Plains, and helped so many inmates with their cases that a "Chanler Club" developed in the Tombs prison. He escaped in 1900 and returned to Rokeby in 1920 after winning back his sanity in court, arriving in a new Pierce-Arrow automobile with a customized bed and field kitchen aboard.

"He told me he was the reincarnation of Pompey," Chanler Chapman said of his uncle.

Among the other brothers, Wintie Chanler had a brief Spanish-American War career when shot through the elbow while standing in the water during a landing. "This is no place for a married man," he remarked, and was back in New York by the middle of July 1899. He carried on a lifelong correspondence with his friend from Harvard days, Theodore Roosevelt, and was among the well-wishers sending telegrams to TR in 1901 when the vice president left Albany on his date with destiny as the successor of William McKinley.

Roosevelt was Willie Chanler's "intense admirer." He saw the adventurous Willie as the rough outdoor hero TR wanted to be. Willie's companion in most of his adventures was the Steen Valletje gardener, George E. Galvin. In 1892, after wrestling alligators in Florida and searching out the Hole-in-the-Wall Gang in the Wild West, Willie left Rokeby on his birthday to lead a long and harrowing expedition into uncharted territory of British East Africa; Chanler Falls was named for him. He ran guns into Cuba and returned a war hero with a new drink for America, the daiquiri. Willie was elected a Manhattan state assemblyman by a landslide in 1897 and made a sachem of Tammany Hall. His sister Margaret, also well known because of the Spanish-American War, joined him in Albany as housekeeper and hostess. During his tenure, Willie sought to ease boxing laws and opposed the Sunday blue laws.

Willie then became a Turkish cavalry colonel (1910–11) who—disguised as an Arab holy man from a district known for its bad Arabic—rallied the desert tribes around Tripoli. Given some poisoned camel's milk, he was kept from the battle that drove the Turks out of northern Africa, but recuperated. Willie was rumored to have lost his leg in a barroom brawl with Jack Johnson, the heavyweight boxing champion. He did lose a leg, probably as a result of a brawl, after he returned to Paris, although the exact circumstances remain unclear. He tried to influence the World War I peace negotiations at Versailles while he was there. He was a prolific writer; in 1921, his novel of Venezuela revolution adventures (*A Man's Game*) was published under the pseudonym John Brent.

Lewis S. Chanler, the most studiously reserved of them all, served on General Emilio Nuñez's staff in the Spanish-American War. He became—informally at least—New York's first pro-bono lawyer and a politician who served as assemblyman, lieutenant-governor (1906–08), and the Democratic candidate for governor in 1908, losing to the incumbent Republican, Charles Evans Hughes. His political life began with a memorable speech at Barrytown in 1888, when he was nineteen years old. The commencement of his gubernatorial campaign, which began as they all did on the steps of Rokeby, was so notable that more than fifty years later an aged Hamilton Fish, Sr., on a visit to the estate, urged J. Winthrop Aldrich to run for office by invoking the great Lewis Chanler.

Robert Winthrop Chanler, an accomplished artist, lived near Rokeby in "hedonistic" pleasure before carrying on an expensive campaign for Dutchess County sheriff. He looked the part—6'5" with a fearless aspect—and got elected. "Sheriff Bob," as he was known to all (including family), was the only Democratic sheriff in the county's history until then. Sheriff Bob was smitten with art while in France and Italy in 1891 and, with the help of many well-off friends, became a reputable modern artist. He was the most notable American artist represented in the 1913 Armory Show; his painted screen, *Leopard and Deer*, hung over the desk where visitors entered. Chanler's *Brooklyn Bridge* panel was the largest item in the show.

The three Chanler sisters grew up under careful tutelage at Rokeby. Elizabeth, the oldest, became disabled with a hip disease while in England at the age of thirteen and spent half a dozen years recovering to the point of being able to walk with difficulty again. She had resigned herself to a celibate life when she unexpectedly fell in love with the husband of a good friend. Margaret realized what happened and spirited her sister away on a round-the-world tour. While in India, they learned that the friend/wife had died, so Elizabeth quickly returned, a respectable romance ensued, and eventually they married. John Jay Chapman (1862–1933), a descendant of the first Chief Justice of the Supreme Court, was a brilliant yet difficult man of unusual passions. In the courtship of his first wife in 1887, after learning that a man he assaulted had been falsely accused he was so abashed he thrust his fist into a coal fire and held it there until it was so mutilated it had to be amputated.

John and Elizabeth Chapman married in 1898 and settled on a farm next to Rokeby. He left the legal profession and devoted himself to criticism and letters, starting with *Emerson and Other Essays* (1898). The writer introduced Oscar Wilde to John Burroughs at Riverby, an interesting visit for Burroughs, who concluded that Wilde was "a splendid talker, a handsome man, but a voluptuary." Chapman was also a playwright and poet. Edmund Wilson once characterized him as America's "best writer on literature of his generation."

Margaret Chanler, called "the Angel of Puerto Rico," received a congressional gold medallion in 1939 for her work as a nurse administrator in hospitals during the Spanish-American War. Her agitation resulted in the creation of a nursing corps within the US Army. At the award luncheon at Hyde Park, FDR joked that he was unable to enlist in that war in 1898 due to a case of the mumps, so the medal rightfully went to "the one [relative] who got there."

Margaret bought out all of her siblings' interest in Rokeby seven years before marrying *New York Times* music critic Richard Aldrich (1863–1937) in 1906. She was a quiet, reserved woman with a rule at Rokeby to never have dinner with a divorcee. Emily Post was among those thus debarred. On the one occasion when she actually had tea with one of them, Margaret pointedly did not remove her hat. Her charming memoir, *Family Vistas*, called "idiosyncratic" in the family's history (*The Astor Orphans: A Pride of Lions*), appeared in 1958.

Alida Beekman Chanler, the eighth surviving child, a woman of such dark beauty it was said that Czar Nicholas II of Russia chose his wife because of their resemblance, fell in love with a descendant of a distinguished Irish family, Christopher Temple Emmet (1868–1957). They married at Rokeby in the fall of 1896. Stanford White supervised the estate decorations for the occasion, a lavish one that involved a special train from New York for two hundred guests. Alida "flopped to Romanism," as her brother Archie put it, and was banned from Rokeby for her Catholicism, the feud between she and her sister Margaret lasting for more than forty years. Alida outlasted all her siblings, however, and was considered "the last of the 400" when she died in 1969.

Rokeby continued to be owned by the family of Margaret Chanler Aldrich, struggling to maintain the 450-acre estate in changed economic times. J. Winthrop Aldrich (b. 1942) had a distinguished public service career with the state Department of Environmental Conservation and as deputy commissioner for historic preservation in the Office of Parks, Recreation and Historic Preservation. Aldrich was a passionate advocate for the region's heritage and natural resources. He was among those incorporating Hudson River Heritage in 1974 and helped establish the Hudson River National Historic Landmark District that extended for twenty miles north of Hyde Park. Wint Aldrich shared ownership of the home with his brother, Richard Aldrich (b. 1940), a shy man of great intellect; a sister; and five young women in the next generation.

One other character in this remarkable tableau served as the representative colorful scion of the Astor orphans well into the twentieth century. Chanler Armstrong Chapman (1901–82) was Elizabeth and John Jay Chapman's son. He lived in "a ghastly pink cottage" (actually a neoclassical chateau) on Sylvania Farms in Barrytown, and published a characteristically brash monthly newspaper called the *Barrytown Explorer* under the motto, "If you can't smile, quit." One of his memorable *Explorer* headlines read: "Kingston Attacked by Giant Mall." Chanler went through three marriages, served as a kind of hayseed local board of education member, and was featured as a Hudson River squire in a 1977 *Sports Illustrated* article by Robert Boyle. He happily terrorized the neighborhood over the years, having purchased six hundred pounds of gravel in 1977 for a five-year supply of slingshot fodder. For a while he had a local radio show sponsored by a dairy. He did the commercials himself, one of which went: "Their man is on the job at five in the morning. You might even see him back at a house for a second time at nine, but let's skip over that."

One of his tenants was Saul Bellow (1915–2005), on a teaching job at nearby Bard College. This was Bellow's second stint at the college, his first in 1953, the year *The Adventures of Augie March* was published. He and Chapman would get into drunken brawls over dinner at times. Chapman was the model for Bellow's eponymous hero of his 1959 novel, *Henderson the Rain King*. "It's his best book," Chapman allowed of the Pulitzer Prize-winning author, "but he's the dullest writer I ever read."

6. "My 300 Daughters"

Study as if you were going to live forever;
live as if you were going to die tomorrow.

—MARIA MITCHELL (1818–89)

The Hudson River Valley was the setting for significant advances in education in America in the nineteenth century. Long before Vassar, the region was a leader in female education. Emma Willard's "Troy plan" spread across the country from 1822 on, her Troy Seminary (renamed the Emma Willard School in 1895) training more than a thousand young ladies as teachers, many of whom went out and founded teaching institutions on the enlightened Willard model. She was as indefatigable as her charges, writing prolifically and traveling the country to organize mothers to "set things right" in their local schools. Seminary-trained educators constituted more than half of the nation's 200,515 public instructors by 1870.

Down in the Highlands, West Point continued to produce first-class engineers—three-quarters of all those in the profession in America before the Civil War came from the academy. Sixty-three new engineering schools were established after 1862 and dozens of major universities expanded their curricula, almost all using West Point textbooks. Rensselaer Polytechnic Institute in Troy, founded in 1824, soon produced graduates of similar note and numbers in engineering fields. Leffert L. Buck (1837–1909, class of '68), built the Williamsburg Bridge in 1903, the longest in the world at the time. But RPI graduates were just warming up when it came to bridge building. John A. Waldell (1854–1938), class of 1875, designed a thousand of them and, in 1893, patented the first vertical-lift bridge.

Mordecai T. Endicott (1844–1926), the "Father of the Civil Engineering Corps" of the US Navy, was the first of fifty RPI graduates to become admirals. William Pitt Mason ('74; 1853–1937), in sanitation chemistry, and Hiram F. Mills ('56; 1836–1921), in water treatment facilities, were world leaders in the development of municipal sanitary engineering. Frank C. Osborn ('80; 1857–1922) and his son Kenneth H. Osborn ('08; 1888–1949) developed the use of reinforced concrete and designed Fenway Park and Yankee Stadium, along with numerous other major league and college ballparks. Garnet Douglas Baltimore (1859–1946), a civil engineer and landscape designer, graduated in 1881 as the first African American to receive a bachelor's degree at RPI. He was a grandson of a Revolutionary War soldier and slave who escaped to Troy. Garnet designed Prospect Park in Troy in 1903.

Alfred Tredway White (1846–1921) was an 1865 RPI graduate who became a pioneer in housing reform. He constructed the first model tenements in 1877—emphasizing aesthetics, safety, open space and ventilation—influenced New York State housing reform legislation, and established the Brooklyn Botanical Garden as a green space for the borough's poor—albeit that practice was not continued over time.

Union College, enriched by a $600,000 trust fund left by Eliphalet Nott on his death in 1866, survived three attempts by Albany alumni and others to move the campus to that city from Schenectady after a "University of Albany" was created by legislative fiat in 1851. Albany Medical College had been chartered since 1839, and only a liberal arts college was wanting for the capitol city. A downturn in the economy made the idea of Union's moving more conducive, but the option was still rejected. The Dudley Observatory, another part of the university puzzle, was chartered in 1852 and begun with great fanfare at the inaugural meeting of the American Association for the Advancement of Science in 1856. Albany Law School was founded as one of the university components and had the distinction of graduating "the first black person to complete a formal legal education in New York State," James Campbell Matthews. Matthews forced the Albany school system to admit blacks in 1872.

Union's troubles were reflected in the unfinished status of "Fort Gillespie," the students' facetious term for the Nott Memorial, a "lynchpin of the campus plan" begun with a six-foot-high stone foundation in 1859 and not finished until 1877. The 16-sided stone cylinder was covered with a dome containing 709 small, colored glass "illuminators." Students referred to the unique memorial as "one end of the bolt that holds the earth together," "The Cheesebox," "Minerva's Breast," and, when it was a library, "The Nipple of Knowledge." Designed by Nott's grandson, Edward Tuckerman Potter ('53), the memorial's only reason for existing was aesthetics. Nott called it his chapel.

The parade of Union College graduates, like those of Vassar and Rensselaer, had strong and lasting influences on America. They included a governor, William Henry Seward ('20); a president, Chester Alan Arthur ('48), a president's father, James Roosevelt ('47), and a campaign manager for two presidential bids, William Bray ('11); two New York State Assembly speakers, Oswald D. Heck ('24, speaker from 1937–59), and Stanley Steingut ('43, speaker in 1975–78); the "Father of American Anthropology" Lewis Henry Morgan ('40); editor and statesman John Bigelow ('35); writers John Howard Payne ('12, "Home Sweet Home") and Seymour Van Santvoord ('78, historical novels); and inventors George Westinghouse ('68, the railroad air brake) and Walter Ransom Gail Baker ('16). Baker was the GE and RCA executive involved in the development of television.

New attempts to have the college relocated to Albany occurred in 1885 and 1895–96, the former effort led by John Boyd Thacher (1847–1909), whose father had convened the 1868 meeting. Thacher was running for mayor and, backed by the local press, used the consolidation of the two cities' educational resources as a campaign issue; he won the election but lost the argument. The second attempt crystallized on January 25, 1896. The New York State Senate passed an authorization bill and a $1.5 million appropriation, yet both were defeated in the Assembly by a 98–16 vote after Schenectady, fighting back, labeled the Committee of Fifty-one "The Forty Kleptomaniacs."

Union rebounded under young President Andrew Van Vranken Raymond ('75) in this decade, the new spirit culminating in the erection of Silliman Hall as a "center of undergraduate life" in 1900. Raymond had "a magnetic personality" that soon endeared him to the college community. As a Union baseball player in 1874, with the bases loaded and a tied score in the bottom of the ninth, he hit the longest home run ever in the college's history.

Sixty miles south of Troy, in 1862, a colorful processional through beautiful fall foliage overlooking the Hudson River at Annandale-on-Hudson marked the presentation of the keys to the Church of the Holy Innocents of Annandale—newly rebuilt after a fire—to its owner, John Bard (b. 1819), by the students and faculty of St. Stephen's Training College. Bard, his uncle-by-marriage John McVikar, and Bishop Horatio Potter (1802–87) had established St. Stephen's some years earlier in a "tripartite agreement" that had Bard donate the land and buildings, McVikar raise funds from among the Hudson River gentry, and Potter involve the church and the Society for Promoting Religion and Learning.

Bard built a parish school at his estate with the aid of wealthy neighbors and friends John Cruger, Edwin Bartlett, and John Aspinwall. The Bards purchased the 130-acre Blithewood estate in 1852 and renamed it Annandale in honor of Margaret Johnston's ancestral Scottish homeland. The college, which opened in 1860 with six students, was formed to train ministers for the church, and in its first hundred years, 663 of the 3,000 graduates had gone on to the Episcopal ministry. Bard's first long-term president, Robert Brinckerhoff Fairbairn (1818–99), arrived in 1862, a former rector of Christ Church in Troy and of Catskill Academy, where he trained Thomas Cole's children. The college offered a baccalaureate degree, a partial program for adults, and a preparatory school for children. The curriculum remained strictly classical, Latin and Greek taking up two-thirds of the students' time over four years. St. Stephen's students lived in a single housing unit, were responsible for their own housekeeping, and never interacted with the faculty socially.

Fairbairn became the oldest college president in New York State and the recipient of many honorary degrees. He continued a strong output of writings on college and Episcopal religion matters. On his death in Brooklyn in 1899, the body was taken by rail to Troy for burial, passing St. Stephen's on a cold January morning. Three hundred students, alumni and others stood on the ice with their hats off in silent tribute to their first and one of their greatest presidents.

Albert Nock (1870–1947) was one of the notable St. Stephen's graduates, "a distinguished and eccentric philosopher and essayist" (in later Bard president Reamer Kline's words) whose libertarian writings, *Memoirs of a Superfluous Man* (1935) and *Our Enemy, the State* (1935), might have become bibles of modern conservatism were it not for the Cold War and emphasis on the evils of Communism.

The New York State Normal School at Albany (the predecessor of the real University of Albany) was the first state-sponsored institution of higher education in New York, starting in 1844 in an old railroad depot on State Street. The first "president"—all administrators previously having been called "principal"—was Joseph Alden (1807–85), who served from 1867 to 1882. Born in Cairo and a Union graduate, Alden was ahead of Vassar College in providing for equal wages for female teachers and for the interest he showed in women students. One of the graduates influenced by Alden was Senzaburo Kodzu ('77), Albany's first foreign-born student and the future leader of Japan's Normal School Movement.

The New Paltz State Normal School was chartered in 1885 by the Regents to train elementary school teachers. Here another grassroots endeavor was at work, albeit without the philanthropic support of a single wealthy benefactor. The college arose from the ashes (literally) of an effort to expand the New Paltz Academy in the year of its 50th anniversary, when the school and a new wing burned down. The community petitioned the state to approve a normal school, the first statewide in eighteen years, which opened two years later following a visit by Governor David Hill and an array of state officials investigating its worthiness. An experimental component was added when the trustees established a department and a four-year program, for New Paltz residents only, for those who did not wish to be teachers. The school's quarters on Huguenot Street were destroyed by fire in 1906, and the campus moved to a ten-acre site east of the Wallkill River and a new "Main Building" dedicated on February 12, 1909. New Paltz innovations, in addition to the "training" department, included a "school city" inaugurated in 1899 and planned by Wilson Gill, who originated the movement. School cities involved the student body in a civic program composed of three "cities" complete with mayors, aldermen, public works, police and courts, and a higher body that included governor, lieutenant governor, attorney general, assemblymen and senators.

Mary F. Bennett founded a college in 1890 in her name in Irvington, which soon moved to a 22-acre site in Millbrook. The Bennett School for Girls had 120 students and 29 faculty and offered four years of high school and two beyond, later becoming a junior college only. The school operated from Halcyon Hall, a 200-room former Queen Anne luxury hotel designed by James E. Ware. The beautiful campus grew with a chapel, dormitories, outdoor theater and science building before being forced into bankruptcy by the coeducation movement in 1978. The 300 students enrolled at the time were invited to nearby Marist College to complete their education. Briarcliff College (1904), a women's college in the village of Briarcliff Manor founded along similar lines, and also with 300 students, fell to expenses and the tide of progress as well in that year. A merger with Bennett was attempted but not successful, so Pace University acquired Briarcliff's assets and established a campus there.

Another women's college was emerging ninety miles to the north in Saratoga Springs, where the Young Women's Industrial Club was founded by Lucy Skidmore Scribner (1853–1931) in 1903. The widow of publishing house scion John Blair Scribner (1850–79), Lucy was a shy, retired woman when she relocated to the Springs in 1900. She saw the need for an institution to help women become self-sufficient, and created the club, which offered practical courses like sewing, typewriting, and dressmaking, as well as music, dance, and textile arts. The club had 436 students by 1908, including a number from adjoining towns. The Regents granted the Skidmore School of Arts a provisional charter on August 31, 1911.

Perhaps the Valley's most famous school grew out of what many considered a vice. In 1807, six years after his father and immigrant farmer James Vassar (d. 1853) had begun an ale-brewing business in Poughkeepsie, Matthew Vassar (1792–1868) ran away from home to avoid being apprenticed as a tanner. He only went as far as Balmville, a hamlet north of Newburgh, and returned in the spring of 1810 with $150 in his pocket, impressing his father sufficiently to be appointed bookkeeper in the family business. A year later, the brewery was destroyed in a fire that took the life of Matthew's older brother, John Guy Vassar (b. 1789). A grief-stricken James retired to farm life while Matthew began brewing on his own in the 1820s, joined by two nephews, Matthew Vassar, Jr. and John Guy Vassar (1811–88), in the Vassar and Company Brewery. The business developed into the largest ale manufacturer in the United States, producing 50,000 barrels a year at Poughkeepsie, with additional breweries in New York City and Lansingburgh.

Vassar was part of a spirited intellectual community that centered around Potter's Book Store in Poughkeepsie in the antebellum years. His country property, Springside, was designed by the age's finest landscape architect, Andrew Jackson Downing. Vassar was president of the Poughkeepsie Lyceum and opened the season on December 3, 1852, by hosting Ralph Waldo Emerson as guest speaker. He was well-read and kept a large library at home; his favorite volume was Herbert Spencer's *Education: Intellectual, Moral and Physical,* and his entry into education represented Spencer's survival-of-the-fittest philosophy applied to the advancement of young women. He befriended his sister Mary's step-daughter, Lydia Booth (1803–54), a teacher with strong ideas on female education, after she opened the Poughkeepsie Female Seminary in 1837. Initially, he wanted to use his fortune to create a hospital, but after Lydia died on November 6, 1854, the seminary, now called Cottage Hill, was purchased by Milo P. Jewett (1808–82), founder of Judson Female Institute in Marion, Alabama, and also a strong advocate for female education. Vassar had long been in the company of admirable, well-read and cultured persons, and here was another exceptional individual who impressed the brewer.

"His thirst for knowledge was insatiable," John H. Raymond wrote of Vassar.

Jewett urged Vassar to abandon the hospital and instead build a women's college—"which shall be to them what Yale and Harvard are to young men." The process involved years of planning and outreach to a broad range of educational and intellectual talent. Vassar purchased a college site after he and nephew Matthew Jr. inspected Mill Cove Farm, where Matthew and his sister had roamed as children, in March of 1859. A substantial building was designed and built in the Second Empire style, resembling the Tuileries Palace in France.

The architect was James Renwick, Jr. (1818–95), who was already at work on St. Patrick's Cathedral in New York City. Vassar brought together twenty-nine friends, business associates, and education leaders to form his first board of trustees, complying with Jewett's stricture that a majority of the board be fellow Baptists.

The state legislature granted a charter for Vassar Female College on January 18, 1861, but not before an intrigue threatened the founder's intentions. Charles Swift, a lawyer and board member strongly influenced by Matthew Jr., drafted a bill to create boys' and girls' high schools and a library—not a college. When he learned of the deception, Vassar angrily pulled the legislation, had it corrected, and ran an article in the Poughkeepsie *Telegraph* that explained the correction and gave a detailed account of the history of the college to date. The incorporation of Vassar Female College was treated well in the national press. Sarah Josepha Hale (1788–1879) of *Godey's Lady's Book* called it a bright moment in the approaching clouds of sectional darkness. *Harper's Weekly* devoted a page of illustrations to it on March 30. *The New York Times* and *Vanity Fair*, however, made fun of the idea of a women's college and treated it cavalierly.

Jewett was elected president at the first meeting of the board of trustees at the Hotel Gregory in Poughkeepsie. Vassar "dramatically" presented "a small tin box" with $408,000 in real estate, mortgages, and rail, bank and public stocks and bonds. William Kelly, a neighbor of Vassar's and wealthy farmer with an 800-acre estate in Rhinebeck, was made chairman of the board. Other members included Vassar's close friend Benson Lossing and Samuel F. B. Morse, a neighbor across the Albany Post Road.

Jewett went on a European trip for Vassar in 1862, made more useful contacts and discovered widespread approbation of the plan, and resumed a deep involvement upon his return. His ego had already elevated his own contributions to the venture beyond anyone else's—lobbying for approval of the charter gave him "quite a reputation in Albany," the aging Baptist exclaimed—and now that ego would be his undoing. Jewett unwisely criticized Vassar in private letters to the college trustees in September 1864, and was forced to resign. The college's first president never had students under him, yet the opening went ahead that year just as he proposed.

Baptist minister and charter trustee John H. Raymond (1814–78) took over the reins with Vassar's blessing and served fourteen years as president until his death. Raymond, a Union College graduate, had been president of the Brooklyn Polytechnic Institute and Madison and Rochester universities. Vassar heeded the urgings of a charter trustee, Elias L. Magoon (1810–86), and his Committee on the Art Gallery, for an appropriation for "living, original American art" and purchased, for about $20,000, Magoon's own collection of more than four hundred oils, watercolors and drawings by the best of the American and European artists; this became the nucleus of the college's art gallery.

Vassar Female College opened September 26, 1865. The Main Building, the largest building in the world for six months, was noted for the wide halls that Vassar asked Renwick to design so that the students could exercise inside in inclement weather. The first 353 students (many of whom arrived on the *Mary Powell*) ranged in age from 14 to 24 and came from 22 of the 36 states of the Union as well as the kingdom of Hawaii. A quarter of the student body lacked formal training or education—"a wretched shame," President Raymond called it—necessitating the creation of a preparatory department that lasted until 1888.

The president's assistant—and soon a legendary figure on campus—was Hannah W. Lyman (1816–71), who was feared for her discipline and "adored from afar" for her "elegance, the majesty of Vassar's first and unique Lady Principal," as the college's fourth president, James Monroe Taylor, described her in 1914. She was "a lady of the old school" crossing "the threshold of a new era." The notion that Vassar girls "have as much fun as the boys at Harvard" was seriously put to the test under Miss Lyman's tenure, yet she grew with the college and was remembered for both her piety and progressive viewpoints. The Lady Principal position was abolished in 1913 and replaced by a "Head Warden" and her board.

A faculty of thirty teachers was appointed, including nine heads of departments and twenty-one women teachers. The men were paid substantially more than the women, an inequity that Astronomy chair Maria Mitchell and Resident Physician Alida C. Avery embarrassed the trustees into equalizing in 1871. Mitchell, the first professor hired at Vassar who actually taught and a necessary but "costly luxury" according to President Raymond, was already famous for discovering the first comet unseen by the naked eye while using a telescope at her family's home on Nantucket in 1847. She and her father, William Mitchell, a mathematician with a love for astronomy given an honorary degree by Harvard in 1860, lived in the Vassar Observatory, the first structure completed on the campus after Main. The observatory's dome used a 12-inch telescope designed by Henry Fitz in Cincinnati. With her students she studied the stars, often requiring their attendance, sleepy-headed or not, in the middle of the night. Their astronomical findings were published in *Silliman's Journal* at Yale and in the local papers. Mitchell invented a means to photograph the sun and stored the plates in a closet, where they were rediscovered, along with her careful, handwritten notations, in 2004. She took her students to Iowa and Colorado to observe solar eclipses, their work attaining national recognition and eclipsing the men's colleges in the field.

Mitchell prodded the administration into opening the campus and the minds of the student body to new and at times radical ideas. The college was "in a ferment" in December 1869 over whether or not Wendell Phillips (1811–84) would be allowed to speak. A fiery abolitionist before the Civil War, he now clamored for the ratification of the Fourteenth Amendment giving blacks the right to vote and wanted the same legal status for Native Americans and—gasp—even women!

"We are about tired of poky lectures," student Ellen H. Richards wrote home about the exclusion of "a man so identified with radical views." George William Curtis, who also spoke on the taboo topic of women's rights, told a friend that his appearance at the college was "one of the most unique occasions of my whole life." Mitchell brought Julia Ward Howe (1819–1910) in to lecture on "Is Polite Society Polite?"—one of several visits by the celebrated activist and poet.

Vassar College in its early years established a tone and rigor of intellectual inquiry matched only by the great men's colleges of the country. Indeed, comparisons with Harvard or Yale became almost competitions among the girls, whose rooms featured one or the other's college banners to show her colors. On a visit in 1870, Harvard president Charles William Eliot (1834–1926) attended the recitations and later confided to Professor Farrar that the students at Vassar were better at their German, French, Latin, "or even in mathematics" than his Harvard students.

The setting that Vassar created, with its remarkable faculty, the revolutionary emphasis on an education in the classics for women, the openness of the campus to new and modern ideas, a bit of Milo Jewett's old-time Baptist sternness, and a student body unquenchable in its thirst for knowledge all con-

spired for a very lively and advanced institution. History was studied using
the daily newspapers of the day. Science took to the field—astronomy experiments in the West, geology girls in a coal mine in Pennsylvania. Trigonometry
students, instead of remaining inside studying rote formulas, surveyed and
developed a standard Vassar map of the campus and surrounding farm used
for many years.

Vassar's views seemed to coincide more with "my 300 daughters" than
the staid notions held by his board of trustees. When Anna E. Dickenson
(1842–1932), a noted abolitionist turned suffragist (Garrison called her the
"girl orator" of his cause), lectured the students in April of 1868, she pointed
out that the law against women suffrage placed them in the same category as
"criminals, paupers, Idiots." Vassar thought this "so shameful a category" that
he urged his "daughters" to apply "the remidy."

The benefactor's death was a poignant moment in the history of the
college. He was nearing the end of his final lecture to the trustees ten minutes
before noon on June 23, 1868, when, according to the minutes of the meeting,
"he failed to pronounce a word which was upon his lips, dropped the papers
from his hand, fell back in his chair insensible, and died." An hour later, the
trustees resumed their meeting to hear the rest of Vassar's speech, read by
Cyrus Swan, the board's secretary.

Lucy Maynard Salmon (1853–1927), the first history professor at Vassar
—and as radical as Maria Mitchell in her pedagogy—succeeded in reducing
the conservative influence of the president and trustees in 1913, when the
faculty was given greater say in Vassar's educational formula. Salmon advanced
the importance of newspapers and periodicals in history studies, took an active
role in Poughkeepsie life, and was a suffragist at a time when such advocacy
was prohibited in the Vassar campus.

In 1865, the students organized the college's first society, Philaletheis
(Lovers of Truth), which invited lecturers famous in their day. The students
were often in awe of the speakers, but never cowed by them. Curtis, of course,
was adored for his charm and urbanity, yet the century's finest intellectual,
Ralph Waldo Emerson, revealed only his parochial roots in a lecture he
delivered on May 17, 1867. The Sage of Concord, "seeing who were to be his
hearers," leafed through the pages of his lecture and omitted passages he thought
were over the heads of women listeners, telling them what he was doing while
he did it. Such condescension was not brooked by this lively and intelligent

group. "There was considerable indignation," one wrote.

Other speakers in the early decades included Edward Everett Hale (1822–1909), the noted short story writer ("Man Without a Country") and founder of the Unification Church in America, and Louisa May Alcott (1832–88), who spoke at the tenth anniversary and the opening of the remodeled Riding School and Calisthenium in 1875. The design of the original riding school building was the first major project for John A. Wood (1837–1910), who began practicing architecture in Poughkeepsie in 1863 and later became a noted Kingston architect.

Poet Matthew Arnold (1822–88) was not greeted well when he lectured on Emerson in 1884. One student wrote that they had "no desire to be led back into medievalism." A senior who sat in the rafters and dangled a toy mouse on a string over Arnold's head was expelled from the college.

Mark Twain, William James, Princeton professor Woodrow Wilson, Jane Addams, William Butler Yeats and his colleague, Lady Gregory, and Booker T. Washington all spoke at Vassar during the height of their careers. Yet, more extraordinary than any of these personages were the achievements of the students themselves. Ellen Churchill Semple (1863–1932), valedictorian in 1872 and the youngest in her class, became a noted international historian of geography whose life outlasted her impact; in time her *Influences of Geographic Environment* (1911), which preached a determinism based on place, was ridiculed by the historical establishment as wrong and passé. Florence Cushing (1853–1927), valedictorian for 1874, became the first woman trustee at the college, and held the position for life after 1912. Math professor Achsah M. Ely ('68) led the drive to create the first women's gymnasium and department of physical education in a college. Laura Wylie ('77) and Gertrude Buck started the first creative writing class in an American college. Elizabeth Williams Champney (1850–1921) scandalized Vassar while a student with a mock-biblical account of Matthew Vassar's life. *The First Epistle of Matthew*, as she called it, was banned from the campus by the "shocked" Lady Principal. Champney went on to achieve enduring fame with a series of eleven "Three Vassar Girls" novels featuring the adventures of endearing coeds on the prowl across Europe and elsewhere. *Harper's Weekly* thought hers "the Best Books for Girls."

A production of *Antigone* by Vassar students in the original Greek at the Collingwood Opera House in Poughkeepsie on May 26-27, 1893—the first airing of the original language play in America—attracted national scholars and reviews from the major metropolitan newspapers. In her senior year, Ida Watson ('01) discovered a new star in the Perseus constellation. Vassar won the first intercollegiate women's debate from Wellesley in 1902, and promptly held a "monster celebration" that lasted two days. Even fudge, "a kind of candy," was a Vassar innovation, in the sense that it was popularized at the college and known as "Vassar fudges" for years after a Baltimore freshman, Elemyn Battersby Hartridge ('92), brought in a recipe in 1888.

Ellen Swallow ('70) entered graduate school at age 28 as the first woman to study chemistry at the Massachusetts Institute of Technology. As Mrs. Ellen H. Richards (1842?–1911), she was a pioneer public health scientist and one of the first to recognize the importance of analyzing drinking water supplies. She led the conference at Vassar that developed the home economics educational discipline. In 1894, she developed a sewage treatment system for Vassar that was seen as a model for institutional sanitation.

Edna St. Vincent Millay (1892–1950) entered Vassar at age 23 after attending a three-month preparatory course at Barnard College. She wrote *The Pageant of Athena*, a play performed in his honor for Henry MacCracken's inauguration as Vassar president in 1915. MacCracken took to this eccentric genius, encouraged her as a poet and playwright, and forgave her many indiscretions regarding the rules. On one occasion, while confined to campus Millay went on a driving tour with three friends, stopping at a tea room near the Ashokan Reservoir and leaving funny notes in the guest book. No one knew of her indiscretion until the next day, when the hall warden herself visited the same tea room and saw the guest book. "All was lost," Millay told a reporter in 1932.

Millay almost missed her graduation in 1917 because she was banned from the campus and had been told she could not graduate. Fellow students protested, so MacCracken, in his only instance of overruling a faculty decision, granted permission for her to graduate with her class. Although Millay broke most of the rules, Vincent and Vassar were a good fit, since "Renascence," the great poem of her youth, was, like Vassar itself, an epiphany on life and the universe.

Adelaide Crapsey (1878–1914) had a crowded career at Vassar, serving as class poet for three years, editor-in-chief of the *Vassarion*, member of debating, basketball team coach, and Phi Beta Kappa scholar. She was a true poetical scholar, author of a learned exegesis on meter and rhythm (*A*

Study in English Metrics, published posthumously in 1918) and inventor of the cinquain, a 22-syllable, 5-line poetic form similar to the Japanese tanka and haiku. Crapsey suffered from tuberculosis for more than ten years, yet composed a phenomenal array of poems during her final hospitalization at Saranac Lake.

Adelaide roomed with Alice Jane Chandler (1876–1916), both graduating in 1901. Alice was Mark Twain's niece, "a shark at English," and greatly liked for her charming personality. She became Jean Webster, the author of *Daddy-Long-Legs* (1912) and other popular books for young women, and credited Crapsey's humorous character as the basis for many of her own fictional ones. Such was the popularity of *Daddy-Long-Legs* that when it became a hit in a theatrical version for Broadway in 1915, at the request of Vassar students it was performed at the Collingwood Opera House that spring. Webster lived at Tymor Farm in Union Vale, not far from Vassar, while pursuing her literary career. She died in childbirth in 1916, at the height of her popularity and fame.

Vassar, Bard, RPI, Union and West Point collectively placed the Hudson River Valley in the forefront of higher education endeavors in the nineteenth century, establishing standards that accrued to the benefit of the public and small independent colleges and universities, and producing some of America's finest intellects in the process. The boundaries of the discipline were extended further than in any other regions of America in the daring and resourceful challenges they presented—advancing past the classical Greek and Roman models of the Enlightenment to the vast new worlds of science and engineering, applying the "remidy" of new thinking and modernism in women's education on a par with men's, steadfastly pursuing education for education's sake whatever the parochial and local impediments might be, and challenging youth to rise to the occasion of a new time and a new way of thinking. Here there emerged the breeding ground for intellectual America in a consistent model for other regions to follow.

7. Saratoga Truncated

Youth, health and beauty are still the trinity of Saratoga.
No old belle ever returns.
—GEORGE WILLIAM CURTIS, "Lotus Eating," 1852

In the late nineteenth century, the Hudson River Valley boasted both America's most democratic grand resort and one of its most exclusive at Saratoga Springs. The "lower" classes of the old United States Hotel mixed at the spa waters with the haute monde of the Grand Union Hotel ilk, each aspect of society disdaining the other's airs as they gossiped about them behind their backs. In 1870, Henry James, 27 at the time, sniffed down his nose at "a democratic, vulgar Saratoga," the people in his crowd complaining about the "dreadfully mixed" nature of society. James was surprised by "the democratization of elegance," and did not care for the clothes they wore, either. For Mrs. St. George, the society dowager who opened Edith Wharton's last novel on the piazza of the Grand Union (*The Buccaneers,* 1938), there was nothing elegant about any of this cluttering of the classes: society, she said, "had grown as mixed and confusing as the fashions."

The rise of the spa as a watering hole for America received a boost on August 14, 1847, when serious horse racing began at Saratoga Springs. The occasion was the appearance of Lady Suffolk, a grey mare granddaughter of the English sire Messenger that faced off against Moscow on a mile-long track with a grandstand of 5,000 cheering fans. The carriages were lined two-deep for a third of a mile at the start of the heats, which the Lady won in the best of five. A month later, on September 16, a crowd of 30,000 that included former presidents Martin Van Buren and John Tyler was on hand for the first of the "running horses" races, won by Lady Digby of New Jersey in straight heats. The Saratoga Trotting Course continued in popularity during the 1850s thanks to Flora Temple, a bob-tailed nag made famous in a song by Stephen Foster (1826–54); Foster's "The Old Grey Mare" was written in tribute to Lady Suffolk.

Southerners who frequented Saratoga were appreciated for the "vim and vivacity" they brought to the spa, but not for the politics they embraced. When Stephen A. Douglas came campaigning in 1860, a barrel of tar his supporters had lit was overturned by a coachman "of a different political party." The flames spread so quickly the meeting had to break up. Southerners departed that same year, when New York outlawed bringing their slave servants with them. But Saratoga continued in full dressage, the cultured old wealth augmented by speculators, war contractors, jobbers and others made newly flush by the Civil War. Even in 1863, when the Union Army was pressed for horses after the tumult of Gettysburg, the course opened to a full crowd. The late Henry Clay's son John came up from Kentucky early that summer and sold some horses, including a $3,000 colt to the former prizefighter John Morrissey (1831–78).

Morrissey, whose nickname was "Old Smoke," was already successful in the casino business in New York, and fulfilled a youthful ambition by coming to Saratoga Springs and opening a gambling house. He became involved with William R. Travers and Leonard Jerome for the first trial meeting at the track. Jerome, a Wall Street financier, former partner of Travers, and associate of Morrissey in the Cornelius Vanderbilt takeover of the Harlem Valley Railroad, became America's premier race track builder in later years; an Anglophile whose three daughters married Englishmen, he was the grandfather of Winston Churchill. William R. Travers (1819–87), who would rise to become the best of the resort wits at both Newport, Rhode Island, and Saratoga Springs, was also a regular at Tuxedo Park and with the Lorillard set in southern Westchester and other high society haunts. He was called "Old Billy" by his friends, and they were legion. Travers, Jerome, and August Belmont created the American Jockey Club in 1863 and built Jerome Park in Westchester, drawing General Grant and the hoi polloi of Manhattan to the opening of thoroughbred racing there.

The Saratoga Racing Association organized on August 26, 1863, with Travers as president and Erastus Corning, Jr. of Albany on the executive committee. The trotting course and an additional seventy-one acres on East Congress Street were purchased for just a little over $10,600, a fraction of their worth and a tribute to Travers' real estate skills. A new course opened on August 1, 1864, with a covered stand (with seats) for 2,000, and a clubroom, salons, and other conveniences built underneath.

The first of the Travers Stakes, the oldest continuous stakes race in America's history, was held that day and won by Kentucky, a horse owned by Travers and John Hunter of Westchester. Steeplechase racing began on the last day of the meet, a horse named Gary Owens winning when Zig Zag, the favorite, fell on the last jump. Trotting became a feature at the Saratoga County Agricultural Society's fair in 1867; a crowd of 10,000 attended. The Travers that year featured Ruthless, the first filly to win the stakes in its long history. The Saratoga Cup race of 1872 pitted Longfellow, "the greatest horse of the decade," against Harry Bassett. Longfellow had easily bested Harry at Monmouth Park in New Jersey, but was distracted by a shoe that had been twisted in an earlier race and lost at Saratoga—and never raced again.

The track fell into decline after Morrissey prohibited horses from racing at Saratoga that had raced elsewhere after June 25. Disrepute followed upon decline under Gottfried Walbaum, owner of an infamous Jersey City track, who proceeded to milk Saratoga for all its worth. A new syndicate came to its rescue and purchased the track for $365,000, electing William Collins "Jock" Whitney (1841–1904) president of the Saratoga Racing Association. Whitney increased the length of the thoroughbred track to a mile-and-an-eighth, enlarged the grounds and facilities, moved the grandstand to save the guests from the unrelenting afternoon sun, and added furlong and mile "shoots," a saddling paddock, and numerous clubhouse changes.

Nine thousand attended the reopening of the track in August of 1902. With New York's high society now involved, the New York *Herald Tribune* forecasted a history for Saratoga as "the Ascot of America." Whitney's sudden death in 1904 did not diminish the enthusiasm, as Saratoga continued to thrive and grow until forced to close in 1912 as a result of new state laws. Fine horses still raced here—the filly Regret was juvenile champion in 1914, and won the Kentucky Derby the next year—and in 1918 a yearling named Man o' War was purchased by Samuel Riddle, starting another golden age in Saratoga racing. Five future Kentucky Derby winners (like Man o' War) were yearlings sold at Saratoga sales.

Saratoga's original attraction was its springs and pastoral beauty. A setting near a small lake and overlooking Bemis Heights, where he had fought for the patriot cause, drew Jacobus Barhyte (d. 1840) after the Revolution, where he built a cabin and enjoyed the local trout fishing. He expanded after 1825 when Joseph Bonaparte (1768–1844), Napoleon's brother and a former king of Naples and Spain, arrived at the United States Hotel to take in the waters.

Bonaparte pleaded with Barhyte to sell his pretty outpost, but the settler refused. Barhyte's trout were a principal attraction to his farm, the number of visitors coming just for the tasty fish prompting him to expand his tavern.

James and Hannah Riley created another popular restaurant at Lake Saratoga four miles from the village. Cary Moon built the Lake House to compliment the Rileys' attractions in 1853. Moon's cook was George Crum (1822–1914), a former Adirondacks guide who learned the art of cooking while working for a Frenchman with a fine regard for culinary perfection. Crum eventually opened his own restaurant on the lake, charged almost New York City prices, and used his five Indian wives as waitresses. He refused to take reservations, the wealthy and the lowbrow waiting together in line for dinner on most summer nights. The inveterate gamblers among the customers whiled their time by dumping sugar cubes in honey and betting on which one would be the first to draw a fly, a game they called Fly-Lo.

Crum's culinary skills were legendary. William Henry Vanderbilt brought a canvasback duck to him and never ate duck elsewhere again because of the beguiling dish that Crum created. He had never cooked the creature before.

A customer in the first year of the restaurant's operation was dissatisfied with Crum's French fried potatoes and sent them back to the kitchen with instructions to slice them thin and cook them longer. Crum, who rarely tolerated such abuses, proceeded to slice potatoes paper-thin, fry them in grease and oil, sprinkle salt on them and serve them to the man. Crum watched in disbelief as his eyes lit up on biting into the fare; others watched and tried the morsels as well, and soon the orders came fast and furious. The Saratoga Chip, also called the potato chip, was born.

The social set at Saratoga Springs were there to be seen, most appropriately in the daily carriage rides undertaken by the wives and daughters to the lake and back. The road to the lake was the social highway of every summer. Water wagons were used at intervals to keep the dust down. All kinds of traveling devices appeared—carts, hay wagons, fine barouches and landaulets, and crowded buses with seats for a dollar or two. Vendors along the roadway offered to sponge a horse's mouth with water for a fee. "Pedestrian amusements" were added to the day, such as track and field events involving even more students than the boating. Among the sideshows was an oarsman dressed in a full suit of armor performing trick sculling to the amazement of the crowds.

The carriage parade went on over a three-day weekend, filling the shores and hillsides around Saratoga Lake with the onlookers.

Elias Jackson ("Lucky") Baldwin, who had made a $30 million fortune in California, had the fanciest carriage. Giula Morosini drove a high gig led by three thoroughbreds who responded to the slightest movement of her reins (made of white doeskin); she was "undoubtedly the best horsewoman in Saratoga," all agreed. Surreys with fringed tops, magnificent Morgans leading buckboards, "basket phaetons with high-stepping, bob-tailed hackneys," the large and heavy Victorias, and the fast sulkies of the "whips" made a daily spectacle of the Saratoga parade. William Henry Vanderbilt was considered the best of the whips of Saratoga, and his Adelina and Maud S. considered the fastest and best bred of all the thoroughbreds in town.

The competition to be first in line on the lake drives involved many of the old-guard families, yet all were often outfoxed by a woman who was thoroughly disdained as not worthy of their set at all. Madame Stephen Jumel (Elizabeth Bowen, also called Eliza Brown, 1775–1865) came to the spa after her husband's death in 1832, appearing in a gold-colored coach drawn by four black horses and attended by footmen in livery, outriders and coachmen. She owned a Greek Revival mansion on Circular Street that she called Les Tuileries. She carried herself like a New York dowager, yet was far from that. The daughter of a prostitute, Eliza Brown had gone through at least three husbands, including an aging Aaron Burr who bilked her of her money before she locked him out of her Manhattan mansion.

Madame Jumel was routinely able to maneuver her coach into the lead position for the carriage parade at Saratoga until 1849, when she led off believing that the other ladies followed. Instead, a single, rundown coach drawn by four "bony horses" came behind with village pranksters mimicking her airs to a delighted crowd. The following day she went to the head of the carriage train again, this time with a pistol in her hand.

Saratoga Springs also drew "fashionable" madams who rented fine mansions for "open house" each evening with their girls. Grace Sinclair and Hattie Adams were among those relocating for the season. The girls rode in the carriage parades and visited the lake, the track, the casino and the spas, advertising themselves in the process.

Among other gaudy revelers was John W. ("Coal Oil Johnny") Steele (1843–1920), who made a fortune in Pennsylvania oil. He came into town on a special train with a full minstrel show and uniformed Negro band, playing and singing "Coal Oil Johnny Was His Name." Steele promptly lost $10,000 to Jim Morrissey at the poker table, and added another $10,000 for drinks all around. Old Smoke's Matilda Street gambling emporium—a "gambling hell," according to a prurient Boston newspaper—was at first feared by Saratoga natives, but the pleasant Irishman won over the staid old crowd by contributing to ladies' charities, always comporting himself as a gentleman, and running an honest den. After seeing the racing venture he entered into with Jerome and Travers through several successful seasons, Morrissey drew boat clubs from Boston, Philadelphia, New York and elsewhere to Lake Saratoga and established regattas. Intercollegiate competitions soon followed.

While serving four years as a congressman, this Irish tough from Troy then outdid himself in planning and creating an elegant gambling casino on thirty manicured acres adjoining the Congress Spring in the village. Local residents were barred from Morrissey's casino. He was always nattily dressed in the best attire, sporting a $5,000 diamond stud, with his wife Susie, adored by Saratoga society, always by his side. Morrissey was rebuffed by Troy's high society, however, when he sought land to build a mansion in that city, and in response had a foul-smelling soap factory built upwind from the mansions of the nabobs who opposed him. He became a state senator representing the "Silk Stocking" district in Manhattan, but contracted pneumonia and died on May 1, 1878, just forty-sevem years old. Yet Morrissey was not finished. An additional comeuppance against his hometown swells came with a huge funeral in Troy; 19,000 mourners followed his casket in a heavy rain to his grave on mansion hill.

The interest in crew and sculling that began in Poughkeepsie spread into the local communities, where neighborhood youths competed in amateur races on streams like the Schuylkill, and eventually at Saratoga Lake. Rowing became so popular at the lake that the New York *Herald* recommended that the new Rowing Association of American Colleges hold its meet there. The first of these, in 1874, involved nine colleges with six-oared boats. In 1875, thirteen colleges in all participated. Regatta and field events returned in 1876, Cornell again victorious in the varsity event while Princeton won the meet. Disputes among the colleges and the horror of college students visiting a den of sin like Saratoga ended the events that year, intercollegiate meets again returning in 1884 and 1898. The National Association of Amateur Oarsmen held its regatta at Saratoga Lake in 1911, ending formal racing at the lake generally until the powerboat era.

A new kind of ostentation arrived in 1872 when Alexander T. Stewart, owner of the largest retail store in the world, bought the Union Hotel and transformed it into the million-dollar Grand Union. The new hotel, which had 824 guest rooms and a dining room that sat 1,400, stretched for 450 feet along Broadway and included two wings a quarter of a mile long. Staircases made of black walnut and Otis elevators run by steam connected the five stories. The United States Hotel was also reborn after its destruction by fire in 1867. It opened in the summer of 1874, u-shaped like the Grand Union, five stories on seven acres, with a bandstand between the wings and a lobby tiled in white marble. The United States had 768 guest rooms and a number of well-appointed cottage suites. The two porches covered more than an acre and held a thousand wicker rockers—the same number placed at the Grand Union.

"This was front-porch life without peer," George Waller wrote. The north piazza was reserved for the very wealthy of the guests, men like Jay Gould, J. Pierpont Morgan, and John D. Rockefeller. Cornelius Vanderbilt, the Commodore, favored whist and racing on his frequent visits. His son, William Henry Vanderbilt, was confronted one day on the United States piazza by a nervous 28-year-old, Hamilton McKown Twombly, who wanted to marry his daughter Florence. Twombly worked as a lowly Western Union clerk, but Vanderbilt approved of the marriage and later made Twombly a Western Union vice-president. Cornelius's grandson, William K. Vanderbilt, when he came of age would always arrive on a special train with his wife Alva Smith.

The drive to the lake might include a pass through the twenty-five miles of gravel roads of Woodlawn Park, Judge Henry Hilton's $1 million, 1,500-acre estate in the town of Greenfield. The mansion and grounds had a score of amusements for Hilton's guests. Augustus Saint-Gaudens' first major sculpture, *Hiawatha*, stood on a pedestal in front of the mansion. The grounds also had a clubhouse for gambling, a ballroom, a sports field with grandstand and a private track. Admission past two burly guards at the gate was by cards distributed by the judge while in town, two hundred or more at a time.

Hilton was A. T. Stewart's estate executor and manager of affairs on the owner's death in 1876. Stewart and Hilton had held the opinion that a drop in attendance at Saratoga's posh hotel was due to the influence of "Israelites." When Hilton decided in June 1877 that Jews were to be excluded from the

Grand Union, Joseph Seligman (1819–80) was the first one barred. Seligman, one of the nation's leading bankers and a prominent member of the New York Jewish community, had been a financial advisor to the administrations of Lincoln, Grant, and Hayes. Animosities existed between Seligman and Stewart as well as Hilton, stemming from Seligman's involvement in the citizen committee that opposed the Tweed Ring, of which Hilton was a member. Bigot that he was, Hilton, in an interview with *The New York Times* on June 20, 1877, characterized Seligman as the prototypical Jew. "He is the Sheeny," he told the newspaper. "His is of low origin, and his instincts are all of the gutter—his principles smell—they smell of decayed goods, or of decayed principle. . ." and so on. The exclusion became scandalous and started the first national debate on the extent and meanness of American anti-Semitism, yet it was only exceptional because of the person of high society who was targeted. Jews were routinely ostracized, marginalized, and treated with extreme prejudice in the Catskills and elsewhere; a Jewish boarding house on the Saxton flats was burned down.

Evander Berry Wall (1860–1940) earned his sobriquet "King of the Dudes" one day in the summer of 1887 when, in response to a wager by John "Bet a Million" Gates (1855–1911), he announced he would appear in forty different changes of outfits between breakfast and dinner, and then did so while the bets accumulated all over town. The display ended with a playing of "The Conquering Hero Comes" as Wall entered the dining room of the United States Hotel in top hat and tails to a round of three cheers led by the heavyweight boxing champion John L. Sullivan. Saratoga also claimed the first appearance of the tuxedo when Berry dressed in a coat without tails for an affair one evening and was rebuffed by the stodgy society of the ball.

The arrival in Saratoga Springs of Richard Albert Canfield (1855–1914), like that of Jim Morrissey twenty-five years earlier, was preceded by a long and fruitful career in gambling and the public's eye. Yet Canfield was already embraced by the *haute monde* of the spa, while Morrissey lived all his life craving a recognition he never received. Dick Canfield purchased Morrissey's Saratoga Club from Albert Spencer in 1893 and transformed it into the Canfield Casino, "the Monte Carlo of America" in its day. He hired a celebrated French chef, Jean Columbin, and charged more than New York City prices for his cuisine, which the customers loved. The Canfield required evening dress, extended credit, and paid in cash, with the office vault always retaining a million dollars to cover any bets. Within two months of opening in the summer of 1894, Canfield won back the $250,000 he paid Stewart for the casino.

Saratoga Springs had more than a dozen gambling houses by the 1890s, and it was becoming of concern to the respectable citizens of town, including Spencer Trask, owner of a great estate and the civic-minded Saratoga *Union* newspaper. Trask appreciated the benefits the summer crowds brought, and once induced Thomas A. Edison to come and install a large version of his incandescent lamp from the roof of the Grand Union Hotel. Yet when Trask aimed his newspaper sights at the dens of iniquity all around the village, the public rejected his sanctimonious outrage. Some church leaders saw similarities between the faro tables and the stock market office that Trask maintained in the hotel, and suggested he clean up his own "game of chance" first.

The fight would recur over the years, however. Nellie Bly (Elizabeth Jane Cochrane, 1864–1922), Joseph Pulitzer's undaunted star journalist, came undercover to expose "the shameful story of vice and crime" that characterized Saratoga Springs. The election of Caleb "Cale" Mitchell as village president added new fuel to the reformers' efforts because Mitchell had a gambling establishment on Broadway. Mitchell was ousted in 1895 and the village secured a year without gambling until a new president was appointed in the spring of 1896. The Canfield and five other establishments—none on Broadway—were allowed to reopen.

The golden age of Saratoga Springs began with Canfield and the society his casino attracted, people like summer visitors Diamond Jim Brady (1856–1917) and Lillian Russell (1861–1922). Known for his jewelry and opulent style, Brady was a railroad equipment salesman who flaunted his millions. Although only 250 pounds in weight, Brady was also the most prodigious of Saratoga Springs epicures, consuming a dozen lobsters with steaks, crabs, oysters, and an assortment of French pastries at a single sitting. He eschewed alcohol but might drink four gallons of orange juice at a time.

After the turn of the century, Brady brought a gleaming new electric brougham, its interior bedecked with the "milky glow" of a hundred small lights. His alluring companion, Miss Russell, the nation's finest operetta singer, had taken on the pounds as well, yet the zaftig look was all the more attractive to the men in those years. Brady had given her a gold-plated bicycle with her initials emblazoned in diamonds and emeralds on the handlebars. Her Japanese spaniel had a $1,800 collar. At Canfield's, Jean Columbin served her favorite foods personally—sweet corn and crêpes Suzette.

John Philip Sousa (1854–1932) and his band led the marches every summer. Enrico Caruso (1873–1921) and (Buffalo born) Irish tenor Chauncey Olcott (1858–1932) came and sang. Victor Herbert (1859–1924) conducted a 54-piece orchestra through his repertoire of songs twice a day in the Grand Union's gardens, and lost his lucrative salary gambling every night. At the end of each season he handed the baton for the final performance to the hotel's son, Edgar Montillion ("Monty") Woolley (1888–1963), "the Beard of the Spa," son of the Grand Union owner, and stage and film star most remembered as the Kaufman-Hart comedy's obnoxious eponym, *The Man Who Came to Dinner.*

Canfield was a connoisseur of the arts and collector of rare European paintings. His library was considered one of the finest in America. He had the finest gambling establishments in Newport and New York, as well as Saratoga, but the reform movement was catching up with the fast world. Canfield saw it coming and closed his casino and restaurant when wary Saratoga officials imposed new restrictions on the trade in 1904. Canfield went to Newport for the season. He reopened again for a few years but finally left altogether as the tide of the reformists grew, selling the casino to the village itself in 1911.

The Saratoga Racing Association, meanwhile, after Waldbaum's scurrilous tenure as owner, had revived under the dignity and style brought to its presidency by Jock Whitney. One of the country's wealthiest businessmen, he was a founder of the Young Men's Democratic Club of New York and helped elect Samuel Tilden governor in 1871. He declined the Democratic nomination for governor while at Saratoga in 1891. Whitney became America's premier horse breeder. His class was unparalleled at Saratoga. For the first Saratoga Special, Whitney had $100 bets placed on behalf of all his guests, employees, and attendants—120 people—on his horse, Goldsmith, to win, which it did, paying 6-to-1. Envelopes marked with Whitney's initials were distributed that evening to all the beneficiaries. The respect he gave to those with him was returned in kind: his bookie, Johnny Walters, took Whitney's lawyers aside after his death and gave them a check to the estate for $150,000, returning a private loan only Whitney knew about.

The village was transformed every August into a carnival of characters and panoply, some of the locals making their annual income in the rentals they provided to the colorful people who came for the races. The season began the day before the track opened, when the Cavanagh Special arrived with a trainload of bookmakers, a modern phenomenon that had grown out of John Morrissey's auction pools at his Clubhouse. "Irish John" Cavanagh led a parade of six hundred or more bookies through the village to their hotels, a band and a crowd of players cheering them on. They set up stalls at a shed near the finish line at the track. A crowd of tipsters also arrived, usually down-and-out ne'er-do-wells who may have stowed away on a train to Saratoga or found their way in some other ingenious manner. They sold tips on which horse would win, not as lucrative a business as a bookie's but productive nonetheless. A good tipster might make $2,500 a season, and then lose it all on the last day on a bad tip he had received.

Bookmaking at racetracks was outlawed by Governor Charles Evans Hughes in the Agnew-Hart bill of 1908, which precipitated an abandonment of Saratoga, although the track did not have to close. The attraction of the spa and the fashion swirl that came each season kept the village and the track active, and the betting just continued in the hotel rooms instead. Finally, in August 1911 the track closed and the entire village remained dormant over the next two summers. Loopholes in the Agnew-Hart law enabled the tracks to reopen in 1913, and the gala season of Saratoga began anew. The Cavanagh Special arrived as usual with its carloads of bookies.

A series of famous horses claimed their laurels at Saratoga, starting with Roamer, a seven-year-old gelding who broke an eighteen-year record for the mile on August 21, 1918. The following August, after a bad start, Man o' War suffered his only defeat in twenty-one races in an upset win by Harry Payne Whitney's Upset at Saratoga. Man o' War's victory in the mile-and-a-quarter Travers in 1920 (beating Upset) set a record that would last until 1946.

As many as 1,500 visitors a week came to Saratoga Springs during its heyday. When changing demographics and falling economies brought about the decline in the turnout of *haut monde* visitors early in the new century, Monty Woolley simply blamed it all on too much of the wanderlust.

"Look at Jock Whitney," he proclaimed. "He's always going somewhere else."

8. Rough Rider at the Ready

This may have been the last generation of Americans who freely indulged a national taste for personal participation in the rough and tumble sport of American politics.

—H. WAYNE MORGAN, 1963

When Theodore Roosevelt, Jr., 23 years old, arrived in Albany on January 2, 1882, to take up his duties as the new assemblyman from the twenty-first district on the east side of Manhattan, he intended only to stay for the one year term to which he was elected. Politics were not savory to the Roosevelt family. His father's indulgence in it had been as a reformist at the 1876 Republican National Convention in Cincinnati and contributed to his early death at age 46 two years later. The sourness of that experience left young Theodore with a score to settle. Roscoe Conkling (1829–88), the state Republican chairman and United States senator whom TR Sr. had criticized in a stirring speech in Cincinnati, helped engineer the defeat of the elder Roosevelt's appointment as collector of customs in the port of New York. The bruising battle led to a lifelong animosity by his son toward Conkling and the man whose appointment to the customs post Conkling had engineered, Chester A. Arthur.

When the young Roosevelt came to Albany, the legislature was still meeting in the old capitol, where Lincoln had spoken. Conkling was an Albany native there in all his presence, a six-foot-three-inch "Viking" with a large square head and what reformer George William Curtis called a "Mephistophelean leer and spit." His father had been a congressman, judge, and Whig Party leader. His wife, Cornelia, was the sister of Governor Horatio Seymour. President Grant had given over the patronage of New York to Conkling, the quintessential Stalwart intent on maintaining the status quo. He considered nuisance reformers like young Roosevelt "man-milliners," which Roosevelt biographer Paul Grondahl termed "a thinly veiled allusion to homosexuals." Yet Conkling's star was already fading, thanks in part to Roosevelt Sr.'s speech—and an extramarital affair with a senator's wife that had become the talk of the town. Conkling resigned his senate seat during that controversy, convincing his colleague from New York, Thomas Collyer Platt (1833–1910), to quit as well, which proved a huge misjudgment when the state legislature failed to return them both to office.

But for now, Conkling had the pipsqueak Roosevelt with which to deal. Teedie, as TR was called within the family, was a Republican even though his uncle Robert and his father-in-law, George C. Lee, were Democrats, as were his good friend Poultney Bigelow and most of the Delano and Roosevelt cousins upriver. Teedie was certainly a family blueblood, yet the Republicanism he embraced and largely helped to define was of a new progressive variety. He was also an intellectual and an author of a highly regarded history (*The Naval War of 1812*). In Albany, he stayed for a few days at the home of a friend, William Bayard Van Rensselaer, before taking rooms with his wife Alice at Delavan House four blocks from the capitol. The politically wizened reporters who hung out at the cigar stand there recognized him as "an uncommon fellow, distinctly different."

"His teeth seemed to be all over his face," George Spinney of *The New York Times* commented. "He was genial, emphatic, earnest but green as grass." His colleagues called him "Oscar Wilde," "Punkin-Lily," and "Jane-Dandy."

That soon changed. On the night of his arrival, Roosevelt declined a carriage ride to his party caucus at the capitol and instead walked up the hill in a biting cold, wearing a top hat and coat with tails, and carrying a gold-headed cane. The most freshmen of freshmen assemblymen, he entered the caucus and immediately went to the front and sat next to the chairman. He refused to support long-time Speaker Tom Alvord of Rochester—"a bad old fellow," TR called him—and instead backed Ulster County Assemblyman General George H. Sharpe. The contest was stalled over a few weeks by eight Tammany Hall Democrats, TR receiving favorable mention in the *New York Evening Post* for his obstinacy.

Roosevelt took long walks around the city and worked out. He hired a sparring partner and did some boxing in his rooms. One day as he was passing by the buffet at Delavan, a fighter named "Stubby" Collins accosted Roosevelt —part of an initiation ritual called the Scrimmage that was inflicted on new members—and took a punch at him. Within a minute Stubby's friends were helping him from the floor, astonished at the little man's power. Roosevelt also offered to step outside when a burly Brooklyn assemblyman, John Shanley, ridiculed a speech he was giving; Shanley immediately shut up. J. J. Costello, the Tammany candidate for speaker, criticized Roosevelt for wearing a girlish outfit when TR was having a beer with two members who were friends. Roosevelt turned and dropped Costello to the floor. Then he helped the man up and bought him a beer.

When a compromise candidate for Speaker, Democrat Charles Patterson, was finally elected in February, Roosevelt used his uncle Robert's influence to secure a seat on the Cities Committee. The chairman, Michael C. Murphy, took a liking to the odd young Republican and made him acting chairman. A bill came up to add a terminal for the Manhattan Elevated Railroad, a particularly scurrilous business owned by Jay Gould. Roosevelt saw corruption in the making, but he knew that the terminal was needed and pushed for approval publicly instead of behind the scenes, as Gould wanted. Roosevelt hid a broken chair leg next to his chair when the bill came under discussion. TR pocketed the bill and declared he would report it himself. This "almost precipitated a riot" and caused Gould's men—"pretty rough characters," TR called them—to move ominously toward him. Roosevelt reached under the table for his makeshift weapon. That ended the confrontation. The bill ultimately made it through the legislature with Gould's payoffs to his friends as promised. Roosevelt was furious but could do nothing.

TR had an ace up his sleeve, though, that eventually brought the leadership to its knees: the press loved him. He was said to have a standing arrangement with the reporters to give any one of them an exclusive interview if they could beat him in a race up the seventy-two stone steps of the capitol. None of them ever tried—most of them were alcoholics anyway—and the gimmick only increased his star power with them all.

Roosevelt blew the lid off the legislature in denouncing a corrupt judge and Manhattan district attorney over another Manhattan Elevated scandal, which prompted universal applause among reformers. His friend Poultney Bigelow wrote from Harvard that his classmates "hailed him as the dawn of a new era, the man of good family once more in the political arena; the college-bred tribune superior to the temptations which beset meaner men . . . our ideal."

Roosevelt received universal applause among reformers. A few days after the end of the session the judge whom Roosevelt had accused, Theodore R.

Westbrook, was found dead in a hotel room in Troy, an apparent suicide.

Roosevelt won reelection in a landslide victory in 1882 and became the minority leader, quickly learning to temper his temper as he worked with his colleagues instead of against them. "I rose like a rocket," TR wrote of the times, as "Roosevelt Republican" became the catchword for the new brand of reformer. Roosevelt's persistent effort to maintain the higher moral ground in time distanced him from the press, however, one reporter joking that Roosevelt kept "a pulpit concealed on his person." He worked with the new Democratic governor, Grover Cleveland, to secure civil service reforms, but the session drained him physically. He decided to visit the Badlands in the Dakotas for some hunting in September to restore his spirits.

Republicans took over both houses in the following year, but Roosevelt lost in his attempt to become Speaker of the Assembly. He would have to be a reformer again after all, and did it with aplomb in pushing through a law strengthening the New York City mayoralty at the expense of the machine-backed aldermen. He also excelled in exposing city corruption as chairman of a special investigative committee. Tragedy soon intervened, however, when his wife Alice (1861-84) developed complications in the birth of their daughter, and his mother "Mittie" (1835-84) came down with typhoid fever. The train from Albany crawled through miles of fog on February 13, delaying his arrival home until midnight. He learned that both women were dying. TR first had to rush to his mother's room, where he and his brother and sisters stood by while she died at age 49. He then went upstairs and held his wife in his arms. Alice had Bright's disease (nephritis), which was not diagnosed until after her daughter's birth two days earlier. She was 22, and this was the fourth anniversary of their marriage; she died on Valentine's Day. A double funeral took place two days later, and the next day his daughter Alice Lee Roosevelt (1884–1980) was christened. The New York State Assembly adjourned in mourning for three days for their colleague.

Politics in the postbellum era was fueled by national issues expounded by the two major parties. Towns in the Hudson Valley were largely Republican, and the Democrats did well in the cities. Republicans were "the party of Lincoln," as well as the Nativist and Protestant parties. Democrats protected states' rights, personal liberties and, even in the North, white supremacy. Vassar College reflected the general drift of political sentiment in its mock elections in presidential years. The students chose Grant over Seymour in 1868, Harrison over Cleveland (twice), and McKinley over William Jennings Bryan both times. Sophomore Harriot Stanton Blatch organized the first political club at Vassar in 1876 with a call for the students to help elect Samuel Tilden to the presidency. The fledgling Democrats paraded through Main declaiming slogans behind "a vibrant comb and jewsharp corps."

Tilden (1814–86) was a New Lebanon boy, son of a local Democratic leader, one of the young Turks of the Albany Regency, and almost a mirror image of Martin Van Buren in his precocious grasp of politics at an early age. He went to New York and secured a fortune representing railroad interests as a lawyer in the antebellum period, all the while keeping his hands in city politics. He wrote most of the platform for the Free Soil Party in 1848, yet opposed granting Negroes the right to vote. His most famous Civil War act was a letter to New York *Evening Post* editor John Bigelow, his good friend (and Poultney's father), chastising America for electing Abraham Lincoln as president. This "War Democrat" manifesto came back to haunt Tilden in 1876.

Like Grover Cleveland and David B. Hill, the national reputation that Tilden acquired as governor strengthened the Democratic Party. Using his friend Republican John Bigelow to chair a special investigations commission, Tilden forced a breakup of the Canal Ring following his detailed account of the graft and corruption in a message to the legislature in 1875. More than a dozen allegations of fraud and corruption listed in the Bigelow commission's February 1876 report were sustained in subsequent court action, and all but two of those indicted were Democrats.

The state did not provide a residence for the governor when Tilden arrived, so he rented a spacious mansion a few blocks away from the capitol on Eagle Street. He brought in a French chef from Delmonico's and made such lavish and entertaining use of the home that his successor, Lucius Robinson, rented the house as well and convinced the state to purchase the estate for every governor's residence. Cleveland, the fourth occupant, still had to furnish the house out of his $10,000 salary.

While Tilden's reputation led to his nomination for president in 1876, his loss to Rutherford B. Hayes constituted a literal theft of the presidency by Republicans in the manipulation of Louisiana electoral votes. Stunned by the loss, Tilden retired to his Yonkers estate, immediately accepted as a martyr by his party and most of the nation. Yet that goodwill wasn't enough to secure the nomination in 1880, and his health failed him in 1884. He died brokenhearted in 1886.

Another prominent New York politician was on the presidential ballot in 1880, this time as the second billing. But an assassin's bullet swiftly moved him into the top job. Chester A. Arthur (1829–86), a Vermont native educated in the Hudson Valley at Union Village near Greenwich and Union College ('48), studied law at Ballston Spa before becoming principal of the Cohoes Academy in 1852. His 1854 defense of Elizabeth Jennings, a black public school teacher assaulted for refusing to leave a city rail car, led to the integration of the New York City rail system. Arthur became an acolyte of Roscoe Conkling after helping to elect Conkling to the US Senate in 1867, and was given the collectorship of the New York Customhouse by President Grant in 1871, the most important party appointment in the state. When President Rutherford B. Hayes sent Theodore Roosevelt Sr.'s name to the Senate in 1876 for the customhouse nomination, Conkling engineered Arthur's reappointment instead.

Arthur was chairman of the state Republican Party in the ensuing years, and named as James A. Garfield's running mate in 1880, mainly as a way to keep Conklin's forces in the fold. Garfield (1831–81) was assassinated six months into his presidency by "Stalwart" Charles J. Guiteau (1841–82), who said he killed Garfield so that Arthur could be president. Stunned and appalled at what the system had wrought, Arthur subsequently became a reform president, presiding over the enactment of the country's first major civil service law, the Pendleton Act, which had been prompted in part by his collectorship machinations at the Customs House. Both his earlier history and new sense of reform prevented his obtaining the 1884 nomination for president, which went to the sitting New York governor, Grover Cleveland.

The Democratic Party in New York experienced a watershed year over a Hudson Valley issue in 1890. For the first time since the Civil War, they secured enough seats in the state legislature to allow a Democrat to be elected to the United States Senate. The achievement was largely the work of Governor David Bennett Hill (1843–1910), Cleveland's lieutenant-governor who succeeded Cleveland when he was elected president and remained as governor after Cleveland lost his reelection bid in 1888. Hill, the statewide chairman, was acknowledged as the Democratic leader even by Tammany Hall. He also retained his seat as US senator from New York.

Hill directed the 1891 campaign that made the Assembly overwhelmingly Democratic, but three seats remained in contention in the state Senate that were needed to control the US Senate appointment vote. He arranged for one local board to declare a victorious candidate ineligible—upon legitimate grounds—and to void the election of another Republican candidate based on a violation of the election law. These actions survived court challenges, but in the third instance, one involving a Hudson Valley election, the maneuvering became messy and ultimately destroyed Hill's budding presidential hopes.

The election in the 15th senate district (Putnam-Dutchess-Columbia counties) seemed to show that Gilbert A. Deane, the Republican candidate, had won by 137 votes over his Democratic challenger, Edward B. Osborne. Deane's victory was not challenged in Putnam or Columbia, but in Dutchess the canvassing board declared a large number of Deane ballots improperly marked, giving Osborne an overall 49-vote victory margin. The Republican county clerk would not certify these returns, so he was promptly fired. The new clerk, John J. Mylod, sent his signed returns off to the state board of canvassers, whom Hill ordered to convene two weeks earlier than usual so that the Republicans would not have enough time to secure a court order. The strategy was not successful; the returns from all three contested districts were restrained and the matter thrown into the Court of Appeals. After Gilbert Deane unexpectedly died, the court issued a decision that forbade the state board of canvassers from acting on the Mylod returns. This order was ignored, however, on the grounds that these were the only returns in the state's possession, and Edward Osborne was declared the winner. This "high-handed" action, apparently taken at Hill's insistence, became known as the "Steal of the Senate" and was seen nationally as an example of political gimmickry gone awry. David B. Hill was denied the 1892 Democratic Party nomination for president as a result.

The Democrats' demise came hand-in-hand with an economic collapse that affected the urban poor badly with a loss of jobs. Tammany Hall and state legislature corruption so disgusted the better interests in New York City that a reform Committee of Fifty, formed in 1893, succeeded in electing a Republican mayor under the Honest Election Party in the following year. In Troy, "honest elections" was the rallying cry for a new Committee of Public Safety. A Committee of Fifty arose in Albany, a Good Government Club in Yonkers, a Municipal League in Schenectady and a Citizens' League in New Rochelle. After Republicans swept the state in legislative elections that year, the Senate instituted an investigation into "Murphyism" in Troy, the practice of buying votes named after the new Tammany Hall leader.

As a result of their legislative victory, Republicans in 1894 controlled the delegate count for the first state constitutional convention to convene since 1867. Elihu Root, chair of the judiciary committee in the Senate, led the historic convention, which established rules for the conduct of the legislature that remained in place more than a hundred years later. A new apportionment plan increased the number of senators from 32 to 50, and the assemblymen from 128 to 150. Bills before the legislature would now be required to "age" three days on the members' desks—presumably so they could read them—unless the governor issued an emergency request that waived the aging mandate. Riders on appropriation bills were prohibited, cities placed in separate classes, the governor's term reduced from three years to two, and the pattern of holding important state and local elections in the same years abandoned.

Former Vice President Levi P. Morton came on as governor in 1894 after receiving assurances from Platt that he could spend his summers at his Rhinebeck estate and not be overly troubled with the business of governance. He already had a national reputation—as Minister to France, Morton accepted the Statue of Liberty in 1884. He wanted to be president and trusted in Tom Platt to get him there. When the nomination went to McKinley in 1896, Morton proposed new civil service reforms that he knew would be popular even though they went against Platt's wishes. Morton also signed New York's first "Australian-style" ballot law, a secret ballot with the candidate names listed with party affiliation that continues in use today.

Republicans shored up their power during this period even as they worked with independents and reformers. Platt instituted a new way to collect campaign funds from corporations, even convincing Teddy Roosevelt that soliciting this way was an "honorable obligation" in which the politicians return the favors by defending big business interests. The practice was not unknown prior to these years, but now it became so successful that it led to payoffs for individual legislators. The system, if not always the chicanery, remains essentially the same in political thinking today.

Local concerns did not always dominate the debate in Albany. The era of American colonialism began after her swift victory over the Spanish at the end of that decade. More than 125,000 volunteers signed on from New York and were spread over a dozen infantry regiment camps like the Camp of

Instruction at Peekskill, where Brigadier-General Peter C. Doyle was in command. TR, who had joined the McKinley administration as Assistant Secretary of the Navy, resigned his post and joined the 1ˢᵗ US Cavalry regiment on Long Island, commanding eight companies collectively known to history as the Rough Riders. They saw their first action at Las Guésimas, the first casualty being Sergeant Hamilton Fish, grandson of the former governor. The Spanish surrender of the city of Santiago was assured when the Rough Riders took San Juan Hill. Twenty-two men under his command were awarded the Congressional Medal of Honor, but not TR, in many ways the most valiant of them all, who spent the remainder of his life trying to secure the award from Congress.

One of the men with Roosevelt on that fateful charge was Jesse Langdon (1881–1975), seventeen at the time he hopped freight trains across America to join Roosevelt's cavalry in Washington. When he found the leader on the steps of the Navy Department building, Roosevelt asked just one question, "Can you ride a horse?" Langdon told him he could "ride anything with hair." He was a tall, large-boned man and extremely strong even in his eighties, one of the fourteen Rough Riders who toured with Buffalo Bill Cody's Wild West Show after the war. In later life, he held several patents and had the distinction of inventing a noiseless toilet known as the "silent john." Langdon settled into retirement in LaFayetteville, left land in a trust that became an attractive county park, and died at the age of ninety-four, the last of the Rough Riders.

Theodore Roosevelt's return to the Albany stage occurred in typically grandiose fashion. His heroics in leading the Rough Riders made him a national hero. After the deaths of his wife and mother, he had retired to the Badlands as a rancher for a number of years, and returned to public service after running unsuccessfully for mayor of New York. He became a crusading reform New York City police commissioner, a hard-nosed federal civil service commissioner, and a prescient assistant secretary of the US Navy. The author of *The Naval War of 1812* was, more than anyone else in America, largely responsible for the country's naval build-up in response to the militarism emerging in Europe in the 1890s.

Just two months after mustering out of the service, Roosevelt was induced to run for governor of New York by now state Republican Party chairman Thomas C. Platt, whose hand-picked governor, Frank S. Black (1853–1913), had become mired in scandal. Black was a Platt confidante and Troy editor and lawyer whose administration was hammered by a special investigation into canal improvements that showed more than a million dollars in "improper expenditures" for an over-budgeted project that the public already generally believed was a boondoggle. In accepting the Republican endorsement, Roosevelt made it clear that his own conscience would be his guide on decisions.

He rejected an endorsement by John Jay Chapman on behalf of the reform-minded Independent Party, and when the Independents criticized TR for going with the Republicans the candidate shot back in kind, claiming Chapman stood "on the lunatic fringe," a turn of phrase that Roosevelt would use again in defending himself against what he called the "Goo-Goos" of the Good Government Club movement. The exchange sorely damaged his friendship with Chapman, a fellow Harvard alumni and brother-in-law of TR's good friends Willie and Wintie Chanler; he did not speak to Roosevelt for twenty years thereafter.

Roosevelt survived a campaign slur by Louis F. Payn (1835–1923), a friend of Black's and corrupt Democrat from Columbia County who claimed that Roosevelt did not have a legitimate residence in New York State because he had lived in Washington for the previous ten years. TR ran a frenetic campaign focused on the evils of Tammany Hall, making 102 speeches in one six-day stretch in late October. Yet he barely won, Republicans in general being heavily tainted by the canal scandal. He defeated Augustus Van Wyck (1850–1922) by fewer than 18,000 votes out of 1.3 million cast. Roosevelt saw in it a victory over "the most corrupt" Republicans as well as "the silly 'Goo-Goos'" and Tammany Hall.

Roosevelt took office in Albany on December 31, stayed out late in celebrating, and had to break a window to get into the Executive Mansion on Eagle Street. Six thousand people greeted the Roosevelts for his inauguration on January 2. The mansion, by now an institution in Albany, had been greatly expanded in Grover Cleveland's first year, the year that TR began as an assemblyman. The renovations were completed under Governor Hill using State Capitol plans and workmen, and included an array of Victorian gewgaws— gables, turrets, balconies, dormers, overhangs—that the *New Yorker* dubbed "Hudson River helter-skelter." The family considered the home, as TR's daughter Alice put it, "a big, ugly, rather shabby house, . . . hideously furnished"—which her stepmother, Edith, quickly changed. The basement

became a menagerie for the animals—both the children's and the president's—
an eagle and a bear cub among the denizens of the mansion depths.

Roosevelt's second wife Edith created a schoolroom in a downstairs wing
and hired a governess for the younger children. Sons Ted and Kermit attended
Albany Academy across from the capitol, their father insisting that they walk
the five blocks to school each morning. Alice, TR's daughter from his first
marriage, now in her adolescence, disliked Albany. She longed to be back in
New York and became, as Paul Grondahl stated, "a self-taught scholar, roaming
the family's extensive library," required only to report to her father at breakfast
each morning something new that she had learned in her readings the day
before.

Extending women's suffrage and creating "forever wild" forest preserves
in the Adirondacks and Catskills were among the lengthy list of promises and
programs that Roosevelt articulated in his inaugural speech. He accepted Boss
Platt's power over appointments—a concession that his earlier self never would
have accepted—and went after Richard Croker and the Tammany machine
with relish. He recognized the threat of "industrial monopoly" rising with the
growth and merger of corporations and their influence on politics and the
courts, and overcame his first major clash with the Republican boss—as well
as his friend Elihu Root, a lobbyist for the industry—in forcing through the
approval of the first franchise tax on the corporations. This was Roosevelt's
most significant finance legislation as governor of New York.

He appointed a bipartisan commission and two prominent Democratic
lawyers to address the canal scandal. He ordered an investigation into the pollution of the Kayaderosseras Creek at Saratoga Lake and required property
owners and the villages of Ballston Spa and Saratoga Springs to end the
discharging of sewage, threatening jail time for village trustees if they did not
comply. The governor followed the Saratoga action with a 1900 mandate to
the city of Rensselaer to provide clean drinking water for its residents. He was
a friend of the farmer, the factory worker, the state employee, and the tenement
denizen. Jacob Riis, a Democrat and intimate of Roosevelt's who often came
calling, "grew to be quite fond of the queer old Dutch city on the Hudson,"
arriving by train in the late afternoons, spending a few hours in conversation
with his friend, and returning on the midnight train to New York. Riis later
credited Roosevelt with initiating a change of viewpoint in the legislature.

Although Roosevelt advocated women's suffrage, he faced a difficult moment in deciding whether to commute a sentence involving a Brooklyn "murderess," Martha Place, who was facing the death penalty at Sing Sing prison. Although it was eleven years since the authorizing law was enacted, this was to be the first case of "electric execution" of a woman in New York history, and it was covered by the national press. The governor refused to make an exception for a woman and allowed the execution to proceed.

To Theodore Roosevelt belonged the honor of applying the cure for "an affliction from which time affords but little hope of relief," as Governor Black stated in 1897—the ongoing construction of the State Capitol. The work had begun auspiciously in 1865 with the hiring of Thomas Fuller, the designer of Canada's Parliament, but a decade later he was replaced by Leopold Eidlitz and Henry Hobson Richardson, who stayed with Fuller's layout for the interior but applied their own designs to the architecture. They were replaced by Isaac Gale Perry, who substantially finished the building in 1899, except for the tower. Frederick Law Olmsted designed the grounds.

The massive building was a combination of French and Italian Renaissance and Richardson's unique Romanesque Gothic, a "battle of styles" made of gray granite. Most of the stone was cut to fit at the quarry in an old plug-and-feather style; transported by boat from Maine, unloaded by hand and steam winches, and carted by horse and wagon up the steep hill to the site. The building rose five stories high, the walls more than sixteen feet thick at the base, the whole structure measuring 400 by 300 feet; its weight was undetermined. The $25 million price tag would have been calculated at more than $500,000 million in Nelson Rockefeller's time.

The Senate Chamber had a ceiling of golden oak and walls with deep cut panels covered in 23-carat gold leaf. Marble was imported from Siena, Italy, for the arches; red granite from Scotland for the pillars, and Mexican onyx for the walls. Two fireplaces six feet tall became convenient meeting places for the senators after central heating was installed, until they figured out that the acoustics carried their voices throughout the room. Portraits of the five architects adorned the five entrances to the room.

The Executive Chamber, called the "Red Room" for the drapes and rug, served as the governor's office until 1885, when it became used only for ceremonial purpose. The Assembly Chamber, the largest room in the building, rose 56 feet above the floor in painted sandstone highlighted with gold leaf trim. As the building settled over time, the stone ceiling started to crack and, after a seven-pound chunk of stone landed next to a senator who was visiting one day, had to be rebuilt. The murals were hidden in the construction of a new wooden ceiling twenty feet below the original. The contractor at the time substituted *papier-maché* for the mahogany beams ordered, causing a huge scandal when discovered.

A famous feature was the Great Western or "Million Dollar" staircase, made of freestone, limestone, granite, and a "corsehill" sandstone imported from Scotland. The structure contains seventy-seven portraits carved in stone, mostly of famous people like Henry Hudson, Abraham Lincoln, and Andrew Jackson, but also including faces of the masons themselves after the list of the famous was exhausted. The third floor landing of the Great Western, which accessed the Assembly Chamber from the rear, became a favored gathering spot for lobbyists awaiting action on their bills in the wee hours of the closing days of the annual sessions a century later. Two smaller but similarly massive stairs occupied the eastern side of the capitol.

TR finished the State Capitol project by the simple gesture of declaring it done, even though a tower dome planned as a central "landmark of the capital city" was not even begun (and was never built). New York became one of the few capitals in the country without a tower. Roosevelt, the twelfth to have occupied the chair since construction began in 1875, was the first governor to work in the building in an atmosphere of peace and quiet.

The death of US Vice President Garret A. Hobart on November 21, 1899, revived Henry Cabot Lodge's feeling that his friend, Roosevelt, should become William McKinley's vice president. The idea was taken up by Boss Platt when he and Roosevelt clashed over the governor's intention to remove Lou Payn as insurance superintendent over a scandal involving a $435,000 "loan" that Payn had received. Roosevelt won the argument—on January 22 Platt capitulated and Payn was replaced—confiding in memorable fashion to an old Assembly friend, Henry L. Sprague, his fondness for a West African proverb:

"Speak softly and carry a big stick; you will go far."

The victory increased the pressure on Roosevelt to accept the vice presidency. Now the insurance industry fell in line with the franchised corporations as a powerful lobby against his work as governor.

"I am expecting to have a good time," Edith Roosevelt told Judge Alton Parker of Esopus over dinner in Albany a few days before leaving for the

Republican National Convention in Philadelphia. Parker predicted that she would arrive "just a bit late" to see TR enter the auditorium and "bedlam" break loose—followed by his swift nomination as McKinley's running mate.

"You disagreeable thing," she purred, once more affirming her husband's lack of interest in the job. Yet the crowd of 18,000 burst into joy when that name was placed in nomination, and Edith looked directly across the auditorium to her husband. He was sitting among the New York delegation, looking only at her. Edith smiled. Years later, TR handily defeated Parker himself in his reelection bid, carrying New York State by 859,533 votes to 683,981.

Roosevelt's campaign manager in 1898 and successor as governor, Benjamin B. O'Dell, Jr. (1854–1926), was a successful Newburgh ice dealer with interests in transportation and utilities. He had served two terms representing Orange, Rockland, and Sullivan counties in Congress. O'Dell was 46 in 1900. He continued to strengthen Republican ties with independents while cooperating with Mayor Seth Low in instituting reforms in New York City. O'Dell repealed a state tax on real estate and introduced a new corporation-based tax structure. He undertook administrative reforms, and generally surpassed his predecessor's record as governor, drawing upon Roosevelt initiatives in doing so. Theodore Roosevelt publicly applauded what his successor did, yet privately ruminated on O'Dell's criticisms of earlier TR proposals, "when Paul was still Saul a year ago," that the new governor now embraced. The president could not take on O'Dell publicly in 1904 because the governor was also party chairman and TR needed New York to win the election.

The new governor was of a breed of progressive Republican politicians, like the new Westchester County Republican boss, William Lukens Ward (1856–1933), who were not above forging ties with Democrats in their time. O'Dell served two terms and returned to public service as the state's ice administrator during World War I. He was perhaps the first modern governor of New York, in the changes he made to the tax structure, shifting much of the burden to business and industry, and the efficiencies he created in government spending. His reorganization of taxes, which he did without bashing corporate money the way reformists, independents and "trustbusters" wanted, constituted a new way of raising significant revenues. Corporations had been paying taxes since 1881, and 4,401 of them contributed $2.1 million in 1896, but the burden still remained on property taxes until O'Dell instituted his changes. The state, to its discredit, still continued with this easy-out solution as the basis for local financing of school districts, which had no choice but to comply; the old eighteenth-century style of quitrent financing simply would not die.

O'Dell had a gruff personality and was not a particularly compelling speaker like Roosevelt, yet he was a thorough party man and every Republican knew it. The party's history since 1896 had shown that going along with reformist thinking was the best way to get along in full control of the government—and the patronage for Thomas Platt as the titular party leader. There was nothing cynical about O'Dell's approach; he won the case on the merits by couching the proposals in a traditional Republican "economy" rhetoric. The corporations, albeit grudgingly, supported the tax changes because Platt's philosophy of supporting the party's financial supporters remained intact. Support was the new mantra in transitional New York State.

O'Dell's initiatives—restructuring taxes and modernizing government— were proposals put forth in the governor's first annual message, and almost immediately enacted into law. They added a popular new moral twist in his new corporate tax structure by financing state government with, as one upstate senator put it, "the wealth of the millionaire who never in his lifetime has paid a tax." The savings to localities were appropriately trumpeted by the towns, increasing O'Dell's popularity. In 1901, the governor went after excesses in corporate privilege by embarrassing the legislature into repealing the charter of the Ramapo Water Company, a thinly veiled raid on New York City's need for water that benefited a few leading Republicans in particular. O'Dell's moves against the railroad were not so successful, but the seeds of change against "grabs" by nefarious characters in industry and business were planted. The changes in government administration led, over the next ten years, to "new and vast undertakings" (according to Comptroller William Sohmer in 1913) in increased spending for education (400%) and highways and public works (470%), a decade when the state's population increased by 25%. By 1912, 23,317 corporations were contributing $10,349,164 toward the financing of a $54 million state government budget.

Benjamin O'Dell cut state spending overall considerably while governor of New York—drawing the support of local municipalities that had struggled with costs for years—but he lacked the power to thoroughly revise how the taxpayers' monies were spent. There was no state budget in those years, no executive controls over spending, merely appropriations made by self-serving legislators for a myriad group of state departments, public institutions like hospitals and schools, and independent agencies. O'Dell tried to compensate for this anomaly in executive administration by publicizing annual appropriations each spring.

The advances were limited to state government. In his 1909 annual report, Comptroller Martin H. Glynn cited "great laxity" in local government administration, particularly villages, and cited $66,000 paid to Westchester County clerks as illegal collections. Albany, Glynn reported, kept $300,000 in taxes and bids in tax sales that the county never paid. The creation of an annual state budget by the comptroller—a reform that Governor Charles Evans Hughes brought to the table—began during the brief eleven months of service by Comptroller (and former Albany mayor) Charles H. Gaus (1840–1909). The budget had previously been a hodgepodge legislative package, and the new system was imperfect because the same office had the task of auditing the budget that it created. Governor Charles Whitman (1868–1947) made the first of the executive's budgets over 1915–18. The comptroller's office remained the conscience of the state during William Sohmer's term; his sweeping recommendations were not adopted but were later incorporated into state finances in the state constitutional changes under Governor Alfred Smith, whose new age analytical thinking finally ushered in the improvements that Benjamin O'Dell's actions initiated.

The spirit of reform that characterized New York State governance in these years sprang as much from the personality of Theodore Roosevelt as from his policies and those of his successors. Cleveland, Tilden and Hill each became nationally prominent as a result of their labors as governor, yet each were restricted in the parochial themes of their tenures, and although Cleveland attained the Presidency he lacked the political support to capitalize on the times. Samuel Tilden's better days—apart from the exposure of the Canal Ring—had centered on his Free Soil Party and down-rent days while an attorney and aide to the legislature before the Civil War, and David Hill self-destructed in his own thirst for power. Frank Black was stymied by the "affliction" of the unfinished state capitol and his own partisan influences. Benjamin O'Dell had the political agility to maneuver a traditionally stalwart governing party into action, using TR as his springboard, and Charles Evans Hughes came along as a true reformer, an outsider really whose accomplishments transcended party loyalties. TR was the true original of the age, a force unto himself who forged new paths of progress on both the state and national levels. He brought New York, as he brought the nation, into modern times.

9. The Grand Parade

> Yet out of this chaos of dreams a new order of things has arisen. This new order is presided over by the genius of Useful Labor. Henceforth Useful Labor, guided by Science, by Art, by Inventive Genius, rules the world.
>
> —NATHANIEL BARTLETT SYLVESTER (1877)

A new century—such promise! And a new dress to adorn that promise, the sturdy new mercantile buildings sporting grand facades of French, Italian, and English influences, their stores brimming with wares and merchandise, the supplies and services fed through sidewalk manholes cut into bluestone, the goods appearing on the counters as if by magic. A sturdy and organized infrastructure to fit the times: streets, cobble-stoned and bricked; the vernacular framed homes of the mill laborers; the fine houses of captains of industry arrayed on the bluffs; the hanging valleys of the Hudson's tributary streams powering the industries and accessories of a new century—a new time. An opera house in every town! So many saloons and cigar makers, candy vendors, milliners, merchants: the streets busy with laborers, shoppers, mothers and children, policemen, politicians, visiting businessmen (some plying wares), all mingled in the life of the Hudson River Valley. The domestic scene tailored to fit the tastes of the times—ready-made clothes for men, the fire-hazard crinoline gone, and women making their own dresses from the tissue-paper patterns produced by Mme. Demorest's Emporium of Fashion in New York City, a Saratoga woman's breakthrough in technology that employed 10,000 women in mass production.

One of the first department stores in the nation, Whitney's, opened on Albany's North Pearl Street in 1859. Owner William Minot Whitney had a wheelbarrow delivery system and installed the first electric lights, elevators, and telephones in a retail enterprise. Horse cars on rails arrived a few years later, in 1863 and 1866, and the novel appearance of a velocipede in 1869. A telephone "exchange" with a hundred members was established in 1878, and the first pay phones went into service on February 2, 1889. The new look spread to the other large communities as well, heralding the new era.

The rise of the mercantile block in the 1880s and 90s, like the department store, emerged in the institutional changes that were transforming society after the Civil War. These were the new revolutions, more spectacular than steam, canal, and rail, driven by the dynamo of progress. To be sure, the Hudson Valley still had its share of sleepy backwaters, places where, as Edith Wharton writes in *Hudson River Bracketed* (1929), "enterprise of every sort had passed by, as if all of its inhabitants had slept through the whole period of industrial development"—its Rip Van Winkle core. Yet even in these cobwebbed corners, the modern was emerging. George M. Cohan (1878–1942), a nine-year-old "Boy Violinist" performing with his family at the local skating rink in Haverstraw in February of 1887, by the end of this period was the "Yankee Doodle Dandy" of a newly remade America and its new form of entertainment: vaudeville.

The times ushered in an expansive economy for an expansive people. The contractions of the 1870s and 1890s were forgotten in the new enthusiasm based on a manifest destiny of exuberance rather than space. The West was gone, but new frontiers were opening all around, even some opportunities arising from the ashes of the past. Glens Falls experienced bad fires in 1864 and again in the spring of 1902, losing 60 stores and 112 buildings in 1864 and 14 buildings in 1902, including the Webb Brothers clothing store (where the fire began) and Joseph Fowler's Shirt and Collar Company, putting 800 employees out of work. Yet within a few years the community rebounded on the backbone of the paper making industries that processed the forests of the Adirondacks.

The connecting link remained the Hudson River, despite the incursions of the railroad on commerce and commuter travel. Sloop and schooner activities disappeared as various forms of steam-driven craft delivered products to the inland communities, hauled their farm goods and other products of the interior in towlines of barges, ferried friends and businessmen between the small ports, and provided ice for the fashionable restaurants in New York City and elsewhere. Magnificent steamboats delivered tourists and everyday travelers and offered excursions from the interior ports. The *Mary Powell* remained in service until 1917. *Sunnyside* and *Sleepy Hollow* were day-boats built in 1866 and converted to night boats in 1870. The *Sunnyside* sank through the ice on December 1, 1875, killing eleven, but more often the captains were able to maneuver through the early ice, the crew throwing Christmas trees on either side to find the thinner ice en route downstream. The steamer *Berkshire* (formerly the *Princeton*) appeared in 1912, at 440 feet the largest river steamer ever built; she could carry 2,493 passengers or 200 autos on the Hudson River line. The excursion boat business thrived in the first few decades of the twentieth century, when the most popular destination was Bear Mountain. These liners continued to ferry passengers to the city into the late 1950s. The 165-year history of sidewheelers on the Hudson ended on Labor Day in 1971, when the *Alexander Hamilton* under Edward Grady was retired from service.

Southern Westchester experienced its first great population expansion during this time. Henry H. B. Angell and his son Stephen began buying Scarsdale lands in 1892, when the town's population was only six hundred. In the same year, Robert Emmet Farley "launched" the ambitious Philipse Manor development in North Tarrytown; his wife was the Hazard Powder fortune heiress. Parkhill in Yonkers and the attractive Pleasantville homes arose in the 1890s. Lawrence E. Vanetten (b. 1865), a Kingston native, became a major park and subdivision developer after settling into New Rochelle as a civil engineer in 1891. His mathematical ingenuity enabled him to design several large attractive residential parks—in Scarsdale, Mamaroneck, Larchmont, Port Chester, Rye, Greenwich, and elsewhere—as lower Westchester lost its rural character and became a tasteful "evolving suburb" in these years. Vanetten contributed at least six important residential parks in New Rochelle, and was responsible for sixty-five in all, ranging from fifteen to 460 acres, over 1900–30. An accomplished athlete and varsity baseball star at Princeton University, he took up golf in 1891 and went on to design several major Westchester courses, including Wykagyl in New Rochelle. He also saved Thomas Paine's New Rochelle house from demolition by having it removed to a new setting in Broadview—one of his park designs—and helping the Huguenot Society to purchase the land. His wife, Elizabeth Barnard Schoonmaker (d. 1943), was a city conservation leader and the founder of the Woman's Club of New Rochelle.

The population growth in these times created new cities—Mount Vernon (1892) Watervliet (1896), Rensselaer (1897), New Rochelle (1899), Greater New York City itself (1898). Eighteen villages were incorporated over

1885–90, and nine more over 1900–17, including Glens Falls (1909), Beacon (1913), Saratoga Springs and Mechanicville (1914). Troy was enlarged by annexation in 1901.

America's "go-ahead spirit" would not be denied even though the destiny of an unbroken continent had been achieved, and like many regions in these new economic times the Hudson Valley was bound on the yellow brick road to good fortune—almost literally in Peekskill's case. The pretty little village with a population of 12,000 in 1909 boasted twelve miles of trolley lines, gas and electricity power throughout, two telephone companies, and business streets all recently paved in yellow brick. Downriver in Hastings-on-Hudson, just 21 miles from Grand Central Station by rail, "a high class residential suburban district" was growing in response to the popularity of the automobile. The Hastings rail station provided easy access to Irvington, Tarrytown and White Plains, and, via scenic Ardsley Avenue, to Scarsdale.

Archibald N. Dedrick introduced the automobile to Albany on December 26, 1899. The Lutheran pastor at Smiths Landing, named Kempner, brought the first Stanley Steamer to that hamlet across from Germantown. The first auto in upper Westchester County was driven by local businessman Harry Barbey. Christina Rainsford, a poet from Katonah in later life, rode in the vehicle when a child, and called it "the panting machine." "Auto-stages" were begun between Newburgh and New York by George E. Davis and Sons in 1916. Historian Alex Shoumatoff assigned the arbitrary year 1914 as "the birthdate of most of the current woods in Westchester" because the automobile was by then displacing the horse, which thrived best in a landscape uncluttered by trees.

The city of Hudson was typical of the new look to the riverfront communities when Henry James and Edith Wharton came "motoring" in 1905. The city announced that year that it had been "merely dozing," was no longer the "finished city" of earlier disrepute, and was experiencing "an awakening, a spurring" forward into the new era. The community had already had its first tragedy in the new climate, a trolley accident in 1902 that killed two children. Ninety commercial enterprises were underway in Hudson by this time, more than half begun after the 1880s and many just within the previous five years. A recession later in the decade doomed some of these, most regrettably in the closing of the local cement works and loss of 300 jobs in 1908, but the arrival of the Atlas Cement Company in 1910 and the Knickerbocker Cement

Company in 1911, which would employ 1,200 workers, changed everything again.

Edith Wharton was already modern, and particularly smitten with the new automobile technology—especially after the rear-view mirror was invented. She took frequent forays by auto from her home in Lenox, Massachusetts. Henry James used the occasion of their drive to record impressions for *The American Scene* (1907). His cultured learning and well-bred New England sense sniffed haughtily at the "zones of other manners" he found in crossing into Columbia County. He was distressed that the eponymous city had no views of the river. He and Wharton, if not their French poodle, were flabbergasted by the animal's rejection at one of the city's fine hotels at dinner time (probably the General Worth); instead, they "found dinner at a cook shop" whose hospitality James praised.

A local commentator, Anna R. Bradbury, out-disdained the grand disdainer's dismissal of her fair city, saying that his attitude only displayed "the smallness of the great Analyst." James's opinion of the "queer old complexion" of Hudson was at least sympathetic toward a "fumbling friendly hand" he found in the layout of the city streets. The visit also revived for Henry James "in the stir of the senses, a whole range of small forgotten things . . . intensely Hudsonian, more than Hudsonian," including a memory from childhood of "a mellow, medieval Albany" and the Rhinebeck estate where he spent time as a boy. His friend Edith's fancy new car made this trip down memory lane possible.

Local interest in producing automobiles developed early. The first Chevrolet brothers car was "launched" in Bronxville. The Walker Locomobile plant in North Tarrytown, designed by none other than Stanford White, was making cars in 1900; by 1914, the plant was purchased by Chevrolet and continued in various manifestations throughout the century. Plans to manufacture five hundred Vaughan Car Company autos to be sold at $2,500 each, instead of the expensive $5,000 models then on the market, were underway in Hudson by the spring of 1913. The operation initially employed twenty-six, but the workforce grew to more than fifty that year. Kingston, Albany, and a few other communities also planned to try the new technology. A Briarcliff Trophy Race in 1908 drew hundreds of spectators for a 300-mile ramble through the dirt roads of northern Westchester.

Although most of America—27 million visitors—had their first exposure to the new miracle of electricity at the Columbia Exposition in Chicago in 1893, the Hudson Valley hosted early electric stations. An 1884 plant that served the city of Newburgh was operated by the Edison Electric Company. Albany had electric lighting in 1888. The Dover Plains Electric Light and Power Company was formed in 1895 by Charles P. Morgan and Charles S. Wyman, with a mill on Ten Mile River and eight customers. The service soon expanded to Wingdale and Wassaic.

Dover Plains was one of the progressive Harlem Valley towns, drawing upon the camping, resort, and tourism trade as well as local industries. Its 1909 high school consolidated sixteen local one-room schoolhouses. A working farm for state prisoners was modified in 1912 to create a mental health institution. The Harlem Valley State Hospital opened in April of 1924 with thirty-two patients; the population would grow to more than 5,000 by World War II. The Dover Stone Church, a geological formation with the appearance of a Gothic arch, attracted visitors in such numbers that historian Benson Lossing created a pamphlet about it in 1876; art historian Kerry Dean Carso has argued that the formation "conferred legitimacy on the American landscape," as if its "medieval" look transcended the European sense of antiquity.

The village of Pawling emerged from the original hamlet of Gorestown with the arrival of the new railroad station in 1849. The population shifted from Hurd's Corners as the area grew. John B. Dutcher (b. 1830) operated Dutcher House across from the railroad, a hotel that also served as an opera, post office, public hall, reading room, and, in 1907, home to the Pawling School for Boys. He became the village's first mayor in 1893. He and Albert Akin (1803–1903) brought a cultural presence to the town after attracting the railroad. Akin organized the Pawling National Bank and served as its president until he was 95. He contributed Akin Hall and Akin Library on Quaker Hill; the library included a fascinating museum of natural history. Akin built the Mizzentop Hotel nearby, the nautical name contributed by his friend, *Monitor* commander Admiral John L. Worden. Another notable Mizzentop guest was Lew Wallace (1827–1905), who wrote part of *Ben-Hur* at the hotel.

Other towns were also changing with the times. Venerable old Dean House on Broadway and Main in Tarrytown had served generations for the one-horse mail rig that came thrice weekly through town and dumped the letters and cards in a large bin that everyone sorted through to get their own mail (and read the doings of others). In 1900, Dean House was transformed into the Far and Near Tea Room by a Mrs. Lowe, who also had an antiques annex.

Gentrification tended to support small, often women-run spin-off industries that served generational needs for a few years and then were gone—torn down like Dean House was in 1912, or otherwise reinvented into the passing scene.

The communities were rural in nature, yet possessed the same national feel. Alfred Beveridge's estimate of "America's destiny" as a world power when the United States claimed the Philippines in 1900 was presaged in the sentiments expressed three years earlier by Hamilton W. Mabie at the 200th anniversary of the Old Dutch Church at Sleepy Hollow. Americans, Mabie proclaimed, were "an imperishable race, to which, in its entirety, are committed the doing of God's work." Speaking on the same occasion was Theodore Roosevelt, who embraced Catholics and other undesirables of the past as fellow Americans.

The Diocese of New York (which included Manhattan) had 132 Catholic schools by 1908, and more than 65,000 students. The core of the 1,400 teachers included Christian Brothers, Marist Brothers, and the Brothers of Mary among men, and women of the Sisters of Charity, Sisters of St. Agnes and St. Dominic, the Sisters of St. Francis, Ursuline Order, and the Felician Sisters. Thirty new schools had been raised in the previous twenty years, most of them for the children of Italian and Irish immigrants. St. Angela's College and Mount St. Vincent were founded for women. Fordham College, established as a seminary (St. John's College) on Rose Hill in 1840, removed the Jesuit school to Troy in later years. St. Joseph's Seminary, which trained Catholic priests, was built at Dunwoodie in Yonkers.

The era of the trolleys touched many Hudson Valley communities, the lines often taking over old plank road or turnpike rights-of-way and extending into the rural areas as more accessible substitutes for railroads. Trolleys were the quick and cheap way to get around the Valley, especially for entertainment. Excursions between Hudson and Albany carried thousands to the Electric Park amusement area at Kinderhook by the turn of the century. Rondout-Kingston had a horse railroad by 1866, replaced by an electric line in 1893. The trolley brought passengers to the river dock for the Rhinecliff ferry (the *Lark*) or steamers going down the river. The steamboat was also affordable; by 1881, with a round-trip ticket on the *Mary Powell*, an uptown Kingston resident could go to New York and back for $1.10.

The trolley from the Wallkill River at New Paltz to the ferry slip at Highland began with the purchase of the New Paltz Turnpike Company by Burhan

VanSteenburgh, a spirited New Paltz public servant who also had his fingers in the water works, the sewer line, and electric lights of the town. The trolley drew tourists to Mohonk and Lake Minnewaska and became tied with the Walker Valley Railroad. The nine-mile ride to the river on the *Minnewaska* took 45 minutes and could accommodate 75 travelers. In the first year of operation, as many as 3,000 people might ride into New Paltz on a fair Sunday.

One express car ran nonstop to Poughkeepsie every day—the trolley line was laid across the railroad bridge to the city—and special cars for the theater were added, with the theater tickets sold as part of the fare. Poughkeepsie students used the trolley to attend the New Paltz Normal School, at a discounted rate of 25 cents round-trip. The "Ohioville," a small electric car winterized with the addition of a stove, was added in December 1897. A new car with a plow capable of clearing five feet of snow from the line in winter was constructed by the company at its powerhouse in Centerville. Despite its successes, the line was sold in receivership in 1899 and became the New Paltz and Poughkeepsie Traction Company. In 2010, a portion of the line was transformed by Charles Merritt's construction company into a rail trail leading to the hugely popular Walkway over the Hudson.

Westchester County proliferated with electric lines as New York Central's ambitious electrification program stimulated growth. The Central's switch from steam to electric power in lower Westchester saved the company $1 million in annual upkeep and maintenance. The New Haven Central was already fully electrified, with a line running from Grand Central 53 miles across Westchester to Stamford, Connecticut. An extension of the New Haven called the Harlem Division was underway, six lines running from Port Morris to accommodate freight and passenger services, and another extension through West Farms to White Plains. A New York Connecting Railroad Bridge was completed by 1908.

The trolley extended 54 miles to Brewster by that year, passing through almost thirty small communities soon lost in the expansion of suburbia—Dunwoodie, Nepperhan, Grey Oaks, Woodlands, East View, and on to Crafts, Tilly Forster Mines, and finally to the far-flung community of Brewster. The electric lines of the Hudson River Division coursed from Highbridge, Morris Heights, and University to Harmon and Croton-on-Hudson, where the steam lines north through the Valley awaited. Real estate prices from New Rochelle to Stamford were rising dramatically. Only about 10 percent of the forty miles of shoreline along Long Island Sound in the Hudson Valley remained available for development, the rest having been bought up by New York financiers and socialites for country homes.

All this development led to opportunities for the inhabitants of the region. Twenty percent of Hudson Valley women over the age of fifteen were gainfully employed in 1900. The birth rate among upper middle class women was falling so rapidly Theodore Roosevelt worried about "race suicide." As material choices increased, so did the scope of creeds and beliefs, and trends in science, law, the arts, and philosophy. Henry George (1839–97) came to America in 1880, asking the same pointed question from his huge 1879 best-seller, *Progress and Poverty*. Why does prosperity breed more poverty? George's remedy was a single tax for all, a notion that Poultney Bigelow embraced after his father gave him their Malden farm and the taxes that went with it, which Poultney viewed in typically chary fashion as a high price to pay for something that "has no value other than sentimental." Bigelow met George on his American trip and remained a friend until the economist's death. He also approved of the single tax scheme because it would have meant that the "vast holdings in land" of the Catholic Church—which he passed on his way upriver—were taxed as well.

To the northwest, where the Mohawk River begins to curl through the Valley, Schenectady remained a relatively quiet canal port until 1890, its large-scale locomotive works having been around since 1851. The Schenectady Gas Works, also begun in that year, became the Schenectady Illuminating Company in 1886, the year Thomas A. Edison (1847–1931) arrived. The gas works measured its success in the rise in numbers of gas ranges, from three in 1890 to 403 in 1894; there were more than 30,000 manufactured by 1930. The works also controlled a trolley company in the city.

Edison's choice of Schenectady followed a search for a suitable large electrical products manufacturing site by his agents in Pennsylvania, New Jersey, and New York. Edison sent Samuel Insall to inquire into the availability of the old MacQueen Locomotive Works, which his upstate agent Harry M. Livor recommended. Edison wanted the property, but thought the $50,000 asking price too high. He offered $37,500, and Schenectady businessmen raised the remainder by June 2. The inventor arrived on August 20, 1886, had breakfast at Given's Hotel, and began arranging the delivery of the machinery he needed for the site. He had John Krueshi supervise the construction of the new plant—Krueshi had built Edison's first phonograph. The Edison Tube Company and Edison Shafting Company were merged into the new Edison Machine Works, which had more than one hundred employees by the end of the year.

"In such a company as this," Thomas Crumerford Martin wrote in *Electrical World* on August 25, 1888, after spending "A Day with Edison at Schenectady,"

> [T]he prosaic and the marvelous jostle each other. Here are six thousand feet of shafting and some fifty thousand feet of belting, driving nearly four hundred separate mechanisms in the production of apparatus whose birth was yesterday.

Eight hundred employees were spread over twenty-six buildings on the flats along the Mohawk River and the Erie Canal. Dynamos, electric motors, insulated wire, and a full range of milling and foundry products were made. New York Central trains routinely stopped or slowed when passing the works, to give passengers a glimpse of the huge electric cranes operating in the plants. Even the workers were amazed by them.

The company consolidated with five others to become the Edison General Electric Company in 1889, when Edison withdrew from active management and monthly revenues were more than $160,000. The company, like Westinghouse, was about to expand its lines from lighting equipment to power machinery and a wide range of electric products, a process that happened quickly mainly because of the origin of these companies as research and development interests and their sophisticated management teams. New products included sockets for lamps, the first porcelain shop, and other wiring devices.

This merger coincided with a wholesale change in power organization generally. Consolidated Edison was created in 1900 by gas and electric companies in New York City, and in 1901 the gas, electric, and street lighting institutions of Poughkeepsie reorganized into the Central Hudson Gas and Electric Company, which grew into one of the largest Hudson Valley institutions in the century that followed.

In 1892, J. P. Morgan helped to engineer a merger of Edison Electric and the Thomson-Houston Electric Company of Massachusetts, a business deal that edged the inventor further off the stage (for a significant cost) and centered control within Thomson-Houston under Edison's company, and with a new name: General Electric, or GE. The company now had two plants, at Schenectady and Lynn, Massachusetts, and would grow into a technology, services, and manufacturing giant with revenues of $120 billion in the year 2000. The first "aerial" photograph taken of the General Electric works in Schenectady was shot from the top of a metal gas storage tank in 1904.

Also in 1892, Edison purchased a Yonkers firm he had been working with, mainly to obtain the services of a precocious young mathematician-engineer, Charles Proteus Steinmetz (1865–1923). This small, misshapen man, who had almost been sent back to Germany by immigration officials at Ellis Island because of his appearance, had begun as an electrical draftsman for Rudolf Eickemeyer in Yonkers. In that shop Steinmetz, as Larry Hart wrote in 1978, "did the work that led to his revolutionary discoveries in the field of magnetic losses, or the law of hysteresis, and which attracted the attention of electrical engineers across the country." Eickemeyer's business was absorbed in the General Electric merger. When the company moved its calculating department in Lynn to Schenectady, Steinmetz went as well, arriving two weeks before Christmas. His calculating (and design) specialty was alternating current. He became known as "the forger of thunderbolts" when he created the first artificial lightning in a huge laboratory using 120,000 volts of electricity.

The population of Schenectady jumped from less than 20,000 in 1890 to more than 31,000 ten years later. General Electric, which electrified the trolley lines in 1891, had control of most of the city's major industries. Seven thousand people worked for GE in 1893. As the operations grew, several hotels were built to accommodate the workers, one of which served 250 lunches a day. The "GE Plot" was purchased from Union College, and fine homes were built for the company. Dr. Willis Whitney established the GE Research Laboratory (later known as the Rest Development Center and the Knolls), which eventually produced two Nobel Prize winners, Irving Langmuir in 1940 and Ivan Giaver in 1973.

Charles A. Coffin (1844–1926) was a founder and the first GE president, a businessman who would be ranked with Rockefeller, Carnegie, Frick, and the Guggenheims among the leaders of the times. He moved GE into the acquisition of steel and copper manufacturing subsidiaries that enabled the company to eliminate its reliance on secondary sources for prime materials. The modern corporation came of age in General Electric, its expansion and growth a response to a vast urban market created by the continuing expansion of the American economy.

As industry grew into the modern age, a broad movement into conservation also characterized the turn of the century generations. The effort to save the diabase of the Palisades—the first great land protection battle in the United States—began when the Englewood Women's Club of New Jersey marshaled forces in 1896 "to preserve land and to provide opportunities for outdoor recreation accessible to all." The ladies of Englewood were much disturbed by the dynamiting of the trap rock and the noise, dust and destruction of the Palisades that came with it. New Jersey Governor Foster M. Voorhees secured an appropriation for a joint commission with New York. The effort was immediately joined by New York Governor Theodore Roosevelt and the energetic and new American Scenic and Preservation Society under its founder Andrew H. Green, the "Father of Greater New York" who led the consolidation of the boroughs. The commission recommended a joint New York and New Jersey Palisades Interstate Park Commission, which was created by acts of both legislatures. The commission chairman was George W. Perkins, Sr. (1862–1920), one of the country's leading life insurance executives, soon to be J. Pierpont Morgan's right-hand man, the eventual campaign manager of Teddy Roosevelt's 1912 presidential run, and a founder of the Progressive Party in America. The quarrying and blasting was irksome to large property owners across the way on the bluffs of Manhattan and the heights from Kingsbridge to Tarrytown, including Perkins, who owned adjoining estates in Riverdale in the new borough of the Bronx.

Perkins secured more than $2 million in donations from his wealthy friends to assist the states. A 700-acre park was created after John D. Rockefeller donated more land along the bluff; his only stipulation was that a parkway be developed. Eventually (over 1901–08), 50,000 feet of frontage and more than 550 acres were quietly added to the district, which stretched from the Fort Lee bluffs to Piermont cliff, almost all of the Palisades that was in jeopardy from industrialization at the time.

In the summer of 1905, 21 permits were issued to campers; by 1909, these had increased to 1,000. In that year Hamilton Twombly and his wife donated the final sixty acres and 3,000 feet of riparian rights, completing the project as far as Piermont. In the same year, the New York legislature set aside 35,000 acres in the Hudson Highlands for a forest reservation that would soon be joined with the PIPC lands. Charles W. Leavett, Jr. surveyed lands for a new Henry Hudson Drive through the park in 1903, but it was another forty years before it was built.

The 1909 state set-aside was prompted by concerns over plans to relocate Sing Sing prison to Bear Mountain. More than a hundred prisoners came across in 1908, cleared land, and put in sewer lines. Yet interest in saving this area had arisen with the 1906 appearance of *The Hudson: Three Centuries of History, Romance and Invention* and the *Hudson River Guidebook* (1907) by Poughkeepsie poet Wallace Bruce (1844–1914). The writings of William Thompson Howell (1873–1916) in New York *Tribune* and *Sun* columns quietly promoted the Highlands as a hiking, heritage and natural wonderland:

> It would also seem as though Nature had purposely created the Highlands for eventual use as a playground [Howell wrote]. She has placed them close to the site of the country's greatest city, and has thus far protected them from the city's invasion, until the time might be ripe for their proper use.

A local Highlands doctor and Columbia University professor, Edwin Lasell Partridge, whose local estate was designed by Frederick Law Olmsted, called for Bear Mountain and all of the Highlands to be declared a national park in an *Outlook* article in 1907. Partridge was a friend of railroad magnate E. H. Harriman, for whom the prison project was particularly irksome because of its proximity to his river estate.

Harriman initiated a proposal to donate 10,000 acres of land he owned adjoining the PIPC holdings on the condition that the prison work stop and that Bear Mountain be purchased by the state and included in the PIPC. The conveyance was executed by Harriman's wife Mary after his death; she included $1 million in cash and convinced the state to contribute $2.5 million toward its development. The parcel was conveyed to New York by her 19-year-old son, William Averell Harriman. The Harriman family followed with $4.25 million in contributions, led by E. Roland Harriman, for the construction of a new bridge from Bear Mountain to Anthony's Nose in 1923. The "parallel wire cable suspension type" bridge featured two 1,632-foot high steel towers connected by two great cables consisting of 37 strands each, each strand consisting of a bridge wire looped back and forth 98 times. The Roebling Company made the cables over a three-month period and attached each to eyebar chains. The bridge remained privately owned until sold to the state in 1940 for $2,275,000. The magnificent structure, the longest suspension bridge in the world at the time of completion, provided a 155-foot clearance for ships using the Hudson River.

A dock was built for steamboats on the Hudson at the base of Bear Mountain, a park constructed around Hessian Lake, and a large playing field added on a plateau 130 feet above the river. Steamboat service began, and in the first year 22,590 visitors came. More than two million visitors arrived in 1922. Winter sports were added over 1922–23, including a "world class ski-jumping" arena. The American Museum of Natural History became involved, and the first section of the Appalachian Trail was built through here.

William Addams Welch (1868–1941), an engineer and environmentalist and the visionary behind the creation of the Highlands parks, was hired by Perkins in 1912. He created the Bear Mountain and Harriman State Parks, expanding the holdings to 40,000 acres, and put his support behind the Storm King Mountain highway in the early 1920s. Welch's work included acres of reforestation, 23 new lakes, and 103 children's camps serving 65,000 New York City kids annually. He added a restaurant on Hessian Lake that accommodated 100,000 visitors in its first year of operation. Artie Shaw, Tommy Dorsey, and Harry James were among those performing at the park's bandstand. Teenager Kate Smith (1907–86) came and sang "When the Moon Comes Over the Mountain," a song composed at Bear Mountain.

The acquisition of the additional lands north of Bear Mountain also involved a race against time with the quarrying operations, not without repercussions from the aggrieved owners. Breakneck Ridge was called St. Anthony's Face for the attractive profile the stone made over the Hudson, but in 1896 Captain Deering Ayers, in an apparent act of spite for having to close his quarry in one blast dropped 2,000 tons of the granite stone, obliterating the face over the Hudson. In 1945, a tunnel was cut through the ridge for the river road traffic—the only highway tunnel in the Hudson River Valley.

The erection of parks, monuments, and recreational amenities typified the bright new era. Natural resources were protected as a logical corollary to the appreciation of the beauty and setting of the state. Theodore Roosevelt led the way with the preservation of the Adirondacks and Catskills as "forever wild." The Saratoga Springs Commission was created in 1909 to preserve the mineral springs from damage by companies that were separating the carbonic acid gas from the waters for profit, diminishing the supplies and affecting the waters chemically. The commission received a setback when Spencer Trask, one of the three members appointed by Governor Hughes, died in a railroad accident at Croton on the last day of the year. George Foster Peabody, namesake for the prestigious media award, was appointed his successor.

The field of archaeology was professionalized under Arthur C. Parker (1881–1955), the state anthropologist whose passion was his own father's Iroquois culture. He conducted the first serious survey of the Valley's prehistoric resources in 1922. In 1924, Parker became interested in Flint Mine Hill in Coxsackie through amateur archaeologist Jeff Ray, who had investigated the hill with Forrest Van Loon Ryder and Grant Van Loan. Three large quarries there yielded more than two hundred flint points. Parker had at least thirty-five informants between Lake George and Dutchess County, eleven with significant collections. His work survived the times: of 735 sites known to professionals in the 1980s, Parker had provided information on 29.5%, or 217 of them. Parker's work enabled his successor as state archaeologist, William Ritchie (b. 1905), to explore pre-Iroquois cultures and in the process develop the taxonomic table used to classify early North American cultures.

Almost two years after Croton Point became a county park in January 1924, the remains of a fortified village and a shell heap were investigated and mapped by engineers associated with the Westchester Park County Commission. Science infused other archaeological digs as well. William F. Stiles of the Heye Foundation explored the Black Rock site in Athens in 1940. Quarrying destroyed a cave containing artifacts on Mount Lookout in Orange County in the early 1930s, but Henry Malley of Middletown remembered playing there as a boy and later provided information leading to the excavation of Dutchess Quarry Cave No. 1 in the early 1960s.

The times were notably propitious for recalling America's past. The state's archival resources had become available in Edward O'Callaghan's translations of the Dutch records in the 1850s, and now attention also fell on local records and tying the strands of the history together. In Kingston, Benjamin Myer Brink (1847–1915), the grandson of the first captain of the *Clermont* and a noted local historian, on January 18, 1905, "launched a new craft upon the sea of journalism" with the first issue of *Olde Ulster*, a monthly history journal drawn from records in Ulster County and Albany that he bound into volumes for each of the next ten years. He published numerous original documents and drew from scholars like retired Navy chaplain Captain Roswell Randall Hoes (1850–1921), a collector of Washington memorabilia whose papers were destined for the Library of Congress.

Local communities spent time finding and documenting the graves of Revolutionary War soldiers, spurred by the Daughters of the American Revolution, which organized statewide in New York in 1901. The Hudson chapter established a free library in 1898 and found a permanent home in 1900 through a donation by Mrs. Marcellus Hartley, a great-granddaughter of one of the city's founders. The home was soon transformed into a multipurpose building complete with theater with orchestra pit for fundraisers. The drop curtain was still in use when featured in a *National Geographic* magazine article in 1962. In 1901, the Quassaick DAR chapter in Orange County dedicated a boulder honoring the construction of part of the chain across the Hudson River in 1776. A monument to Chief Ninham and seventeen Stockbridge Indians who died in a battle in the Bronx on August 31, 1778, was erected by Mount Vernon DAR on June 14, 1906. The New York chapter, at the urging of Mrs. Robert J. Davidson of Rockland County and as part of the Hudson-Fulton Celebration, led the dedication of a large stone Memorial Arch at the Stony Point Battlefield State Reservation; almost 24,000 visitors came to the reservation in 1909. Trying to take advantage of the publicity, Francis Bannerman III, a Brooklyn scrap metal dealer and purveyor of military hardware who owned an island in the Hudson, sold what he claimed to be authentic links in that chain for up to $350 apiece. (They were actually British made.)

New York, the first in the nation to acquire a historic site in Washington's Headquarters at Newburgh, embraced its role as protector of parks and monuments. The American Scenic and Historic Preservation Society, which managed the sites, was actually a government agency created by an act of the state legislature. The society took over the André Monument in Tappan in 1905, was active at the Stony Point dedication, and placed a granite marker in Weehawken near where Hamilton fell. (The actual dueling site was obliterated by the arrival of the Erie Railroad Company.) Philipse Manor Hall was conveyed to the state in 1908, but remained in use as Yonkers city hall until a new one was built.

The Society of Colonial Dames honored Anne Hutchinson, the Rhode Island dissenter whose family was massacred nearby in 1643, with a plaque at the Split Rock in 1911—it was later removed to St. Paul's Church in Eastchester.

A large granite slab marking a Continental Village site behind Garrison burned by the British was unveiled in 1921 in honor of "Mothers of the Revolution." In 1923, the Sons of the American Revolution purchased Freeman's Farm from Mrs. Jennie E. Wright, placing the 193-acre site of the first of the Saratoga battles with a nonprofit patriotic organization and fulfilling a five-year campaign by Lake George Battle Park custodian Stewart MacFarland of Glens Falls. In the same year, Poultney Bigelow and Congressman Hamilton Fish regaled a crowd as guests of the Dutchess County Historical Society, the New York Public Library purchased the original 1630 deed for the patroonship of *Rensselaerswijck* (signed by Pieter Minuet), and historian Dixon Ryan Fox (1887–1945) helped Westchester County establish an eighteenth century museum.

Fox, like young Franklin D. Roosevelt, was the personification of a rising interest in heritage and history by young intellectuals of these times. After graduating school in 1907, he started his career as the principal of the district school in Sherman Park in Westchester County. Fox joined the New York Historical Society in 1918 and a dozen years later became the first professional historian to become its president. He was joint editor of *New York History* when it appeared in 1919. His Ph.D. dissertation, *The Decline of Aristocracy in the Politics of New York, 1810–1840*, became "a minor classic in American history," according to Richard V. Remini, when published by Columbia University that year. Fox, the first historian to attempt a voting analysis using statistics and graphs, was writing at a time when most historians agreed with James Madison's dictum that political party divisions resulted from unequal property divisions, but the young Westchester scholar added a twist by concluding that parties continued "more from memory and habit" than "calculated differences of interest," a sentiment that continued to characterize American politics in modern times. He lived in Valhalla until his appointment as Union College president in 1934, where he set about establishing the Mohawk Drama Festival, the first cooperative effort between a college and a professional stage. He nearly tripled library appropriations and doubled the college capital.

Remini suggested that had he lived, what Fox might have accomplished "at the conclusion of [World War II] when colleges were entering a new era of expansion and growth can only be surmised." He was meeting with General Electric officials about support for a special postgraduate summer session in physics when he had a heart attack and died on January 30, 1945.

Interest in local history blossomed all over the Valley in these years. The Holland Society gathered in Kingston on December 15, 1923, dined on Spanish mackerel and Maryland turkey, and enjoyed learned talks by their president, DeWitt Van Buskirk, and A. T. Clearwater, the county judge and author of a history of Kingston. They met to discuss forming a Kingston chapter of the society, which happened with another grand dinner six months later. A society member, Franklin Roosevelt, helped revive interest in Hudson Valley Dutch culture that year, when he drove Helen Wilkinson Reynolds through the nooks and crannies of Dutchess County for her pioneer study on rural homes.

The Chappaqua Kiwanis Club asked Arthur W. Lawrence, president of the Westchester County Park Commission, to deliver the address at the village's 200th anniversary celebration on September 7, 1930. More than 5,000 attended. Chappaqua, which was part of the John Richbell patent of 1666, certainly had cause to celebrate the village history, but the real occasion for applauding was the opening of the new Grade Crossing Elimination Bridge that relieved congestion caused by the Saw Mill River Parkway and New York Central Railroad passing through at the same location. The new bridge was just west of where Horace Greeley had his country home seventy years earlier, on the old editor's celebrated swamp. The ribbon was cut by Greeley's daughter, Gabrielle Greeley Clendenin (1857–1937), with a statue of Greeley erected at its western end. Gabrielle, who was active in Herbert Hoover's presidential campaigns, was the youngest of seven Greeley children, five of whom died before their father's death in 1872, and she and her husband lost two children as well. They lived in a reconverted barn on the farm, the first such structure said to be built of concrete. This was her only public event that year because her husband had died just a month earlier.

A revival of interest in early Dutch-American architecture after the turn of the century had already resulted in a new style, called Dutch Colonial, that spread from New Jersey into the Midwest. Oddly, the Dutch Hudson Valley was hardly touched by it. The exception proved the rule, at least in the exterior of the home built in 1909 for Edgar and Kate Eames by architect Frank E. Wallis in a secluded forest near Woodstock. This came to be known as the Martin Comeau property after the daughter, Marion Eames, 51 at the time, married a 34-year-old lawyer, Martin Comeau, in 1931. Comeau, the town attorney and civil defense director during World War II, negotiated the agreement that saved the Woodstock Golf Club. He became a recluse on Margaret's death, and never entered their living room again. The town bought the attractive 78 acres in 1979, established the town hall in the home, and created a picturesque natural setting for townspeople and visitors.

The state legislature was eager to get into the historic preservation act. Senator Abraham Palmer, who had briefed President Lincoln on his experiences as a prisoner of war in the South in 1864, delivered an impassioned plea for $5,000 to purchase cases to house the state's collection of Civil War flags. Governor Sulzer's wife had a floral spray laid in front of his desk on the Senate floor, depicting the American flag in red and white carnations and stars made of daisies. Palmer got the money and the state protected a remarkable collection of flags.

The idea of a celebration linking Henry Hudson's 1609 voyage of discovery and Robert Fulton's 1807 steamboat success was first raised by the Rev. J. H. Suydam of Rhinebeck in a letter to the New York newspapers. He had been impressed with the 1893 Columbian Exhibition in Chicago and wanted a similar convention in New York City. Public hearings over the winter of 1905 led to the idea of celebrating all along the river over a two-week period coinciding with Hudson's visit dates. New York City still played the major part, divided into 53 districts for pageant activities, and with a volunteer corps of eight hundred. The event was given a formal tone with the dedications lists, a prohibition on commercials or advertisements, and a well organized committee structure involving the finest members of society. Franklin D. Roosevelt served on the Public Health and Convenience Committee.

The Hudson-Fulton Celebration Commission was created under state law in 1906. The commission included thirty trustees and members of the American Scenic and Historic Preservation Society. During the event, the society dedicated the Palisades Interstate Park, played behind-the-scene rolls in much of the historic and scenic activities, and provided assistance, verifications, and inscriptions for memorials. Its longer-term contributions included a remarkable collection of scholarship and translation unrivalled until Charles Gehring's appearance in the 1970s. The society's *Fifteenth Annual Report, 1910*, included appendices containing Robert Juet's original text of the voyage of the *Halve Maen*, not available in accurate form since 1842, and the first appearance in America, in English as well as the original Italian, of Giovanni da Verrazzano's account of his visit in 1524, each accompanied by learned exegeses. Edward

Hagaman Hall (1858–1936), secretary of the society since 1897, arranged the publication and contributed a comprehensive essay on Hudson that included technical drawings of a *Half Moon* replica under construction in Holland. The Verrazzano "codex" was purchased by J. P. Morgan for his library collection. Italian Americans installed a large bronze of their explorer looking toward the Narrows from Battery Park, and Italian sailors participated in New York's first Columbus Day celebration three days after the Hudson-Fulton event.

The Hudson-Fulton extravaganza included a groundbreaking exchange of art between the United States and Holland, the opening of which coincided with the opening of the Palisades Interstate Park's gala. The Metropolitan Museum of Art created the first large-scale exhibition of American art in a museum; the works were purchased by Margaret Slocum Sage on behalf of the museum, and later became the heart of the American Wing.

The celebration began in New York on September 25 and ended sixteen days later in Cohoes. A 1,500-ship flotilla sailed into the Hudson Valley and included, in addition to a Dutch replica of the *Halve Maen* and a replica of the *Clermont*, battleships from naval rivals Germany and Great Britain and the ill-fated *Lusitania*. The sail and steam provided the largest pageant in the history of the state and probably the nation, with communities all along the river participating. Cornwall-on-Hudson, after some bickering among who should be on the local committee, marveled at the exhibitions of sail and hosted the *Half Moon* and *Clermont* locally for two weeks. Governor Charles Evans Hughes praised the Poughkeepsie pageant—a two-day display of parades, historical displays, dinners, concerts, church events and, at the conclusion, "a dazzling variety of aerial bombs" shooting over the riverfront—as "the climax in beauty and completeness" of all the local celebrations. In Hudson, with the entire courthouse outlined in electric lights, the October 7 celebration drew 30,000 people and was preceded by weeklong events, including an Armory service and parade of 1,200 school children. Seven torpedo boats were on hand for visits and inspections by the crowds. Hudson was the only locale where "the famed historical floats" were hauled out of the river for the parade down Warren Street. After the parade, a dinner for 300 featured Governor Charles Evans Hughes as the keynote speaker.

The Hudson-Fulton festivities ended on the evening of October 9, 1909, with beacon fires with searchlights and fireworks for more than three hours from New York to Troy. The New York Evening Line had two packed excursion boats out for the occasion, at $2.50 a person with a private stateroom on the return.

In April 1924, Governor Al Smith signed a law giving the replica of the *Half Moon* to the city of Cohoes, which underwrote its restoration and care in promoting the city's waterfront heritage. The ship had been moored in Popolopen Creek near Newburgh, where Brooks Atkinson saw it in 1922, but a West Shore Railroad trestle across the creek eliminated access. The Holland Society secured the support of Edward Hagaman Hall and Franklin D. Roosevelt of the Ship Model Society to save the vessel, and lobbied the legislature and the governor for its new home on the waterfront at Cohoes.

In all of this celebration of the past and the heritage resources of the Valley, West Point Military Academy continued as the stalwart sentinel of the Hudson Highlands, producing class after class of military men and expert engineers and surveyors whose work continued to transform America. The lofty hills themselves, whose renown was likened to the castle-strewn Rhine by so many past generations of European visitors, remained sufficiently insulated by their own isolation to appear sublimely distant and aloof as the second great wave of industrial expansion spread throughout America and the Hudson River Valley.

II. TWILIGHT OF THE GODS

Corporation. N. An ingenious device for obtaining individual profit without individual responsibility.

—AMBROSE BIERCE, *The Devil's Dictionary* (1911)

10. Sam and Sam

> Our readers may thus . . . be entertained by the most
> charming fictions which fancy has ever created.
>
> —INTRODUCTION,
> *Personal Memoirs of U. S. Grant* (1885)

M ount McGregor lies twelve miles from Saratoga Springs and, geologically at least, was not a part of the Hudson River Valley, yet its most famous resident during a few months in 1885 made it a community of the nation in which all resided. Ulysses S. Grant (1822–85) came to the Mount to die.

The eighteenth President of the United States did not deserve even an honorable mention for his executive services to the nation, his two-term administration having dissolved in scandal and controversy so badly he was pitied more than reviled in the ensuing years. In fact, remarkably little of U. S. Grant's life commended itself to the ages. He spent four uncommitted years as a cadet at the United States Military Academy. He failed in businesses and progressed only fitfully in the military until his own dogged persistence and President Lincoln placed him at the head of the Army of the Potomac.

Grant tried to support President Andrew Johnson in Johnson's fight with the Radical Republicans over the Negro question and the South after the war. In 1866, he toured the Hudson Valley with the President, William Seward and other cabinet members. The entourage stopped at West Point, Newburgh, Poughkeepsie, Peekskill, Albany, and Schenectady. Johnson was criticized by the Radical press in Schenectady on September 4—they were chary toward Lincoln, too, when he came through in February 1860—but vowed to press on; he did not know how to go backwards into America's future. Yet Northern sentiments also reflected a "fly in the ointment" criticism that unfolded at West Point in 1870 when Mississippi's new black senator, Hiram R. Revels, appointed a black youth to the academy who subsequently failed the entrance examination. An editorial in *The Nation* cautioned that this should have been expected.

Grant's connections with the Hudson Valley were limited mainly to war and political connections, and a few wealthy families. The choice of Mount

McGregor for his final days evolved through the assistance of Dr. George Shrady (d. 1908), otherwise known for having convinced the New York State legislature to license doctors. Dr. Shrady never did believe in germs. He had a farm at Kingsbridge and was connected to Grant through Chauncey Depew (1834–1928). Grant had other wealthy friends in the Valley, like William S. Dinsmore, the "tycoon turned horticulturalist" who had expanded Henry Brockhulst Livingston's Dutchess County estate, the Locusts, into the 2,000-acre Dinsmore Place. Grant visited Dinsmore with General George A. Sharpe (1828–1900) of Kingston during his 1872 campaign against Horace Greeley. Sharpe was the head of Grant's Secret Service team during the war, his Surveyor of Customs at the Port of New York, and a major Republican Party figure in the Valley. Grant noticed the Overlook Mountain House from Dinsmore Place and resolved on a visit—which the newspapers quickly turned into an affair of state.

Overlook Mountain House had been managed by John E. Lasher as an elegant mountaintop establishment when built over 1870–71. Three years after a fire destroyed the hotel on April 1, 1875, it was rebuilt by the Kiersted brothers of Saugerties and leased to Colonel James Smith of Poughkeepsie, who established a proper, family-oriented establishment that did not sell alcohol. Future president Chester A. Arthur was a guest that year. In Grant's time, however, John Lasher had scorned the temperance fervor that gripped the Woodstock community below the mountain and catered to a crowd more amenable to Grant's kind of conviviality.

Several national reporters were on hand in July 1873 to question the President about his interest in pursuing a third term, now that he had just been elected handily to a second. Grant had come upriver on the *Chauncey Vibbard*, was joined by General Sharpe at Rhinecliff, and crossed over on the tug *Sandy* while dozens of steamboats saluted his arrival. The party was greeted by the Rondout Cornet Band and an elaborate parade to Sharpe's Kingston home. A special train waited at the Kingston & Syracuse rail depot. Another band and a great crowd greeted him at the West Hurley station, where he spent more time shaking hands and greeting people before a barouche with four fast horses spirited his party off to Woodstock and another fancy greeting by the prominent townspeople there.

The party moved to Mead's Mountain House and then proceeded up the Overlook trail in a dense fog, finally arriving at the hotel to the huzzahs of another large crowd. Rockets were set off and immediately disappeared in the fog. "Showers of flowers and favors" landed on and around Grant as he entered the hotel. When he appeared on the veranda, the fog broke and the celebrated landscape of a unique Valley perspective greeted the President of the United States, as if on a royal cue. The music was provided by the Wagner brothers from New York, whose violinist, a Mr. Eisner, played a solo version of "Yankee Doodle Dandy" that pleased the President. Several members of the Hutchinson Family Singers, a famous group vacationing at Overlook, joined black Civil War veterans, black students from Lincoln University, and the waiters and kitchen help in serenading Grant with old war songs. The next morning, accompanied by two young girls in white dresses, he led a parade to Hopper's Rock, where the whole party sang "America."

Sharpe and Grant had an opportunity to climb the rocks at Devil's Kitchen, and enjoyed cigars together overlooking Platte Clove. John Lasher was said to have given the rock they sat on to the President for shipment by Dinsmore's Adams Express Company to Washington—but Grant declined the offer. The monument has been known as Grant's Rock ever since. Crowds lined the way when his barouche sped through the hills to West Hurley and the railroad later that day. Grant spent two hours shaking hands at Sharpe's home and finally bid the crowd goodnight from the balcony at midnight. The hateful (to Republicans) Rhinebeck *Gazette* claimed Grant was "redolent with the stench of the back pay swindle and cheap whiskey" of Washington, and "was, as usual, drunk." But the pro-Republican Kingston *Daily Freeman* claimed the President, whose heavy drinking had been a campaign issue for Greeley the previous year, was not even tipsy.

Twelve years later, Ulysses S. Grant returned to the Hudson Valley, this time to Mount McGregor because he was broke and dying. The cottage where he stayed was owned by Joseph W. Drexel, a financier, philanthropist, and co-owner of the Balmoral Hotel next door. The location was considered a good one for the mountain air, and acceptable to Grant, who wanted to remain in New York. Chauncey Depew arranged for a special train on behalf of his boss and Grant's friend, William H. Vanderbilt. A locomotive, dining car, and Vanderbilt's own private coach were used. Grant boarded at Manhattan with his wife, his son Fred and Fred's wife Nellie, five grandchildren, and Grant's personal transcriber, N. E. Dawson. There were also three medical personnel on board because of the cancer.

The train left New York on a hot day in the middle of June in 1885. Grant's cancer had spread deeply into his throat and ate away at his tongue and mouth. He was 63 years old, his beard whiter than his years, and "literally starving to death" because of the constriction on his throat. Crowds were everywhere along the journey through the Valley; veterans of the war stood at attention while he passed. Julia woke him as they passed West Point. Five hours after departing New York, an honor guard waited at Saratoga. Grant walked with difficulty to a train pulled by the *J. W. Drexel*, and tried to walk to the cottage from the train stop, but could not. He was carried up a steep grade to the porch. The two-story house was large and airy, and had an open porch on three sides. Grant's room, which had large windows, was off the porch near the front of the house. Here he remained, limited to only tea and soft drinks through much of June, restful yet wasting away.

Grant had been bilked of his money by a pair of charlatans, James Fish and Ferdinand Ward, and was desperate to provide for his wife and children. He had recalled some admiring words a journalist said to him about dispatches he had written during the war, and decided to take up the writing of his own autobiography in the hopes that he might leave his family something of value after all. A concerned friend, Mark Twain, who like Grant went by the nickname Sam, saved him from the machinations of a greedy publisher. Twain had a good eye for talent, and convinced Grant to let him handle the manuscript. He was a publisher as well as a famous author and promised full royalties on any money made so that his family would be spared further embarrassment. He spent the time at Mount Gregor with Grant, and occasionally visited the Saratoga Springs casinos and horses, attracting a following wherever he went. He was already well known and celebrated there when he came up with Grant.

Mark Twain was as much a Hudson Valley institution as an American one. He lived in Hartford, Connecticut, and had married Olivia Langdon of Elmira, where they spent their summers and where Twain composed most of his major works. The trip usually involved a trek across the Hudson Valley, enabling Twain to give talks and stay with relatives or friends along the way. His nephew Charles L. Webster (1851–91) lived in Amenia. (Webster's daughter was the novelist, playwright and Vassar graduate Jean Webster.) The two men created a publishing company together.

Twain's 1869–70 speaking tour—the subject was "Our Fellow Savages of the Sandwich Islands"—included several local venues: Collingwood Opera House in Poughkeepsie ("a fine audience," the *Daily Eagle* reported); Mount Vernon, Amenia, Cohoes, Albany, Union Place Hall in Troy, Rondout, and Cambridge. "His introduction of himself was remarkably Twain-ish and placed him and his hearers upon good terms at once," *The Cohoes Cataract* reported, although the turnout at Egbert's Hall was low. The talk was sponsored by the Sons of Temperance and the Grand Army of the Republic. The house was full for Twain's West Troy speech.

"Roughing It" was the topic at Rand's Hall in Troy on February 1, 1872. When Twain spoke at Tweddle Hall in Albany on November 28, the *Argus* opined that he was America's best humorist because he appealed to "the idea, and not in the mere use or misuse of words or phrases," as with Josh Billings or Petroleum V. Nasby. Twain was at Newburgh and the Troy Music Hall in 1885 and at West Point in 1881, 1886, 1887, and 1890. At Vassar College, he read "Trying Situation" and "Golden Arm."

His local correspondents included Joel Benton of Amenia (1832–1911), a poet and essayist who used Charles L. Webster & Co. for Benton's *The Truth about "Protection"* (1892). Benton also entertained as houseguests John Burroughs (a close friend whom he called "our Prophet of Outdoordom"), Horace Greeley (the first speaker for Benton's Amenia Literary Society), Margaret Fuller, Wendell Phillips, and Elizabeth Cady Stanton.

Twain was on hand for Horace Greeley's sixty-first birthday dinner in New York on February 3, 1862, and Greeley was featured in some of *Roughing It.* Twain wrote humorously about the "Private Lives of Horace Greeley" in 1868, and was thrown out of the publisher's office after entering uninvited in 1871. Twain lived near Riverdale at Wave Hill one summer, but probably did not know Greeley in Chappaqua. Letters from Greeley to John Bigelow (1868) and from John Hay to Bigelow (1871) concern some Twain matters; Bigelow, the Highland Falls squire and Tilden Fund manager, wrote to Twain at least six times during Bigelow's later years. Twain was the guest speaker at a dinner honoring John's son, Poultney Bigelow, in England on January 31, 1897, and published at least two of Poultney's books, including Bigelow's only worthwhile endeavor (with *Seventy Summers*), the delightful *Paddles and Politics down the Danube* (1892). He also kept Bigelow apprised of his European and African speaking tours, and remained in touch while in New York and Connecticut.

Ulysses Grant finished his memoirs on that mountain porch and died on July 23, 1885. His body was removed to New York on August 6, the bier led by General Winfield Scott Hancock, a classmate from West Point and the head of the US Army's 4th Infantry. As the train passed, the corps of cadets at West Point saluted. More than 300,000 came to City Hall for a last view of their general.

Mark Twain made good on his promise. The first books he and Webster published were *Personal Memoirs of U. S. Grant* (1885–86) and *Adventures of Huckleberry Finn* (1885), and each became bestsellers. To sell the *Memoirs*, Twain had shrewdly kept the public aware of the general's last battle, and carried out a brilliant campaign involving ten thousand book agents, many of them Civil War veterans, who spread across the country with a patriotic message composed by Twain. All the profits—$450,000, or about 30 percent—went to Julia and her family. The book has been continuously hailed as one of the best military biographies ever written; Twain himself considered the *Personal Memoirs* comparable to Julius Caesar's *Commentaries*.

Julia Grant (d. 1904) was protected by Twain as promised, and lived on to become close friends with Jefferson Davis's widow, Varina, when they both lived on Sunset Hill in Bronxville in later years. They played cards and rode the trains to New York together. Grant's first-born, Frederick, a well-known New York Republican, was buried a major-general at West Point on his death in 1912.

11. Extractive Resources

The public be damned; I am working for my stockholders.

—WILLIAM HENRY VANDERBILT (1879)

As the new age of industry dawned in the post-Civil War era, resources that once seemed endless were devoured in the rush to progress throughout the Valley. Wood, the main energy source for America, was also the pre-eminent Hudson Valley industry. Wood fires made the potash that enriched farm soils and cooked the broken limestone into cement. Wood ashes were the source of household soaps. Wood was as essential as leather in farm labors, accounting for the wagons, carriages, barns, stalls, and all the appurtenant structures. In 1846, the brickyards of Rockland County consumed 10,800 cords of wood harvested from the hills behind Stony Point. A hundred thousand cords were burned annually by steamboats on the river. Farmers were the main suppliers, selling almost four million cords in New York State in 1864, in addition to what was used for their own needs.

The harvested timber of the Adirondack forests flowed into a two-and-a-half-mile-long lumber district at Albany, "the white pine distribution center of the world." The log-driving industry became so large that sorting booms were created along river tributaries, the goods of the various lumber companies distinguished by "log-marks" or the stamps of a "marking hammer." The industry commenced about 1813 when Norman and Alanson Fox began to move Brant Lake logs down the Hudson River to Glens Falls. In the eighteenth century, Abraham Wing—a Quaker from the Oblong in Dutchess County—established saw and grist mills and devised a system for channeling logs into a large holding area on the river. A Big Boom was added in 1849 across the Hudson above Glens Falls to hold the hewn logs until the docks downriver were ready to process the product. Agile sorters and log movers culled the marking hammers to extract logs for the shipments. The entire operation—with some two hundred workers involved—was managed on the river from a makeshift shack constructed on a floating log foundation. By 1870, production peaked to almost 214 million board feet—more than a million market logs sorted and handled by the Great Boom company for sixty lumber companies along the river.

Thousands of logs on the river created a perilous life for the drivers, who were known for their agility and fearlessness. Some were crushed at the banking grounds, some drowned in rapids or the icy river water, and some were pulled under while breaking the great jams that developed. Heavy rains and melting snow prompted the Boom's collapse in 1859, scattering half a million logs along the Hudson River shorelines between Fort Edward and Troy, yet the industry would not be deterred. The industry, like the harvesting of the hemlocks for tanning in the Catskills, brought forth the best and worst of nineteenth-century American ingenuity and resource, the destruction of vast old forests in the creation of a vast new empire.

Glens Falls companies turned logs into pulp and paper products for ship-ment by canal boats downriver to Albany and New York markets. Millions of logs were directed past the city, and Fort Edward and other paper-processing sites, down the river to Albany. Forty-six firms operating along Albany's north end in 1854 turned logs into lumber at the city's sawmills, employing Irish laborers who lived in Limerick, as the north end was called, and formed social clubs like the Lumber Handlers. After 1866, when the Hudson River Pulp and Paper Company was founded at Corinth, wood production expanded with a new technology for making paper from pulp instead of rags. Hudson River Pulp merged into the International Paper Company in 1898 as paper became cheaper and more abundant, requiring even greater draws upon the resources of the northern forests.

The great hemlock forests were gone by 1850—the "purple glens" (in George William Curtis's phrase) lost to the Catskills foothills, the sun no longer setting "still and solemn over the purple hills" of the Kayaderosseras, the "purple mountains' majesty" of southern song lost to these mountain glens as well. Yet tanning continued as a viable industry after the Civil War in the small vil-lage or hamlet operations that persisted. Henry Bange's Lackawack Tannery in Kerhonkson produced 15,000 hides of "union crop leather" annually by 1871; F. S. McKinstry's Sole Leather Tannery along the Shawangunk Creek in Gardiner transformed 7,000 hides. A delightful folklore tradition developed around the tanners and the strange lives they lived deep in the forest. Tannic acid was yellow, sticky, and smelly, so foul that the gatherers often did not leave the woods until the work was done. It was said you could smell a tanner coming from a mile off. Many of the stripped trees were used for burning and construction—the huge ice houses along the banks of the river, the framed mansions like Greenbank in Saugerties—but many also were left standing, shorn of bark, the stark skeletons of the once majestic forests now a cemetery of phthisic steles.

At the southern end of the Valley along the Palisades, enterprising men bought up woodlots and had the logs cut and pitched down "gutters" to the river—which became convenient hiking trails in the twentieth century. "Un-dercliff" squatters might have a small pear orchard or use shad fishing, stone quarrying, and other part-time pursuits to make ends meet, all of it in sight of a metropolis darkened by soot, smoke, and the soiled hopes of generations. By century's end the Palisades too would be transformed dramatically because wealthy estate owners who lived just across the way were looking back, and were not pleased.

Bluestone production advanced at a rapid pace after the Civil War, deconstructing miles of Valley ledges and speckling a rearranged topography with rutted roadways, abandoned quarries, and miles of slag piles. The isolated "Irish villages" of the 1850s were subsumed in worker communities that followed the stone for the next forty years. The bluestone industry denuded all cover on the Ashokan flagstones along a productive ridge from the Ulster-Greene county line and down the Esopus valley to Marbletown. The quarries stretched westward to the mountain crests in some areas along this parallel. Shaffer Vredenburg recalled in the 1950s that the entire Bearsville Flats in Woodstock was fully cleared "halfway to the top" of the bowl of hills around it. In 1920, a man could stand at the Highwoods intersection and look across a barren landscape five miles distant to California Quarry Road, nary a tree in sight. Winding roads down from the hills and on the steep grades near the river docks were laid with stone cut to hold the wheels and keep the wagons from skidding, a practice called "Belgian bridges."

The handling and cutting of bluestone for shipping, the cement industry, and brickmaking along the extensive clay beds of the Hudson contributed to the growth of the Rondout area. The little community on the river had more than 10,000 residents by 1870, greater in size than its sister village three miles west at Kingston. Led by the Newart Limestone and Cement Company agent, James G. Lindsley, Rondout applied to the state legislature for a city charter in 1871, prompting a Kingston committee to propose a consolidation. A ferocious courtship ensued over the next two years, as historian Alf Evers reported in *Kingston* (2005), "followed by the press, on street corners, in barrooms, at dinner tables." Surely no greater distance among couples contemplating marriage existed in the nineteenth-century Hudson Valley, the populous and working-class Rondout asserting its disdain for "a Kingston clique of old family members, and a surplus of lawyers, bankers, and real estate owners" while Kingstonians decried Rondout's exaggerated population as composed of poor, non-voting immigrants and their children. When the two finally merged in 1872, Rondout did not invite Kingston to the cornerstone laying of the new city hall on John O'Reilly's hill, prompting Kingston officials to come the next day and lay their own "half corner stone." Although outnumbered, "uptown" or the old Kingston area dominated the city for fifty of the next seventy years by appealing to Rondout friends in the elections of mayors.

A separate Town of Ulster was created, almost surrounding the new city, and a separate and tiny Town of Kingston, once called "the chin whiskers" of Woodstock, while the hamlet of Zena was taken from Kingston and given to Woodstock. These changes were a gerrymandering created in the wake of the Panic of 1873 by Kingston Republicans with the help of General George H. Sharpe in the state legislature to disengage their jurisdiction from colonies of poor, unemployed, mostly Irish bluestone workers in favor of the "taxpayer district," the city itself, which was paying out more than $15,000 a year for poor relief in the outlying areas. (Elsewhere, Ulster County towns in total paid less than $500 a year for poor relief.) In essence, the tax issues notwithstanding, the uptown crowd consolidated its control of the city by divesting of erstwhile Rondouters on its fringes. Zena taxpayers complained of their burden as well, and the rowdy workers exacerbated the situation by forcibly preventing Republicans from voting in their districts.

The city of Kingston had to face upgrades of its infrastructure to accommodate the expansion brought about by the merger with Rondout. Sewage was diverted to the Rondout Creek—considered the technological solution in its time—and the city contracted with the owner of a water supply behind Woodstock in Mink Hollow for a dozen years before purchasing the whole system, modernizing a reservoir at Cooper Lake, and running a line underneath Woodstock to avoid contamination of the water by the hamlet's tannery.

James Lindsley's New Jersey company had been chipping away at the limestone ridge behind Rondout, called the Vleitberg, and finally demolished a notable peak that had been useful for mariners on the Hudson River. The Rondout Valley was already developed industrially with a dozen cement plants, the Laflin and Rand Powder Works at LeFever Falls, and the Rifton Carpet Mills. At Rifton, Jeremiah Dimick's extensive works was a family operation that had by its presence created one of the nicest villages in Ulster County. When workers attempted to unionize, J. W. Dimick, Jr. closed the plant, to the region's astonishment, and the workers moved off to carpet works at Yonkers and Amsterdam. Rifton became a virtual ghost town for decades thereafter.

Hugh White's kilns at Whiteport and Greenkill in Ulster County, where the rich Rosendale cement beds were first tapped around 1850, supplied the cement for the Croton Aqueduct in 1871. The industry developed quickly when it was discovered that certain strata of the Rosendale rock hardened under water (due to calcium silicate oxides in the stone), and thus became useful for lock-building and bridge abutments. The limestone extended across the village of Rondout to the Hasbrouck Avenue heights over Ponckhockie, where caves were pumped of water while small railroad cars carried men to their depths for the quarrying of the stone.

The Hudson Valley brick industry—the largest in the world—virtually rose and fell in the thirty years after 1890. Although the industry's fate remained tied to the growth of New York City, whose population increased by 1.5 million from 1890 to 1910, hundreds of small brickworks operated wherever clay could be found, many one-, two-man, or small family operations that took advantage of a local supply until that was gone. Although Rockland was the largest brickmaking county from 1870 to 1906, dozens of brickmaking operations developed on the river above and below Kingston, from the large Washburn Brothers works six miles north in Glasco to the Christian Schleede operations in Port Ewen. Sixteen to twenty works operating along here in the 1880s employed a thousand workers. The adjoining neighborhoods of Ponckhockie and Rondout in Kingston hosted large Hutton, Terry Brothers, Charles S. Schultz, and George Washburn operations by the 1890s. More than 250 million bricks were produced in this vicinity in 1895.

In Rockland County, most of the brick industry's energies concentrated along a two-to-three mile stretch around Haverstraw that was first developed by James Wood (b. 1773) in 1815. Wood became "the father of the brick industry in the Hudson Valley" in 1836 when he patented a process that introduced coal dust into the clay and produced a better, harder brick at a faster rate than anyone else, cutting the kiln time from fourteen to seven days. Richard Van Valen increased industry production in 1852 by introducing a machine that filled the brick molds more quickly and in a stiffer manner than by hand.

In 1880, sixteen Haverstraw landowners leased lands to brickmakers, while another sixteen ran their own yards; Haverstraw had thirty-eight yards by 1900, producing 326 million bricks a year. Among the larger operations upriver were the Rose and Jova brickmaking works at Danskammer Point north of Newburgh, where a community of several thousand arose at Roseton, and quickly faded once the clay works were abandoned.

In 1893, when a serious economic depression hit the nation, 126 brickmakers served the New York market along the Hudson River. Within a year, the wholesale brick price dropped by 30 percent to $4.25 per thousand—at a time when the breakeven price was $5 per thousand. The Palatine Hotel in Newburgh (later the city library) hosted manufacturer get-togethers in which the depression of the market was studied and debated. Some of the larger manufacturers engaged in more aggressive industry belt-tightening—the Brockway yards in Beacon, for instance, which could undercut the competition by up to a dollar per thousand bricks. The industry also became influenced by New York City money and experimented with eliminating the commission brokers who sold the bricks on the market.

Financier Charles R. Flint attempted to consolidate the industry, but the manufacturers distrusted his New York City money. Oakleigh Thorne, the president of a switch and signal company in Pennsylvania and owner of a Millbrook estate, sought to create a 700-million-brick combine in 1899, hoping to control the prices on the New York market, but he too was seen as an outsider among the upriver companies. Thorne bought two companies and sold them back at a 20 percent loss a year later. The most significant consolidation effort came with the John B. Rose Commission House. Rose, a Yale graduate who took over his father's business, also owned the largest works on the river at Roseton, a few miles above Newburgh. The Commission House represented fifty manufacturers and controlled 600 million bricks a year, employing 130 barges and ten sailing vessels on the Hudson; forty barges could be berthed at once at their West 52nd Street docks. The industry strengthened further when a trade organization of 126 manufacturers, the Hudson River Brick Manufacturers Association, formed in 1902.

The worst accident in the Valley's brickmaking history occurred on January 8, 1906, when part of the village of Haverstraw collapsed into a clay bank, killing twenty people. The Rockland Street business section and a number of homes were destroyed, the resulting fire threatening the entire village until a heavy snowfall came in the night. As a result, the center of the industry shifted from Rockland to Ulster County, where more than thirty yards were in operation. Danger lurked on those shores as well; two men were killed at the Washburn works in Glasco after 1920 when a clay hillside shifted and collapsed.

A third of the Hudson Valley brick production remained unsold in 1910; a year later, twenty-five manufacturers went out of business. The Greater New York Brick Company was created in 1911 to stabilize the prices by using commission men from Haverstraw and nearby Grassy Point who were on good terms with local manufacturers. This was successful for a number of years, but the pressures on the industry to produce at the lowest possible cost inevitably led to its continued decline. The John B. Rose Company, the largest in the world twenty years earlier, was sold at bankruptcy in a Newburgh court in 1919. Only fifty-two manufacturers of brick along the Hudson River remained in 1922.

At the Washburn Brothers works, the workforce consisted of Italian Catholic immigrants who were treated with prejudice by the Washburn family —kept "below the hill" where the Protestants lived—but the success of the operation made such nuisances tolerable. By the second decade of the twentieth century, the works had become the largest manufacturers of bricks, producing 250,000 a day with around 400 employees. A strike developed in 1920 over the pay, which varied from as low as $1.85 a day to $3. The workers wanted a twenty-five-cent increase, but when the strike came R. C. Washburn, the son of a founding brother, went south and returned with forty or fifty workers, "all colored people" in John Buonfiglio's recollection sixty years later. The Italian workers ended the strike and went back to work. The two groups got along well, the blacks looking to the Italians as "kingpins" of the industry and the Italians finding in the African Americans willing workers eager to learn. Long and close relationships developed among some of the families.

"It wasn't as hard as doing it alone," Buonfiglio recalled.

The Glasco Italians retained much of their Old World culture while working the bricks. Napolitano families worried about "some Calabrese" who came down from Cementon after learning that Italians were there. A family named Ferraro had a son who "got stuck" on one of the girls and proposed to her. The girl's parents talked about it at home, and found someone to compose a letter (since they could not read) and sent it to a parish priest in Naples. The boy had some education and came from a good family of common, working people like themselves. The priest made inquiries and reported back—the family gathered round while the translator read the response—and the marriage was approved.

The Washburns had farm fields that stretched for two miles over to Barclay Heights, called the Track Farm because of a racing oval that was there. All of the goods the Italians purchased were through the company store, which worked on a 20% profit margin, higher for clothing and pharmaceuticals and less for butter. The Washburns also paid some family medical bills, but eventually the numbers that were "carried" by the company became too much. By 1939, when more than $50,000 was due the company on the books, the local town poormaster refused to help because they were "niggers and Guineas." The prejudice of the local white establishment in the nearby village, some of it expressed violently, continued over the years, the Italians reciprocating in their kind and the whole paradigm continuing in muted fashion for years.

The industry benefited from new technology when David Strickland created a low-pressure steam dryer in 1912, followed by the Strickland Automatic Brickmaking machine in 1920. He also introduced the coloring of commercial bricks for the New York market, and served as manager of the Denning's Point Brick Works in Beacon after 1920. A million Hudson Valley bricks were sold in 1926, the last of the boom years after a new competitor, Belgium, flooded the market in 1927. Joseph Mayone, who owned brickyards in Glasco and Athens, was one of the producers who supplied bricks for the Chrysler building in New York in 1933—and for dozens of other buildings in New York, Long Island, and Connecticut—yet in time he fell under the weight of the Depression. Some brickmakers who had invested in new technology for cooking and drying the bricks (like George Hutton and Terry Staples) survived those years—a half million bricks were made in one year in the decade after WWII—but by 1980 only one maker of Hudson River bricks remained. The last of the Hudson River brickmakers closed in 2007.

The great Ice Age depositions also left thousands of tons of sand in the northern Valley, the best of which—the molding sands—were harvested for industries for 150 years. The fields lay between Glens Falls and Marlboro, the best in the Albany-Coeymans area. Albany and Troy stove makers used the local molding sand during the period of greatest stove production between 1840 and 1870, the most successful being the North River and Crescent (Half

Moon) brands. Albany molding sand was also used in manufacturing marine engine parts in Europe.

Almost pure dolomitic limestone was shipped from quarries in Tuckahoe and Pleasantville. Henry Marks had a quarry at Ossining, the stone used for many years as flux in Newark blast furnaces. The Sing Sing Lime Company stone was suitable for lining Bessemer steel converters. These were the only locales in the region with pure dolomite, which was also ground into the fineness of sugar to extract its carbon dioxide. The Pleasantville quarry dust was known as "snowflake marble."

Somers, Amawalk, Hastings, and Verplanck also had limestone quarries. The limonite iron ores of eastern Dutchess County were fairly depleted by 1900. Thomas A. Edison had magnetite mines in the gneiss behind Annesville Cove in Peekskill—and more famously in Edison, New Jersey— intent on creating bricks of magnetite for blast furnace flux. The entire $2 million effort fell apart in 1899 with the discovery of the Mesabi iron range. The last of twenty-six magnetite mines operating in a five-county area in 1880 closed in 1931.

The cement industry hit the brick business hard and virtually ended the bluestone era. The Rosendale stone at East Kingston was the setting for early experiments in Portland cement (the term was coined in 1824), samples of which were exhibited at the Philadelphia Exposition in 1876. An attempt to make Portland cement in Croton later that decade failed because of the high sand content of the clays used, but related beds of limestone proved fruitful at the Cementon plants seventy miles upriver twenty-five years later, possibly because the new rotary kilns provided greater heat than the upright ones. A successful operation by the Wallkill Portland Cement Company at South Rondout began in 1880 and extended until 1889, when it was destroyed by fire.

A boom in block manufacturing developed when it was discovered that the Portland cement process significantly lessened the time needed to dry the product. One concrete block replaced twelve bricks; poured foundation walls were easier, quicker, and cheaper to build than brick ones. Samuel D. Coykendall tried to outlast the new competition by consolidating thirteen cement companies in the Rosendale area, but could not keep up. The making of Portland cement grew from 454,813 barrels in 1891 to 3,602,284 in 1898 in the United States, and then at a rate of 18 percent a year in the first half of the twentieth century. The Glens Falls Cement Company's Iron Clad and Victor brands—established in 1894—contributed to these numbers by utilizing the exposed Trenton limestone along the Hudson, but the stone had to be picked through carefully, the discarded pieces reserved for building stone and quick-lime. Hoosick Falls also had extensive outcrops of this stone, some of which was used for flux locally and in Troy.

Although Andrew J. Snyder Jr.'s Century Company at Cottekill and Tillson below Kingston continued well past World War II, scientists at the time predicted that the center of the industry would develop in the mid-Hudson limestone ridge outcroppings between East Kingston and Catskill-Ravena. The first successful new plant was built by the new Catskill Cement Company in 1899 under superintendent Herman C. Cowan, who changed the name of Smiths Landing to Cementon to commemorate their arrival. (The old name was resumed after the collapse of the industry a century later.) Cowan built a bucket cableway over the highway to move the stone and clay to two kilns, which could produce 300 barrels a day.

A New Jersey company built the adjoining Alsen plant (later called Lehigh Portland) in 1902. The Acme followed two miles further north by 1919, becoming a Seaboard, North American, Marquette, Gulf & Western, then Independent and St. Lawrence company plant in future years. Acme had pioneered the use of the rotary kiln cooking process for the stone. St. Lawrence, a Canadian company owned by a Swiss conglomerate, virtually doomed the industry on its arrival in the 1970s by undercutting the prices well below its own costs for the first several years. Alpha Portland Cement Company, which adjoined Lehigh Portland on the south and became the qualitative representative of the industry in the 1970s, was the most prominent casualty of the new economics. Alpha shipped by rail and truck—delivering as much as 700,000 pounds a day to New York and New England markets in the summers—while Lehigh included a barge system that provided millions of pounds for major construction works in the Bronx, Brooklyn and Rhode Island. The trucking industry collapsed as well.

In Albany County, the Indian Ladder along the escarpment of the Helderbergs rose in 700-foot-high cliffs of Pentamerus limestone. Becraft lime-stone was quarried west of Catskill and from Becraft Mountain across the river in Hudson, which also supplied Troy furnaces with flux in the late nineteenth century. A Pentamerus bed was quarried on the northeastern edge of the city for road materials for many years, and then for Portland cement. The Callanan Road Improvement Company operated a limestone quarry in South Bethlehem. The Ravena-Coeymans area had five different operations. Limestone was quarried and used in eastern Dutchess County, following the line of the Harlem Valley Railroad. The Ketcham brothers sold dolomite at Dover Plains. In South Dover, a marble company quarried a fine-grained white dolomite and brought it to the railroad on a private trolley line. Orange and Saratoga counties had several operations, and the Tomkins Cove Stone Company still drew from the extensive beds of limestone beneath the Tors in Rockland County.

Cementon became a tough little hamlet after the cement plants arrived, isolated by north and south railroad overpasses and occupied mainly by Croatians who came to work the stone. The hamlet that Rufus Smith (1782–1859) settled in 1835 had grown to about 1,200 people with fourteen saloons and at least two murders by 1910. The Alpha Clubhouse was built on the ridge, providing boarding for workmen, foremen residences, and a dance hall. The community was also hotly political; when Herbert Hoover won election in 1928, enthusiastic Catskill Republicans started a parade to the south that ended when Democrats stoned them at the first Alsen overpass.

Farmers also had it tough in Cementon/Alsen, although some, like John Bulich, Sr., persevered. Bulich established a new industry, mushroom growing, by using the rich dirt the limestone dust fallout created. Peddlers hawking fish, meat, butter and cheese, books visited the community often, and even a clothing wagon sent up by Amrod's Department Store from Saugerties. Petey Amrod outfitted the Catholic children who attended St. Mary's Elementary School in that village, allowing the whole school year for the bill to be paid if the family was poor, and absorbing more than one of those accounts himself over the years.

As agriculture faced its own new set of priorities, industries proliferated in the Hudson River Valley while rising to the new economic challenges of the times. A thriving foundry and rolling mill employed several hundred workers in the new lower Westchester village of Spuyten Duyvil (renamed from Fort Independence in 1872) by the 1880s. The mill was started when three farms were purchased and consolidated by Troy businessmen Elias Johnson, David B. Cox, and Joseph W. Fuller in 1852. More than thirty new businesses were attracted to the area, including Isaac G. Johnson's malleable iron foundry. North of Spuyten Duyvil, a cluster of houses called Cooperstown grew on part of the 356-acre Van Cortlandt estate after 1853. Country tracts of important individuals from the city were developed in the vicinity in the postwar years, among them Riverdale, which had the first fire-engine house in old Yonkers (and "a melodious old Spanish bell" cast in 1762). In 1856, Henry F. Spaulding laid out a village composed of beautiful country estates on 100 acres that William G. Ackerman had purchased. Theodore Roosevelt played on one of the estates as a boy.

By 1871 the Co-operative Cutlery Company at Ellenville in Ulster County was producing fine knives. Across the county near the river in Esopus, the Laflin & Rand Powder Company had mills in the western woods that made six hundred kegs of powder a day and employed fifty-four men. The night sky off Saugerties, Newburgh, Poughkeepsie, Cold Spring and elsewhere was lit with the fires of the older furnaces, the wood fuel replaced by bituminous coal sent over on the Ulster & Delaware Canal from the Pennsylvania fields. The *Henrietta Collyer*, a schooner built at Nyack in 1880, was one of about a dozen vessels hauling ore and limestone to the downriver blasts and bringing out the pig iron and potash.

Albany, the oldest incorporated city in the United States, boomed during this period. The capital city had 76 churches, including a dozen each of Roman Catholic and Baptist. Eight daily, eleven weekly, and three monthly newspapers served the community. Major structures included a new US government building that cost $500,000. The new capitol, authorized in 1865, had already cost $14 million, with the final price rising to $20 million by the time the construction was finished.

Twenty-seven-hundred men worked foundries along Ferry Street in Albany in 1885, producing 220,000 stoves a year. In Troy, the Burden Iron Works, which started as a nail factory, made the spikes that connected the railroads across America. One of its products was a replacement for the Liberty Bell in Philadelphia. In 1887, standing on a hill over the Wynantskill, Nathaniel Bartlett Sylvester looked down upon "more than fifty chimneys" fueling "as many furnaces," the lumps of malleable iron rolled into bars "that seem to wind their way like fiery serpents through the works." Two men at an anvil and forge could fashion seventy horseshoes a day. Sylvester marveled at the water wheel that Henry Burden invented, "sixty-four feet in diameter, over two hundred feet in circumference, and twenty-four feet in width," the water passing through "an immense conduit . . . Revolving before me was the largest water wheel in the world."

Troy's collar industry had the greatest proportion of women laborers in any city in the Northeast—a large majority of them Irish. The industry dated to 1827, when Hannah Lord Montague, tired of washing her husband's shirts when only the collars were soiled, snipped one off and washed and reattached it. The Montagues opened a factory with Austin Granger in 1834 and soon developed the "bishop's collar"—upright and tight against the neck—as well as dickies and detachable cuffs. A spin-off industry arose in cleaning the collars, beginning with Independence Starks' first Troy Laundry in 1835. By 1880, the industry had spread nationwide and given rise to the image of the "white collar worker" in American business. Troy employed 15,000 workers, mostly women, in the industry heyday in 1900.

The Collarworkers' Union, one of the first women's unions in America, was formed in 1864 from the indignation felt by three laundry workers—Kate Mullaney, Esther Keegan, and Sarah McQuinlan—over the low wages and bad working conditions they endured. Three hundred women industry workers walked out on the city's commercial operations for a week in February and won their demands. Kate Mullaney (1845?–1906) and friends led several other uprisings over the next few years, the women aided by the all-male iron-moulders union of Troy. The invention of the paper collar affected the industry significantly at this time, but Mullaney continued to represent women's interests in industry and became the first woman ever appointed to a national union office. US Senator Hillary Clinton placed a plaque of honor on her house on Eighth Street in 1999.

A fine shirts manufacturing business was run by Jesse and Adelbert Maxon in a factory across from the Civil War statue several miles east of Troy in Berlin in Rensselaer County. A central drive shaft ran the length of the building with large leather straps running from it to power the sewing machines. The industry was another one that employed skilled women workers, whom the Maxons obliged with hours suitable for each women's particular home needs. Jesse took frequent trips by train to Boston to take orders for their custom-made products.

In Rockland County, the Pierson Mills, which produced a million pounds of nails a year in 1810, built the Nyack Turnpike to the river and began shipping steel to Piermont along the new Erie Railroad in 1841. The sea wall along the New York Central Railroad was built from quarries at Clarkstown in the 1840s. The New York Trap Rock Company, begun by Daniel Tomkins in 1838, became the largest crushed stone industry in the world, with operations at West Nyack, Haverstraw, Tomkins Cove, and Suffern. John Suffern called his village New Antrim when he created his iron mills at a neighborhood the locals called Point of the Mountain; Suffern also had mills at Ramapo and Garnersville. J. E. Brausdorf developed a small dynamo that became a source of power for lighting the US Capitol and Pennsylvania Avenue in Washington. William Hyenga created the first industry for manufacturing smoking pipes in Spring Valley. In 1906, F. C. Koch patented a precision gauge for machine parts that became a standard of the industry in the making of typewriters, automobiles, lathes and other products (including caskets). Koch's small Nyack factory made thousands of these gauges for the government in World War I.

Rockland was the home of Avon Products, Inc., called the California Perfume Company when founded by David Hall McConnell at Suffern in 1886. McConnell began and perfected the direct sales approach to domestic products that made "Avon calling" a familiar sound in housewives' doorways in the next century. He started with perfumes and expanded to 350 products by the early 1940s, with 40,000 sales personnel around the country. The Suffern plant employed 600 during these years. Duncan Studio was another curious Suffern industry, where William Ireland Duncan began manufacturing Tatterman marionettes early in the 1920s. These dolls were conducted through 45,000 performances over the next twenty years—advertising sketches for the most part—and were featured in one motion picture.

Man's wonder at the ancient world expanded in the discovery of the remains of the Cohoes mastodon in the excavations for Harmony Mill No. 3 (since called "the Mastodon Mill") at Cohoes Falls in 1867. Harmony Mills represented the latest in cotton mill technology for its day. Begun in 1836 by Peter Harmony, the first of the textile mills was erected in 1837, three years after the Mohawk River was dammed and a raceway built to direct water to power the mill. The company was sold at a sheriff's auction in 1850 to Thomas Garner (d. 1867) of New York and Nathan Wild of Kinderhook. At least three dams were eventually built, and ten canals to direct the water to the various mill sites; the water was used six different times before flowing back into the river. The Mastodon Mill, the largest in the world when completed, included a huge bronze statue of Garner standing with plans in hand, done by Boston sculptor Martin Milmore (1844–83). Eight hundred horsepower turbines were installed in the basement to draw the water hydraulically from the old Erie Canal bed to power the works. A papermaking mill was added and converted for jute and cotton bag manufacturing in 1872. The complex included a large meeting and Sunday school hall with a small library for the employees.

The company built forty-three tenement buildings for the workers that survived as an intact neighborhood on the north side of Cohoes. Harmony Hill, a seventy-acre farm site west of the city, provided more housing accommodations (as many as 600-to-900 tenement houses and at least five boarding houses for unmarried workers) and a company store that accommodated a community of six thousand. Garner had $2.5 million invested in the property by the early 1860s. He also had a printworks for the calicos in Newburgh and warehouses in New York City.

Harmony Mills produced cotton fabric for calicos and fine muslins, its most productive period running from 1860 to 1880, and survived until 1932. The Mastodon Mill alone employed 2,500 workers making 700,000 yards of fabric a week. The mill was managed from 1850 to 1894 by a British father and son, Robert Johnston (1807–90) and David J. Johnston (d. 1894). Robert Johnston convinced Garner and Wild to purchase the site, and was considered one of the country's finest industry leaders; Samuel Slater, called the "Father of the American Factory System" by Andrew Jackson, "admired his spinning." Johnston had manufactured the first worsted fabric (*mousseline de laine*) ever made in America while superintendent of a cotton works owned by Alfred Wild, Nathan's father, in Valatie. In 1863, he returned with three chartered ships carrying 5,000 workers and their families, all new tenement housing awaiting their arrival.

Harmony Mills compared well against the finest textile mills of New England in size and production. In 1863, the *Cohoes Cataract* reported, Harmony had more manufacturing machinery operating than any mill in the country. Engineers from Europe and the Far East studied the water system that Canvas White developed. The labor force included English, Scots, Irish, and French Canadians. A 72-hour week was required, the wages for the unskilled workers amounting to 50 cents a day.

The "harmony" of the ownership's arrangements with the workers (two-thirds of the 3,500 employees were women) and the wider community—as late as 1937, the mill still owned three-quarters of the city of Cohoes—precluded significant labor disputes and other disruptions during its years of production. The Panic of 1857 led to a three-week strike the following year because the company lowered wages by 25% in order to maintain full production, and the workers got half the wages back as a result. Weavers walked out for a week in 1863, but returned when the management held firm because of the high price of cotton at the time. Harmony Mills remained fully employed during the national depression of 1873–77; wages were reduced but so were the rents on the tenement housing. Additional wage cutbacks led to a one-day wildcat strike in 1876.

A walkout by women weavers in February 1880 precipitated a well-organized strike by 5,000 workers. The Mule Spinners' Association, the Card Room Union, and the cotton-twisters joined the weavers' protest. They won their demands, but management proceeded to penalize the leaders over time. This led to a second strike that drew support from Troy iron molders and textile centers in Massachusetts. Another outbreak in 1882 drew the attention of the New York media and the national labor press. Samuel Gompers (1850–1924) was among those who came to Cohoes in support of the workers. The strikers returned to work after several months, yet joined the national Knights of Labor. Their leader, Joseph Delahanty, became an assemblyman and state labor leader following the strike.

David Johnston became mayor of Cohoes and served for 39 years as superintendent of the Harmony Union School. He was a model citizen and philanthropist who walked to work with the workers every day. The company was worth $22 million in 1890, yet faced severe competition from other mills. After David's illness and death, his nephew, David Stuart Johnston, became manager and briefly revived worker enthusiasm and production. When he left, the Garner interests were sold, a hydroelectric plant was built, and the innovative canal system became obsolete. The company survived under new Massachusetts ownership, but with the onset of the Great Depression Harmony Mills, "one of the largest cotton plants in the east," lost 70% of its production and was forced into "orderly liquidation" on May 24, 1932.

Specialized industries proliferated in the Valley, the communities developing in sophistication as their workforces grew. Communities became identified with specific industrial activities—stoves and iron products in Troy and Albany, paper making and coating at Saugerties, plows and stoves at Peekskill, patent medicine and stone quarrying in Ossining, Irvington's greenhouses (thanks to the presence of Lord and Burnham) and road-building industry, ironmaking (mainly the Abendroth Foundry) at Port Chester, bricks from Cortlandt, Verplanck, Haverstraw, Kingston, Glasco and other river towns; and Yonkers with its carpet mills, sugar refining, hat and rubber manufacturing, and the Otis Elevator Company. Thirty-five major manufacturing interests located in Yonkers between 1852 and 1895. The Waring Hat Company, which returned in 1884 after starting in the city thirty-five years earlier and leaving after two years, was the largest of its kind in the country, producing 1,200 hats a day by 1898. The Yonkers Hat Manufacturing Company thrived for nearly a decade in the 1880s until a fire forced the company to relocate to Peekskill. Two more hat firms were located in Yonkers as well.

Elisha Graves Otis (1811–1861) began with a small shop along the river in 1854 and, like Fulton with the steamboat, was not the inventor of the elevator but the first to make a practical application of the device. He invented the movable lift with a safety device and a hydraulic gear to run it, the basis for all later elevator technology. Ever innovating, Otis Elevator introduced the escalator at the Paris Exposition of 1900.

The largest of the Yonkers industries was the Alexander Smith and Sons Carpet Company, which ran out of the old Waring Hat Factory building on Vark Street and used new power looms invented by Smith and Halcyon Skinner, who revolutionized carpet manufacturing worldwide. By 1909, Smith and Sons produced almost forty miles of carpet a day using 6,500 workers— one-third of the city's total workforce—almost all of whom lived in the city and walked to work.

John Masefield (1878–1967), later England's poet laureate, was one of them. The hard economic times at the close of the century forced him out of work for six weeks. "We did not know the cause of the closing," he wrote:

> we judged, vaguely, that it was due 'to the depression,' whatever
> that was; the effect upon us all, and upon the town itself . . . , was
> black indeed. . . . Most of the married workers could not see beyond
> the mill; it was their life. Few of the unmarried men ever saved
> money. Few of either party had expected any horror of this kind;

their ship went from under their feet. . . . I shall never forget the universal sympathy in that stricken town; how kind all people were in those days; how gladly they shared what they had, and how the tradesmen, the restaurant-keeper, the dairyman, the Chinese laundryman, and two or three more, alike lowered their rates at once, to the cutting off of all possible profit to themselves, so that their clients should not have too hard a time. . . .

Alexander Smith (1818–1878) died at the age of 60 on the evening before his successful election to the House of Representatives representing Yonkers constituents. The Alexander Smith Carpet Mills Historic District—which comprises eighty-five buildings in Yonkers—was added to the National Register of Historic Places in 1983.

Pleasantville had several private schools by 1875, including the Belmont Seminary for young women and a county Alms House where fifty children were taught. Lamps were placed around the community in 1874; the telegraph came in 1883, and the Mount Kisco Electric Light Company in 1889. Two newspapers were published—impressive for a community of under 1,200. In Mount Kisco, the making of needles and women's shoes became productive local industries. The largest concern at Newcastle Corners was the Spenser Optical Works, said to be the largest in the country at the time; the Works burned in 1877 and was promptly rebuilt, but left the region eleven years later.

The range of products and skilled labor was immense. Westchester, the most populous Hudson Valley county although only seventeenth in the state in manufacturing, had more than five hundred concerns in 1880 and employed more than 10,500 workers. The county's assessed value went from $52 million in 1879 to $179 million in 1901, largely due to industrialization.

Irish workers building the West Shore Railroad in the 1880s remained and lived in the vicinities of their labors, some in shacks along the tracks and some joining enclaves of local factory workers. The experience was similar for the Irish who came to Albany to work the mills. The founder of Albany's Sacred Heart Church, Father Francis Maguire, used a whip and "a powerful fist" (in William Kennedy's words) in keeping the peace while making his parish rounds on horseback. One of Father Maguire's successors, the aptly named Father Fearey, "thrashed" a husband for beating his wife, declaring to the astonished miscreant "that the laying on of hands was the province of thy God and my God, the Father."

Overland progress advanced in fits and starts in the late nineteenth century. Some of the fits were predictable, like the persistence of a few plank roads long after their usefulness had dissipated. A stage ran along one in the 1870s from the Glens Falls terminus of the Delaware & Hudson Railroad to the new tourism at Lake George. The railroad industry expanded across the counties, and added attractive amenities (as finely outfitted sloops once did) for the passenger trade. Some of the starts were dramatic: in 1874, the six-mile-long Hoosac Tunnel was breached through the narrowest ridge in the Berkshire Mountains in Massachusetts, connecting Albany with Boston by rail. An engineering wonder of the world in its day, the tunnel symbolized man's conquest of geography itself in the making of America.

Rural towns were still building roads under an eighteenth century labor assessment system that involved men in the local neighborhoods working as crews under an overseer or "pathmaster," who was usually one of their neighbors. In 1873, a state law allowed towns to convert to a "money system" run by an annual tax, but only the rise of the good roads movement drew serious attention to the conditions of the internal road system that provoked real change. That movement was driven by the bicycle.

The League of American Wheelmen was influential with wealthy community leaders and as a political force. Governor David B. Hill opened public parks to wheelmen after their national organization (200,000 strong) promised to support his reelection. This legislation was the beginning of a good governance trend that advanced in the administration of Benjamin O'Dell after the turn of the century and culminated in the modernization of state agencies by Governor Alfred E. Smith. The bicycle's influence was also felt in areas that attracted tourists—a Catskill-Palenville run was created in Greene County and eleven miles of good roads were constructed between Gansevoort and Glens Falls in 1893. The commencement of rural delivery of mail that year also promoted the good roads movement.

Cyclists advocated road improvement through alliances with the newly emerging motorists and the railroads. Yet the issue was not clear for any state legislators. The traditional antagonisms of Democrats toward internal improvements still lingered, and upstate Republicans had to face the conservative farm vote. The appeal of a good road to a farmer (and a railroad) was the speed by which products could get to market, but farmers knew that road taxes would be derived from real property assessments, and they had the most land. Cyclists lived in populated areas and paid little by comparison.

The state gave counties the authority to create and maintain roads in 1892. County highway boards were created and local investments in stone-crushers and other heavy equipment authorized by referendum, and the farm communities usually lost out to the more populated hamlets in these votes. The Higbie-Armstrong Act of 1898 provided 50% in state aid for highways, the counties contributing 35% and the towns 15%; the first highway built under the new law ran from Waterford to Mechanicville. Yet only $34,518 was spent on new roads, at an average cost of $3,000 a mile, and only 59 miles of new state roads were built over the next five years—compared with petitions requesting 1,308 additional miles. Route 9W through West Park remained a dirt road until macadam was laid in the World War I era.

The advent of concrete in construction work led to the building of the Fenimore Bridge across the Hudson River between Moreau and Hudson Falls in 1907, at 1,025 feet "the longest reinforced concrete structure in the world" at the time. The federal government stepped in with the Post Office Appropriation Act of 1913, offering $500,000 for mail roads that rose to $75 million under the Federal Aid Road Act of 1916. A six-arch bridge was erected at Glens Falls that year, a steel truss bridge at Schuylerville, and another in Ballston.

Meanwhile, the "pathmasters" were still in charge. A typical pathmaster in the years after the turn of the century was Will Voerg (1882–1948) of Saugerties, a village farmer with some homegrown engineering skills. He had a reliable group of locals he could call out in an emergency or for maintenance work. He was a transitional figure who became an overseer of larger crews as the state assumed more control over highways maintenance. Voerg used his own Cadillac as the overseer in the early 1920s, the top lopped off and the rear converted to a pick-up style box for the roadwork. He had a sideline selling fresh fish and produce from the riverboats to the boarding houses in the mountains.

12. Rails Trails

Fierce-throated beauty!
Roll through my chant with all thy lawless music,
    thy swinging lamps at night,
Thy madly-whistled laughter, echoing, rumbling like an
    earthquake, rousing all,
Law of thyself complete, thine own track firmly holding. . . .

—WALT WHITMAN, "To a Locomotive in Winter" (1881–82)

When Coeymans native Niels Sears (1825–1907) decided to move his family to California in 1869, he made a reconnaissance trip over the new transcontinental railroad first. He had already been west, practicing law in Missouri and California and returning in 1853 to marry March C. Niles, the daughter of the judge with whom he had boarded while studying law at Rensselaerville. Sears left New York for the West again on the Erie Railroad on May 9, 1869, two days before the golden spike completed the railroad at Promontory Point, Utah. His passage to Sacramento cost $238. He arrived in California on May 19, returning to New York two weeks later. Sears was the first person to travel across America completely by rail.

Railroad growth, both before and after the Civil War, was both spectacular and chaotic, rails sprouting like spring legumes in all the counties, ready for the commodities and travelers of the new modern times. In Westchester the lines followed the geography, the Hudson River Railroad along the river; the Putnam (or New York City and Northern) Railroad following the Saw Mill River, the New York and Harlem through the Bronx River Valley, and the New York, New Haven, and Hartford mimicking the shoreline of Long Island Sound.

The Hudson River Railroad, built from 1846 to 1851, was popular in its early years, carrying almost 50,000 passengers in the fall of 1847, the year the line reached Peekskill. At first considered an impossible engineering task— Thurlow Weed suggested that "a 'Railway to the Moon' was scarcely less preposterous"—the rail was conceived as competition to Boston's plans to run a line from there to Albany. The projected $4.5 million cost in the end became the most expensive railroad in America, at $9.3 million or $80,000 a mile. A wood-burning locomotive could make the 143-mile run from New York to Albany in four hours. The road lost money initially because Erastus Corning shipped his New York Central produce and goods to the city on Daniel Drew's Packet Line of steamboats in the summer, only resorting to the rival rail for shipments when the river was frozen over.

The New Haven and Hartford Railroad ran through Rye, Harrison, Mamaroneck, New Rochelle, Pelham, and Eastchester, and in 1873 added part of the Harlem and a small Port Chester rail line. The future city of Mount Vernon developed quickly and in a novel form after the rail arrived in 1851. A contingent of working families that were fed up with city rents came north, purchased five Eastchester farms totaling 370 acres, and within six months subscribed a thousand members to their nascent organization called the New York Industrial Home Association, No. 1. The post office ruled that the community's new name, Monticello, was already taken in New York State, so they settled on Mount Vernon instead. The group erected a railroad depot, and within another year 300 houses were up or on their way.

Despite an emphasis on passenger use in the accounts of these railroads, more than half of the New Haven revenues came from freight. The lower suburban county was largely built on the goods brought in by the New Haven. The New Rochelle area, heavily wooded and barely settled when the line came in late 1873, was soon transformed into an industrialized region. The Northern Railroad was built for the farmers in the Saw Mill River valley. Most of the twenty-five early stations disappeared with the communities they represented, including Lincoln, Dunwoodie, Bryn Mawr Park, Nepperhan, St. Andrews, Mount Hope, Woodlands, Worthington, and Baldwin Place. A Yonkers branch served six stations in the Van Cortlandt-Fordham Heights area. Yet most of the revenues—which were never enough—were derived from freight services, not the passengers. A New York, Westchester and Boston rail was planned and partially built—with lines to White Plains and Port Chester—but only operated from 1911 to 1938.

The New York and Harlem, chartered in 1831 to serve the village at the top of Manhattan, wisely secured the right to enter Westchester County as well. The train reached Chatham in Columbia County in 1852, but was never financially successful because of the $7.9 million expense. The Harlem added a small line between Lake Mahopac and Goldens Bridge in 1872, and was then incorporated into the New York Central.

Erastus Corning, working with his niece's husband and fellow Albany financier, Democratic Congressman John V. L. Pruyn (1797–1882), consolidated eleven railroads between Albany and Buffalo into the New York Central System in 1853, creating a $30 million corporation. The swift growth of the venture received a tongue-in-cheek nod of appreciation in 1858 when 86 signers petitioned the state legislature to hold a constitutional convention to abolish the executive and legislative branches of government and vest their authorities in the board of this railroad. In 1855, 350 acres three miles west of Albany in Spencerville was purchased and transformed into Corning's principal eastern rail yard. A workforce of almost a thousand was employed in these "West Albany" fields under master mechanic Edward H. Jones. Onsite clay was used in making a huge brick roundhouse for a locomotive, passenger, deck and platform car shop; the roundhouse could store thirty cars and engines inside. Within the first decade, using thousands of cattle, sheep, and hog cars built here, West Albany became the largest wholesale cattle depot in the United States, managing 700 cars a day. By 1867, Central's yard stretched between Albany and Schenectady, where a new locomotive works would soon be erected.

The New York Central defined railroad progress in these years, but Corning's Achilles' heel became access to New York City because his line ended at Albany. He needed the Hudson River Railroad to ship his goods south in the winter. Vanderbilt closed that avenue to Corning when a new railroad bridge opened across the Hudson in 1867 (a second, double-tracker followed in 1872). He stopped his trains at Greenbush and made the passengers rent sleds or walk across the ice to the city. The confusion and uproar that resulted led Corning to agree to Vanderbilt's terms for passage of the Central's goods, and within two years the Commodore forced a merger, creating the New York Central and Hudson River Railroad. A connecting link with the Harlem River Railroad at Chatham was made in 1871.

In the fever of the post-Civil War era, the Poughkeepsie & Eastern Railroad was built over the 43 miles from the Hudson River past the Ancram lead mines to Boston Corners. The Dutchess County Railroad ran from Fishkill to Millerton until 1898, serving iron mines at Clove Valley after 1869. By the end of the century, the Rhinebeck & Connecticut Railroad had a terminus at

Rhinecliff, with a bridge across to the Rondout planned but never built. A railroad bridge across the Hudson at Poughkeepsie was built from 1873 to 1888. Ursula Burroughs roundly chastised her husband for walking their eight-year-old son across the unfinished span in the dead of winter one year. The first train came across on December 29, 1888, and a direct line opened to Hartford the following year, all to move Pennsylvania coal into New England.

The Delaware & Hudson Railroad, started by John B. Jervis in 1846, expanded north and west into upper New York, and remained independent until 1870, when taken over by Vanderbilt's New York Central. In time the railroad extended to Montreal, and by the 1940s was operating over 846 miles of track with 6,700 employees. A $2.2 million repair shop was established on 110 acres at Colonie in 1912. Among its subsidiary lines were the Schenectady & Duanesburg, on which George Westinghouse served as a director, and, also fourteen miles long, the Greenwich & Johnsonville in the rich farming region of Rensselaer County; the G&J extended to Schuylerville with the acquisition of the Battenkill Railroad in 1903. While a pattern of rail distribution among farming and population centers prevailed in most counties, north of Albany the recreational resources at Saratoga Springs, Ballston Spa, and Lake George also kept the industry busy. The northern D&H branch, a short stretch from Glens Falls to Lake George, was built for tourists and appropriately became a bikeway in the Lake George State Park late in the next century.

West of the Hudson, the Rondout and Oswego Railroad had forty miles in operation in Ulster County in 1871, running to Kingston via Hurley, Olive, and Shandaken. The Walkill Valley was a branch of the Erie that connected the R&O through Shawankgunk, Gardiner, New Paltz, and Rosendale. The New York and Oswego Midland had a branch from Middletown to Ellenville. Port Jervis in western Orange County had two rail terminuses and shops, comprising a huge rail center. In 1875, an "ice gorge" in the Delaware River knocked out two bridges and carried away several of these buildings.

A railroad united Troy and Schenectady in 1843. In Rensselaer County, George E. Greene (1860–1943), the "dean" of the legal profession in the county, led the construction of the Hoosic Valley Street Railway (a trolley line) and its expansion to Bennington, Vermont, and North Adams, Massachusetts. By 1874, six railroads crossed Columbia County: the Hudson River (1851), Harlem (1852), Boston & Albany (1838), Harlem Extension (1869), Pough-keepsie, Hartford & Boston (1872), and Rhinebeck & Connecticut (1874).

The 57-mile-long Lebanon Spring Railroad ran from Chatham to Bennington, Vermont (1869–1953).

The Becraft Mountain cement industry began with a railroad built by Frederick W. Jones (d. 1901) to carry the stone and marble rubble to Hudson River docks. The railroad crossed South Bay as it came down from the quarries, offering tourists pleasant perspectives of Hudson, the river, and the Catskill Mountains along the way. Jones's business survived until 1900, when the Colonial Construction Company built a cement factory to take advantage of a relatively pure limestone found in the quarry. Eventually the property fell to Universal Atlas Cement, which added a roadbed, and St. Lawrence Cement, which dismantled the railroad in 1990.

Western Rockland County hosted the railroad fitting yard of the East with the Ramapo Iron Works and the Ramapo Wheel and Foundry Company. By the mid-1930s, 300 men were employed at Hillburn. The rail for New York's subway trains was manufactured here. The foundry made four hundred railroad wheels a day. The community included a company store, a school, and housing for the workers.

The New York, West Shore & Buffalo line, organized in early 1880, initially forecasted at $40 million, cost over $50 million and bankrupted the line before it reached Buffalo. West shore towns along the way were delighted, however; at Kingston, judge Frederick Edward Westbrook crowed that its arrival meant an end to Rondout's "former sense of superiority" over the river's freight trade. The railroad turned west at Coeymans and used the D&H to access Albany, with the Central also cooperating despite the apparent competition with the HRRR, by leasing a Schenectady-Athens spur that gave access to the Hudson River. The West Shore was considered "one of the most substantially built and elegantly equipped railroads in the country," laid with heavy double tracks of rail, bedecked with iron bridges and ballasted with stone drawn from the Tomkins Cove Lime Company. A five-hour run to Albany opened on July 9, 1883, and included Pullman cars that went on to Saratoga Springs via the D&H. The Central picked up the pieces in the financial collapse of the West Shore in 1885 and became the owner.

The growth of an inter-urban surface rail system run by electrical power quickly followed upon the development of rail in many counties. Westchester County trolleys connected Tarrytown with New York and Connecticut and included Tuckahoe, New Rochelle, Mount Vernon, and White Plains.

Peekskill and Ossining ran small lines for their own cities. With rail and trolley combined, Yonkers soon had twenty stations for travelers to use. Trolleys were initially powered by horses that pulled cars along tracks in the streets, but a pathogen that destroyed many horses in the eastern United States in the 1880s led companies to explore the new technology of electricity. Individual lines soon consolidated into larger concerns, county trolley systems were created, the demand stayed high and the prices low. By 1893, more than 5.8 million riders were served by the Westchester County trolley system; in 1894 that number rose to eleven million. Railroads were also good for the taxpayers: their property tax assessments often comprised a quarter of all of the assessed value of the communities they served, and in some communities more than half.

Ned Harriman entered the railroad business through his friend, Stuyvesant Fish, who was a Garrison neighbor of William Osborn. President of the Illinois from 1855 to 1865 and director until 1877, Osborn had revived the line using his own personal credit after the 1857 panic. Osborn brought Fish in, first as a director of the Illinois and then as secretary of the Central's rail line to the Gulf of Mexico. Harriman purchased bonds offered by Fish in 1881 and took a personal interest in the Illinois at a time when the odds in the high stakes rails game were beginning to shift in an unexpected direction.

"I don't like that man Harriman," said Sam Sloan, an old railroad man and summer neighbor of Fish and Osborn at Garrison. "He and Stuyv Fish are going to get Osborn in trouble with the Illinois Central if he don't watch out."

Harriman continued to purchase the stock despite the consternation of conservative Wall Street bondsmen, telling his customers that the Illinois was "the best road in the country." The line had the best credit, thanks to the management of Osborn from 1875 until his retirement in 1882, and greatly expanded after Harriman became a director in 1883, increasing its mileage by a thousand over the next five years and proving to be a very good investment indeed. By 1885, Harriman was able to retire from his brokerage business and buy an estate near J. P. Morgan's at Highland Falls, across the river from Garrison. Harriman's acumen as a railroad manager came with the Panic of 1893, after he had advised his board against a large expansion program they had advocated. The panic forced the bankruptcy of more than 150 railroads, but not the Illinois. Bankers across the country gave the credit to the Central's president, Stuyvesant Fish, who quickly acknowledged that Harriman's foresight had saved the day.

One of those gone bankrupt in the panic was the Erie Railroad, which Harriman now took on his daily jaunts from his new Rockland estate to the city. When the Erie was forced to organize under terms that Harriman had proposed, it responded in petty fashion by denying Harriman his request to have the Chicago make a special stop at Goshen so that he could attend the races there; he outwitted them by having a friend buy a Chicago ticket at Goshen, necessitating the flagging of the trail. A few years later he would bail out the Erie, then owned wholly by Morgan, with a $5.5 million loan. Harriman also trumped Morgan in acquiring control and undertaking, in less than four years, a $25.6 million reconstruction of the Union Pacific Railroad, singularly ranked as perhaps the greatest engineering feat in America until that time. The market value of Union Pacific shares increased from $25 in 1898 to $185 in 1906.

The squalid nature of the railroad industry first drew the young J. Pierpont Morgan into its web in 1869 when Jay Gould, of the same age, attempted to take over the small Albany & Susquehanna Railroad. Gould had "prodigally bribed" New York State legislators in gaining control of the Erie, a line that had developed in fits and starts after Governor DeWitt Clinton offered its franchise to Southern Tier industries as a trade-off for the Erie Canal. The railroad had only reached Goshen by 1841, a prodigious achievement given the nature of the Hudson Highlands. The line was completed to Dunkirk on Lake Erie in 1851, and after the Civil War Gould wanted to sell coal to New England and take some of the New York Central trade on the Great Lakes.

The A&S, founded in 1852 by Joseph H. Ramsey, had a railroad bridge across the Hudson at Albany that Gould coveted. Ramsey was still in control in 1869, but because of Gould half of his directors aligned against him. At the annual A&S board meeting in Albany on September 7, 1869, Ramsey had the rail's subscription books (which he had been hiding in a cemetery) lowered into the room through a back window to keep them away from Gould's forces. Ramsey was said to have dealt with Gould's trusted henchman, "Jubilee" Jim Fisk, by hurling him down a back stairs. He brought J. Pierpont Morgan in as a supporting stockholder, and when the Erie slate was finally ousted from the A&S board Morgan directed Ramsey to join the Delaware & Hudson line. The D&H then constructed a rail connecting line with the A&S, opening an avenue that the original D&H board members had deemed desirable back in the 1820s.

The A&S became Morgan's first corporate board seat, which he took in partial payment for his pains. In doing so, he established the standard of "relationship banking," whereby bankers assumed board membership in corporations as ways to ensure their investments and also control the boards. The maneuver also raised Morgan's annual income to $75,000, allowing him to purchase the huge estate south of West Point that he named Cragston.

In 1879, when William Henry Vanderbilt (1821–1885) chose to sell a large block of stock in his father's New York Central Railroad to avoid newly imposed taxes he asked Pierpont Morgan, then 42, to broker the sale. William had inherited the line from the Commodore, who died in 1877 leaving a fortune of $100 million. The crude and vulgar Commodore never thought well of his son, whom he considered "a dunce," yet he left him 87 percent of the New York Central stock. William had shown confidence in acquiring the Harlem Valley Railroad station in Manhattan and bringing all his father's lines under one roof there, calling it Grand Central Station, yet he seemed to live up to his father's estimate during the sale of the stock, running afoul of the public in damning it so publicly. Morgan masked the high-volume sales and made a fortune himself in the bargain.

Morgan stepped in on New York Central's behalf again in 1883, when a rate war broke out with the Pennsylvania Railroad over the West Shore Railroad, which opened another, easier route to market from the Midwest. The scheme was complicated by an interest of D&H Canal president Thomas Dickson (d.1884) to abandon the canal in favor of rail by connecting Albany and Jersey City via the Wallkill Valley Railroad and a new, $4 million line running north from Orange County. The Wallkill was now under the control of Thomas Cornell, who also had his designs on the Hudson River line. The elephant in the room was the Vanderbilt's New York Central line that the West Shore would parallel up the Hudson River. Dickson despised the Vanderbilts and the rates they charged for the D&H's freight, but also worried that William would respond by building a rail to Saratoga to compete with the D&H's lucrative line there. But the Central was more interested in undercutting the Pennsylvania line. New York Central was now sorely tried by the loss of revenues and had to defer needed maintenance of its tracks. A war could prove to be calamitous.

Morgan worried that the machinations within the rail industry were seriously harming commerce, yet he also had a personal interest in resolving the dispute. In 1882, his children, while playing at Cragston, were menaced by Irish workers on the West Shore, and the estate itself was pelted with stone from dynamite blasts during the construction. Morgan brought together Chauncey M. Depew, president of the New York line, and his Pennsylvania counterpart on Morgan's yacht, the *Corsair*, on July 20, 1885. While the ship sailed the Hudson, he chastised the men over the concerns his investors had in America's railroads, and allowed them to broker their own solution. The two railroads agreed to buy out their competing lines and end the war. Cornell benefited by selling the Wallkill to the Vanderbilts. The D&H Canal, although it had its own rail line following the canal to tidewater, never realized Dickson's dream of shifting entirely over to rail, and instead quietly drifted into senescence over the next 20 years. The days of the great canals were done; the only substantial improvement to the D&H in the waning years was the addition of an elevator system at the Rondout receiving point to handle more product. The West Shore became the Central's second track on the Hudson River highway and Morgan was lionized by the news media for engineering the Great Railway Treaty of 1885, also known as the Corsair Compact.

"Pierpont handled the West Shore affair better than I could have myself," his father, Junius Morgan (1813–90), said from England—high compliment indeed for a father so parsimonious in his praises.

13. The Takings

The destruction in reality fills one with awe. What a lovely village is being laid waste.
—WEST SHOKAN correspondent,
Kingston Daily Freeman, January 22, 1913

An old Indian myth about the origin of the Catskill Mountains told of a giant monster that had drunk dry the Great Lakes and, still thirsty, was heading toward the Atlantic Ocean when Manitou, exasperated at the creature's gall, rose up and struck it dead. The Catskills formed where the monster fell, North and South lakes representing its eyes, a solemn Indian's head appearing in numerous unmistakable Valley views of the Plateau Mountain range, and the torso and legs stretching down the northeastern front like a sleeping giant. That was the old Indian myth. A new one might instead have the monster slouching from the south, this time to drink dry not the ocean but the great water resources that Manitou held in its benevolent Catskills palm, only now no god arose to strike the monster dead.

A modern-day manifestation of Manitou's revenge happened, in a sense, at the end of the twentieth century when New York City agreed to expend hundreds of millions of dollars on improvements in the mountain communities to ensure the continued purity of the "west-of-Hudson" watersheds. It was a Hobson's choice for the city, not one generated by neighborly friendliness, since the alternative was to construct a multi-billion-dollar water filtration plant. The cure was only partly successful, however; the construction of the Ashokan Reservoir and the massive new Catskill Aqueduct (1907–17) imposed collateral impacts on communities that did not benefit from the improvement.

The city's water distribution system from Croton to below Yonkers, created over 1837–42, remained a model in architectural adaptation well into the twentieth century. Over its original 57 miles, the Croton River drained 378 square miles of the lower Hudson Valley. Before the system was built, the river current had moved swiftly enough to prevent an accumulation of marshes and sediment near its outlet to the Hudson, but once a significant draw occurred sedimentation poured into the river's delta. Riverside commerce all but ended, and the Hudson River shore in Westchester County was significantly redefined. Van Cortlandt Manor, its once-conspicuous porch immediately accessible from a riverside dock before the reservoir, now lay far inland and out of view.

Fifty years after the Croton Reservoir, with 70 million gallons of water a day for New York City no longer adequate, new storage was added at Quaker Bridge, four-and-a-half miles below the first one, and the Bronx River watershed was tapped with a 45-foot-high dam at Kensico. The New Croton Dam, completed in 1907, was the largest hand-hewn masonry project in the world at the time. The construction displaced a world of farms, pastoral trails, covered bridges and hidden estates owned by wealthy part-time residents. Part of the "Old Put" Putnam Division of the New York Central Railroad was engulfed in the process. Unable to run rail from the Hudson River line, the city used barges and teams of horses to haul tens of thousands of barrels of Rosendale and Portland cement and tons of coal to the site. Frequent changes to the plans extended an eight-or-nine year project to more than fourteen in duration—and created windfall after windfall profits for the contractors with each new change order.

The New Croton Dam Lake was spanned at its deepest part by the 2,000-foot long Hunter Bridge, obliterating the once thriving hamlet of Huntersville. The $4 million dam held 32 billion gallons of water over 3,635 acres, draining 361 square miles into a 19-mile-long lake. Five major bridges were needed to accommodate north-south traffic, the largest the four-lane Taconic State Parkway span, which crossed near the future Catskill Aqueduct right-of-way. A 12-foot-round water conduit was laid over 26.5 miles to the Harlem River, almost all of it through a rock tunnel; the conduit could carry 250 million gallons a day for 29 miles over a 23-foot fall to Central Park.

As many as 1,500 workers were employed on the project. As the work proceeded, the state of labor-industry relations generally helped provoke a national incident in a short-lived walkout by a small group of blacksmiths at Croton Landing. The men wanted the current $1.35 company minimum wage rate to be the same as New York's minimum wage, $1.50 for 10 hours. The company refused, which led 600 of their fellow workers to join the blacksmiths. The metropolitan newspapers did not approve of these immigrants, and there was little sympathy for the action locally. Tensions came to a head thirteen days into the strike when (unfounded) rumors spread of a plan to dynamite the dam. The contractor brought in a hundred "deputy sheriffs" (the local papers knew them as common thugs), armed them, and sent them to the site. Enraged workers stoned them on the bridge to the dam. After the melee, they offered to relent on the extra hours in return for $1.50 a day, but by now the county sheriff wanted the militia. The edgy governor, albeit sympathetic, was increasingly troubled by rumors of violence, so on Easter Sunday Theodore Roosevelt ordered two infantry companies and 350 cavalrymen to Croton Landing.

The companies marched north from the New York Armory on Monday, April 16, running ammunition and camp wagons in the rear. The first of the troops arrived by train just before nightfall, each man outfitted with twenty rounds and three days' rations. In the warm spring evening, they made camp and pitched tents outside the village while the children of the workers walked among them. Shortly after 8 p.m., under moonlight, a detachment led by Sergeant Robert Douglass, a tall twenty-eight-year-old Scot known for his basketball prowess, was relieving sentinels along a guard line. At the ninth station, standing alone, Douglass cried out and collapsed. No weapon was heard or seen, yet now a man lay dead. His squad wanted revenge, but they were restrained while the workers stoutly denied killing the sergeant.

A tense night ensued, followed by a rainy Tuesday as the workers' community was cut off and guards posted all along the nearby roads. The Seventh Regiment moved on Thursday, the infantry in a long line in the front with fixed bayonets, the cavalry behind them. Soldiers used their bayonets to probe gardens, pigsties, and woodpiles for incriminating evidence. All the homes were searched for weapons; only three guns were found. The strike leaders were arrested and led off in handcuffs, eighteen men charged with inciting to riot and eight others seen by the sheriff at the stone-throwing incident. Four labor agitators who came into the village urging the men to remain on strike were later arrested.

Sunday was a quiet day at the soldiers' camp. Their sweethearts and wives arrived from the city and a daylong picnic ensued. Some of the laborers, worn out and half-starved, returned to work on Monday, April 23, joined by fifty Hungarians brought in by the company as scabs. It took another two years, but by the summer of 1902 the workers achieved their goals, an eight-hour day rather than ten and a three-cent increase in the hourly wage, from 14 to 17.

A number of the immigrants who built the new reservoir lived at the base of the new dam on Yorktown Road in a temporary town dubbed the Bowery, notable for its twenty-three saloons and brothels. Italians and Irish lived in separate enclaves at the Bowery. A local mafia developed around Mount Kisco in an enclave called Sutton's Row (the Shoppers' Bazaar area of modern times), managed by *agenti* who arranged their passage and board and became the equivalent of *padroni* or neighborhood overlords of the immigrants. One of them, a scoundrel named Petrillo, was said to have charged $12 board for a man who only made $14 a week. Around 1900, a keg of dynamite exploded under his porch, and that was the end of Petrillo. Other swindlers persisted, though. In 1904, Westchester Sheriff James Merritt succeeded in ending a Black Hand extortion ring that preyed on the Croton workers.

After the dam was built, many Italians worked the factories at Mount

Kisco or became premier masons for architecture and domestic landscaping needs. Part of eastern Westchester County's charm is attributable to the quality work that they did, and one of three Westchester County residents in the 1960s was a descendant of the original reservoir builders. Italian families also populated enclaves of other cities where the work was available, notably Troy, where the community along the Poestenkill was called Little Italy. The neighborhood, although made of tenements, sported the characteristic Italian patches of tomatoes and arbors of grapes. Little Italy bakeries produced flaky pastries and breads that were sold on the street and to the wealthy families in the fashionable brownstones along Albany's Washington Park.

Twelve reservoirs in all eventually made up the Croton system, including the Boyd's Corner, Sodom, and Titicus built before the New Croton. Villages at Pine Bridge, Cross River, and parts of Croton Falls and Goldens Bridge disappeared, and Purdys Station and Katonah were relocated away from the water. Old Katonah's loss was particularly egregious, a fine village beautified by one of the old Improvement societies, with factories and mills, two hotels for visitors to a ninety-acre racetrack complex, a newly-enlarged school, three churches, a small home-based women's garments industry, and a railroad station. The finer houses were raised onto timbers and relocated—some while the stubborn residents still lived in them. Some workers coming home at the end of the day found their house moved fifty or a hundred yards away without notice. Six cemeteries were emptied and 1,500 remains distributed elsewhere. The Village Improvement Society supervised the creation of the new Katonah, tanneries, breweries and slaughter houses banned, temperance established (sending the saloons a short distance away across the new town line), and new roads provided by the city of New York, but it was no longer the pastoral jewel of a bygone era.

Two impoundments followed the New Croton, at Cross River and Croton Falls, adding another 25 billion gallons in storage capacity, yet the need for more water prompted a search for new sources to serve the city. Ultimately, the city would turn to the land of the Manitou west of the Hudson. In 1876, Poughkeepsie businessman Harvey G. Eastman offered a plan to pump Hudson River water into a reservoir above Poughkeepsie—which had a new slow sand filter plant to draw river water for its residents—and then distribute it to Croton River streams along fifteen miles of piping through the Highlands. In lower Westchester County, the Merchants Association called for a dam across the

Sawmill River at Philipsburgh for a fifty-mile-wide lake to allow water to flow by gravity through an aqueduct to the city. A March 1900 report by engineer John Ripley Freeman (b. 1855) to city Comptroller Bird S. Coler suggested that Ten Mile River in Dutchess County or the upper Housatonic in Connecticut be dammed for New York City water. Freeman optimistically suggested that a new state boundary line could be drawn giving New York the Housatonic watershed it would need. He dismissed the use of the Ramapo River, the Popolopen and Moodna creeks, and the Wallkill River as suitable reservoir watersheds. Two dams behind Fishkill were also suggested. Charles Armstrong recommended a Great Lakes source in 1905. As late as 1950, to avoid the need for the Cannonsville Reservoir in the deep Catskills, Lawrence T. Beck suggested a dam at Haverstraw, over which Thruway traffic would pass. Beck's dam would block the salt from flowing upriver, while allowing fresh water from upriver to pass over on an aqueduct.

New York City's needs prompted the Municipal Board of Public Improvements to enter into a contract in the summer of 1899 with the Ramapo Water Company, a paper corporation created in 1895 that promised to provide 200,000,000 gallons of water a day for $5 million a year. The *Katonah Times* reported on September 1 that the company was planning to own all the water rights along the river between Peekskill and Yonkers and to run two pipes under the river at Peekskill and Hastings. As far as real holdings, the company held some options in the Esopus watershed but otherwise was not land-rich and had no sources of water. The exorbitant nature of the contract prompted city Comptroller Coler and the Vigilance League and other reformers to fight its implementation, inevitably drawing Governor Theodore Roosevelt into the fray. In his 1900 annual message, the governor flatly declared that New York City should own its own water supply, not deal with private contractors. The Ramapo Water Company Act was repealed in the following year, but by now New York was moving forward with a new plan.

Problems with pollution continued to be of concern in the east-of-Hudson system, despite the Webster Act cleanup of 1894. A 1903 commission recommended that the New Croton Aqueduct be fitted with a slow sand filter near Tarrytown, the mechanics of which caused a delay in the construction of the Jerome Park distributing reservoir. A filter system was recommended for the Catskill Mountains watershed plans then under consideration—terming it much more economical than waiting until a retrofit was needed—but that interest waned as the new science on chlorine and other chemical purifiers developed. Possible sites for filter plants were included in early Board of Water Supply reports to Mayor George B. McClellan—the 30-year-old son of the Civil War general's administration also initiated the first New York City subway— but the matter was soon dismissed. Yet the city was experiencing leakage of some 40 million gallons a day, enough water to serve 380,000 people, and would experience a water famine in the event of a major drought.

The 1900 John Ripley Freeman report had suggested that the Schoharie Creek watershed be investigated and that test borings be done at Bishop's Falls in Ulster County to see if a high dam could be built there. This was where the Ramapo Company had held extensive rights and was planning a series of small reservoirs, none more than fifty acres in size, to draw the Catskills waters. The Freeman recommendation percolated among municipal officials until a survey was done in 1902 and a commission formed that included Freeman, sanitary engineer Rudolph Herring (b. 1847), and, as chairman, William Hubert Burr, an RPI graduate ('72) and professor. The Fishkill and Wappingers creeks in Dutchess County were also studied, and the Roeliff Jansen Kill in Columbia County. Initially, five reservoirs were under consideration, including ones at Lake Hill and Wittenberg in Woodstock. The commission rejected a reservoir for the Catskill Creek, since its water was harder in terms of mineral content than the Esopus. Reservoirs further north, at Preston Hollow in Albany County and Oak Hill and East Durham in Greene County, would have fed the new Catskills reservoir via an aqueduct through Purling, Palenville, and Saugerties but were also set aside as unnecessary.

A commission recommendation to draw Hudson River water at Pough-keepsie and sand filter it into the Croton system was dismissed, despite engineer assurances, as undesirable because of the public's perception of the river as unsanitary. At the same time, residents of Dutchess County objected to the siting of any reservoirs there—ones were under consideration at Hibernia (north of Millbrook), Clinton Hollow, and Rochdale (the latter covering an area a thousand acres larger than the Ashokan Reservoir), and from south of Pine Plains to Ancram in Columbia County. These were all stillborn because of the Smith Dutchess County Act ban of 1904, which ended any thoughts of extending the Croton system northwards.

Although the Rondout Creek was not extensively studied, that water-shed was considered second only to the Esopus in the quality of the water, and its use for a reservoir was implicitly written into the city's thinking. Mayor McClellan moved on the Catskill system idea, recommending that the city's power of eminent domain be extended and water bonds be exempted from a municipality's debt limit. Statewide voters approved the water bond limit extension in November 1904. The Dutchess County experience led the legislature to approve new protections for Westchester and Putnam county residents affected by the Croton system, and all municipalities within the city systems were given the right to draw water at the same rate as city users.

In May 1905, Governor Frank W. Higgins approved laws to establish a water supply commission and select McClellan's plan for a large reservoir in Ulster County. J. Waldo Smith began as chief engineer on the project on August 1, 1905. The newly created Board of Water Supply developed plans for reservoirs in the Esopus, Rondout, Schoharie and Catskill watersheds, received approvals for a $161.8 million appropriation to draw 500 million gallons per day, and had drilling crews working at Bishop's Falls and Tongore within two months of the board's appointments. Among the early casualties was the grist works of David Bishop, "the blind miller," who was said to have never erred, despite his infirmity, in the amounts of grist he produced.

When the Ramapo Company ideas first emerged, the *Daily Freeman* had opined that several new lakes would add to the picturesque quality of the area, but now, with the size of the new reservoir appearing to be so invasive— more than twelve square miles of water surface—the reaction upstate to the plan when announced was stunned disbelief. Edward Coykendall, the general manager of the Ulster & Delaware Railroad, called the McClellan Act "one of the most outrageous acts of confiscation ever passed by a legislature in a civilized country." The State Water Commission convened seven hearings, the first and most heated at Kingston on November 27, 1905. One hundred and twenty-six objections were received, ones from Kingston and more than twenty towns and villages in Ulster, Greene and Schoharie, as well as Yonkers, Peekskill, and affected corporations and utilities. The commissioners made the dubious conclusion that opposition statements—mostly made by lawyers—were "apparently intended as a basis for claims," whereas "personal inquiry of many inhabitants" showed that "the vast majority of [the people] are favorable to the project." Testimonial statements from those inhabitants were not included in the record, and in the end the state approved the plan as "justified by public necessity." Amendments to the McClellan Act that year provided more protections for property owners, including the payment of indirect damages in confiscations, and authorized delivery of water to towns and cities along the route. A total of 674 properties were to be taken in the Ulster County plan.

Dozens of appraisal commissions were created, each containing three members at least two of whom had to be from upstate counties, 129 in all; their proceedings created chaos in the Kingston courthouse when claims were filed by property owners. The commissions used 101 "expert" appraisers whose valuations and expertise were discredited broadly in time. Although officials generally believed that the McClellan Act protected the rights of the owners, New York City's Corporation Counsel John J. Linson (1850–1915)—a member of the bar in Ulster County and former state senator—used numerous ruses to defraud families of their property. When the county commission, which included popular Kingston attorney William D. Brinnier, decided to consider losses associated with business removals as well as their structure, Linson termed the idea of compensating for lost businesses "absolutely monstrous." Another, less liberal commission refused to let Mrs. Tina B. Lasher of Brown's Station testify about the cost of her lost boardinghouse and small store business, and reduced her payout a thousand dollars less than what the city offered—which was itself almost half of her actual claim. She died before a Supreme Court judge ruled that the city needed to recognize her claim for indirect damages due to loss of business.

A group of local lawyers led by Judge A. T. Clearwater—a constant and persistent opponent of the city's efforts—proved too wily for the city and secured significant payouts for their clients from the Shokan area. Clearwater was also a persistent advocate for reforms to the McClellan Act, none of which ever satisfied local concerns.

Hearings at the Ulster County courthouse might run for hours or days and draw crowds; some lasted through the summer and into November. Finally, Sheriff Zadoc P. Boice (a West Shokan sawmill operator and claimant) ordered them ended except on days when the court was not in session, prompting the city to threaten to take them to West Shokan. Boice stood his ground, however, and the city capitulated and conducted more regular hearings at more appropriate times. In the end, however, many property owners were distraught and discouraged by the delays the city threw in their way when it came to paying. The city also went onto properties before they acquired them and forced owners off their lands.

One hundred and forty-one claims were adjudicated by the appraisal commissions by February 1908, yet no one had received their money. Of $44,399.25 charged to property acquisition by the Board of Water Supply in March, only $3,328.50 went to property owners; the rest went to the city's lawyers and surveyors. In 1909, the *New York World* reported that John Linson had disbursed $231,337 over 1907–08; a 1914 lawsuit against him and fellow Kingston attorneys Everett Fowler and Augustus H. Van Buren for $100,000 in alleged overcharges was dismissed in Supreme Court in Kingston. Each of the defendants' attorneys was awarded $500 for their troubles.

Work on the Ashokan Reservoir and Catskill Aqueduct began in 1907, the year the New Croton Reservoir was finished. Three city departments were created—at Kingston, Poughkeepsie, and White Plains—for the reservoir itself, the 62-mile underground aqueduct, and the 17-mile connection across Westchester County. Plans also began for new Kensico and Hill View reservoirs in Westchester. The key planning component for the northern section of the aqueduct was a thirty-mile span needed to cross the Hudson between Storm King and New Hamburg. Inverted siphons would be needed at the river—226 test borings were made from a ship, a total of 28,000 feet—and also to span the Esopus, Rondout, and Wallkill valleys, and Shawangunk and Marlboro mountains. From Hunter's Brook to Hill View, the southern section would run for 26 miles under a difficult suburban terrain.

The $187 million, gravity-fed aqueduct system included 314 square miles of the Schoharie Valley watershed and 257 square miles of the Esopus watershed; the Ashokan Reservoir component cost $30 million alone. Groundbreaking for the aqueduct took place at an 11-mile section in Garrison; the mayor and 350 dignitaries arrived at Cold Spring on the steamer *Albany* and were shuffled by automobile to the site. The aqueduct crossed five counties and required seven pressure tunnels to breach valleys and rivers, seventeen miles in all. Included were the longest tunnel, a four-mile stretch under Rondout Creek, and the most complex, from the river through Garrison in Putnam County. The Garrison tunnel, which came through Cat Hill, took five years to complete, partly because of financial problems experienced by the builder, Thomas McNally Co., as a result of the 1907 panic. Pressure tunnels ran between 300 and 700 feet deep, except for the Hudson River tunnel between Storm King and Breakneck Ridge, the most complex of all.

The borings for a tunnel under the Hudson River dropped five hundred feet through silt without reaching bedrock. The tunnel, 11,430 feet in length, was carved 1,114 feet below the surface of the river by up to 300 workers per shift. A thirty-man police force was brought in to handle 1,500 workers housed on either side of the river. A highlight on the Cornwall side was the courtship and marriage of a local "millionairesse," Antoinette Gazzam, to a project engineer. A constant danger in the construction was the falling "popping rock," which required steel roofing at thirteen locations along the tunnel. Opposing crews reached each other under the Hudson River when the last nine feet of granite was blown open in a ceremony on January 20, 1912; the city's new reform mayor, William Gaynor, pulled the switch. Cheering workers scurried through from the Garrison side. A concrete tunnel was then built to wall the shaft.

In 1911, when two-thirds of the Ashokan reservoir work was completed, T. A. Gillespie & Co. was awarded a $1.6 million contract to complete the Hudson River siphon. Historian Charles H. Weidner termed this feat "one of the miracles performed by the Board of Water Supply's engineers" and "the greatest siphon yet built by man." The siphon was a gigantic tube used to convey water from one level to another by no other power than atmospheric pressure, a round, 14-foot, 5.5-mile-long tunnel framed in steel and lined in concrete, stretching for 3,022 feet through solid granite more than a thousand feet below the surface of the Hudson River at the start of the Highlands.

On Christmas morning, 1911, eight men working the Hudson River tunnel were trapped in a cramped space for several hours after a steel sheath fell and severed air and electric lines. Accidents also occurred with cave-ins at Hunter's Brook near Croton Lake and the Reynolds Hill Tunnel between the Sawmill River and the Bronx. More than 200 men died in the ten years of the project's life, and more than 3,800 accidents were recorded. Malaria struck the worker camps at Storm King and Peekskill because of the swamp vectors around Constitution Island; 633 cases were reported one summer.

Italian, African-American, Hungarian, Russian and other workers were housed separately to avoid conflicts, but fights and troubles occurred nonetheless. In May 1913, a melee broke out in White Plains over 400 workers brought in to replace 300 men who went on strike. Eventually the men got the pay increase they were seeking.

The aqueduct was horseshoe shaped, 17 by 17½ feet in size, and capable of handling 550 million gallons a day, the largest linear municipal water conveyance in the world. The Esopus cut and cover tunnel, built by Stewart-Kerbaugh-Shanley Co., connected the reservoir outlet with the 3,470-foot Peak Grade Tunnel near High Falls. A funicular railroad was installed at the base of Bonticou Crag to convey quarry and crushed stone rubble in the building of the tunnel. At Atwood, a rock cut 25 feet deep and 900 feet long was required. The Rondout Pressure Tunnel shaft (498 feet deep) struck veins of sulfur water that limited the work to three-hour shifts because of hydrogen sulfide gas.

The line entered Westchester County east of Van Cortlandville, and passed through Crompond, Millwood, and Pleasantville before emptying into the Kensico Reservoir at Nanny Hagen Road. The new Kensico, which was finished in 1915, blocked thirteen miles of the Bronx River watershed and included a spillway and conduit to carry excessive rainwater to the corner of the Kensico Dam Plaza, although the spillway never came into use. The waters flowed to the Hill View in Yonkers and Jerome Park Reservoir in the Bronx, a fall of more than 200 feet from the Ashokan. The project was completed in 1917.

The official bid award on building the Ashokan Reservoir was made on August 31, 1907, to MacArthur Brothers Company and Winston & Co. of New York and Katonah for $12,669,750. The actual work was delayed over a bid dispute, but once settled the project went forward. Heavy equipment was hauled upriver from Katonah, where James O. Winston had just finished the Cross River Dam, including steam-powered rollers, shovels, crushers and mixers. Eight narrow-gauge train locomotives, called dinkeys, were also imported to the site, small coal-burners in the 12-to-18 ton range that had been taken out of service on the city's elevated lines. The initial work in Ulster County involved a new narrow-gauge rail section from the Ulster & Delaware at Brown's Station to Olive Bridge, and one built to a bluestone quarry that required a 390-foot steel trestle across the Esopus Gorge, creating a main section rising at Brown's Station, two wings on either side, 2.3 miles of Beaver Kill dykes, and waste and dividing weirs, the project resulting in two separate basins capable of holding a total of 128 billion gallons of water. The clearing and burning of the Beaver Kill Swamp resulted in skin rashes from the poison ivy and poison sumac that hospitalized many of the workers—twice, when the material was cleaned in the spring and then burned in the fall.

"The smoke from these burnings produced a heavy, autumnal haze that hung for weeks over the valley," Frank L. Du Mond wrote. "At night those slow-burning fires made a frightening, eerie picture across the devastated landscape."

A central power station provided the compressed air needed to operate four huge cableways (the first of many), plus all other power equipment. Alsen Portland Cement of Greene County supplied the cement for a storehouse of 4,000 barrels capacity; the mix was produced by a 275-horsepower steam engine. In time, 33 locomotives and 579 rail cars would be used on the reservoir and its dykes.

James Overton Winston (d. 1947) was a Virginia Military Institute graduate who had served on the First Virginia Council of Defense in 1917. His family was in a line of foxhound and horse breeders that included a younger brother, Thomas, who was a partner with his brother in the construction industry. "J. O.," as he was often called, lived in Kingston while overseeing the reservoir project, taking his own daily train car to and from the work site. He became a familiar and well-regarded member of the Kingston community and a trustee of the Senate House. He cultivated his "old Virginia" background in entertaining friends and acquaintances. On one occasion in early 1913, he hosted a dinner at the Wiltwyck Inn Hall that featured Polk Miller, a banjo player whom Winston brought up from Virginia to relate tales of the old plantations before the Civil War. Polk was accompanied by a quartet "of his own plantation negroes," two of whom had been born into slavery.

While in Kingston, Winston began accumulating parcels of hardscrabble farmland a few miles from his friend Poultney Bigelow's estate in Saugerties that he turned into a model livestock farm of more than 800 acres. He took advantage of the property's natural beauty and developed it in the analytical fashion of an engineer, laying ceramic water pipes underground to serve several houses and barns, adding two small, attractive stone dams to drain a large earthen dam he converted from a wetlands on the ridge behind the farm, and creating a huge bluestone mansion designed by Gerard Betts of Kingston that looked down and across the fields to the Saugerties road to Cairo. In March 1913, he appointed Townsend "Crip" Ackerman (1888–1984), a Lloyd native and future Harness Racing Hall of Fame jockey, to manage his thoroughbred horse herd, then consisting of forty-five animals, at Saugerties Farms. Ackerman was superintendent of horses at the Ashokan site; he had lost a leg as a boy, yet raced for Winston on local courses in Rhinebeck, Goshen and elsewhere around the Valley.

The Southern Planter considered J. O. Winston "one of the best informed students of blood lines and pedigrees in this country" when it came to thoroughbred horses. His dairy herd was recognized in the *Guernsey Breeders Journal* from the early 1920s through the '40s. In March 1921, the *Journal* called the Winston Farm "one of the largest and best kept stock and dairy farms in the Hudson River Valley." In 1941, the *Journal* included two of his bulls among the "Great Production Sires" of America. One of the milk cows, known as "The Saugerties Flower," was said to have fetched $30,000 when sold in the 1930s.

Winston was a large man, often seen in topcoat and hat with a cigar in his mouth, looking remarkably like Winston Churchill in wartime, and rode in a chauffeur-driven Peerless automobile while living in Saugerties. At the Ashokan site, he created a village for 4,000 laborers that included its own sewer plant, paved and lighted streets, a hospital, bank, three churches and police and fire stations. A 1908 census listed 2,455 men, 178 women, and 301 children—and 200 mules. Rates for laborers were between $1.20 and $1.60 for an eight-hour day. Board and lodging was $22.50 per month for a single room, and $20 if shared. The bakery produced 5,000 loaves a day. Half the laborers were Italian; the force also included African-American mule handlers whom Winston brought in from Virginia. The work on any given day involved 1,900 men and more than 350 animals, and the use of fifteen locomotives and 120 dump cars.

An abiding problem at the Ashokan construction site, as in the Croton system, was the incidence of criminality ranging from assault and murder to burglary and drunkenness. The city had to establish a police bureau with stations in Peekskill, Garrison, Brown's Station, and High Falls. Douglas McKay (West Point '05) served as chief for three years after 1908. The force grew from an initial 49 patrolmen to 280 officers and 69 sergeants by 1910, when 1,519 arrests were made, including 138 felonies. Several new precincts of city police were added. The "most spectacular" case involved the murder of Mary Hall of Yorktown Heights, wife of a city engineer, by a gang of Italian workers looking for $3,000 supposed to be stashed in the house. They were captured and convicted, and all six electrocuted at Sing Sing in July 1912. The undertaker who secured their bodies charged admission for people to see them.

Many of the Italian community were experienced stonemasons who had come up from Katonah, at times followed by unsavory characters. Luigi Fogia, a shady Calabrian who fell afoul of the Black Hand mafia at Katonah, established a saloon that was too close to the Brown's Station camp. The case involved undercover work by the Chief Humphrey's Detective Agency of Albany. In December 1909, Fogia, who used the alias Demetrio Zema, was convicted of arson in the first degree for attempting to burn down the camp officer's home, who had prohibited his men from drinking at Zema's, and was sentenced to twelve years hard labor at Dannemora. Luigi's wife, who tried to draw a gun on the arresting officer, also went to jail.

With 1,519 arrests in 1910, the need for policemen grew as the project progressed. New DEP precincts were set up at Mohonk, Hurley, Gardiner, Pleasantville, Kensico, Valhalla, Elmsford, and Yonkers, and three-man stations created for eight other communities. The police force grew to 262 patrolmen and 77 sergeants, its greatest numbers, in 1911, when arrests fell to 1,285; by 1917, with the completion of the reservoirs, the police force was reduced to 34 patrolmen and 16 sergeants, although fears of German saboteurs brought in the National Guard in 1918.

In addition to the Ashokan project, Winston was awarded the contract to move a 13-mile section of the Ulster & Delaware after the city settled with the railroad owner, Samuel Coykendall, to make way for the water. As a concession, Coykendall was given the job to build the new rail line needed to skirt the reservoir as long as the work was completed in two years; the U&D contracted with Winston and the tracks were finished on June 8, 1913, seven days before the deadline. The next day, while trying to make up time, the *Rip Van Winkle Flyer* came roaring through Brown's Station and collided with the private train that had just dropped Winston off at the worksite, killing the 54-year-old operator, Curtis Peters.

A curious situation arose with the disposition of the Methodist Episcopal Church of Glenford in the U&D matter in 1914. New York condemned the property and awarded $5,600 to the trustees, but after the U&D line was relocated the property was transferred to the railroad. The church trustees then approached the railroad for the right to move the church, and were given permission by Winston, who had all the salvage rights on the job. After the church was moved to the corner of Ohayo Mountain Road, the city ordered them to return it on the grounds that the church lay mostly on city, not railroad property, or pay $1,700 for that portion that had been on city property. During the trial it came out that Winston Superintendent M. J. Look had asked a city engineer about it in 1911 and been told the church could be moved—but that engineer had not consulted with his superior. A jury brought in a sealed verdict of $45 as the value the church owed the city, which served as a small but fitting response to the many takings the city undertook at undervalued prices.

The Ashokan Reservoir job involved the relocation of 2,000 people who lived in eight hamlets and numerous farms in the Esopus Valley. A total of 15,222 acres of land was condemned and either purchased or taken through court action by the end of 1909. More than 1,500 barns and outbuildings were removed, along with 504 homes, ten churches, ten schools, seven sawmills, smitheries, stores, mills, general stores, boardinghouses, shops and other structures. The remains of 2,637 bodies in cemeteries were relocated off site; 897 were moved in 1909 alone.

People in the Shokan, West Shokan and Broadheads vicinity were required to vacate their properties by May 1. Although it had been a bad spring for construction work, the extent of the progress allowed the city to begin filling the dam with water behind the west weir by September 1913. The weir, which rose 250 feet over the cleared Esopus Creek valley, divided two basins, one fed by the Esopus watershed and one by the Beaver Kill watershed. Bids were awarded for a new road system around the reservoir on February 3, 1913, which the *Daily Freeman* touted as likely to draw thousands of tourists because of the beauty of the setting. Forty miles of roads and six new bridges were part of the project, but the work was delayed by the city Board of Estimate, which did not want the responsibility of maintenance and upkeep. Local fears were also fueled over legislation pending in Albany to save the city harmless of all taxes for the reservoir and road improvements. New York City paid 50-to-85 cents for every dollar of taxation in the Croton district, and the Ulster County towns wanted the same arrangement.

The construction work formally ended on June 24, 1914, when steam whistles across the work zone blared for an hour in celebration, but more work needed to be done. The final touches on the construction took place over 1915; Winston's men laid a new brick, concrete and macadam road over five-and-a-half miles on the dam and dike, and completed the cover for the dike. Zadoc Boice had the contract for eighteen miles of fencing and guardrails around the dam and headworks. A fire on February 24, 1915, destroyed a barn at the construction site where more than a hundred mules were kept, killing eighty-seven of them and also destroying a locomotive that had just been rebuilt in the shop. Winston kept his stock of mules at Saugerties Farms over the winters thereafter, removing the shoes and allowing them to romp inside a large barn.

The entire Ashokan project ended with the completion of the Storm King pressure tunnel on November 13, 1915, after a serious crack in the tunnel was discovered and repaired. The final water impoundment had begun that February, filling both basins to 55.3 billion gallons or 42 percent of capacity (128 billion gallons) by year's end. Bishop's Falls disappeared under a hundred feet of water, but the slowness of the water's rise prompted the Poughkeepsie *Evening Star* to wonder if the reservoir was worth the trouble. The filling of the reservoir created a 12-mile-long artificial lake with a water surface of 12.8 miles and forty miles of scenic shoreline. The ten-year project resulted in the loss of 283 lives—blasting and rock and earth slides causing the principal mishaps—and 2,883 men injured. When water was finally released to the city aqueduct after months of testing, it took twenty-two hours to reach the Kensico Dam, on November 22, 1915. The filling of the Kensico and Hill View reservoirs ensued. In 1916 the Breakneck tunnel was dewatered to repair cracks that were leaking 221,760 gallons a day, the "most serious defect" in the system once it was completed.

A huge disparity developed in courts that were largely sympathetic to the city's interests between the claims of the property owners ($626,000 in 1913) and the final awards ($123,000 in that year). New York City newspapers had been badgering the city about payouts, claiming they were exorbitant when in fact they were very low. Thirty-five business claims were settled in April 1913 with payouts of between $125 and $700. The city bitterly protested an award of $15,000 to Winchell's General Store in Shokan. One of the largest claims was from the Ulster and Delaware Bluestone Company, $33,000 for a loss of product and business. The largest award, after that to the U&D Railroad, was ordered by a Hudson judge to be paid to John I. Boice of Bishop's Falls for $112,303.18.

A 1904 state law protected Westchester County from any further dam building after the New Croton and required New York to furnish water to towns and villages where their facilities were located, and to pay property taxes. More than a decade later, the city initiated a spate of lawsuits against local towns for over-assessing more than 21,000 acres of city properties in the Ashokan system, establishing a pattern that would persist throughout the century; overtures were also made to the state legislature for relief of local taxes, usually without success. The pattern was malicious and unethical; if the city lost in court they would merely reword their claim and file again, and again and again until the worn out and financially depleted communities gave up.

Another issue arose over men who worked in factories or businesses affected by the reservoirs. The McClellan Act allowed for compensation for these workers of half a year's pay if they were employed from 1905 until the condemnations. Sheriff Boice's worker at his sawmill, Samuel Thompson, made a test claim for $235.50 in 1910, which was dismissed with the admonishment that it should be settled out of court. The city did so, settling eighty-six wage claims in 1913.

The first of the claims for lost riparian rights downstream came from the Eastern Dynamite Company below the Olive Bridge dam. By the middle of 1913, the city paid four property owners, including Horace Boice and Pratt Boice of the town of Ulster, more than $12,000 for decreased property values on the Lower Esopus Creek. Four years after the completion of the reservoir, a Troy judge denied four downstream waterpower claims against the city of New York. Judge Howard's "caustic" opinion nullified a commission decision awarding $540,000 in damages to these local mill properties, including three in Saugerties and the James H. Sands claim at Glenerie Falls. The judge acknowledged that the Saugerties companies had to divert more water to generate the steam to operate their mills, but dismissed outright the Sands claim (he was a speculator, not a manufacturer), noting that no business had operated at what was called "the Deserted Village" for twenty-five years.

The completion of the Ashokan Reservoir had the effect of turning the Esopus Creek into two separate water bodies, upper and lower, that significantly changed the natural cycles of the lower creek. The principal casualty in the lower creek's new evolution was the wild trout, which much preferred the colder waters of the mountains. The state tried to compensate in later years with annual stocking programs. Over time, the hanging valley from the spillway channel where the excess water flowed developed a unique habitat in sandy drifts and gravel bars; Fowler's toad (*Bufo fowleri*) and the hognose snake (*Heterodon platirhinos*) adapted to the altered ecology. On the flats of the lower Esopus, different patterns of silting encouraged algae growth and increased accumulations that led the US Army Corps of Engineers into studying lower creek flows to determine ways to protect farming, fishing, and ecological resources.

Over time, each of the lower creek towns developed individual problems associated with the changed flows and natural systems, and the turbid water impacts from severe storm events in the early twenty-first century drew fishing, ecological and other nonprofits into the discussion.

Jurisdictional and other problems resulted for the towns affected by the new reservoir, just as in Westchester County the new impoundment at Kensico effectively divided the northern county from its southern neighbors. In Ulster County, the picturesque village of West Hurley, which had united the township in the past, was wiped away along with the remains of the Beaver Kill Swamp and the muskrats, ducks, snakes and mosquitoes that called it home. The day after the last church service was held in that hamlet its demolition began and the materials was trucked to Zena, where a smaller edifice was erected. West Hurley and Glenford were separated from their fellow hamlets by the reservoir, the schism accelerating in West Hurley after that hamlet became strongly identified with Woodstock with the arrival of Hervey White on the Maverick. Political arguments over representation complicated county legislature reapportionment efforts in 2012, leaving few satisfied with the results.

The new Kensico Reservoir (completed in 1915 by 1,500 workers to replace an 1885 structure) was designed to hold a fifty-day supply of the Catskills water. The reservoir occupied parts of three towns, Armonk, Harrison and Mount Pleasant; villagers tried to stop the reservoir but without success. The burning of one of the barns was used as a background for a motion picture filmed at the time. A downward spiral in agriculture resulted in the displaced land and changed transportation pattern that was never reversed because the farmers, given the penurious payments they received, were only rarely able to find suitable land to start over. If the Ashokan was built for practicality and only incidentally became a breathtaking venue for travelers and tourists to visit, the Kensico was designed for its visual impact as the monumental terminus of the Bronx River Parkway, decorated with a landscaped plaza and ornamental stone that a hundred Italian stonecutters worked a nearby granite quarry for two years to produce. A highlight of the Kensico construction was a blast of 32.5 tons of dynamite—the largest charge in history to that point—on March 21, 1914. The explosion created more than 200,000 yards of rubble and dust. Here as at the Ashokan, accidents claimed a number of lives. The worst incident involving eight Italian workers who died after their supervisor discharged eighteen sticks of dynamite; he was arrested for the act.

Five hundred American Society of Civil Engineers members and a contingency of the American Water Works Association visited the Kensico project during construction. George Washington Goethals, the chief engineer of the Panama Canal, came in 1915. Five hundred residents, including most of Kensico and part of Valhalla, were displaced by the project. In contrast, the Hill View Reservoir—a ninety-acre holding tank for 929 million gallons used to "equalize" the aqueduct flows and the draw into the city system—did not require such numerous condemnations of private property. The city was able to find a largely unoccupied glacial hilltop on the highest ground in Yonkers capable of holding the new container. With the completion of the Hill View, water from the Catskills finally reached Manhattan on November 29, 1916.

The Ashokan system experienced significant storm events in 1913 that raised the reservoir levels to 12,400 million gallons impounded. The water flooded a temporary railroad tunnel and the aqueduct's Screen Chamber floor, as well as overflowing onto the highway and into the Beaver Kill waste channel, which fed the Lower Esopus Creek. On November 9, part of the highway washed out and driftwood knocked the Shokan bridge from its piers, ending any vehicular traffic (and communications) into the West basin area and across the reservoir footprint. The rain, the bridge failure, the end of travel to neighbors across the way, and the sudden appearance of no trespassing signs in New York City property in this area was seen by some locally as a fitting curtain on life in this part of the Hudson River Valley.

By 1928, when the full Catskill system was in operation, 614 of the total daily city consumption of 879 million gallons a day were fed into the system from west of the Hudson, and the Board of Water Supply was once again looking for new sources of water. Initially, the Dutchess and Columbia county watersheds were again considered, but attention in due time fell on the Delaware River and the idea of developing a new reservoir on the Rondout—partially within the Hudson Valley—and tapping the Delaware's east branch in the mountains.

The commencement of a new Delaware system was delayed for more than two years while New Jersey and Pennsylvania pursued a lawsuit against New York through the US Supreme Court, and in the end was approved for a limit of 440 million gallons a day and other amenities, including the construction of a new sewer system for Port Jervis along the Delaware. A second Catskills aqueduct line was constructed through Gardiner in Ulster County between 1937 and 1945 and connected with the Catskill line. Three small villages were consumed in its construction. A huge mixing plant was built in the hamlet to receive trains from up and down the Valley carrying sand, gravel and bulk cement. A water tank built for the construction had to be heated in winter to allow the work to continue. The new aqueduct—the most spectacular tunnel of all in terms of difficulty—eventually carried water from four new reservoirs the city built in the Catskills, starting with the Rondout Reservoir straddling the Ulster-Sullivan line between Wawarsing and Neversink.

Collateral damages created by the city's failure to prevent huge clay depositions from dumping into the Lower Esopus Creek as a consequence of major storm events were minutely examined over several years in discussions among city, state and local officials and environmentalists, the local advocates calling for reduced reservoir levels to control the runoff and the city steadfastly clinging to its prime directive, the delivery of clean water to its customers, as the rationale for dumping the "chocolate" water. Ironically, a solution was already in place in the addition of aluminum sulfate, an inert chemical, to the waters entering the Kensico Reservoir, and that was grudgingly allowed to resume by the state regulatory agencies while the discussion ensued. It turned out that the upper Esopus Creek watershed was probably not a good place to site a reservoir after all, at least when major storm events came into play, since the mountain reaches of this world-famous trout stream contained a particularly egregious clay that did not settle out of the water once introduced by runoff and erosion.

14. Franklin Plays with Fire

Humboldt, the great traveler, once said: "You can tell
the character of the people in a house by looking at the
outside. This is even more true of a community. And
I think I can truthfully say that of all the villages of
Dutchess County—and I have been in pretty nearly
every one—there are very few that appear as favorably
as Pleasant Valley."

—FRANKLIN D. ROOSEVELT,
on the campaign trail, October 1910

The ornate Senate Chamber on the third floor of the "stiff Renaissance
palais" that held the capitol of the State of New York at Albany was a fitting
setting for Courtney Massengale, the nefarious schemer in the grand military
novel *Once an Eagle* (1968) by Anton Myrer of Highwoods in Ulster County.
In the novel, while serving in the South Pacific with Myrer's hero, Sam
Damon, Massengale recalled his childhood of privilege and wealth. The boy
was taken regularly to the State Capitol by his mother and aunt Harriet after
his dancing class with Monsieur Charbet, "a very correct Frenchman with
black satin pumps and a pince-nez with a lovely long blue ribbon." Looking
down upon the assembled senators, Myrer wrote, Massengale "listened to the
voices of the legislature thundering like the voices of the gods . . ." His uncle,
appropriately named Senator Schuyler, smiled, shook the boy's hand, and
asked if he would like politics as a future career. Around them, men "stroked
their mustaches" and exchanged polite small talk with the ladies who had come
to view the session. Young Massengale remained quiet, "but standing there
holding his mother's hand he knew that one day he would rise and speak in
that great hall." The character that Myrer so deftly drew was an insufferable
egoist who saw himself as naturally fitting within the company of nabobs, and
was commensurately appalled when the family lost its fortune and poor Courtney had to settle for West Point.

Myrer's characterization in this sprawling novel captured the core of the
New York state legislature in the early twentieth century, men described by

historian Robert H. Wiebe as "of intense partisanship and massive political indifference." Decorum and polity held sway, politics being little more than "a grand recreational device" for them. An interregnum of progressive republicanism arrived in the governorship of Charles Evans Hughes (1862–1948), who broke the hold of the political machines and large corporations on the state's public services, but otherwise it was business as usual—and the business usually involved their own special interests.

Hughes, the son of the Glens Falls Baptist minister, rose to the governorship after exposing abuses as counsel to highly publicized committee investigations in the gas and electric lighting and life insurance industries in New York City in 1904. His meticulous unmasking of the finance capitalism of J. Pierpont Morgan and E. H. Harriman revealed extensive political graft—Chauncey Depew and George W. Perkins were among those stung in the scandal—and led to Hughes's recruitment for the governorship by the very party that he exposed. Depew's days as the United States Senator from Peekskill were numbered when he could no longer proffer railroad stocks for favors, yet he was still lionized as the best after-dinner speaker. When Democrats joined Republicans in trying to undo Hughes' reforms, the people saw through the two-party charade and rallied behind the governor.

Hughes was a complete innocent at politics. Nominated by acclimation at the Republican convention in Saratoga Springs in 1906, he conducted his administration with little regard to party interests. He was the only Republican on the state ticket elected that year, by 57,897 votes over the Democratic-Independence League candidate, William Randolph Hearst (1863–1951). His lieutenant governor was Democrat Lewis S. Chanler, the Astor orphan and Red Hook town supervisor. Hughes made the first spirited attempt at reorganizing state government along executive lines. His most lasting achievement was the transformation of the governor's relationship to dozens of state agencies in the creation of the Moreland Act in 1908, which authorized commission-level investigations of any agencies of the state. Eighteen other states created similar commissions in the twenty years after the Moreland Act's enactment. In New York, a dozen subsequent governors used more than thirty-five commissions of investigation—albeit not all of them effectively. A 2013 Moreland Act investigation convened by Governor Andrew Cuomo turned sour when he abruptly terminated it, saying the goal had been met through legislation; a stream of political scandals followed soon thereafter.

The Republican marriage with independents and reformers since 1896 was institutionalized in Governor Hughes' alliances, including a new public services commissioner he appointed, Thomas Mott Osborne (1859–1926). Osborne, a wealthy Progressive, founded the Democratic League of New York, a group of anti-Tammany Democrats who would gain several assembly seats in the 1908 elections. To his later chagrin, Osborne was initially aligned with Tammany Hall leader Charles F. Murphy (1858–1928) through an antagonism toward Theodore Roosevelt's "New Nationalism" that Osborne shared with John Jay Chapman.

Franklin Delano Roosevelt, aged 28 at the time, came to the New York State Senate in 1911, and although he looked and often seemed to act the Courtney Massengale–type his sincerity was much, much deeper. Roosevelt had been considering public office for some time, was involved in civic service in other ways, and was not happy in the legal work he did in New York City. When Dutchess County District Attorney John E. Mack (1874–1958) approached him to run for office in the heavily Republican district in March, he accepted the challenge even though he knew he had little chance of winning. No Democrat had won the district since 1856. Yet times were changing and he was the bellwether of that change, the improbable winner in the 26th senatorial district of Dutchess, Putnam, and most of Columbia counties.

After accepting the nomination on October 10, 1910, FDR rented a red Maxwell touring car, "bedecked" it "with flags," and took along perennial Democratic Congressman Richard Connell on a whirlwind campaign that covered 2,000 miles in a month. His first campaign speech was at Bank Square in the city that would later be called Beacon, where he was introduced by Morgan Hoyt, the editor and publisher of the *Matteawan Journal* and a Democratic state committeeman. Morg Hoyt would introduce Roosevelt (at FDR's insistence) at the same place at the start of eight more campaigns. While in Fishkill, Roosevelt stayed at the home of Major James Forestall, whose son Jimmy, just 18, was on hand for that first speech. James Forestall, Jr. went on to become Assistant Secretary and then Secretary of the Navy under President Roosevelt in World War II, and the first US Secretary of Defense, under Harry S Truman in 1947.

In 1910, the candidate spoke wherever he could, railing against Tammany Hall and GOP Albany County boss William "Billy" Barnes and his local ally, Lou F. Payn of Columbia County. Payn, who Elihu Root once termed "a stench in the nostrils of the people," had been accused of "voting tombstones" in Teddy Roosevelt's days as governor. ("We always respect a man's conviction," Payn famously replied.) TR dismissed him as a corrupt state insurance superintendent, and faced considerable criticism for the action until it was revealed that Payn, whose state salary was $7,000 a year, had received a $435,000 "loan" from a New York City trust company. Barnes, the Harvard-educated grandson of Thurlow Weed and owner of the Albany *Evening Journal*, was called the "Boy Leader" of the upstate Republicans. His grip on state affairs, despite this setback, remained firm until 1921, when a scandal publicized by the *Times-Union* revealed that $18,000 in coal bound for Albany city hall instead wound up in the bins of his Republican cronies.

Roosevelt's opponent, incumbent Senator John Schlosser, was a Barnes-Payn ally and one of the partisan "Black Horse Cavalry" who had fought against Teddy and opposed all of Hughes's reforms. One of FDR's early campaign themes was support for the direct election of US senators, which Tammany Hall and most Republicans disdained with fervor. Franklin won the vote by 1,140 out of more than 30,000 cast. He won his own town of Hyde Park, a feat that he would accomplish only once more in the nine general elections he participated in during his lifetime, and never as a presidential candidate.

Upon arriving in Albany the following January, Roosevelt was thrust almost immediately into the national spotlight when he humbled Tammany Hall over a hot political appointment. Tammany leader Big Tim Sullivan (1862–1913) might have anticipated the trouble the new upstart would cause: on learning of Roosevelt's victory, Sullivan pondered whether it might be better to drown him because of the trouble, "sure as shooting," that he would bring to the Albany stage. Yet, although he came in on a platform of reforming the political structure in Albany and was an admirer of Governor Hughes, Roosevelt was not a diehard reformer at heart. He tolerated the temperance and anti-gambling forces, but considered them obstructionist. In the Senate in 1911, he chaired the Forest, Fish and Game Committee, and proposed legislation restricting timber cutting on private lands after hearing Gifford Pinchot (1865–1946) talk about deforestation disasters in China. Conservation, which he practiced on the Hyde Park family estate, became a major issue throughout Roosevelt's political career.

In one of his first political tests, Roosevelt had to tread carefully over the merger of Matteawan with Fishkill Landing into the single municipality of Beacon. Matteawan did not want to lose its name and individual identity and at first did not agree with the new name, but eventually had to support it. Beacon received its charter on March 15, 1913, and Morg Hoyt created a new Democratic newspaper, the *Beacon Journal.* FDR "worked" for the paper under editor Ed Hayden in 1921, writing a weekly column at no pay that was quoted around the nation at times.

Meanwhile, Albany was in uproar over delays in crucial government building projects. A new state education building under construction across the street from the capitol since 1908 was delayed past its January 1, 1911, opening date. The state's library, virtually filled when the new edifice opened in 1889, was crowded across the entire western front of the third floor of the capitol. New York's official library history went back to 1818 when Governor DeWitt Clinton appointed John Cook as the first state librarian. The first collection included 669 volumes and nine maps. New York became one of the best libraries in the country with the purchase of a $1,000 first edition of John Audubon's *Birds of America* in the 1830s, although the edition was worn out through overuse a decade later.

When the Regents took over as trustees in 1844, the library had 10,000 volumes. Its collection was greatly augmented by the work of Nicholas Marie Alexandre Vattemare (1797–1865), a famous and remarkable ventriloquist whose particular passion (encouraged by the Marquis de Lafayette) was inducing states and governments in Europe and America to exchange volumes of their library collections. The collection was further enlarged by an accumulation of European books by David Bailie Warden (d. 1845), formerly the private secretary to General John Armstrong when Armstrong was Minister to France. Warden had also been principal of Columbia Academy in Kinderhook and head tutor of the Kingston Academy; John Vanderlyn did a portrait of him that came with the collection. Hermanus Bleecker's 2,700 volumes (he had been charge d'affairs at The Hague) was donated by his widow. With the addition, in 1850, of the papers of Sir William Johnson and Governor George Clinton, the state library achieved national status, especially when the Clinton papers were found to include those carried by the British spy John André when he was captured in 1779.

A new library was built in 1854 with a corridor connection to the capitol for the use of the members. Governor Fenton, other state officials, and members of the legislature convened there on April 26, 1865, and proceeded through the corridor to the assembly chamber to view the casket of President Lincoln lying in state.

Thomas Fuller, the first architect of the new capitol, planned on filling the top two floors with the library. His successors in 1876, Leopold Eidlitz and Henry Hobson Richardson, moved the library from the east side to the west to accommodate the needs of the Court of Appeals. In 1883, the library and its 126,600 volumes were evicted altogether because of the construction, and the collection housed on makeshift shelves along the "Golden Corridor," an Eidlitz-designed passage linking the east and west sides of the capitol.

A new architect, Isaac Perry, began the construction of the Western Staircase, which passed by the new library area on the third floor. The collections were moved in a fairly helter-skelter fashion, and the staff settled into what they expected to be an excruciating but brief hiatus. Two years later, in 1886, when Governor Cleveland was elected president the capitol construction appropriations were severely reduced. In February 1888, the *New York Times* groused that the library was still "cribbed, coffined, and confined in quarters never intended and entirely unsuited for it," so it was finally moved to its new quarters in 1889, while the construction continued all around.

Melvil Dewey (1851–1931) had been hired to organize the library and as secretary of the Board of Regents. In creating his Dewey Decimal System, he studied this state library and others in 1873, concluding that their arrangement of books alphabetically without regard to subject was inefficient and wasteful. Dewey brought to Albany a library school he had created and then made controversial at Columbia University by admitting women. The New York State Library School was provided a classroom on the fifth floor of the new capitol and served thirty-two students the first year. "The very elect go there," a librarian at the national association convention said in 1902. "No drones are admitted."

Dewey expanded the state library's mission by bringing the Albany Medical College and State Medical Society collections into a state Medical Library and creating a library for the 5,000 blind residents of the state. He created an Education Alcove that later became a full library, a Children's Library (which he "most reluctantly" abandoned due to space needs in 1900), and a separate Legislative Reference section for the elected officials and branches of government. His Women's Library came about as a result of New York's donation of 2,500 books by female authors to a special exhibit of the World's Columbian

Exposition in Chicago in 1893; he built up the collection by reaching out to new women authors. Although Governor Flowers vetoed a $10,000 appropriation for the program, Dewey's 1,000-volume "peripatetic" collection for a traveling library came into use in early 1893 in Charlton, where twenty-five people had subscribed.

Dewey was to many "the Edison of the library field," creator of a standardized card catalog system, a long-distance "paid help" research program for scholars, a photography collection, and an early advocate of the long-distance telephone as an inter-library tool. His work was praised by Theodore Roosevelt when he came in as governor in 1899. His eccentricities included a passion for the metric system and for simplified spelling; he shortened his own first name, but the Regents declined to allow him to reduce his surname to "Dui." (A typical vestigial Deweyism survived in the word "catalog.") Dewey was also a physical fitness advocate, one of the first to purchase a new safety bicycle in Albany. He convinced the city to pave the bumpy cobblestones with asphalt and bought five of "the librarian's horse," as he called them, for his staff to use.

He enjoyed taking the library school students, almost always young women, on carriage rides around Albany, and continued the practice when the automobile arrived. After 1904, Mevil and Annie Dewey made Lake Placid into a world-renowned winter sports community, but the club caused such a pattern of anti-Semitism in the resort hotels of the Adirondacks that a political uproar led to his resignation as librarian in September 1905.

The library was the brightest, the most beautiful room in the new capitol, yet it looked haggard and ugly in the unending accumulation of materials, almost all of it paper, collected over the first twenty years of the new capitol's operation. Shelving was added wherever stacks could fit, stopping up windows and doorways, tucked into corners under slanted ceiling and roof lines, stacked in new, narrow, crowded aisles, turning the library into a "chaos of convenience" and the biggest fire hazard in New York State.

"Hundreds of thousands of feet of oak have been used in shelving and interior finish," Dewey wrote in his 1900 annual report, which listed holdings of 437,733 volumes, "and in spite of careful installation for electric wires, we cannot avoid the fear that some day this woodwork in some room will be accidentally set on fire and priceless material destroyed."

Governor Frank W. Higgins signed the law providing for a new $3.5

million State Education Building. Architect Henry Hormbostel designed a striking Greek neo-classical edifice fronted by thirty-six Corinthian columns stretching for a long, dramatic city block, the longest colonnade in the world. Ground was broken in July 1908, but it was still unfinished almost four months after the scheduled opening.

Tuesday, March 28, 1911, was an interesting day in the capitol. The legislature was in the midst of a fierce fight over the appointment of a new junior US senator from New York to replace the inimitable Chauncey Depew. Depew was a Peekskill native and "the highpriest of the railroad interests" (in Louis Auchincloss' words), but had to step down as Senator over his unilateral attention to those interests. Assembly Speaker Alfred E. Smith (1873-1944) and Senate President Pro Tem Robert F. Wagner (1877–1953) were committed to the appointment of William F. "Blue-eyed Billy" Sheehan, a notorious politician and the choice of Tammany Hall leader Charles F. Murphy. Smith had come to the assembly from the Lower East Side in 1904, sat in the back row and said nothing for a year on orders of Tom Foley, Murphy's predecessor; he soon became the best bill writer in the legislature and, except for the Sheehan mistake, a keen judge of Democratic horse flesh. When New York's Peter Pan, James V. Walker (1881–1946), was elected to the assembly in 1910, Smith, eight years his senior and a friend since Walker was fifteen, took him under wing, brought him with him on the train every week, and installed him in rooms near Smith's at the Ten Eyck Hotel. When Smith was elected governor in 1920, Walker—by then a "gallery god" and state senator—became his president pro tem.

Billy Sheehan, whose corruption while lieutenant-governor and boss of Buffalo had helped elevate the independent reform sentiments of the state in the 1890s, was a law partner of Alton B. Parker of Esopus, the failed presidential candidate. The decision on the appointment would be made by both houses voting together, but Wagner was opposed in the Senate by a group of party upstarts led by the new senator from Dutchess County, Franklin Delano Roosevelt. Roosevelt's refusal to attend a party caucus to nominate Sheehan in mid-January drew others to the cause. The in-fighting and arguing went on for weeks until March 27, when Murphy released his caucus from supporting Sheehan and overtures were exchanged with Roosevelt on finding a compromise candidate. On the following day, March 28, Al Smith declared that a vote would be taken the next day. He caucused with his Tammany supporters in the library on the third floor that Tuesday evening, while Roosevelt and the insurgents met at FDR's home. The meetings went until after 1 a.m.

Louis McHenry Howe (1871–1936) worked late in the capitol that night. Born into a family of privilege and prosperity, Howe's parents were descendants of Indiana's founding families. His father lost his fortune in the Panic of 1873 and had to settle for a relative's home in Saratoga Springs, where he wrote for *The Saratogian* and later became owner and editor of the Saratoga *Sun*. Louis became assistant editor at the age of seventeen when his father was appointed Saratoga Springs postmaster by President Grover Cleveland, and co-owner and co-editor four years later.

Captain Howe was also a correspondent for the New York *Herald*, a job that Louis took on from time to time, meeting notables and personages in the process, men like Richard Croker, Roscoe Conkling, and Big Tim Sullivan. The young reporter scooped the nation with an interview with Theodore Roosevelt near Lake Tear of the Clouds when President McKinley was shot. Howe's keen feel for political campaigns led Thomas Mott Osborne to bring him within Osborne's new Democratic League, and to use Howe's talents for Osborne's gubernatorial ambitions.

Physically, Howe never fit the political mode. Frail and tired-looking most of the time, not a handsome man (except for the large brown eyes), Howe had suffered a bicycle accident in youth that left his face pocked by a shadow. As a young man he had become involved in theater at Saratoga Springs, collaborating with Franklin Dowd (son of Dr. Charles Dowd, "originator of our system of Standard Time"), and later with Clarence Knapp, a future mayor of that city. Howe and Knapp wrote and staged a naughty production called *Pink Dominoes* that upset some of the straitlaced local families. In November 1898, before going to the Philippines to cover the Spanish-American War, Howe eloped with Grace Hartley, a Vassar student who had come to Saratoga on a vacation with her family two years earlier. Howe's freelance writing expanded and by 1905 he became Albany correspondent for the *Herald*'s evening paper, the *Telegram*, like his father had before him. Osborne put him into frequent contact with young Roosevelt.

The delay that Roosevelt and his twenty insurgents had created over the US Senate vote was worthy of national attention in this machine town. Most of the political wags who looked young Roosevelt over probably felt as Howe did at first, at wit's end to explain how this "spoiled silk pants sort of guy" had beaten Lou Payn. This was not an unenlightened crowd, this Park Row bunch. Park Row was the informal name given to the cramped quarters that the press used in the capitol, off the middle of the third floor hallway a short walk to either chamber's main entrance. None of them had expected Roosevelt to win the senate election, since Democrats were losing ground elsewhere around the state and the nation, and besides, the district was solidly Republican.

Howe, alert to Osborne's view of the man, saw something in Roosevelt as he watched him take the traditional Dutchess seat at desk number 26. The wizened reporter liked the young man's spunk and personality, but wondered at his patrician airs and the snobby way in which he wore a pince-nez—as a compliment to his more famous cousin—giving Roosevelt the appearance of always looking down his nose at people. Still, he saw something special and soon confided to his wife that "nothing but an accident could keep him from becoming president." After Roosevelt challenged Tammany Hall and won that spring, the "gnomelike and slovenly" Howe became FDR's most trusted aide and companion, engineering a farmer's friend and boss-fighter image that garnered the candidate a 1,631 vote plurality in his reelection bid in 1912— while Roosevelt lay prostrate with typhoid fever the whole time!

The Howes rented an apartment in Albany for the legislative session in 1911. It was not a long walk from the capitol in the late evening for Louis, so he had remained in Park Row to file his report after attending Roosevelt's caucus. With him at Park Row into the wee hours were a *New York Evening Post* reporter and a sleepy telegraph operator waiting for their stories. One assemblyman continued working after the Al Smith caucus was over in the library on the west side, and two night watchmen were making their rounds.

The central reading room in the library where Assemblyman Aaron Levy worked was a space exactly the size of the Senate Chamber (73 feet by 42 feet, with a 56-foot-high ceiling). The library spread for three hundred feet across the entire western front of the capitol, reading rooms adjoined on either side by a pair of intricate stacking blocks of endless rooms of paper. When completed the building, which covered three acres, was considered "completely fireproof."

Levy left at 2 a.m. but returned to the library before leaving for his rooms. He looked through the window and, without entering, saw flames leaping from his desk. He ran through the Assembly Chamber, calling for help. The reporters responded and Howe rushed to the scene. Mullins, one of the night watchmen, hurried to assess the situation, and then ran to street level to pull the alarm. It was 2:46 a.m. The first unit was on the scene by 3 a.m. The men had to hook the hoses to steam-driven pumps connected with the hydrants at street level and carry equipment and hose up the three flights to the third floor.

At 3:20, the heat from the library exploded a glass transom into the hallway at the top of the stairway. The airshaft adjoining, where the elevators were installed, served as a perfect draft for the fire. The north windows of the library burst from the heat, and soon a north breeze prevailing outside also encouraged the fire. By now, Chief William W. Bridgeford had arrived and was pressing his men to move closer. He saw the danger as the fire approached an oak-and-glass partition that separated the reading area from the library's full collection.

"Jump at it, men," urged Bridgeford. "If she cracks those windows, we're done for."

Mullins was fumbling with his keys outside the library at 3:35 a.m. when the partition exploded into a collection of 175,000 volumes of dense, dry, packed-in paper. The men watched as it leapt from shelf to shelf and ran up the mezzanine stacks with such heat the iron of the framework melted. Within twenty minutes, the library was fully engulfed and Bridgeford had to pull his men back to safety. The fire spread from the third to the fifth floor, completely destroying Melvil Dewey's library school in the northwest tower.

Governor Dix, Al Smith, and dozens of state officials and bureaucrats gathered outside, waiting for an official to arrive with the combination to the safe on the first floor. The official, named Draper, was reached by telephone but refused to give the combination over the wire and instead sent his son rushing to the scene with the numbers in hand. Carolyn Warner ran into the hall and secured the papers. Men were entering and leaving the capitol on both sides of the first floor now, carrying out furniture and documents.

At 4 a.m. another huge crash brought down the roof south of the northwest tower. The tower collapsed inward onto a huge granite chimney that also fell, crashing through the fifth floor, and the fourth, to the third. The skylight over the Million Dollar staircase exploded, sending men scurrying out of the way of the falling debris. The flames were now exposed to the sky, the fire inside pushing eastward toward the legislative chambers. The firemen managed to hold its progress just short of the Senate Chamber, but in the Assembly it entered the ceiling area and was spreading quickly. Walter Arnst watched a huge section, including two chandeliers, fall onto the floor.

The Assembly ceiling, called "the scandal ceiling" when constructed because *papier-mâché* was substituted for oak, actually saved the building from complete destruction. When water poured in, the *papier-mâché* became soaked, and the fire abruptly ended. Park Row wags claimed the capitol was, fittingly, saved by corruption.

By 7 a.m., Bridgeford and his men had the fire under control, although flare-ups occurred for a couple of more days. The seat of the government was ruined. One man was missing, old Samuel Abbott, 78, the second night watchmen, found two days later under six feet of debris on the fourth floor. As soon as the building was secure, the state architectural inspector, Franklin Weir, was on the scene. His examination revealed that the structure could be rebuilt, at a cost estimated at $5 million. The cause was not Mr. Levy's cigar, he declared, but most likely defective wiring, most of it twenty-five years old, which Governor Dix and others before him had tried without success to have the legislature replace. And so the government continued, without a capitol, the legislature and the Court of Appeals crammed into Albany's City Hall with the city government. The *Times-Union* lauded the quick recovery of the state in an April 3 editorial, as did the media generally for the manner in which the legislature took an accounting and commenced the needed repairs. Nevertheless, it was four years before the fourth and fifth floors were once again ready for occupancy.

The destruction of the library provided a bitter irony to a time when New York State was addressing its heritage needs so profoundly in publications, dedications, celebrations and restorations. Director James Wire cabled the Library of Congress that "a clean sweep" had occurred, one that "could not have been worse." The recovery of materials was begun by Arnold Van Laer and I. N. Phellps-Stokes, and they received some reassurances in the discovery that the collapse of the mezzanine area had actually helped preserve materials trapped under all the debris. Some documents were blown from the building —one landed six miles away in East Greenbush—and fell to the streets. Many were returned but many also lost to collectors or souvenir-hunters. Among historic materials destroyed were thousands of Dutch manuscripts, including most of the archives of the colony of Rensselaerswick, which had been moved from the patroon's home to the Albany County Clerk office in 1899 and relocated to the west wing of the capitol in 1906.

A heritage was lost. In all, of the 300,000 manuscripts held in the State

Library collection, more than 270,000 were wholly or partly destroyed. A half-mile of books, more than 450,000, were incinerated. Worst of all, the card catalog that maintained the record of all the holdings was also fully destroyed. These were many of the ordinary records of the colonial period that, as researcher Chris Kolakowski observed, were essential to historians in understanding and reconstructing early American life.

Restoration work on materials that were saved continued for decades under the direction of Peter Nelson (1875–1944), the Supervisor of Public Records and Director of Archives, until 1936. His specialties included Hudson Valley history. Oddly, Nelson and his wife, who also worked there, were married on the evening of the fire.

The political fight—the vote on the new United States senator from New York—was delayed three days in the turmoil over the fire. When it became apparent that the Roosevelt insurgency could not be overcome, Tammany leader Charles Murphy offered several other choices, including a party loyalist who was known to be independent. On March 31, 1911, State Supreme Court Justice James Aloysius O'Gorman (1860–1943) was elected on the sixty-fourth ballot with the support of the insurgents, who would soon regret it.

A traditional rapprochement among Democrats resumed the next year when New York's congressional delegation supported a constitutional amendment circulating among the states for the direct election of US senators by the voters. The amendment was approved by the state legislature in May 1913, crowning more than a decade of beneficial changes that came with the new progressive era.

Benjamin Odell's innovations as Republican governor a decade earlier, the rise of Charles Evans Hughes and a sense of ethical leadership that he brought to governance, Teddy Roosevelt's far-sighted tenure as America's conservationist president, and even the appearance of the ship of state once the library damages were repaired all fell together in the spirit of the times. A crowning symbol was the magnificent new Education Building faced with its thirty-two Corinthian columns along Washington Avenue and adorned within with a breathtaking Rotundo and Will Hicok Low's twenty large murals.

Low's variation on the New York State seal fittingly depicted the Hudson River with a three-masted ship and a sloop, representing both the foreign and inland trade—via New York's harbor and the Erie canal—that made New York the Empire State. "Aspiration" struck a note for the new thinking in displaying

Hermes guiding a beautiful young woman through mist toward a star, the powers of darkness overcome in the rise of co-education. The finest of all was Low's rendition of the architectural element that inspired the design of the building itself, the Corinthian column of Callimachus, here standing at the basket of a beautiful maiden's mementos, the weight of which spread the leaves of an acanthus into volutes of support for the structure all around.

15. The Last People's Man

> I'll tell you what I want. I have got to go on the stand and tell my story. I've got to tell the truth, and I am going to tell the truth about the $10,000 . . . I gave you $10,000 one afternoon in my private office. We went uptown in a taxi-cab to my house. When I left you, you went on to Mr. Murphy's house and gave him the money. Murphy told me so the next day.
>
> — GOVERNOR SULZER, to John F. Delaney (September 24, 1913)

One day in 1975, in the first few months of his freshman year as a New York State assemblyman from Ulster County, Maurice D. Hinchey (b. 1938) was waiting in the Assembly Parlor on the second floor of the State Capitol for his colleagues to arrive for a press conference. Standing just inside the room with his legislative aide, future Albany city court judge Thomas Keefe, Hinchey wondered aloud about the figure in the unusual painting that hovered over them. This was the hall where the Assembly Speaker portraits were hung, and the first one as one entered was the youngest speaker of them all, William Sulzer (1863–1941). The aide, who had taken the colorful capitol tour, related the mournful tale of the "people's man" of 1913 who fell afoul of the railroads and Tammany Hall and became the only governor of New York to be impeached and removed from office.

The assemblyman had reason to wonder just by looking at the portrait. Here was a striking semblance of a man—a tall, thin body, ungainly like Lincoln's but in a studied way, with a pair of steely sharp blue-grey eyes and a sternly formal face that faintly couched a politician's guile. William Sulzer could be alternately innocent, shrewd, grim or friendly in appearance, a signature wad of tobacco usually protruding from a cheek like a pivot to his smile—the tobacco was all that was missing in this portrait. A verbal portrait of him a few weeks after his inauguration as governor in the *Kingston Daily Freeman* described him as "in manner, pose, even dress, the absolute artistic appropriateness that only a stage manager of genius could apply," a man who spoke only of his own accomplishments. "You are adrift on the Sulzer sea" when talking with him, the newspaper said.

Henry Morgenthau, a friend of his, recalled Sulzer well in 1921:

His greatest pride was his resemblance in face and figure to the immortal Henry Clay. This physical resemblance was not fanciful. Sulzer had his high forehead, large mouth, and deep-set eyes—he bore, indeed, altogether a quite remarkable likeness to the Sage of Ashland . . . He had grown a long forelock, and had trained it to fall over the forehead after the Clay style. And he had cultivated a gift for ready speech into as near an approach to the eloquence of Clay as his limitations of mind permitted.

Sulzer was that *rara avis*, a warbler crow among the jackdaws who flew from Tammany Hall's cage. Told by a fortune teller (so he claimed) that he would grow up to become the youngest speaker in the history of the New York State legislature, governor of New York, and president of the United States, Sulzer had the misfortune of proving that, at times, two out of three *was* bad. His studied demagoguery ultimately collided with a railroad crew bill and an all-powerful political machine that tossed him off the track of his projected fate. Yet there stood the man in the painting as he once stood in the flesh, in that room in the capitol he would rule ever so briefly, more confident and sure of himself than any before or since.

All through his life, as he told it in his own inimitable if ungrammatical style, William Sulzer made it a habit of being "direct" with people:

My headquarters are under my hat [he said in an October 7, 1912, campaign speech for governor]. I never had any use for a campaign manager, or a campaign money collector, and I shall not have any use for them during this canvass. I shall deal with the people direct.

As a boy, he ran away from home and toured the West Indies as a hand on a tramp schooner. Returning in 1882, instead of going north he rejected the sage advice of his companions and entered the land of the Seminoles, widely believed at the time to be cannibals; Sulzer befriended them and became a blood brother. He met Geronimo in 1885, helped with his transfer from a Florida prison to Fort Sill, Oklahoma, and was given a silver ring in appreciation by the Apache. It was the only ring Plain Bill ever wore.

He took the same stubborn attitude to his politics. In 1884, as a 21-year-old with a riveting style, he campaigned too well for his childhood hero, Grover Cleveland, and boss John Kelly threw him down the steps of Tammany Hall. In 1889, on only the second or third day of his first campaign for election, Sulzer walked brazenly into his district's toughest neighborhood, Mackerelville, and was beaten up by thugs; he won the election by eight hundred votes. In the same year, he was almost arrested for supporting the free speech of anarchist Emma Goldman (1869–1940).

If William Sulzer was anything, he was "direct," except for that one time, that most crucial moment when he faced the trial of his life. Failing to directly confront the charges brought against him by a scheming and malicious legislature, Sulzer's decision not to testify at his own impeachment trial lay at the heart of the decline and fall of the last "people's man."

The trouble with Tammany Hall only started with John Kelly. The Gordian knot was cut in 1896 when Sulzer bucked Tammany leader Richard Croker (1843–1922), forced a primary, and won reelection as congressman from the Lower East Side. Croker did not want Sulzer to run for a second term; he would defiantly serve seven more. He had already attempted and failed at getting the nomination for governor. He would continue trying every two years for eighteen in all, until finally awarded the plum by a worn-out Tammany Hall in 1912. He had fulfilled the fortuneteller's first prophecy, becoming Speaker in 1893 (he was Minority Leader the following year), and now would fulfill the second.

Sulzer was a budding progressive as an assemblyman and a congressman. He called for a Jewish state in Palestine, condemned Jewish pogroms in Russia, and supported Cuban independence. He created the legislation establishing the Department of Labor with a cabinet-level secretary. He introduced the law declaring war against Spain and one to raise the wreck of the *Maine*. He sponsored the federal income tax amendment, a resolution reestablishing the merchant marine, and a national good roads resolution. Plain Bill was the people's man, to be sure, yet how he went about his business only distanced him from the people's friend, Tammany Hall, and others who saw him for the demagogue he truly was.

Sulzer was elected the 41st governor on November 5, 1912, by a 205,454-vote plurality—the largest up to that time. He was well known for a commendable progressive record and his congressional hijinks, a poseur of "the people's" cause who had a nose for grabbing headlines and was practiced at its art. William Stiles Bennet (1870–1962) of Port Jervis, who served with Sulzer in Congress, claimed he became governor because Bennet was drunk one day in 1908 when a key vote took place on a rules agenda. Sulzer failed to vote with the Republicans as all the other Tammany Democrats were doing, which damaged relations between Republicans and insurgent Democrats and led to an effort to dump him in 1910, when Sulzer outwitted them by threatening to make Bennet's drunken event public. Denied the chairmanship of the ways and means committee in the next Congress and given foreign relations instead, he promptly offered a resolution to sever commercial relations with Russia over that nation's pogroms of the Jews. The resolution passed both houses and was hand-delivered to President Taft by Plain Bill himself. Two years later (as Bennet saw it), when Democrats were unsure of their strength compared to the Republicans and Progressives, Sulzer was chosen as a sure vote-getter, especially among Jews.

His detractors quietly condemned him when he declared the governor's mansion "the people's house" and opted to walk to the capitol for his inauguration —smoking a cigar, wearing a slouched hat and grey overcoat, and joking with the "rabble" walking with him—instead of riding in a regal carriage or a new automobile. He was "a constant player to the galleries—in short, a demagogue," it was plainly seen, "an exasperating bag of bombast and 'hifalitin' oratory, best summed up in the effective slang word 'bunk.'" Yet Plain Bill was "direct" with the people, and they loved him for it.

Congressman Sulzer was one of the sponsors of the constitutional amendment by which United States senators were elected by direct vote of the people, and in his inaugural address as governor urged New York to ratify the amendment. Sulzer's first two months were spent in rooting out corruption by replacing department heads, a pattern that gradually tested Tammany Hall's patience. His need to satisfy the patronage requests of Thomas Mott Osborne created more difficult situations with Tammany, whom Osborne often just wanted to embarrass. The governor managed to improve the operations of several departments and institute significant reforms to the Stock Exchange, although the Exchange balked at the changes and having itself regulated by the state banking department.

The "full crew" bill (Sulzer's term; it was called the "extra crew" bill by the railroad) would have required additional brakemen on rail runs on weekends and holidays, a total of six men per train when the railroads had traditionally cut personnel to save overtime money. Nine railroad presidents signed a statewide advertisement that appeared on March 31 claiming that a $2 million annual "waste" of dollars would be required to meet the terms of the bill. The railroad had had considerable say on the idea in the past; Governor Hughes and two other chief executives had vetoed similar legislation, but Sulzer approached it as a safety measure because of the accidental deaths and injuries among workmen when the railroads were undermanned. The bill was enacted following a strenuous campaign that likely signaled the beginning of the governor's undoing.

His veto of hydroelectric power legislation drew the ire of the lieutenant-governor, Martin H. Glynn, the former state comptroller and Columbia County editor and publisher who had an interest in a project that would have benefited from the new law. Rumors began to circulate around Albany that the railroads and the hydro-power lobbies had amassed a war chest of $500,000 for Sulzer's removal.

The governor's style consisted of a persistent rant against the Democratic machine as the deepest evil to be overcome. He fixed on the direct primary and drew a line in the sand, unlike Governor Hughes, who spent almost two years trying to convince his legislature in more politic ways to enact the same bill. As Sulzer's tone and invective increased, the members' disgust with him mounted. His reform bill only received two votes in the state senate, and then he recalled the legislature knowing that the bill did not have a chance. His operatic collapse began quietly when a Joint Legislative Investigating Commission chaired by Senator (and Tammany Hall stalwart) James Frawley of New York was formed to investigate state departments. In a reaction to Sulzer's attacks, the Frawley Commission began to look into how Sulzer was pressuring legislators into backing the direct primary bill, as well as his handling of campaign finances. The Commission recommended eight articles for impeachment in all, the most telling of which were allegations that Sulzer diverted more than $12,000 in campaign funds to his own personal use in the stock market. His stock agent, Frederick L. Colwell, refused to answer questions when first called before the Commission, and on the last day of the hearings he disappeared, last seen headed north after picking up a bag of clothing at the Yonkers rail station. Sulzer would not allow his secretary, Louis Sarecky, to testify and claimed the entire affair illegal because the state constitution only allowed extraordinary sessions to deal with the legislation given them by the governor. His huffing and puffing could not blow the house down, however. The vote to impeach, taken about 4 a.m. on August 14, with "only a technical quorum present," was 79-45, 76 of whom were needed to impeach. Fifty-one of the 79 were from New York City.

The 1846 state constitution amendments that redefined the nature of the Court for the Trial of Impeachments (the first one had been created in 1784) prescribed that a judge who was thus impeached could not continue the perform his functions until acquitted after trial, and the argument was made against Sulzer. Yet he continued as governor, albeit much impaired by the situation that had developed. The Court for the Trial of Impeachment (made up of the Senate and the Court of Appeals) convened in September with former state senator Edgar Truman Brackett (1853–1924) the chief counsel to the Board of Managers against the governor. Brackett was a local philanthropist whose generosity extended to Skidmore College, the Saratoga Hospital and the First Methodist Church; he developed an 18-hole golf course in Wilton. Alton B. Parker also joined the managers. During the trial, several donors—including Jacob Schiff and Henry Morgenthau—insisted that the money they gave was not particularly for campaign expenses. Morgenthau was amazed at the knowledge the prosecution had of a telephone call he took from Sulzer while in New Rochelle, unaware that lines in the governor's mansion were tapped.

The governor was urged to testify but could not get corroboration for the claims he wanted to make. He secretly recorded a conversation in his mansion's library with John H. Delaney, a Murphy operative whom Sulzer had given $10,000 for delivery to Murphy. The money came from Allen Ryan, a shadowy character whom Sulzer claimed Murphy told him to contact. Delaney would not budge, however—"There's one fellow who never squeals, and there will never be two ways about it"—and subsequently Ryan testified only that he gave the money to Sulzer, not for Murphy, and it became unaccounted for in Sulzer's financial reports. Ryan (according to Sulzer) later contacted the governor under an alias and offered to help him, but Sulzer declined. Ryan told him, Sulzer said, that a source close to Murphy told him that the case against Sulzer was "cut and dried" and that he "did not have a chance in the world."

The trial made it clear that the governor or his wife Clara diverted campaign money to investments in stocks and tried to cover it up. Other charges, including the allegation that Sulzer unduly pressured members for their votes, were not sustained. The law that proscribed the use of campaign funds for personal uses had been enacted in 1911.

Sulzer's fall was dictated—depending on the source—by Murphy's failure to get the state appointments he demanded; by the Catholic Church (thanks to his successor Martin Glynn), or just the Irish (he was "a political traitor," which they were said to be very good at dispatching); by "the kept newspapers" in New York City; or variously by "the Gashouse Gang, Wall Street, and the Dirty System." The New York Historical Society's voluminous collection of Sulzer papers included several anonymous and signed notes and letters claiming that the fix was in and that Frawley, Assembly Majority Leader Aaron Levy, and Senator Samuel J. Rampsberger of Buffalo were paid large sums to secure Sulzer's conviction and removal from office.

The management of the charges and the impeachment of William Sulzer were undertaken under the leadership of Assembly Speaker Smith and Senate President Pro Tem Wagner, two young and rising political stars whom the Legislative Correspondents Association's Red Book for the year called Murphy's "Gold Dust Twins." They lost their reelection bids that year, as did every other member who voted against Sulzer, and Sulzer himself was elected to the Assembly by a huge majority a month after his downfall. His popularity with the people never waned.

Six years later an attempt to reopen the proceedings through an appeal to the Senate Judiciary Committee failed, as did a lawsuit brought by Sulzer. New information was put forth claiming that Smith had large piles of money on his desk late in the night of August 13 and that eight Republican assemblyman who voted for Sulzer in the first round of voting earlier that evening changed their votes after visits to Smith during the night. Two of these men were from the Hudson Valley: slater Eugene R. Norton of Granville in Washington County and coal and ice dealer Myron Smith of Millbrook in Dutchess County. Emil Kovarik claimed he saw the money, but not the Speaker. His deposition was tainted, however, by the fact that he became Sulzer's bodyguard around the same time and was still with him all these years later. A more credible witness came forth in the person of O. R. Miller, the state superintendent of the New York Civil League, a moral reform lobbying organization.

Miller said that his legislative superintendent, Charles L. Boothby, told him about seeing the money when he entered the Speaker's office while seeking a pass to attend the Assembly proceedings. He said Smith was at the desk and looked "frightened" when he saw Boothby, but was reassured by the man that he would say nothing about what he saw. Boothby refused to step forward, Miller said, although William J. Hough also said that the statement Miller made about Boothby was accurate. Nothing further came of the matter, and even a commission of inquiry into the impeachment proceedings that Assemblyman Hinchey created in the 1980s dropped the subject after learning that Sulzer had also been a bagman for Tammany Hall, routinely bringing money across town for Charlie Murphy during campaign years. Guilty or not, he did not deserve a resurrection.

Sulzer spent the rest of his life attempting to vindicate his name and reputation, to no avail. Martin Glynn, his successor, got the credit for the direct primary law and New York's ratification of the direct election of US senators. He changed the look of the election ballot to emphasize the offices sought instead of the political parties of the candidates, and considered his finest achievement the enactment of the state's workmen's compensation law.

The railroad full crew law persisted as a thorn in the industry's side over the next fifty years, and was finally repealed in the 1960s. Today, a hundred years after Sulzer's downfall, only two crew members are needed for any railroad train in New York State, the conductor and the engineer. The federal railroad authority has proposed reducing that number to only the conductor.

16. Suffer the Children

The Foreign Minister of Germany once said to me your country does not dare do anything against Germany, because we have in your country five hundred thousand Germans reservists [emigrants] who will rise in arms against your government if you dare to make a move against Germany. Well, I told him that that might be so, but that we had five hundred thousand and one lamp posts in this country, and that that was where the reservists would be hanging the day after they tried to rise.

—James W. Gerard (1867–1951)

Douglas MacArthur (1880–1964) arrived at the United States Military Academy at West Point by train from Weehawken, New Jersey, on a Tuesday afternoon, June 13, 1899, a boy from Milwaukee who came under privileged circumstances. His grandfather had been a member of the Supreme Court of the United States. His father, Arthur MacArthur, was the commander of the 2nd Division of the VIII Army Corps in the Philippines, and was at that time preparing an advance against the army of Emilio Aguinaldo that would lead to the revolutionary insurgent's capture and MacArthur's appointment as military governor of the Philippines.

Young Douglas wore a Stetson hat. With him was his mother, Mary Pinkney Hardy ("Pinky") MacArthur (b. 1852), daughter of a wealthy Virginia cotton merchant, who moved into Craney's Hotel on the edge of the West Point campus. A fellow Craney's resident and friendly rival was Mrs. Frederick N. Grant, whose son U. S. Grant III ranked second behind MacArthur in the plebe class.

West Point remained traditionally old in MacArthur's day. Almost immediately he came to the attention of a congressional committee over a hazing incident in 1900, and gave a full accounting as "the so-called victim" of the incident, but refused to name names. The congressmen were startled at his maturity and thoroughness. He knew that if the committee demanded disclosure and he refused to name his abusers, he would be cashiered out of West Point. Yet, bolstered by his mother's poetic charge to her son—

"Remember the world will be quick with its blame /
If shadow or shame ever darkens your name"—

he knew what to do.

"I would be no tattletale," Douglas MacArthur declared to himself. He was asked to divulge the names, but pleaded with the distinguished panel to consider his position, his background, his father's good name— all the while quaking with fear and experiencing a terrible nausea. The court ordered him to his quarters, where he waited for the adjutant's footsteps and the dreaded decision, which never came. The names were made known to the court through other means, and MacArthur's further testimony was not needed.

Young Douglas was harassed by the middies of the Naval Academy of Annapolis in the stands over his father's high position while playing left field in the first baseball game between the two academies on May 18, 1901:

Are you the Governor General
Or a hobo?
Who is the boss of this show?
Is it you or Emilio Aguinaldo?

The young man took the catcalls in stride and "squared it up," as he put it, by "working the Navy pitcher for a base on balls" with the score tied at 3-3, stealing second and third on the catcher's wild throw, and "trotting home" when the outfielder's throw went over the third baseman's head. Army won, 4-3, and later the middies, "those fine sportsmen," treated MacArthur "as though I really was the governor general."

Douglas was not averse to the occasional prank while studying at West Point. In his plebe year, on April 16, 1901, a cannon was rolled to the super-intendent's lawn and pointed at his door. MacArthur was suspected of being among the youths who rolled the reveille gun across the plain and hoisted it to the roof of West Academic Building; it took a week with block and tackle to haul it down.

He recalled a recitation on "the space-time relationship" that Einstein would soon unravel in his theory of relativity, how incomprehensible it was to young Douglas, and how he merely memorized the pages of text and recited them when called to address the subject in class. Did the young man know what it all meant, the instructor, a colonel in the army, asked. "No, sir," MacArthur replied, certain that his ignorance would be his undoing.

"Neither do I, Mister MacArthur," Colonel Feiberger said slowly. "Class dismissed."

MacArthur's rise to First Captain of the Corps in his senior year surprised himself, if his memory is to be trusted. He claimed to be "astonished" that his grade at West Point was the best in twenty-five years. His cumulative point count of 2424.2 out of a possible 2470 was a 98.14% score, third ever (by mere tenths) in the history of the academy. He had perfect 100s in law, history, and English. He led the class in math, drill regulations, ordnance and gunnery, and military demeanor. He achieved the highest ranks available each year. The First Captain honor gave him the privilege of living in the octagonal tower room, which had a fireplace and a view of Craney's from the window.

MacArthur's classmates recalled his ego and a confidence that never betrayed any misgivings. At graduation on June 11, 1903, Secretary of War Elihu Root cautioned the students that before they ended their army careers, "you will be engaged in another war. It is bound to come, and will come. Prepare your country for that war."

MacArthur saw service in the Philippines at first, where he fell in love with the island country and its peoples. He would go on to become military attaché to President Wilson and command the 42nd Division in France in World War I, serve as West Point superintendent from 1919 to 1922 and as the Army Chief of Staff from 1930 to 1935, become supreme Allied commander in the Pacific from 1942 to 1945 and of the occupation forces in Japan over 1945–50; and command United Nations force in Korea in 1950–51. Along the way his illustrious career would be tarnished—in 1932 by his brutal suppression (with Dwight D. Eisenhower by his side) of the makeshift "Hooverville" Bonus Army of veterans gathered in Washington to demand their bonuses, and in 1952 by his dismissal from Korea by President Truman— yet his mother's admonition would never be forgotten.

During MacArthur's early years in the army, West Point joined in the grand parade of the new century, adding a Catholic chapel in the Norman Gothic style, designed by Hynes and LaFarge, in 1900. A new Cadet Chapel for Protestant faiths was finished in 1910, 200 feet long by 72 wide, capable of seating 1,500, and hosting, at 18,000 pipes, the largest organ in the world. The stained glass behind the Chancel depicted the 27 military leaders of the

Bible; the Revelations of St. John the Divine occupied 21 panels above the main entrance. Cadets would march to mandatory services there for the next 63 years.

Among the outstanding cadets at West Point in the early twentieth century was George S. Patton Jr. (1885–1945; class of '09), a football star and the first American to participate in pentathlon competition in the 1912 Olympics. Dwight D. Eisenhower's class was lionized at West Point, even though he was indifferent to his studies. The 1915 graduates were known as "the class the stars fell on" because of the 59 generals they produced, two of a five-star rank, Eisenhower (1890–1969) and his fellow company member and friend Omar Bradley (1893–1981).

At 21, Eisenhower had been too old to enter Annapolis, so he settled for West Point, scoring 87.5 in the opening exam. A tackle at Abilene in 1910, he only wanted to play football, and showed great promise in the few months of his sophomore year. He was said to have All-American potential, but twisted his knee in a game against Jim Thorpe and Carlisle College, and in the following week was severely injured in a drill with a training horse. His tendons torn and ligaments and cartilage permanently damaged, Eisenhower's football days were over—the injury also led to a slice in his golf drive made famous by the protruding "Eisenhower Tree" (d. 2014) at Augusta National in Georgia. A friend commented that he seemed to have "lost interest in life," but Ike soldiered on, as a cheerleader for the cadets and a member of the yearbook staff. He spent much time exploring the old forts areas in and around West Point. He was given to pranks, like other senior cadets, and occasionally went "over the wall" for sandwiches or ice cream at night—an expellable offense—and smoked cigarettes against the rules. Ike was once punished for fast dancing, and he ended his college career ranked 125th in discipline while graduating near the top of the second third of his class, 61st in a class of 164, and became a first lieutenant in the nineteenth Infantry at Fort Sam Houston, San Antonio, Texas.

While Douglas MacArthur was off stoking American imperialism elsewhere, America girded for troubled times while watching the shadows of war rising on the European continent. Although the high percentage of German-American populations tempered the response in the Hudson Valley, fears over German infiltration and influence fueled anti-immigrant feelings against anything that sounded Teutonic. President Wilson gave as well as he received when criticized by "disloyal" German-Americans in 1916 over America's sympathies for the English cause, even though the "hyphenated" vote was important in his run against Charles Evans Hughes that year.

German-American loyalties were deconstructed up and down the Valley just as strenuously if not as vociferously as elsewhere. In Ulster County, Overlook Mountain became suspicious to patriotic Woodstock men because Morris Newgold—obviously a German!—had purchased the mountain house site in 1917, and Max Schrabisch (1868–1949) was excavating Native American rock shelters on the mountain's side—obviously emplacements for machine guns! A guest at the hotel had a wireless radio—another spy! The xenophobia brought the otherwise-distant Byrdcliffe and hamlet communities together to some extent, as both looked over their patriotic noses to watch the doings on the mountain. At one point the patriots stormed Overlook, convinced that an aurora borealis display was really signals to German u-boats off the coast.

Schrabisch was the New Jersey state archaeologist for four years and a friend of Judge Alphonse T. Clearwater. He was a contributor to Reginald Pelham Bolton's anthropological papers on *The Indians of Greater New York and the Lower Hudson* in 1909. He came to the Hudson Valley with an interest in Native American rock shelters, excavated five shelters on Overlook and two on Ohayo Mountain. In Napanoch, Schrabisch was looking into shelters in the Shawangunks for the American Anthropological Association when he was arrested under suspicion of being a German spy on June 10, 1918. The local constabulary, afraid that he would abscond with national secrets if released, subjected him "to third degree measures" before tricking him into pleading guilty to "being a tramp" to avoid further suspicion; the local justice of the peace, Daniel Fitzgerald of Warwarsing, promptly sent him to the Ulster County jail for five days. Furious, Schrabish employed Saugerties attorney Frederick Darrow to have the conviction reversed and almost brought action against his accusers, but was persuaded otherwise by friends.

In Schenectady, questions about the loyalty of Frank Coe Barnes and even Charles Steinmitz arose during the war. Steinmitz, who became thoroughly American after arriving in New York, had left Germany partly because of his writings advocating socialism, so he was not about to be counted among the sympathizers of the Kaiser. (Rod Steiger played Steinmitz in his socialist days in a 1959 CBS television series, *The Joseph Cotton Show*.) Barnes (1862–1934), a short, stocky, cigar-smoking professor of modern languages, was called "Dutchy" by his Union College students, a sure sign to some that he too was tainted.

Barnes wrote an article for the *Modern Language Journal* urging schools not to stop teaching German, and Vassar refused to discontinue their German language course, but they were working against the grain, as books with German compositions were removed from schools and people demonized anything German. Sauerkraut became "liberty cabbage," hamburger was transformed into "Salisbury steak," persons with German names were often humiliated, and ministers preached the war against the Teutonic horde from their pulpits. Theodore Roosevelt turned citizenship oaths into blind loyalty statements and insisted upon only "one American mold." The attitudes were less prevalent in Valley communities where strong German roots had grown, but was present nonetheless, even among some Palatines descendants.

New York contributed more than 500,000 soldiers to the war effort, 190,000 from the sixteen counties bordering the Hudson River; a total of 14,093 casualties from the state were recorded. The war took its toll of Hudson Valley men. The first soldier from Kingston to be killed in action was George F. Schirick, whose brother was a state supreme court justice. Schirick was in the first American division to arrive in France. LeRoy Eltinge of Kingston, a brigadier general and career officer since the Philippines insurrections, served on General John J. Pershing's general staff in France; they were both West Point graduates. Several Kingston men were among the 550,000 Americans involved in the St. Mehiel Drive in September, which was the beginning of the end for Germany. Three lieutenant colonels, four majors, and ten captains were among the other officers who served from Kingston. Six Kingston High School students who joined—Aubrey Arnst, Ulysses G. French, John A. Joyce, Percy T. Keator, J. Geoffrey Strugnell, Leonard E. Woodrow—died in action.

Henry Lincoln Johnson (1897–1929) was a redcap porter at Union Station in Albany when he enlisted in the all-black New York National Guard army unit in June 1917. His unit—now the 369th Infantry Regiment, called the "Harlem Hellfighters"—arrived in France on New Year's Day. On May 14, Henry repulsed a German attack of two dozen soldiers while on guard duty in the Argonne Forest and rescued fellow guard Private Needham Roberts after he had been captured. Both men were seriously wounded, yet Johnson came at the Germans with his rifle, grenades, and in hand-to-hand fighting with his bolo knife. He was wounded 21 times. The Germans called him

"Black Death" after this incident; he was promoted to sergeant and became the first American soldier to receive the French Croix de Guerre with Gold Palm. Johnson's image was used to recruit black soldiers later in the war, and Theodore Roosevelt wrote about his exploit in stories of the war.

Johnson died penniless in Illinois in 1929, officially unrecognized by the Army for his extraordinary service. His cause was revived in the 1970s, with a monument erected in his honor in Albany and a posthumous Purple Heart awarded in 1997. In 2002, the US Army conveyed upon Johnson the Distinguished Service Cross, the second-highest honor in the service, for extraordinary military service while engaged with the enemy. He was exhumed and re-buried in Arlington National Cemetery.

The 369th was given its nickname by the Germans. They never lost ground while in the war, never abandoned a trench, and never had a captured soldier, not even Needham Roberts.

Jefferson Feigl of Mt. Kisco was killed in France on the first day of the German push from St. Quentin, March 21, 1918. He was a second lieutenant who had volunteered while at Harvard, the first American artillery officer killed in the war. A year later his parents received his handbag with a touching letter written to them as he lay dying. Jefferson Feigl Square was named for him by a grateful hometown. Among the White Plains casualties of the war was Private James Francis Lunney, who arrived in France on May 1 and died on August 30 of a gunshot wound during an engagement in Belgium. Infantry Captain Frederick W. Cobb (acting major at the time of his death) was killed by a shell on a hill in France on September 29, 1918.

Clifford B. Harmon left Harmon Park, the development in Croton-on-Hudson he had created, and became a pilot in the war, en route to a career as an aviation pioneer. Kingston native Washington Irving Chambers (b. 1856), a noted naval commander, was the first American to design a reliable gyroscope for torpedoes, and, in 1912, produced a catapult to send airplanes off ships that became useful during the war.

Dr. Rudolph Diedling of Saugerties went to France in 1917 as a lieutenant with the 32nd Division of the American Expeditionary Forces. There his fate ultimately did cross with that of the great ex-president, not in the promise or bright expectation of the age, but in a sadder way. Theodore Roosevelt's son, Quentin, gave the ultimate sacrifice that summer, and he was in Diedling's company. Diedling also had lost a son, nine-year-old Dudie, in a sledding accident on January 30, 1915. Diedling was honored as a war hero for several small hospitals he created for soldiers along the front. A few years after the war, a man named Henry Zahn came to Saugerties to take a job with Central Hudson Gas & Electric. He had been shelled in a foxhole and had to crawl for safety, where he was immediately treated by a doctor—the same man whom he now met practicing in this sleepy Hudson River village.

Albert Cashdollar (b. 1891) was typical of the young men who left their homes, wrote poignant letters to their mothers and other kin, fought in a number of battles, and mercifully returned home. Cashdollar was wounded in the Argonne and continued fighting until relieved by replacements. He opened the first automotive garage in Woodstock when he returned, and went on to serve as town supervisor and commander of the Ulster County Defense Council in World War II. Philip Buttrick was a Woodstock youth with a Yale degree and specialty in cork forests. At the outset of World War II, Buttrick helped organize the first American chapter of France Forever in Woodstock. He was with the Red Cross in France in 1917, became a French officer, and was awarded the Croix de Guerre.

Poultney Bigelow, the childhood friend of the Kaiser, fueled the war fever by writing about the dreaded horde and the supposed frequency of railroad cars being derailed, munitions factories blown up, and threats to bridges. Most of Poultney's rants were exaggerations, but his fears were shared by those living closest to the city. Howland Pell (1856–1937), whose family once owned most of the county around Pelham, was a captain in the First Provincial Regiment assigned to guarding the New York City water supply over 1917–19. The Croton aqueduct had sentries posted for a hundred miles within sight of each other. City police at the new Ashokan Reservoir kept a watchful eye west of the Hudson. The national guard patrolled both sides of the river at the Cornwall-Garrison tunnel. The Poughkeepsie railroad bridge was also considered a sensitive security risk during the war.

New York joined with the nation in creating a war industry to sustain the effort, with numerous factories retooling and otherwise upgrading to meet the new production demands. General Electric led in these efforts in its extensive Schenectady works. A US Naval Ammunition Depot created by Congress at Iona Island in 1899 was outfitted with a hospital, telegraph system, fire department, generating plant and water works. Two hundred Navy employees assembled shells and canisters for battleships. Special "sparkless compressed-air locomotives" were used to move the materiel safely to the docks for shipment to Fort Lafayette at the Battery. Iona continued as a federal defense facility until 1967, when it became part of the state parks system.

The New York Council of Defense organized county home defense committees in May 1917 under a $1 million appropriation approved by Governor Charles S. Whitman and the legislature. State and county agencies assisted in the civilian war efforts, the packaging and shipment of medical supplies, clothing, writing implements, and foodstuffs. Home-front actions were begun under a Committee of Safety in Westchester County, led by Col. William Boyce Thompson of Yonkers. Westchester already had men in the field in the 27th Division, a National Guard unit on active duty along the Mexican border under Major General John F. O'Ryan of Salem Center; they went to South Carolina first for training, and then to France in May 1918. The 27th played an important role in the British assault on the Hindenberg Line. The 77th and 42nd Westchester divisions saw action in the Argonne Forest, when more than 3,600 men of the 77th fell. In all, Westchester lost 467 men during the First World War.

Arthur William Lawrence (1875–1937), a major real estate developer who co-founded Bronxville with his father, William Van Duzer Lawrence, became the Food and Fuel Administrator for Westchester County. Appeals for pay allotments for families of servicemen went through the adjutant general's office in Albany. Mrs. William Mumons of Hoosick Falls wrote a letter pleading for support on January 25, 1918, after months waiting for the government to act. Her husband, Private William Mumons, had reported to the Depot Brigade after being drafted the previous October, and she was almost destitute.

The war was fought at home in the factories and mines where materiel was produced at huge rates to support the expeditionary forces. New York harbor was the major shipping port for the war. Twelve 9,000-ton steamers were under construction in the Newburgh shipyards in the spring of 1917. Marvel Shipyard retooled and sent products to France by transports loaded at the Newburgh docks. Iron and steel mills in the Albany area contributed heavy materiel; elevators shipped tons of grain from the interior farmlands; textile manufactures produced uniforms, boots, and other necessities; and scows and tugboats were built for overseas shipment.

An explosion at the American Hand Grenade Loading Corporation plant south of the village of Port Ewen on November 15, 1918, left one dead and several injured. It happened on a Friday evening where the firing apparatuses for grenades were assembled; a man carrying a tray of them apparently tripped or dropped the tray. Fifty-to-sixty workers in the building at the time escaped, including a number of young women workers whose skirts were torn off in the blast.

Edith T. Jones was one of thirty women from White Plains who served, a public school teacher and volunteer with the Y.M.C.A. canteens in France; she spent a year in Paris and was involved in a number of engagements in the war. Ladies of the Cornwall area had a special tie with French soldiers through Mrs. Pauline Sands Lee, who was in Paris with American Aid for French Wounded; they contributed 79,237 surgical dressings to the cause. Frances Hoppin cared for up to sixty Belgian children a year through her brother's Red Cross connections in France. Squads of local women from Cornwall and Newburgh met troop transports at Cornwall Landing (when refueling) and distributed refreshments for up to 10,000 soldiers a day. On Memorial Day in 1920, "the only captured cannon of the Great War ever presented to an American community" was given to Cornwall by Captain Pierre Lecomte du Nouy of France.

Miss Eloise Payne Lucquer, who painted very good watercolors of flowers, with her friend Miss Delia Marble began a native plant garden at Ward Pound Ridge Reservation and organized teams of "farmerettes" to harvest vegetable and milk the cows while the men were off to war. Daisy Suckley sold war bonds door to door in the summer in Rhinebeck, and volunteered in the winter as a nurse's aide at Ellis Island. Her eldest brother, Henry, "the handsome, capable son on whom their father had pinned the family's hopes," was killed when a German bomb hit his Red Cross ambulance near Salonika, Greece.

Vassar girls raised $2,100 for an ambulance and $4,600 for a tuberculosis hospital in France by mid-December 1916. When the country entered the war in the spring of 1917, 638 students were already enrolled in a dozen preparedness courses, ranging from first aid and home nursing to surgical dressings and motor repair. Alice Campbell ('17) led a dozen farmerettes in replacing men on the Vassar farm, earning 17½ cents an hour and paying their board from those funds. More than 200 students stayed on campus the following summer. A farmer reassured them that milking a cow was "just like learning to play the piano." A Vassar Relief Unit was organized by the Associate Alumnae and sent to France to run eight Red Cross huts for convalescing soldiers; they later undertook relief work at Verdun.

The college ran a Training Camp for Nurses in the summer of 1918, in which 435 student nurses from 42 state and 115 institutions of higher learning participated. The project was organized by Minnie Cumnock Blodget ('84) and run by professor Herbert Mills. The college also provided President MacCracken with a leave of absence to attend to his duties as National Director of the Junior Red Cross. A total of 150 Vassar alumnae were in service in France from 1914 to 1918; one of the casualties of the war was Lieutenant Alvin Treadwell, son of the college's zoology professor.

Henry Noble McCracken set up the Junior Red Cross nationally to help with the war effort. Red Cross and Liberty Bond drives were popular throughout the Valley. The Rensselaer County drive was led by the county's most prominent lawyer, George E. Greene (1860–1943). Law committees were formed among the attorneys in each of the counties to dispose of the unfinished cases of their colleagues who entered the service. Reports were provided to the defense council on the county activities for Saratoga, Albany, Rensselaer, Schenectady and other Hudson Valley counties. At what came to be called Flag Hill in Mount Pleasant, just west of the Pleasantville railroad station, someone climbed the hill each day and erected the flag, yet no one ever knew who it was.

Mohonk Mountain House sponsored a Country Fair to benefit the French War Relief victims in August 1918 that was so popular it continued into the 1970s. In the hamlet of Woodstock, women in costume set up booths to sell food, plants, and flowers, and to craft objects for the war effort. They too became popular and were continued as the Market Fair for another sixty years. As befit the colorful arts community, innovations in adapting to a nation short on supplies became Woodstock novelties. Bolton Brown (1864–1936) solved the rubber shortage by making tire wheels of wood and steel springs, his loud arrival in the hamlet remembered for years thereafter. Edward ("Ned") Thatcher taught wounded veterans how to make toys from old tin cans, and published a popular book about the craft, *Making Tin Cans Toys*, in 1919. A number of Woodstock men went to Rondout to work the war industries at the shipyards in those years.

When Florence Ballin Cramer heard of the armistice by telephone from a friend in New York (there were more than eighty phones in the town by then), she wrote that it "was like seeing sunshine after having spent years in a cave, we became dazed. . . . Konrad and I rushed out doors and danced around madly in sheer joy." They drove through the hamlet with fellow artists Andrew Dasburg, Caroline Speare, and Paul Rohland, proclaiming "Peace!" to all. They picked up some wine in Saugerties and had a grand time all evening.

"West Point is forty years behind the times," Chief of Staff General Peyton March told Douglas MacArthur on June 12, 1919, in appointing him superintendent of the academy. It was actually far worse, as MacArthur discovered. The four-year curriculum had been abandoned in favor of a one-year training course in the headlong need for officers to replace the 9,119 who were killed or wounded in France. The academy was also under attack again, as it had been in Andrew Jackson's time, but now as an unnecessary appendage to a world in which war had become an anachronism. People genuinely believed that "the war to end wars" would do that, just as they did after World War II. MacArthur faced that challenge by force of logic and an appeal to reason in congressional budget discussions and other forums. When there are no fires they do not disband the fire departments, he reasoned.

MacArthur undertook a massive restructuring of the academy, convinced that a "psychology of command" needed to be inculcated in the raw new recruits. He modernized the curriculum along a whole new plan. With no upper classmen to provide the traditional discipline that made West Point work as a model educational community in the past, a cadet initiative development structure was constructed that became the modern West Point model. The summer program of a week in artillery practice that had been standard in his days at the Point was replaced by a month in an actual army camp situation, the brutal inculcation of all new plebes that became known as "Beast" in later days.

The commander also required every student to participate in every sport offered at West Point, creating an intramural model that was adopted by other colleges in future years. This dramatic change in sports expansion did not go unnoted over time; in 1927, he took leave of his regular duties to accept appointment as president of the American Olympic Committee, leading the team to an overall victory over Germany in the Netherlands games that year. During his stay in Amsterdam, MacArthur enjoyed dining with Queen Wilhelmina and listening to her discourse with expertise on the Dutch Hudson Valley history of the seventeenth century.

Douglas MacArthur served only three years before moving on to another high command, yet in his vigorous remaking of the West Point model he created a whole new military school concept and a new American military officer corps. On his recommendation, the cadet body was increased from 1,334 to 2,500.

The war took its toll on the young cadets of the region, but the sickness the servicemen brought back with them did even more damage. In 1915, four months had elapsed before Edward P. McCormick, the night supervisor at the Diamond Mills on the Saugerties waterfront, recorded another Saugerties child's death in his daily notebook, after the passing of six-year-old Ruth Conaley in a fire in Glasco on June 1. By November of 1918 he was recording several a day for weeks, all victims of a worldwide influenza epidemic:

Nov 5 Bradley Margaret died 3 Yrs East Bridge
Nov 6 Montano Eula died 3 Yrs Partition St
Nov 6 Kerbert Mrs. George died 24 Yrs Montgomery St

Conditions for children improved over the war years, with advances made in controlling diphtheria, typhoid, and other contagions that typically struck children. New York, on both the state and local level, was becoming more diligent in the care and treatment of the ill and infirmed, particularly children and those below the poverty level. In 1914, Scarborough millionaire and philanthropist Valentine Everit Macy (1871–1930) was elected Superintendent of the Poor of Westchester County with Progressive and Democratic support. He undertook the reform of children care services, cleaned up the almshouse at Grasslands, and, with the advise of social worker Ruth Taylor, ended the commitment of children to institutions under a regressive system that financially rewarded any of the 128 city and town judges with the power to do so. Many children were sent home, sent to relatives, or brought into respectable foster homes. Macy then made a commitment with Republican Party boss (and fellow Columbia graduate) William Lukens Ward to become a Republican in return for Ward's support for a new county welfare department. Ward, the Republican boss from 1900 to 1933, was the first politician to bring together the county's cities and towns, which was key to the system of parks, roads, and expanded social services that Ward pursued over the years. Macy created a chain of newspapers that supported Ward and his policies over the decades.

When the influenza epidemic struck in 1918 at Rensselaer Polytechnic Institute in Troy, 650 students in the Student Army Training Corps were just moving into temporary barracks. As the campus went into quarantine, the Spanish flu was followed by diphtheria; the two illnesses claimed fourteen lives. Vassar had remained in quarantine since opening in the fall of 1918 because of the spread of the epidemic. The students helped with relief work at nearby Arlington by raising $600, making masks and swabs for the Red Cross, amassing clothing and blankets, and donating orange juice that they squeezed from hundreds of oranges every day in the Students' Building basement. When news of the impending Armistice arrived at 3:30 a.m. on November 10, 1918, the night watchman, hearing the whistles of the city blowing in celebration, rang the fire alarm and started to pass the word. The entire campus turned out.

The Valley, like the country, shut down because of the influenza, government offices closing or staggering hours, schools closing, as well as theaters and other places where people might congregate. Pastors protested when local officials asked that church services be curtailed or postponed because of the threat of contagion. Many wore masks when on the streets or in public places, and still the death toll rose. Cornwall undertaker Edward L. Sylcox "ran out of coffins and had to commission a local carpenter to make them," Janet Dempsey reported. "Sometimes an entire family was stricken."

Hervey White, the founder of the Maverick colony in Woodstock, worked as an assistant to Dr. Mortimer Downer in nursing influenza patients. Downer asked if he liked "taking chances at death," referring to the notorious contagion of the disease.

"Life is not so sweet that I can't do my duty," White said.

"That's the way I feel about it," the doctor replied. Hervey nursed Will Peper, the blacksmith Henry Peper's son, until his death. Will's brother, who was deferred when the draft came to allow him to remain at home to help at the shop, returned from France to help the father again. Another dying young man, delirious in his fever, supposed that Hervey was an angel nursing him; they both had a hearty laugh.

Another victim of the Spanish influenza, in a way, was the physician Julius Hammer, sentenced to Sing-Sing Prison in 1919 on a manslaughter conviction for performing an abortion on a woman who subsequently died. She had the influenza, as well as heart problems and nephritis. Hammer's trial was badly managed by his lawyers, according to his son Armand (1898–1990), and became a populist cause that led the New York medical community into calling for changes to the state's restrictive abortion law.

The son described the shock of seeing his father in Ossining "in prison uniform, surrounded by thieves, murderers, rapists and gangsters," at a time when the boy was completing his own medical studies at Columbia University. The visits to the prison were arduous—a full day to make the trip from Manhattan in 1921—and almost cost the young Hammer his education because of classes he missed. Yet he graduated with honors, and in the six-month interim until his internship Hammer made a decision that would change his life. He would go to Russia to help fight the typhus epidemics there, in the land of his father's birth; he would do this to please his father.

III. EVERYTHING GONE CRAZY

The lighter the snow, the more it drifts; and the more frivolous the people, the more they are blown by one wind or another. . . .

—JOHN BURROUGHS, *In the Catskills* (1910)

17. John Burroughs: An Appreciation

> The universe is a more amazing puzzle than ever. . . the hazy
> butterflies, the carved shells, the birds, beasts, fishes, insects,
> snakes, and the upheaving principle of life everywhere incipient,
> in the very rock spring organized forms. Not a form so
> grotesque, so savage, nor so beautiful but is an expression of
> some property inherent in man the observer. . . . I feel the
> centipede in me—cayman, carp, eagle and fox. I am moved by
> strange sympathies; I say continually "I will be a naturalist."
>
> —RALPH WALDO EMERSON, 1833

John Burroughs (1837–1921) came down from Roxbury in Schoharie
County as a young man in the 1850s and worked as a teacher, first in Olive,
while energetically pursuing attempts at nature essays like those of his idol,
Ralph Waldo Emerson.

"I had just begun to get hold of myself with my pen," Burroughs wrote;
"I was like a young bird just out of the nest. My flights were short and rather
awkward." His writings were so much like Emerson's that James Russell Lowell,
who published his first essay in the fledgling *Atlantic Monthly* in 1860, initially
thought he had plagiarized the Concord Sage. Burroughs married Ursula
North (1836–1917) of Troy in 1857, and confided to her that his would be
the life of a writer and that he expected in time "to have my name recorded
with the great and the good." His most famous poem, "Waiting," was a
prescient prediction of his fate and one of the most popular poems of the
nineteenth century—

> Serene, I fold my hands and wait,
> Nor care for wind, nor tide, nor sea;
> I rave no more 'gainst time or fate,
> For, lo! my own shall come to me.

Burroughs had begun as an imitator of Samuel Johnson and other
Enlightenment writers, but he became engrossed in Emerson on his second

reading of the *Essays: First Series* (1841), learning valuable lessons in style, pace, and sentiment. He met Emerson after a lecture of his at West Point in 1863. In the same year, Burroughs found a copy of John James Audubon's *Birds of America* in the West Point library. The fledgling naturalist likened his first encounter with the *Birds* as "bringing together fire and powder," and added ornithology to botany and natural science among his passions.

His writing craft further improved thanks to Walt Whitman (1819–92), who told him to write what he knew instead of imitating Emerson, and in time John became a revered figure of the Hudson River Valley. His first collection of nature essays appeared in 1871; *Wake-Robin,* the title suggested by Whitman (and part of the book strongly influenced by him), is a common name for the white wildflower (*Trillium grandiflorum*) whose arrival harkens the first of the birds in spring. The essays kept coming over the years, almost three hundred in all collected in twenty-four books. Burroughs bristled at some of the early compliments he received—from Henry James, for instance, whose review of *Winter Sunshine* (1875) praised his "originality" and "real genius for the observation of natural things," yet suggested that he "sees sermons in stone and good in everything."

"I do not look for sermons in stone," Burroughs wrote. "I paint the bird for its own sake, and for the pleasure it affords me, and am annoyed by any lesson or moral twist."

He eschewed any transcendental Emersonian implications, even though he also wrote philosophical essays, and differed with Emerson on a basic level. Emerson considered nature as secondary to man in the scheme of things, while Burroughs, echoing a Native American viewpoint, considered "nature" and "the boy" to be essentially the same. Burroughs had a similar view of Henry David Thoreau (1817–62), although he praised *Walden* (1854) as "our first and probably only nature classic" and "certainly the most delicious piece of brag in our literature." Burroughs felt that Thoreau like Emerson was seeking "intently for the bird behind the bird,—for a mythology to shine through his ornithology." The antebellum trust and faith in God's light shining on the American experiment receded in Burroughs' view of nature, as it did in the age of sheen in which he wrote. Burroughs, as a result, is often considered a "literary" naturalist, and indeed his writing is as accessible to the reader in modern times as it was in his own. Yet there were depths to his efforts that belied this simplistic view.

"We talk of communing with Nature," Burroughs wrote in his journal on November 27, 1877: "but 'tis with ourselves we commune. Nature has nothing to say. It all comes from within. The air supports combustion, but 'tis the candle that burns, not the air. Nature furnishes the conditions—the solitude—and the soul furnishes the entertainment."

The freshness and immediacy of Burroughs' first published essay, "The Return of the Birds," characterized many of those that followed. The writer himself acknowledged that he was a lesser stylist than the "crisp, tart, snappy" Thoreau, but he added, "I think it probable that my books send people to nature more than Thoreau's do." Much of what the general public knew and took for granted about nature in later years came first from Burroughs.

Whitman's recognition as America's most important poet began with this budding naturalist and the book he wrote about the man and his poetry. Burroughs first learned of Whitman's unusual poetry from a close friend, Myron Beecher Benton (1834–1902), whom Burroughs met in 1862. Benton had written to Burroughs in admiration of one of his early essays, so John came over on the Highland ferry when Myron saw his brother Charles off at Camp Dutchess, where the 150th New York Volunteers were waiting to enter the Civil War. The two men became engrossed in conversation, and in the afternoon Benton drove Burroughs by carriage the thirty miles back across Dutchess County to the Benton home in Amenia. Troutbeck—its name taken from Samuel Coleridge's district in England—lay in the Oblong on a terrace up against Connecticut, with long southerly views of the Webutuck Valley. Myron's early writings appeared in the Cincinnati *Dial* and the Boston *Commonwealth*. His *Songs of the Webutuck* (published posthumously in 1906) was mildly favored by the critics. He and Burroughs became greatly attached and tramped the Valley hills together. They were together at Benton's home when Emerson died on April 27, 1882. Myron Benton's death on November 25, 1902, had a heavy impact on Burroughs, who called his friend "gentle, genial, mellow, unobtrusive; his own native, meandering Webutuck in human form."

While out gathering nuts near Troutbeck during one of their early visits, Benton read from the third edition of *Leaves of Grass*. Myron was not a committed Whitman fan, but for John there was no other book that made such an impression. Burroughs was 26 and Whitman 44 when they met at Charles Pfaff's beer cellar in New York.

"Walt kissed me like a girl," Burroughs wrote.

He composed the first substantial essay in support of Whitman, "Walt Whitman and His Drum Taps," published in *The Galaxy* in December of 1866. *Notes on Walt Whitman, as Poet and Person* (1867)—which was probably written with Whitman's guidance and support—was Burroughs' first book, the first critical study of Whitman, and the book that ignited both Dante Gabriel Rossetti and the Pre-Raphaelites' interest in Whitman and Algernon Swinburne's attack on him in England. A contemporary critic, Moncure D. Conway, called the *Notes* "the best critical work ever produced in America."

Whitman apparently had a hand in several Burroughs works, particularly those in which Whitman was the subject. John's essay, "The Flight of the Eagle," was drastically revised and retitled (from "The Disowned Poet") by Whitman, who also wrote to Burroughs that he especially liked that chapter in *Birds and Poets*—since it was about himself. The two men became very close, but did not share the physical passion that Whitman had for other men. He was a frequent visitor and often stayed at the Burroughs house when both were in Washington, and when Burroughs came north in 1872 to establish a farm in the Hudson Valley he admonished Ursula to treat Walt as she would himself. From Burroughs, Whitman derived the image of the hermit thrush (*Turdus ustulatis*) to invoke the grief he felt over the death of Lincoln ("When Lilacs Last in the Dooryard Bloomed"). Whitman composed "The Dalliance of the Eagles" as a tribute to the birth of his friend's son in 1878. The poem drew upon a Burroughs journal entry about the sighting of two eagles, so enraptured with each other that they clasped claws in the sky and swung around and around in a freefall toward earth, "like school-girls a-hold of hands."

Whitman made three trips to Riverby, walking the woods with Burroughs as they had in Washington (where John also came with Whitman on visits to wounded soldiers). In *Specimen Days* (1892), Whitman wrote of a visit he made with his nephew Albert E. Johnson on June 21, 1878, while Whitman was not feeling well:

> The place, the perfect June days and nights, (leaning toward crisp and cool,) the hospitality of J. and Mrs. B., the air, the fruit, (especially my favorite dish, currants and raspberries, mixed, sugar'd, fresh and ripe from the bushes—I pick 'em myself)—the room I occupy at night, the perfect bed, the window giving an ample view of the

Hudson and the opposite shores, so wonderful toward sunset, and the rolling music of the R.R. trains, far over there—the peaceful rest—the early Venus-heralded dawn—the noiseless splash of sunrise, the light and warmth indescribably glorious, in which (soon as the sun is up) I have a capital rubbing and rasking with the flesh-brush —with an extra scour on the back by Al. J. . . . all inspiriting my invalid frame with new life, for the day.

Young Johnson recalled the "pre-breakfast" swims in the river, he and Burroughs "listening to Walt declaiming passage after passage of Shakespeare, particularly from 'King Lear,'" and watching the Albany boats pass from the veranda in the evening.

On Whitman's last visit to Riverby in the spring of 1879, he and Burroughs stopped on one of their country drives to listen to a wood thrush singing. They visited a waterfall, where Walt sat on a fallen hemlock making notes about the setting with its "rich underlay of ferns." Burroughs chose the locale for his cabin in the woods a few years after Walt's death. He wrote the first chapter of his second book on Whitman there (*Whitman: A Study*, 1896), starting with the waterfall scene.

John Burroughs often entertained school groups, and had a special friendship with the Vassar College Wake Robin Club, who came to Black Creek and Slabsides often over the years. He came to Poughkeepsie with Whitman in 1878 for commencement and to visit Frederic Louis Ritter (1834–91), the head of Vassar's School of Music, on invitation of Ritter's wife, Fanny Raymond Ritter. The two writers traveled to the commencement over the Highland ferry in a buggy with a lame white horse.

"We didn't come in style, but we got here," Burroughs told a Whitman Centenary audience at Vassar in 1919. At the time, Ritter was the only one at Vassar who knew of the poet. The composer told the naturalist that when he wanted to evoke a mood for writing music, he always read from *Leaves of Grass*. Ritter composed a Whitman "Poem for Recitation" in the following year, dedicating it to Burroughs. The attitude was not always as friendly toward the controversial poet, however; Burroughs recalled that Herbert Gilcrest, a Vassar artist whom Burroughs visited on one occasion after Whitman's death, experienced a disgusting sneer from an old faculty member when Gilcrest spoke of his admiration for Whitman.

Fanny Ritter was, according to Clara Barrus, "perhaps the first musician to publish a critical account of the musical elements in Whitman's poetry." Fanny continued a correspondence with Whitman in 1880 over his poem, "Two Veterans." Vassar ultimately acquired fifty volumes of Burroughs journals for its library. In one entry, he described a conversation with Whitman in which the poet saw nature writing as on the same level as his own, "inspired as well as poetry":

> So many ways by which Nature may be come at; so many sides to her, whether by bird, or insect, or flower, by hunting, or science— when one thing is really known, you can no longer be deceived; you possess a key, a standard; you effect an entrance, and everything else links on and follows.

In addition to Whitman, Burroughs hosted Oscar Wilde at Riverby in August 1882. Wilde had toured New York in 1881, staying downriver at John Bigelow's Highland Falls estate, and was back for the staging of a play, *Vera, or The Nihilists*. He came upriver to see Henry Abbey, the Kingston poet, who took him to Riverby. They sat on the porch in rocking chairs, enjoying the summer, talking about how America had failed to harness industry properly and was now destroying nature. Wilde helped four-year-old Julian gather berries for lunch, and was an instant hit with Ursula once he expressed admiration for the bread she made. Burroughs considered him an exceptional thinker—they were both admirers of John Ruskin—"a splendid talker, a handsome man, but a voluptuary."

At Riverby, Burroughs welcomed the romance of the river and its brawny winter face. To him, the preternatural whine of the shifting ice sounded like an old man snoring "in his winter sleep":

> It is a singular sound. Thoreau calls it a "whoop," Emerson a "cannonade," . . . A cannonade indeed! As the morning advanced, out of the sunshine came peal upon peal of soft mimic thunder. . . . As noon approached, the sound grew to one continuous mellow roar, which lessened and became more intermittent as the day waned, until about sundown it was nearly hushed.

The river came alive with the breakup of the ice in the spring, "great masses" moving in a huge traffic jam on the watery highway, "crowding and jostling each other, and struggling for the right of way." The incoming tide carried the ice in the reverse direction, flowing upstream "as if sure of escape in that direction," he wrote. "Thus they race up and down, the sport of the ebb and flow; but the ebb wins each time by some distance."

Burroughs discovered and reported the sublime, in passages such as this, yet never pursued beauty as an end or goal as had the Hudson River School painters. "Beauty without a rank material basis enfeebles," he wrote. He also avoided sentimentalizing nature—but was not averse to the occasional pathetic fallacy in calling birds "widowed mothers" and the like—and began a national controversy in March 1903 by attacking "the yellow journalism of nature" practiced by "nature fakers" who anthropomorphized animals by attributing intelligence and reasoning to their behaviors. Burroughs was reacting to a new genre that had emerged in fiction, his attack precipitating a seven-year controversy that raged in the journals and drew in President Roosevelt. Burroughs and Roosevelt had met in New York City in March 1889 through a mutual friend, Rhinebeck essayist and political independent John Jay Chapman. TR sent Burroughs a letter in 1903 praising his position on the nature fakers.

The President had Burroughs join him on a jaunt to Yellowstone that spring, and TR came with his wife Edith by presidential yacht to Riverby on July 10, 1903.

"How are you, Oom John?" said Roosevelt, using the Dutch "uncle" familiarly as he landed. Teddy, Edith, and John hiked to Slabsides together for a lunch of chicken, potatoes, the ubiquitous celery, and Ursula's cherry pie. A large crowd gathered at the river when the president left, and Burroughs made a point of introducing each of them by name.

In 1907, Roosevelt engaged fully in the nature writing controversy with an article supporting Burroughs in a national publication. TR included Jack London's *White Fang* in his attack, which prompted the author to respond that he took pains to describe animal reactions as instinctual. Burroughs returned to warnings and admonitions about "the 'yellow' reporter abroad in the fields and woods" often in his later writings. The irony was that Ernest Thompson Seton (1860–1946), whose *Wild Animals I Have Known* (1898) drew Burroughs' initial ire, later became friends with Burroughs, who considered him a reliable naturalist; Seton's four-volume *Lives of the Game Animals* led to his receipt of the John Burroughs Medal for nature writing in 1927.

Burroughs built Slabsides in the woods a few miles from Riverby (to escape "domestic tyranny," he told Benton) to provide a writing and contemplation space away from the unexpected visitors who were always calling upon him at home. He saved Woodchuck Lodge, his boyhood home in the mountains near Roxbury, thanks to a Henry Ford gift in 1913, and spent his summers there for many years. Both became National Historic Landmarks; the 180-acre John Burroughs Nature Sanctuary developed around Slabsides and has had a year-round resident naturalist in-house since 1977.

"My retreat is covered with the bark of young chestnut-trees," John wrote, "and the birds, I suspect, mistake it for a huge stump that ought to hold fat grubs (there is not even a book-worm inside it), and their loud rapping often makes me think I have a caller indeed."

In time, Burroughs experienced a changed attitude toward the river setting of Riverby. Although he still appreciated how "it idealizes the landscape" and "multiplies and heightens the beauty of the day," he now considered the Hudson a distant and aloof acquaintance, its size bloated by the estuarial coming and going of the tides, a presence that diminished man and his surroundings: "I think one might spend a lifetime upon its banks without feeling any sense of ownership in it, or becoming at all intimate with it: it keeps one at arm's length." He much preferred the small and intimate settings of nearby Black Creek or the swampy forest where he and Julian dug out his celery bog.

John Muir (1838–1914), who came in 1896, was one of the first of Burroughs' Slabsides guests; John and Julian rowed over to the Hyde Park railroad to pick him up. Burroughs visited the well known naturalist whenever in California, and the two joined E. A. Harriman's Alaska scientific venture in 1899. Burroughs differed significantly from Muir in his concentration on the close and intimate as opposed to the sublime panoramas of Muir's "playground" and the latter's strenuous efforts to save unique natural resources like Hetch Hetchy Valley in Yosemite National Park.

John and Myron Benton first attempted a hike up Slide Mountain, the highest peak in the Catskills, in the summer of 1884, coming at it from the east, and had to return the next year to reach the summit, this time by a more likely path through Woodland Valley. Burroughs was not there in 1886 when his upriver neighbor Judge Alton B. Parker joined the state's forest commissioner at the Slide summit to announce the creation of the Catskills Forest Preserve, yet it was Burroughs 1888 essay, "The Heart of the Southern Catskills," that sparked the public's interest in the region.

Burroughs did not engage in the emerging politics of conservation, like his friend Muir, even though in his journal he worried about "what a sucked orange the earth will be in the course of a few more centuries." In the same passage he spoke of the mills and industries of Pittsburgh as "the devil's laboratory," and looked forward to a day when the delivery of power arose "above the surface for the white coal, for the smokeless oil, for the winds and the sunshine. . . . Our very minds ought to be cleaner."

Burroughs transformed into a modern commentator over his interest in Darwin and Bergson. Although he rejected Bergson's *Creative Evolution* idea of the *élan vital,* or creative energy of evolution, as an admixture of "metaphysics and natural science" inadequate to explain the "final mystery" of life itself, he accepted that the mystery remained to be resolved. "Where there is no vision," he once wrote, drawing on the new automotive technology, "science will not save us. In such a case our civilization is like an engine running without a headlight."

Frank Bergon considered Burroughs a pioneer ecologist in his interest in "the interactions of organisms with their environments." The new science—the term "ecology" was coined in 1873—was advanced by young scientists whom Burroughs met on the Alaska trip and remained in touch with for more than twenty years. James Stapleton, the resident naturalist at Slabsides, speaking at a Bard College symposium on Burroughs in 1978, discussed ways in which he anticipated later ecological and ethological science advances in his observations.

After the turn of the century, Burroughs was known for his acquaintances with the rich and famous, including Henry Ford, Harvey Firestone, and Thomas Edison. The men frequently went on camping and other trips together and became well-known public friends. Ford gave Burroughs a Model-T in January 1913, which Julian learned to drive first so he could teach his father. But Burroughs proved to be a terrible driver. Poultney Bigelow wrote that he was "as little fitted for the role of chauffeur as a nursery maid in the conning tower of a destroyer." Bigelow and his wife had just come down from western Ulster County, the car weaving abruptly at any unusual bird sightings, Burroughs and Henry Ford more engrossed in their passion than the road.

Burroughs was already in his sixties when he met Clara Barrus (1864–1931) in Middletown in 1901. She was a medical doctor at the psychiatric hospital who, like many other young women of the day, was taken with

Burroughs' writings and his personal charm. By now he was a celebrated American writer and a part of the conservation movement that developed after the Civil War publication of Reginald Marsh's *Man and Nature* in the year that Barrus was born. Clara became his personal companion and amanuensis, traveling with him virtually everywhere. His name and lore preceded him wherever they went, and his appearance in the long beard (already growing whiter), his slow walk, congenial attitude and friendly disposition, especially toward the young, ingratiated him to people wherever he went.

Their friendship was controversial within the confines of family and close friends. Clara's persistent questions about the Benton-Burroughs correspondence irritated the family and his brother Charles at Myron Benton's funeral; Julian thought she was "ambitious." The family's traditional Christmas dinner with their father ended in 1913 when Barrus, without asking, brought her two nieces. Burroughs enjoyed the company of young women and was probably quite a flirt, but the family felt it unlikely that he and Barrus were intimate despite the time they spent together. Her presence around Riverby irritated Ursula, who became bitter and resentful, and when Barrus helped to care for Ursula during her terminal illness, it was as if drawing a curtain across John's past.

Burroughs subsequently sent her all of his journals through the 1880s, made her his literary executor, and gave her his Whitman collection. After his death, she gave away his clothes without consulting the family, and kept his notebooks close but could not get the journals after Julian locked the study door. Clara produced several books after his death (her own limited selections from his journals), and an abbreviated biography. The best of the posthumous works was *My Boyhood, with a Conclusion by His Son Julian Burroughs* (1922), written by John and Julian. To her credit, Barrus saved his heritage and sold her holdings to the Berg Collection, which is now housed in the New York Public Library.

Burroughs outlived many of his contemporaries, but not his own fame. He became a revered and friendly figure in America's imagination, the aged grandfather ever ready to afford an afternoon's conversation about birds or the forest or some other natural subject with a stranger, a child, or a President for that matter. Troutbeck burned down just before Christmas, 1917, ending the legacy of his old friend Benton, and the house in Olive in Ulster County where Burroughs composed "Waiting" was torn down to make way for the new Ashokan Reservoir. An age, a century and a world war were passing, and he was still called upon for speeches and appearances across the country.

Burroughs and Barrus were returning by train from one such engagement in California on March 29, 1921, when he awoke abruptly at 2 a.m. and asked: "How far are we from home?" He quietly died before the reply, near Kirbyville, Ohio. The guests for his funeral were put up overnight at Holy Cross Monastery—the former Payne estate which Julian had managed—and accompanied the body to its unique resting place on the hill above Woodchuck Lodge in Roxbury. For all his fame and famously wealthy companions, Burroughs left a modest estate of which, according to Ulster Surrogate Court Judge Kaufman's decree, "Mrs. Clara Burroughs" was entitled to roughly a third.

Alf Evers, the historian of the Catskills, a boy of fourteen attending New Paltz schools, saw John Burroughs one day, then well into his seventies, driving up Main Street in his Model-T Ford. "He was hanging on for dear life to the steering wheel," Evers recalled, his beard blowing in the wind, giving the appearance of "a very tense driver." Late in life, Evers was interviewed by Roberta Josephson for her SUNY New Paltz dissertation on Burroughs and the Shawangunks. She concluded the interview with a pointed question about the meaning of John Burroughs for future generations:

> JOSEPHSON: "How can each one of us carry on the tradition of Burroughs in our own lives?"
> EVERS: "Well, I think it's to be aware of the natural world always, always. . . and then to cherish it, to treasure the natural world. But to me this is enormously important. I can't get through a day without it. I go out into the woods many times everyday, lie down on the earth, look at things, and feel renewed. That's how I've managed to hang on for eighty-five years."

Alf Evers "hung on" for fifteen years more, and died on December 29, 2004, less than one month before his one hundredth birthday.

18. Modern Times

> In politics, in religion, in economics, in sociology, everything seems
> to be out of date, and is being re-examined! . . . Nothing is safe—
> nothing is sacred from the clamor of the reformers, from the
> outcry of the radicals, from the intrusion of the iconoclasts. . . .
>
> —SEYMOUR VAN SANTVOORD, February 2, 1924

M odern times in the Hudson River Valley officially began in Albany on
May 29, 1910, when Glenn Curtiss (1878–1930) took off from a
makeshift airport on Westerlo (Castle) Island and flew for two hours and 51
minutes to Manhattan, demonstrating the viability of long-distance air travel
to the world.

Curtiss, aged 32, came to collect a $10,000 prize offered by the *New
York World* for the 152-mile flight. He built his "monster violin" at his home
in Hammondsport on Keuka Lake, called it the *Albany Flyer,* and shipped the
plane by barge to Albany for the occasion. It was a curious contraption, a
double set of wings covered in rubberized silk with a balloon cloth attached
containing five inflatable bags and metal drums on the underside of each wing,
all for flotation in case he crashed into the river.

"It was the world's first seaplane," historian Reed Sparling wrote, although
the flotation devices were not put to the test.

Curtiss reconnoitered the river by boat to determine wind currents
and find potential landing sites. His principal fear concerned the Hudson
Highlands and its notorious winds. The *World* allowed for two stops on the
route, but he thought he could make the flight with just one stop for fuel. He
chose a field just south of Poughkeepsie. Bad weather delayed the takeoff for
three days, enough to sour the interest of thousands of onlookers who had
come to see the plane. Fewer than a hundred spectators were on hand on the
fated day, although downriver the audience of shoreline watchers grew sizeable
with anticipation.

Curtiss averaged 52 miles per hour, "going like H—!" as a telegraph operator related when the plane flew over Catskill. Six-year-old Elizabeth Bur-

roughs heard the plane fly past her schoolhouse in West Park, but did not rush out with the other children to see because the teacher (who also rushed out) had not given permission. Curtiss toyed with the idea of flying under the Poughkeepsie railroad bridge, but flew over instead and landed at his designated site. His fuel supplier failed to appear, however, so Curtiss topped off his ten-gallon fuel tank with eight gallons provided by two New Jersey motorists who were on hand for the occasion. The *Poughkeepsie Daily Eagle* likened the takeoff to a partridge "running to get its wings," the noise of the aircraft even mimicking the beating of the bird's wings.

He had been flying at 700 feet, but rose to 2,000 for the Highlands and still experienced jolting gusts of wind that forced the craft into a 200-foot fall at one point, "the worst plunge I ever got in an aeroplane," Curtiss later said. As cadets on the plains at West Point saluted the airman flying by, Curtiss mused at the ease with which he might drop bombs on them from the air.

An oil leak forced him to land in Manhattan just south of the Spuyten Duyvil kill, where a startled homeowner was enjoying his Sunday papers on the porch. The brief stopover turned the man's back lawn into a "fairgrounds" as people came rushing to watch Curtiss take off for the last three miles of his journey. All Manhattan was out on the rooftops, the tugs and larger boats hooting in the bay as Curtiss flew around the Statue of Liberty and landed on Governor's Island. *Scientific American* gave him a trophy for his deed.

Later that year, Molly Ahearn reported, the big event at the Dutchess County Fair in Washington Hollow was a race involving a small Curtiss biplane, piloted by Eugene Ely, and Ralph DePalma's 45-horsepower red Fiat. The local paper called Ely "man bird" and "birdman," but he was not that on this day. He lost all the heats to the Fiat, and on the last one crashed in a nearby field, breaking a rudder and some of his pride.

Twenty years after the Curtiss flight, four major airlines were in business (including the predecessor of American Airlines, founded by W. A. Harriman in 1929), and aviators with licenses were giving passenger rides and performing parachute jumps at ball fields and cow fields all along Curtiss's route. LeRow Field in Westchester County featured parachute jumps as well as charter flights; a German chutist named Paul Wintermeyer was killed there in 1929. Eddie DeAlmo contracted with Harry Beers to run his Waco 10 plane next to the Driving Park in Saugerties in 1929. Twenty-year-old Alice Voerg (1909–90) got two rides that day, one with each of her younger brothers because her father Will refused to ride in such a contraption but did not want them to ride alone.

Castle Island hosted the first important long-distance air field in America, thanks to Curtiss. The field that he used was named the Quentin Roosevelt Memorial Field after 1918 and operated until 1928. After returning from France, Colonel Charles A. Lindbergh landed the *Spirit of St. Louis* here on July 27, 1927, while undertaking a 22,000-mile hopscotch across America, a feat considered even more astonishing than his Paris flight because he was never more than ten minutes late for any stop along the way. Mayor John Boyd Thacher II showed Lindbergh a Shaker farm on the Albany-Shaker Road where Thacher was planning a much larger airport. The remains of Shaker founder Mother Ann Lee and her brother William were removed to a nearby Shaker cemetery when the construction began in the following year. The Albany Municipal Airport opened as a mail run on June 1, 1928, and by October passengers were flying to Montreal and Newark.

Greater Albany expanded its water-borne footprint into the oceans of the world when the dredging of the Hudson River with a 27-foot channel as far south as Hudson allowed for the creation of the Port of Albany in 1931 on 200 acres along the river in Albany and thirty-five in Rensselaer County. The "Deeper Hudson Movement" addressed one of the grand transportation challenges of its day, led by Congressman (and former governor) Martin Glynn, who obtained $5 million in dredging appropriations. Albany became a shipping port for petrochemicals bound for the north and west, for greater wheat shipments from the interior, for machinery and other manufacturing goods from New England, and for Canadian products in those long, cold months when the St. Lawrence was frozen at Montreal.

On October 10, 1929, the *Munsomo*, the first ocean-going vessel to depart from the Port of Albany, sailed for Gulfport, Mississippi, with a cargo of 2,400 tons of machinery. The machinery had come to Albany through the Barge Canal and by rail from Taunton, Massachusetts, and Pawtucket, Rhode Island. On June 5, 1930, the *Irland*, a ship of the Danish-French Line, arrived with 3,400 tons of wood pulp from New Brunswick, Canada. The port handled 700,000 tons of cargo that year, mainly petroleum stored in a mile of new storage terminals along the river. Six main rail lines were connected with the port through five miles of switching yards and a float ferry, providing a total handling capacity of 20,000 cars a day. A grain elevator with a million tons per year capacity was one of the largest in the country. Three hundred new manufacturing, distribution and mercantile businesses came into the Albany area in the late 1920s.

In Troy, the Ford Motor Company built a dam and hydroelectric plant to serve its company works. The city pressed to have the federal government extend the deepwater channel six miles north of Albany by removing bedrock and replacing the Albany-Rensselaer Bridge with a tunnel. Henry Ford intended to establish major works at Green Island at the time, and contributed staff and his own testimony before congressional committees in the effort. The effort was never realized, despite the city's energetic advocacy and persistence, and only experienced setback after setback from engineers and congressional committees. Fellow communities in the Tri-Cities Area applauded the city because of the goodwill that Troy continued to express toward the success of the deepwater project, regardless of how far north it extended.

Greater attention to the transportation system's capacity arose in the congestion of railroad traffic that strangled war commerce over 1916–18. Freight needed to be diverted around Albany—the drawbridge had to be opened often forty times a day, and to avoid a heavy rail grade eastward from the Hudson. A better scheme evolved with the Castleton Cut-Off Bridge, which was built for $20 million and opened on November 24, 1924. The bridge connected the New York Central system with the Boston and Albany line. A six-mile-long, 10,760-car capacity railyard was created between Feura Bush and Selkirk to handle the new traffic.

If Curtiss' air flight were not the inciting event, another phenomenon might best describe the advent of modern times in the Hudson Valley, perhaps as a harbinger of the climate change crisis to come a century later. Following an unusually warm 1912–13 winter, a wind and sleet storm hit on Good Friday, March 21, followed in two days by the nation's "most devastating natural disaster." Torrential rains came on Easter and continued for four days, affecting a twenty-state area from Oklahoma to Maine and dumping in the capital region of New York as much as four weeks of normal rainfall. More than four feet of water covered lower Broadway in Albany, but Troy was hit hardest with an inundated business district; Watervliet had five feet of water on its streets. The Mohawk River at Schenectady rose sixteen feet in three days—within forty-eight hours, the combined flow of the Mohawk and Hudson exceeded that of Niagara Falls.

The Quackenbush pumping station, which purified the city's water supply by sand filtering, passing the water through Prospect Reservoir, and chlorination, was overwhelmed when barriers burst and half of the city's supply became contaminated with fecal coliform from the Hudson River. More than 180 cases of typhoid developed two months later despite warnings in all the city newspapers on Holy Saturday—before the flooding began—to boil water before using. When Prospect Reservoir was determined to have high levels of *e coli*—the gate valve shutting off the flow of river water back to the city was stuck open—the city dumped bags of powdered bleach into the waters, eliminating the pollution and demonstrating the effectiveness of chlorine for the first time in purifying large bodies of water.

Albany had experienced serious flooding prior to this event because of ice gouging on the upper river as the spring thaw came. Large blocks of ice would block the river, forcing the meltwaters to flood the plains and communities around them seeking outlet. The 1913 flood led to the construction of the Great Sacandaga Reservoir (and fourteen others), starting in 1922 and culminating in 1930, which effectively eliminated seasonal flooding thereafter.

Or perhaps modern times actually began in the kitchens of the Hudson Valley. Most homes had two-tiered iceboxes that held large blocks of ice delivered weekly by local dealers; the iceman was also often the fuel dealer for the community. In 1930, Christian Steenstrup (1875–1955) invented the General Electric refrigerator, which had a condenser on the top that gave the appearance of the Civil War ironclad *Monitor*. Although some old iceboxes remained in use into the early 1960s, the era of ice harvesting was effectively over and a new age begun.

Air flight, automobiles, an explosion in business and growth, the emergence of women as a political and intellectual bloc, and the beginnings of accommodation with African Americans were startling new aspects that fit with the new "flapper" age, a time of change so dramatic and universal everyone noticed and nobody cared. Upriver, a new sense of confidence led Troy businessmen to finance a new hotel, the Hendrick Hudson, from stock raised locally in 1925–26; the establishment quickly became "the city's social center." Closer to the city, New Rochelle's per capita wealth was as high as any community in the United States. White Plains had a plethora of works, factories, manufactories and plants producing everything from pearl buttons to corsets and macaroni; its workforce was served by nineteen bus lines into the city. *Reader's*

Digest settled in Pleasantville in 1923, providing jobs for five hundred local residents. Property values in Yorktown rose by 25 percent in one year. Cortlandt and Mount Pleasant experienced 90 percent growth rates during the decade; Yorktown's population grew by 89 percent. As if to celebrate the new times, Somers welcomed "John," a Barnum and Bailey Circus elephant draped in gardenias and orchids and wearing galoshes on a 53.7 mile walk across Westchester County, honoring the trek Hackaliah Bailey's Old Bet made a hundred years earlier. Everyone rushed forward as if tomorrow was already behind them.

Incidents of crime increased with the expanded population growth, not always in the urban areas. In Ulster County, a section of High Falls was known as Pistol Row until cleaned up by the Citizens League in 1913. Dutchess County was subjected to a band of house thieves called the Candle Gang. Sylvania, one of the Chapman estates in Barrytown, was robbed, and Margaret Aldrich was rescued by the sheriff and his deputies while under a siege at nearby Rokeby. Her brother Archie (whom the family considered crazy) suggested that she have the windows fitted with galvanized sheet iron that could be removed and folded for storage during the day.

New York continued to maintain Sing Sing Correctional Facility on the Hudson River in Westchester County, but that too was entering into modern times. Thomas Mott Osborne, the Democratic League leader who helped secure Woodrow Wilson's election in 1912, became the Sing Sing warden under Democratic Governor Charles Whitman (1868–1947). He introduced the Mutual Welfare League, a model for prisoner self-government, and survived a 1915 attempt to indict him on criminal charges before being forced out by his political enemies in 1917. The 1915 action was raised against his method of prison management and led to a Westchester district attorney investigation in which Osborne was exonerated. Dr. Rudolph Diedling of Saugerties, a prison commissioner, brought charges against Osborne in a report that the *Cornell Daily Sun* said was "sensational" (yet kept secret), and which a majority of Diedling's fellow commissioners opposed and had tabled. Diedling offered testimony against Osborne and, in March 1916, was severely criticized by Assemblyman Hamilton Fish during Fish's futile attempt to have the state assembly investigate the entire prison system in the state. Throughout the controversy, Osborne retained Governor Whitman's support even as the Sing Sing warden was battling with his own state superintendent.

One of the inmates whom Osborne encouraged was Charles Chapin (1858–1930), an editor of the New York *Evening World* who murdered his wife in 1918. He became known as "the Rose Man of Sing Sing" for his cultivation of the flowers and the plantings around the prison.

Almost all of the reforms Osborne advocated were instituted by a later warden and perhaps Sing Sing's finest administrator, Lewis Edward Lawes (1883–1947). Lawes was an opponent of the death penalty and a strong advocate of rehabilitation. He resumed the system of self-government that Osborne initiated, and was particularly known for the trust he imparted to his prisoners; he loaned them money and was always repaid. His first wife, Kathryn Lawes (1885–1937), called "the Angel of Sing Sing," helped many of those incarcerated and their families. When she was killed in a car accident in 1937, Lawes scheduled a service at a funeral home outside the prison. The inmates objected because they could not pay their respects, so the night before the funeral Lawes opened the south gate and the men marched in double file a quarter of a mile to the wake, without guards or any guns trained upon them, and later that evening regrouped and marched silently back to prison. Lawes continued as warden for another four years.

Some crime was institutionalized in the politics of the era. Westchester County government in those days was under the grip of "the boss," William L. Ward, chairman of the Republican County Committee and his "sub-boss," as he liked to call himself, Henry R. Barrett, the county committee secretary and chairman of the White Plains committee. Ward was generally straightforward and honest in his political dealings, but Barrett was also general counsel for the Westchester Parkway Commission and counsel for the Westchester Lighting Company. A scandal developed involving Barrett and four cousins—two brokers, an appraiser, and the chair of the budget and appropriations committee—when they sold land for three times its value to the county on speculation, reaping a half million dollars in profits. The county board of supervisors was charged with neglect of duty just in time to affect the general election.

In Albany, muggings and other crimes on the street were a factor in overturning decades of Republican Party domination of City Hall—and commencing almost a century's worth of Democratic Party domination. The two warring newspapers included the old *Albany Evening Journal*, run by William ("Billy") Barnes (1866–1930), who was also the Republican leader (and grandson of Thurlow Weed), and the *Times-Union* under Democrat Martin H. Glynn. Patrick E. ("Paddy") McCabe was the Albany Democratic leader at the time, but an ineffectual one. Barnes, a Harvard graduate called "The Boy Leader" when he came into power in 1900, was propelled into the spotlight (and called "President-Maker") by helping the engineer the renomination of William Howard Taft and defeat of Theodore Roosevelt in the 1912 election. This was payback of sorts for Barnes, who helped Republican state leader Thomas C. Platt elevate Roosevelt to the Vice-Presidency in 1900, which backfired when McKinley died and TR became President.

Glynn (1871–1924), a Valatie native and son of a saloon owner, had worked his way up the ladder into the ownership of the *Times-Union* after taking degrees at Fordham University and Albany Law School. He was elected a congressman in 1899, became state comptroller and then lieutenant governor, succeeding William Sulzer as governor on his impeachment and removal from office. Glynn was the first Roman Catholic to hold the office, and a man who, despite his Tammany Hall support, accomplished a great deal for the state in his various roles. Glynn was also largely responsible for the statue to Philip Sheridan in Capitol Park. Franklin Roosevelt liked him and lionized him when unveiling his portrait as governor in the capitol in 1931. "His admiration for Sheridan was supreme," Franklin would say.

Glynn's greatest accomplishment occurred on the international stage when he served as the intermediary in bringing Eamon de Valera and David Lloyd George together in the creation of the Irish Free State in 1921. George himself took the podium at the state legislature in Albany in 1923 to describe Glynn's role in effectuating the agreement. Glynn's early death followed years of suffering crucial back pain as a result of a childhood accident.

The spat between the newspapers over 1919–22 was purely political, yet it touched on the crucial issues of the day for Albany. Billy Barnes, who also had an interest in the J. B. Lyons Printing Co., defended a corrupt and inactive city administration under Mayor James R. Watt, while Glynn hammered away at the mayor's failure to support the police in controlling crime. Barnes had come under investigation in 1911 over police corruption and the state printing contracts. "The Albany Inquiry," as it was called, exposed the city's vice district (called "the Gut") and extensive Republican corruption, but was unable to bring Barnes down. He was losing influence by 1919, however, in part because he supported the Prohibition bill. Mayor Watt retained his job (until 1921), but only by 1,500 votes compared with a 10,000 plurality two years earlier.

One Democrat won in Albany that year: Daniel P. O'Connell (1885–1977), a 34-year-old working-class Irishman who campaigned in his Navy uniform and was elected county assessor. Within a few years, "Assessor Danny" replaced Paddy McCabe and, with a brother and a cousin, established a powerful Democratic political machine. Barnes lost the printing contract, sold his interest in the newspapers in 1924 and left Albany forever, moving to Mount Kisco.

William Kennedy (b. 1928) captured the spirit of these colorful times in his "Albany cycle" of novels and his wonderfully entitled *O Albany! Improbable City of Political Wizards, Fearless Ethnics, Spectacular Aristocrats, Splendid Nobodies, and Underrated Scoundrels*. He evoked the language of the young toughs on Colonie Street in his second Albany novel, *Billy Phelan's Greatest Game* (1978):

> Would you work for Billy Barnes? Never. Packy McCabe? Sure.
> Who's the man this election? Did you hear how the Wally-Os stole
> a ballot box in the Fifth Ward and Corky Ronan chased 'em and
> got it back and bit off one of their ears?

The novel also evoked King Jazz and his Orchestra playing at Baumann's Dancing Academy and McEnelly's Singing Orchestra and the dances they ran in Sacandaga Park. "'They put pins in our heels for the prize waltz,' George [Quinn] said. 'Anybody bent the pin was out. I won many a prize up on my toes and I got the loving cups to prove it.'"

Dances were held at the pavilion at Snyder's Lake in Rensselaer and the Al-Tro Park on the Hudson in Colonie. The Al-Tro, formerly Lagoon Island and at first called Pleasure Island when it opened in 1895 (and later called Dreamland), was built up by P. J. Corbett near the river at the foot of Garbrance Lane. Another amusement venue, called the Mid-City Park, developed on the Troy Road with a rollercoaster, merry-go-round, pool and skating rink. The Mid-City was next to Hawkins Stadium where the Albany Senators, a class-A team in the Eastern League, played professional baseball in the 1930s. Baseball was also featured at Island Park near the Menands Bridge.

The Irish neighborhood was called Gander Bay—"good old Gander Bay, where George Gilmore's geese did the rhumba every day"—and stretched along Canal Street, later called Sheridan Avenue. Dinny Roman's was the last of the Lumber District saloons. His son Andy kept up the grocery store (the largest in the North End), and was close to Dan and Ed O'Connell who came up every Sunday to conference with the North End Dems—which included Will Cook and Kennedy's great-grandfather Big Jim Carroll (1858–1939). Cook nominated Al Smith for governor at Saratoga and took a trolley to get there.

Revolutions in fashion, attitudes, economics, and beliefs were all caught up in the heady times, and especially among young people. "The youth of the twenties," Paula S. Fass wrote, "were at once the product of change and the agents of change, because they existed at a strategic point in history when their actions really did make a difference." At Vassar College the changes arrived early, the daring among the students coming into Poughkeepsie more and more often after 1902 sporting the look of the Gibson Girls as the century deepened. The turtleneck sweater became *de rigueur* in the same decade, followed by the V-neck and heavy coat-like sweaters. Skirts remained close to the ground in 1910—an attractive element in the annual daisy chain tradition at Vassar—but coat fashions (including striped blazers) changed and became more comfortable. Even a hat or two appeared on campus in that year, and were commonplace by 1916. By the end of the decade, plain skirts had given way to plaids and prints. The customary white pleated skirt was introduced in the 1920s, when white became the characteristic spring color of the college. By 1921, seniors and juniors were allowed to go to the Poughkeepsie movies unchaperoned, "even with men," and take drives as long as the drivers were approved by the warden. The appearance of knickers on the girls drew a complaint from a Poughkeepsie newspaper that they should not be allowed in town. More pronounced waistlines, the bob hair-do, and corsages worn on the hip also were popular. The coonskin coat was accepted by 1922, for those who could afford one, but noisy galoshes were barred at the library's door—in Latin, Greek and a dozen other languages. When sunbathing became popular, discrete places on campus were provided until the physical education hall and its solarium were completed in 1933.

By the end of that decade, bare legs, bobby socks, sweater sleeves rolled above the elbow, and colorful rubber boots for winter were the standard lady student's fare. Alumnae criticized the new student, her attitudes and dress—permanent waves and fur coats!—as eroding Vassar's democratic style, but the students defended the new ways as marks of their maturity. Some women at first thought the "unbeautiful and uncomfortable" French fancy for bare legs would die quickly, according to fashion expert Marian Clarke, but welcomed the bobbed hair, shortened skirts, end of the corset, low-backed bathing suits, and street dresses.

The excesses of this new age were identified with youth, and had their representatives in women like Edna St. Vincent Millay, whom the New York media pounced upon for her shocking views and opinions. "Vincent," as she liked to be called, could not understand why sex was not treated as openly and freely as other bodily needs, like dinner. Novelist Floyd Dell saw the changed sexual proclivities of the youth as emblematic of man's evolution as a species.

The growth of tourism that accompanied an interest in the Valley and the Catskills was a direct result of improvements in transportation. Airports did not proliferate, but the automobile not only flourished but improved over the years. With its popularity came access to new summer colonies, usually established along ethnic lines, as progressively distant from the metropolitan area as advances in auto technology and roads allowed; one could chart their settlements by transportation industry changes. By the mid-1930s, Ulster and Greene counties had supplanted the southern counties as the new vacation-land, and in the next decade became as established as Sullivan County; the main street of Leeds (and most of East Durham) got reputations for boisterous taverns when the Irish came in droves. Purling thrived as a mini-Jewish Alps of lodges, boarding houses and "manor" estates—Jimmy Durante and Frank Sinatra were among the celebrities who came and performed. These centers also drew the locals out on the weekends, and remained as old and established colonies throughout the century. But more change was on the horizon that would eventually steer these towns back to their roots.

19. A Conference at Troutbeck

How appropriate that so tremendous a thing should have
taken place in the midst of so much quiet and beauty there
at Troutbeck, which John Burroughs knew and loved
throughout his life, a place of poets and fishermen, of
dreamers and farmers, a place far apart and away from the
bustle of the world and the centers of activity.

—W. E. B. Du Bois

Joel Elias Spingarn (1875–1939), the oldest son of Elias and Sarah Spingarn,
was expected to pursue a legal career, but his austere and aloof manner led
him to become a scholar, academician, and self-styled "aesthetician" instead.
Yet he was "a passionate and often electrifying speaker" and a Republican Party
progressive who ran unsuccessfully for Congress in 1908. In the stuffy pre–
World War I years, Spingarn encouraged his students at Columbia University
to cultivate spontaneity and original genius. Joel's brother Arthur (1878–
1971), the jovial son, was the one who became the lawyer. The brothers admired each other, both developed early and intense interests in the plight of
African Americans, and both were involved from the start in the National Association for the Advancement of Colored People.

Joel was considered the less ambitious brother—ruined by family money,
some in the disdainful set surmised, becoming a country gentleman instead
of a businessman. His wife, Amy Einstein Spingarn (1883–1980), was the
daughter of a wealthy New Jersey mill and real estate owner. She fell in love
with Joel and proposed marriage to him. When he joined the NAACP leadership in 1911, she became involved in the suffragist movement in Dutchess
County; Amy knew that elected legislators "pay little attention to anything
but a vote."

Joel and Amy purchased Troutbeck, the former Benton family homestead in Amenia in the Harlem Valley, in 1910. Four years later, he created
the Spingarn Medal of Achievement, given annually by the NAACP to a
prominent black person. Two years later, Joel and Amy hosted at Troutbeck a

key conference on Negro rights that spurred the NAACP onward in the decades that followed. Spingarn helped the African American cause in the war by coaxing the army into establishing an officer-training school for blacks. He served as chairman of the NAACP's board, and later held the association together in the early years of the Depression—sometimes with threats of his own resignation. With his brother Arthur and young men like Thurgood Marshall (1908–93)—who helped create the NAACP Legal Defense and Educational Fund and was its first chief—Spingarn promoted a strong legal profile that culminated thirty years later in *Brown v. Board of Education of Topeka, Kansas* (1954). Arthur was chairman of the legal committee from 1911 to 1941, directing all their court battles over those decades, and he served (overlong, to be sure) as president of the NAACP until 1967.

The need for the Amenia Conference of 1916 arose extemporaneously with the death of Booker T. Washington (1856–1915) and the onset of the war in Europe. Progress in race relations had been stunted since the compromise of 1877 that ended Reconstruction in the South, and the only presidents remotely considerate of African American issues, William McKinley and Theodore Roosevelt, had disregarded the subject of prejudice while in office. Even Booker Washington treated blacks as second-class citizens. Yet in almost that same period of time, the black population doubled, literacy among blacks increased from 18.6% to 55.5%, and blacks began organizing their own banks.

Both Joel and Arthur Spingarn knew and revered W. E. B. Du Bois (1868–1963), author of *The Souls of Black Folks* (1903), although Du Bois' difficult personality led the Spingarns to treat him with "kid gloves," as Amy recalled. "He carried himself like a French aristocrat," she said, not disparagingly. Du Bois recalled with warmth their sensitivity in the planning of the Amenia Conference, as Joel coaxed him "with a speculative eye and tentative intonation" into inviting the editor of a Negro paper who had violently disagreed with Du Bois and his politics.

"He was important," Du Bois wrote about the undesirable editor, "and Mr. Spingarn was pleased to see that I agreed with him in this."

The invitations went out under Joel's name, and he, Amy, and Arthur "worked long and assiduously" (in Du Bois's words) to ensure a private and pleasant stay for their visitors:

"A tent colony will be pitched on the shore of a three acre pond," Spingarn wrote in "The Call" to the conference, "equipped with cots and bedding, a commissariat, and a mess tent where the conference can be held in case of rain. It will be camp accommodation and fare, but we believe the more enjoyable because made an informal gathering in the open air. Everyone is advised to bring a bathing suit."

The conference unfolded over August 24-26, 1916. The concept worked to perfection, at least for Du Bois. More than fifty national leaders arrived, the first morning "misty with a northern chill in the air and a dampness about it," and were visited now and then by notables like the governor, the local congressman, education and military leaders, and Negro businessmen and politicians. They established their tent community on a lake a half-mile south of Troutbeck homestead, where grand feasts "appeared, miraculously steaming and perfectly cooked, out of the nothingness of the wild landscape" each day.

Du Bois' tentmate was James Weldon Johnson (1871–1938), one of Booker Washington's Washington friends, lyricist for "Lift Ev'ry Voice and Sing" (1903), former diplomat under President Theodore Roosevelt, and the future executive secretary of the NAACP and Harlem Renaissance leader. "The thing was too intimate and small to allow for partisan outbursts or continued disaffection," Du Bois wrote. "We were too near each other." The magic of the place created "a rollicking jolly time" that breezed past the "sense of stiffness" among otherwise competing leaders and spread goodwill among all.

The conference drew NAACP president Morefield Storey (1845–1929); Dr. Ernest E. Just (1883–1941), a noted Negro biologist and Spingarn Medalist; "social investigator" and *Nation* and *Crisis* writer Martha Gruening (1887–1925); several friends of Booker Washington, Southern leaders like J. C. Napier of Tennessee, Midwest standard-bearers, representatives from Pennsylvania, Maryland, and New England, and a dozen or more Washington notables. William Bennet, the Republican congressman from 1905 to 1911 who would be elected again that November for a two-year term, came over from Port Jervis. Democratic Party politicians were not invited because of President Woodrow Wilson's racist attitudes toward blacks.

The daily programs included topics like "Education and Industry," "The Negro in Politics," "Civil and Legal Discrimination," "Social Discrimination," and, on the last day, "Practical Paths" and "A Working Programme for the Future." Eventually the conference produced a statement of principles that stood as a hallmark for Negro aspirations at the dawn of a new age. All seemed to realize that the old enmities must be set aside so that the new hopes could be realized. All the efforts of the past, including the radical Niagara Movement that Du Bois himself helped to found, must yield to the new coalition of black power that was emerging in the wake of Washington's death. The conferees aired their various difficulties, held private sessions to ensure that all emotions could be vented, and finally declared their intentions. The Amenia Conference of 1916 resolved that Negro education in all forms and aspects should be advanced; that political freedom was essential to the Negro's advancement in America; that the leaders of the race must organize to be effective and must set aside the old suspicions and arguments they had about each other.

The NAACP became a powerful force in litigation against Jim Crow laws in the South in the years following the 1916 conference, but as W. E. B. Du Bois lamented, "if the world had not gone crazy" during and after those days, its aftermath might have been more dramatic. The immediate consequence of Amenia was the achievement of its original purpose, a closing of the ranks of Negro leadership in America. The setting at Troutbeck, "how appropriate" as Du Bois wrote, allowed the passing from the pre-modern to the modern in race matters in America, from the naïve innocence of a Booker T. Washington to the stern realism of a W. E. B. Du Bois, a transformation that happened within a context of convivial friendship.

Joel was elected president of the NAACP in 1930, despite criticism over his race; Langston Hughes was among those writing to congratulate him. Spingarn remarked to the organization's leadership in February 1932 that the NAACP lacked the support of "young colored intellectuals" who needed to be brought within the movement. Progress had brought more bitterness with it: the local black Baptist pastor in Greenburgh was elected to the school board in 1932, but not before a cross was burned on his lawn by the local Ku Klux Klan. The Great Depression, the rise of fascism and communism, the frustrations over Northern prejudice and ending Jim Crow laws, lynching and other black atrocities in the South, and dissensions within the black leadership led to the convening of a second Troutbeck Conference in 1933. Spingarn had to threaten to resign as president to gain support for the conference, for which Du Bois was finally appointed chairman. Ralph J. Bunche and Roy Wilkins

Frederic E. Church, "Sunset Across the Hudson Valley," September 1870

Hallway in Lindenwald,
Martin Van Buren National Historic
Site, Kinderhook

Armour-Stiner House, Irvington.
Also called the Octagon House,
designed by Orson Fowler and the
residence of Carl Carmer when he
wrote *The Hudson* (1939) as part
of his Rivers of America series

U. S. Grant from West Point to Appomattox, commemorative engraving on the occasion of his death

"Haying Near New Rochelle" by Fort Ann artist John Henry Dolph (1835-1903)

New Croton Dam and Spillway *(Acroterion photo)*

East shaft descent under Hudson
River, aqueduct construction,
Ashokan Reservoir c 1912
(Acroterion photo)

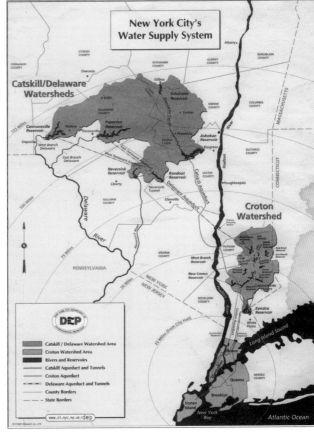

NYC DEP depiction
of New York City
Water Supply System

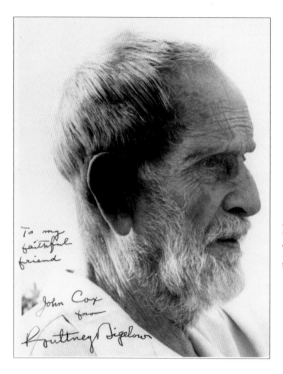

To my
faithful
friend

John Cox
from
Poultney Bigelow

Poultney Bigelow, Malden squire,
world correspondent and friend of
the Famous Four, 1947

Robert Chanler's
"Leopard and Deer,"
painted screen,
1913 Armory Show,
New York City

Lowell Thomas of Pawling

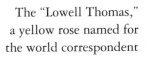

The "Lowell Thomas,"
a yellow rose named for
the world correspondent

New York State Capitol, framed by Alexander Calder stabile,
Empire State Plaza, Albany

Catskills Escarpment and Kingston Rhinecliff Bridge, from Ferncliff Forest firetower

(*Daniel Case photo*)

The Hudson River from Breakneck Ridge

(*Jeffrey Pang photo*)

Newburgh from downtown Beacon *(Daniel Case photo)*

Hot air balloons over the Hudson, view from Walkway Over the Hudson
(Julian Colton photo)

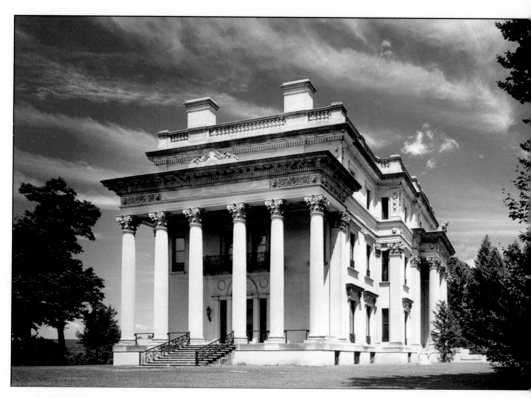

Vanderbilt Mansion National Historic Site, Hyde Park

West Point Cemetery in winter

Above: Opus 40, Harvey Fite monumental sculpture, Highwoods (Ulster County), 2007

Frances Dunwell, Hudson River Estuary Program Director

Richard B. Fisher Center for the Performing Arts, Bard College, Annandale-on-Hudson
(Daniel Case photo)

Hudson River Sloop Clearwater   *(Anthony Pepitone photo)*

I-287 and I-87 Interchange, New York State Thruway, Suffern

Hickory Edwards and Two Row Wampum paddlers passing the Indian Point nuclear complex in the Campaign to Renew the Two Row Wampum, a 1613 agreement between Haudenosaunee and Dutch to travel on the path of life together in parallel paths, honoring and respecting each other without trying to impose either party's special interests on the other. *(Tom O'Reilly photo)*

were among the new young leaders who came, an average age of 30 years (according to Du Bois) and including social workers, professors, teachers, attorneys, artisans, a physician, and two librarians.

Lewis Mumford caught some of the intellectual flair of that conference when he stopped by to partake of one of the camp dinners. He was delighted with the assemblage of "jolly, hearty, strong, confident, chattering, good-natured people," all surviving happily despite the camp-style arrangements. As with the first conference almost twenty years earlier, the spirit of the occasion helped all to forego the inconveniences of a single huge tent for thirty-three cots and only Troutbeck Lake to bathe in. They swam and played baseball, even in the rain. The young professionals ("the coming leaders of the race," in Mumford's words) were engaged in a "keen discussion," he wrote, "tussling with the eternal dilemma of all intellectuals today: how to be a communist without willfully swallowing the fierce ignorances, the blind hatreds, the willful dogmatisms of the orthodox revolutionists."

The second Amenia conference focused on economic issues. No speeches or pontificating took place, instead a steady and detailed discussion of the problems that blacks faced, leading to a "general consensus of agreement that was rather startling." The system of private property and economic power was questioned. The government's attempts at reorganizing the country under a partnership of capital, labor and government support might lead to increased wages, fewer hours of labor, and a control of the commodity and labor markets, but were not likely to effectively create economic stability for the Negro. A new labor movement was needed, the conference concluded, one with political as well as economic goals to ensure that the reforms would be accomplished.

"It was withal a very beautiful experience," Du Bois wrote.

20. Miss Diedling's Last Photograph

Be a good sport about it. No more falling off the water wagon.
Uncle Sam will help you keep your pledge.
                                    —WARREN H. ANDERSON (1919)

Four inches of snow fell on the mid-Hudson Valley on January 19, 1920, the night the Volstead Act went into effect and a total prohibition on the manufacture and sale of alcohol became law. It was a bitter cold day; Ed McCormick recorded a temperature of twelve below on the third floor of the bookbindery in Saugerties when he went to work at 7 a.m., and that was inside. More than forty saloons that crowded along the main streets of the village from the waterfront to the railroad station a mile and a half away went out of business that night, crowded to the end, a pattern replicated in villages and towns around the state and nation. In a room warmed by a coal fire on Montgomery Street, a Knight of St. John named John H. Kerbert (1854–1941) took pen in hand and cursed the calamity that Congressman Andrew J. Volstead of Minnesota had caused to befall upon the world:

> To the Land of the She
> And the Home of the Knave
> That Fanatics and Crooks
> Would completely enslave
> The thoughts of its future
> Bring little of cheer
> Til the Devil take Volstead
> Who shut off our Beer.

The implementation of the Eighteenth Amendment to the US Constitution caused a precipitous rise in crime when a black market engulfed the country in a sea of country stills, bathtub gin works, speakeasies, and roadside barns filled with barrels of illegal hooch waiting for transport. Shakedowns, beatings, armed threats by gangsters, and more than a few killings followed suit. Men who had toiled ten hours a day in factories suddenly made much better money as bootleggers—if they could stay out of trouble. The business was legitimized in the local neighborhoods, even if banned nationally. Governor George Pataki's mother, six or seven at the time, affixed the "gin" labels on her father's homemade hooch, which her sister then delivered to customers around their Peekskill neighborhood. Alternatives to saloons like the "poor man's club" at the Broadway Gospel Mission in Albany could not satisfy the need. Cynics like Croswell MacLaughlin, a former drunk and editor of Cornwall's weekly *The Courier* for twenty years until 1922, treated Prohibition as a joke. Local police often sympathized and looked the other way—in Albany that was the rule—as many also did with the numbers gambling practiced in the cities and towns. The social life that accompanied alcohol use was accepted as naughty but nice, even respectable in some ways. Polite, upright, proper families remained disapproving behind their curtains, and preached a standard of upright living in their private lives, yet were powerless to affect the changes that were upon them.

Albany, Hudson, Newburgh, Poughkeepsie, White Plains and other centers of commerce suffered with the lost booze business—some more grievously than others—and the increased crime that avoidance of the law provoked. C. H. Evans & Company Brewery in Hudson was forced to close, leaving the city entirely depended on the cement industry for an economy. Hudson became better known for its thriving prostitution business, where Diamond Street gained a reputation as "the Northeast's bordello," a common enough industry in the previous decades yet one now tainted with a brand of permanence.

Not all the crimes were committed by criminals. Attorney General A. Mitchell Palmer's raids rounding up supposed anarchists and their supporters in November 1918 and January 1919, in part a reaction to the influence of socialism, impacted the Hudson Valley in the enthusiasm with which the jingo press and Nativist anti-immigrant sentiments supported him. When three "detachments" of I.W.W. agitators, as *The New York Times* called them, arrived in Tarrytown to create "riotous disturbances" protesting the Rockefellers and the 1914 Ludlow, Colorado, massacre, fifteen were arrested after chasing them through the streets of Tarrytown, and the rest "given severe 'football' treatment before they were placed aboard a train for New York." (The police used the "playfootball" technique by pushing, jostling and knocking down the demonstrators whenever they tried to assemble to speak.) *The Times* reported that "hundreds of citizens and the entire police force participated." Rebecca ("Becky") Edelson (1892–1973) led the protestors in their appearance in court, was sentenced to Blackwell's Island prison, and went on a twenty-seven day hunger strike until released, the first recorded hunger strike in American history. The day after the disturbances ended, John D. Rockefeller Jr. caught the 8:24 Tarrytown train for New York, as usual.

A Socialist Party administration was swept into office in Schenectady in 1911 behind the Rev. George R. Lunn (b. 1873), a former First Reformed Church pastor who dominated progressive efforts in the city, but that was an aberration compared with the rest of the Valley. A virulent anti-socialist bias infected the New York State Assembly when the ultra-conservative Union League Club petitioned for a joint legislative committee "to investigate seditious activities in the State" in 1919. The committee held no hearings, conducted summary searches and seizures, arrested more than a thousand people (only twelve were convicted of any crimes), and proposed new state laws requiring loyalty oaths by teachers, licensure of schools, and an independent state secret service.

To add to the reactionary spirit, Assembly Speaker Thaddeus Sweet (1872–1928) suspended five assembly members of the Right Wing Socialist Party in January 1920 on a 140-6 vote, and tried to outlaw the party. Sweet was chastised in "biting" criticism by former Governor Charles Evans Hughes, and coldly responded that Hughes, now a respected jurist, was merely giving aid to the enemy in his comments. Governor Al Smith vetoed the draconian bills the legislature approved, but each one was subsequently enacted after he was voted out of office in 1920. The joint committee issued a report in the spring of 1921 that exacerbated upstate-urban relations; its chairman, Clayton R. Lusk, was found to be accepting graft and soon disappeared from the scene. Smith charged back in 1922 and the Lusk laws were all repealed in the following spring.

Local police "red squads" that formed during the war continued into the 1920s. A "red scare cinema" developed with D. W. Griffith's signature xenophobia and racism in films like *Orphans of the Storm*, crudely mislabeled "one of the great creations in US cinema of the early 20s" by Leon Barsacq and Elliott Stein. Griffith (1875–1948) directed his stars, Lillian and Dorothy Gish, on an elaborate 14-acre set created by Charles D. Kirk in Mamaroneck. Griffith also shot *America* there, his last "historical spectacle," with battle scenes filmed in the fields of Brewster and Somers in September 1923.

Prohibition had its supporters, of course, the most vociferous of whom was William H. Anderson (1874-c. 1959), the leader and principal lobbyist of the Anti-Saloon League and acting secretary of the Yonkers Committee of 1,000 for Law Enforcement, which Anderson used to create the Yonkers Plan to support the new law. John D. Rockefeller and V. Everit Macy (1871–1930), a Westchester industrialist, philanthropist and commissioner, were among those pledging thousands. The plan had a national corollary that Anderson created in the Allied Citizens of America, 200,000 strong. Although the Yonkers Plan goals were to uphold Prohibition, encourage enforcement, and oppose repeal, Anderson was not a fair player. He came to New York, "the liquor center of America," at the beginning of 1914 after having closed a thousand saloons in Baltimore, and applied tactics of character assassination, false rumor, fake documents, and personal intimidation against his enemies. He was able to secure a home rule law on prohibition—wherein individual towns and villages could vote it out—and then promoted gerrymandering to increase the number of communities that joined. When the war came he offered the argument that ending drinking was patriotic for all Americans. He blamed foreigners—especially Jews, Irish and Italians—and targeted Catholics, who responded that Anderson's tactics were enabling the resurgence of the Ku Klux Klan (which also supported prohibition). He did not deny the allegation, and indeed there were cross-burnings in Westchester, in 1923 in Park Hill, Yonkers, and in New Rochelle in 1924. Most of Anderson's activities in gaining state support occurred before Prohibition went into effect, and when the legislature turned cold toward his interests he went after them as well. One of them was Assembly Speaker Sweet, who said Anderson's methods "make your blood run cold and your hair stand up." The lobbyist committed a *faux pas* and was disparaged when he spread a rumor to three hundred newspapers that "liquor interests" had a "slush fund" to buy state legislators for their cause. He finally fell from grace in 1924 when convicted of forging financial records of the League, and served two years in Sing Sing.

The first Prohibition raid in Albany, at John J. Maxwell's Saloon on Broadway on February 6, 1920, was conducted by federal police. More than a hundred agents swooped down on 34 saloons in Yonkers on October 27, 1921, arresting 35 and destroying a truckload of elixirs even though nine of the saloons, which had been forewarned, had no alcohol on hand. Similarly, numerous parties were cancelled on New Year's Eve in 1922 when warned that raids were imminent, although a hotel near the White Plains Fair Grounds and an Elmsford saloon did not get the messages in time. Hundreds of gallons—two casks of port, fifty bottles of sherry, 1,180 quarters of malt liquor and 200 of moonshine—were among the casualties dumped by police between the jail and courthouse in White Plains that night.

The New York State Police and the state's courts did not get statutory authority to enforce the Volstead Act until April 5, 1921, when Governor Nathan Miller signed the "Baby Volstead Act" into law. Arrests for intoxication increased, from 1,037 in 1919 to a high of 4,118 in 1924. In 1923, the law, which was never popular, was repealed under Al Smith's administration, but not without casualties. Smith himself was indifferent toward the repeal while it worked through the legislature, wary of a political backlash, and did not advise his supporters in the Assembly one way or another. ("Work it out among yourselves," he said.) Even though Tammany leader Charles F. Murphy and State Senator Jimmy Walker strongly supported repeal, the bill was approved in the Assembly by only one vote. ("In other words," James A. Farley of Rockland County wrote, "each member of the Assembly of New York, including myself, had held the balance of power without realizing it.") When Governor Smith signed the repeal into law, the hoopla that followed made him the national leader of the anti-Prohibition sentiments, but locally the responses were ambiguous. Farley, who supported repeal, was among the casualties, his brief one-year career as a state assemblyman ending that fall in his rejection for reelection, "and thus Rockland County reaffirmed its faith in Volsteadism."

Police in the federal Prohibition bureau continued to work independently under J. Edgar Hoover (1895–1972), and in January 1929 a "flying visit" by 70 of his agents led to 135 raids in one month alone. Some local communities stayed the course on enforcement when their own prohibition laws were violated, like Mount Vernon in 1922. A White Plains "protective league" hired detectives to root out violators that year, and Mamaroneck waylaid a $100,000 stock of whiskey, brandy and gin bound for New York on the Boston Post Road. On the same day, New Rochelle police seized a boat launch with $50,000 in illegal booze. Four major stills were shut down in that city in 1927, their proprietors charged with tax as well as Prohibition violations, which elevated the activities to felony status. The most stringent penalty in Westchester County fell to Andrew Blanco when his Peekskill speakeasy was raided; he was sentenced to three-and-a-half years in prison because he was a parolee.

Many more than those caught got away with their illegalities, however, some in unusual ways. Arthur Flegenheimer (1902–35), also known as Dutch Schultz, ran the Yonkers Brewery in William Anderson's town under a pseudonym, the State Cereal and Beverage Company. Schultz and his family lived in Bronxville on the future campus of Concordia College, where he kept a low profile. He had a license to make "near" beer and augmented his operation with ice cream making because it required the kind of cooling apparatus that was used in bootlegging. On September 29, 1930, his operation unraveled when a hose was discovered carrying mash into a city sewer line. On investigation under Mayor John J. Fogarty (c. 1898–1954) it was learned that Schultz's beer hoses were run through the sewer lines to offsite locations where the product was barreled and shipped. The lines were burned and the license for near beer revoked, but in 1932 the system had revived, the local paper announced. Product worth $50,000 was dumped into the Nepperhan River, leaving a notable aroma of beer on the city streets. The brewery reopened legitimately after Prohibition ended. Local contractor and Democratic state committeeman Thomas Brogan attempted to operate the facility, but Schultz's wife brought suit and he withdrew, fearing a revival of interest in ties the locals may have had with the mobster.

Crime other than the manufacture and sale of illegal spirits came with the times, some of a comical nature. When state police stopped two men and a woman with their Christmas turkey in White Plains on December 25, 1920, they found a bottle of whiskey in the bird, a bottle of grain alcohol in a head of lettuce, and another in a pineapple. In Ulster County, an inebriated local on his way home was pulled over by a constable who asked where he was headed; he tried to say Unionville, an old name for the hamlet of Veteran, but it came out "Toodlum." He then proceeded to make a song of it ("Toodle-um, toodle-lee, toodle-um-dum-dum") that survived as a folk name for the hamlet throughout the century.

Novelist William Kennedy, who cut his writing teeth as a reporter for the Glens Falls *Post-Star* and Albany *Times-Union*, interviewed Democratic boss Daniel P. O'Connell in 1974 and pieced together the details about "Legs" Diamond's death in a second-floor flat on Dove Street on December 18, 1931. Jack "Legs" Diamond (1897–1931), born John T. Nolan in Philadelphia and also called Gentleman Jack, was an early niche marketer of the Hudson River Valley, except that his agricultural "product" was illegal booze. In New

York, Diamond was a colorful nightclub character, often accompanied by a showgirl named Marion "Kiki" Roberts (née Marion Strasmick), whose character later figured in Kennedy's Albany cycle novels. Diamond was in Cairo in the late 1920s, after being driven out of New York City by Dutch Schultz and his gang.

Diamond had stills and storage barns in a sixty-mile area from Catskill to Highland that fed his extensive bootlegging business in New York. He came down once a week from his farm in Greene County and inspected his holdings, stopping for a haircut at the same barber in Saugerties and always leaving a $5 tip. He also visited a beautiful young woman on Montross Street, Myrtle Whitaker (d. 1995), whom the New York *Daily News* labeled "The Woman in Red" in a front-page photograph of them leaving a speakeasy in Brooklyn. Called "the gangster who couldn't be killed" and "the clay pigeon of the underworld," Legs was shot three times at close range, and narrowly escaped an assassination attempt by Dutch Schultz's gang at the Aratoga Inn in Greene County in April 1930. Gangsters raked the place with machine gun fire, leaving two bystanders dead and Jack wounded three times.

He was in Albany in the summer of 1931 to answer charges brought against him over the beating of a Catskills trucker named Grover Parks, who probably refused to deliver Diamond's booze or maybe even stole it. Jack was acquitted of that crime, and then decided to elbow in on the Albany beer trade, even after being nicely advised by Dan O'Connell to get lost. O'Connell told Kennedy that Sergeant William Fitzpatrick had warned Diamond to leave town or Fitzpatrick would kill him. One night the sergeant and a detective climbed the second floor of the Dove Street townhouse where Diamond was sleeping off an evening's outing after the Troy trial and "took care of that matter," as O'Connell put it, with five bullets in the gangster's head. Fitzpatrick became police chief shortly thereafter, and was murdered by a detective while in his office in 1945.

Despite Dutch Schultz's Yonkers operation, much of the Westchester County booze traffic was controlled by Louis Pope (d. 1950) out of White Plains. His network included rail, truck and boat shipments from the Thimble Islands in Long Island Sound off Connecticut to various county locations. A good deal of the local business was unorganized, however. Farmers, here as elsewhere, produced applejack, as their forefathers had before them, which was derived from fermented cider that had been frozen, separating the alcohol

content. Homebrewed beer, often made in a basement tub, was also commonplace, especially among the provincial Irish.

The violent nature of the illicit booze business created a heightened sense
of danger in the mid-Hudson in those days, one of the collateral impacts of
Prohibition that colored its history. A number of communities had local tales
of young men from otherwise respectable families who became involved in
the business and met unsavory fates: Danny "Rube" Dargan, a local cut-up,
was one of them, found by the side of a road in rural Saugerties. Eventually
the real toll of the law became understood, not just in the lost jobs and failed
lives, but in the hypocrisy of those who opposed it as well.

Many Valley residents found unorthodox ways to get their drink during
Prohibition. Henry Noble MacCracken, the young president of Vassar, was
out walking the campus at dusk one night near a tank that had been given to
the college by a grateful France for the service of Vassar women during World
War I. The tank was shipped by steamboat to Poughkeepsie and unloaded by
the tennis courts, near a dormitory. As he approached, a young woman
dropped out of a window in her bathrobe, stole over to the tank, opened the
turret and removed a bottle of bootleg. She had difficulty climbing back into
the open window until MacCracken came over and gave her a boost. "In she
went," he recalled.

Margaret Elizabeth Barrett Diedling (1903–23) of Saugerties was the
quintessential small village belle, one of a new breed of young women whose
lifestyle loosened with the manners and moral attitudes that ushered in the
Roaring Twenties, yet quieter than most. Margaret was no Vassar girl—in
dress, mores, or intelligence—yet young people around the Valley were becoming smarter as well, or at least trying to, the proportion of high school
graduates among 17-year-olds rising from 16.3 to 27.5 percent from 1920 to
1929, and the number of students in college (nationally) growing by 50,000
a year. Miss Diedling came from good stock. She had studied painting, could
play a little piano, and dutifully looked after her younger cousin on Hudson
River Day Liner trips to join her mother and sisters in the city. Her father, Dr.
Rudolph Diedling, had come down from Catskill in 1898 to wed Caroline,
the prettiest of the four prominent Bruckner sisters and the only one to marry;
his parents had a fashionable house built for them on Market Street. Diedling
was a prominent young doctor decorated for service in World War I, and a
member of the state prison commission. The village long remembered him

for having cured a Yonkers man, James C. Eqing, who had tried to poison himself with laudanum. The doctor walked the man all night, not knowing what else to do, and in the morning the man was cured.

Margaret, Diedling's twenty-year-old delight, ran with the best of the local society, the sons and daughters of the mill owners and plant managers, a classy crowd for a small town but "fast," as they later said. The origin of her illness was officially unknown, but it was clear it came from drinking bad alcohol. A uremic infection struck quickly in the early days of June 1923, barely a month after her twentieth birthday. The doctor called in specialists from New York, but there was no time. It rained every day that month, until the morning of June 9 when she died in her Market Street bedroom room with the rose-colored satin drapes and bedcovers, the mahogany furniture, and a table made from a spinet piano. Recollections of her nine-year-old brother Dudie's fatal sledding accident eleven years before allowed the village to share in the couple's grief, and most of them came out for the funeral, entering the house and filing up the stairs to see her, the girl laid out on her own bed, a sleeping beauty they had known all her life. Peter ("Petey Qua-Qua") Campanella, the kindly and half-witted village street sweeper, picked some wild daisies in the woods and brought them with him, and they and the roses were the only flowers the stricken parents allowed in the room.

The flush of life was drained from the parents' features, the bright promise of the century having lost its sheen. Caroline and Rudolph knelt by the bed, their faces streaming in tears and devotion, their gazes fixed on their daughter in the last photograph ever taken of Margaret E. B. Diedling.

21. A Parkway through the Bronx

Those who can, build. Those who can't, criticize."
—ROBERT MOSES (1888–1981)

In 1895, a commission that included the mayors of New York, Yonkers, and Mount Vernon was formed by the state legislature to study the feasibility of a sewer line through Westchester County. The county had become dense with communities as the encroaching city expanded, and one of its most attractive assets—the Bronx River corridor—was befouled. The river traversed twenty-five miles of Westchester, dividing Yonkers, Greenburgh, and Mount Pleasant from Eastchester, Scarsdale, White Plains, and North Castle before running for seven miles in New York City. Its "very serpentine" form was tidal to West Farms, and thereafter rose through "a succession of beautiful lakes, waterfalls and woodland streams almost primeval" through modern Bronx Park and a picturesque gorge between Greenburgh and Scarsdale, all of it stinking of sewage. With the waters from the northern watershed came the "unsanitary and foul-smelling contributions" of "barnyards, privies, cesspools, gas-house refuse, the watery part of White Plains' sewage disposal works, [and] drains from houses in Tuckahoe, Bronxville, Mount Vernon, Woodland and Williamsbridge" along the way.

In 1893, the Webster Act authorized "for the sanitary protection of the sources of water supply" large-scale condemnation and land acquisitions that culminated in a cleanup of all the lands within three hundred feet around the reservoirs. As many as 529 "principal nuisances" were removed the following spring, and 33 estates surveyed for condemnation. Seven mills, a tannery and a slaughterhouse were among the businesses "sold and removed." Finally, the cleanup of "many nuisances. . . in a single spot" at Katonah, including "a large number of privies," cleared "all direct objectionable drainage" into the Bronx River. Yet the people disliked the haste and how they were treated by the city, and it was true: a disregard for local interests, as historian Charles H. Weidner has pointed out, established a pattern that became typical of the city's approach toward its upstate neighbors in later years.

The solution to the lower river pollution was to divert the discharges through a trunk tunnel from the Bronx Park to Long Island Sound, picking up the waste streams of the Hutchinson River and Westchester Creek communities of Mount Vernon, Eastchester and Pelham, and relying upon the ebb tide to carry the waste away. In 1895, the mayors commission considered but dismissed the idea of a highway as a secondary consideration, but in 1905, when the Bronx River Sewer Commission was created, the package included a picturesque 25-mile-long highway between Hunt's Point and a new dam planned at Kensico.

Transportation improvements were high on the agenda of progressive thinking in these years. New York voters passed an unprecedented $50 million transportation bond issue—the first such bond issue in the nation—at a time when only 8,625 motor vehicles were registered in the state. "Road No. 1" built with this money was a two mile section of the Troy-Schenectady Road. The bond issue benefited rural upstate communities and was not particularly good for Westchester, which only had 868 new miles added to its system; two small rural upstate towns, by comparison, added more than 2,000 miles each. Westchester was seeing the light, however. The county's population grew by 54 percent between 1900 and 1910, from 184,257 to 283,055, and by 1906, with the Bronx River trunk sewer line "rapidly advancing," 2.2 million visitors came to the New York Botanical Gardens and Zoological Park.

New upscale communities underway at Bronxville and Scarsdale showed the need for better management of county resources, and with fears rising about city interests of necessity subordinating "local differences for the sake of metropolitan advancement" some now felt that all of Westchester to North Castle would soon be subsumed within the metropolis. A Bronx River road would provide relief from that paradigm, potentially offering a "direct, level, and attractive boulevard to the city from the open countryside." The highway's designer, German landscape architect Herman W. Merkel, sought to emulate the "transverse drives" across Central Park as a model that would also create green buffers for the travelers. Progress seemed to be moving hand-in-hand with aesthetics, since the Palisades Parkway Commission was already considering a limited access highway "on a similar scale" across the Hudson River.

An additional $1.65 million in land takings would be needed to build the Bronx highway, commissioners concluded in 1907; the actual costs for land exceeded $2.5 million by 1914. More than 1,200 parcels were involved, the largest fifty acres in size, the smallest forty-three square feet, and more than 620 homes and other buildings removed in the construction, including the glut of advertising and other unsightly amenities along the way. More than six thousand trees were trimmed and 1,314 dead ones removed; chestnut, cherry, hickory, and hemlock were eliminated because of blights they bore at the time.

The Bronx River Parkway, the longest and perhaps the most beautiful of the early limited access picturesque thoroughfares serving suburban areas, was approved by the state legislature in 1907 but not built until the early 1920s. A lengthy wrangle on cost sharing resulted in New York City picking up 75 percent of the parkway's cost. The parkway consisted of four lanes, two in each direction, following the undulating path of the Bronx River in Westchester County and roughly paralleling the New York & Harlem Railroad, which had 72 passenger trains a day in operation in the 1890s. The new road formally opened on November 5, 1925, when the last connection tying the Botanical Gardens and Kensico Dam was completed. More than 35,000 cars used the highway in 1928, and an extension was already planned for the juncture of the new Saw Mill River Parkway at Hawthorne. The Bronx River Parkway served as an example of the "townless highways" that Lewis Mumford and Benton McKaye were advocating to relieve congestion and ensure the flow of traffic around and through populated areas.

The Westchester County Parkway Commission, established in 1925, added ninety-eight miles of parkways and freeways to the county's extensive recreational areas over the decade. The projects were presided over by Madison Grant, a New York society figure and anti-Catholic racist who also dabbled in eugenics. The commission built three other modern highways—the Hutchinson River, Saw Mill River, and Cross County parkways—the expansion of the county's transportation access following in natural order the creation of the Croton Water Works for New York, the steam rail for Mount Vernon commuters, and the telegraph, telephone, electric lights, and trolleys that constituted the root system of the new suburban modernism. The system, constructed by state and county appropriations totaling more than $47 million, had seven major parkways by 1928, a total of 16,671 acres of roads and abutting lands, or 140 miles for cars.

A proposed Croton River Parkway was abandoned because the land became too expensive, but even as the county grew in highway mileage, it was failing to keep up with the times. By 1923, a three-mile stretch of the Boston Post Road in Rye had the heaviest traffic in the nation, rising to 50,000 cars a day. Most of these were commuters. In 1927, Westchester had more residential building permits than any other place in America; Yonkers was seventh among cities in this category. By 1930, all of Pelham in southern Westchester was considered fully developed, with no large tracts remaining; the town population, 11,851, had more than doubled in the previous ten years. Residential growth in Westchester was twice as busy as eight upstate cities combined. Westchester also created country clubs and recreational parks to go along with a mobile society, also more than any other county in the nation. The county was already transformed into an automobile suburb.

Westchester had nine miles of waterside parks, including Crugers, Croton River, and Kingsland Point along the Hudson River, and Glen Island Park, Rye Beach, and Manurising Island Park along the Sound. In Rye Beach in 1926, "Playland" was rising as a large-scale recreation and amusement park with a boating lagoon. Kingsland's 80,000 visitors that year dropped to 33,000 the next because of the Playland competition, but soon rebounded as more and more tourists came for the attractions.

An extension of the Hutchinson River Parkway through Pelham to the Connecticut state line, completed on January 30, 1937, led to the demise of the Pelham H-Line Trolley, the inspiration for the "Toonerville Folks," a nationally syndicated comic that ran for almost fifty years. The creator of the comic, Fontaine Talbot Fox (1884–1964), and 5,000 fans came to Pelham for the July 31 celebration ending the trolley's life. A dozen silent films and fifty-five comedy shorts were spin-offs of the popular comic. Wilna Hervey (1894–1979), a painter and enamellist living in Bearsville by 1927, played the role of Powerful Katrinka in the series; Dan Mason (born Daniel L. Grassman) was the trolley skipper. The shorts made the young actor who played the hero kid, Mickey McGuire, famous and gave him his stage name. Joe Yule Jr. could not continue using the name professionally after Fox objected, so the boy settled on Mickey Rooney (1920–2014) instead.

22. From Troutbeck to Yaddo

What are we coming to now? Are we going to disregard all idea of beauty in our art. You see exhibition after exhibition of the "Modernists" here in N.Y. and "sales" of their horror. Perhaps we are all going crazy!
—F. S. CHURCH to William Launt Palmer at Albany (April 24, 1914)

The Hudson River Valley attracted artists for the beauty of the scenery and access to the Catskills since before Thomas Cole's time, and from time to time small, short-lived arts communities or neighborhoods developed among artists and intellectuals who followed in Cole's footsteps. In a few cases actual colonies or preconceived settings for the advancement of creativity also arose, and in Woodstock's case this spawned a sense of community that redefined the town and outlasted the century.

Lawrence Park in Bronxville drew well established authors and artists, including muralist, stained glass artisan and writer Will Hicock Low (1853–1933); William Henry Howe (1846–1929) of the Old Lyme, Connecticut, art colony; and William T. Smedley, who ranked with John Singer Sargent as a portraitist in his day. Low, an Albany native, undertook the series of large murals for the Rotunda of the new Albany state Education Building in his Bronxville studio over 1913–18, each of them done in the grand Academism style of the Ecole de Beaux Arts in celebration of the gods of the Greeks and Romans and their associations with all that was good and just about society and civilization.

This was not an art of Armory Show sentiments, nor was Bronxville a community that drew artists together under a common cause or the genius of a single benefactor even though William Lawrence's sense of high culture set the tone, and the economic bar. Artists gravitated to other Hudson Valley locales, usually not intentionally to join with other artists even though their works often bore similarities. In the Harlem Valley, for instance, a local group known as the Dover Plains Four practiced "from well before the Depression" to mid-century, following a tradition established by Asher B. Durand. Paintings of Walter C. Hartson (1866–1946), G. Glenn Newell (1870–1947), Arthur J. E. Powell (1864–1956), and Harry F. Waltman (1871–1951) remained on display at the local school library in the next century.

Troutbeck, Joel and Amy Spingarn's Dutchess County homestead nestled in the foothills of the Berkshires on the eastern edge of Amenia, provided a setting for intellectuals as well as Joel's horticultural interests. The Harlem Valley town was described by Horatio Nelson Powers in 1889 as:

A pleasant vale; bright fields that lie
On gentle slopes and knolls of green;
Steep mountains sharp against the sky;
Clear streams and tiny lakes between.

The farm was already a literary and aesthetic landscape nurtured by three generations of the Caleb Benton family. Eight hundred acres, a property the size of Central Park, were farmed around a "cold closet" the Bentons made of a pool fed by limestone springs at the headwaters of the Webutuck River. The grounds, planted with sycamores, lilies, scilla, ajuga, and primrose, were a principal attraction for Joel Spingarn, who was a world-class horticulturalist. When the old farmhouse, a Gothic structure modeled after Andrew Jackson Downing's writings, burned in 1917, the Spingarns built a stone house with a slate roof in a style propounded by William Morris.

Spingarn, who had a hand in creating the 1913 "International Exhibition of Modern Art" (commonly called the Armory Show) and supported the "new criticism" in literature in the 1920s, was one of "the American Promise generation," as Lewis Mumford called them. Spingarn, Mumford, and nearby Bridgewater, Connecticut, resident Van Wyck Brooks (1886–1963) met at Troutbeck over a long weekend to discuss the decay of civilization in working up their individual contributions to editor Harold Stearns' controversial multivolume *Civilization in the United States* (1921).

Lewis and Sophy Mumford—by now he was a noted public intellectual and regional planner—settled into a farmhouse in nearby Leedsville in 1926. He wrote *The Golden Day* (1926) there that summer. The book defined the antebellum cultural explosion and encouraged a revival of the Hudson River School of Art in the process. Mumford liked the rural setting and daily swims in Troutbeck Lake and the rambles over hills and pastures, the place seeming to give the book "a kind of crystalline clarity, like the water from Troutbeck Spring."

Spingarn published a series of Troutbeck Leaflets that described and celebrated the intellectual scene that he cultivated. Amy Spingarn was a painter and poet fluent in four languages and as involved as her husband with the bohemians, writers, and artists of the times. She once sponsored a show of antilynching paintings exhibited in East Coast communities. Her art was shown in New York and Dutchess County galleries and included local scenes along the Webutuck River and the old Amenia Inn.

Amy maintained an atelier in Manhattan, where she recited Wordsworth and Shelley to Langston Hughes (1902–67) over cinnamon toast and tea one evening in 1925. Later that year she committed $300 to his Lincoln University education—agreeing with Hughes that the small black university in eastern Pennsylvania was preferable to Harvard. (The top student in his class was Thurgood Marshall.) Hughes briefly vacationed at Troutbeck after the 1928 school year, and looked to Amy for the advice and friendship that a patron could provide. A testament to the Spingarns' respect and admiration for

Hughes was reflected in four mahogany beams at Troutbeck in which they had carved tributes to the peoples of the world—Nordic, Jewish, Indian, and African—the last modeled after Hughes. Hughes dedicated his first novel, *Not Without Laughter* (1930), winner of the Harmon Gold Medal, to the Spingarns. Amy published a slim volume of his poems, *Dear Lovely Death*, on a small hand press she bought in 1931; the numbered edition of one hundred copies had a frontispiece of Hughes done by Amy, and was said to be Langston's favorite book. Amy did his portrait in oils before he left for Paris and the anti-fascist revolution in Spain in 1937.

Other Hudson Valley intellectuals besides the Spingarns had ties to the Armory Show. Arthur B. Davies (1862–1928), an artist who had an attractive farm in Congers and helped in The Eight's revolt against the National Academy in 1907, spent much of 1912 organizing the French Impressionist paintings among the 1,600 works shown at the Armory. A man so shy and withdrawn that he had to be pressured to show his own art, Davies became a "Terrible Ivan" when he took over the presidency of the show's planning because of his interest in the European art. He and John (1869–1953) and Mary Horgan Mowbray-Clarke (1874–1962) mortgaged their farms in Rockland County to help subsidize the $28,000-a-month rental. They were all, like Spingarn, deeply involved in William Morris's Arts and Crafts thinking, and antipathetic to capitalism and industrial views of the modern world.

Mary Mowbray-Clarke, an art critic and landscape architect, co-owned the Sunwise Turn Bookstore in Manhattan. Her daily commute began with a walk over the mountain to the Mount Ivy train station. One of her houseguests from the Sunwise Turn crowd was the Sri Lankan aesthetic anarchist and "metaphysician" Ananda Coomaraswamy (1877–1947), who coined the term "postindustrial" in 1913. John Mowbray-Clarke's range as a sculptor—a stone torso of his was included in the Armory Show—was often pointedly political. The couple entertained at their Pomona home, called the Brocken. Harold Loeb (1891–1974) spoke of "the group around Brocken" as "in revolt against 'our commercial age'." He may have brought his sparring partner, Ernest Hemingway (1899–1961), or his cousin and her friend, Peggy Guggenheim (1898–1979) and Abby Aldrich Rockefeller (1874–1948), on visits to the Brocken.

Henry Varnum Poor (1887–1970) came upriver in 1919 at the invitation of the Mowbray-Clarkes. He bought a farm site for $500 and built Crow

House in the Arts and Crafts style on South Mountain Road in Clarkstown. His pottery established his reputation in the 1920s, although he was also a noted WPA muralist in the New Deal. A huge fireplace, a spiral staircase of tulipwood and oak, and the integration of a tributary of the Hackensack River into the design added to the drama of the house. A swimming hole that he created channeled the water through a mill to grind his pottery glazes. The house was immediately recognized for its beauty, how well it was integrated into the landscape, and as an early model for sustainable living. Poor also built or worked on homes for friends, including actor John Houseman (1902–88) and cartoonist Milton Caniff (1907–88).

Clarkstown and Nyack were magnets for creative people from the city. The marriage of Helen Hayes (1900–93) and playwright Charles MacArthur (1895–1956) was considered problematic, by Brooks Atkinson at least, because of her demure personality and his womanizing and alcoholism, yet their love survived even his reputation over the years. MacArthur had returned to Nyack in 1927, where he attended Wilson Memorial Academy as a youth, and rented the old Nyack Girls Academy with Ben Hecht (1894–1964) to work on plays and movies together. (Henry Poor designed Hecht's poker room.) Helen would come up with her friend, Ben's wife Rose, to deliver food and other supplies, and the four of them filled the academy hall with laughter as *The Front Page* emerged, the finest comedy ever written about the hardboiled newspaper business. MacArthur and Hecht also collaborated on *Twentieth Century* (1932), a number of other plays, and nine movies while in Nyack. One of the films, *Once in a Blue Moon* (1934) was shot in part on location in Tuxedo, using the estate of J. Pierpont Morgan's sister, Mrs. Morgan Hamilton, to depict the Russian countryside. It was the most expensive film ever shot in New York until then and a box office flop, but MacArthur and Hecht could not have cared less. They spent most of the time engaged in marathon backgammon games during the filming.

Maxwell Anderson's relocation from New York to a rustic home a few miles north of Nyack near Haverstraw drew special friends with similar backgrounds whose creativity was nourished by the sylvan setting. When Anderson (1888–1959) first visited New City in the spring of 1921, the sleepy Rockland County town forty miles north of New York was rife with the stories and legends of old Dutch sailors passed down by the families of old-timers. He had learned of a small artist's colony along South Mountain Road three miles north of the village from Mary Mowbray-Clarke. Here the rents were cheap, the lawns never mowed, and the neighbors quiet and interesting. A noted editorial writer with the *New York World*, Anderson borrowed $500 for a down payment and bought an old farmhouse with a waterfall behind it for $3,000. The house lacked electricity, a well, or plumbing. He called it Seven Fields, after the seven stone walls on the three acres he owned, and he and his wife Margaret "camped out," as he put it, for several summers before expanding the house and adding services. From the attic window, where he made his study, he could see both precipitous High Tor rising 850 feet behind the village of Haverstraw three miles distant and a grand cataract that coursed through a deep ravine below him. He made the daily trip to the *World* by bicycling to the Weehawken train in Haverstraw. Anderson quit the *World* and expanded his New City tract to thirty acres after achieving success on Broadway with *What Price Glory* (1924), a play he wrote with fellow journalist Laurence Stallings about Stallings' bitter recollections of World War I.

Anderson had the house renovated by Carroll French, a painter-sculptor and itinerant puppeteer. French decorated boards and beams around the farmhouse with whimsical carvings of the local flora or fauna and storybook characters reminiscent of the region's Dutch folk history. The neighborhood where Anderson lived took on a "free-love colony" reputation in nearby Haverstraw, because of the incidence of unmarried couples and the predilection of some, including the Andersons, to occasionally swim in the nude.

Creative neighbors included fellow playwrights Eunice Tietjens (also a novelist, journalist and poet; 1884–1944) and Harold Hickerson (an Anderson collaborator on *Gods of the Lightning* in 1928); Cubist painter and sculptor Hugo Robus (1885–1964), and painters Morris Kantor (1896–1974) and his wife (after 1928) Martha Ryther (1896–1981). Ryther taught for twenty-five years at the Rockland Center for the Arts, which hosted a large retrospective of her paintings in 1981. Kantor's oil-on-linen masterpiece, *Baseball at Night* (1934), was made from sketches he did while watching one of the earliest lighted games at a field in West Nyack.

Burgess "Buzz" Meredith (1907–97) and Paulette Goddard (1910–90) were the most prominent of the actors. Having risen to fame in Anderson's *Winterset* (1935), Meredith lived in "Treason House," the home of the Arnold co-conspirator Jacob Hett Smith. Pulitzer-prize winning cartoonist Bill Mauldin (1921–2003) lived on South Mountain Road, as did Milton Caniff, who created "Terry and the Pirates" and "Steve Canyon." Marion Hargrove (1919–2003), a writer who was discovered by Anderson, moved there after World War II, as did musical composer Alan Jay Lerner (1918–86), who collaborated with Kurt Weill on *Love Life* in 1948, and his wife, movie actress Nancy Olsen (b. 1928).

Anderson's closest friends were Kurt Weill (1900–50) and Lotte Lenya (1898–1981), neighbors during the last fifteen years of Weill's life. They bought Brook House in 1935, which was nearby along the creek, and Weill and Anderson were soon working on theatrical projects together. They completed *Knickerbocker Holiday* (1938) and *Lost in the Stars* (1949) in New City, the latter based on Alan Paton's 1948 novel *Cry, the Beloved Country*. Weill had written five "enchanting" new songs for a third collaboration, *Adventures of Huckleberry Finn*, when a severe cold kept him in bed at Brook House for a few days before turning for the worse. He died of a coronary thrombosis on April 5, 1950. Anderson eulogized Weill as someone who "had more to give to his age than any other man I knew."

"As a composer he was a magician," Anderson wrote. "He would take a lyric from my hands, run upstairs to a piano, spend an hour or so alone, and reappear with three different musical settings for me to choose among." With the passing of the man whom Anderson considered "the only indisputable genius" he had ever known, the creative output of the playwright diminished dramatically.

The proximity to New York was congenial for artists and intellectuals in general, many of whom lived upstate while working in the city. Lillian Hellman (1905–84) had a farm at Pleasantville, which she shared in the 1940s and 50s with Dashiell Hammett (1894–1961), the creator of the Sam Spade detective novels. Brooks Atkinson (1894–1984), the theater critic and writer, and his wife, writer Oriana Atkinson (c. 1895–1989), had a summer cabin north of Piermont in Rockland County before retiring to a farmhouse in Greene County.

Clifford B. Harmon (1866–1945) developed his namesake "New City on the Hudson" as an artists' community in the first few years of the new century. Harmon drew movie stars like Mary Pickford (1892–1979) and Douglas Fairbanks (1883–1939) to the area, and attracted Wilbur Wright to Croton for a demonstration flight. A colorful figure, Harmon founded the International League of Aviators and in 1926 established the Harmon Trophy, honoring aviators around the world. He built Nikko Inn and Playhouse, designed after a Japanese tea house, where Pickford and Fairbanks stayed. The setting lay on the cliffs overlooking Deep Hole, a popular Croton swimming place that he decorated with gondolas. Others with homes in Harmon included actress Gloria Swanson (1899–1983) and Isadora Duncan's sister Elizabeth, who founded a dance school there (albeit not in Isadora's tradition).

Harmon and the hamlet of Mount Airy were incorporated into the village of Croton-on-Hudson in 1932. A group of old frame houses on Mount Airy Road were rented out by friends and acquaintances from Greenwich Village who were deeply involved in socialist, suffragist, and anti-war causes before and after the First World War. A central figure was Max Eastman (1883–1969), editor of *The Masses* who became a rabid anti-communist and staunch defender of Senator Joseph McCarthy in the 1950s. Eastman's assistant at *The Masses* was Floyd Dell (1887–1969), a novelist and political writer who came to Croton in 1919 after marrying Bertie Marie Gage. He had somewhat famously described the "seven" manifestations of Greenwich Village, the last being in his own time, the bohemian years of 1912–18. Dell wrote ten novels, the best of them based on his own experiences in depicting rebellious youth. His other works included *Looking at Life* (1924), a collection of his radical writings; a 1927 study of Upton Sinclair; and *Homecoming: An Autobiography* (1933).

Also from the Greenwich Village *Masses* group were John Reed (1887–1920) and Louise Bryant (1885–1936), who came to Croton in 1916. A year later, they left for Petrograd and the experiences that resulted in Reed's first-hand account of the Bolshevik rise to power, *Ten Days That Shook the World* (1919). Eugene O'Neill (1888–1953) was living in Croton at the time of their arrival, and became smitten with Bryant. He gave her a love poem, but she told him that she and Reed had already married. O'Neill became a virulent critic of Reed after the bestselling *Ten Days* shook the world.

Max's sister Crystal Eastman (1881–1928) and her husband, Walter Fuller, an anti-war activist as well as a British poet, were Croton regulars. Crystal, a large and beautiful woman, was a Vassar graduate ('03) with degrees from Columbia and New York City University Law School, and a noted sociologist, suffragist, pacifist, and radical journalist. She was among the organizers of the American Civil Liberties Union in 1920. Doris Stevens (1892–1963), a friend of Crystal's, invited Edna St. Vincent Millay as a houseguest in 1923. Millay, the precocious poet known for her free-spirited lifestyle, fell in love with an Eastman colleague, Eugen Bossevain (1880–1949), at a charades game on Mt. Airy Road; they married at Croton on May 19 and spent the summer there. On April 30, a *New York Evening Post* reporter came up on the steamboat to inform her that she had just been awarded the $1,000 Pulitzer Prize for Poetry, a remarkable achievement since she was only the second-ever recipient and a woman to boot. Later the Boissevains lived for two years in Croton Falls before purchasing a farm tucked against the Berkshires in eastern Columbia County and naming it Steepletop.

The Hudson Highlands continued to attract creative individuals. Russel Wright (1904–76), the noted industrial designer, established a design center on a 75-acre estate he called Manitoga in Garrison in 1942, and spent the next three decades creating his home, Dragon Rock, and four miles of beautiful landscaping. Dragon Rock was built on the edge of a water-filled quarry in eleven different levels, using the large slab rocks of the quarry as stairs.

Aaron Copland (1900–90) had the use of Mary Churchill's Briarcliff Manor home in Westchester County in the spring of 1929, to which he happily escaped in order to work on the *Symphonic Ode*, "my first big orchestral piece" and his most ambitious work to date. In 1930, Copland rented a small house on Hook Road in Bedford and began his *Piano Variations*, "my first major piano piece." The writer Gerald Sykes (1904?–84), whom Copland had known since 1925, took an upstairs room to work on a new book of his own. They came up in a snowstorm on January 1, Copland driving, and almost crashed into the Kensico Dam. Sykes was not disturbed by Copland's work, even though the composer had hauled along "'tons' of music" to play as he composed. The range astonished Sykes, from 15th century compositions through works by Mozart, Haydn, and on to Brahms and Schumann. Sykes felt he was present at the Creation as the *Variations* unfolded in Bedford.

"Something special was happening," he wrote. "I was seeing Aaron in an inspired moment, and yet he was tranquil and even-tempered, even though he was pressured by time and responsibilities. I lived with the Piano Variations for months. It was a wonderful experience—Aaron at his best."

Copland, Sykes, and the music critic Harold Clurman (1901–80) had become fast friends. The *Variations* was not finished until after the three gathered at Yaddo for the first time in the summer of 1930. When Clurman met them at the train station at Saratoga Springs, he shared with Copland a note he received from the Yaddo director, Elizabeth Ames (1885–1977), telling him "not to monopolize" Copland's time. The artists got to know Mrs. Ames as a force to be reckoned with, especially her habit of leaving blue notes in the artist boxes if she had a complaint or special concern. It was during this season that Copland suggested promoting younger composers by hosting a festival of contemporary music at the retreat.

Copland felt he had a perfect setting at Yaddo for work on the *Variations*—"the first of my works where I felt very sure of myself." He was given the "turret studio" that reminded him of "the Tower Scene in 'Pelléas'" and enabled him to work "extraordinarily well because of it. For the rest," he added about life at Yaddo, "one lives like a wifeless bourgeois—eats well, sleeps in a soft bed, and relaxes in cushioned chairs."

The *Variations* was panned by the New York critics at its premiere in 1931, yet the reception of the work exploded after he played it at Yaddo the following year. "One feels its author the composer of the coming decades," Paul Rosenfeld wrote in 1936. The piece, "new and strange" as Copland later wrote, in time was accepted as one of the seminal music works of the 1930s.

Paul Bowles (1910–99) joined Copland at Yaddo in 1930, took harmony lessons from him, and traveled to Europe and North Africa with him the following year. Although Bowles was not there, all the members of a new Young Composers' Group that Copland helped to start were present at the First Festival of Contemporary American Music at Yaddo on April 30 and May 1, 1932. Charles Ives (1874–1954) contributed seven songs to the Festival, Bowles sent five songs from Morocco, and Virgil Thompson (1896–1989) provided a musical setting for a Max Jacob's work, *Stabat Mater*, all at Copland's request. Oscar Levant (1906–72) played parts of an unfinished *Sonatina* that Copland urged him to complete for a Yaddo premiere. Copland stepped in to perform his *Piano Variations* at the last minute after George Antheil had to cancel, and repeated the performance on Sunday evening after receiving numerous requests to do so.

The Ives songs were chosen by Copland, who accompanied on piano. This was "a turning point in the recognition of his music," Copland wrote of the composer. He later arranged for their publication, the first of Charles Ives' songs to become commercially available. Copland also included Ives' "Where the Eagle Cannot See" as a song for the Second Yaddo Festival, and arranged for his full (and revolutionary) *114 Songs for Modern Music* to be published in 1933.

Copland bought Shady Land Farm in Ossining in 1952 while he was working on *The Tender Land*, an opera that premiered two years later; he lived there for eight years, spending part of this time in Europe as well. He moved to Rock Hill in the town of Cortlandt in 1960, where he remained for the rest of his life. Aaron Copland, who barely survived being blacklisted in the McCarthy era, was eventually awarded the Presidential Medal of Freedom, the National Medal of the Arts, and a Congressional Medal of Honor. He died at Phelps Memorial Hospital in North Tarrytown in 1990. Five years later, a local coalition organized a grassroots movement to save the home for posterity, and in 1998 Copland House opened under artistic director Michael Boriskin, offering a range of composer residencies, music, and educational programs—the only composer's residence in America so dedicated.

Rita Smith, who worked for *Mademoiselle* and was one of the models for Holly Golightly, brought Truman Capote (1924–84) home to meet her widowed mother and sister in their weathered old house in Nyack in 1945. Smith had in effect discovered Capote when she published his first story in *Mademoiselle*. Her sister Carson McCullers (née Lula Carson Smith, 1917–67) became an overnight literary sensation when her first novel, *The Heart is a Lonely Hunter*, appeared in 1940. The sisters and their mother, Marguerite Smith, had taken a spacious apartment at Graycourt Manor on South Broadway the previous fall, and purchased the large Victorian house next door the following spring. Marguerite took to the neighborhood as if it were a cozy Southern town, and frequently visited the Nyack Library just down the street. Carson and Truman were alike not only in the precocious success they enjoyed, but in appearance and mannerisms as well. They became enchanted with each other; McCullers considered the young Truman "her very own private little protégé." Her family remained "wildly Southern" while living over the Hudson—all the better for Capote, who easily slipped into the New Orleans patois of his childhood.

McCullers was already seriously ill, and was often bedridden when revelers and family arrived. John Huston (1906–87) recalled meeting her while in New City on a visit to Paulette Goddard and Burgess Meredith:

> Carson lived nearby, and one day when Buzz and I were out for a walk she hailed us from her doorway. She was then in her early twenties, and had already suffered the first of a series of strokes.

I remember her as a fragile thing with great shining eyes, and a tremor in her hand as she placed it in mine . . . But there was nothing timid or frail about the manner in which Carson McCullers faced life. And as her afflictions multiplied, she only grew stronger.

Carson's interest in Yaddo had been sparked in 1941 by the violinist-composer David Diamond (1915–2005), who was attracted to her "magnetism and strange sickly beauty," and drew her to the colony because of McCullers' interest in Katherine Anne Porter (1890–1980), to whom she expressed her unabashed admiration that summer. The moment turned into an embarrassment when Porter, mistakenly believing that Carson was homosexual, rudely ignored and stepped over her when Carson lay on the floor outside her door hoping to accompany her to dinner one evening. McCullers wrote "The Jockey," her short story set in the Worden resort bar at Saratoga Springs, while at Yaddo that year; it was taken to *The New Yorker* by her new Yaddo friend, Edward Newhouse (1911–2002), who presented her with a check for $400 after returning from the city. Carson carried it around like a trophy while slumming in the Congress Street nightclubs that week. The check figured into divorce proceedings against her husband that Carson initiated in New City later that summer after he forged her name and cashed it for himself.

McCullers returned to Yaddo for two days in November 1944 for a reunion with Newton Arvin and Elizabeth Ames, and returned again for Christmas with Ames in the winter. Her story, *The Ballad of the Sad Café*, was included in Houghton Mifflin's *Best American Short Stories* that year. She remarried James Reeves McCullers Jr. (1913–53) in Nyack in March of 1945 and maintained a stormy relationship with him until his suicide in November 1953. McCullers suffered several strokes in the mid-1940s (and an attempted suicide) that left her debilitated and in despair over her future recovery while in Nyack. Following her recovery, Carson and Capote acted like brother and sister when ensconced for a season of writing at Yaddo in 1946.

"Nothing could keep Carson from her desk at half-past nine in the morning, and she stayed there throughout her stay," Elizabeth Ames wrote of her writing habits. "She was very, very disciplined. She could turn against or grow cold toward anyone who was ever thoughtless enough to try to break in on her."

Yet she started every day with a glass of beer in hand—Ames called it "a quietening" that gave her focus—and turned to sherry later in the day and cognac and cocktails in the evenings, the alcohol consumption that would so disrupt her final years quietly growing upon her in these years. Carson—whose usual "dress-up city garb," as her colleagues called it, were men's trousers and a buttoned white shirt, at times accompanied by a cigar only partly smoked—was a startling figure to the other Yaddo residents, particularly at the Sunday evening buffets, and on one occasion while in the gardens she convinced her fellow residents to act like insane asylum inmates for the crowds of tourists frequenting the grounds, thereby confirming, as Virginia Spencer Carr writes, their assumption that the artists were all crazy.

Porter, who was famous and aloof toward all the Yaddo crowd except David Diamond, later regretted her chary estimate of the young writer in 1941, and was once again the resident older writer in 1946, but McCullers had by then eclipsed her and Capote quickly became the star. Carson had used her influence to have him admitted (it was long after the application deadline), and he became an immediate attraction for the other creative denizens of the old mansion.

"He walked as if every step were choreographed to some music that he alone heard," Marguerite Young (1909–95) recalled. "I remember him as being absolutely enthralling that summer, high-spirited, generous, loving. We all thought he was a genius." The colony was just what he needed, since he was finding it increasingly difficult to write with his mother's alcoholism constantly disrupting his home.

The writers and artists were expected to work until four in the afternoon —box lunches were left outside their rooms—and then dine together and enjoy the evenings. The 500-acre estate included four trout-stocked lakes, a rock garden and fountain, rose garden filled with marble figures (and open to the public), and several hundred thousand stately trees, most of them planted by Spencer Trask himself over the years. Romances flowered. Enormous amounts of alcohol were consumed, games played on the lawns, and stealthy visits into the village for movies or more fun undertaken. Capote worked on *Other Voices, Other Rooms* and wrote a short story, "The Headless Hawk," while staying in the tower room where Copland had composed and Katrina Trask had always gone to write poetry. He had an affair with Howard Doughty (1904–70), a 42-year-old Harvard professor and biographer of Francis Parkman who tried to hide his dalliance with "the little one." Doughty, who was said to have looked like James Stewart, was also having an affair with Newton Arvin (1900–63) of Smith College, a bald, undistinguished looking biographer with a head full of ailments, who arrived on June 12. Arvin, who was close with McCullers, was also on the Yaddo board. He and Capote immediately fell in love, which led Doughty to leave for Boston although he later expressed "the warmest delight" at what had occurred. He last glimpsed Newton and his "Precious Spooky" walking hand-in-hand to their rooms.

McCullers made herself at home in Capote's company, dancing awkwardly with him in Yaddo's huge kitchen and wondering aloud where he came from.

"From *Harper's Bazaar*," Elizabeth Ames replied.

Once, while rummaging through Truman's clothes for something to wear for dinner at Yaddo, McCullers discovered a paper in his drawer that had his real name—Truman Streckfus Persons—and playfully threatened to out him.

"You just go right ahead, honey chile," he said, "and I'll tell them your real name is Lula Smith" (which it was). In later years, Truman remained "very, very fond" of McCullers: "She was a devil, but I respected her." Gore Vidal's estimation of the Rockland writer was a bit different: "An hour with a dentist without Novocain is like a minute with Carson McCullers," he wrote.

At Yaddo, Jean Stafford (1915–79) safely recovered from a fever in the early fall of 1943. She had "a hard but I think triumphant time" completing a novel (*Boston Adventure*, which became a bestseller), her husband Robert Lowell (1917–1977) wrote to friends. Among the guests whom Lowell got to know was Flannery O'Connor (1925–1964), working on *Wise Blood* (1952). "She had already really mastered and found her themes and style," Lowell wrote to Elizabeth Bishop after O'Connor's death, "knew she wouldn't marry, would be Southern, shocking and disciplined."

Lowell's 1947 visit at Yaddo included the company of Arna Bontemps (1902–73), whom Lowell described as "a colored librarian from Hashville who writes juveniles"; Theodore Roethke (1917–99), "a ponderous, coarse, fattish, fortyish man; well-read and likes the same things I do, and quite a competent poet"; J. F. Powers, a Catholic novelist and poet later imprisoned as a conscientious objector during the Vietnam war; and Marguerite Young once again, whom Lowell uncharitably termed a "really crucifyingly odd and garrulous, poor thing!" Malcolm Cowley and Elizabeth Hardwick came in 1948. Writing to Ezra Pound that year (he was being held in a mental institution in Washington), Lowell termed Yaddo "a sort of St. Elizabeths without bars—regular hours, communal meals, grounds, big old buildings etc." He produced five hundred lines toward a long poem that winter.

An "explosion" at Yaddo (Lowell's term) occurred with Lowell and Elizabeth Bishop's unfounded allegation that Elizabeth Ames was supporting communism in her management of the center. A friend of Ames's, former Yaddo guest and active communist Agnes Smedley (1892–1950) was under Federal Bureau of Investigation surveillance as a suspected spy in 1949. Lowell, Bishop, poet Allen Tate (1899–1979) and others started a smear campaign against Ames and sought an investigation by the board. The story had broken in *The New York Times* that February. The board conducted a thorough review and exonerated Ames of any involvement in communist activity.

Lowell urged Hardwick to come to the colony in 1947, the year he and Stafford divorced. A liaison ensued and the two married in Boston on July 28, 1949, and a week later moved into a "picturesque and ancient" Red Hook farmhouse where Israel Putnam had had his headquarters for a while in the American Revolution. They expected to be in residence for the school year at Bard College, but Lowell was at the Payne Whitney Clinic in Manhattan by September, experiencing the first manic episode of an illness that would eventually drive him mad. Lowell was at Bard again in 1956, when he gave a paper "on art and bad characters," and visited with a friend, Bard's 17th century literature scholar Andrews Wanning (d. 1997).

The colorful array of well-known artists, writers, actors and intellectuals who came north to enjoy the Hudson River Valley experience merely reflected the cream of a vast new crop of creativity in the region. People of varied degrees of talent came, as did the general public, in the serendipity of casual associations with particular geographic locales, or by virtue of family associations or other special circumstances—even as tourists initially—and practiced their crafts while enjoying the settings. The region was also a place where talent could be cultivated formally by utopian thinkers or those, usually wealthy ones, interested in cultivating particular viewpoints or theories about aesthetics and society. New "Hudson River schools" of a regionwide nature did not emerge, but the colonies left their stamps on time and fame nonetheless.

23. Byrdcliffe and the Maverick

There is only one way to paint a masterpiece, and that
is to become a master.

—BIRGE HARRISON

The Woodstock arts colony in Ulster County was begun by a wealthy Englishman, Ralph Radcliffe Whitehead (1854–1929), who had come to
America in 1892 to establish a utopian colony of artists and craftsmen along
the lines of John Ruskin's Guild of St. George. Whitehead had studied under
Ruskin (1819–1900) and was influenced by the Arts and Crafts movement,
in particular its rejection of industrialism as demeaning to the spirit of man.
The creation of Byrdcliffe coincided with the establishment of several other
important art colonies in the country, including Taos, Provincetown, New
Hope, and Carmel, and was the last important large-scale project of the Arts
and Crafts movement during its early years.

The planning began in Indianapolis in the spring of 1902, by Whitehead
and Bolton Coit Brown (1864–1936), who had founded the art department
at Stanford University in 1894. Hervey White and two of his friends, Fritz
van der Loo and Carl Eric Lindin (1860–1942), became involved after meeting Radcliffe at Hull House in Chicago. The name for the colony came from
the middle names of Whitehead and his wife, Jane Byrd Whitehead.

The Whiteheads were not likely to have settled here—Jane disliked the
place—but for the enthusiasm of Brown, who had had an epiphany upon first
seeing Woodstock from Mead's hotel. Brown had been in the Catskills for
three weeks when, one spring morning in 1902, he came out of Mink Hollow
past Cooper Lake and took an old wagon road up the back side of the Overlook range, coming to Mead Mountain House with its view of an apple orchard in full bloom and a community of farmers and tradesmen below.
Whitehead came at Brown's behest, toured the town extensively, and finally
said, "Well, all right, let's have it here." His wife arrived, had a frustrating time
dealing with the rough country, and left in a fury.

Ralph Whitehead purchased 26 acres on the side of a mountain from Levi Harder for $400 on September 1, 1902. He continued buying land and, over a month, spent over $14,000 for 1,000 acres on Mount Guardian. Brown laid out the roads and began building houses for himself and Whitehead; the Whitehead home was called White Pines. The community grew to more than thirty-five structures and included an opera, theater, casino, and living and studio accommodations. Byrdcliffe's Studio was the casino, which was connected to the Loom Room and White Pines by a "Covered Bridge." The Studio was the location for the art show, dances, concerts and other social events. The Villetta was created as a dormitory and "reflectory" for students on scholarship. Off-campus, so to speak, in the "lower" Byrdcliffe area closer to the Glasco Turnpike, a barn and farmhouse were joined in a "lodging club" called the Lark's Nest, where White and Lindin would live. The Lark's Nest was managed by Elizabeth Krysler, a Chicago artist who had illustrated White's novel *Noll and the Fairies* (1903). Lindin, White and van der Loo at first lived in the town's former Lutheran Church, sleeping on the pews while Lindin used the pulpit as an easel. He and his wife, bookbinder Louise Hastings (1882–1968), remodeled the church into a permanent home after they married in 1905. White wrote a novel about Lindin at Byrdcliffe, disguised as a *roman-a-clef* set in California with fictitious names.

A prospectus for the Byrdcliffe Summer Art School was put out for the first season in 1903. Brown, Herman Dudley Murphy (1867–1945) of Boston, and Dawson Watkins of Quebec were the first art instructors. That spring, the first gala dinner was held, but by the end of the season Brown was fired for arrogance. In later years, he commented how the sudden appearance of this formalized crafts and arts colony drew people to the Woodstock area:

> [A]rtists oozing out of Byrdcliffe or drifting in from the world at large, [who] set up all over the region their widely varying establishments. Thus, it was that the Art Colony entirely outgrew the original idea—a chosen and selected group—and became instead a large free public movement that has been growing steadily for thirty years and is likely to grow thirty more.

Watkins left at the same time as Brown. The colony added metalworking taught by Edward Thatcher, a protégé whom Whitehead had discovered and sent through Pratt Institute. Woodcarving was taught by Giovanni Battista Troccoli (1882–1940), a Murphy apprentice. Lovell Birge Harrison (1854–1929), a Canadian artist, was brought in to teach painting with Murphy in 1904. Among the new crop of artists were Vivian Bevans (1881–1947), who married Hervey White that winter, and Bertha Thompson (1882–1974), a metalworker who rented a cottage at Byrdcliffe from 1908 until having her own house built in 1914. The most important photographer at Byrdcliffe was Eva Watson-Schütze (1867–1935), a founder with Alfred Stieglitz (1864–1946) of the Photo-Secession.

The colony drew the attention of the wider cultural world. A 1909 article in *American Homes and Gardens* by Poultney Bigelow was well placed and particularly notable because of the remarkable photographs by Jessie Tarbox Beals (1870–1942) that accompanied it. Bigelow frequently came up from Malden-on-Hudson—he and Jane Whitehead apparently knew each other in England, before she married. John Dewey (1859–1952) and John Burroughs (with his companion Clara Barrus) were summer visitors.

"The large solid library was a surprise to me," Burroughs wrote. "Few colleges have as good. " Dewey and his children constructed a playhouse at Carniola (Brown's farmhouse) in 1906. Clarence Darrow (1857–1938) and Thorstein Veblen (1857–1929) came to see their friends from the Chicago days.

Furniture produced at Byrdcliffe soon became its principal product, although the industry was short-lived. The adventure got off to a good start but faltered after the first year, partly due to Jane Whitehead's pre-Raphaelite attitudes and practices. The hillside became a refuge for her from all things modern, including "mechanical forms of progress" like the new automobile. In an arrangement of patron and underlings described as "benevolent despotism," the rules were virtually medieval and the artists much too restless to put up with her peccadilloes. Students and instructors were expected to participate in Morris dances and other fancies of Jane's imagination every evening, as if they were what White called "toys for rich people" who preferred to "dally" on "poetic and sensitive" clouds. To compound the problem, the beautiful furniture was too expensive to produce for a common market.

The community changed when a faction broke with Whitehead over the rules and regimentation at the colony. The school was virtually "given up" by the winter of 1905, when furniture making also ended. Harrison's influence continued in the landscape style of painting that developed when he brought in the Art Students League in 1906 for summer programs after an initial attempt at an ASL summer school failed in Lyme, Connecticut; by 1914, 137 students were enrolled. Harrison had his students painting in the outdoor light of the *plein air* style practiced by French impressionists, and conducted criticisms on Saturday mornings. The availability of cheap accommodations, the forty-cent stage ride from the West Hurley train station, and the general buzz about this special new place for artists fueled an interest in the colony.

One of those who came that first year was Marion Rorty Bullard (1878–1950), who was smitten by art in her youth at the Wallkill Academy in Middletown, where she was born. She settled in Woodstock permanently and, by 1911, was part of a "Rock City group" of artists who included Henry Lee McFee (1886–1953), Eugene Speicher (1883–1962), and John Fabian Carlson (1874–1945), among others. McFee and Speicher were also early League students, and Carlson came as the principal instructor in 1915. Carlson later described Rock City's as the "highbrow group":

> [A]ll seated on the famous stone wall [at the Rock City four corners], or around the cummunity pump, busily talking shop, singing and playing the harmonica. Gayety [sic] was a habit with these, and most of them owed their creature-comforts and happiness to the ministering angel embodied in a dear old soul, the famous Mrs. [Rosie] Magee, [who] stood ready to serve the youngsters with shelter, food, and sympathy.

Bullard's first impression of these impressionable artists—from "high up in the horse-drawn stage coach" while she waited for the driver to have a haircut at the general store—was startling. Three men came from the store with their new haircuts, one in plaid, one in polka dots, and one "a face— eyes, nose and mouth done in black hair!"

The League students, and many of them stayed on through the winters, all became enchanted with what Helen Shotwell called "the dark power of the Catskills." Bullard "broke away" from the early style, Shotwell reported, "and painted directly, out of her own deep feeling for the world around her." She became a popular children's books writer and illustrator, her stories often set in the neighborhoods around her.

The ASL was not the only school in town. Established artists took in students, and some came north and established formal training programs. Winold Reiss (1886–1953), an ASL lecturer and German immigrant, established a well-regarded school in Greenwich Village in 1915 and moved it to Woodstock over 1916–17. He drew Wilna Hervey, 21, to the colony, who drove up with her roommate Molly Pollock and a mattress tied to the roof of her Dort in 1918. Wilna only stayed for the summer, however, for within a year she was cast as "the original Katrinka" in a highly popular series of films of Fontaine Fox's Toonerville Trolley cartoons. She returned on several occasions and purchased land in Bearsville—with "a $300 shack" for a studio, as Dan Mason put it—but did not settle for a number of years as her film career expanded to California and a new series with Mason. By June 1923, Wilna was in Bearsville part-time with her companion, Dan's daughter Nan Mason (d. 1982), who also became an artist. Four years later, they had accumulated 47 acres and a 200-year-old farmhouse on Cooper Lake Road called Treasure Farm.

Wilna was an exceedingly large woman, the perfect choice for "powerful" Katrinka, who once yanked her stonemason, Walter Shultis, by his overalls from a ditch for having stolen her stash of applejack and replacing it with tea. The girls became locally famous as subjects of filmmaker Gustave Schrader, who came to shoot their bucolic farm and was treated to a show that included Wilna milking a cow directly into a cat's mouth, Nan's display of tricks with their collie, and a horse that "rolled on the ground like a dog," as Joseph P. Eckhardt described it. The film was shown throughout the area in 1928. That June, the Big Girls, as they were now called, hosted a housewarming party that soon turned into evenings of raucous entertainment that served as more localized versions of the Maverick Festivals once that tradition was abandoned. Their friends and "mentors" included Wilna's old friends (since 1918) Eugene and Elsie Speicher and Charles and Jean Rosen; Speicher (and Henry Lee McFee) encouraged Wilna's naïve art style, "for which she became famous," and Rosen influenced Nan's early art. Nan also studied under George Bellows in Woodstock.

The influx of young artists began the transformation of Woodstock's visual sense of place as a home to the modern art movement, although Whitehead's influence remained important throughout his life. Artists at Byrdcliffe continued to make jewelry, pottery, baskets, rugs, music and art, holding annual exhibitions every August. Whitehead made pottery and exhibited around the country through most of the 1920s, he and Jane maintaining well on their Byrdcliffe perch, serenely aloof from the crazy bunch cavorting below. They lost their son, Ralph, Jr., in a sea disaster in 1928, and the dispirited father died in the following year. Jane Whitehead continued to make writing, theater, crafts and painting important at Byrdcliffe, their son Peter assuming the management on her death in 1955. He subsequently donated the estate to the Woodstock Byrdcliffe Guild, which transformed it into a thriving art and historic heritage venue.

The town's reputation in the early decades attracted intellectuals from fields other than art. Wallace Stevens (1879–1955) visited in 1915 and 1917. Walter Weyl (1874–1921?) and his wife Bertha—she was a Hull House alumnae —took a house on Ohayo Mountain. Weyl was author of a seminal progressive tract, *The New Democracy* (1912), and editor of *The New Republic* from 1913 to 1919. English poet Richard le Gallienne (1866–1947) lived on Plochmann Lane before buying Harrison's old house near Byrdcliffe. Hart Crane (1899–1932) came for two months in 1923, staying at the original George Plochmann home as a guest of Slater Brown (1896–1997) and Edward Nagle (1893–1963). Crane was driven over from Eugene O'Neill's Connecticut home by Oona O'Neill; he wrote detailed accounts about his own experience and the ordinary lives of the artists of Woodstock. Thanksgiving that year included drop-in guests writer John Dos Passos (1896–1970) and sculptor Gaston Lechaise (1882–1935).

Anita M. Smith (1892–1968) became the quintessential Woodstock bohemian after arriving in 1912. Wealthy, as Jane Whitehead had been, she rebelled from her Philadelphia family and used money intended for a ball gown to come to the colony. She was an impressionist who studied under John Carlson and exhibited at the Maverick as well as the National Academy of Design, the Art Institute of Chicago and the Pennsylvania Academy of Fine Arts. A noted herbalist and folklorist, Smith "chronicled the bohemian life" in *Woodstock: History and Hearsay* (1959). Stonecrop, the house that she had built at the base of Overlook Mountain in 1934, became an observation post during World War II.

Hervey White drew Hull House friends and admirers of his early novels to Woodstock. A true modernist, White wanted only to write "the dithyramb of noise and of speed." He considered painting and sculpture to be dead arts because they were not practiced by common artisans. His fatal flaw was his belief that he should not profit from his writing and painting because that would give him "advantage over others." His beauty was the spirit and talent he would bring to his creation, the radical new arts community at the Maverick.

In 1904, after White became disenchanted with Byrdcliffe and spent some time in New York, he and van der Loo bought a 102-acre farm on the other side of Woodstock hamlet in a lowlands near Zena that he called the Maverick. The Maverick was in many ways the antithesis of Byrdcliffe, an "entirely unpretentious" colony in tune with the free spirit of the times. If Whitehead was the Ruskin of America, White had in common with Arts and Crafts founder William Morris an interest in printing and the writing of epic poetry. After his marriage ended in 1909, White built summer cabins and invited talented friends to come and live in them; the first was a cellist named Paul Kefer. Hervey printed seven of his books while at the Maverick, as well as two magazines or journals, *The Wild Hawk* (1911–16) and *The Ploughshare* (1916–20); *The Hue and Cry* was another Maverick publication, surviving from 1923 to 1926. In 1936, when White was 72, James Cooney took over his press operations and produced *The Phoenix* (1938–40), another interesting literary magazine, in which Henry Miller served as European editor; the experiment lasted two years.

White built five more cottages on the property, and in 1915 sponsored a festival at the Maverick to raise funds for a well. This "annual gala" was repeated every year thereafter until 1931, drawing the attention of the New York newspapers for its gaiety and irreverence. The festival was held on the full moon in August, climaxing with a production of "Scheherazade" and followed a month later by a pig roast for the artists. After the honored guest was eaten, the artists gathered in the concert hall to reenact the festival in comic imitation.

A battle that the *New York Times* saw as one between a bohemian art colony and the respectable community of businessmen and conventional churchgoers arose over festival excesses and the people who came to watch the "crazy artists" during those days. Six-to-eight thousand appeared one year. In 1929, a broadside issued by a new "Committee of Fifty" complained of the festivals and called for their end. The fifty were actually only four staid residents, two of them ministers, yet the times were changing for Hervey White and his unorthodox method of raising money to pay for the colony he built. The Festival lasted another year and then folded, and with it any further expansion of the Maverick.

White initiated chamber recitals in 1916, built a music hall, and started a restaurant—called the Intelligentcia—that lasted a few years. The cook was Hippolyte Havel (1871–1950), a Greenwich Village bohemian who called the nabobs who came slumming "capitalist pigs" while serving them; Arnold and Lucille Blanch managed the place. White's casual approach allowed him to borrow money and supplies and construct small homes for cheap rentals to those who came.

"The Maverick is a dream valley," Hughes Mearns (1875–1965) wrote in 1927. "Houses are built while you wait."

The colony grew into a little art village, White adding the Maverick Theater in 1924. Dudley Digges ran the theater. Helen Hayes and Edward G. Robinson (1893–1973) performed at the opening on July 4, 1924, in Lady Gregory's *The Dragon*, to great acclaim. Woodstock became a special place for theater people as well as artists, writers and musicians. Ben Webster started the Phoenix Players at Byrdcliffe that year. The Woodstock Playhouse was built in dramatic style near the entrance to the hamlet in 1938 by Robert Elwyn, who also served as producer and director. A "battle of the theaters" ensued with the Maverick for a few years. The Playhouse's popularity extended into the late 1960s; one of almost the same design was later built on the site in 2001.

The Maverick's "one monument" was a huge carved horse sculpture made with an axe from a single tree by John B. Flannagan (1895–1942). "Everyone on the Maverick was watching," sculptor Hannah Small (1903–92) recalled:

> They were fascinated. We loved everything that Flannagan did and we were terribly excited about it. I remember seeing him working; he was working frantically and he was doing the whole thing with an ax. It was the fastest work I'd ever seen. When it was finished he went off and had another drink.

Hervey paid Flannagan his standard 50 cents per hour for the job. John Bub of Saugerties, 19 at the time (and working at the same rate as Flannagan), was on the crew that installed the 18-foot tall horse at the entrance road to the Maverick, where it remained for thirty-six years before being placed in storage by Emmett Edwards. In 1979, the sculpture was moved to the

Maverick Concert Hall and mounted on a stone base by sculptor Maury Colow.

The first of the Maverick musicians were Paul Kefer, Pierre Henrotte, and Horace Britt (1881–1971); Isabelle Byman (1907?–82) and Inez Carroll also became regular performers. Henrotte, concertmaster at the Metropolitan Opera House, did a violin recital at the first concert in 1914, held in the Fireman's Hall in Woodstock; he organized the programs until 1926.

"From the very beginning, music at the Maverick was a unique effort of professionals and amateurs," wrote Leon Barzin (1900–99). "I mean amateurs in the finest sense of the word: lovers of the art." White delighted in talking with outside reporters about his "high finance" way of making his "music chapel" successful—he bartered with the local sawmill operator and storekeepers for goods and materials, promising to pay everyone back in time.

The Maverick Concert Hall is the oldest continuous summer chamber music festival venue in America, and has made music history in the process. Writing in 2013, Leon Botstein described the 1913 Armory Show as "the beginning of a century-long rise to dominance of the visual arts in American culture," a transformation that had no comparable movement in music. The "Armory Show moment" in music, he wrote, came in the 1920s, notably with the rise of jazz. The Maverick has been the exception that proves the rule, remaining fresh and vibrant while drawing upon a modern classicism throughout its history.

One of the most notable (or notorious) events in modern music history happened one rainy August evening in 1952, when pianist David Tudor (1926–96) walked onstage, sat at the piano before a large audience, and did nothing for four minutes and thirty-three seconds except to open and close the keyboard cover three times as a way to mark the movements of the "music." The sound of the rain, the rustling of the trees, and the people getting up to leave in disgust became the music of the evening. This was the world premiere of "4'33"," called "the silent piece," the most famous work of composer John Cage (1912–92).

"Cage was always better received among artist than among all but the most radical experimental musicians," Kay Larson wrote in *The New York Times* in 2001. Botstein wrote of Cage's influence on the arts and "the realm of ideas" through his writings, more so than any other composer "since Richard Wagner." Fittingly, Cage's archives and materials remain in trust at Botstein's Bard College, placed there by his friend and executor, Merce Cunningham.

Cage and Tudor had come to Woodstock at the call of a friend and fellow experimental composer, Henry Cowell (1897–1965), a music anthropologist who had a radio program ("Music of the World's People") on WBAI in New York during that decade. Cage called Cowell "the open sesame for new music in America"; fittingly because of Leopold Stowkowski's early interest in bringing his music to the general public, Cowell was celebrated by the American Symphony Orchestra at Avery Fisher Hall at Lincoln Center on January 29, 2010. Cowell composed his "Hymns and Fuguing Tunes" at his Shady home, on the other side of a small hill where Sonia Malkine's strains of European folk songs rose over the valley. In the same neighborhood were Louise (1907–92) and Brock Brockenshaw (1912–2004), potter and painter respectively, whose studios were in the original glass company store. Brock, as he was universally known, became famous for his hospitality to strangers, his wine parties, his nudes and portraiture, and in later life his magnificent still lifes of flowers. Alf Evers came to live a mile up the road in later years and took Cage hunting for mushrooms in the vicinity during one of his visits.

These were the decades after the first wave of artists and craftspeople had come and gone at Woodstock. Harrison died in 1929, eulogized by Bigelow as the virtual founder of the colony—or at least (according to Evers) its transition from sedate Byrdcliffe to "the lusty, uninhibited art colony of Woodstock." Harrison's style fell into conflict with the new art of the 1920s, which Harrison tolerated (and applauded), but which his successor as old guard landscape painter, John Carlson, detested as "ultra-modern." Carlson, the first scholarship student at Byrdcliffe years ago, "stalked out" of the Woodstock Artists Association meeting in 1921, done with that bunch. The WAA soon had a hundred members, others of the old guard as well as new artists, although Bolton Brown, the colony's best lithographer, was not a member. The first WAA show in November 1923 involved many of the younger artists, and when taken up by the New Gallery in New York they became known as the "Woodstock School." The landscapes—some influenced by cubism, some by Cezanne—were often drawn from the industrial and riverfront settings of the workingman.

Raymond Steiner credited Konrad Cramer with bringing cubism to the colony. Cramer (1888–1963) was an early associate of Alfred Stieglitz and Herman Moore (d. 1968) and an advocate of modernism who studied at the Woodstock School of Painting and Allied Arts after working in Germany under a Rockefeller grant in 1920. Although he turned to textiles and representational styles in later life, Cramer showed at the Whitney Museum's breakthrough "Abstract Painting in America" exhibition in 1935. His wife, Florence Ballin Cramer (1884–1962), who met her husband while an art student in Munich, was a noted Woodstock landscape and still life artist. Both were represented in the first and second Whitney Biennials in 1933 and 1935. Konrad administered the Federal Arts Project for the Woodstock region with Judson Smith, and turned to photography in 1935. Cramer taught photography at Bard College in the 1940s.

The Whitney Museum took more than a passing interest in the Woodstock scene in these years. Moore, the second director, summered at the colony. He was assistant director under Juliana Force (1876–1948), the close friend and buyer for Gertrude Vanderbilt Whitney from the late 1910s. Juliana started buying Woodstock art for the new museum in 1929, her annual arrival in time proclaimed by the first artist she visited ("Mrs. Force is immanent!" the cry went forth), which invited artists to bring out their best works for her review. Eugene Ludins (1904–96), who lived permanently in Woodstock from 1929 on, was an artist of special interest to Force; on one occasion, in a hurry so as not to miss her train, Juliana climbed into the window of his studio and took a landscape painting, leaving a $250 check for the artist. Force also bought Lucille Branch's *August Landscape* (1932) for the first Whitney Biennial, and George Bellows' most famous painting, *Dempsey vs. Firpo* (1923), from his widow Emma for $200,000.

Henry Gottlieb, who arrived in 1921, was the first artist to live year-round at the Maverick. Others included Carl Walters (1883–1955) and painters Arnold (1896–1968) and Lucille Blanch (1895–1981) and Austin Mecklem (1894–1951). Mecklem, one of the artists in the Whitney Museum's first Biennial Exhibition in 1932, taught at the Woodstock School of Painting in the mid-1930s and married one of his students, Marianne Appel (1913–88), who had begun painting while at Sarah Lawrence College. She arrived in Woodstock in true artiste style, accompanied by her mother in a chauffeur-driven car. Appel found residence on Chestnut Hill Road, where she enjoyed standing on the roof of her cottage target-shooting with her .22 pistol, a beautiful weapon with a polished reddish wood handle. She painted in oils and gouaches and worked as a muralist along with her husband in the Federal Arts Project. Appel won the Woodstock War Memorial competition for the Village

Green that Wilna Hervey spearheaded, and in later years she turned to commercial art and puppet-making with Bill Baird and Jim Henson.

Mecklem and Appel, both accomplished swimmers, were among those who popularized Big Deep, a swimming hole and iconic Woodstock setting a quarter-mile east of the hamlet off the Saugerties road. Appel was also "an indomitable rope jumper," Polly Kline wrote.

During these years a "battle of the hotels" emerged involving the Overlook Mountain House, the Colony on Rock City Road, Twaddell House on the Village Green (transformed into the Old Woodstock Inn by Stephen B. Ayres), and the Woodstock Valley Inn, which burned in 1930. Whitehead had an interest in the Valley Inn, which, like Ayres' new place, catered to "conservative" values in the community. The Colony was dressed in a pretentious Spanish style that many of the art colony folks considered inappropriate for Woodstock. Overlook was being rebuilt along grand mountain-house lines by Morris Newgold and survived partly because of Newgold's business sense. He leased the hotel in 1918 to a membership organization called the Unity Club that was an offshoot of the International Ladies Garment Workers Union, bringing hundreds of young women "swarming" into Woodstock. The locals called them "the bloomer girls" for their characteristic dark bloomers and white blouses, but distrusted them because most of them were Jewish. A few miles down the Saugerties road, a colony called Shagbark, for Christians only, was organized for its proximity to the Woodstock setting.

An interesting pattern seemed to develop of artists who only remained for a short time yet left a significant presence on Woodstock. Robert Henri (Robert Henry Cozad, 1865–1929, "pronounced Hen-rye, like buck-eye, and he never let you forget it," according to Van Wyck Brooks via Russell Lynes), a distinguished modernist artist and teacher, was here for the 1923 season. He was the leader of the Ash Can School of painting and had sparked The Eight in their 1907 spontaneous objection to the staid National Academy of Design. Henri established the Society of Independent Artists, which drew Woodstock-related artists like Louise Kamp (1867–1959) and Milton Avery (1885–1965) among exhibitors in the 1930s.

Eugene Speicher, an Ash Can painter and student of Henri's whose reputation grew in later years, had been visiting Woodstock since 1909, settled in the 1920s, and remained until his death in 1962. Henri and Speicher's presence drew George Bellows (1882–1925), "the most prosperous" National

Academy artist in his time. Bellows became very active in the community, serving on the WAA board and enjoying his Sundays as first base coach at the Rec Field.

Yasuo Kuniyoshi (1893–1953), who came in the 1920s, was one of the colony's finest painters and an inspiration to generations of young artists. Sculptors included Italian immigrant Alfeo Faggi (c. 1885–1936) and Alexander Archipenko (1887–1964). Craftspeople included potters and ceramicists Zulma Steele (1881–1979) and Carl Walters, weaver Marg Little, furniture makers Iris Wolven and Arthur Stone, and metalworker Edmund Rolfe. Steele became a lifelong resident of Woodstock. Hughes Mearns was a trailblazer in exploring the creative outlets of children in his books, *Creative Youth* (1925) and *Creative Power* (1929). Matthew Josephson (1899–1978), while working on *The Robber Barons* (1934), came to Woodstock's art colony in the summer of 1932, feeling as if "a great blight" was on the place because of the Depression; Arnold Blanch denounced the nation's art as having fallen into decay during those years. WAA members also included prominent illustrators like Cushman Parker and Ivan Summers (1889–1964). Summers came in 1919, taught at the Art Students League, and was known for books of medical illustrations as well as his *plein air* landscapes, several done in Saugerties and Rondout.

Robert Chanler, the Astor orphan featured in the Armory Show in 1913, was called "a raucous Matisse" in his early years in Woodstock and was best known for his parties. Chanler was admired in modern art circles for his screens and murals. When in his fifties, he made a summer studio from a mill he bought in town. He had a heart attack in the summer of 1929, tried recuperating in Bermuda and New York, and returned to Woodstock the following summer with a valet and nurse. The oppressive heat led him to have his bed moved into the garden, where he could hear the gaiety of the art colony across the way. He was hospitalized in Kingston again, where he died on October 24, 1930. Sheriff Bob was fifty-eight years old.

Charles Rosen (1878–1950), an Art Students League instructor and one of the New Hope Impressionists when he moved to Woodstock in 1920, was in the first WAA show. He produced remarkable industrial paintings like *The Roundhouse, Kingston, New York* (1927). Rosen, who developed a lifelong friendship with Wilna Hervey and Nan Mason, was one of the more colorful players in the Maverick festivals over the years. Rosen, Cubist Henry Lee

McFee, and Andrew Dasberg founded the Woodstock School of Painting in 1922. Austin Mecklem also depicted the Kingston roundhouse, and did paintings about the cement industry on the Hudson. Both were among numerous WPA artists from Woodstock—Rosen's murals are featured in the Poughkeepsie Post Office and elsewhere, and Mecklem's in Connecticut and Alaska public buildings.

Anton Refregier (1905–79), a Russian émigré muralist, printmaker, sculptor and painter, came upriver to study under Archipenko. After six years at the Mount Airy art colony at Croton, Refregier found work in the WPA in 1936. For the standard salary of $23.86 a week, he created murals in public spaces that he identified with the revolutionary socialist spirits of his European roots. His most important work, the twenty-seven-panel *History of San Francisco* for the Rincon Post Office, was the largest WPA mural in the nation. The award was controversial in Woodstock, where Refregier's only real competition arose.

Harvey Fite (1903–76) built a cottage at the Maverick in 1930, and a few years later purchased an abandoned quarry in High Woods, a hamlet about five miles away where his monumental bluestone sculpture, Opus 40, would rise. Among his first visits in the neighborhood was one to Henry Wilgus's store, where Fite inquired about old stone workers who might still be around. Wilgus directed him to a neighbor on the corner of Fite's road, Lewis Snyder (c. 1894–1943), with whom Fite struck up a friendship. Snyder, who died of lung disease caused by the stone dust, gave Fite his tools, including picks, feathers, drills and all, some of which remained at the museum that Fite's stepson, Tad Richards, maintained at Opus 40 well into the next century.

Fite scavenged some chicken wire from the Cramers and built his first studio at the quarry. He fit well into the neighborhood, taught sculpture at Bard College, and took under wing a young Baltimore artist, Jean Lasher, who in time married a local neighbor, Berthel Wrolsen and settled into a nearby High Woods home. Jean and Henry Wilgus went fishing in the Ashokan every Thursday for years. Wrolsen assisted Fite in his bluestone work, and discovered and supervised the extraction of the Opus 40 signature monolithic stele from the Sawkill Creek years later.

Like Tomas Penning, Fite had been carving the notoriously difficult bluestone into figurative forms, and realized after several years of creating settings for his individual works that the setting itself was the subject. "He made the pedestal the sculpture," Walter Randel, a former student of his at Bard College, said in 2011. "The monolith [at Opus 40] represents man in an abstract sense. This was not like the earth works of today."

Randel characterized Fite's masterwork as "democratic" in the sense that the visitor "was a participant" who experienced the sculpture by walking on it. Fite's transformation was in the John Flannagan tradition of spontaneity in art and abstract expressionism. The legitimacy of the non-figurative as an art theme was affirmed in much of the Woodstock art in these years.

In 1939, part of a 38-acre parcel of land donated by the Kingston Water Department a mile east of the hamlet was transformed by the National Youth Administration into a complex of attractive artisan workshops, including a foundry, weaving center, and textile, carpentry and wool shops, known as the Woodstock Resident Work Center. The NYA was a youth agency of the Works Projects Administration created in 1935 to employ artists and crafts persons under the New Deal. The new center was inspired in part by Eleanor Roosevelt's Val-Kill Industries themes of artisans working at practical tasks, and was meant to employ youths in meaningful work instead of riding the railroad boxcars as fledgling hoboes or otherwise leading lives without promise or hope. The students themselves did the construction using stone from local quarries, the only instance of such work in NYA history. Franklin Roosevelt's preference for the medium and its prevalence in Woodstock-area construction informed the use of local bluestone. The Clark Neher Building Company (later called Woodstock Building Supply) constructed the dramatic arched window over the stone foundry building. The overall design of the camp may have been done by Edmund Cloonan, a local resident and WPA engineer who had worked for the Kingston Water Department, although Alber Graessner (the woodworking shop), Tomas Penning (the forge/stone shop), and Eugene Caille (the textile shop) were credited with various aspects of the design. Cloonan was likely influenced by the department's Sawkill Road treatment plant a few miles away, the construction of which in 1897 created a small and beautiful lake below a Devonian ridge.

The first Resident Work Center director was Richard S. Wallach, who presented Mrs. Roosevelt with a trowel made by the students for the cornerstone laying in 1939. The Center accepted students between the ages of 18 and 24, as many as ninety working here over the years. Products included fireplace utensils, tables, benches, domestic items, and blankets; they also learned husbandry and domestic and household practices. Female students were admitted for wool-processing and weaving, and lived in rented quarters on Baumgarten Road a mile away; the men at first stayed at a boarding house in Lake Hill and then in adjoining boarding houses on Hillcrest Avenue in Woodstock. Instructors included sculptor Tomas Penning, woodworkers William Green and Earnest Brace, master blacksmith and ironworker Eliot Fatum of nearby Veteran, and Norman Tower Boggs, who served as director of education and arranged programs for the students.

Tomas Penning (1905–82), a bluestone sculptor from High Woods, supervised the work and became instructor in stone carving and masonry. At times he used his home studio in High Woods to teach bluestone sculpture to his students. Penning came up from New York in 1933 to train with Archipenko, who lived nearby. Like another High Woods denizen, Harvey Fite, Penning was inspired by Mayan art in his stone sculpture. He often worked on commission in religious themes, resulting in Liturgical Art Society works in Verplanck, Chautauqua, Esopus, and Saugerties. His signature works at the center include the flagpole base and a thin bluestone sundial donated to the Woodstock School of Art by Petra Cabot and installed by Angela Gaffney Smith in 2011. The base contained carved relief scenes depicting the activities at the camp, triptychs on metal working, agriculture, carpentry, pottery, and spinning and weaving.

Elizabeth Penning was a Palmolive heiress and friend of Eleanor's. She and Tom entertained the President and the First Lady in their home and attended Roosevelt affairs at Hyde Park. Tom and Eleanor danced together on occasion, to FDR's delight. Eleanor and her friend Eleanor Morganthau visited the center several times, and Eleanor mentioned the Woodstock school in "My Day" columns in 1939–40. She hosted several students at her home a month after an August 1940 visit (and had "the boys" for picnics and swimming from time to time), and arranged a meeting with her Val-Kill weaver (and former housekeeper), Nelly Johannsen, over problems they were having with the wool they were producing. The weavers produced 800 yards of cloth a year.

Penning brought the students into town for projects like the carving of a headstone on Hervey White's grave and the construction of a chimney and fireplace in Willow (at the future home of the James Cox Gallery). They also worked in Kingston, driven down in a flatbed truck, where an adjunct center was created that hosted a school and also produced furniture. Kingston provided for movies and roller skating on Saturday nights at times, and young Kingston and Woodstock women were invited to the Resident Work Center on Friday nights for round and square dances and on Monday night for dance classes. The center continued until 1942, when three-quarters of the students enlisted in the war on one day. Three years later, the Kingston Water Department offered to release the federal government from its lease, provided the buildings and structures were demolished, but no action was taken.

The evolution of the Woodstock art colony had come full circle, from the arrival of the Art Students League and Radcliffe's utopian colony to the institutionalizing of a particular focus on art that drew as much from the free-spirited Maverick ways as the hallowed traditions of Ruskin and Morris. The gaiety and charm of the community was infused with a serious sense of purpose in the making of fine art, a characteristic that carried over into the music and art scenes of the second half of the century.

24. Hallelujahs All Around

> I am here and I am there and I am everywhere. I am like the radio voice. Dial in and you shall always find me.
> —GEORGE BAKER (Father Divine)

Charles and Georgianna Lewis of Albany had reason to celebrate how their children did in life. Walter Elijah Lewis (1875–1926) was a bandleader and tightrope walker in a vaudeville act. Percival Bowie Lewis (b. 1877), the most favored, was a founding member of the Young Men's Colored Republican Club who later became a Roosevelt Democrat. Virginia May Lewis (b. 1881) and her family were the first African Americans in a new suburban part of Delmar. Their boys scored the highest marks on the Regents exam in the school, and Virginia became statistical supervisor in the state Department of Motor Vehicles. Georgine Sheldon Lewis (1887–1970), the fifth child, became assistant professor of English at the Washington, DC Teachers College. Henrietta Bowie Lewis (b. 1891) was the first African American permanently appointed school teacher in Albany and, because of "a good fight I had put up," the first permanently appointed civil service worker—white or black—in the city. She later became Senior Social Worker in the state Department of Social Work. Her husband, Charles Howard ("Carl") Van Vranken, was one of the first three black state appointees under civil service and a founder and first treasurer of the Albany Interracial Council. All the children of Charles and Georgiana Lewis followed in their father's footsteps, in a sense. Charles F. Lewis (b. 1852) was the first African-American mailman in Albany, but he left after nine months because the pay was so low. He assisted Albany lobbyist William H. Johnson in convincing the state legislature to enact "Janitor Johnson's Law" in 1873, which prohibited insurance companies from charging blacks more for policies than whites.

The record of African-American achievements was not limited to Albany or a few families. Mrs. Mary Harden and her daughter Bessie Harden Payne (1895–1991) started the Poughkeepsie Neighborhood Club in 1913, Mary serving as president until her death in 1948. The club's purpose was to uplift women and provide civic work. They brought many good speakers to the city, and sponsored the first Lincoln-Douglas dinner in 1917. The club became part of Mary McLeod Bethune's United Federation of Negro Women in later years.

Sarah Breedlove (1867–1919) arrived in Dobbs Ferry in 1917. Widowed in 1887 by a lynch mob in Mississippi that mistook her husband for another black man, she remarried and divorced because her second husband could not keep pace with her ambitions, which involved inventing new and revolutionary hair care products for black women. Sarah remade her image in her second husband's name (as Madame C. J. Walker), developed a hair lotion that made her famous, and became the first black millionaire in America. Sarah trained a battalion of 3,000 "beauty culturists" who took her products door-to-door and made Madame Walker's a familiar name, throughout South America and the Caribbean as well as in America. She also broke ground in defeating prejudice by using her money to force theaters to stop charging black folks more than white folks to see the new technology: moving pictures.

At Irvington-on-Hudson a next-door neighbor walked two pet elephants up his driveway, but nothing in showmanship compared with the arrival of Madame Walker. She brought in Vertner Tandy (1885–1949), the first black architect in New York, to design and build a classy white stucco mansion she called Villa Lewaro. The interior French ballroom rivaled those of Versailles. Above the marble staircase off the main hall was an oil painting depicting the heavens. Austrian chandeliers, arched stained-glass windows, and an expensive Estey Organ Company pipe organ were other touches in the house. The grounds included a marble reflecting pool with water lilies and exotic fish, a lion's head fountain, statues of nymphs and marble urns, and a stucco carriage house with Walker's collection of expensive cars. Sarah was a gracious hostess who became well known in the community for her philanthropies. She died, at age fifty-one, of hypertension developed during a lifelong habit of overwork. The auction of her estate drew thousands of the curious and those looking for bargains in gilt, red velvet, and fine wares. The property was sold to two sisters, also millionaires, who established a home for elderly women called Companions of the Forest.

Yonkers had all the signs of a progressive community in the progress African Americans had made. By 1905, when blacks paid taxes on a quarter of a million dollars in real estate, the leading businessman was F. J. Moultrie, whose property was assessed at $100,000. A. A. Thornton was a successful black undertaker, and the Thomas S. Lane Company was a black-owned tailoring business since the 1880s. The city also boasted three barber shops, several grocery stores, taxi and express concerns, a black-owned unemployment agency, and a caterer. Yonkers also had a chapter called the Invincible Order of Colored Co-Operators of America (IOCCOA), a self-help community group that bought land for investment, built and sold homes and businesses, provided education for resourceful students, and helped factories get started. Yet when John E. Bruce rented a home in Yonkers in 1905, he learned how the subtle evil of "the microbe of prejudice" worked in the suburban cities. Bruce was publisher of the New York *Chronicle* and one of the most important African American Republicans in the state. He moved into the house in June but had to leave by July when the house went up for sale. By October, not having been sold because whites did not want to live in an emerging black neighborhood, the house was rented to Bruce again, but at a higher rate.

African Americans nationwide were flush with excitement in the first decades of freedom after the Civil War, yet equal status quickly proved illusionary, nor was it improved appreciably with Booker T. Washington as their only representative leader nationally. Many found inspiration and hope in W. E. B. DuBois's "Credo," a Nicene Creed for blacks first published in 1904 that hung on the walls of many Negro homes in the early twentieth century. The formation of the National Association for the Advancement of Colored

People and the Amenia Conference of 1916 helped to refocus black aspirations and establish a militancy needed to assert rights and identity.

That identity was strengthened in peculiar ways in the years that followed. George Baker (1880?–1965), a Georgian preacher in Sayville, Long Island, went by the title Father Divine after becoming an overnight sensation when a judge who had sentenced him to prison died three days after the sentence was overturned. Divine said he regretted having to make an example of the man. His mission was a magnet for many in need of spiritual support, white believers as well as black. The diminutive evangelist (standing just 5'4") established fifteen "kingdoms" in New York City, and then moved upstate, creating more than twenty small farms run by his faithful (usually reformed female drunks or addicts), which he called "heavens." Some of the believers remained in these heavens for decades after Divine's death, continuing to make small products like jams and jellies and selling them from roadside stands. At Hope Farm in Saxton, ten-cent meals and low-priced gasoline were served by Divine's followers. An immaculate 1937 Cord automobile (only brought out for his visits) remained in storage in a rundown barn until it was sold with the property long after his death. Families who came upriver to be near friends or family members in the heavens often remained and settled as farmers, business people, postal employees, and other industry and agriculture workers and professionals.

Father Divine created a Cooperative Plan to finance purchases and improvements, never holding a mortgage on any of his properties. He owned five properties in New Paltz, including a heaven a mile west of the village on Route 299. Father Divine's followers in the New Paltz area went by the names Sweet Pea, Sarah Love, Reliable Willie, and Handyman Amos. They were often known in the community as honest and trustworthy folk. A Lloyd heaven was kept at North Eltings Corners Road, and a successful farm was also managed in High Falls. The Krum Elbow heaven, which he obtained from Roosevelt hate-monger Howland Spencer, was especially popular for the "20 cent chicken dinners" dispensed to "bus loads of people" who "came from the surrounding area." When he visited each "kingdom" or "heaven," Divine always served "his flock" individually in massive dinners "in the grand style of a maître d'hôtel." Local realtor Elting Harp, who came to Krum Elbow with his daughter Delia and her husband David Shaw to advise Divine on his various holdings in the town, was struck by the numbers he found enjoying dinner at the farm.

Individual instances of success and even accommodation between whites and blacks did not represent the picture as a whole. African Americans remained underemployed, unconsidered in culture or community ameliora- tion, and badly treated as a rule in the Hudson Valley. Even among enlightened thinkers, often the best that could be managed was a condescending attitude, and few whites understood the damaging effects on society that vaudeville's depiction of black humor had on their thinking. "The Jazz Singer," Al Jolson's blackface film about a white singer who overcomes his father's admonishments to become a music hall performer, had its world premier in Schenectady in 1928.

Union College was a case in point when it came to educating African Americans. The first black graduate was William C. Scott in 1946, almost 150 years after the school's founding. Students in the 1920s and '30s enjoyed minstrel shows like Delta Upsilon's "Harlem Night," in which the invitation offered "cullud music, cullud entertainment, and above all folks, don' ferget a strictly STRICTLY cullud crowd's s'pected to attend." At least the college president himself, Dixon Ryan Fox, did not wear blackface, but he came. Fox's successor, Carter Davidson, while extending "a welcome hand" to "the so- called 'minority groups'" in response to the state's new Anti-Discrimination Act of 1948, displayed his own condescending attitude by disparaging the idea of "a college of minorities" in agreeing to abide by the law.

The suffrage movement, another cause for hallelujahs, developed some- what differently in New York because the state enacted a voting law for women two years before the constitutional amendment went into effect. Susan B. Anthony (1820–1906), whom William Henry Channing called "the Napoleon of the women's rights movement," spent much of her childhood in Battenville in Washington County; the home is now on the National Register of Historic Places. When her father's cotton mill fell under hard times and the family had to move to nearby Hardscrabble, Susan took up teaching to supplement the family income, and taught in New Rochelle for several years before moving to Canajoharie. She was shocked to find that women were paid less than men. She became radicalized in 1852 when denied an opportunity to speak at an Albany temperance rally and formed the Woman's New York State Temper- ance Society with Elizabeth Cady Stanton, her mentor in suffrage interests.

The cause was a frequent topic in community settings in the Hudson Valley, often involving formal speakers and, as elsewhere, was not popular among the men. An 1883 debate on suffrage sponsored by the Athena Society of Chappaqua drew a spirited discussion. At the Dutchess County Fair in September 1900, Governor Theodore Roosevelt told a crowd of 30,000 that women's rights "should be left to the men to think about and the woman should think of her duties." Some did, since emancipation was not of interest to many post-Victorian young ladies, frequenters of Mrs. Lowe's Far and Near Team Room in Tarrytown and similar sedate establishments for example. If the bright promise that ushered in the century for these polite, intelligent, often vivacious young women was tarnished by prohibitive attitudes, their accomplishments in the domestic setting, at least as far as they were concerned, eclipsed the times.

As the movement accelerated, Westchester had a number of quality organizations dedicated to women's issues—the Women's Christian Temperance Union and Women's Institute in Yonkers, the Woman's Civil League of Tarrytown, and Woman's Clubs in Mt. Vernon and Port Chester—the latter opening with 299 charter members in 1903. The county became one of five in the state with a public health department, on the encouragement of the county branch of the New York League of Women Voters in 1926. Mrs. Kenneth B. Norton of Bronxville, the founding president of the Westchester County Federation of Women's Clubs, became a director of the Westchester Lighting Company and trustee of Consolidated Edison Company in the 1930s. Caroline Goodwin O'Day (1869–1943), founder of Rye's LWV chapter, was a force in the state Democratic Party, served four terms as New York's first female representative in Congress (albeit never winning in Rye).

Inez Mulholland Boissevan (1886–1916), a Vassar graduate, was a natural leader of the suffrage cause in its penultimate stage because of her imposing presence (appearing as Lady Liberty in parades) and ability to address the issue. Unfortunately, she died of exhaustion while on a national speaking tour. Among her colleagues in these activities—and on one occasion before President Woodrow Wilson—was Josephine Baker (1873–1945) of Poughkeepsie, whose mother had been in the first Vassar class. Josephine became a doctor whose work resulted in a dramatic reduction in infant mortalities in New York City, from 676 to 111 per 1,000 births between 1909 and 1923. Like Amy Spingarn, she was good with the cutting phrase, noting during World War I that it was "six times safer to be a soldier in the trenches of France than to be born a baby in the United States." Josephine produced a highly regarded memoir of her experiences in public service.

Amy Spingarn led the suffragist movement in Dutchess County, serving as chair of the Women's Suffrage Association in the first assembly district. She maintained a notebook during the critical years 1915–17, assiduously recording responses to the objections to giving women the vote. Women were too emotional, the critics said, or would neglect the home by participating in politics; they would only duplicate what their husbands did. Since they could not bear arms, they did not deserve the right to vote, to which Spingarn responded: "Every time a soldier is born, a woman risks her life. And no man can do that."

The workplace, child labor, pure food, schools, sanitation were all subjects of intense interest to women like Spingarn. She corresponded and met frequently with political candidates and officeholders and joined, often as a leader, public demonstrations in support of the vote. At the Poughkeepsie Fair in 1917, her organization distributed slices of apple pie to the drafted men of the Home Defense League. Their work was validated with New York's passage of women's suffrage in 1917. In March of 1918, seventy-three women of Corn-wall—which had supported suffrage when it failed the first statewide canvas in 1915—were able to vote for the first time.

There were few hurrahs for the poor in the optimism of these years. The encroachment of the railroad on farmlands and other private properties affected those who remained near its lines after easements and other rights were attained. Cassie Calhoon was a poor, uneducated Pangyanger who lived in a shack on a hillside where the main West Shore Railroad line passed through the town of Lloyd. "Pangyangers," as the locals called them, were the town's poor folks, remnants of a band of families who had come across on the ferry in 1819 with Jemina Wilkinson (1752–1819), a Quaker and religious leader known as the "Publick Universal Friend." Communities like the Pangyangers existed in pockets around the Valley, usually in hollows, hidden vales, or tucked away in the hills, some dating to Native American days. In Rockland County, they were known as the Jackson Whites. In northern Dutchess County, a community of Native American survivors included youths whom the local state police watched for burglaries and other small crimes. "Eagle-Nesters" occupied a ridge overlooking the Esopus Valley in Ulster County. In the foothills of the Taconics in Columbia County, they were called Bushwhackers or Pondshiners, and may have been descendants of early down-renters. Originally treated as peculiar sociological units, many of these communities developed over the years and became respectable business and community resources.

Jemina was taking new converts at New Jerusalem, her community on Keuka Lake in western New York, but died on their arrival in Lloyd. Some families in the group continued on; some remained and settled the hills north of Marx Pond and behind Lily Lake Pond. They grew to include thirty families or more during the century, and included Betsy Ruger, "The Witch of Pang Yang," an herb doctor from Litchfield whose witchcraft was of "the old Connecticut variety." The local moniker derived from Penn Yan, Pennsylvania, another Wilkinson community.

As Clintondale farmer John Jacobs related the story to the Ulster County Historical Society in 1996, Cassie Calhoun's cow came through a hole in the railroad fence one day and was killed by a train. She went to the railroad office to be recompensed but was rudely refused. That day, she boiled off a pail's worth of lard from the dead animal, and with brush in hand painted the tracks up and down the hill behind her shack. The next train that came through was the "Million Dollar Meat Train" from Chicago, making its daily run to supply the restaurants of New York City. The Million Dollar almost reached the top, but then slipped, skidded, and slowly slid back down. Three times the train backed up and tried to crest the hill, three times the little engine that could just could not. The railroad had to bring in two locomotives from Croton to pull the Million Dollar over the hill. The next day, they paid Cassie for the cow.

As women became more involved, Monday Clubs began to appear in local communities, not specifically restricted to women members but serving as venues for mature ladies of the communities to exercise educational and informational programs for their own edification. The effects of women's initiatives reached the upper Valley when the Salem Women's Club formed on January 10, 1923, and had more than fifty members by the end of the year. The club was admitted to the state federation in 1924. Its notable speakers included Eleanor Roosevelt, authors Frances Parkinson Keyes and Pearl Buck, and artist Norman Rockwell.

The implicit support given by upstate newspapers to the birth control movement was characteristic of the change in thinking in the new age. Local papers not only reported local news about the movement but also provided information about birth control from elsewhere from time to time. Birth control had been classified as obscene by the Comstock laws of 1873, but new attitudes emerged in the new century. A Middletown article viewed birth control as the latest "technological advance" (in historian Robyn Rosen's words) to protect mankind from overpopulation. The topic became a cause in 1914, when Margaret Sanger (1879–1966) was arrested in New York City for illegally dispensing birth control information; she fled to Europe and returned by 1916, when she was arrested again, this time with her sister, Ethel Bryne, and sentenced to thirty days in jail on Blackwell's Island. The Middletown and Kingston newspapers carried four articles on Bryne, who went on a hunger strike in prison—she was released in February 1917. In the same month, the *Irvington Gazette* carried an article about the Tarrytown Equal Franchise Society's complaint about society's official disapproval of contraception and how that contrasted with its lackadaisical attitude about "the pleasures of men" in consuming too much alcohol.

Sanger had called for a "birth strike" as early as 1910. When the 1917 case came before the New York Court of Appeals in 1918, the judge confirmed the sisters' convictions but also ruled that physicians were exempt from the obscenity code when they prescribed birth control for their patients. This chink in the armor of conventional thinking led to a new era of discussion and agitation. Mary Ware Dennett and the National Birth Control League were often in Albany during this time, lobbying the New York State legislature to remove contraception from state obscenity laws altogether.

The subject attained a kind of unofficial imprimatur when Sanger was chosen to deliver the keynote address at the first annual Summer Institute of Euthenics at Vassar College in 1926. The term "euthenics," which generally dealt with the science of improving society through the improvement of living conditions, had been coined by Vassar professor Ellen Swallow Richards in 1905 and was now promoted by the new college president, Henry Mac-Cracken. The *New York Times* called the get-together a workshop on "child development and race improvement," but in Sanger's hands it took on the aspect of a race cleansing movement as well. She had been advocating a new science of "eugenics" in the *Birth Control Review*, which she founded in 1917, as the best way to "improve" humanity over time.

"The American public is heavily taxed to maintain an increasing race of morons, which threatens the very foundations of our civilization," she said in a Vassar speech that became infamous. Sanger went on to bemoan the outrageous expense of asylums, prisons, and institutions for the care of the defective and diseased. One of these was the Eastern Institution for Mentally Defective Delinquents established at Napanoch in Ulster County, where docile inmates were jobbed out to local farms and other low-level work in the surrounding communities. "Happy Nappies," as they were called, also worked at crafts and, during World War I, paraded with wooden rifles around the grounds.

At the time of her advocacy for eugenics, Sanger's focus represented a more respectable approach to the subject than birth control for population growth because it came from a fiscally conservative viewpoint. She approved of strict immigration laws on the same regressive principle, namely that keeping out the woebegone and unfortunate would protect America's gene pool. Scientific attention to genetics began at Union College with a course on "The Cell and Heredity" in 1927, which expanded after Ernest Dale joined the faculty in 1929 and worked on the genetics of petunias and radiation effects on plant genetics.

The earliest birth control clinic in the Hudson Valley was established at Grasslands Hospital in Valhalla in 1929. The Albany Birth Control Committee was created in 1934 and opened a clinic at Albany Hospital; another was established in Poughkeepsie in 1935. Representatives of the Birth Control League spoke in Goshen before the Twentieth Century Club, signifying the movement's coming of age. By 1936, the Westchester County Medical Association was opening lines of cooperation with local clinics, although it was another three years before the American Medical Association endorsed contraceptives.

Clinics were established at Newburgh, Millbrook, Beacon, Middletown, and Hudson in 1937, and at Rhinebeck in 1940. The Poughkeepsie clinic, which opened in 1935, had 703 calls in 1939. A Hudson River Maternal Health Center was established at Yonkers without a problem that year. The inevitable backlash came from Cardinal Hayes of the Catholic archdiocese, who called the birth control advocates "prophets of decadence" and attacked the ABCL's call for federal dissemination of birth control materials. Catholic opposition erupted in Middletown after a state subsidy was established there in 1940. This was one of fifty-five clinics statewide, 40 percent of which received some type of state support, yet in Middletown the opposition was significant. A similar problem erupted in Albany in 1941, even though the Maternal Guidance Clinic had been operating since 1935. Albany Hospital discontinued the service in 1942 when Bishop Gibbons threatened to withdraw the Catholic agencies from the Community Chest.

The Yonkers birth control center served 350 women in the first eleven months, women from Dobbs Ferry, Irvington, Hastings and Tarrytown as well as Yonkers. By 1943, the Westchester group was affiliated nationally as the Hudson River Committee for Planned Parenthood. Eleanor Roosevelt's support for the movement in 1940 helped to legitimize it in the war years.

These were indeed hallelujah years for the untended aspirations of the American scene, an "April" in the springtime of national aspirations in the same way that T. S. Eliot characterized that "cruelest month" in the "waste land" of modernism in his poem of this same period, a hard struggle and bursting-forth of the flower of democracy. African Americans, thanks in part to Amenia and the support of some—a few—in white society, divested of their hyphenated status and affirmed more forcefully their full roles as free men and women. Youth flowered forth in all its brash attire, defining a era of excess and frivolity and enabling a radical transformation in pedagogic thinking to follow. Women found both a vote and a voice in affirming their rights and status. And American art finally came of age, commencing a process that would soon eclipse its abrupt emergence in 1913 from the example of the Europeans. Modern times was born.

25. A "Golden Age" in Education

> The whole purpose of education is to turn mirrors into windows. —SYDNEY J. HARRIS

Dr. Frank Parker Day (1881–1950), president of Union College, gave the address at the fall get-together at Poultney Bigelow's river estate in Malden-on-Hudson on October 5, 1929, proclaiming to a crowd of a thousand about a "glimmer in the east of the golden age of education" that was forthcoming. The era was already underway, in radical changes among institutions of higher education as well as the quality of the intellectuals that academia was producing. Even West Point Military Academy, which stood, in the words of Brigadier General (Ret.) Lance Betros, "like granite against the tide of social currents" in emphasizing continuity instead of change during this period, experienced its own revolution in academics under Douglas MacArthur's tenure as superintendent.

In his first year as Union president, Frank Day led an Association of American Colleges commission on organizing school curricula and "encouraged" a revision of Union's academic structure in radical new ways. But the impacts of the Great Depression and his own health problems forestalled major changes at the college at that time; an honors program was tried and failed (and did not become established at Union until 1966), scholarship funding dropped significantly, and his efforts at reforming athletics to eliminate the rising commercialism of the practice among colleges generally was stillborn. Ultimately, because of his health and intrigues among board members, he became the only Union president to be dismissed. A new Union Plan that restructured the academic program was begun in 1934, but Day's successor, Dixon Ryan Fox, was not a radical education thinker and did not encourage the changes that Day had begun.

In 1950, *Harper's* editor Frederick Lewis Allen attributed the rise in the numbers of children in high school since 1900 to the technological changes that came with a growing industrialism, yet the old school also had its day. Local grade school education benefited in new ways as a result of John Burroughs' writings, after Mary E. Burt's series of *Little Nature Studies for Little People* debuted in 1895. "A Brave Mouse," "A Wolf in Spider's Clothing," and other small and intimate Burroughsian glimpses into the natural world appeared in these little books in both large and small type for a range of elementary school classes and ages for almost four decades.

Greater attention was paid to private education, both formally and in specialized training. Westchester County remained home to exclusive boarding schools for the sons and daughters of the wealthy but also had a history of support for labor education. The first school for workers of enduring importance in America was the Brookwood Labor College at Katonah, founded in 1921. The American Federation of Labor supported the college until 1929, but thereafter, bereft of funds, the school declined until it closed in 1937. About five hundred graduates from Brookwood entered the labor force with significantly better training than other workers. The Hudson Shore Labor School, a resurrection of the failed Bryn Mawr Summer School for Women Workers in Industry of Pennsylvania, rose on the shores of West Park briefly, and also quietly expired because of the economic times.

Although not associated with a particular school, the consolidation of the medical profession occurred during and after the war, and physician income grew significantly as a result. These were the years in which quackery was finally subdued—its thorn in the medical profession dating to before New York's decision to admit non-educated physicians as professionals in the early American period. Membership in local medical societies became the entryway to privileges at local hospitals. The profession could not control the rise of prenatal and child care services, however, whose advancement was driven by educated women with social interests and a new political influence after gaining the right to vote. Studies leading to a 1932 national report on medical care (led and run by doctors) revealed the high and unequal distribution of medical costs, yet limited the sinecures to strictly medical solutions. Root causes of illness in nutrition, hygiene, living conditions and other social indices were pointedly ignored. At the same time, the insurance industry grew hand-in-hand with medicine in per capita costs and remained private. Some doctors even denounced voluntary as well as mandatory health insurance as promoting too much competition. The omission of compulsory health insurance from the Social Security Act was one of its "conservative" features, and yet a 1938 Gallup poll showed that seven of ten doctors favored mandatory health insurance.

Edward Pulling began his "Project Pullingsburg" search for a suitable preparatory school site in 1928, and was given a personal tour of the Springwood holdings in Hyde Park by the governor himself, Franklin D. Roosevelt, who came down from Albany to show him around. Pulling had taught FDR's sons at Groton. Roosevelt offered him a right-of-way to the river and would build a boathouse for him as well. "Although his enthusiasm was contagious and his offer tempting, we decided not to accept it," Pulling wrote, because the school site was too near the main road and, he felt, the clientele would likely be limited to Democrats.

Pulling's wife was a childhood friend of Betty Flagler, whose wedding she attended in Millbrook, and Betty's mother recommended Millbrook for their school. After the Depression began, in November 1930, Pulling visited a former Millbrook Hunt Club house that had gone under, on "the old Stephenson Farm near the road to Amenia" and established the Millbrook School in the following year. Henry Harkness Flagler became the first trustee board president of the Millbrook School and the school's greatest benefactor. The school was incorporated in 1932. In 1936, Millbrook's first biology teacher, Frank

Trevor, established the only zoo located on a high school campus at Millbrook.

New York's Board of Regents began looking more closely into "what the educational system of the State is accomplishing" in 1935, focusing on "major issues" such as the importance of a high school education in the molding of an American, how school personnel are developed, adult education, and school financing. The normal school in Albany was renamed the New York State College for Teachers in 1914 and charged with preparing teachers for secondary education using a liberal arts base, emphasizing that it was a "college for teachers," and not a "teachers' college." Enrollment remained around a thousand students through the next few decades, began rising in the 1950s, and totaled 2,500 by 1962.

The benefactions of Margaret Olivia Slocum Sage (1828–1918), in addition to providing social and economic philanthropies nationwide through the Russell Sage Foundation, expanded West Point's footprint with her donation of Constitution Island to the academy; created a new campus for the Emma Willard School in Troy in 1910 and established Russell Sage College in 1916 as a women's vocational institute on the old Willard School grounds.

Rensselaer Polytechnic Institute graduates, including the first holders of degrees in electrical and mechanical engineering, listened raptly to a commencement address by Admiral Robert E. Peary in 1911. Peary likened his 23-year quest for the North Pole, which he reached in 1909, to that of the future that awaited the graduates, wishing that they, like him, could say at the end, "I have made good." His speech was interrupted by applause for several minutes. RPI had changed, around 1910, from an old Board of Examiners method of testing students to a system where professors themselves monitored the finals. After 1912, Harriet Peck, the first school librarian, created a card catalog for the school's 9,000 volumes, and quadrupled the size of the collection over her 34-year tenure. Miss Peck was a recognized "pioneer in library science," and also the characteristic lady librarian of her day, wearing wire-rim glasses, her hair tucked in a tight bun, enforcing the rule of silence with a stern look and demeanor. A dozen new degree programs were instituted under the 33-year tenure of President Palmer C. Ricketts, who also oversaw the addition of ten new academic buildings and a million dollar grant he obtained from Mrs. Sage. The number of faculty increased from 15 to 129, and included a number of internationally famous professors. The development of the "Ricketts Campus" climaxed with the completion of a large laboratory for aeronautical and metallurgical engineering courses in 1935, subsequently named for him.

More than 250 representatives from colleges and educational associations around the country (including 72 from 23 other countries) joined RPI officials for the college's 100th anniversary celebration on October 3, 1924. Alumni chartered the steamer Berkshire and came up from New York, using the craft as their hotel for the occasion. Herbert Hoover, the US secretary of commerce and holder of an honorary RPI degree, offered the keynote address. The community of Troy contributed $167,000 toward a new campus building for the civil engineering department. A plaque for the RPI Approach, as the marble entrance to the college from Broadway was called, was dedicated by a lineal descendant of Stephen Van Rensselaer III, Mrs. Elisabeth Van Rensselaer. Over the next few years an auditorium named for Amos Eaton and a new clubhouse were added, an architecture department building in 1929, and one for metallurgy and aeronautical engineering in 1934, named for President Ricketts, who died that year. His widow left their $300,000 estate to the college after her death.

Of all the Hudson Valley institutions of higher education, Vassar College in Poughkeepsie remained on the cutting edge of innovation and change as the new thinking emerged. Henry MacCracken, only thirty-five when he became the college president, was enthusiastic about the "new consciousness" in women's thinking as early as his arrival in 1915, when he startled the Poughkeepsie community by endorsing women's suffrage. Over his long tenure, he transformed the old institution into a modern college in which students participated as "colleagues" with the faculty in pursuing their studies. At Vassar, the transformation became an aspect of the new pedagogic thinking—educating women to be proactive in the contemporary world— although MacCracken's initial application of the new direction, a school of "euthenics" on the domestic and family sciences, was not well received. The Vassar Summer Institute for Family and Childcare Services, on the other hand, became an important federally sponsored center for women and the family in World War II.

St. Stephen's College in Annandale-on-Hudson, having survived a weak attempt by Eliphalet Nott Potter to become warden after his tumultuous Union College years in the nineteenth century, expanded its elective courses under its fourth warden, the Rev. Lawrence Thomas Cole (1869–1955). Over three years (1898–1901), forty new courses were introduced, with particular strengths in the sciences. The preparatory program for high school students deficient in their studies was eliminated, as it had been at Vassar, precipitating a drop in enrollment from 54 to 42 students that necessitated the program's restoration after a few years. St. Stephen's developed fitfully in the early 1900s, plagued by money problems and changes in wardens, until 1909, when William Cunningham Rodgers (1856?–1921) took over the leadership and the warden became the college president. President Rodgers, the rector of wealthy Grace Church in Millbrook, was hired for his fundraising abilities. Ten months into the term, he hosted the college's 50th anniversary celebration in a grand affair at Trinity Church and the Astor House in New York. More than twice the usual numbers of bachelor degrees were awarded that spring. The college was modernizing—electricity throughout the campus, new water, sewers, and heating infrastructure, a new president's house (the first new build-ing since the Hoffman library in 1895), and renovations to Aspinwall Hall—creating pride and enthusiasm among the faculty and supporters.

By 1915, one sixth of the members of the Episcopal Church in America were under the pastoral care of St. Stephen's graduates, 455 of whom had be-come clergy (380 still living at the time) in the 55 years of the college's exis-tence. One of them was the Rev. Thomas Cole (d. 1919), son of the Hudson River School painter, noted amateur paleontologist, and rector of Trinity Epis-copal Church of Saugerties for forty years. The church is noted for its William Morris and Louis Comfort Tiffany stained glass windows.

Rodgers' enthusiasm and that of Haley Fiske (1852–1929), a board member since 1905, and the retirement in 1913 of conservative George B. Hopson (of the "founding" fathers generation of St. Stephen's), helped sustain the college in these years, but enrollment was again dwindling as the new war hysteria began to turn people away from higher education and its goals. Plans for a gymnasium were postponed. The college had only 32 students over 1917–18, seventeen of them already serving in the armed forces. When St. Stephen's became a unit of the Student Army Training Corps, the numbers rose to just under a hundred, although most of the "civilian" students in min-isterial studies declined to join the new Corps. Since all expenses were paid by the government, St. Stephen's emerged from the war years strengthened by the experience, yet with only 30 members again in the student body.

Bernard Iddings Bell (1886–1958), at 33 half the age of any of his predecessors, arrived at St. Stephen's in July 1919 to assume the role of the presidency. Reamer Kline later described him as "great in his gifts and great in his faults," a man "ultramodern, dynamic, controversial, eloquent." Bell found, in his own words, "9 professors (6 incompetent), 29 students, a run-down set of buildings, no laboratories, a laughable library, no endowment, a big debt," and a message from the State Education Department threatening to annul the college's charter "on grounds of utter incompetency."

"How could we ever stand living here?" his young wife asked. Yet Bell quickly brought the campus into order and the enrollment to 49, writing: "A new epoch in the life of St. Stephen's is now at its birth." He was a churchman who worked with the Episcopal clergy trustees in pursuing "a broader, more secular mission." He became an important national figure in traditional conservative philosophy, hailed by Russell Kirk (1918–94), the founder of modern conservatism, as "an Isaiah preaching to the Remnant." Yet for all his conservatism, Bell's faculty included one of America's first sociologists, Lyford ("Trotsky") Edwards (1882–1984), and "new humanist" Albert Jay Nock (1870–1945), an 1892 St. Stephen's graduate and, like Poultney Bigelow, advocate of Henry George's theories about economic class.

Bell led St. Stephen's into an affiliation with Columbia University, taught religion there while Donald G. Tewksbury (1894–1958) of Columbia served as dean upstate, and brought about the change in the college name to Bard, honoring its founder. The Columbia affiliation, modeled after the university's arrangement with Barnard College, came about because of traditional affiliations between the two institutions and Bell's attention to fundraising. The merger brought in generous donations (he had "gotten together and spent $830,000" by March 1929). Governor Roosevelt joined the board. Herbert Lehman, his lieutenant governor, promised $2,800 for the endowment fund in 1928, gave another $1,000 in 1929, and maintained a close interest in Bard and its students over the years.

Bell worked closely with the noted Episcopal bishop, William T. Manning (1866–1949), the chairman of the Bard board of trustees. With the Columbia connection, he developed an intimate triumvirate with Manning and the celebrated Columbia president, Nicholas Murray Butler (1862–1947), a Nobel Prize winner and arguably the greatest educator of the twentieth century. Close ties already existed between the great university and the small minister's college through John McVikar, one of the founders of Columbia University and an uncle of John Bard. Three times in the past St. Stephen's had seriously considered merging with Columbia. Butler saw the merger as consistent with the development in America of an Oxford model of an umbrella university overseeing several different independent colleges. The merger, in addition to donors, brought to St. Stephen's the universal approval of the college rating authorities, ended "denominational restrictions" in the faculty and students of the college, and carried small, provincial Bard College to the heights of higher education. Bell wrote that the two institutions had set up:

> an experiment which the whole educational world is talking about —the experiment of conducting individualized higher education . . . with a definite attempt to combine fearlessly scientific instruction and a real consideration of aesthetics, philosophy, and mystical imponderables. The College is placed by this in the floodlight of educational observation.

The merger lasted until 1944, when Bard separated and became co-educational.

On its own again after World War II, Bard added émigré scholars from Europe to its faculty, including painter Stefan Hirsch, political writer Felix Hirsch, Budapest String Quartet founder Emil Hauser, and philosopher Heinrich Bluecher, the husband of Hannah Arendt. These were joined in the ensuing decade by influential American thinkers like Mary McCarthy, Ralph Ellison, Anthony Hecht (Bard '44), Franco Modigliani, Theodore Weiss, Saul Bellow and Dwight Macdonald. Although an affiliation with the Episcopal Church continued and a strong religious studies program remained a core unit of Bard, the college became better known generally as a nonsectarian liberal arts college of the first rank in America.

A need for a Catholic college in the Diocese of Albany led to the establishment of Siena College at Loudonville in 1937. The discussion was initiated by Edmund F. Gibbons, the Albany bishop, and the Orders of Friars Minor in New York City, as a result of Bishop Gibbons' friendship with Thomas Plassman, O.F.M. The 38-acre Walter Garrett estate a few miles north of Albany was purchased through a third party because of the neighborhood's known antipathy toward Catholics, and the school established as an extension of St. Bonaventure College by the St. Bonaventure dean, Cyprian Mensing, O.F.M. The school became St. Bernardine of Siena College in 1938, and simply Siena

College thirty years later. A student body of 778 in 1940–41 was reduced to 294 two years later, rebounding (with numerous other colleges) in the GI Bill years after the war.

The Franciscan Friars community at Siena was a formal convent ruled by a Praeses and two discretes in 1943. The college included two lay teachers initially, both émigrés from Hitler's Germany, a sociology professor named Egon Plager and biologist named Albert Uffenheimer (d. 1941). Plager, a favorite of the students, became a distinguished professor of criminal justice in later years and vice-chairman of the New York State Probation Board. The founding friars (assigned in 1937) included Benjamin Kuhn, O.F.M. (1905–88), whose infectious enthusiasm for Siena delighted both the college and the wider community for decades.

Kuhn was remembered as the instructor in biology for liberal arts students, who demonstrated the difference between static and kinetic energy by hoisting his 300-pound frame on top of a desk while quietly telling the students, "This is static energy." He then jumped while loudly proclaiming, "And this is kinetic energy!" Students or professors rushed in from other classrooms in fear that an earthquake had occurred; "Oh, it's just Father Ben," they would say, and return to their studies.

And thus it was that the modern times that arrived in zany notions of people flying and devil-may-care partying crossed a threshold from the static energy of a Victorian past to a kinetic embrace of new times and possibilities, and retained a sense of humor as a kind of divine grace to carry the whole notion forward. Yet the new era also bore its own implicit demise, in a smug complacency over the tatters of great poverty and an even more ferocious war than the one that ushered it in. America's heroes would emerge in these times, too, and the Hudson River Valley would contribute its share.

IV. THE AGE OF ROOSEVELT

[E]verything in me cries out to be back in my home on the Hudson River.

—FRANKLIN D. ROOSEVELT (1944)

26. The Roosevelt Heritage

> This generation of Americans has a rendezvous
> with destiny.   —FRANKLIN D. ROOSEVELT

Sara Delano's father, the "autocratic" yet "lovable" Warren Delano II (1809–98), owned a forty-room country estate called Algonac overlooking the Hudson on the northern edge of Newburgh. An early Republican, he was "a daring businessman" in the tea and opium trades in the Far East. Private tutors, summers in the country, winters filled with sleigh rides, skating, hot cider and doughnuts, and family trips to Europe and the Orient—these were the norm for Sara Delano (1854–1941) and her sisters.

Warren Delano at first discouraged a marriage between his daughter and a man twice her age, yet Sara had developed a fondness for "Mr. James," as James Roosevelt (1828–1900) was known to all. His first wife (and second cousin), Rebecca Brien Howland (1831–76), died after twenty-five years of marriage; they had a son, James Roosevelt Roosevelt (1854–1927), whom everyone called Rosy. Mr. James was a tall, slender man, handsome in muttonchop whiskers, who was born at Mount Hope on the Hyde Park bluff. He had an estate of $300,000 based on refinery and railroad investments, modest but certainly of the economic elite of his day. He speculated grandly and shielded his inherited wealth. Mr. James raised cows, enjoyed the horse races, and hunted fox. A Democrat in a heavily Republican town, he served as town supervisor, vestryman, and warden of St. James Episcopal Church.

Newly married, on October 7, 1880, Mr. James and Sara came up from Algonac by carriage, crossed on the Poughkeepsie ferry, and moved into Springwood, the rambling river house he purchased twenty years earlier after Mount Hope burned down. They were in a distinguished neighborhood. Archibald Rogers, their nearest neighbor, was an associate of John D. Rockefeller. Ogden Mills, the Wall Street financier, and Vincent Astor lived upriver. Frederick W. Vanderbilt was in the middle, more or less, in a 54-room mansion that cost $660,000. Mr. James once declined dinner there because, he told Sara, they would then have to invite the Vanderbilts to Springwood.

Sara was 26 when their son, Franklin Delano Roosevelt, was born on January 30, 1882; James was 54. The birth was a miracle of sorts, the mother having been given too much chloroform. A maid was astonished to see the tiny boy breathing. As young Franklin grew, James enjoyed taking his son around to the horse races in the county. Locally, the racing set gathered at the Doty Union Park in East Poughkeepsie, later purchased by Matthew Vassar for his college, and the Poughkeepsie Driving Park, a half-mile track run by A. Stoutenburgh "a short distance from this city on the plank road." The Union Corners race track in Pine Plains was another of Roosevelt's favorites, run by a local racing celebrity named Daniel Wiggs, who diversified on the side by selling Whirlbone Liniment for man and beast.

In the summer of 1890, the Roosevelts returned from a Paris trip with a governess, Jeanne Sandoz, 19, who taught the eight-year-old son French and an unusual repertory of science subjects. She was also outspoken in her liberal political views. Franklin also had a male tutor, Andrew Dumper, with whom he became fast friends. Dumper encouraged the boy's interest in collecting, which had begun with stamps and expanded to the natural environment around Springwood. FDR kept a meticulous bird-sighting diary and began a collection of stuffed specimens of male and female species in Dutchess County that grew to become "most comprehensive." Franklin insisted on stuffing the first one himself.

The nearest neighbors, the Rogers boys, were his most constant companions. Franklin and Edmund built a sailboat of sorts "on the top of a hemlock tree" and played at seafaring with the toy. They hewed and tied logs into a makeshift fishing raft, but when they boarded she sank. Plans for a yacht club were drawn up; a field was cleared and flooded, and a dam and part of a clubhouse constructed. Young Franklin was outfitted with a small, lateen-rigged iceboat called the *Hawk*, with which he became adept. Franklin went to Groton School in 1896, two years later in age than most boys, and was teased by the other students because of his age and aristocratic air. At Harvard, which he entered in 1900, he was an average student yet perfectly fitted to the Harvard spirit. His senior thesis topic was "The Roosevelt Family in New Amsterdam before the Revolution."

Sara's highest ambition for her son was that he become "straight and honorable, just and kind, an upstanding American," just like his father. Franklin's experiences in these early years likely contributed, as it had for his father, to his sense of commonalty with the average farmers and businessmen of his town.

Franklin grew to know the back roads well from his father's peregrinations and his own as a young politician and historian. In the 1920s, he drove through the wood trails of the county to determine the best route for a parkway. In 1943, he drove Eleanor and Daisy Suckley "at 50 miles an hour to Cruger's Island" in Annandale-on-Hudson, along the railroad track for part of the way, and then sat facing the swamp and watching thousands of migratory birds; his wife was bored to death. Another favored stop was his maternal uncle Warren Delano III's home, Steen Valetje, off the River Road in Red Hook. Roosevelt would come over to see his first cousin Lyman (1883–1944), a year younger than Franklin, who kept red setters and Norwegian ponies. After Lyman inherited the estate, President Roosevelt brought Queen Wilhelmina and the Netherlands foreign minister there for tea. He also liked visiting the Locusts, Lytle Hull's home, where President Grant was once photographed playing chess on the piazza. FDR signed himself into the visitors' book as "successor to President Grant at 'The Locusts,' Sept. 6, 1942."

His interest in Dutch colonial architecture, deeply felt and genuine, sprang from his ancestry, his uncle Frederick A. Delano's passion for geology, and his own studies as a member of the Holland Society and a charter member of the Dutchess County Historical Society when it formed in 1914. The 1915–16 additions to Springwood mixed "a dash of Hudson River Dutch" with Georgian styling that architects Hoppen and Koen provided. Franklin persuaded his mother to expend the additional money to have the wings built of native fieldstone. The walls were laid out the same as the superintendent's cottage on Thomas Newbold's estate next door, a structure that FDR admired.

After his 1911 victory in the fight against Billy Sheehan, Senator Franklin Roosevelt represented his district's and his own interests, yet otherwise remained a marginal figure on the state stage. His special interest in mental health arose with the Poughkeepsie hospital, the site of which was sold to the state by his father. As a fledgling politician in Albany, Franklin had not developed the confident savoir-faire that came to characterize the President of later years. Frances Perkins (1882–1965), then a labor lobbyist and social worker, considered young Roosevelt a man oblivious to his colleagues, possessing an "artificially serious" demeanor and a habit of throwing his head back as if he were "looking down his nose at most people." His height only added to the seeming disdain, but he was maturing nonetheless. By mid-1912, Franklin had met Woodrow Wilson (1856–1924) and endorsed his presidential campaign—over the esteemed "Bull Moose" TR and incumbent Republican William Howard Taft. Franklin and Thomas Osborne developed the Wilson campaign in New York. The young man and the candidate shared a disdain toward the whole New York political machine, yet were careful about state politics, shying away from the Sulzer impeachment, for example, even though both sympathized with the harassed governor.

Roosevelt's move to the position of Assistant Secretary of the Navy occurred through a chance meeting with the President-elect's new Secretary of the Navy on the post office steps in Washington. The secretary, Josephus Daniels (1862–1948), asked Roosevelt if he wished to be his assistant—the same post that TR had held under an earlier president. This was the one post in the national government that Franklin Roosevelt really wanted. Daniels's genius was in appointing FDR as his second-in-command without worrying about the consequences. New York Republican senator Elihu Root (1845–1937) advised him against it ("whenever a Roosevelt rides," he told the secretary, "he wishes to ride in front"), and Root had a point. Yet Daniels, a canny Southern newspaper editor, was the craftier politician and had better judgment on most naval tactical matters than Roosevelt.

When word reached Park Row in Albany that Roosevelt was taking Louis Howe along on his Navy work, one reporter suggested that now that Howe would be "exposed to water," he should take "a dozen cakes of soap and maybe he'll finally come clean!"

Roosevelt's name came up as a potential US Senate candidate in 1914. The *New York Sun*, perhaps inspired by Howe, ran a flattering article about him in December 1913, noting his early support for the direct primary bill that passed that year. FDR threw his hat into the ring after learning that the President would support his candidacy. Howe conducted intensive behind-the-scenes work with the Democrats on his behalf—mailings, leaflets, news stories—and set up a three-week speaking tour. In the end, Roosevelt lost the nomination to a popular German ambassador, James W. Gerard (1867–1951), who went on to lose in November to James W. Wadsworth, Jr. (1877–1952), a former Republican state assembly speaker. Wadsworth was reelected in 1920 but lost to Democrat Robert W. Wagner in 1926.

By the fall of 1915, FDR had mended fences with Tammany Hall and went to the state convention at Saratoga Springs with a promise from President Wilson to leave New York City's patronage to the machine in return for the nomination of Judge Samuel Seabury, a noted jurist, as governor. Roosevelt invited Charlie Murphy and Judge Olvaney, another Tammany Hall leader, to join him on an inspection of the Iona Island Naval Arsenal, returning so late in the day, or so enjoying it, that they stayed overnight at Haverstraw's New Main Hotel.

FDR was seriously considered for governor in 1918. He favored Osborne, but when Al Smith emerged as a candidate FDR supported the New Yorker. Smith was elected, and relations between Al and Frank grew warmer. FDR went as a delegate to the 1920 Democratic Party convention in San Francisco intent on helping Smith's national aspirations. In the end, James Middletown Cox (1870–1957), the Ohio governor, was nominated to run against Warren G. Harding (1865–1923) for president. Cox surprised the convention by insisting on FDR as his running mate. Smith seconded the nomination the next day as Josephus Daniels beamed with pride from the rostrum. Roosevelt received a rousing cheer from 2,000 employees when he resigned his position with the Navy Department (he was succeeded by Colonel Theodore Roosevelt, Jr.) and started the campaign to become the vice president of the United States.

Louis Howe wanted to use Smith's success in beginning a reorganization of New York State's government by urging efficiency in government as the Democratic platform—Republican Benjamin O'Dell had had some success with that theme in 1900—but Cox and Roosevelt resurrected the unpopular League of Nations, in hindsight a gross *faux pas* given the overwhelming rejection of their candidacy by the voters, yet not so apparent an error at the time. Eleanor and her new progressive friends were strongly in support of the League.

Cox and Roosevelt crossed the country campaigning by separate trains, an enlightening experience for Franklin's wife, who was taken under wing by Howe and educated in the fine points of politics along the way. Harding swept in on a 61% landslide (carrying the Vassar straw vote as well, 594–301), but Roosevelt remained "lighthearted" over the loss and went about the train cars giving each member of his traveling party a set of cuff links. The gift established a tradition every year thereafter, as each of the entourage joined FDR for his birthday in what was known as the "Cufflinks Club." Howe was not distressed by the loss, since his boy was now firmly and absolutely a national political figure.

Yet Roosevelt, thirty-nine years of age, was about to face his darkest hour. On July 27, 1921, he toured a new Boy Scouts camp at Bear Mountain State Park and swam with the boys in a pool below Hessian Lake. He was photographed marching in the scout parade, the last photograph of Franklin D. Roosevelt walking unassisted. Two weeks later he was at the family home in Campobello, Maine, when his left leg, then his right, became paralyzed. The illness was not diagnosed as infantile paralysis for another ten days.

Franklin, like so many parents, knew about polio personally. He felt the parent's fear in 1916 when an outbreak at Campobello led him, as the assistant secretary, to have a Navy ship bring his five children to Hyde Park for safety. He had fallen ill with typhoid in 1912, had a throat infection in 1917, and influenza and pneumonia in 1918, and now faced something worse when it came to his political health. Only a week before the Bear Mountain swim FDR had learned that a US Senate subcommittee had accused him of perjury in a Navy scandal case involving the use of civilians to bait homosexuals. *The New York Times* headline read: "Lay Navy Scandal to F. D. Roosevelt. Details Unprintable." He rebutted the allegation effectively, however, and his reputation was undamaged in the long run.

Louis Howe carefully managed information about the affliction in a way that did not harm Roosevelt's political status. He elicited Eleanor's involvement in working to restore Franklin's morale and spirit. Howe's strategy kept Roosevelt in the game of politics, his dramatic and popular return to the stage (at least briefly) occurring when he nominated Al Smith for president in 1924. Smith's first campaign for the office was also Eleanor's coming-out as a political force, thanks in part to the tutelage of Louis Howe. Prior to the convention she and her Todhunter School colleagues, Nancy Cook (1884–1962) and Marion Dickerman (1890–1983), traveled around the state exhorting women to vote and supporting numerous social causes. She invited Smith to Hyde Park—Sara was appalled by his coarseness—and worked closely with him on the presidential nomination. She faced down Charlie Murphy and forced him into allowing the women's caucus to name the women delegates, and then led the women's platform committee at the party convention in New York. She was embittered and appalled in the end when the resolutions committee flatly refused to consider the social platform for which she had campaigned. As the deadlocked convention ensued in the hundred-degree heat, she sat so engrossed in her favorite pastime that Will

Rogers asked if she was "knitting in the names of the future victims of the guillotine."

Howe, meanwhile, convinced Smith that having Franklin Roosevelt nominate him would be a dramatic national moment. FDR worked for three weeks at Hyde Park to be able to walk the fifteen feet to the podium at Madison Square Garden. When the time came, wearing his steel leg braces, and with a cane in his right hand and the arm of his sixteen-year-old son James on his left, carrying on a banter as they walked, Franklin Roosevelt returned to the national stage—dripping in sweat, but he had made it. The sun broke through the clouds above the skylight at the Garden and flooded him in light. In a soaring pitch for party unity across the country, Roosevelt called for the nomination of "the Happy Warrior of the political battlefield." The two men who had become nationally famous when at odds with each other a dozen years before, stood together once again in the limelight, the nation cheering for both of them now.

Al Smith lost the nomination but ran again for governor that year and defeated Theodore Roosevelt, Jr. by a mere 100,000 votes in several million cast. The victory was another satisfying moment for the Hyde Park Roosevelts. Eleanor and her two friends traveled to campaign stops in a car absurdly outfitted with a teapot, to remind voters of Ted's near-complicity in the Teapot Dome scandal that rocked the Harding presidency.

Roosevelt spent six years of hard effort to win back his legs, a period of such grueling regimen those around him marveled that he could do it. Hamilton Fish (1888–1991), a friend at the time, said that, absent the battlefield, he had never seen such courage in a man. Roosevelt's search for a cure led him to a spa and resort in Warm Springs, Georgia, which he eventually purchased and turned into a polio treatment facility. Four years after the Garden speech, Franklin Roosevelt could stand in steel braces and "walk" with a cane and a helpful arm by his side, without perspiring. His fate was what it was; his future was before him.

In 1928, when Al Smith was nominated for president, he needed a strong Democrat in the race for governor to help him win New York over Herbert Hoover (1874–1964). He wanted Franklin, but Roosevelt (and Louis Howe) felt Democrats would not fare well in the general elections, so his best position was to wait until 1930, then serve two terms as governor, and be placed well for the 1936 presidential nomination. He was not finished with his recuperation, and the baths at Warm Springs required his attention. He avoided several calls from Smith over the matter and went south to be out of touch. His assistant, Marguerite "Missy" LeHand (1894–1944), sent a long telegraph to Smith at the end of September explaining why Franklin did not wish to run. Finally, Smith importuned Eleanor, and she phoned her husband on October 1, knowing that Franklin would only take a call from her. She handed the telephone to Al Smith, and FDR became the gubernatorial nominee. One factor in his favor was his GOP opponent, Attorney General Albert Ottinger (1878–1938), a short man with a Napoleon complex. When Ottinger offended his Erie County running mate, Republicans and Democrats there made an agreement that led to FDR's securing 20,000 more votes than he deserved.

Roosevelt was also fortunate in his running mate, Herbert H. Lehman (1878–1963), a colleague of Smith's who as a colonel in the Navy had worked with Roosevelt during World War I. A highly successful Wall Street investment banker, he left private service to work with the governor, becoming perhaps the most effective lieutenant governor in New York history. If Eleanor was FDR's legs, Lehman was "that splendid right hand of mine," Roosevelt said. He served in a similar capacity as governor of New York to President Roosevelt during the Great Depression, and became a United States senator who early and vocally opposed Joseph McCarthy during the Red Scare of the 1950s. His years of business expertise enabled Lehman to create efficiencies in purchasing and state agency practices. He also took to special interests of the governor's, like the creation of a health resort at Saratoga Springs and state mental hospitals.

Roosevelt called for a two-cent tax on gasoline when he came into office in 1929, a revenue-raiser that Smith had rejected a few years earlier. Roosevelt used the gasoline tax to promote rural relief programs and reorganize funding support along more equitable lines. Rye, the wealthy lower Westchester town, had been receiving $1,500 a mile in state aid compared with only $25 per mile for the very rural counties; FDR raised the minimum to $100 a mile. He also sought basic changes to the ways in which local government worked. "The counties are governed under the same form, the same offices, and the same business methods as were established under the Duke of York in 1688," he complained in 1929. "Most things have improved since then. Local government has not."

Highway construction in New York boomed with the onset of the Depression (and would become a centerpiece of the New Deal) because of the jobs it created. The governor secured $65 million for roads and $75 million for at-grade rail crossing improvements. The work was not without its troubles. A strike at a Westchester County construction site arose in June 1931 after several contractors agreed among themselves to cut wages from 50 to 40 cents an hour. Westchester contractors were already undercutting labor gains by running "commissary rackets" at company stores, so the pay cut served as insult piled upon injury for the workers. Two hundred men with the Peckham Road Corporation marched through White Plains and Greenburgh in protest on May 21. The next day, North Castle police arrested 27 men involved in inciting other workers. Four hundred men meeting at the White Plains Union Hall that night voted for a $5 wage for an eight-hour day.

Workers brought in to replace the strikers were harassed by 500 union men on July 13. The strikers became violent, throwing stones at men crossing picket lines at a Valhalla sewer project. Two hundred and fifty workers at Elmsford walked off the job of one of Westchester's largest contractors, Petro Lucianni. One man was shot in the arm later in the week in a confrontation with the police. When the wives became involved by pleading with scabs to leave one job site, Manuela Laocus and Theresa Binon, each holding their babies, were arrested. Nine hundred men were now involved in the strike. White Plains Mayor Frederick C. McLaughlin recalled his public safety commissioner from vacation and brought in two US Immigration Bureau officials. Two hundred and fifty workers were rounded up and twenty of them held as illegal immigrants. The American Civil Liberties Union condemned the actions. The state labor department tried to broker a deal but was unsuccessful. Nineteen more men were arrested while picketing; Harry Allen, one of the strikers, went home and returned with his rifle. Five of the small contractors agreed to the wage demands, but fifteen large companies held out and brought in African Americans as replacement workers.

Finally, internal union strife led to an end of the crisis and the creation of the Westchester Construction Laborers' Union (WCCLU), a more conservative group that had removed its communist and progressive members. The WCCLU united with Local 60 of the Laborers and Hodcarriers' Union, yet the strike persisted when AFL teamsters joined the cause. Attempts by the American Federation of Labor to help with the negotiations were rebuffed by the WCCLU, even though the national union had been active in Westchester for over ten years. The AFL had helped in 1921 in the founding of the Brookwood Labor College of Katonah, but in 1931 the union complained about the school's director, radical pacifist A. J. Muste (1885–1967), who helped organize the leftist Conference for Progressive Labor of Action (CPLA).

Contractor Lucianni agreed to the five-dollar, eight-hour day on July 29, but the AFL could not reach the two other major county contractors, Will Peckham and Arthur Riegel. Four more union groups recognized the AFL in early August—the Drillers, Blasters, Rockmen, Shores & Wreckers locals, and fifteen more contractors agreed to the terms. Jailed strikers were freed, the strike ended, and the county Board of Supervisors authorized the county engineer, Jay Downer, to meet the strikers terms but exclude alien workers.

Howe began Roosevelt's reelection campaign several months before the vote, aided by James A. Farley (1888–1976) of Rockland County. Farley had run Smith's later governor campaigns and would be Roosevelt's representative on the floor in the 1932 Chicago presidential convention. A talking pictures program of FDR, Robert F. Wagner, and Herbert H. Lehman was created and shown in two hundred community cinemas. Henry Morgenthau—both Sr. and Jr.—speechwriter Samuel I. Rosenman (1896–1973), and Mrs. Caroline O'Day were on the campaign team. Roosevelt's Republican opponent in 1930 was "Tiger Tamer" Charles H. Tuttle (1879–1971), President Coolidge's United States attorney who had taken on Tammany Hall and even sent Albany political boss Dan O'Connell to jail on a contempt charge. Tuttle's running mate was Caleb H. Baum of Newburgh, a dry with Prohibition Party support who would not agree to his own party's plan to revise the eighteenth amendment.

The governor had initiated daily press conferences and numerous radio appearances to keep the public informed about the state's activities. To accommodate his disability, he had a special elevator to his office installed in 1929, replacing a "secret stairway" built into the original structure and remodeled in 1916. He had Farley appointed state Democratic Committee chair over objections by upstate delegates. Planks were inserted, with Frances Perkins' recommendation, to study unemployment insurance and stabilization measures to stem the tide of a rising Depression. FDR came out for fair pay for teachers, an eight-hour day for laborers, and a minimum wage advisory board. He called for a bond issue for state hospitals, expanded home rule opportunities for local governments, and established utility rate fixing by contract. Al Smith put FDR's name in nomination at the Democratic convention in 1930, even though the relations between the two men had cooled over Roosevelt's failure to take Smith's advice—and his advisors—in running the government.

FDR ordered investigations into several judgeships—a canny move during the campaign—including ones in Westchester and Saratoga counties. He was the consummate campaigner, never mentioning his opponent by name, stressing just one subject in every address, using his roots as a Dutchess County squire to identify with the farm interests, developing a uniquely personal tone with the electorate, and emphasizing his opponent's inability to cope with the times. The voters knew that he did not cause the Depression. He opposed the Eighteenth Amendment, yet was, the *New York World* declared wrongly, "personally dry" and "temperamentally favorable to the dry point of view." At the 1930 governors conference in Salt Lake City, Roosevelt called for national unemployment insurance and old age security. He won reelection by 725,001 votes, including the first-ever Democratic plurality upstate (167,784) and his first victory in his own hometown.

Roosevelt experienced a number of frustrations in trying to cope with the politics and the economy. In January 1931, he invited the governors of six neighboring states to meet with him on unemployment insurance, public works planning, labor and workmen's compensation laws, a fruitful event although the New York State legislature delayed any action on unemployment insurance until 1935, the year that FDR secured the Social Security Act from Congress. The struggle against the problems of the Depression led Roosevelt and Lehman into extraordinary actions to stem the economic losses. At the governor's request, Lehman set about accelerating the state's jobs program by increasing state construction over the winter months. He also led the effort to establish a Temporary Emergency Relief Administration that created the first unemployment relief program in the country.

The governor also acted on matters closer to his own heart, such as a reforestation program to employ out-of-work men. He pushed for the development of Saratoga Springs "as a real health resort." A million dollars was appropriated and a commission created in 1929 that recommended a seven-year program to upgrade the baths, concluding that daily patronage would rise from 2,700 a year to 5,000 if the facilities were there. Noting that "thousands" already benefited from the waters, the state found "sound medical justification" in the investment. A total of $2.2 million was spent overall, including a $500,000 administration building, pavilions, inviting walks, and $300,000 in landscaping upgrades, a million-dollar drinking hall, and a $300,000 bottling plant—and the commission added that a sanitarium was needed.

With the expansion of the waters use, improvements were also made in transportation in Saratoga Springs, even though the city objected to plans to run the state highway through, instead of around their jurisdiction. The Delaware & Hudson Railroad undertook a $169,000 grade crossing project at Fort Edward that affected both Saratoga Springs and Ballston Spa. George Foster Peabody, the chairman of the Saratoga commission, saw these changes as essential to improving the entrance for tourists into the Adirondacks.

Franklin D. Roosevelt nominated his lieutenant governor for governor at the state Democratic convention in 1932. Herbert H. Lehman won that election by more than 820,000 votes and worked with the president over the next ten years in implementing a "Little New Deal" for New York State—despite opposition from Republican-controlled houses of the state legislature for nine of those ten years. When Lehman moved to purge the food stamp rolls of hangers-on and deadbeats in 1938, he was criticized by the Socialist Party at a press conference at Camp Three Arrows in Putnam County. In 1942, Roosevelt asked Lehman to join him in Washington to head a new State Department office to assist liberated refugees and help nations affected by the war to rebuild. The governor resigned his office a month before the term ended to accept the position.

Roosevelt maintained close ties with home during his presidency, returning to "the Little White House" on two hundred occasions over the years. The Rev. George Anthony, rector of St. James Episcopal in Hyde Park was a long-time confidante. His local contacts included Eleanor's cousin Robert "Reggie" Livingston, chairman of the Columbia County Democratic Party, J. P. Hardy Steehold, a Salt Point judge who ran against Congressman Fish at Roosevelt's behest, and William Vincent Astor (1891–1959). Despite his wealth, and even during the thick-and-thin of the class acrimony over Roosevelt policies, Astor remained a close friend of his neighbor downriver. Roosevelt took a cruise after his election in 1933 on his yacht, the *Nourmahal*, and at other times on the Chesapeake and Hudson.

Franklin Roosevelt's sense of place about Hyde Park and the Hudson

River Valley was deeply rooted in the soils and local ties, and that came across in his closeness with the American people. In some ways, money distanced the family from Hudson Valley squires, yet Eleanor herself was mystified by the wealth of the Vanderbilts. She once inquired of Mrs. Frederick Vanderbilt what she did on her daily carriage drives around the Hyde Park estate, alone except for her coachman. Mrs. Vanderbilt said she spent the time in intellectual exercises recalling the kings and queens of England, then the presidents (all "forward and backward"), and if she had time, the monarchs of France.

Roosevelt was hardly aware of his status as a latter-day patroon, even in adulthood. In a 1943 discussion over "class consciousness," Daisy Suckley found "very interesting" FDR's lack of understanding of the distinction between "river" and "village" people then common among his fellow vestrymen at St. James and elsewhere along the river in those days. The President was not disingenuous in these sentiments. The Roosevelt heritage embraced the common man.

27. Eleanor's Day

Do one thing every day that scares you.
—ELEANOR ROOSEVELT

The world of Eleanor Roosevelt (1884–1962), fragile already, collapsed entirely one evening in September 1918 when she discovered a packet of love letters from Lucy Page Mercer (1891–1948) in her husband's luggage. An affair had been going on for some time and was widely known in Washington circles, thanks in part to Eleanor's mischievous cousin Alice Roosevelt Longworth (1884–1980), who invited Lucy and Franklin to her parties to help move the romance along. Eleanor knew that a distance had come between she and Franklin, but regarded its origins in their separation for so many months. And she told Alice in one of her letters, "I did not believe in knowing things which your husband did not wish you to know"—which was perfectly fine with Alice.

Terribly hurt by the correspondence she read, Eleanor immediately offered Franklin "his freedom." She was ready for divorce, but her mother-in-law was not. Sara declared that if their marriage fell apart she would cut Franklin off from his inheritance. Divorce was unthinkable for budding politicians in those days, and Franklin's boss, Josephus Daniel, a fundamentalist Christian, would have certainly fired him had he known. Louis Howe cautioned FDR against divorce and persuaded Eleanor that Franklin needed her to succeed. The five children and their complicated lives together also worked against separation. The children later claimed, when grown, that the revelation ended the intimate relations between Franklin and Eleanor, yet they already had significantly different views about sexuality.

Franklin seemed to understand the damage he had caused and increasingly defended his wife from any criticism. Their bond seemed to grow as a result of this pain, perhaps not in love so much as in partnership. Franklin took Eleanor to Europe with him in January after the end of the war, and both became dedicated to the creation of the League of Nations after seeing the devastation the war had caused in Europe.

The pain lingered. Photographs of Eleanor with Sara in 1920 showed a thin and dejected woman who had become anorexic. It was an improbable marriage from the start, Franklin the outgoing and gregarious young man, Eleanor the shy and withdrawn "wallflower." Her mother, Anna Rebecca Hall (1863–94), had been a New York fashion belle who disliked her daughter's plain looks and called her "Granny," slights that had a terrible impact on the child's development. Her father, Elliott Roosevelt (1860–94), Franklin's godfather, was a hopeless alcoholic who doted on his daughter. As problems with her husband developed, Anna and the children spent springs and summers at Tivoli while Elliott cavorted in New York and Long Island. In time he was banished from the home, as devastating for Eleanor as it was for her father.

Her mother died when ER was eight, she lost a brother a year later, and her beloved father died when she was ten. She and her brothers, Elliott, Jr. and Hall, were packed off to "a stern and repressive grandmother" in the country. Oak Terrace was the estate overlooking the river just a few miles north of Tivoli that the grandfather, Valentine Hall, maintained in addition to his West 37th Street townhouse. Valentine died at age 46 in 1880. Eleanor had to cope with five unruly siblings and a widow, Mary Livingston Ludlow Hall (1843–1919), ten years younger than her husband, who knew little about maintaining a country estate.

Eleanor had some tutoring in French, but could not read. Elizabeth Ludlow, her grandmother's sister, made the discovery, and promptly started daily lessons that soon extended to sewing and cooking. The girl lived a highly regimented life, yet was able to escape into the countryside and into fantasies about her father from time to time.

Mary Hall, although still in her early fifties, became reclusive, alone in her room except to issue orders and conduct prayer services to which the entire household, including the servants, was required to attend. She was particularly stern toward Eleanor, while at the same time indulgent and agreeable toward her own six children. ER's aunts and uncles helped to open her life, encouraging her to join in their frivolities, to ride pony and jump horses, to play at tennis and other games, to learn shooting, bicycling, and rowing. Her aunts Maude and Pussie became special friends, Pussie leading her into an enjoyment of poetry and Maude into an enjoyment of herself.

Eleanor's grandmother, thinking the child's spine to be crooked, forced her to wear a metal brace for a year. Yet over the years, Eleanor expressed only warmth and thankfulness for her grandmother and her Tivoli home. The hard treatment gave Eleanor a confidence that she had been denied under her mother's dilatory care. She remained in Tivoli until she was fifteen, when her grandmother sent her to London to the Allenswood finishing school, run by Marie Souvestre (d. 1905). Marie had known Elliott and Anna and had taught Eleanor's aunt Bye (TR's sister, Anna Roosevelt Cowles, 1855–1931). Here over the next three years, Eleanor Roosevelt's life changed dramatically. She gained self-confidence, learned European fashion and ways, and became the school leader and an "intimate favorite" of Madame Souvestre's.

"Never again would I be the rigid little person I had been theretofore," Eleanor wrote about her travels around Europe with the Madame and even on her own. On one of the solo trips to Paris, she was seen without a chaperone. Word was quickly sent back to her grandmother, who demanded her return to America. Eleanor spent a miserable summer and fall at Tivoli, beset now with the alcoholism of her uncles Eddie and Vallie instead of her father's. Vallie especially had gone over the limit with his "sprees." He would on occasion poke a shotgun out of a second-story window and fire toward visitors coming down the lane. The door to Eleanor's room was fitted with three locks for her protection that year.

When they were children, Franklin Delano Roosevelt had ridden her around a nursery floor on his back at one time. ("Purely a matter of hearsay to me," Eleanor recalled.) They danced at a family Christmas party when she was fourteen; Franklin was impressed with their conversation. They met at other times at family affairs, yet the spark that ignited a love between them apparently occurred in a chance encounter on the New York Central Railroad the summer of 1902. They sat together and talked for almost two hours, and on reaching Poughkeepsie went to the parlor car to greet Franklin's mother, whom Eleanor knew as "Cousin Sally." Sara was still wearing mourning from her husband's death two years earlier.

In November, Eleanor, eighteen, and Franklin a junior at Harvard, dined with other Roosevelts in the James Roosevelt "Rosy" Roosevelt box at the annual horse show at Madison Square Garden. Eleanor was among those mentioned in *Town Topics* and *Herald* society columns the next day. That evening, Franklin entered Eleanor's name in his diary for the first time. They saw each other more frequently over the next two years.

The winter of her eighteenth year was Eleanor's coming out as a New York debutante. In later years she often wrote and spoke of how she felt like such a wallflower, especially with the memories of her vivacious mother and society belle in her thoughts, yet these views were not shared by her contemporaries from those times. Three of her dance partners at the debutante ball, whom Eleanor believed signed her card out of duty and honor to the family, were in fact competing over the privilege. And Alice, the acerbic cousin from Oyster Bay whose wit often cut both ways, disliked Eleanor intensely because some in the family considered her "more like my father's daughter than I was."

"She was always making herself out to be an ugly duckling but she was really rather attractive," Alice once wrote. "Tall, rather coltish-looking, with masses of pale, gold hair rippling to below her waist, and really lovely blue eyes. It's true that her chin went in a bit, which wouldn't have been so noticeable if only her hateful grandmother had fixed her teeth."

Eleanor engaged in settlement work on the Lower East Side in the summers and spent winters in Washington visiting Aunt Bye—"a publicly admired intellectual and salonist" whose home was called "the little White House"—and her husband, a rear admiral from the Spanish-American War, William Sheffield Cowles (1846–1923). Eleanor engaged in the life of capitol society and acquired a level of "social ease" and understanding of Washington that would serve her in years to come, but not in its politics. "I lived in a totally nonpolitical atmosphere," she later wrote. The pitiable children, not the injustice of poverty, were the motivation for her settlement work. She was only dimly aware when her uncle became president on McKinley's death, and did not think much of his election in 1904.

People in the Valley who knew her called Sara Roosevelt "Mrs. James"; Eleanor did too, even after she became her daughter-in-law. Sara was shocked when Franklin told her over Thanksgiving of 1903 that he intended to marry Eleanor. She convinced him to put off the announcement for a year so they could take a Caribbean cruise, which she thought might enable him to forget about his distant cousin. Yet Sara had in a way been the encouragement of the bond as well. She had invited Eleanor to house parties and had her at Campobello when FDR returned from a trip to England.

The marriage of Eleanor and Franklin at her cousin Susie Parish's house on East 76th Street on March 17, 1905, was on her mother's birthday, not intentionally but to accommodate the schedule of her uncle the President (inaugurated for his second term thirteen days earlier), who came for the St. Patrick's Day parade and to give the bride away. The wedding happened just as the parade was proceeding along nearby Fifth Avenue, the singing of "The Wearing of the Green" by the Ancient Order of Hibernians almost drowning out the service. At the end, President Roosevelt stepped forward and exclaimed, "Well, Franklin, there's nothing like keeping the name in the family." He kissed the bride and turned to the refreshments, most of those attending following him. Soon the young couple was alone, as they were when they cut the cake, Teddy holding forth with amusing stories elsewhere in the apartment.

Sara left Springwood to the couple and visited her sister at Tuxedo Park for their first week together. A European honeymoon began after the Columbia semester that fall (Franklin was studying for the bar exams, which he failed twice), three months of travel and visiting with family and friends. On their return, Eleanor, now pregnant, was appalled at her mother-in-law's control over their living arrangements in Manhattan. Eleanor's most fervent wish was to have a home of her own, yet Franklin did not see her anguish nor respond to her complaints about his mother. At Hyde Park, Sara made no allowances for the new wife at all, neither a privileged place at table, nor a study of her own, nor even a chair to join Franklin's and his mother's by the fireplace. Eleanor dutifully tried to win over her mother-in-law's affections, yet knew that she could never be satisfied. Eleanor had no responsibilities, not even the rearing of her own children, which Sara appropriated perhaps with some justification since Eleanor had no notion of child-rearing at all. She retreated into depression and withdrawal, refused to communicate for long periods of time, and felt betrayed by her husband's casual indifference.

The first child, Anna Eleanor, was born on May 3, 1906. James came on December 23, 1907. In 1908, Sara had "Siamese-twin town houses" built for them on East 65th Street—one for Sara and one for the couple, with sliding doors and passageways intricately connecting the floors, as maddening an arrangement for Eleanor's staff as for herself. Franklin, Jr. arrived on March 18, 1909, a robust infant but fated with heart problems; he died on November 1. Elliott came on September 23, 1910, the year of Eleanor's most intensive depressions because of Franklin's frequent absences.

Two weeks after his son was born, Franklin embarked on an election campaign that changed the course of his life. Eleanor was thrilled because her life was changed, too, first in the home they chose at 248 State Street in Albany, where Sara would come only as a guest. Eleanor also experienced her first political awakening in moving to the capital. She brought a new staff, three servants and an English governess for Anna and James, and was completely moved in on the first day, January 1, 1911. She hosted an Inaugural Day "open house" lunch for 250 the following afternoon. Eleanor became a part of Albany's political world, universally liked and enjoyed. She also became a much better mother in the process.

Albany brought Franklin and Eleanor closer, as in their carefree early days. Her new acuity in political matters was valuable to her husband, her opinions sound and sensible, and her contacts even more widespread than his. She also knew the protocols and postures of politics, retiring upstairs with the children when the men took up cigars and caucused over the Billy Sheehan case, for instance, and always supported her husband's efforts. She did not begrudge Tammany Hall as an institution, and instead focused on the individuals, their views and speeches; some of her friends were Tammanyites. As the insurgency of 1911 waned after Gorman's appointment to the US Senate, Eleanor's connections helped bring Franklin back into the Tammany fold, at least on speaking terms. Roosevelt himself skillfully walked a trail to better Tammany relations that came to benefit the Wilson administration in the ensuing years.

Franklin Roosevelt was not a reformer at heart and had little interest in the plight of the poor and the downtrodden when he came up the political ladder. The investigation into the Triangle Shirtwaist Company fire of March 25, 1911, led by Robert Wagner and Al Smith with Frances Perkins as chief investigator, produced thirty-two labor reform laws in New York that FDR took credit for in campaigns in later years, but as a state senator he had little to do with them. Roosevelt claimed that his lack of an interest in social causes happened solely because he had an agricultural constituency, not a labor one; it likely had patrician origins as well.

Another Roosevelt claim, that he came out for women's suffrage in 1911 as a result of a visit to his office by the beautiful and glamorous suffragette Inez Mulholland, was refuted by Eleanor in later years. He made the decision at least two months earlier, she said, and she was surprised by his action since the women's vote had not been a subject of interest to her, a woman. Eleanor readily accepted her position in the world as inferior to men and only became a suffragette because of her husband's advocacy. (She joked to a cousin that a suffrage parade during Wilson's inauguration "was too funny.") Nor was Eleanor a progressive, but in time all of the reformers who drafted her uncle's Bull Moose progressive platform of 1912 became her close allies.

Eleanor contracted typhoid along with her husband just as the 1912 political campaign began. Wilson was the presidential nominee, and Franklin would be running for a second term. ER had difficulty with the strategist called in to run FDR's campaign, Louis McHenry Howe, because he was a heavy smoker of Sweet Caporals, cigarettes that were unusually smelly. Thanks to Howe, Franklin sailed through his own campaign from his bed while also leading, with Thomas Mott Osborne, the Wilson campaign in New York. When he received the appointment to the Navy post, Eleanor visited Aunt Bye in Connecticut for pointers on becoming a proper spouse in official Washington.

Franklin went off on a European inspection tour in July 1918 and returned to New York on September 12, a victim of double pneumonia on a ship that was also afflicted with the new influenza that was gripping the world. Eleanor, still in her Red Cross attire, met him at the dock with an ambulance and physician. It was while unpacking his bags that night that she discovered the Mercer love letters. Once resolved to retain the marriage, both Franklin and Eleanor changed their habits—ER went to more social events in the capitol, and Franklin stayed home more with the children—and became dedicated to the League of Nations struggle. Eleanor set about redefining her role as an independent thinker.

Her legacy as a champion of racial justice, world peace, economic security, housing for the poor, education, and human rights developed slowly and in contrast with their lifestyle and contacts. The Palmer Red Scare raids of 1919 were not of interest since the Roosevelts were friends with the Palmers, who lived across the street, and their own home was damaged when the Palmer home was dynamited on June 2 of that year. Yet the death of Grandmother Hall at Tivoli the next month led ER, now 34 years old, into an introspection about women's lives and their independence. At Hyde Park she asserted her authority over her own family, causing tensions with Sara that were only relieved when she left with the children to visit the Delanos.

ER's conversion to social causes occurred over time. She began to appreciate socialism after seeing Palmer's crackdowns on workers and poor people, but did not speak out in these early years. The white backlash to race riots in Washington that summer involved a mob of mostly sailors, yet neither Daniels nor Roosevelt intervened. Eleanor's only concern was for her husband's safety.

"Do be careful not to be hit by stray bullets," she wrote Franklin at one point.

Eleanor was pleased with Franklin's nomination as the vice presidential candidate in 1920, "but it never occurred to me to be much excited," she later wrote. Instead, she "felt detached and objective, as though I were looking at someone else's life." She was more sympathetic toward the imposition the campaign caused on her mother-in-law's space, her "lawn being trampled by hordes of people" during FDR's acceptance speech at Hyde Park, than the glory of his running. She might have been marginalized even further, except that Franklin insisted, for the first time, on her joining him on the campaign train. The experience was painful at first—Eleanor was barred from the heady political planning and discussions—but gradually the experience became another element in her political maturation, thanks to Louis Howe. He spent time with her during the cross-country campaign, educating her on politics, local leaders, and the intricacies of an extended national campaign.

In the summer of 1924, FDR announced that his wife needed a cozy "shack in the country" to pursue a women-owned business venture she had been discussing with Marion Dickerman and Nancy Cook. He suggested the place where they picnicked along the Val-Kill, a stream a mile-and-a-half east of Springwood (and still a part of the estate), and worked out the cabin details with Henry J. Toombs, a new draftsman with McKim, Mead and White, for whom this would be his first commission. The "shack" would have a modern contemporary interior and an exterior all Dutch-Hudson Valley inspired. Marion would be staying there, and Eleanor would have a place of her own away from the mansion. Marion, the principal at Todhunter, the private school in New York City where Eleanor taught and assisted in the management, moved into Val-Kill when it was ready in January 1926. Nancy Cook had been working with local boys on learning jobs and skills. Together, they formed Val-Kill Industries to train workers by producing furniture and other crafts at economical prices. The industry survived for ten years, with increased difficulty after the onset of the Depression, producing modest and attractive furniture and other household items.

ER's role in Val-Kill Industries almost led to an involvement with the American Crafts Council through Aileen Webb (b. 1892). Aileen inherited great wealth from her parents and married into even more. Aileen's efforts at marketing handmade items had started the Crafts Council movement. She wanted to open a shop in Manhattan using Val-Kill furniture, but nothing came of the venture. The Val-Kill model was a part of the theme for the National Youth Administration experiment in an arts-and-crafts school in Woodstock that Eleanor promoted at the end of the 1930s.

Now a wiser and more experienced political operative, Eleanor became immersed in Al Smith's 1928 presidential campaign, even giving stump speeches herself from time to time. She was said to have made one of her first political speeches in support of Smith on the terrace of Aileen Webb's Garrison estate. Smith recognized her unique abilities and used them well, and although Eleanor was deeply discouraged by her treatment by the Democratic leaders she was there for Smith at the crucial moment when he needed her to help convince her husband to become the gubernatorial candidate. When Franklin was elected she was again off to Albany, this time much more progressive in her thinking and attitudes.

Eleanor had her own group of friends and associates, and often had close relationships with the help. Mabel Haley Webster, her personal maid, was with her when the affair with Lucy Mercer was discovered. Her personal secretary Malvina "Tommy" Thompson, with whom she shared Val-Kill in later years, came via the Red Cross and the Democratic Committee in New York. She introduced Eleanor to Lorena Hickok, an Associated Press reporter. They did not hit it off immediately but became close friends when Roosevelt first campaigned for the presidency. The "masculine looking" houseguest and Eleanor had a sharp break that may have been precipitated by Hickok's advances.

Earl Miller (1897–1973), a former New York State Trooper who became FDR's bodyguard at the governor's mansion, spent time with Eleanor over the years until her death, suggesting a "touching romance of younger man and older woman" in their playful and endearing friendship. Henrietta Nesbitt was the Dutchess County housekeeper whom Eleanor refused to be without. Eleanor also took Joe Lash (1909–1987) and Trude Wenzel Pratt (1908–2004) under wing when their courtship began in the White House, where they had come as part of the youth movement of the 1930s.

Eleanor's involvement in America's interests was greater than any other First Lady. Her genuine interest in the plight of minorities fostered many changes during the Roosevelt years, directly in terms of policy and indirectly by her example. She resigned her membership in New York's most exclusive club, the Colony, when they blackballed Elinor Morgenthau because of her Jewish background. Her confrontation with the Daughters of the American Revolution in Washington over their refusal to allow Marion Anderson to perform at the DAR hall led to her resignation from that organization and a White House invitation to Anderson to perform at the Lincoln Memorial instead.

Yet Eleanor's influence did not always sway her husband's decision. FDR's most egregious actions included the notorious internment of American citizens of Japanese descent during the war and the administration's tacit acceptance of the forced deportation of as many as 100,000 Mexicans in the 1930s, more than half of whom were US citizens. President Roosevelt's relief policies also tended to harm African Americans more than help them. The black man was always the first to lose his job, the lowest paid worker when he managed to keep one, the one denied his full share of public support because of his race, and always discriminated against wherever he went. Blacks represented 12% of the population but suffered 30% of the harm in these years.

Eleanor often pressed FDR to his annoyance about discrimination and the needs of the black community. She had met Asa Philip Randolph (1889–1979) in Albany—he was a Socialist State Comptroller candidate in 1920 and a Secretary of State candidate in 1922—and developed a close relationship with him when her husband came to the White House. When Randolph and other civil rights leaders threatened a march on Washington over discrimination practices in war industries in 1941, Eleanor pleaded his cause. FDR relented and ordered full participation in the defense industry without regard to race, creed, color, or national origin, a policy that Eleanor convinced Randolph to accept. The President's decision not to extend the ban into the armed forces itself was not acceptable, however, leading Randolph to initiate a new campaign in 1947 that led to President Truman's ending of racial segregation there as well in 1948.

Eleanor's actions were often challenged as inappropriate by conservative, anti-Roosevelt, and traditional Christian family-value interests. She supported and abetted the progressive approach to incarceration that developed from the Smith administration through Roosevelt's years as governor, and assisted in the planning and design of Woodbourne in Sullivan County and Wallkill prison in Ulster County, both built by 1932. The Wallkill Correctional Facility "façade looks more like a gothic monastery than a prison," Mike Wise wrote in *The New York Times* in 2003.

Eugene Luther "Gore" Vidal (1925–2012) had occasion to visit Eleanor Roosevelt at Val-Kill in 1959, while he was living in Barrytown. Vidal was born in West Point, where his father (Eugene) was an instructor in aeronautics and a former football hero and Olympics competitor. Eugene Vidal served as President Roosevelt's first director of air commerce, and now his son, who renamed himself by taking his mother Nina's maiden name in 1939, wanted to run as a Democratic-Liberal candidate for Congress in Dutchess County. He needed Eleanor's advice and support. Vidal was expected, and when he found the front door of the cottage open he walked in and called, but there was no answer. He opened the first door he came to—a bathroom—and there stood Eleanor Roosevelt arranging a dozen gladioli in a toilet bowl.

"Well, now you know *everything!*" she said. Vidal was struck by her candid attitude. "It does keep them fresh," she added.

Eleanor was initially cool to Vidal's candidacy, but when the polls rose in his favor, she took to the prospect and held a tea for the women campaign workers at her home. He was fascinated by her "shrewd, grey-blue eyes" which he felt seemed to stare back at people until they looked the other way.

Vidal was at her funeral in 1962. Four presidents also attended.

28. What Francis Phelan Saw

It takes two Smiths to make a cough drop, but only one Hoover to make a clean sweep.

—Saying, attributed to Bill Kick's father

When John Mack of Poughkeepsie placed Franklin D. Roosevelt's name in nomination for president at the Democratic national convention in Chicago in 1932, the nation had been dealing with the effects of the Great Depression for almost three years. The next morning the candidate broke tradition by flying from New York to Chicago—the plane stopped twice for fuel—and accepting the nomination personally at the convention. It took four ballots for the campaign to achieve the two-thirds vote necessary to claim the nomination.

"I pledge you, I pledge myself, to a *new deal* for the American people," he told the cheering crowd.

Six months later, the day after giving his first inaugural address in March 1933 ("the only thing we have to fear is fear itself"), Roosevelt ordered a bank holiday to check the progress of the decline, and over the next hundred days fashioned a legislative structure to fight the Depression that gripped the land. In Westchester County, 47 commercial and about a dozen savings banks closed during that holiday; ten of the commercials never reopened. Credit was extended, theaters took IOUs for tickets, and the railroads accepted checks. A $7,500 payroll for five hundred emergency relief workers ($3 each for three days) was delayed until March 10. First National in Hastings-on-Hudson took extraordinary steps to reassure the public. The bank asked the local clergy to announce from the pulpit that the bank was still solvent, and had their staff deliver change to local stores to help ensure that weekend shoppers would be served.

Roosevelt's "brains trust" (the term was coined by *New York Times* reporter James Kieran) met in Albany and Hyde Park during the spring and summer of 1932, formulating campaign positions that would later translate into New Deal policies. The core group consisted of three Columbia University professors: Raymond Moley, who coined the "New Deal" phrase and drafted the "Forgotten Man" speech with Roosevelt; Rexford Guy Tugwell, an economist and agriculture expert; and Adolf A. Berle, Jr., who co-wrote with Moley a Commonwealth Club address that called for an "economic constitutional order." Moley became FDR's principal economic advisor after the election and handled the interface with Hoover's treasury secretary, Ogden L. Mills of Staatsburg.

As governor, Roosevelt was a states-rightist who advocated self-reliance instead of appealing to the Hoover administration for assistance in the aftermath of the 1929 stock market crash. A 1931 conference on unemployment in the state enabled him to create the Temporary Employment Relief Agency in New York, but by the following February he understood the vast nature of the Depression and joined other governors in calling for federal aid. After legislative controls over spending were finally overcome in a Court of Appeals decision in 1929, Roosevelt was adept at utilizing the new executive budget in pacing the legislature into approving deficit spending as the state's fiscal difficulties accelerated. He met every Monday morning with Democratic members about pending legislation and used the contacts to overcome Republican challenges to his budgets.

The state budget grew by $44 million over 1929–33, to $271 million, the fixed government charges and contributions to other governments rising from $36 million to $169 million since 1920. New taxes included retail sales and, with the end of Prohibition, beer, liquor and wines (and their manufacture); Comptroller Morris S. Tremaine (1871–1941) brought in dozens of T.E.R.A. workers to process the new paperwork. Motor vehicle fines could not be collected because few could afford to pay them, and when they were paid some communities kept the money for themselves. Several local town justices were arrested for failing to turn over fine monies; the state pursued Ossining to the Appellate Division of the state Supreme Court to recoup its motor vehicle revenues. Money that flowed back to municipalities from special taxes like these fines and franchise and bank fees dropped to $36.7 million, down from $52.6 million just two years earlier. In contrast, aid for emergency relief, spiked by $21.9 million in federal money, rose from $129.6 million in 1931 to $162.8 million in 1933, ranging from $77,136 for Putnam County to $1.3 million for Westchester.

The Great Depression struck nationally, but in some ways the local economy was still moving along before the new times caught up. While national unemployment rose to 25 percent, Troy, which had 104 wholesale businesses employing almost 900 people in the 1930s, hovered at a 5 percent rate, and one third of those out of work were women whose jobs were taken up by men. Wage cuts were instituted in most establishments, however, the workweek shortened, and banks postponed mortgage payments to avoid foreclosures. Westchester County was involved in a construction boom in 1930, as it had been at the start of each of the previous three decades, and, in 1934, still maintained strong municipal assessment valuations (fifth in the state among counties). The median value of a Westchester home was $13,701, compared with $4,720 statewide. A new sewer district expansion was underway; a new armory was coming to New Rochelle, and the National Guard was about to spend $50,000 on Camp Smith in Peekskill. Almost $1.4 million was put to work on the Bedford Reformatory and Sing Sing Prison. A $12 million office building was planned over the Putnam Railroad tracks in Getty Square, and construction on a new high school began in Yonkers.

Hiram J. Halle (1867–1944), an oil magnate and inventor, became the personal mentor to Pound Ridge after moving there in 1928 at age 61. The community was on the progress skids, its population having dwindled to 515 in 1920 as progressive Westchester passed it by. In 1933, Halle financed the first year budget of the New School for Social Research's University in Exile campaign to save European scholars from totalitarian regime persecution. In the late 1930s, he brought numerous Jewish exiles to Pound Ridge to refurbish thirty-three homes that he purchased; thirteen are on the National Register of Historic Places. His contributions to the community served as a virtual one-man WPA for Pound Ridge. He purchased numerous family farms and gave the owners the option of leaving or staying and working the farms for him; many stayed. Halle's impact on the community virtually saved Pound Ridge and attracted wealthy entertainment figures, among the first of whom was Benny Goodman (1909–86). The Pound Ridge Historical Society hosted a tribute to him ("Hiram Halle and His Legacy") in 2015.

Cornelius A. Pugsley (1850–1936) was a former president and chairman of the board of the Peekskill bank, which was a hundred years old in the spring of 1933. He was a congressman in his early fifties and, through the American and Scenic Preservation Society, established the Pugsley Award in 1928 to honor achievements in parks and recreation. Pugsley was confident about the nation's ability to bounce back from the calamity when it hit. He invested $200,000 in a town park and $40,000 for a college in Florida. He had 1,040 share of bank stock that was valued at $1.5 million before the crash, but on May 21 the bank had to reorganize and he lost it all.

Doing what was necessary, feeding cash into the disrupted economy, the National Bank of Wallkill was able to stay open during the banking crisis when farmer Simon DuBois (d. 1932) and other contributed $30,000 to secure deposits. In Rockland County, Garnersville lost its print works to textile interests in South Carolina in 1930, creating a void in the workforce until 1934 when William F. Larkin converted his Garnerville Ice Company house into a holding company. He partnered with 91 local businessmen and had 16 knitting and dye goods factories employing 1,500 workers ensconced in the building by the start of World War II.

As governor, Roosevelt signed a law that allowed Peekskill to assume financial responsibility for hospital services to the poor and accident victims, a measure that Peekskill voters approved as the only recourse to the hospital's dissolution. The county established its own TERA, following the governor's model, and created one work bureau for the county and individual ones for Mount Vernon, Yonkers, New Rochelle, and White Plains. By November 1933, more than half of the 18,807 applicants for public relief were approved; "make-work" type jobs that the county created included indexing the county registrar's office, creating a land-value map of the county, and doing park work on trails, picnic areas and in plantings. A new almshouse was opened at Grasslands in 1934 with the federal government's assistance.

Yet even as America rose to the challenge, the casualties of the times were severe. One was the Elm Tree restaurant chain that two of the polite, post-Victorian sisters from Saugerties, Louisa Bruckner (1881–1930) and Emma Bruckner (1874–1941), had started in New York City. The Elm Tree, like Mrs. Lowe's Far and Near Tea Room in Tarrytown, served young unmarried women professionals, but Louisa became too heavily invested in stocks and lost it all with the crash. She jumped from a Wall Street window a few days after the fall.

Frank Sinnott was another Saugerties resident whose success was curtailed by the crash. He had a speakeasy in the front of Simmons Dairy during the 1920s and did well by it, living in a comfortable Washington Avenue home and always buying a new car every year. Sinnott lost $30,000 in the crash and later sold fish out of a truck for a living.

Some escaped the crash. Richard Gunnison, an advertising executive, sold his stock early in 1929, and then amused himself on the commuter trip from Scarsdale by calculating how much money he would have lost on Black Tuesday. He paid off his new home and rode out the crash with assets intact, investing again a few years later at considerable profit. Alfred Loomis and his partner and brother-in-law, Landon K. Thorne, made their fortunes in the 1920s devising ways for utility companies to underwrite the kinds of large investments needed to construct generating plants and electrical distribution systems. These types of financial inventions helped build the automobile, appliance, and telephone industries. Yet Loomis and Thorne quietly sold off their assets and converted to dollars or long-term bonds.

Loomis made $50 million in the first few years of the Depression. His neighbors in exclusive Tuxedo Park did not fare so well. The "smug citadel of inherited wealth" was devastated by the Depression, many of its grandiose homes soon boarded and empty, some even burned to reduce real estate taxes. Loomis helped several neighbors cover their losses, gave loans to others, and refused to allow the Tuxedo Park Association to reduce wages as recommended by the general manager. Seven members of the Loomis family staff who had eavesdropped at dinner conversations among Wall Street nabobs and then invested their money also lost badly. Loomis was annoyed but there to help. He gathered them together, gave them each one thousand dollars, and lectured them severely against investing unwisely.

Franklin Roosevelt, in this sense the last Jeffersonian to hold presidential office, had roots in agriculture as a gentleman farmer. His farm was run by a tenant, yet he avoided the label manor lord by concentrating on forestation as an agricultural pursuit. He advocated reforestation as a state senator before the war, and as governor championed a 1931 state constitutional amendment that converted 169,943,035 million acres into state forests at an average cost of $3.85 an acre; the lands remained taxable for town purposes. As president, Roosevelt created the Civilian Conservation Corps to employ young men in natural resource conservation. More than three million workers each made

$30 a week, most of which was sent home to their families, while creating parks, planting trees, building flood and erosion control projects, and otherwise improving America. Roosevelt took a design interest in model bungalows for the CCC camps, having the first built near his home at Norrie Point; they still exist and are rented out to campers by the state park service. The northern camps were integrated for the first two years, but in 1935 all of them became segregated, whites and blacks in their own camps instead of together. The camps were operated by War Department area commanders under General Douglas MacArthur, who complained about their drain on the regular army even as they proved to be a great informal training ground for officers and enlisted men. The CCC was the most popular of all the New Deal programs. Among the young enrollees were Stan Musial, Aldo Leopold, Archie Moore, Raymond Burr, Walter Matthau, and Robert Mitchum. New York oversaw 67 Corps camps, one of them in Cornwall-on-Hudson.

Roosevelt conducted thirty-one fireside chats between March 1933 and January 1945, not on a regular schedule and tending to cluster during periods of crisis. He traced their origin to his governorship of New York and the times he had to "go over the heads" of the legislature and the press to provide information and appeal to the people directly. The chats were brief, from fifteen to forty-five minutes in length, averaging twenty-six minutes. All were given from the White House, except two from Hyde Park. Up to 83% of America's radios were tuned in on those evenings.

Like his father, Franklin was deeply attached to the larger community in Hyde Park and firmly convinced that agriculture was the backbone of America. In affirming his roots, in 1933 he established the President's Cup for the best horse or pony at the Dutchess County Fair. Yet America's backbone was strained for more than a decade. Farm prices fell from $17 billion to $9 billion over 1920–32, and farm income dropped 20 percent more precipitously than the economy, to $5 billion nationally. Roosevelt forestalled riots in 1933 with radical legislation that protected farmers against foreclosures and subsidized reduced production as a way to raise prices. Farmers were especially helped by the Rural Electrification Administration, which more than tripled the number of farms with electricity over the next five years. Rosetta Winchell, "the mayor of West Camp," blessed the advent of electrification into Ulster County not for its power or illumination, but as a fire preventive that would finally do away with the dangerous gas lamps.

Rosetta was one of the housewives who never denied the anonymous hoboes who "came over the hill" from the mountains to the river, stopping at her back door for a drink of cider, a little charity and some food if she had it. The young men whose families could not continue to feed them often left home each summer and "rode the rails" in boxcars across America, dodging Pinkertons and other rail yard agents and police in the camps that proliferated on the edges of cities like Albany. Thousands of men became desperate with the times, and walked the rail yards while waiting for the next train to nowhere. William Kennedy's Pulitzer Prize winning Albany cycle novel, *Ironweed* (1983), focused on one of these men, whom Kennedy called Francis Phelan, beset with his own demons—as the country was then, too—about a failed and tragic try at life.

Peddlers were other itinerant travelers. Marcy C. Allen recalled an old Armenian carrying his pack through Hurd's Corners in Pawling with silks, laces, braids, and threads on a route that he had followed every year since early in the century. He took orders from the housewives for special goods they wanted and showed up a few weeks or months later with the goods. Some country folk sold berries in season at the mountain boarding houses. Average housewives living within the shadows of the Catskills, Shawangunks, and near other productive forest hillsides, often spent Sundays walking to huckleberry outcroppings with neighbors, their arms swaying with baskets containing cheese sandwiches for lunch, collecting a crop for pies, breads, and some sales back home.

Governor Lehman placed Robert Moses as head of the Emergency Public Works Commission in 1933. The creation of the Saratoga Springs Authority and expansion of the baths and the construction of the Rip Van Winkle Bridge at Catskill were Hudson Valley components of the commission's vast works. The first project of the 1932 New York Bridge Authority, the $2.5 million Catskill-Greenport span across the Hudson River could handle five million cars a year when it opened on July 1, 1935, at $1.20 a car each way. Pedestrians had to pay ten cents to cross the Rip Van Winkle Bridge, but pigs and mules could cross on their own. One of the side benefits of the bridge was an end to the perilous car trips men took across the river on the ice in winter to the pleasure houses on Diamond Street in Hudson.

During the 1930s, Governor Lehman routinely fought with the legislature over control of the new executive budget process. The press created the row; newspapers around the state criticized the wholesale changes in state government management of the Governor Smith years and called for a return to lump-sum budget practices instead of the line-item model that was pioneered by Governor Charles Whitman in 1914. Lehman prevailed in the protracted court struggle over funding control, even as he failed to win the record spending approvals he needed. Still, by the end of his term in 1940, the Democratic governor left New York with a sizeable budget surplus, the first since before the Depression, which became important in meeting the "defense emergency" that now replaced the economy emergency with the outbreak of World War II.

The Works Projects Administration, created in 1934, was more efficient and better funded than FERA. A Historical Records Survey was organized over the winter of 1935–36 to create jobs for white-collar personnel out of work; lawyers, historians, teachers, researchers and clerical workers were hired. A Historic American Buildings Survey employed out-of-work architects like Oscar Vatet, who had designed many buildings in Pleasantville and now went about measuring Westchester County buildings. The Federal Arts Program employed 3,750 artists who produced more than 15,600 works, including numerous Hudson Valley commissions, at a cost of $1.3 million. Tom Barrett of Poughkeepsie, who formed the Dutchess County Art Association in 1934, executed the murals for the Millbrook Memorial School. Harmon Neill (1893–1980) painted one at the Bowne Memorial Hospital in Poughkeepsie. Charles Rosen was among the Poughkeepsie Post Office muralists; and Olin Dows at Hyde Park and Rhinebeck. Several Woodstock artists participated, including Austin Mecklem, Marianne Appel, Ivan Summers and Anton Refregier. Henry Billings (1901–85), who was briefly associated with Woodstock, contributed several murals, including one in Wappingers Falls. An art class at Poughkeepsie High School was created in 1937 under the slogan, "Arts for the Millions." The entire national program benefited from the interest of Dutchess County neighbors and friends of the Roosevelts, Treasury Secretary Henry Morgenthau and his wife; at Treasury, Morgenthau initiated the first large-scale government arts project in the nation's history.

The private sector also stepped up to aid the creative community. The Humanities Division of the Rockefeller Foundation, founded in the late 1920s, sought to reformulate the humanist tradition in ways that made it "directly relevant in Depression-era America." Community theater, educational film and audio, and local and regional history and folklore were seen as ways to combat "the sense of rootlessness and the crisis of authority brought on by the boom-and-bust rhythm of unregulated capitalism." Vassar College, one of three colleges nationwide, benefited from a $10,500 foundation grant "to underwrite a summer institute" for those involved in the Federal Theatre Project. The college was a good choice, since Vassar had been the first college to offer drama after English professor Gertrude Buck started a course in playwriting and created the Vassar Dramatic Workshop in 1916. And besides, Hallie Flanagan, the director of the college's Experimental Theatre, was a friend of Eleanor Roosevelt's and the outspoken director of the WPA's venture into theater.

"We need a theatre," she wrote in *Theatre Arts* in 1935, "adapted to new times and new conditions; a theatre which recognizes the presence of its sister arts." The FTP survived for three years, created a thousand productions, and gave salaries to 12,000 out-of-work professionals. When Hallie Flanagan appeared before Congressman Martin Dies' red-baiting anti-New Deal investigations committee in November 1938, the audience burst into laughter when she had to explain that Christopher Marlowe, Shakespeare's contemporary, was not a Communist.

As the nation emerged from its prostration during the Depression, new ideas took root, some tied to international affairs. Rosendale in Ulster County thrived on an unusual form of tourism in the later years of the Depression. Norwegians from Brooklyn brought their Telemark Ski Club and Nordic skiing to Joppenbergh Mountain on the north side of Main Street and held their first tournament in January 1937. The novelty of a summer jump down a hill covered with borax was attempted, using an array of mats and carpets covered with straw and borax as a landing; in 1941, the jump was enlarged to 50 meters. The war ended the novel sport, but Nordic skiing was revived in the 1960s, a 70-meter jump opening in 1966. Olympic skier Franz Keller (b. 1945), a German who won the gold medal in 1968, came in 1969. The competition ended in 1971.

The *Saugerties Daily Post* reported in November 1940 that a new airplane parts factory was planned near the old Driving Park north of the village, but it was never built. When General Motors developed plans for a large automobile manufacturing plant along the railroad, the local industry leader, Martin

Cantine, quickly bought up the property needed for a siding. He did not want to lose the workforce at his paper-coating mill. GM went on to Tarrytown instead and the Cantine railroad property became the village dump. Barrels of spent cleaning fluid were dumped in an adjoining wetlands, using village trucks, of course, since all considered the arrangement with the benevolent Cantine the least they could do. In the 1990s, the toluene and aromatic hydrocarbons had to be cleaned up under new strict liability environmental laws. Village taxpayers and new property owner Rotron Inc. of Woodstock each paid $1 million toward the bill.

Westchester County spent two decades attempting to develop a charter form of government, until final approval came in 1937. Carl Pforzheimer, a Scarsdale investment banker and treasurer of the National Municipal League for thirty-five years, chaired the commission that produced the acceptable charter. Home rule was protected for the towns and villages that feared the elimination of the old board of supervisors. After being approved by the state legislature and the governor, the charter was accepted by the county voters by a 60–40% margin. Retired judge William Bleakley, the first county executive (elected in 1938), undertook a reorganization of county government in the consolidation of services and agencies.

The revival from economic collapse became apparent when the national government expanded its depository resources. On March 27, 1937, the Treasury Department disclosed that bids would go out in a few weeks on a depository at West Point to provide greater protection for its silver. *The New York Times* reported that the $600,000 "strongbox" would be wider and longer than the new one for gold at Fort Knox, Kentucky; up to twenty steel vaults could be accommodated. Office and security space, and "a force of machine gunners" concealed in niches in the walls, were among the amenities. The depository would hold two billion ounces (seventy tons) of silver, or $900,000,000 "at current rates" (i.e. 1937), almost twice the Treasury's capacity at the time.

29. Lowell Thomas of Quaker Hill

FDR to portly Republican Casey Hogate: "Mr. Hogate, they tell
me you have to hit a home run to make it to first base."
Casey: "Yes, sir, Mr. President, that's what any American businessman has to do under the New Deal. Let's play for a bit
of a stake: if your Packers win, you double the income tax;
if we win, you abolish it."
FDR: "I have no more confidence in my team than in the
Supreme Court."

—LOWELL THOMAS, *Good Evening Everybody:*
From Cripple Creek to Samarkand (1976)

L ike the city to the region and the river to the Valley, Franklin Roosevelt
dominated America in his dozen years as President by the sheer force of
his presence. Yet America and the Hudson River Valley were not otherwise
empty landscapes. An opposition, loyal and otherwise, made up of moderates,
critics of varying strengths and persuasions, and some who truly hated the
man—some of them his own relatives—were part of the setting as well.

Dixon Ryan Fox of Scarsdale was one of the moderate Republicans who
questioned Roosevelt's policies yet remained loyal to the presidency. In June
1938, wondering if social security would actually harm "the moral and physical
wealth of the world," he warned Union College graduates to be ready to eliminate
the program "if and when it becomes clear that ambition is being penalized,
that personality is rotting through disease, that strong men are content to be
carried—but carried at last by whom?"

Roosevelt's standing with another Dutchess County squire, Joel E.
Spingarn, might have led to a different approach toward African Americans
had they been closer. Joel and his Leedsville neighbor, Lewis Mumford, like
Edna St. Vincent Millay at Steepletop, were not far distant from FDR's sense
of international urgency as the decade of the 1930s neared its fateful conclusion. Joel in particular had taken the measure of both "pacifism and cynicism"
twenty years earlier, warning his fellow Americans that isolationism was a bur-

row to hide in, not a cure for America's personality problems with the rest of the world. He saw a time of tyranny at hand, just before his death in 1939.

Mumford would live to blame America's pacifism for the "state of civic rottenness" that he saw in the decade. National narrow-minded cynicism of this sort and the more ubiquitous notion of isolationism increased in the 1930s, paradoxically since air flight, the radio, and the intrepid Lowell Thomas expanded America's contacts with the outside world. And Mumford, although he appreciated Roosevelt's greatness "as a symbol," never could forgive the president's careful balancing act in mollifying the forces of retrenchment as he nudged the nation toward the European war.

Casey Hogate's friendly repartee with the President over the income tax at a softball game was the tip of a very deep and cold iceberg that existed between Roosevelt and the wealthy class. Frank Bailey (1865–1953), a banker and Brooklyn developer from Chatham, wrote about his rise in the business world with the deliberate title *It Can't Happen Here Again* (1944), meaning that his success never could be repeated because of FDR's graduated income tax. Bailey applied the same conservative approach in his long service as Union College treasurer and trustee, frustrating progress at the college along the way despite his generosity.

Bailey and Hogate were on the outside looking in at Roosevelt's economic policies. Many in the President's own cultural world, and in his bloodline in some cases, were aghast at what he was doing to the rich. He was "a traitor to his class" to a distant cousin like General John Ross Delafield (1874–1964), a wealthy antiquarian appalled by the 1935 call for an inheritance tax and large tax levies on personal fortunes. Howland Spencer lived across the river from Hyde Park and claimed the Krum Elbow reach for his side of the river's crook, not Roosevelt's, calling himself the Squire of Krum Elbow. In time, he sold his property to Father Divine in a racist slap at the President he hated. Spencer, so the story goes, was so incensed with FDR's policies and the war that he went to the Bahamas (where the King of England was said to have given him an island), only returning after the President's death.

The American Liberty League was the principal conservative voice against FDR and New Deal policies during his first term. The League's most prominent member and the one with the deepest personal grudge against Roosevelt was Al Smith, who claimed in January of 1936 that the president had begun a class war in favoring the poor. Yet the League never had substantial support in the nation, and Smith's joining it damaged his name more than helped its mission. The administration used the Smith allegation to great effect in defeating the Republican candidate that year, Alfred Landon, who called the League's endorsement of his candidacy "the kiss of death." Roosevelt himself thought that Smith, who "made possible the dominance of our party in this State," had simply become "a different man" with "a different viewpoint," and refused to join the castigation of him by Democrats over his changeover.

James A. Farley of Rockland County, the Postmaster General, state and national Democratic Party leader and campaign manager for Al Smith in 1922 and for Roosevelt's gubernatorial and presidential campaigns, experienced a "blizzard of mud-balls hurled in my direction" by Roosevelt haters across the country in the months prior to the 1936 election—and characteristically responded to none of them. He accurately predicted the size of Roosevelt's victory over Kansas Governor Alf Landon that year, and coined the phrase, "As goes Maine, so goes Vermont"—they were the only states, as he predicted, to support Landon. His esteem for the President was unmatched, yet he broke with FDR over a third term, partly because of Farley's own ambitions to become president. Eleanor Roosevelt attempted to patch the differences between the two men, but Farley demurred even though he remained close friends with ER and their son Jimmy.

During the war, Roosevelt readily accepted an overture from one of his potential detractors, the young and wealthy Hudson Valley neighbor Nelson A. Rockefeller. A Rockefeller memorandum on the need to bring Latin America together under a single leadership model to prevent the insinuation of Nazism there led to his appointment as a special envoy to the continent. Roosevelt knew Rockefeller was Republican, of course—Rockefeller pointedly asked the President if that would be a problem before accepting the post—but FDR believed, apparently erroneously, that Rockefeller had contributed to his Democratic campaign. Rockefeller had given Alf Landon $33,000 four years earlier, and before commencing his work in Washington he surreptitiously met with Wendell Wilkie, who encouraged him to work with the President regardless of politics. He was the right man at the right time: Rockefeller's impact on South America was electrifying.

Lowell Thomas (1892–1981) was the most famous fellow Dutchess County resident in Franklin Roosevelt's day, often even more beloved than the President before the nation. He was already internationally celebrated when he took up residence on Quaker Hill in Pawling in 1926, the man who "discovered" T. E. Lawrence ("the King of Arabia," as Frances Thomas called him) and made both men famous in doing so. A great radio personality, Thomas was also famous as the historian for the first round-the-world airplane flight in 1924.

Young Thomas had a cub reporter's luck in Chicago in 1914 when he got a tip on Carlton Hudson Biggs, a man who was conning wealthy patrons along the North Shore. Biggs was known as the "Count of Coxsackie" in police circles in New York, where he had similarly victimized naïve ladies. Thomas gleaned information about the character from Charles A. Whitman, the district attorney of New York and, back in Chicago, eventually learned where Biggs was holed up. He returned to New York, met again with Whitman, now the governor, and arranged the Count's capture in return for a Chicago *Evening Journal* scoop on the action. The North Shore was jolted by the revelations about the former playboy, and Thomas was given full credit for exposing him.

Thomas moved to Quaker Hill two years after *With Lawrence in Arabia* was published. His family lived initially at Clover Brook Farm, a 37-room frame farmhouse built by Isaac Akin along the bluff. The story goes that Beulah Bondi, an actress and somewhat of a clairvoyant, saw the Thomases in her dressing room on Broadway one evening and told them of a vision she had of them living in a white house in the country. In 1926, after leaving Lowell, Jr. at a country home preparatory to another tour of Europe, Lowell "suddenly remembered" Beulah's prediction as the train came into Pawling. He and Frances rented a car and drove around until they came upon an attractive home. A butler answered the door and presented them to a Mrs. Wise. When Thomas asked if the house might be for sale, she was astonished. She had lived there all her life and just that morning had decided to sell. After their return from Europe, they drove Beulah into the county and asked her to identify the house she had seen in her vision, and she immediately identified Clover Brook Farm.

A next-door neighbor (at Glen Arden Farm) was Benjamin B. Hampton (1875–1932), a former magazine publisher who made a fortune producing early Zane Grey movies. Kenneth Craven "Casey" Hogate (1897–1947), president of Dow Jones and the *Wall Street Journal* and the gentleman critic with whom FDR bantered on the baseline, bought the Hampton farm and sold it to famed war correspondent Edward R. Murrow (1908-65) when Casey moved to Scarsdale.

Pawling was already a land rich in history and lore, where George Washington's army had encamped in the year after Saratoga. The grand Old Mizzentop Hotel, a hostelry of the 1890s, drew the rich and famous in its day. Admiral John Lorimer Worden (1818–97), the Civil War commander of the *Monitor*, named the Quaker Hill prominences for the masts of a ship—Mizzentop, Maintop, and Tiptop. One of his friends was Lew Wallace (1827–1905), who courted his wife and wrote part of *Ben Hur* on Quaker Hill. The principal community benefactor was Albert John Akin (1803–1903), a Quaker whose family dated to colonial times who made a fortune in drawing the Harlem River Railroad to Pawling. His donations included the hotel, a $100,000 community endowment, and the Akin Free Library, a ponderous yet beautiful stone edifice containing the Olive Gunnison Natural History Museum.

Thomas became so influential in Pawling that he caused a makeover of the geography of Quaker Hill. Over 1936–37, he used some arm-twisting to "convince" the board of trustees to have Akin Hall moved to the site of the Mizzentop, which was torn down in 1929 at mostly Thomas's expense. The Hall was given a new steeple and portico in the relocation. Colonnaded windows were added over 1941–42 and a new interior in 1948–49. Thomas asked Dale Carnegie (1888–1955), his former colleague and business manager in England, to donate an avenue of elm trees, and had the county change the access road to Quaker Hill to better accommodate the new church setting. Thomas also helped Carnegie promote his phenomenally successful self-improvement book, *How to Win Friends and Influence People* (1936), and more or less embodied the positive philosophy that Carnegie fostered. Thomas's other highly successful neighbor, Norman Vincent Peale (1898–1993), preached a new kind of manifest destiny for Americans in his 1952 bestseller, *The Power of Positive Thinking*.

Sunday attendance became a Quaker Hill event and drew many of Thomas's world-famous friends, including President Herbert Hoover, Bishop Fulton J. Sheen, and neighbors Peale and US Senate chaplain Dr. Edward Elson. Hoover came to Clover Brook to relax and fish after turning over the White House to President Roosevelt in 1933. At the time, Hoover was, as Thomas put it, "then at the nadir of his popularity, forsaken, even reviled" by

Americans generally. Thomas considered him "the wisest" of all the men he knew. Hoover had roots in the Hudson Valley; his mother was descended from the Winnes of Ulster County. He co-wrote *The Problem of Lasting Peace* (1942) with Hugh Gibson, his former ambassador to Belgium and a Quaker Hill regular, and knew Thomas through the Explorers Club of New York. In time the estimate of Hoover changed; when Thomas took him to the Army-Cornell football game at West Point several years later, "all forty thousand who were there stood and applauded" when they rose to leave. "It was a thrilling moment [for Hoover]," Thomas wrote, "for it was the first time he had been given such an ovation since he had left the White House."

Thomas came to Pawling for the quiet and to write, but his life changed dramatically again when he joined CBS Radio in 1931. He had made his first broadcast, an hour-long show about his round-the-world air travel, in 1925. In 1930, Thomas made the first network newscast, which was carried for a year by both NBC and CBS. William S. Paley convinced him to audition as the replacement for Floyd Gibbons on the new Literary Digest news program, and that began a 46-year relationship that made Thomas one of the most popular men in America. At first he commuted by train to the CBS studios in Manhattan—on one occasion stopping the train after skiing ahead of it during a snowstorm—but then the company acceded to his request to broadcast from the country, the first such experiment in radio history. A barn that he converted into his studio was so large that it became the subject of a newsreel account.

In 1936, Thomas became interested in acquiring the 3,000-acre Hammersley Hall estate on the north side of Quaker Hill. The property (named for the original colonial era owner) was under consideration for sale to a group of developers to be broken up into pricey estates. It was the home of Fred F. French (1883–1936), "the skyscraper builder" who erected Tudor City and Knickerbocker Village. "A tall, thin man," French had built the mansion in 1929 and accumulated 3,000 acres that included Quaker Lake, the largest water body on the hill. The house had some of the same structural features as a skyscraper, as well as a 45-foot sunken living room and a hand-carved cherry paneled library. Strapped at the time because of the costs of moving Akin Hall, Thomas arranged loans from his radio show sponsors, the Sun Oil Company and the Pews of Philadelphia, to acquire the estate. He retained a thousand acres and the 35-room Georgian mansion until his death, and donated 1,500 acres to the Nature Conservancy. A 1939 study of the flora of the area by Henry F. Alderfer reported thirty-five species of trees, including hemlocks up to eighty feet tall.

Thomas cleared a hundred miles of horseback trails and installed eight gates on the Quaker Hill ridge, and had a ring built for the neighborhood children to perform in what came to be known as "the world's smallest horse show." He maintained a softball diamond and a "stand of small 'squioias' (from deepest Lynan province)" that did not survive the years. He had a ski run built for himself and his son, both avid skiers, on nearby Strawberry Hill. He tried a dairy farm, planted thousands of trees, added a gymnasium, two swimming pools, a tennis court, two underground water systems, and started a mink and fox farm with C. C. Avard, a Canadian fur farmer. Avard provided the animals and the rancher, Fred Ward, who moved to Pawling with his family. Ward's daughter Electra married the radio engineer, Gene Nicks, and became Thomas's secretary for the next forty years.

"I was in the money now, and with every passing day I became more expert at getting rid of it," Thomas wrote.

Robert Trent Jones (1906–2000) designed a nine-hole golf course at Tiptop, at 1,600 feet the highest point in the Hudson Valley between Long Island and Albany. The course included "the longest hole in the world" at 790 yards (listed as 800 on the scorecard). Gene Sarazen (1902–99), who had a dairy farm nearby in Harrison (where he was born Eugenio Saraceni), was an honorary member of the country club board and frequent player; he opened the course for Thomas. Sam Snead and Presidents Nixon and Eisenhower played there. Snead, who had a neck problem at the time, played the "trick nine-holer" and "broke the course record with a 30," but declared himself not ready for the National Open the following week. He had a birdie six on the ninth.

"Back home we'd call that cross country golf," Snead declared. "That's when you see how many strokes it takes to hit the ball from one town to the next!"

Active members of the Quaker Hill Country Club in 1949 included Governor Thomas E. Dewey as honorary president, and Edward R. Murrow, a CBS colleague of Thomas. Murrow was chair of the entertainment committee's "Saturday Nights subcommittee." A barn that was transformed into the country club featured a unique Thomas contribution, a "History of Civilization

Fireplace" built with stones collected from around the world by his friends. Herbert Hoover once smuggled a stone out of Hitler's bunker for Lowell's fireplace. Egypt, the Parthenon in Greece, the Church of the Holy Sepulcher, St. Peter's Basilica, the Taj Mahal, the Great Wall of China, the Panama Canal, Notre Dame Cathedral, and Machu Picchu and Cuzco were all represented. The clubhouse was adorned with a Sanskrit motto urging the practice of generosity and the enjoyment of life's pleasures. No alcohol was allowed.

Thomas set up a film studio in the 1940s and made more than a hundred commercial films and all the prologues for his Cinerama productions. In 1975, Thomas donated Hammersley Hall to his alma mater, the University of Denver, which eventually sold it into private hands. The home included the studio, golf course, roads, ponds, landscaping, and 15,650 square-foot mansion with steam heating plant and electrical transformer vault, all appraised at $3.55 million.

Thomas was a phenomenon of his times. His half-hour travelogue program came on at 7 p.m., just after dinner, when families across America crowded around the radio in the parlor for a visit to some forgotten corner of the world. When he did a broadcast on Western Union one evening and the company offered free telegrams in response to the show, Thomas received 265,657 in one night. He intended to answer them, and stored them in a barn that he loaned to his brother-in-law Raymond Thornburg and Norman Vincent Peale, to use for their new publication, *Guideposts*. When all went up in flames one night, including the *Guideposts* subscription lists, an appeal by Thomas led to Peale's publication immediately tripling in the number of subscribers. His CBS show, "Lowell Thomas and the News," became the longest-running program in broadcast history. He was the first ever to broadcast news on television.

He had a mountain range in the Antarctic, an island in the Arctic Ocean, and a Tibetan refugee school named after him, among other places. The "Father of Cinerama," Thomas was inducted into the Ski Hall of Fame (in both Canada and America), the Journalists Hall of Fame, and the International Travelers Hall of Fame, alongside Neil Armstrong.

Thomas also issued fifty-eight published works, many of them colorful stories of the people he knew and the places he had seen. His working companion and co-writer was burly Prosper Buranelli (1890–1960), who made a fortune writing crossword books that sold more than 100 million copies and launched the Simon & Schuster publishing house. They worked in a fourth-floor study at Clover Brook, a room sixty feet long by twenty-five wide, with four desks, each one containing a book in progress.

Thomas actively recruited his world-famous friends to visit Quaker Hill, to live there and speak on behalf of Thomas's various local fundraising efforts. Most of them were subjects of Thomas books. Sam Woodfill (1883–1951) was a World War I Congressional Medal of Honor recipient whom General Pershing considered "the outstanding soldier of the war." Woodfill had taken out five machine guns at the Meuse-Argonne; Thomas's *Woodfill of the Regulars* was his tribute to the man. Fred Harmon was one of fourteen survivors of a doomed ship who survived for 1,300 miles in the Pacific, eating their engineer along the way; *The Wreck of the Dumaru* was another Thomas bestseller. Prince William of Sweden (1884–1965), a "fellow hunter" (at 6'8" in height), came up from New York for a three-day visit on January 7, 1927, while on a lecture tour of America. Although the winter was harsh that month, Thomas arranged for him to speak at the Pawling School and then deliberately "forgot" the prince's text so that he would need to speak extemporaneously, which he accomplished with charm and flair.

One of the first friends to purchase a neighboring farm was Dewey, the New York district attorney who had made a name for himself jailing criminals. The DA and his wife Frances Hutt (a star in musical comedy who died in 1970) came up in 1938 from Tuxedo Park, which was then too exclusive for a man with budding political aspirations. Their farm, in the old Hurd's Corners neighborhood on the north side of Quaker Hill, was called Dapplemere and included a horse racing track built by B. L. Haskins that may have been antedated by one frequented by James Roosevelt in his day.

Thomas served on the board of the Pawling School since 1933. The school had ninety-five students and was run by a board of trustees composed of major corporate heads of America. He was instrumental in transforming the school grounds into the Number One Air Force Rehabilitation Center, a convalescent home for wounded US airmen during the war. He invited them all to come and ski when they could, installing a thousand-foot tow, a chalet, a jump, a downhill and hundreds of acres of wooded trails to accommodate the veterans and his other friends. The golf course also came into play during the war, an international event that found members of the Quaker Hill Country Club hosting as houseguests luminaries like the British ambassador, while similar dignitaries came out in England on the same weekend. Scores were wired across the Atlantic and trophies exchanged.

In 1940, the *Pawling-Patterson News-Chronicle* reported on a visit to the Greer School, in which Thomas suggested that preparatory schools like Greer bring in men of experience in world affairs to lecture and teach. Dutcher House, the hotel that John Dutcher built in Pawling, was a training school for cryptographers and a convalescent hospital for wounded servicemen, thanks to Thomas. His work led to the creation of the Army Air Force Technical Training School in Pawling and lectures by important figures in the war effort. A weekend in August often began with a benefit softball game for the National War Fund, followed by a parade of Air Force training school personnel under Commander Gene Tunney (1897–1978) and notable veterans like Ted Shane (1900–67), the co-author with Thomas of *Softball, So What?* in 1940.

Commander Wade McClusky (1902–76), a hero of Midway, gave an evening talk in Thomas's barn. The first speaker for the summer 1943 series was the school's commander and "our new neighbor," Colonel Loving Pickering. In September 1943, Major Everett "Brick" Holstrom (b. 1916), a pilot with Doolittle and now instructor at Stewart Field, spoke on the bombing of Tokyo. Bradford Washburn (1910–2007), "America's foremost mountain climber," talked about Mount McKinley in September 1942. Herbert Hoover came a week later and spoke on world affairs. Branch Rickey (1881–1965), owner of the Brooklyn Dodgers, was another speaker. Norman Peale was featured several times. Lowell and Fran also went on the road locally to spread the word about Quaker Hill. The *Scarsdale Inquirer* reported in June 1942 on an attendance of 150 for the local Women's Club's hosting of the Thomas's and their film presentation on their home, the skiers, and the "Nine Old Men" softball team.

The story of the Nine Old Men began in the hot summer of 1933, when Thomas made a call to Marvin McIntyre, one of President Roosevelt's secretaries, to invite a few members of the President's entourage—a press group of 130—over to the hill to enjoy the cool breezes. They all came, including the President, his four sons and daughter Anna; FDR dipped into Lowell's applejack before adjourning to the coolness of the Clover Brook wine cellar. Thomas had a bright idea and invited them outside for a softball game. He phoned his teammates and some of the Pawling businessmen who had joined in games before, and a contest ensued in the summer heat while the President remained enjoying the fruits of the wine cellar.

"It was a hilarious game," Thomas reported. The Correspondents went to a 10-0 deficit before the combined "Debtors and Creditors," whereupon they all stopped keeping score. Two men slid into the same base. Several writers "wandered together under a fly ball until it hit one of them on the head." A columnist swung so hard at a third strike his belt popped and he fell entangled in his pants. After enjoying hearing about the salacious details, FDR invited Thomas and his team to Hyde Park for a game, staging it in Staatsburg at the estate of his "implacable foe," Ogden Mills. Major Jarvis and his Secret Service laid out the diamond. Roosevelt parked his touring car next to first base and managed his team from there, while Eleanor sat on the running board, "stoically knitting."

The game hit national headlines. FDR had pulled Rexford Tugwell as pitcher, which prompted Chicago *Daily News* editorialist Frank Knox to suggest he should "finish the job and get him out of the administration altogether." Every summer thereafter, FDR sent a challenge to Quaker Hill, where all the ensuing games were played drawing crowds of a thousand or more. Core players for Thomas included Metropolitan Opera tenor James Melton, actor Robert Montgomery, General Eddie Rickenbacker, Howard Morgens of Proctor and Gamble, President Eisenhower's future Secretary of Defense Neil McElroy, Casey Hogate, and boxer Gene Tunney. Chase Taylor (1897–1950), another regular on the team, came as his popular alter-ego, Colonel Stoopnagle, and commented humorously on Thomas and his Quaker Hill doings. Among the occasional umpires were opera star Geraldine Ferrar, Gloria Swanson, Sally Rand ("sans fan or bubble"), and Anna May Wong, who was once knocked unconscious by a line drive.

William Harrison ("Jack") Dempsey (1895–1983) came and played a few times, but confessed that when other kids were playing sandlot ball he was out riding the rails or involved in a brawl. Tunney was a pitcher; he bought his chauffeur a catcher's mitt so they could warm up together. A Marine Corps veteran who preferred the polo set of the Greenwich, Connecticut, area (not far from Pawling), Tunney had defeated Dempsey for the world heavyweight boxing championship twice, in 1926 and a year later in the famous "Long Count Fight," in which Dempsey's failure to move to a neutral corner after knocking down Tunney cost him the fight. The two worked together in promoting Roosevelt's New Deal in later years.

Thomas's Debtors and Creditors played almost every Sunday, often doubleheaders, and frequently for charity. One game at Madison Square Garden drew 15,000 spectators. The Akin Hall organ was purchased with proceeds from another game. Among their opponents were Robert L. Ripley's Believe-It-or-Nots from Westchester County, the Connecticut Nutmegs, the New York Artists and Models Guild, the Circus Saints and Sinners from down in the Harlem Valley, Tunney's Boxeroos, and a team of Republican Roosevelts from Oyster Bay led by TR's son Ted and called as "the Oystervelts." Heywood Hale Broun, a Nutmeg, became a favorite at Quaker Hill when he introduced the practice of having a woman run for the batter—in his case his beautiful wife who stepped up in short shorts—"during the pre-shorts era," Thomas pointed out later.

"We always had trouble getting a cap or hat big enough for Heywood Broun," Thomas joked. In one of the Oystervelt games at Quaker Hill, Thomas brought in Bill B. Van (1878–1950), a vaudevillian who did an imitation of FDR. The grandstands were packed, with Ted Roosevelt at the plate. He had been let in on the joke. A black open touring car appeared in the outfield, flanked by state troopers on either side. Roosevelt ran to the car, jumped on the running board, and shook the "President's" hand. Thomas had it all caught on Super 8 film.

In 1937, when Franklin Roosevelt tried unsuccessfully to pack the Supreme Court with his own judges, Thomas changed the team's name to the Nine Old Men. They appeared in their first game in Danbury, dressed in goatee beards and Geneva gowns and "introduced" by Geraldine Farrar. When Roosevelt heard about Thomas's new team name, he showed up at their next game in Pawling with his players wearing a new name on their shirts—the Roosevelt Packers.

Hamilton Fish often played first base for the Old Men. Roosevelt knew him well, of course. Fish was the oldest living descendant of Pieter Stuyvesant, a friend of the Roosevelts in their youth, and an implacable foe after FDR recognized Russia. He was a vocal leader of the isolationists in Congress and a diehard arch conservative in his later years. At the Quaker Hill game, FDR facetiously asked who Lowell's first baseman was, and when told, said he was a better baseball player than a congressman, and offered to buy his contract for thirty cents.

Roosevelt knew where he stood with the Lowell Thomas crowd. He told the world traveler in the summer of 1940, just after Wendell Wilkie was nominated to run against him, that he knew he would never get a vote out of Quaker Hill. He had tried once, back in 1910, when he drove all the country roads in his senate campaign.

Tom Dewey came to play on one occasion in his best suit, since he was on his way to a speech and did not have time to change. Thomas put him in as a pinch hitter. Dewey turned a left field blast into a sizzling double, and tore his pants when he slid into second. Thomas later opined that Dewey would have beaten FDR in the 1944 election if someone had taken a picture of that slide. Lowell considered the governor "the warmest guy in the world but, some said, [he] projected the public image of a suspicious department-store floorwalker."

Among those joining the Nine Old Men at times were Jim Thorpe, Vice President Henry A. Wallace, and James H. "Jimmy" Doolittle. Thomas's best pitcher at Pawling was Captain Frank Hawks (1897–1938), a speed flyer and carnival high-dive artist. Hawks and Winthrop Rockefeller had a friendly tussle during one game, each throwing the other into the pool. Hawks left his last game in "an experimental plane" en route to Buffalo, struck high-tension wires after refueling, and died in the crash. Thomas wept at his funeral.

George Herman "Babe" Ruth Sr. (1895–1948) was on the Believe-It-Or-Nots team when they faced the Debtors and Creditors before 14,000 at Madison Square Garden. He struck out, and no wonder; Thomas had brought in a ringer, "Cannonball" Baker, the country's fastest softball pitcher. When Thomas substituted Tunney as pitcher, the Babe blasted a three-run homer. Ruth, who always enjoyed a good party, rented a house in Putnam County and made frequent forays around the lower Valley. One of his stops was Glenmere, a sprawling Italian villa that Robert Wilson Goelet built in 1911 in the Sugar Loaf hamlet of Chester. Goelet attracted the wealthy sporting set to his grounds, including the Duke and Duchess of Windsor in their day, and established an annual New Year's Day horse race on the ice that drew gentry like Averell Harriman and Pierre Lorillard as participants. His youngest son, Peter Goelet, began WGNY, the Newburgh radio station, at Glenmere in 1920.

Thomas loved the friendly ribbing that he and Roosevelt shared over the softball games. He was a tried-and-true Republican in his voting ways (he thought FDR gerrymandered Ham Fish out of office in 1944), yet he was apolitical for most of his public life. Thomas held softball games to support Dewey's run for president in 1948, but his only political speech, and a brief one at that, was on behalf of Herbert Hoover before the county's Non-Partisan League at Fishkill at the home of (stalwart Democrat) Henry Morgenthau in 1928. Thomas's appeal lay in that wide-eyed boy's innocence that he brought with him from the Midwest, the go-ahead philosophy that echoed that of his friends Dale Carnegie and Norman Vincent Peale, as well as his radio expertise and as a world reporter. As Hattie Swan, an old-timer on the ridge once put it, "If there is anyone on Quaker Hill who doesn't like Lowell Thomas, it must be the other person's fault."

Roosevelt communicated with Thomas on other matters besides softball. In a 1933 "Dear Lowell" letter, he praised Thomas's leadership of the American Platform Guild, a speaker's bureau that Thomas had created. Eleanor Roosevelt knew Lowell well, having traveled over to Quaker Hill for speech lessons from him from time to time. As the softball season approached in the spring of 1942, Roosevelt cabled Thomas to express his regrets that "Hitler has ended our ballgames for the duration" of the war.

In 1976, Lowell Thomas looked back on the golden era of Quaker Hill as if it were just yesterday. He drove by the fields and heard the crowds. He looked across Strawberry Hill and saw Tom Dewey putting on skis for the first time. He recalled the improvements he had made, all the changes and how the hill looked when he first came. "There was a golden age on Quaker Hill in the years before the war," Thomas wrote:

> It was no longer the sleepy, shut-away little community of Colonial days, nor was it the summer resort that boomed just before the coming of the automobile. Instead, for a favored handful, a few old-timers and those, like us, who came to blend our lives with its orderly rhythms, the high ridge above the Harlem Valley became a haven of unblemished tranquility. It cast a particular spell.

30. "The Largest Standing Army in the World"

> It's come at last. God help us all.
>
> —FDR, on word of the *blitzkrieg* of Poland (1939)

Gunner's Mate 2/C Walter E. Bowe of Staatsburg thought about it for a moment. "If you are wrong about this," he said to himself, "you could face a firing squad." He was standing on the deck of the destroyer *USS Tucker* behind a 50-caliber machine gun on the port side.

It was a beautiful morning in Pearl Harbor, Hawaii—Sunday, December 7, 1941—and Bowe had been at his gun station, waiting that last, endlessly long five minutes until eight o'clock to raise the ship's flags for the day. He had a coffee beside him. He saw an airplane come down the lock into the channel at the entrance to the harbor. The plane dropped a "fish" as it came to the *USS Utah* and pulled up, followed by two more planes that also unleashed torpedoes. The *Utah* exploded and sank. Walter yelled to a group of soldiers on the fantail who had not seen the attack. Frustrated, he ran into the gun shack, turned on the water pumps to cool the 50-caliber, and pulled back the bolt handle.

The first one was in silhouette, but when he saw the red ball painted on the wing when it banked, he knew what was happening and began to fire. Walter Bowe hit one plane and it fell on the crane boom of the *USS Curtis* off Pearl City. He fired until the gun overheated and then jumped to the next one and began firing without the trainer sights. By now a crew was helping him. "They scored a direct hit on one aircraft," Oscar Roloff, a shipmate, recalled in a 1955 *Our Navy* magazine article.

Walter Bowe, a neighbor of Franklin D. Roosevelt's, was the first American to return fire against the Japanese in World War II; Admiral Chester W. Nimitz noted the fact in giving him a commendation on March 22, 1942. Bowe's ship, the *Tucker*, sank the following August after a radio operator failed to detect a minefield the destroyer entered while escorting a supply freighter off an island in the New Hebrides. Bowe and all but six of the other crewmembers were able to swim to safety on a nearby island.

Two other Hyde Park men were at Pearl Harbor that day. Sergeant Clifford W. Crispell and Mess Sergeant Raymond J. Collins of East Park were stationed at airfields elsewhere on Oahu. One of Al Palmatier's brothers was on the *Enterprise* in the Pacific, one of the three aircraft carriers and their escorts that were all away from the harbor supplying island outposts around Hawaii at the time of the attack. Harold Kipp was on a cruiser that had left the harbor on a routine mission two days earlier and returned that evening.

Crispell, his tour of duty having ended at 4 a.m., fell from his bunk onto the floor when the attack came. He stayed on duty for the next seventy-six hours, in charge of four machine guns that succeeded in forcing the enemy formations to scatter, giving a brief moment for America's planes to launch. Crispell described the Japanese pilots as "unpredictable fighters. One of their planes caught two of us in a field. They could have gotten us, but they didn't try." In the months after the attack, Crispell's activities were restricted and the nightly blackouts ended the islands' social life. He salvaged some metal from the *USS Arizona* and made a ring with a crest carrying the ordnance department's flaming bomb emblem and sent it to his father back home.

Ray "Fat" Collins, 25, returned home for a fifteen-day furlough in June 1942 and was interviewed by Helen Myers (1901?–1975) of the *Poughkeepsie Journal.* He was an army cook at Wheeler Field, twenty miles from Pearl, a corporal at the time, and was wounded in the attack. He was still in the hospital when he was promoted to mess sergeant, a position that supervised six cooks for the troops.

"You can make a pretty darn good coleslaw with dehydrated cabbage," he told Ms. Myers.

Collins confided that he "had often wondered what war was like," and "certainly found out in a hurry that morning." When he heard the bombs he quickly shut down the kitchen. Then a bomb landed "just right of me," behind two concrete walls that collapsed, pinning him in the wreckage. Four bombs in all hit the barracks, yet Collins was dug out by his buddies twenty minutes later. When the wounded were carried off to the hospital, "the Japs swooped to machinegun the ambulances," he said. He spent seven days recuperating.

Ray's younger sister Ruth quit her job as a staff nurse at St. Luke's Hospital in New York and joined the Army Nurse Corps when she learned that her brother had been injured. By mid-1942, she held the rank of second lieutenant and was serving in England. Ray was killed in Italy, one of nineteen Hyde Park men (including Commander-in-Chief Franklin D. Roosevelt) who died while in service during in the war.

In Hyde Park as elsewhere the families were stunned when they heard the news about Pearl Harbor over NBC or CBS radio at 2:30 that afternoon. Some were listening to a Giants-Dodgers football game that was interrupted with a flash announcement by the Mutual Broadcasting System. John Watson Golden, 17, went over to Zeph's Soda Fountain when he heard the report, meeting his fellow Roosevelt High School buddies who now all wanted to enlist. (John would in 1943.) Seven members of the school's championship basketball team, along with coach Robert Smith, were drafted within two years. Newt Hover, the team captain, was killed in action in Belgium on January 28, 1945. Six members of the football team enlisted or were drafted. All five of Charlie "Smitty" Smith's brothers joined the war, but Smitty had to wait until he was old enough before enlisting in 1952. All the brothers survived and returned home after the war.

Franklin Roosevelt was working on his stamp collection at the White House that morning, but that pleasure only belied the tense fears he and his advisors felt about the whereabouts of the Japanese fleet. He had struggled for years to aid the Allied efforts against the Axis powers in the face of severe isolationist calls from prominent people ranging from Charles Lindbergh to Congressman Hamilton Fish. He could not rely on manpower—as late as 1939, the US Army had only 135,000 personnel, the seventeenth largest army in the world, even though 280,000 were authorized. Lend-Lease programs for ships and supplies became the principal means for Roosevelt in helping Great Britain face the German onslaught in 1939–40, which Roosevelt had secured in the face of such opposition.

He was not alone among Americans in seeing the need to help the allies. Americans across the country relied on their president—their friend—to do the right thing, and implicitly trusted his judgment. From her Steepletop aerie in 1940, Edna St. Vincent Millay cautioned that "There Are No Islands, Any More":

Dear Islander, I envy you;
I'm very fond of islands, too;
And few the pleasures I have known
Which equaled being left alone.
Yet matters from without intrude
At times upon my solitude;
A forest fire, a dog run mad,
A neighbor stripped of all he had
By swindlers; or the shrieking plea
For help, of stabbed Democracy.

Roosevelt and Harry Hopkins were having lunch when the secretary of the Navy called with the news about Pearl Harbor. He called the secretary of state, Cordell Hull, who was meeting with the Japanese ambassador at the time, and then Roosevelt sat quietly for eighteen minutes alone before dictating the news bulletin that press secretary Stephen Early sent out to the radio media.

As the emerging conflict developed, the president relied upon a West Point ('07) graduate, Henry H. "Hap" Arnold (1886–1950), to build up the nation's military power through aviation and allocate its flight resources to help other countries fighting Germany. Arnold had come to FDR's attention through a dramatic flight of new B-10 bombers from Washington to Alaska and back that Arnold created for the publicity. He became a member of the Joint Chiefs of Staff in 1941 and was FDR's personal representative to Chang Kai-shek in 1943.

The notion that Roosevelt deliberately provoked World War II by ignoring information about the Japanese attack on Pearl Harbor—Charles A. Beard put forth the theory in his 1948 *President Roosevelt and the Coming of the War, 1941: A Study in Appearances and Realities*—was identified as a form of errant reasoning called "the furtive fallacy" by historiographer David Hackett Fischer. The fallacy assumed that because some signals suggested chicanery, chicanery happened. In fact snippets about the coming attack were present in the thousands of pieces of information that came before intelligence and army sources in the days and weeks before Pearl Harbor, and Roosevelt was certain in December that an attack would take place, but expected it in the Philippines. Roosevelt also knew, through an old Harvard friend, Otohiko Matsukata, of a plan the Japanese had developed in 1934 for land and sea conquests over the century, none of which included the United States.

The chicanery notion was repeated by Hamilton Fish and other isolationists, yet Fish lost his reelection bid in 1944—after thirty years in elective office —and did not serve again. *Life* magazine revived the fallacy in 1948, claiming that Thomas Dewey had "authentic information" that showed that the Japanese radio code was cracked prior to December 7, 1941, and information obtained of an impending large-scale attack. Stanley High reported that Dewey was importuned by General George Marshall not to reveal the knowledge, since the Japanese were still using the same code. The Republican candidate, *Life* maintained, lost to Roosevelt in a much narrower margin than the gross numbers appeared; had 750,000 votes out of 48 million cast been shifted in key states, Dewey would have taken the electoral college and, with it, the election. The *Life* implication was that had Dewey used the information, he might have defeated FDR.

The prosecution of the war relied on huge quantities of salvage for war industries, most notably in iron for ships and armaments. Among the more dramatic contributions was the sixty-foot-diameter Burden Iron Works water wheel in Troy, which was broken up for its scrap value. The supplier of horseshoes for every Northern horse in the Civil War had continued operating until 1938, employing 1,100 as late as 1923 in the production of horseshoes and other products. Like other cities, Troy went through energy conservation, rationing, merchandise shortages, blackouts and pricing and rent controls as part of the war effort; the controls on rent were not lifted until 1961.

Westchester County's foresight produced a model of government planning in the local war effort. The board of supervisors took up Governor Lehman's recommendation in September 1940 that it create a county council of defense along the state council model. The county body was authorized in October and first met on December 13, 1940, almost a year before the war began for America. The state also authorized each town and village to appoint defense councils, which forty-five government units in the county did, excepting only five villages that fell under their towns' aegis. The cities of Mount Vernon, New Rochelle, Peekskill, White Plains, and Yonkers created their own councils, and all of them deferred to the county council in integrating the planning effort. The county's plan included surveys and studies, inter-agency cooperation, active subcommittees, and information and data collection. Council purposes included civilian protection and protection of war industries, health and sanitation, morale, welfare (originally called "women's activities"), legal matters, and relations with state and federal defense bodies.

Industrial production was not a significant defense matter for the county, since most of the essential industries were located further upstate, but the council eventually was led by a representative of one of its most important industries, utilities vice-president and chief engineer George Cornell of Westchester Lighting. The county's principal task was to prepare for a likely evacuation of New York City in the event of an attack. A master warning system was needed, housing and services had to be available for those fleeing the city, and the level of emergency needs was likely to accelerate significantly. The welfare committee focused on food training, first aid, community help, nursing and sanitation issues, and immediately set about devising a survey of vocational interests to ensure a sufficient workforce for an emergency. Mrs. Frederick Godley of Rye organized a Women's Participation Committee that soon became very active. Uniforms were designed (for women at least; men wore armbands), which were neither obligatory nor popular except among the speakers that the council sent around the county.

The public was initially apathetic to participating in a strenuous defense program—the enemy was 3,000 miles away, after all—but warmed to the task as the prospect of war became clearer. The war council set up offices in the county building, obtained a quarterly budget allotment of $5,820, and went into action. The telephone bill the first year rose to $3,900; in time, the budget was $1,400 a month, and that included more than 18,000 volunteers. The mobilization was so swift and comprehensive the entire county became involved.

By November 1941, 358 defense training courses were in progress in Westchester County, 197 involving the Red Cross and first aid and 171 in home nursing, auto mechanics, radio technology, rescue work, child care, map-making, and auxiliary police and fire instruction. The 360 licensed members of the Amateur Radio Association made themselves available in communications for the defense effort. The shocking event on December 7 led to the first full-scale army alert and blackouts in several areas two days later, the initiation of a Civilian Air Raid system and a "Turret System" of communications warnings on the 11th, and the first of the air raid sirens with a two-minute test on December 13. A housing survey of upper Westchester was begun on January 29, 1942.

The defense councils, locally and statewide, were replaced by a War Council and Office of Civilian Protection under the state's War Emergency Act of 1942, the state adopting Westchester's recommendation that the two functions be bifurcated for more effective and efficient management. Civilian Protection assumed the army system of general orders, special orders, regulations and circulars under the direction of Herbert Gerlach of Ossining, the county executive, taking on a paramilitary aspect that left no doubts about the seriousness of the effort. The office also had a small women's staff called the Flying Squadron, whose function was to sweep down on towns and villages and establish and maintain municipal control centers (with the locals' vigorous support). A War Emergency Radio Service was established under Henry B. Lockwood; Dr. J. W. H. Randall trained new Gas Reconnaissance Agents; and municipal police trained as UXB Agents to handle unexploded bombs. A blackout of the industrial plants was carried out on February 11, and a countywide blackout on March 8. A signaling system in the event of a power failure and a Dim-Out program, requiring cars to run with parking lights so as not to be seen from waterways, were begun. Deputy Civilian Protection Director Rossiter Halbrook waxed effusive over "the finest drill Westchester County has had" on November 19, 1942, a countywide blackout that involved 97 reporting agencies and only two fines for violators.

By September 1942, 682 nurse aides had been trained by the Red Cross. A Nutrition Committee gave instructions to 4,927 householders; 759 were trained in food preservation techniques. Westchester had 552 nurses who enlisted in the war, 518 of whom performed their service in the county. Three of these nurses died during the war, two in accidents and one of pneumonia; seven who saw service were awarded bronze stars, and two remained "in charge of overseas hospitals" at the end of the war. Almost 850 of those who took the Red Cross training enrolled in schools of nursing after the war, Westchester producing more than 370 nurses over 1945–47.

As with other counties, much of the work of the War Council was taken up in drives and collections of precious war materials. All the towns and villages participated. A salvage committee (originally called materials conservation) had its first campaign six months before Pearl Harbor, an Aluminum Drive following a month later. Ten to fifteen pounds of metal per capita were collected in more than a hundred salvage depots involving more than 2,000 workers. "Win with Tin" campaigns over 1942–45 collected 1,742,281 pounds, Pelham contributing the most among towns and Bronxville among villages. Waste fats (due to the loss of Middle East oil), waste paper, and hosiery also involved spirited collection campaigns. The War Council celebrated the community's efforts in the spring of 1943 with a two-day "Warfair" exposition in the county office building auditorium under the theme, "Your County at War." More than 8,900 attended.

The war also called attention to the failed and defunct railroads that now yielded precious resources. Trolley tracks dormant on town and city streets for decades were taken up and the metal melted down. The New York, Westchester & Boston had maintained a regular commuter service (108 trains a day) from Willis Avenue in the Bronx to Mount Vernon, where it separated into lines to New Rochelle, Larchmont and Port Chester and to White Plains. The venture was a failure because through-travelers had to leave the train in the Bronx and take the elevated into the city. The line was abandoned, its rails and bridge girders melted for weapons, and sales of the railroad lands led to several development projects and the erection of Donnybrook Lodge where the Heathcote station in Scarsdale was located. The lodge became a popular stop for motorists in later years.

New York's water system was protected by National Guard troops, men stationed within sight of each other along the aqueduct and around every reservoir and important facility just as in World War I. General Electric and the RCA Corporation established spin-off industries in several of the river towns to provide parts for military applications. Kingston, a city of 28,589 in 1940, was important for its transportation nexus and skilled labor force. Rondout harbor was busy with work on vessels of various sorts (including sub-chasers and mine-sweepers). The hydraulics for Navy fighting planes were made by 550 workers at a sprawling round-the-clock Electrol Inc. plant—the work commended in the naval aircraft battle of Midway. Electrol expanded with the addition of the local Apollo Magneto plant noted for its reliable impulse starters. Across the Rondout in Port Ewen, the Hercules Powder Company was spread out over several acres and its powder storage guarded by armed men.

The *keekuten* (overlooks) along the river and on the promontories, some of which once kindled with the bonfires of the patriots, became lookout stations for a civilian corps of volunteers watching for the silhouettes of the sky. Westchester County had more than thirty of them. The volunteers worked from small, often unheated cabins, identifying the passing aircraft by their shapes and radioing the information to Stewart Airport, where a register was maintained of the air traffic. The local training extended to high school students as well as housewives and retired persons. Anita Smith, the Woodstock artist and writer, was the chief observer for the town's observation post of the Aircraft Warning System at its onset in 1941, and secretary of the France Forever organization formed in the same year. She had a small structure erected on stilts on her property (with a potbellied wood stove); Wilna Hervey was one of the volunteer spotters, at times in temperatures as low as thirty degrees below zero. Rita Gavigan, at the time the author of a racy gossip column in the *Saugerties Daily Post*, was the chief observer at Nanny Goat Hill in Saugerties, a promontory that took in a thirty-mile downriver corridor. Thomas Townsend, the Carmel postmaster for forty years starting in 1933, was a civilian spotter on Seminary Hill; he used a shed for the first few years and then a thirty-foot tower. Miss Christina Burns, the sister of Major General James H. Burns, was the Pawling post observer. The Rhinebeck post was atop Mount Rutsen in the Ferncliff Observation Tower, built by the Army Corps of Engineers in 1942; six men from the Army Air Corps, including John Ochs, arrived that year and manned the post round-the-clock. A number of the outposts were revived in the late 1950s in the Second Red Scare.

Local women, like their husbands, sons and brothers, were stirred to the war effort after Pearl Harbor. In Schenectady, the American Locomotive Company was awarded the government contract to manufacture tanks in 1941, and soon the production was so huge the traffic was stopped on a daily basis to accommodate the metal mastodons. Aline Gilbert (Steyer), 18 at the time, recalled impatiently standing on a State Street corner during her lunch hours in 1943, waiting for the tanks to pass. Twenty or thirty came rumbling out and crossed Erie Boulevard, testing the apparatus for war-readiness. Aline, who later studied at the Woodstock School of Art and became a portraitist and graphics artist, was one of a number of bright young women who took up the industrial slack when the men went off to war.

"I graduated [from high school] on Saturday [in 1943], and on Monday morning was on a bus to Schenectady," Aline recalled. She lived for the first year near Proctor's on State Street in The Foster, a girls' hotel where men were not allowed above the first floor. Later she took an apartment on her own. She worked in the General Electric engineering department and soon transferred to radar in a cavernous underground building on Campbell Avenue, reviewing designs in the drawing department and packaging small parts for the assembly line. She took engineering courses that GE offered at night, spending about four years there. The radar units she worked on were "monstrous things," she recalled, "the eeriest looking box-shaped things" that were assembled outside. After leaving Schenectady, she worked at a GE plant in a former bookbindery in her hometown, Saugerties. The local school superintendent, here as in numerous other communities, was the point person for the defense industry, handled the hiring and firing and managing of the personnel, and ran a tight ship. Aline was atypical in that she retained her job even after the boys returned from the war and took up their places in American industry.

Joan Waters (Keefe), also 18 and just out of Catholic high school, worked at the Edgewood Arsenal in Baltimore in the summer of 1939. All of her sorority sisters went. She worked in two other WWII industries and served in the first company to be mustered into service of the Women Army Auxiliary Corps (later shortened to the Women's Army Corps or WACS). Like the other girls who felt constricted by gender stereotyping, Joan bristled at the office work she was relegated to perform, and quietly dreamed of driving a supply truck on the front lines of the war. After serving in the first of the WACs, she took a job with Bell Aircraft in Marietta, Georgia, where they made B-29s. Bob Hope came and performed on one of the plane wings. Years later, an 87 year-old Ulster County activist dubbed "Saint Joan" by the local Saugerties paper for her take-no-prisoners antiwar advocacy, Joan Keefe recalled her fierce patriotism in those times.

"I wanted to kill Germans!" she said, laughing.

Lucy Abbott of Saugerties was assigned to a medical unit in Fort Polk, Louisiana, where she helped treat former Japanese prisoners of war. Shirley Crotty Hunter was a nurse cadet who trained in Kingston. Pat Canaughton was one of the WAVES (Women Accepted for Volunteer Emergency Services) who did clerical work at the headquarters level. Honor Mulligan, also a WAVE, took boot camp at Hunter College.

Rosetta Winchell of West Camp had a job at the Saugerties GE plant, and since she was older than many of the girls she was somewhat indispensable. The school superintendent, Dr. Grant D. Morse, became upset one day with Rosetta's work habits. Her son was home from his work as a state trooper assigned to Franklin D. Roosevelt at the president's quiet resort in the Virginia mountains (which a subsequent president named Camp David), but Morse was unaware of this when he demanded to know why she was leaving work early. She marched into his office and told him that her business concerned important matters and she would not take any guff from him about it. The superintendent was a stern taskmaster, and a wise administrator. He expressed his appreciation for what Rosetta was doing, and told her to handle the job anyway she wanted.

Jean Anderson, later a Highwoods artist and writer, worked the defense industry just before the war came to America. She was critical of the nation's isolationism before the war. "The surprise element was ridiculous, because we had been preparing all along," she said in 1998 of the months before Pearl Harbor.

Secret Service efforts around Hyde Park accelerated dramatically to ensure the protection of the President at the northern White House. A secure tunnel had been built into the Poughkeepsie post office for such an emergency. The local towns were alerted to the need to be prepared, and businesses and industry responded accordingly. Violet and hybrid anemone growers in Rhinebeck removed the glass from their greenhouses so German bombers would not be able to locate FDR's Hyde Park by its proximity. The greenhouses at Mills Mansion were dismantled for scrap metal during the war.

Enthusiasm for the war effort was commonplace. At Vassar College, the educational community initially went through the motions of organizing and preparing for blackouts, air raids and emergency measures while still in shock in the several weeks after Pearl Harbor; the air raid shelter was established in the halls of Main. Eventually drives for war relief kept the community focused while leave rules were relaxed to allow students to see off siblings, fiancés and family friends who were going overseas. In 1942, the students organized entertainments for British soldiers on rest leave at Camp Smith at Peekskill, and the faculty entertained them with dinners on campus. One night Jo Gleason saved her ration coupons to serve their guests fine steaks, but none of them ate when the meals were served. "I bet they want their meal well done," warden Elizabeth Moffatt Drouilhet said. Once the steaks were removed from the table and "browned to shoe leather . . . they ate every bit."

The faculty divided bitterly over a call for reducing the four-year curriculum to three because of the wartime emergency, as other schools were doing with the permission of the state Board of Regents. Returning to the four-year model after the war proved equally divisive, as many in the faculty wanted to keep the three-year program option. The trustees, led by Skidmore College president Kathryn Starbuck, preferred the three-year program followed by a year in pre-professional service.

The Victory Gardens program was very popular, each county organized under VG Councils. Governor Dewey had a law passed authorizing the killing of animals that fed off the gardens out of hunting season. The state had 1.5 million gardens in 1943, constituting about 200,000 acres at $20 value per acre of farm products produced. Local newspapers reported unusual backyard productions and local yields, as well as collection efforts for produce bound for Camp Shanks, Camp Smith and elsewhere. When FDR gave his first fireside chat since Pearl Harbor, he asked the people to have a map on hand while they listened. The map business boomed. He spoke at 10 p.m. on Feb. 23, 1942, to an audience of sixty-one million Americans, and quietly described the Allied situation in all parts of the world. It was his most effective fireside chat since the first one in 1933.

The impacts of rationing, especially of gasoline, affected all local travelers, and effectively eliminated casual long-distance travel. Nan Mason petitioned the local rationing board for an increase in her allotment for trips to her candle factory in Kingston, and when she and her partner Wilna Hervey went the few miles from their Bearsville farm into Woodstock hamlet they hitched their mule to a small cart in the summers and a sleigh in the snows of winter. Early in 1943, Governor Dewey created the New York State Emergency Food Commission, which handled fuel needs as well as food. Serious gasoline shortages in the spring and summer resulted from an unusually long winter on the Great Lakes. The shortages led the commission to alert the Petroleum Administration for War (PAW), which provided gallons to needy local areas. Dewey created a farm machinery repair program—fifteen agricultural engineers fitted with trucks and tools—that addressed some local farm needs. Food shortages had become a critical concern that necessitated a strict enforcement of the rationing limits. The production of milk and eggs was assisted by the import of two-and-a-half tons of grain from Canada. The New York State Farm Labor Program addressed shortages in farm manpower, especially critical when garden and fruit crops matured together in the fall. In 1944, 120,000 adults and youths and 20,000 out-of-state workers were employed.

The Valley provided vast resources for the war effort. Although the county's timber industry had all but disappeared by this time, pilings used in the building of the 45,000-ton US battleship *Iowa* in 1944 were drawn from the Hudson Valley Lumber Company of Nanuet, which had also contributed the rudder post to Admiral Byrd's Antarctic flagship. A War Department request for landing strips led Saratoga County into using its highway department to build an airport north of Saratoga Springs. The project was funded by the Civil Aeronautics Authority. The Tilly Foster Mine in Brewster, which became a reservoir following a tragic mining accident in 1895, was used to test diving equipment by soldiers in the war. Inwood marble was quarried by 200 workers for its magnesium at Wingdale, and the quarry was considered in later years as a source of the mineral for the space program. Emery mines abandoned on Colabaugh Road in Cortlandt were reopened. Carborundum (the second hardest mineral after diamond) was also mined there. The emery, once used in making the steps to the lower level of Grand Central Station because of its slip-free surface, was now used in industrial flooring in the defense industry. The Hudson River became the conduit for titanium taken at the National Lead Company's mine on Tahawus Mountain near the origin of the river, where a fifty-foot vein of iron ore had been mined in the nineteenth century. When the ore proved tainted with the titanium impurity, the mine eventually shut down, but with the war effort came a shortage of the metal, which was useful in making pigments and until now had been mined in India. The lead company revived the mine in 1941, and it became the major source of titanium in the United States.

The Hudson Valley was uniquely situated to serve as a transfer point for men and materiel in mobilizing and maintaining the war effort. Schenectady rolled out dozens of tanks and other armaments. Brewster Junction handled tanks, half-tracks, and other military vehicles shipped from Detroit and bound for overseas. Here the vehicles were transferred to the Putnam rail line, where clearance restrictions did not apply, allowing oversized freight to be taken to New York. The Patterson rail station became a regular stop for the military trains carrying these heavyweight beauties.

Camp Shanks in Rockland County, informally called "Last Stop USA," was the major east coast disembarkation point for troops going to Europe and North Africa. Named for Major David Carey Shanks (1861–1940), the Orangeburg Army installation at the terminus of the Erie Railroad handled 50,000 troops at a time and processed 1.3 million servicemen, including three-quarters of the

D-Day soldiers. Rail worker Joe Benjamin (1911–91) recalled the thousands of soldiers leaning from the rail car windows, many with tears in their eyes, their final letters home in hand, pleading for the rail workers to mail them. Somehow the pennies for postage were found, Benjamin said, and all of the letters were mailed. Many of the 400,000 prisoners of war were also processed through Camp Shanks, the first a group of Italians, spending from two weeks to several months there at a time. Camp Shanks also hosted exhibition games involving half a dozen major league teams, including the Brooklyn Dodgers and New York Yankees. Sergeant Joe Louis (1914–81), the heavyweight champion, jogged the streets of Orangeburg while stationed at Camp Shanks. Dozens of entertainers came to cheer up the troops. More than fifty regiments, brigades, divisions, and fighter and operations wings and group were stationed there.

By the summer of 1938, Alfred Loomis (1887–1975), an extraordinary avocational scientist who used his own fortune to finance his experiments and sponsor many professionals with their own, ended his laboratory work at Tuxedo Park on brain wave functioning. He donated most of his equipment to the Harvard Medical School and began to explore the emerging field of microwave radio technology. When Hitler invaded Austria that year, Loomis made notes on the tank models and artillery and the decimation caused by Luftwaffe bombings. He recalled Thomas Edison's charge to the nation to develop the finest in modern weapons when the first war broke out twenty-five years before, knowing that hard scientific research was at the core of any munitions advances. He himself developed the Loomis chronograph at Aberdeen during the First World War, which accurately measured the velocity of shells and remained standard equipment in the military.

In early 1939, Loomis received Edward Bowles (1898–1990) at Tower House, his Tuxedo Park estate. Bowles was an MIT radio specialist with fifteen investigators under him working on high-frequency microwave projects. Loomis was already involved in military work through his first cousin, Henry Stimson (1867–1950), an aide to two Republican administrations whom Roosevelt would soon name Secretary of War. Stimson had recommended Alfred for appointments on key boards and government committees. His science connections included Ernest O. Lawrence (1901–58), the Berkeley scientist who had invented the cyclotron, and Vannevar Bush (1890–1974), former director at MIT and now the head of the Carnegie Institute in Washington, D.C. Bush frequently drew upon Loomis' expertise, financial capabilities, and connections, and Loomis had already begun his own investigations by transforming Tower House into a military-applications lab and recruiting several fine young minds to help him carry out experiments.

Loomis and Bush studied "the matter of distance finding by radio" in a series of letters over the winter of 1938–39. By the spring, Bush had fleshed out a project to build "a plane detector" that he described in detail to Loomis. He added that "the trigonometry involved is not bad." England had pioneered early radar in the first years of the war, but was baffled by use of the technology at night and the need to keep the instruments small enough to carry on a plane. Loomis had concluded that the microwave spectrum might allow radio sets to become small and portable and detect airborne craft with accuracy at any time.

By April 1940, Loomis was convinced that the country would soon be drawn into the war. He brought Bowles' group of somewhat astonished MIT and private industry scientists to Tower House, paid their salaries, and provided a state-of-the-art scientific laboratory. Bowles was not comfortable in the company of the Wall Street tycoon, especially since Loomis was such a "gadgeteer" who "pretty much called the shots." Yet he could not object to working with a close friend of the MIT president. Loomis was delighted with the new opportunity, which would take him to the highest levels of government security. They resolved the problem and were soon working with British scientists in employing the new radar applications in the field.

Loomis' friend and former laboratory intern George Kistiakowsky (1900–82) passed along information about German efforts to develop a fission bomb out of uranium. Loomis played a role in the Manhattan Project as Bush got him involved in a National Defense Research Committee "to correlate and support scientific research on mechanisms and devices of war" that the president approved two days before German tanks rolled into Paris.

FDR was at Hyde Park in 1944 when he decided to reverse a decision he had made at Quebec the year before to have the United States develop an atomic arsenal independent of Great Britain. A Hyde Park Aide-Memoire completed on September 18, 1944, rejected the urgings of Danish physicist Niels Bohr (1885–1962) to proceed with an atomic arsenal alone on the grounds that the Russians would likely do the same. Vannevar Bush, who supported Bohr's initiative in some ways, concluded that Roosevelt preferred to "control the peace" over an embrace of international controls on nuclear energy.

President Theodore Roosevelt
(*Library of Congress*)

Naturalist John Burroughs in 1914

North River Bluestone Works, c. 1883, Malden-on-Hudson, Ulster County

(*Library of Congress*)

"Female Torso,"
John Frederick Mowbray-
Clarke, 1913 Armory Show

Dorothy and Lillian Gish in
D. W. Griffith's *Orphans of
the Storm* (1921), filmed on a
14-acre set in Mamaroneck
(*Library of Congress*)

William Henry Johnson and Needham Roberts, 369th Infantry Regiment ("Harlem Hellfighters"), 1918

Bronx River Parkway view, c. 1923; the first of the aesthetic parkway designs in America

Margaret Sanger
(1879-1966), advocate
of birth control and
genetic cleansing
(*Library of Congress*)

Hamilton Fish III
(1888-1991),
newly elected member
of Congress
(*Library of Congress*)

Franklin D. Roosevelt at
Groton, April 1900

Eleanor Roosevelt
school portrait

Louis Howe and FDR
in Albany, c. 1932

Eleanor Roosevelt
in 1954
(*NARA photo*)

Poet Edna St. Vincent Millay
of Steepletop, Columbia
County, in 1933
(*Library of Congress*)

Gore Vidal in 1948
(*Library of Congress*)

General Douglas MacArthur,
commander of U.S. Forces
in the Pacific Theater, World
War II

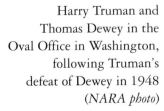

Harry Truman and
Thomas Dewey in the
Oval Office in Washington,
following Truman's
defeat of Dewey in 1948
(*NARA photo*)

Composer Aaron Copland at his desk in Westchester County

Grandma Moses in 1953
(*Library of Congress*)

Betty Friedan (1960)
(*Fred Palumbo, World Telegram*)

Vice President Nelson Rockefeller, National Security Council meeting, Washington D.C., c. 1975

Frances Reese of Scenic Hudson (Robert Boyle to her right), signing Hudson River Peace Treaty with Consolidated Edison, ending Storm King controversy, December 1980

Winston Farm Alliance dedication of the "Not Here Never" mural by Kate Boyer and
F. Tor Godmundson, Saugerties, 1989

Bob Dylan and
Albert Grossman, 1965
(*Michael Saporito photo*)

Pete Seeger performing at
the No Nukes Concert,
Saugerties 1978
(*Michael Saporito photo*)

Robert F. Kennedy Jr.
and Maurice D. Hinchey
(*Michael Saporito photo*)

Helen Hayes celebrating her
90th birthday at her home in
Haverstraw, March 17, 1990
(*Michael Saporito photo*)

31. Sleigh Rider

> I never realized the full scope of the devotion to him
> until after he died—until that night and after. Later, I
> couldn't go into a subway in New York or a cab without
> people stopping me to say they missed the way the Pres-
> ident used to talk to them. They'd say, "He used to talk
> to me about my government."
>
> —ELEANOR ROOSEVELT

Franklin D. Roosevelt was most uncomfortable in his public role when he was attending church.

"I can do almost anything in the goldfish bowl of the President's life," he once remarked, "but I'll be hanged if I can say my prayers in it. It bothers me to feel like something in a zoo."

When he attended the National Cathedral on March 4, 1934, to join in a celebration of the first anniversary of his swearing in, he found the pews already filled with tourists gawking and pointing at him. To add to his annoyance, they talked all through the service.

Roosevelt did not attend services regularly. His Sundays were spent as leisurely as possible, with no appointments before noon and the usual friends over for dinner. The menu was always the same: scrambled eggs cooked in a chafing dish with sausages, a salad, dessert and coffee. If there were guests, he enjoyed telling stories about his great-great-grandfather, Isaac Roosevelt, leading Washington's horse in the first inaugural parade, or his own father's acquaintance with Sam Houston before Texas became a state. Roosevelt's reading tended toward naval history, biography, American history, and children's books. He worked at the "hilltop" cottage plans with Henry Toombs in those presidential years. He collected materials for the Dutchess County Historical Society, and he still worked at his other hobbies when he could, especially his stamp collection, which had become so overused that Grace Tully suggested a leather replacement for its wooden case. Minnie Astor (Vincent's wife) had one made for the president's birthday, but his death intervened.

Roosevelt had an uneasy relationship with the Episcopal bishop of Washington, the Rt. Rev. James E. Freeman (1867–1943), because of Freeman's persistence in trying to get FDR to agree to be buried in the crypt at the National Cathedral, where Wilson lay. A few months into his second year, Roosevelt drove around Springwood with Frances Perkins on one of her visits to the Hyde Park White House, and stopped at the hemlock hedge enclosing his mother's rose garden.

"That's where I'm going to be buried, Frances," he said. "Don't you ever let anyone try to bury me in any cathedral."

In 1937, the night before Bishop Freeman interred the former secretary of state Frank Kellogg in the cathedral, Roosevelt took pencil and paper and wrote out a detailed description of his funeral and interment. The document was sealed in his personal safe and not opened until a few days after his death in 1945. The family was already engaged in almost exactly the instructions that the President had left, knowing for many years of his dislike of the bishop's interest in securing the body for his church.

He was a senior warden at St. James in Hyde Park, and his son James a vestryman. Franklin's father had gone over from the Dutch Reformed to the Episcopal faith after his first marriage and become a vestryman and occasional senior warden. The red brick church had Gothic overtones, but was meant to look like a typical country church in England, tucked within evergreens and ivy. The Roosevelt pew, which originally bore a brass nameplate ("J. Roosevelt"), was third from the front on the left side. The local church, unlike the grand cathedral, was circumspect about calling too much attention to its place in the president's life, but finally, during the war, a small sign was added to the lawn on the Albany Post Road: "The Church of the President." While going to service one Sunday, Roosevelt noticed that someone had added a postscript to the sign that read: "Formerly God's."

FDR roared his appreciation.

Franklin Roosevelt's time with Daisy Suckley provided an outlet for the burden he bore as America's leader. Often this was in the form of a drive in the country, getting away from it all, at times in delightful romps eluding Secret Service cars that followed. Daisy was a part of the many social events on the President's calendar, some of which involved other family members as well. A relaxing ride on the presidential yacht, the *Potomac*, on the first weekend in September in 1937 involved "Cousin Alvey" and Reggie Livingston, as well as uncle Fred "who is a dear" (as Daisy wrote). Roosevelt urged "all" to be there at noon to embark on time.

Roosevelt began a day in August 1942, with a relaxing few moments with Daisy at Wilderstein, returning to Hyde Park with her for the reception of former Empress Zita of Austria and her daughter, the accomplished Archduchess Adelaide, 28, who held a doctorate and taught at Fordham. Later that day he and Daisy spent time at Crumwold, the huge stone chateau that Archie Rogers had a half-mile north of Springwood. This was where Daisy first set eyes on FDR, in 1910, and on this day so many years, so many burdens later, she watched him rest.

"The President has many worries about the world just now," she wrote, "when in repose his face is over serious & drawn. His moments of relaxation are few."

They drove south after leaving Crumwold, the Secret Service behind them. Roosevelt abruptly turned into a field, the guards following and trying to overtake him. "He put on the gas," Daisy wrote, "& there was a regular small boy race. . . . The Pres. lost all his worries for about two minutes and was driving at full speed & having a fine laugh." The escort loved the sport as well, she wrote, although normally they became upset on the back roads rides when Roosevelt sped ahead in his smaller roadster, knowing the twists and turns so well, and then pulled over and waited with a big grin while they furiously caught up.

Their cousin, Laura "Polly" Delano, offered another relaxing outlet for the couple: she made a great Tom Collins. On November 27, 1942, after touring his "plantation" with arborist Nelson Brown (Roosevelt would have 30,000 more trees planted in the spring) Franklin and Daisy stopped at Polly's Rhinebeck home for a visit. Polly was shockingly fashionable, the first in her circle to collect Erté, the first to use red nail polish (a sister asked if she had been "disemboweling a rabbit"), her hair dyed blue, then purple, bedecked in pearls and gold, wearing a silk blouse "open to the waist" at galas and the like.

As usual, three of her huge dogs lay among her guests. They could not stay long because Polly disliked screens, which prompted hurricanes of insects to visit on hot evenings. Besides the Tom Collins, Franklin enjoyed the visits because Polly disdained Eleanor and welcomed his flirtations. She herself maintained a "lifelong" liaison with her chauffeur, who was also an expert dog trainer.

Daisy reported that on the way home the president of the United States confessed to feeling "*ivre*" after three of Polly's concoctions. Daisy was "the little mud wren" to some of the White House staff, a "prim spinster" to herself. She was actually closer by blood to Eleanor, a fourth cousin on the Livingston side. Her father, Robert Bowne Suckley, was the son of a Hudson River gentleman who inherited a fortune in real estate at age 32, most of which his sons lost in bad investments. She was called "Daisy" after the French word for that flower, *marguerite*. She gave no clues to the deep relationship she had with the President, and never confirmed that she kept a diary. In 1991, after her death at age 100, thousands of pages were found in a battered black suitcase tucked under her bed, personal writings about FDR that dated from 1933. Their old-fashioned love affair most likely came to fruition on a splendid September afternoon in 1935 on the wooded hilltop where Top Cottage rose. There, he told her of his dreams for the house and the two of them.

When FDR arrived back at Hyde Park on February 7, 1943, after a few days of rest at Washington following the grueling Casablanca trip to see Churchill, Daisy was working in the library. He came in and gathered up his dog Fala and spent the next few days in the library attic, sorting through the "horrors" of his term and the "ugly gifts" that had accumulated and that he would set aside for discarding or melting down for the war effort. His free time, what little there was of it, seemed more and more consumed with the past, the memories and the little pieces of his life that he kept as talismans to touch and feel and contemplate at times.

Daisy was with the President at Warm Springs on the afternoon when the terrible headache came on. So was Lucy Mercer Rutherford, who quickly left after he died. Roosevelt's death caused Lewis Mumford, living across Dutchess County in Amenia, to pause and ponder the man in a letter to Van Wyck Brooks. Mumford's chronic underestimation of Roosevelt continued even in his death:

> He was too divided a man ever to win a clean victory: his magnificent physical courage, perhaps unparalleled in our time except in actual warfare, was never equaled by his moral courage. The chances are that he would have fumbled and compromised the organization for peace far more pitiably than Wilson did.

On the funeral train coming north to Hyde Park, Eleanor Roosevelt lay awake all night thinking about "The Lonesome Train," the poem about Lincoln. Awaking at one point in the middle of the night, Bess Truman pulled the shade on the vice president's car and was startled to see the people, so many of them, lining the track as the train moved along, silently paying their respects. She quietly drew the shade, embarrassed at having interrupted something intimate between America and its President.

All during the presidential years, the weight of the nation on him, Franklin Delano Roosevelt was also physically disabled, the burden of a useless pair of legs seeming to express but a tip of the true measure of his humanity. He was as bullish as his wife's uncle Teddy in facing his infirmity, working for years in the vain attempt to overcome it, yet his frustrations were also Rooseveltian in scope. He had been physical all his life—the boy who could kick his leg higher than the others, the walker of the woods who leapt over the rail fencing, the Navy man who once climbed the rigging of a sail ship in an inspection tour. He even used to sleepwalk as a boy.

Roosevelt found ways to cope, some of brief, and some of longer duration. One that stayed with him over the years was a ritual of bedtime, how he evoked the image of Franklin the boy standing in the bright crisp air at the crest of the hill that swung down from the south porch at Springwood. A deep winter's snow folded to the bluffs below, beyond which the Hudson lay frozen and still. He crouched, Flexible Flyer sled in hand. He shifted the runners into line and dove forward, collapsing on the fine weathered wood as the craft spilled into the whiteness, the breeze, and the sound of the runners whistling through the snow. He maneuvered deftly into the lower curves and around the billowed clouds of whiteness to a fine and graceful stop near the tree stand at the bottom. Standing, he grasped the sled rope, turned, and walked back up the hill to sleigh again.

The great hill beckoned every evening to the grown-up boy. He fell into sleep each night playing that boy again, facing the hill with the Flyer under arm—the dive, the fast ride, the curves and swells of snow parting before him, rising in satisfaction at the conclusion, trudging again with sleigh through the snow to the top, and the ride again.

V. THE POSTWAR YEARS

It's all little villages up there, dairy farms, shit like that,
spread out. A lot of people rent summer places up there,
a lot of New Yorkers have weekend places there. It's not
the kind of territory I know.

> Barney Buler's description of the Hudson Valley
> DONALD E. WESTLAKE, *Smoke* (1998)

32. Grandma of the Hoosic

EDWARD R. MURROW: "What are you going to do for the next
    twenty years, Grandma Moses?"
GRANDMA MOSES: "I am going up yonder. . . ."
MURROW: "So this is something that in a sense you have no fear
    about or no apprehension?"
MOSES: "Oh, no. Go to sleep and wake up in the next world. I
    think that's the way. Did you ever know when you went to
    sleep?"
MURROW: "No, I don't think so."

—*See It Now* (1955)

Art has always been commonplace in the Hudson River Valley, thriving
among the ordinary people in educational, social, and community settings, engaging in lively folk traditions that often transcend parochial origins,
and defining a sense of place unique to the region. Yet rare were the instances
when fine and folk art merged in the public's eye—the *Van Bergen Overmantle*
a singular example in the eighteenth century—until a delightful genius was
discovered in 1938 in a little old lady from the Hoosic Valley.

The Hoosic is one of several eastern hanging valleys that drain the
bowl that is the Hudson Valley. Like Schenectady or Woodstock, the
Hoosic lies within both the Hudson River Valley and another region, in
this case the Green Mountains of Vermont. Perhaps the unusual artistic
sensibilities of Anna Mary Robertson Moses (1860–1961) comprised only
a natural corollary to the Hoosic's geographic distinction, the exception
that proved the rule, since this unique individual easily deserved a region
of her very own.

"Grandma" Moses was born in Greenwich and lived much of her life
on a farm in nearby Eagle Bridge. She was discovered as a great artist by a
vacationing art gallery owner, Louis J. Caldor (d. 1973), when she was already
77 years old. Caldor came across landscapes that she had painted for friends
and family on panels in her kitchen and on exhibit at Thomas's Drugstore in
Hoosick Falls. Subsequently, three of her paintings were shown in the
Members' Room of the Museum of Modern Art in 1939, and a "one-man

show" entitled "What a Farm Wife Painted," mounted by Caldor, appeared at the Gallery St. Etienne in 1940.

The response was extraordinary. As with most great works of art, Moses' paintings jumped from the canvases when viewed in person, only the busy and agreeable nature of her scenes, not their sonorous tones, appearing in reproductions. This was an art that, for all its primitive charms, was distinctly wedded to a sense of place, yet shared an affinity with modern art in the geography depicted—for example with Louise Blanch of Woodstock, who exhibited in the Whitney Museum's First Biennial Exhibition in 1932 and whose "August Landscape" of the Woodstock hillsides might well have been painted in the Hoosic Valley.

Otto Kallir (d. 1978), the dealer who had brought Egon Schiele and Gustav Klimt to America and who once sold a painting to Adolph Hitler, published a groundbreaking study, *Grandma Moses: American Primitive*, in 1946. Three years later she was given a Women's National Press Club award "for outstanding accomplishment in Art" by President Truman at the White House. Truman sent her a birthday card every year thereafter. *July Fourth* (1951) was made for the president and donated to the White House. Fifty paintings of hers were shown across Europe in 1950. Russell Sage College granted Grandma Moses an honorary doctorate—she was so thrilled with the cap and mortarboard they gave them to her. Thomas J. Watson befriended her and became a supporter, acquiring several paintings for the IBM collection. Eleanor Roosevelt, Irving Berlin, Walt Disney, Lillian Gish (who starred in a dramatization of her autobiography), and Thornton Wilder were other visitors and admirers. A film narrated by Archibald MacLeish followed, and another honorary doctorate from the Moore Institute of Art in Philadelphia. Her autobiography was published in 1952.

Moses did two paintings of President Eisenhower's Gettysburg farm at the request of his cabinet, which presented them to the President in a ceremony led by Vice President Nixon on January 18, 1956. Eisenhower, who had sent a postcard view of a painting of his own to the artist in 1952, was delighted, especially with the size of the golf green she included on the front lawn.

The 1955 "See It Now" interview may have been the most unique encounter in Edward R. Murrow's popular and incisive series. The interview took place after the film crew stayed in Eagle Bridge several days to record her making a painting at age 95. People in the Valley who had televisions and could receive the show were riveted by Murrow's style, the directness of his questions and the way he chain-smoked through the show. Anna Mary turned the tables on him by "pushing aside" her painting and asking Murrow pointed questions as well. She insisted that he attempt drawing himself and challenged him on the afterlife. After that brief exchange, Murrow sat gazing at his guest as if at a loss for words, his head rested on his hand, the smoke of his cigarette rising above his fingers.

In 1961, Governor Rockefeller declared her 101st birthday "Grandma Moses Day" in New York. She painted her last picture, *Rainbow*, in June of that year, and died at 101 years of age on December 13 at a nursing home in Hoosick Falls.

33. The Last of the Seine Fishers

> But the Hudson is bad; it is really bad. I saw a fisher-
> man today. He turned his back and his worm made a
> break for it.
> —JOHNNY CARSON ("The Tonight Show")

Toward the end of the war, nine-year-old Richard Joseph (b. 1935) joined his dad in the spring when he took his vacation from the New York Central Railroad and became a commercial shad fisherman. They lived on River Road in Port Ewen, a mile below Tucker's Beach and just above the old and unused Sunoco oil dock. The work really began in February when the cotton netting arrived from Connecticut and they soaked it in a large tub of linseed oil to preserve the cotton cord; the nets were hung out to dry until the spring. By the end of the 1940s the nets were replaced with new nylon ones that were not stiffened by the dried oil and could catch more fish. The nets were several hundred feet long, thirty feet wide, and hung thirty-five to forty feet under the water, and in each case they had to be fitted with sim lines tied with cork on the top and weighted on the bottom with rings. The laborious process was undertaken by the family in the house, one end of netting tied to the stairs banister and run twenty feet at a time through the bedroom.

"I was pretty fast at sewing the net," Richard wrote in a 1997 memoir, "so lots of times I got to stay home from school to work on the nets. I'd do that all day long, day after day, until we got it all done."

In March the family came down to the river and cleaned and painted the boats that had wintered over on the shore. The boats were left in the water tied to a buoy for a week so the wood would expand, and any leaks repaired using oakum and cotton. The main boat was fitted with an old gasoline engine they called the knuckle-buster, until Richard's dad geared up to a Johnson five-horse that was "fast enough" for them to get into the river and strong enough to "flag the ships away from our nets."

The boys set up the gear at the oil dock beach, cleaning it first of weeds and debris. The nets were carefully packed in special "cuddy" boxes on the boats and strung out in section over the river flats, dragging the bottom and collecting the fish as they drifted downstream when the tide changed. Ronnie's dad reduced the number of damaged fish by changing the old way of pulling them into the cuddy, spending a longer time on the river separating them from the cuddy and, as an added benefit, improving their appearance. Also unlike the old-timers, who only fished during the day, the Josephs fished through the night to take advantage of all the tides. They made that change in the 1940s when the state restricted fishing to from Sunday morning to Thursday evening.

The meshing was large enough for the undesirable and smaller males to swim through, trapping the larger roes with their eggs. The Josephs, working in pairs in two boats, collected the nets back into the cuddy, throwing the fish into boxes they had on board, and when the boxes were full they just continued to fill the boat with the fish. If there were too many in the boat, the males were thrown back into the river because their market value was too low to care. The Josephs became so good at it that in time they had their own truck and delivered the crop to the Fulton Fish Market twice a week, collecting from other fishermen in the area as well. Richard's dad dressed them smartly in boxes, "tail-to-toe on their backs so their bellies would be up," layered with ice, always getting a much better price because the fish looked so attractive to the buyers. In time they delivered seventy-five to a hundred boxes at a time, each box containing more than twenty fish that sold at $1.25 each. Richard's mother also sold them at home, packaged up nicely for each customer, and kept those proceeds for herself.

"Her side money," Richard said. "Which was okay with us. She earned it."

Everett C. Nack (1928–2004) of Claverack worked for the buck shad that he and John Bicus collected after Nack came home from the service in 1953. After two years, he traded eight muskrat skins for an old linen gill net and went on his own, making enough money the first season to buy a nylon net. In time, Nack ran three boats and became a well-known river character and environmentalist concerned with species loss on the Hudson River. One year he and his crew tagged four thousand shad for the Canadian government, and the next year captured them in the same place, the fish having traveled as far north as the St. Lawrence River bay and south to North Carolina.

Nack especially enjoyed catching smelt, the small diadromous shiners that came up the river first, before the shad and herring and striped bass, and were collected in scap nets in the tributaries. He took these "really tasty little fish" in the runs of the 1950s, when the practice was illegal and the locals had to avoid the local game warden; making it legal "took the fun out of it," he said. Nack was among the "forty or fifty guys" who fished the Columbiaville Creek; Tyke Ransom, Bill Mergendahl, and others took smelt with scap nets in the Esopus below Cantine Dam, and others fished the many other tributaries where the smelt came. Then came the shad, herring, and striped bass; Nack and other upriver old-timers called herring "sawbellies" and used them for bait for the stripers and also to prepare crocks of them in cream or wine sauces.

Everett Nack was the last of the commercial seine net fishermen on the Hudson River. "There was nothing ordinary about Everett," Tom Lake wrote in 2004. "His card offered goldfish, snails, driftwood and live bait." He was famous for his "all girl crew," as he put it, family and friends who were available during the weekdays and enjoyed getting out on the river. It appeared that even the fish respected him. Lake accompanied Nack for several hours one Christmas eve in the late 1970s in tagging shortnose sturgeons for the Boyce Thompson Institute where the fish wintered over in shallow waters so cold that ice formed on the boat's gunwhales while the two men worked. The creatures were "stacked like cordwood" and tagged using a 100-foot-long gill net; they never pulled up the same fish twice.

Downriver, one of the finest of the seine fishermen was a contemporary of Everett Nack's, Henry Gourdine of Crotonville, who might haul 4,500 pounds of fish a day with his crew of twelve. When he was a boy, Gourdine was on hand when a 500-pound sturgeon was pulled from the river, producing a hundred pounds of roe at $4.50 a pound. He was still catching sturgeon in fifty-foot nets in the 1950s, "perhaps a dozen in a season," as well as shad, enough to pack fifty boxes with crushed ice for hauling to the New York market.

The Hudson River was highly polluted during these years, as were all of the state's rivers, a Special Committee on Pollution Abatement reported in 1949. Bill Wolf wrote in *Sports Illustrated* of a river doused in municipal sewage for its entire length in the Hudson Valley, with industrial wastes from textile, milk, and tannery operations polluting the upper river and slaughterhouse dyes, laundry and metal plating wastes in the estuary. New York City dumped 800 tons of sewage a day into the river. Paper plants in Glens Falls and Fort Edward, chemical plants in Troy and Rensselaer, dye and manufacturing operations and a hundred other industries used the river as their ready-made sewer. The state response was limited to a modest planning grant to encourage municipalities to cure their sewage disposal problems, a model sanitation code, and a recommendation that sewage plants be built for twelve state institutions operating in the Valley. New York set limits on fishing for shad to try and protect the species, but by the end of the century their run had diminished to a trickle. One of the last of the locals still working the nets was Richard Jackson of Saugerties, a former IBMer, biker and bar owner, who went out before dawn every morning and complained bitterly by days end of the sparse catch.

When the commercial fishing ban came along in the 1970s, the abundant eel catch was the first to go because they were bottom-feeders—Hudson River eels (*Anguilla rostrata*) were a delicacy in Europe, where the great markets were. The loss of the eel fishery was a blow to many local families. Ivar Anderson had to move his operations from Tivoli to Rhode Island to survive, and eventually took a job as a cement trucker on the Hudson to maintain his family back home. He was bitter about the ban and the lost income, of course, but mostly he missed the lifestyle that he so enjoyed sharing with his sons.

34. An Era of Great Developments

GIANT MALL ATTACKS KINGSTON
—CHANLER CHAPMAN headline, *Barrytown Explorer*

The end of World War II finally brought about the growth and expansion of the lower New York–northern New Jersey area that was expected when the George Washington Bridge was completed in 1931, but never came because of the Depression. New York State's population grew to 14,830,192 in 1950, including more than 1.2 million in the Hudson River Valley. Population density ranged from 44 persons per square mile in Greene County to 682 in Schenectady and 451 in Albany counties. Fifty percent of the population resided in the cities, with Albany the largest at 135,000. Manufacturing accounted for 34% of the Valley workforce; wholesale and retail 17.5%, and 10% professionals. The wartime budget policies created large surpluses that enabled Governor Dewey to avoid the dreaded "narcotic spending" habit of using bond issues— $94 million in 1944 and as high as $323 million in 1945.

The growth was fueled by an aversion to city life—just as in the past those who could afford it came upriver to escape the "miasma"—only this time it was the white-collar industries and not just the wealthy who found the "hushed change" of the country preferable to the city smog. General Foods' 1954 relocation of a thousand executive workers from Park Avenue to suburban White Plains heralded the shift into the Valley by adding large windows to their new headquarters to take advantage of the sunlight. Almost immediately an advertisement appeared in *The New York Times* offering "6.6 Acres, Opposite General Foods," a sign of the great developments and profound changes to come.

Lower Westchester almost bucked the trend—or complicated it—when consideration was given for the siting of a United Nations headquarters. The home for all nations might well have been in the Valley had Franklin Roosevelt lived. Daisy Suckley recalled his thoughts about a postwar peace organization when they talked at Top Cottage on April 2, 1943. "The P. was relaxed & peaceful," Daisy wrote in her journal, "& talked mostly about his hopes for future peace. He has it all worked out in his mind already—The problem is to get the selfishness out of the conference." He wanted to be chairman of the new organization and the whole structure done "simply" with a secretary-general and a modest staff, "a small group of houses" for other nations, and "a good airfield," Daisy wrote. He wanted it to be in the Hudson Valley, near Hyde Park of course.

After a European location was rejected in the fall of 1945, as many as a hundred United States locations were considered, including ones as far north as Esopus in the Hudson Valley, but Westchester became the more likely target in February 1946, when the General Assembly established a commission to find five alternate sites in Westchester and Fairfield, Connecticut, counties. Westchester County officials wanted Rockwood Hall north of Tarrytown. Rockefeller family interests were not specific as to location—although Junior at one point drafted a letter donating Pocantico Hills for the project—but were deeply involved in keeping the headquarters close. Nelson Rockefeller had attended the UN organization conference in San Francisco in the spring of 1945 as Assistant Secretary of State for Latin America, and joined the UN Committee for the City of New York with his brother Winthrop and the family architect, Wallace K. Harrison.

Strong opposition to a Westchester site arose among suburban homeowners for a number of grassroots reasons, including fear of a separate sovereign state in their midst and xenophobia toward foreigners; property values would surely soar. A UN ballot initiative was roundly defeated. Nelson Rockefeller then seized the initiative and secured office space for the organization in the Empire State Building, a critical need at the time. The UN briefly flirted with San Francisco and Philadelphia again before returning the focus to New York. When a location at Kip's Bay on the East River became available, Nelson expressed his support and convinced his father to make an $8.5 million gift to allow the UN to purchase the site. Wallace Harrison designed the final structure.

With or without this grand new home, a boom in building fueled by a "boomer" generation of new babies gripped the Valley as it did the nation. Soon after the war, Thomas Callahan's Colonial Acres emerged as a huge tract in Scarsdale. In 1947, twenty families formed Usonia Homes, a cooperative in Pleasantville, and developed 97 acres with fifty one-acre homes on circular lots and a community farm. Their leader, David Henken, had seen a Frank Lloyd Wright-designed home at the Museum of Modern Art in 1940 and became engrossed in the project. Wright was one of the ten architects who designed the homes (he did three of them), and he wrote about the Sol Friedman home in the January 1950 *Architectural Forum.* Wright designed a home in the prairie tradition on Manursing Island in Rye five years later. Among other major architects, Philip Johnson's Oneto in Irvington was "set like a sculptural object in its landscape," as Frank Sanchez wrote, and Marcel Breuer's Newmann house in Croton was a Bauhaus-style masterpiece.

In the 1950s, a thousand new people moved into Corning Homes, an Albany city housing project "right in the middle of the hills," as William Kennedy recalled, "where the Gully and the Cowboy Ladder used to be." The pace quickened into sameness and uniformity, residential outcroppings appearing wherever industry and business expanded, and a growth in schools and services following. Housing "kit" plans from a Sears-Roebuck catalogue were still available, as they had been in the 1920s; popular magazines like *House Beautiful* and *Better Homes and Gardens* advertised architectural plans that could be purchased for a few hundred dollars and used with competent local contractor-builders. Very few took advantage of architects, because of cost and an antipathy toward the profession that dated to the 19th century, the new ranch style out of California being preferred in many cases. Some of the older and desirable stately homes of captains of industry and community leaders who passed on were moved *en toto* to new sites. Martin Cantine's home on a hilltop in Saugerties was rolled across the fields on logs to Washington Avenue and left there as it arrived, the front door now facing on the backside of the block. Although the Valley avoided the imposition of a Levittown, cheap new developments did proliferate, badly framed and boarded without insulation and with interior layouts of thin panels or even plywood. For low-income families, mobile home parks expanded, uninhibited by zoning and lacking municipal services like water or sewage, and were only gradually brought into better standards by complacent local officials and an uninformed electorate who resisted the increased costs that progress caused.

Lewis Mumford saw the irony in the spectacular regional growth, how the original impetus for the flight to the picturesque country as an asylum to escape the excesses of civilization while still enjoying its benefits turned that country into "a low-grade uniform environment from which escape is impossible:

As soon as the motor car became common, the pedestrian scale of the suburb disappeared, and with it, most of its individuality and charm . . . The suburb needed its very smallness, as it needed its rural background, to achieve its own kind of semi-rural perfection. Once that limit was over-passed, the suburb ceased to be a refuge from the city and became part of the inescapable megalopolis.

Dutchess County, its agricultural acreage diminished by 30 percent since 1930, had 1,027 farms in 1959; ten years later, there were 491 working farms left. The 1970 census reported a county population of 222,295, up by 75,000 over the previous decade. Yet as the number of farms and working acreage diminished, the sense of Dutchess as a farm county continued in its scenic qualities, attraction for a wealthy horse set among its "hilltopper" second-estate owners, and, each summer, by the Dutchess County Fair. The Fair prospered and expanded (from a 50,000 attendance in 1950 to 175,000 in 1972) while agriculture declined. Several large merchant buildings were added in 1968, keeping the semblance and spirit of farming's importance, and in time the Fair adapted to the changes by expanding its programs into other venues.

"We're still trying to emphasize agriculture, but we're really living in the midst of an urban area," Fair manager Sam Lloyd told Harold Faber of *The New York Times* in 1972.

By mid-century, dairying accounted for 60% of the Valley's farm business, although Columbia and Ulster had significant apple industries and Ulster County was a leading poultry producer. Orange County farmers drained thirty-five square miles below Mount Lookout, displacing a major bear habitat, creating a huge market for celery, onions, and sod. The "Black Dirt" region began producing 40 percent of the state's onions. In time, farmers tailored their crops to meet the new demands and developed new "niche market" themes for the metropolitan region. When a grape juice factory came to Clintondale, the orchards were promptly abandoned for vineyards; the apple harvest resumed as the premium fall crop once the new industry was gone. In beautiful Washington and Rensselaer counties, farmers took matters in their own hands in the 1960s by creating a farm land trust, the American Stewardship Association, that succeeded in saving 99 farms containing more than 15,000 acres from development by 2014.

Changes to the agriculture and markets law in 1971 created districts with lower tax assessments, protecting 371,000 acres by July 1973. Over time, as the interests of farmers, environmentalists and heritage promoters merged a fuller mix of support amenities developed, including open space and viewshed protections, the encouragement of a more varied agriculture-related mix of uses, and an embrace of nostalgic thinking prompted by the beauty of the settings. The Hudson River Valley was seen for what it had always been—a rural paradise that New Yorkers wanted to protect—yet the upsurge in wealth that brought in the suburbs, new factories, transportation networks and the ubiquitous automobiles also chipped away at the pastoral beauty and profoundly affected the lower Hudson River Valley. "Conspicuous consumption," a C. Wright Mills 1953 coinage to describe the times, became available to most if not all.

Traditional industries held on for a while, but ultimately yielded to the new times and new ways. Pasquale Lucchese's marble quarry in Thornwood was sold in 1938, yet continued to produce marketable stone until 1973. O'Brien and Kinkel still mined and crushed feldspar in northern Westchester, shipping the rock by train from Bedford Hills to a fine China manufacturer. Oliver quartz, usually mined for radio oscillators, had a rose strain that was favored in China for statues. The red-toned Oliver quarry yielded feldspar containing cryolite, a radioactive compound, as well as twelve-sided garnets, emeralds, aquamarine, and mica, the latter used in making isinglass windows for coal stoves. These stone businesses were all folded by 1960.

More than 22,000 suburban shopping centers were built nationally over 1950–70—a thousand in the Hudson Valley—the impetus driven in part by an IRS tax code manipulation in 1954. "Accelerated depreciation" changed a forty-year norm of straight depreciation to seven years, its implementation enabling a spate in the cheap production of malls owned by chains and franchises. The practice went on for thirty years until the Tax Reform Act of 1986.

The Martin Cantine Company, a paper-coating concern that was the principal employer in Saugerties for seventy years, continued to produce "the Tiffany of the trade" after the founder's death in 1935, but its days were numbered. Production in the Cantine plant slowed to a trickle in the 1960s. The noon whistle no longer ushered the men past the turbines through the mill's great doors to their homes or local bars for a lunch break, storefronts in the adjoining village became empty as the workforce moved on. The village lay desolated until an antiques trade sparked by Joan Keefe kickstarted the local economy in the 1990s, attracting a new, younger population, mostly transplants from the city. Albert Grossman, the Woodstock music impresario, took over the dam used by Cantine's and the Diamond Mills Paper Company, but died before pursuing a restaurant complex at the Cantine mill site; a restaurant and upscale hotel were finally built in 2012.

The postwar era produced advances in the status of African Americans due in part to President Truman's dramatic (if short-lived) embrace of a civil rights platform in 1948. *Brown v. Board of Education of Topeka* (1954) was a defining moment of the Eisenhower decade, precipitating the rapid integration of schools and changes in educational thinking. In some Hudson Valley districts, local school children came home and reported that it was no longer proper to call blacks "niggers" around the family dinner table, no matter how friendly the intent; remarkably, given the extent of prejudice, the new stricture set in and the terms "blacks" and "African Americans" came into general use. Local sports participation increasingly involved black athletes, but only partly because of Jackie Robinson and the integration of professional baseball. Black ballplayers had talent, and that was all that mattered on the local diamonds.

The era signaled a quantum shift in the correctional industry in the Hudson Valley, the "enlightened" approach of the Al Smith-Franklin Roosevelt times giving way to a formalized institutional management system influenced by the growth in housing near prisons and the community's security needs. Gardening, animal husbandry, education, sports competitions—"demonstration" games, as they were called—with outside communities, and other useful activities continued at rural prisons, but without the energy of the earlier times. The new prisons cost more and had greater manpower needs. The savings realized by the loss of the farm industries of old were expended in more jobs for the locals. An era *was* gone, and a new one begun.

An infusion of 1944 Federal Highway Act monies of 60% of the costs of building new roads prompted a rush in unstructured, even chaotic growth in some areas. A profusion of mixed uses related to the automobile dispersed jobs throughout the suburbs, devoured open space, and led to a decline in traditional land uses like farming and forestation. Automobile traffic grew 64% in New York State over 1946–53. Motor vehicle registrations rose from 2.8 million to 4.3 million in less than a decade. With the growth in strip malls came greater traffic and a profusion of limited access highways replete with cloverleafs, jug-handles and flow-through inventions to serve the new style. Parking lots became huge, yet families still clung obstinately to the belief in malls as the new form of "door-to-door" shopping.

Although a mix of service industries would arise in time and eclipse the industrial base of the Hudson Valley economy, manufacturing remained strong after the war. Papermaking industries were concentrated in Saratoga and Washington counties; apparels in Rensselaer, Dutchess, Orange and Ulster; machinery manufacturing in Dutchess; and textiles in Columbia and Orange. The electrical industry grew by leaps and bounds in Schenectady County. Small, rural operations survived in some industries—fasteners, for instance, who served the aeronautics industry—and more often folded under higher costs and the competition from cheaper goods made elsewhere. An entire underclass of working housewives developed in the sewing industry in many Valley cities and towns, led by entrepreneurs like Albert Giannotti in Saugerties and Kay Stacio, a beautiful and tough businesswoman in a Cadillac convertible who dominated the Kingston industry with a large local operation in the 1950s and 60s.

The arrival of the IBM Corporation transformed sleepy backwaters into bustling bedroom communities and made Route 9 between Poughkeepsie and Fishkill into a long commercial strip. Upriver a new bridge across the Hudson River was built to accommodate the regional impacts of an IBM plant in Kingston. With the Kingston-Rhinecliff Bridge came an explosion of residential growth on both sides of the river and a mall-building frenzy around the new facility north of Kingston in the town of Ulster. The city of Kingston—albeit contributing significantly to the workforce—lost most of its uptown business core and faced hard times because of IBM's arrival. The city was saved in a way by a Woodstock artist, watercolorist John Pike (1911–79), who demonstrated how the look of the Wall Street-North Front Street commercial neighborhood might be improved by drawing a colonial-style rendering of the storefronts on a napkin over lunch one day. The design was subsequently rendered into an attractive and popular drawing card for shoppers to return to uptown; it mattered only to a few purists that Pike's colonial facade was imposed on rows of Victorian architecture.

Adjoining towns experienced dramatic changes, usually in bedroom-community growth. A dramatic shift in shopping patterns doomed traditional business districts, leaving storefronts that once featured various specialties and departments empty and bare. Eight to ten butchers in the business area of a small village before the war were reduced to two who worked the sawdust floors of the A&P and Grand Union—until those businesses moved on as well. A family shoe store, local pharmacy, bus station, a florist or two, a dry-cleaner and a few undertakers, soda and sandwich shops and some bars survived the hard times—along with the local movie theater.

Arthur and Austin Simmons turned the cornfields of Barclay Heights where they hunted fox in the fall into hundreds of new homes for the industry of tomorrow. They added a mall, and soon two more developments came along. The town, still rural in its thinking, rejected an offer of a new sewer district as part of the developer package, and paid the consequences twenty-five years later when an expensive and much larger district had to be built. In Saugerties as elsewhere, taxpayers and governments resisted expenditures on infrastructure until spurred by state and federal funding, and by legal censure when necessary in subsequent decades. A mayor who resisted local sewer plant improvements in 1975 complained after the project was built that his name did not appear on the plaque dedicating its completion.

The Valley was hit by two hurricanes in the spring of 1955 that resulted in the most severe flooding of the century. Main Street in Rosendale was covered with five feet of water from a Rondout Creek awash with the overflow of the Rondout Reservoir, prompting a major US Army Corps of Engineers flood control project that extended to 1969. The Wallkill River overflowed, dousing farmlands from Plattekill to Tillson. At the Ashokan Reservoir, young and old alike came to see how high the turbid waters flowed over the spillway into the Lower Esopus Creek—eight, ten feet some claimed; some claimed more. The water flowing over Cantine Dam near the Esopus outlet at the Hudson 24 miles to the northeast crested at more than sixteen feet above the dam itself.

Science moved with the new sensibility of the era. Pioneer research in seismology and marine geophysics carried on by Professor William Maurice "Doc" Ewing (1906–74) at Columbia University found a home for the testing of sensitive scientific devices when Torrey Cliff, the 125-acre Palisades estate of Thomas W. Lamont (1870–1948), was donated by his widow, Florence Corliss Lamont (1873–1952), to her alma mater on his death. She presented the deed to then-Columbia University President Dwight D. Eisenhower. A year later a laboratory in a basement root cellar in one of the estate buildings formed the nucleus of the Lamont Geological Observatory, a world-class science institute renamed Lamont-Doherty in 1969 following a major donation by the foundation of Henry Latham Doherty (1870–1939). Its database in seismology and marine geosciences became the most comprehensive and accessible in the world.

An atomic research center for naval propulsion, the Knolls Atomic

Power Laboratory, was established in Niskayuna and West Milton during this decade. The 3,905-acre Kenneth A. Kesselring campus in West Milton operated two submarine nuclear propulsion plant prototypes to test new designs and systems under operational conditions. The submarine *USS Seawolf*, the second nuclear powered submarine built for the Navy, was powered by a unit developed here. Four reactors were constructed and tested at Kesselring between 1958 and 1992; two of these were deactivated and defueled by 2000. The 180-acre Niskayuna site designed reactor cores and propulsion systems, including the Trident submarine system. The work began under a General Electric Corporation contract in 1946, first in the design of an electricity-generating plant, and, starting in 1950, for the Navy. A process for extracting plutonium and uranium from irradiated fuels was developed at the Knolls Separations Process Research Unit Facility over 1950–53. Knolls also began producing a Chart of the Nuclides in 1956, which detailed the nuclear properties of every radioactive element. Almost 50,000 Navy officers and enlisted personnel were trained in nuclear submarine operations at these facilities.

Support industries expanded in response to the expansion in growth. Central Hudson Gas & Electric built a pair of new steam generating plants at Danskammer Point in 1950, sending power to customers on both side of the river via the first high voltage submarine pipe cable in the United States, this one laid under the Hudson River in 1948. In 1951, Niagara Mohawk introduced a cleaner and cheaper fuel by purchasing the New York Power & Light Corporation coke plant in Troy and manufacturing natural gas. Growing power needs led entrepreneurs into searching for natural gas pockets in the Marcellus shale that stretched to the Hudson River across northern Ulster County. The Gas and Oil Land Leasing Company drove deep exploratory wells in the shadow of Platte Clove in West Saugerties in the late 1950s, and at the Winston Farm in 1962. One of the Winston Farm wells was driven 2,808 feet deep, passing through a fault line; some gas was found but not enough to exploit given the technology of the time. Fifty years later, a renewed interest in extracting natural gas—now called "fracking"—arose in the country's search for cheap, clean power, but found no safe haven in the Hudson Valley. Local communities conscious of the environmental and health downsides of fracking resisted it strenuously.

The burning of coal led to Danskammer's retirement in the 1990s, although it was revived again twenty years later as a likely generator of electrical power during peak summer hours close to the metropolitan region, now powered by natural gas. Two smaller plants on the site were also planned with a fuel oil backup in case natural gas became unavailable. After a negative environmental declaration was made, Riverkeeper took the EPA to court over impacts of water withdrawals and the hot water dumping impacts on fish spawning areas in the river.

In the lower Valley in 1900, the Hackensack Water Company acquired the small (one employee and 81 customers) Spring Valley Water Works in Rockland County, a wise expansion that included most of the upper Hackensack River watershed. When plans to expand services in Rockland County were initiated, critics claimed the company was trying to steal the resource for New Jersey. A legal wrangle went on until 1957, when a new source, DeForest Lake Reservoir, went into service near New City. Smaller companies were bought up and added to the deForest system, until the supplier was providing 100 million gallons a day by 1969, more than twice the output of 1950. The company reorganized as United Water Resources Inc. in 1983 and expanded into water quality testing and municipal water service operations, developing two million customers in fourteen states.

Upriver towns were taking advantage of the immense water resources of the region, including the aboveground runoff and the water left in the wake of glaciers. Kingston was drawing from the Catskills behind Woodstock. Four miles to the north, the Plattekill flowed down from Platte Clove into tiny Blue Mountain Reservoir in Saugerties, which drained a 17-square-mile watershed with a potential yield of more than thirty million gallons a day. The upper reaches of the Normanskill flowed into the Watervliet Reservoir after its construction interrupted the creek at French Hollow. (The local bass fishing improved.) On the other side of Albany, the city of Cohoes discovered a deep series of aquifers while drilling for artesian wells near the future site of Albany Airport. The Latham water district tapped the water resources of the Colonie Channel in the early 1930s, pumping two million gallons a day by 1942. These wells went on stand-by in 1953, when a surface-water system was begun. Clifton Park, Guilderland, and Bethlehem all drew from substantial well resources in the 1940s in the same buried valley areas.

America and the Hudson Valley were moving into a new epoch, yet the style and flavor of the Valley's character was not lost in the transition. A girl could ride a horse for thirty miles overland from Clermont to Glenco Mills on a brisk day in 1959, crossing farm fields and a few roads but rarely seeing a car, and it was not uncommon to see farmers on tractors coming down Warren Street in nearby Hudson a few years later. By the same token, the Valley's sense of modernism arose in the new architecture of the southern Valley. Jackie Gleason's Round House near Peekskill, designed by Silverman and Cika, was a dramatic $600,000-plus elaboration on the flamboyant entertainer's life and lifestyle pointed out to curious travelers on the Hudson Valley Airporter route along Route 9.

In southeastern Dutchess County, the Albermac Sweet Shop was the hottest spot for Pawling teens in the '40s and '50s—featured in *Life* magazine! Beautiful Holiday Hills had waterside and wooded park trails and hosted the annual Harlem Valley Agricultural Fairs. A convalescent home on the grounds that Consolidated Edison operated was purchased and turned into a camp and conference center for the Metropolitan YMCA of Greater New York in 1947.

Norman Vincent Peale, the "positive thinking" guru of Pawling and a personal friend of Richard Nixon, fell under criticism in 1960 when he led 150 Protestant ministers in protesting the presidential candidacy of John F. Kennedy (1917–63) because Kennedy was Catholic. Theologian Reinhold Niebuhr, Episcopal Bishop James Pike, Paul Tillich, President Truman, the national Board of Rabbis and more than a hundred ministers were among those taking exception to Peale's extremist view. His syndicated column was withdrawn from a dozen newspapers, and he was forced to resign from the political committee he created. Some recalled Adlai Stevenson's estimation of Peale when the minister challenged Stevenson's candidacy in 1952: "Speaking as a Christian, I find the Apostle Paul appealing and the Apostle Peale appalling," Stevenson said. He lampooned Peale in stump speeches for Kennedy, turning it into a criticism of Richard Nixon's candidacy.

John Kennedy's history in the Hudson Valley had roots. The Kennedys lived in Bronxville in southern Westchester from 1929–36 and were parishioners of St. Joseph Church, where Teddy married Joan Bennett in 1958. Jack's wife, Jacqueline Bouvier (1929–94)was related to Gore Vidal, a Barrytown squire in these years who moved in the same social circles in Washington. In 1957, Vidal wrote that he "knew" that Kennedy would be elected President because he narrowly missed being the vice-presidential choice in 1956. Jack campaigned in the Valley for President, riding through Troy in a convertible with Rep. Leo W. O'Brien to a Democratic reception on September 29, 1960; Richard Nixon arrived the next day for a testimonial in that city. Robert Kennedy also made a political speech in Troy in 1960, and returned in 1964 to Brookside Park. His reception at several stops in the Valley during his 1968 campaign drew several thousand well-wishers.

Vidal shared his opinion about Jack's chances with his Barrytown neighbor, journalist Richard Rovere, who "patiently" explained that that was not possible, "ever." Vidal, "as it turned out," was correct. He also wrote that Kennedy was "obsessed" with Nelson Rockefeller as a potential opponent, even though around Washington (Vidal claimed), Rockefeller was considered "muddle-headed" and "stupid."

"I can beat Goldwater," Vidal said Kennedy told him, "but Nelson is something else." After the 1960 vote—when Vidal had himself run unsuccessfully for Congress from the Hudson Valley—the President-elect joked with Gore that his having received 20,000 votes more than Kennedy in Vidal's district was "the most humiliating experience of the election."

35. A Short Man with a Mustache

Who nowadays ever goes to Albany?
—*The New York Times* (February 4, 1938)

The record of Thomas E. Dewey (1902–71) as New York State governor included the passage of the first civil rights law in the country, building the New York State Thruway, creating the State University of New York, and reducing state taxes for eleven of the twelve years he served—not to mention leading New York during the war. The state debt fell by $100 million under Dewey. During the war, he was diligent in securing federal contracts for the private industries that took over the war effort in 103 of the 113 federal plants in New York. His administration helped 130,000 small businesses to get started. A million more jobs existed in New York in 1949 than in 1939. A hardliner on labor—he barred utility workers from striking—Dewey increased unemployment benefits as governor and was a champion of a right to work for all. He ushered the first mandatory driver insurance law through a reluctant legislature. World War II left New York State with a $310 million surplus that the governor diverted to a postwar reconstruction fund for public works, mainly highways. Dewey was a highly capable administrator and an opponent of what he called "narcotic government," that bane of deficit spending that he himself would have to resort to in finishing the Thruway. He was able to finance on a pay-as-you-go basis $840 million of the roads program, but that was not enough for the behemoth moving through the Valley.

His record as a racketbuster from his New York City district attorney days was marred only by a failure to unseat the O'Connell machine in Albany, although he did reduce corruption in voter registrations, assessments, and some contracting work. His Election Frauds Bureau reported in October 1943 that 50 of the 128 polling places of Albany, and 6 of 13 in Watervliet, had flagrant incidents of votes being "bought," double voting and double registration, and registering "nonexistent persons," among other irregularities. In response, Albany County settled that by admitting that the allegations were "technically correct," and opened its own investigation of the state legislature, spreading the innuendo that it would continue until the district attorney ceased his; the siege was raised.

After losing by a respectable 64,000 votes to the incumbent, Herbert Lehman, in his first bid for governor in 1938, Thomas Dewey came back two years later when Lehman stepped down after four terms and won the election by ten times that plurality—640,000 votes. He was an early frontrunner for the GOP nomination for president in 1940, but his young age and isolationist viewpoints pushed him aside in the frenzy over Wendell Wilkie's candidacy. Dewey lost badly as Roosevelt's opponent in 1944 (3.6 million votes and a 432 to 99 Electoral College margin), but did better than any predecessor. The campaign, due in part to the influence of his friend John Foster Dulles (1888–1959), changed Dewey into a leader of the liberal element of the Republican Party and an internationalist who supported a United Nations.

Dewey was particularly stung by Alice Roosevelt Longworth's 1944 characterization of him as "the little man on the wedding cake," an allusion to his mustache and smart dress. He was overly sensitive about his height and joked in 1948 that the last thing America needed was "another short man with a mustache" (at 5'8", he was two inches shorter than Truman). He also had more substantial drawbacks. Dewey was abrupt and thoughtless in dealing with subordinates, and disdainful toward his betters. He told his state college presidents to "sacrifice some of your standards" in admitting as many thousands of war veterans as applied after 1946.

"A blunt fact about Mr. Dewey should be faced," John Gunther wrote two years later. "It is that many people do not like him." Yet he was easily reelected in 1946, becoming the first Republican governor to serve for more than four years.

Thomas Dewey kept a symbolic pair of scissors, for cutting red tape, on a "gadget-free" desk. He golfed in the low eighties. His passion and his pride was Dapplemere, his Pawling farm, which he worked with his hands. "I work like a horse five days and five nights a week for the privilege of getting to the country on the weekend," he once remarked. His drives to Albany, if not up the Taconic in haste, often followed second-class roads to a ferry at Kingston, where he would stop for visits with Arthur Wicks and other Republican town and county leaders, moseying through the towns to the capitol while gathering small notices in the weekly papers. Sometimes a big shot or two visiting at his farm would join him—in September 1949 it was Robert Schuman, the French foreign minister—whom Dewey would introduce along the way.

Life magazine pictured the governor entrenched at Albany as a bastion against the "bitter leftist medicine" of "communist and fellow traveler persuasion" groups. Such was his sway over his party that once, when Republicans held a majority in the assembly, a bill dear to the governor's interests but opposed by the teachers' lobby was declared passed by the clerk even though Democrats were sure they had the majority needed to kill it. They stormed the desk to demand a recount. A whispered discussion ensued between the floor leaders, after which the Democrats allowed the bill to pass. Republicans were actually one vote short, but Irving Ives, the GOP majority leader, told minority leader Irwin Steingut that an Ossining Republican had left for home and would be recalled, forcibly by the state police if necessary, unless the Democrats agreed on the bill. It was already after 2 a.m., so Steingut relented.

In Dewey's tenure as governor, General Electric became a major war industry at Schenectady and Niskayuna, employing a huge workforce, mostly women, in building tanks and other materiel. IBM's rise as America's computer giant began in the Dewey era and prospered partly because of his farsighted Thruway project.

Dewey chose Governor Earl Warren of California as his running mate for the presidential campaign in 1948. He benefited from Dwight D. Eisenhower's refusal to become the Democratic Party candidate, ignored serious conservative Republican reservations about him, endorsed President Truman's foreign policies, promised to retain FDR's New Deal programs, and watched with Republican glee as the Democrats lost Dixiecrats and Progressives within their party. The Alsop brothers in Washington called him the standard-bearer for "the forces of modernity in the Republican party." His diminutive stature, a mustache that he himself thought ugly, and his non-photogenic looks were liabilities offset, in *Life*'s opinion and that of many New Yorkers, by his abilities as an administrator. He was also a powerful speaker and had a way of drawing talent from private industry into working for the government at huge salary reductions. He cooperated with the legislative leaders—meeting once a week with them over dinner to go over the bills under consideration—and regularly postponed projects until he had secured approval from them.

Dewey fully anticipated with the rest of the nation that he would glide into the presidency on a bed of Harry Truman foibles, and so did nothing about it, losing in effect on the merits. He avoided controversy, did not answer questions posed by the press, and made vacuous statements that were immediately seen as gratuitous and unworthy of a presidential aspirant. Truman rocketed across the country in a whistle-stop campaign while Dewey sat back, contented with his margin of lead. He was as shocked as the rest of the country when he lost by 2.2 million votes, yet he quickly congratulated Truman and went back to being governor.

Governor Dewey served another term and then returned to Dapplemere, opened a highly successful law business, and became the young elder statesman of the Republican Party. The racketbuster had a pastoral heart after all, and on his tenth visit on Governor's Day at Rhinebeck in 1952, he spoke to visiting foreign students about the local county fairs in Americans:

> In this Dutchess County Fair, you are viewing a typical American institution, one we have developed here, and all over the United States. We bring out fine products to our fairs to help show others how to do a better job. This fair is a characteristic American institution where we all meet as equals regardless of race, color or creed. It is a place where we come together as farmers, workers, as neighbor to help neighbor.

Dewey helped Eisenhower secure the presidential nomination in 1952 and urged the designation of his running mate, Richard Nixon of California. Both Eisenhower and Nixon visited Pawling. Dewey was antipathetic toward a fellow Republican, Nelson Rockefeller, even though they shared a progressive spirit in politics. He declined to even attend the 1964 Republican convention because conservatives were taking over the party. Dewey was also a friend of Democrats, and especially close with Hubert Humphrey, whom Dewey helped secure the Democratic nomination for vice president that year. In 1968, he advised Lyndon Johnson on ways to avoid a showdown with Robert Kennedy over the presidential nomination.

The governor was not averse to change when change was needed. The old rule about counties purchasing rights-of-way for state highways was holding up ten road projects in Westchester County in 1939, yet the rule was not seriously challenged until 1944, when the highways agenda became a top defense goal. Dewey promptly made the rights-of-way purchases a state responsibility. He argued that counties no longer had the funds for such acquisitions, which was certainly true in Westchester's case. The county had built 160 miles of parkways after the Bronx River drive was completed, creating a $68 million debt by 1933.

But perhaps Dewey's most lasting legacy is a stretch of asphalt and cement, a new artery for the region in an age when the river wasn't enough. A "superhighway" from New York City to Albany proposed by Democrats was ridiculed in a *New York Times* editorial in 1938, but the war demonstrated that the existing network of highways was completely ineffective in moving materials to the front. Plans for a "Thruway" emerged in 1942 when Assemblyman Abbot Low Moffat and Senator William H. Hampton sponsored bills calling for a 200-foot right-of-way on the west side of the Hudson River. This was not to be a simple meander through the pastoral countryside, as it was for the Palisades Interstate Parkway, which began shortly before the Thruway and was touted as a superhighway but was built along the old parkway concept thinking of the 1920s. The Thruway drew upon those early designs by including wide rights-of-way, controlled access, an end to grade crossings with other highways and railroads, and beautification through the banning of billboards and attractive landscaping along the way. Yet the new "superhighway" replaced the parkway concept as appropriate for moving business and commerce as well as for recreation, leisure and commuter uses— Dewey saw it as another Erie Canal, which it would largely parallel from Albany to Buffalo. The new road had its antecedents in the Lehman administration and was completed under Democratic Governor Averell Harriman. Governor Dewey deserved the honor of having the highway named for him—in 1964, after Harriman rejected the idea—because his administration established the project, found the money, and largely built it. When Herbert Lehman became a US senator, he endorsed the Thruway as "one of the best postwar projects under consideration."

Arthur Wicks (1887–1985), a Kingston laundry owner, state senator, chairman of the finance committee, and majority leader of the state legislature, was such a power broker in his day that he redirected the route of the new Thruway from the east side of the Hudson River, where Governor Lehmann wanted it to follow the Taconic State Parkway, to the commercial west side, including an exit at his hometown along the way. Working with him as an aide in this effort was Westchester County Assemblyman Malcolm Wilson (1914–2000), a Yonkers resident and White Plains lawyer. Wicks ensured a $2 million appropriation in the 1944 budget that started the process of acquiring the rights-of-way. Described as a "bantam rooster walking up and down the aisles" of the Senate Chamber in Albany, he was a Dewey champion who was named lieutenant governor in 1953, but was forced to resign six weeks later over the frequent trips he made to Sing Sing Prison to visit a jailed labor leader, Joseph S. Fay.

Dewey "got rid of him," according to Senate secretary Albert Abrams (1915–1993). "It was quite a pathetic scene," he added, Wicks "now relegated to the back row as a junior member" of the Senate, supported only by a few of the more principled senators, like Thomas Desmond of Orange County: "He was drummed out, the Dreyfus from Kingston."

Wick's protege and successor as Ulster County Republican Party chairman, Kenneth L. Wilson, also succeeded him in the ability to get big projects done. The former Woodstock town supervisor and assembly member shepherded through the legislature the creation of the Belleayre Ski Center and its expansion in subsequent years. A small state park in Wittenberg was named for Wilson.

The initial planning on the Thruway in 1943 included a Berkshire spur to the Massachusetts Turnpike at West Stockbridge and a New England Thruway extension through the Bronx and Westchester. Complaints from some Westchester residents that the huge road projects had "already ruined some of its lovely little towns" fell on deaf ears. These were new times. The control of highway projects, as well as the evolution of planning, shifted from the influence of individual legislators and their constituencies to the engineers alone, in planning, design and execution. The process, in Michael Fein's words, coincided with "a new kind of federalism," in which "engineers consolidated their control over road-building politics" and local protections and oversight disappeared. The broader transportation agenda looked upon local issues as "trivial by comparison."

Governor Dewey endorsed the change as professionalizing the road-building science; he also needed the federal dollars that came with such large-scale thinking. The culminating moment was the creation of the New York State Thruway Authority. Bertram D. Tallamy (1901–89), the fourth state public works superintendent since 1939, oversaw this transformation and later became the first federal highways administrator under President Eisenhower.

There were unintended consequences to the new way of thinking. The transformation of public works projects from local and legislatively driven to a businesslike professional operation complete with a sophisticated and slick public relations component made good sense in achieving the goals of miles built, yet also turned highways management into a "closed system" that limited consideration of the social and political context in which it physically happened. Arterial road designs around communities looked good on paper, but often became intrusive interruptions of hamlets and neighborhoods in the execution. Rural roadwork was harmed by budget restraints created by the emphasis on large-scale thinking, since state aid to towns did not rise proportionately with the rise in major highway costs.

At the same time, technology changes were encouraging better roads and more local road building. An attempt to used Rosendale cement on the Thruway near Mount Marion yielded frustrating results because of the month-long drying time required. Bertram H. Wait, who appreciated the durability of Rosendale in the construction of New York City's Catskill Aqueduct from the Ashokan Reservoir to Westchester, developed a method of mixing the lime-stone with synthetic cements that shortened the setting time. The Thruway tried it with success in New Paltz, and it soon became a popular and durable road-making product. Local communities benefited when a new hot asphalt-concrete mix developed in 1949 that created better highway pavements and streamlined the construction by preparing the mix off-site and hauling it to the road site by trucks fitted with turning mixers. As counties began to upgrade their rural byways, the state created a ten-year highway program to help. By 1952 road modernization was underway for 788 of the state's 932 towns, which generated goodwill for the governor but did not fully meet the need.

Governor Dewey broke ground on the first section of the Thruway on July 11, 1946. The construction proceeded into the fall of 1949, but money and supplies were the bane in the early years. A shortage in steel forced a 30% cutback in construction in 1948; by 1950, fewer than 13 miles had been completed. The logistics of two railroad crossings delayed the Route 28 interchange at Kingston. In Saugerties, the Lane Construction Company completed the bridges and, by October, was preparing the lane approaches at the interchange at Byrnes Corners. Dewey came to town and formally opened the New York State Thruway—six miles of it at any rate—early the next year. Democrats called it his "luxury boulevard" and "Dewey's pork barrel," but his opponent that year, Senator James M. Mead (1885–1964), could not effectively use the issue because the new road was popular.

The Thruway was initially organized as a free roadway to be financed by general revenues, but Bertram Tallamy changed that with the creation of the Thruway Authority. The residue of postwar thinking also played to the highway's advantage. In July 1950, while Dewey was presiding over the opening of the Catskill-Saugerties section, President Truman had just authorized the use of US forces in Korea. "If anyone ever drops a bomb on New York City," the governor proclaimed, "you won't hear any more arguments about whether New York City needs the Thruway." This proved a prescient statement fifty-one years later when the attack on the World Trade Center closed the airways and necessitated the transferal of stored records of many destroyed businesses by truck from Iron Mountain facilities around the country.

The Thruway project was closely entwined with the construction and real estate industries, Wall Street financiers, and motorist organizations. Friends of friends in high places also benefited. Harold J. Senior, a former partner of Tallamy's, received $830,000 in contracts. M. J. "Jack" Madigan, a member of the committee that recommended creating the Authority, became a major advocate for the Tappan Zee Bridge and obtained the contract for his firm to design the bridge.

In addition to creating the Authority to handle the operations and develop the revenues for its long-term viability, Dewey's "grandest stroke," a $400 million bond issue to move the road forward, made him the "narcotic government" leader he never wanted to be. In 1951, Superintendent Tallamy cleverly turned the need for voter approval of the bond issue to the Thruway's favor by calling it "the opportunity [for voters] to vote themselves lower fees." The bond issue passed in a 4 to 1 margin despite Democratic Party opposition. The record-low 1.1% interest rate saved voters $120 million due to the Authority's good practices. Democrats also fought a prohibition on billboards within 500 feet of the right-of-way that became law. By that year, 140 miles of the roadway were completed.

The parkways of Westchester and the New York State Thruway fostered new, more diffuse suburbia that depended completely on the automobile to accommodate the new families. Downtown areas ignored by the superhighways declined, shopping centers proliferated along routes near the exits, and a surge in communications and power needs spurred suburban growth. The fresh-blowing breezes and picturesque scenery of the country may have served well in an earlier time, but these values disappeared in the hurly-burly expansion of the development years and the new mantra of long-distance truck commerce.

Herbert Gerlach could do little as Westchester County's executive as dozens of potential Thruway routes through the county were considered. The Board of Supervisors supported the route finally chosen in a 32 to 9 vote, largely out of frustration over the national traffic crunch in this region, a 65% jump over 1946–51 alone. The board acted against local community wishes, but needed the state money promised for the Cross Westchester Parkway after the state itself refused to take over interregional transportation corridors from the county—as originally conceived in 1943. The Thruway Authority bifurcated the local opposition by laying out one section of the plan at a time, performing a sleight-of-hand so deftly that individual properties affected badly by the highway became marginalized in the debate; Lisa and Margaret Hein stubbornly remained in their home near Tarrytown while the nearby blasting broke the windows around them.

The Yonkers North Broadway Citizens' Association took the state to court over the destruction of the city's storefronts for the New York City approach of the Thruway. The courts threw out the baby of a lawsuit with the bathwater of the people's overall control over this public matter in accepting a blanket claim that the routing was strictly an engineering decision. This was still a prehistorical era when it came to government interest in environmental and heritage protection. The cultural resource management programs that resulted from the national Highway Salvage Act (1958), National Historic Preservation Act (1966), National Environmental Policy Act (1969), and the state Environmental Quality Review Act (1979) and Historic Preservation Act (1980) would establish a new paradigm for man's impacts on the earth—an imperfect one as governments and developers continued to conspire to get around the rules to foster economic development projects. New York State under Governor Rockefeller gave archaeologist Paul Huey and his team a grudging two frigid winter weeks to excavate and document Fort Orange's rich heritage while the Empire State Plaza transportation network construction waited.

Like the Yonkers area of Westchester, Rockland County was completely transformed by the Thruway, losing its pastoral charms and much of its history and identity as a county in the construction. South Nyack's business district was wiped away. In Suffern, where the Thruway was planned through a narrow Ramapo Mountains gap that already had two railroads, two highways, and the Ramapo River, the Thruway Authority's insensitivity to local needs led to an attempt to divert the river over three of the town's reserve wells. Crews were stopped by the local police and a local trustee, John C. Petrone, but by November 1953 the road moved along. The pattern was the same in the northern counties; in Plattekill in Ulster County, a picturesque setting typical of the rural and historic Hudson River Valley was removed in the relocation of Route 32 to accommodate the Thruway. Changes in the natural environment were not anticipated or clearly understood when the planning took place. Numerous new wetlands were created where the new highway interrupted small waterways. These changes altered natural life in several ways, mainly by cutting off former corridors of travel for animals. The impacts on biodiversity caused by the Thruway interruption were never measured. Attention to these issues might have softened and humanized the behemoth highway, while still moving commerce along gingerly as desired.

Swathes of archaeological resources were swept away all along the construction route. Upstate farm fields were cut in half, roads connecting neighbors and families stunted into dead ends, hamlets destroyed, and whole villages left bereft of income in the loss of main traffic thoroughfares. Mumford's idea of a beneficial highway system connecting communities from a distance was cruelly sublimated by a juggernaut passing by or obliterating old economic centers of life. Intersections and grade crossings were eliminated in a profusion of bridges, exits and entrances, and the simple abandonment of old crossroads.

Mumford in his naivety once saw the automobile and electricity as new technologies that would finally relieve the congested cities and spread the population in a "regional system of distribution" as envisioned by Benton McKaye in 1929, but now he was sadly disillusioned that the pathway of the new state road merely paralleled the same transportation pattern the railroad had created (in following the path of the river). The automobile crowded out the railroad just as the rails had crowded out the steamboats, and Mumford's decentralized regionalism became a quaint and rickety Model-T from a forgotten planning era that collapsed in the enormity of the growth that the new highway precipitated.

Not all local impacts were deleterious, at least not for all affected, and for many communities the Thruway meant new business, new incomes, new potentials and possibilities. Once the Tappan Zee Bridge was built, the White Plains Trust Company took in the $234 million assets of the National Bank of Tuxedo, the first instance of banks crossing county lines as well as the Hudson River to merge. The Cross County Shopping Center in Yonkers was the result of a complex, probably non-conspiratorial arrangement that nevertheless dealt a drastic blow to that city's commercial center. The state Department of Public Works was able to realign a dangerous turn, the Thruway got a better route through the area, and Cross Properties Inc. put in a $30 million shopping center. Tallamy's chicanery lay in keeping the arrangement from the public's attention: he was cautioned by his public relations director Bob Monahan to avoid the term "impact" in any public utterances; his job was to "build," not "destroy."

Thanks to Senator Arthur Wicks, Kingston in Ulster County found itself on the "right side" of the river when a boom in business resulted—and just in time. Hardly a single new house had been built in Kingston since before 1930—more than 70% of them were built before 1920—and now IBM came into the adjoining town with a plant that employed 5,000 in the making of the components of the AN/FSQ-7, a super-computer (the largest in the world) housing the Semi Automatic Ground Environment (SAGE) system for tracking and intercepting enemy bomber aircraft. IBM had come to the region with the purchase of Cliffdale, the Kenyon family estate in Poughkeepsie in 1944, where the company produced aircraft fire control systems and the Browning automatic carbine rifle. The first typewriters and printers were built there as well. A huge facility developed around Cliffdale before IBM expanded into Ulster County. The company established itself as one of high integrity based on Thomas Watson's three guiding "Basic Beliefs"—respect, service, and excellence.

Kingston 459,200-square-foot plant was dedicated on November 2, 1956, on two hundred acres of a former Boice family farm, where 5,268 workers were soon employed. The typewriter division transferred over five years later. The SAGE project—along with the development of a sophisticated airline reservations system and support for the Apollo space flight control system—translated Watson's guiding principles into a first-class business model. The SAGE project enabled Kingston to take on greater importance in the IBM community. In time, teams of programmers and specialists were traveling the world installing and maintaining system stations that monitored the Thin Red Line of Soviet airspace. SAGE was never completely adequate, especially after the Soviet Union replaced its long-range bombers with intercontinental ballistic missiles, but its development represented a quantum leap in computer science. IBM's role was in the manufacturing of the computer itself, which used ferrite-core memory chips supplied by hundreds of subcontractors in the Hudson Valley and elsewhere. SAGE was a major reason why IBM dominated the computer industry in later decades. One of the systems was deployed at Stewart Air Force Base near Newburgh.

In a pattern that was echoed elsewhere, land values rose by an average of 50% in surrounding towns as well as the city of Kingston. New "bedroom communities" developed as local housing tract developers, in partnership with contractors, engineers and lawyers, rose to the occasion.

The town of Ulster population grew from 4,411 in 1950 to 8,449 ten years later. Seven new schools were built in the Kingston-Ulster area in the twenty years after 1960. By 1985, IBM Kingston was employing 7,100, and ten years later, because of changing economic times, IBM was gone. The company retained a Hudson Valley presence at Armonk and Fishkill and gradually rebounded in the succeeding decades.

The Tappan Zee Bridge and its $80.9 million price tag was a highly volatile issue because of its location and the number of people the construction would affect. More than 200 homes in South Nyack and Tappan had to be relocated. Bertram Tallamy defended the location as placing the general public's interest above any local ones. "It's not the width of the body of water you want to cross but the number of people who want to cross there," said Emil Praeger, the design engineer, RPI dean, and former Navy captain. Actually, the location was determined in part because it was just outside the jurisdiction of the Port Authority, which asked that it be far enough north so as not to interfere with the George Washington Bridge traffic. The Thruway had originally been designed to end at Suffern, but the Authority decided to build the bridge and extend the highway to New York City. Plans for a span in the Dobbs Ferry-Tappan Slote area were recommended as early as 1920, and seriously considered by the Port Authority of New York in 1950, when Governor Dewey moved the location a few miles north to avoid the Authority's jurisdiction.

The bridge connecting Nyack and Tappan across the second-widest area of the Hudson River extended 16,013 feet, its cantilever span of 1,212 feet (the ninth largest in the world) providing a 138-foot clearance for river traffic. The length of the span added to the construction costs, while the use of hollow concrete caissons to support the load helped to reduce the expense. Paul Windels of the Regional Planning Association thought the use of caissons "a basic error" and the whole bridge of "freak design"—yet it worked.

The first of the steel pilings were driven in June 1951, construction was then delayed by another steel shortage, this one brought about by the Korean War. Actual work was resumed over 1952–55. The caissons (eight in all) were built in a clay pit at Grassy Point ten miles north of the bridge in Rockland County, a staging and assembly ground for the whole project ("the largest natural dry dock in the world" at the time). They were then floated to the site by barge, the first arriving in October 1953, filled with water, and sunk to a depth of 42 feet where a blanket of sand and gravel had been prepared. The water was pumped from the caissons as the steel bridge rose above them, the pumps continuing to provide buoyancy to the bridge as needed during the life of the span.

At the daylong celebration on the opening of the bridge on December 15, 1955, the destroyer *U.S.S Rizzi* served as an escort for Governor Harriman and the dignitaries who gathered for the ribbon-cutting. Standing by silently were sixteen housewives from Piermont, Grand View-on-Hudson, and Sparkill, each wearing shirts bearing a single letter to illustrate their protest against a planned connection to New Jersey: "Save Our Villages!" The construction would come back to haunt the eight-mile Tappan Zee Bay shoreline a dozen years later when an accumulation of silt aggravated by the bridge threatened to close down marinas and boatyards and turn the Piermont Mole, a mile-long pier into the Hudson, into a causeway.

The housewives of Rockland County were not the only residents displaced by the mammoth state project. Commuters—those who were meant to benefit the most—suffered almost as badly. Even before the bridge was completed, New York Central Railroad was petitioning federal and state authorities to discontinue the West Shore's passenger service. Rockland County fought the move throughout the decade, but ultimately the railroad was able to discontinue twenty-eight of the forty-four daily passenger trains, remaining with only eight each way between West Haverstraw and Weehawken, New Jersey.

Governor Harriman signed the law naming the Tappan Zee Bridge in early 1956; the span was named for former Governor Malcolm Wilson in 1994, but the name was never used in practicality. Everyone called it the Tappan Zee, and the bridge became the principal Hudson River crossing between the George Washington and Newburgh-Beacon bridges, the Bear Mountain Bridge having evolved into a local traffic corridor because of its isolation in the Highlands. With interstate connections at both ends (Suffern and Port Chester) and access via Route 17 to the Southern Tier, the Tappan Zee became a "vital link" in the Northeast regional transportation system. The bridge also provided a direct connection between Rockland and Westchester counties, and a modern through-traffic corridor for New York City traffic into the state's interior.

Eighteen thousand vehicles passed over in 1956; fifty years later, 135,000 per day used the bridge, the total expected to rise to 175,000 by 2025. Tappan Zee Bridge traffic increased by 11% between 1980 and 1996. In 1999 the state Department of Transportation added 2,400 new park-and-ride spaces in Westchester, Putnam, Rockland and Orange to encourage ride-sharing as a way to reduce the traffic flow. Moveable barriers to add a fourth lane during peak usage hours, electronic toll collection (E-Z Pass), variable pricing for commercial vehicles, and a significant rise in express bus traffic were other tools that helped reduce congestion.

Changing attitudes by the public toward the transportation infrastructure had begun appearing as early as the $2.8 billion highway bond referendum of 1955. A $500 million bond issue that included a penny-per-gallon gasoline tax dedicated to highway uses was approved in 1952, and the record showed that the Thruway had recorded a fatality rate of 2.44 per 100 million vehicle miles, better than Pennsylvania (4.2) and the national average (6.5), yet the New York Automobile Association campaigned against the measure because it did not dedicate all the revenues to highways. Governor Dewey himself supported it, but the bond issue went down by a two-to-one margin.

Four new expressways were recommended in 1954 as a result of the Thruway's success, including the 333-mile Adirondack Northway from Albany to Canada, built between 1957 and 1967. A pair of identical steel arch bridges spanning the Mohawk River between Colonie and Halfmoon, formally named the Thaddeus Kosciusko Bridge, were informally referred to as the Dolly Parton Bridge by motorists delighted with the design and beauty of the spans. Saratoga County was transformed into a virtual bedroom county for the capital city, and when Governor Nelson Rockefeller dedicated the final connection north of Glens Falls on May 26, 1961, a quicker connection to the Adirondacks region for metropolitan-area travelers was achieved.

The "rhetoric of national defense" used to promote road building during World War II continued in Eisenhower's Interstate Highway Act of 1956, which resulted in a 42,000 mile national system. The New York Thruway, its 535 miles completed by that year, was an impetus for this program, which also had antecedents in the New Deal era Federal Aid Road Act of 1938 (revived in 1944) and in Eisenhower's own experience as a young officer taking a military caravan across the United States. Daniel Patrick Moynihan, an aide to Democratic Governor Averell Harriman at the time (and a confirmed urbanist), drafted a stinging rebuke of the interstate highway idea over its failure to address mass transit instead; these words too fell on deaf ears.

The act changed the federal highway dollar share from 50% to 90%, which allowed for the addition of a parallel span to the 1963 bridge across the river north of the Highlands. The first Newburgh-Beacon Bridge, a 6,870-foot span, was built for $24 million with a promise from state Transportation Commissioner Raymond T. Schuler that tolls would end after the investment was recouped. By mid-1975, the 2.2 million vehicles the first year had risen to 8.7 million, the need for toll revenues eclipsed any prior promises, and the new span was begun. A partisan dispute in the state legislature over the next several years resulted in the naming of the bridge after Congressman Hamilton Fish, the isolationist nemesis of President Franklin D. Roosevelt, for whom the Mid-Hudson bridge at Poughkeepsie was named. The Newburgh crossing was eventually tied into the interstate system through I-84 between Boston and Scranton-Wilkes Barre.

The Thruway and the Major Deegan Expressway into New York City were incorporated into the new federal system, and I-684 was built to connect the cross-Westchester Expressway (I-95) at Port Chester through Purchase, Armonk, Bedford and Brewster to I-87. In the 1990s, I-287 became a convenient New York City bypass for commercial traffic from New Jersey into New England. An interstate connection between I-90 in the city of Albany and the Albany County Airport was built despite public opposition—largely because of Mayor Erastus Corning's strong support—and soon criticized for cutting the city off from the Hudson River. A new Hudson River Expressway planned for the east side of the river between Tarrytown and Beacon, a pet project of Governor Rockefeller's, was never built.

Within forty years of its completion, the Thruway suffered under the very congestion problems its construction was meant to alleviate. In 1997, after a high-occupancy lane was rejected by commuters on the Cross Westchester Expressway, Governor George Pataki created a Task Force of the principal involved agencies to come up with a better traffic plan for the lower Hudson Valley in general. The Vollmer Associates study took two years and looked at the forecasted traffic to the year 2020. Restoring the West Shore Railroad commuter traffic was rejected because that would not extend a rail connection between Stewart Airport and the Connecticut border at Port Chester. A $1.3 billion price tag for a 13-year project to rehabilitate the Tappan Zee Bridge emerged. The plan included a "bus guideway system," popular in Europe, along a separate electronic lane during peak hour periods, but did not allow for an expansion in traffic or expanding transit services in the lower Hudson region. Any capacity expansion would require a new bridge.

Criticism of the concept included a rejection of a rail amenity, since only 3% of commuters used rail at the time, and a call for a tunnel instead. The "Tappan Tunnel" idea was raised by Alexander Saunders in the October 2000 issue of John Vargo's *Boating on the Hudson*, and immediately drew the support of environmentalists and regional planners. Saunders envisioned three tunnels side-by-side, each carrying three traffic lands and two rail lanes, the last for freight as well as commuter traffic, at a cost of $700 million not including access to the tunnels at Suffern and Tarrytown. The potential grade needed to move traffic and rail was considered an obstruction to the tunnel idea.

Eight years after the Vollmer report, when plans for a new bridge and its amenities were announced by Governor Andrew Cuomo and a public review commenced, the cost for it all had risen to $16 billion and the state and the Metropolitan Transit Authority were again facing serious citizen opposition. A consensus was finally reached among the authorities in September 2008 on a $6.4 billion double span incorporating eight vehicular traffic lanes and bus rapid transit (from Suffern to Port Chester), and a shared bicycle-pedestrian path— but postponing a rail line until a vaguely later date because of excessive costs. The project was fast-tracked for funding support by the Obama administration and construction begun in 2013.

36. The New Red Scare

Lately I've been thinking that the Cold War is almost worse for art than the real thing—for it permeates the atmosphere with fear and anxiety . . . An artist fighting in a war for a cause he holds just has something affirmative he can believe in. The artist, if he can stay alive, can create art. But throw him into a mood of suspicion, ill-will and dread that typifies the Cold War attitude and he'll create nothing.

—AARON COPLAND, March 1949

"It was a queer, sultry summer, the summer they electrocuted the Rosenbergs, and I didn't know what I was doing in New York," Sylvia Plath (1932–1963) wrote in the opening lines of her novel *The Bell Jar*, published a month before her suicide.

After a two-hour search on an "unbearably muggy" Friday afternoon, at 4:22 p.m. on June 19, 1953, FBI agents from Kingston located Joseph P. Francel working as an electrical contractor in Cairo, Greene County. They were a hundred miles from Frankel's job site, yet there was time enough for him to be there and prepare. Joe Francel, 57, was the fifth executioner at Sing Sing since the electric chair was installed there in 1890. The last one barely escaped a firebombing at his home; the one before was a suicide in his own cellar, and before him the man became a recluse; the first of the executioners dropped dead in the warden's office. Joe did not know it at the time, but this would be his last $150 job down the river.

Warden Wilfred Denno was there to meet Francel when he arrived. The death house at Sing Sing was built in 1922. Above the door carved in stone the word "Silence" greeted all who came, and the house had seen some use over the years. The electric chair at Sing Sing was made of kiln-dried red oak. The protocol consisted of a 2,000 volt charge for three seconds, 500 volts for fifty seconds, 2,000 more, then 500 again, then 2,000, three final jolts administered intermittently to prevent the cooking of the flesh. The body temperature might rise to 130 degrees Fahrenheit, the brain almost to the boiling point. A leather face mask was fastened to the victim as "a palliative for the witnesses" to prevent the eyes from popping out.

The Rosenbergs would be the 567th and 568th to meet their fates in New York State since 1890. Ethel Greenglass Rosenberg, 37, was on death row for 801 days; her husband Julius, 35, for 767 days. A flurry of attempts to halt or delay the executions took place all day in Washington, Connecticut, and New York. The Rosenberg lawyer, Manny Bloch (1901–54), had succeeded in postponing the fated day for two years, but now time, like the minutes of their lives, was running out. This was already the day after the third date that the original presiding judge, Irving R. Kaufman (1910–92), had set. President Eisenhower rejected a direct appeal to his office on the grounds that the Rosenberg's espionage had threatened tens of millions of Americans.

US Supreme Court Justice William O. Douglas (1898–1980) had granted the couple a third reprieve to allow Chief Justice Fred Vinson to convene an extraordinary session on an argument put forth in yet another appeal, that the death sentences for the Rosenbergs were invalid because the Atomic Energy Act of 1946 superseded the Espionage Act of 1917. The Douglas stay was vacated at noon that Friday and the executions rescheduled, at first for 11 p.m. They were always at 11 p.m. at Sing Sing, but usually on a Thursday.

Another last-minute appeal by attorney Daniel Marshall came before Judge Kaufman because the Rosenbergs were Jewish and it was likely they would die on the Sabbath. Kaufman, who was also Jewish, called the prison at 3:15 to see if the executioner had been summoned; he had. He asked the warden to consult the prison's rabbi, Irving Koslowe (1920–2000), on the actual time of sundown that day (the Sabbath starts eighteen minutes before sundown). Koslowe, appointed to the post in 1950 by Governor Dewey, was a recent Yeshiva University graduate who needed the work at the time. He witnessed seventeen executions over his career. Koslowe had a wry sense of humor—his congregation of a little more than a hundred Jewish inmates, he once said, was unusual in that it "doesn't mind losing members."

Manny Bloch thought they had another reprieve, but instead the judge rejected the final petition at 7:45 p.m. The date of the execution of a person in New York was set by a judge, but the actual time of the executions was up to the discretion of the warden, so Denno set these for 8 p.m. The public was not notified. The President wanted this done; it had gone on too long. "They were to be killed more quickly than planned," Arthur Miller later said, "to avoid any shadow of bad taste."

The day before, Thursday, June 18, was the condemned couple's fourteenth wedding anniversary. They were able to celebrate together, in a sense, since their cells were separated by a wire mesh screen. Ted and Joan Hall drove past the prison just before sunset, on their way to a dinner party in Ossining. He had been suspected himself of being a spy, and actually did have a Soviet handler, so the couple, Joan later recalled, felt "that there, but for some inexplicable grave, went we."

The FBI had a secret command station nearby to contact their boss immediately in case the Rosenbergs finally broke down and talked. They both maintained their innocence and had said nothing to implicate anyone else during the entire ordeal. Julius went first because he was the weakest and the closest to the chair. Ethel offered no final remorse; she still lived after the first two jolts. Afterwards, Rabbi Koslowe was given a police escort to his home in Mamaroneck, where he entered a birthday party underway for his son, seven years old like one of the Rosenberg boys.

The trial and executions were controversial at a time when many Americans were tired of the distasteful House Un-American Activities Committee (HUAC) hearings and the relentless snooping of J. Edgar Hoover and his Federal Bureau of Investigation over supposed Communist sympathizers. None of the other individuals implicated in the spy ring were executed, although each of them confessed under scrutiny. Harry Gold, the courier, served fifteen years in prison. Morton Sobell, tried with them as a spy, testified against Julius regarding his delivery of classified materials, including information about the atomic bomb, and was sentenced to seventeen years; he finally admitted he was a spy in 2008. Ethel's brother, David Greenglass (b. 1922), who provided the documents from Los Alamos and testified against his brother-in-law, received ten years; fifty-five years later, he admitted that he had wrongly implicated his own sister in the espionage.

When records in the former Soviet Union became available for Western scrutiny after 1989, the facts became clear. Julius was a recruiter and courier for the Soviets who helped pass along information on the Manhattan Project. Ethel, who typed some of the information for her husband, was otherwise less involved, yet was mentioned sympathetically along with Julius in Nikita Krushchev's memoirs when published in 1990.

In a sense, the most damaging aspect of life in the 1950s—the Red Scare—was also FDR's fault anyway, as everything else wrong with America was said to be by his enemies now that he was gone. Henry Steele Commager captured that sense of the hysteria—that and how the Red Scare protected racial segregation in America—in one of the first responses to the conservative and right-wing hysteria that was sweeping the nation. His September 1947 essay in *Harper's Bazaar*, "Who Is Loyal to America?", chastised the Republican-Conservative thinking that demonized the New Deal as an infection that had spread "various shades of Communism" throughout the land. Harry Truman railed against "these reactionaries" on the campaign trail at the Schenectady railroad station in 1948. FDR's old enemy, Hamilton Fish, was also stumping the Valley, preaching an Americanism to veteran groups who had fought the very war that as an isolationist he fought against. A dark and nasty latter-day nativism directed toward ideologies instead of geographies prevailed, and hateful of all were the socialist values associated with the New Deal years. The damnation extended to the local level in practice. John Kingsbury of Shady, once the administrative consultant to Harry Hopkins and chairman of the National Council of American-Soviet Relations, was condemned locally as a subversive over his support for a national health plan. Anton Refregier's social realism mural in the annex of the San Francisco post office was targeted by Congressman Richard M. Nixon in July 1949 as "very objectionable art, of a subversive nature" that he felt should be removed, along with all other art "that is found to be inconsistent with American ideals and principles."

Although Dixon Ryan Fox, the Union College president, was a critic of FDR's policies, he was a rare-breed educator for the times, hewing to the tradition of liberal thinking that encouraged free expression and an openness toward ideas. Fox stood firm for academic freedom. He criticized conservative attacks on high school history books, and put a label on the demonizing in an article entitled "The New Red Scare" in *New York History*. His successor as Union president, Carter Davidson, had to contend with its most important trustee, Frank Bailey, whose diatribes against communism led to two faculty resignations in the 1940s. Bailey became shriller as he aged; in January 1952, at age eighty-seven, he convinced fellow trustees to approve his resolution on teaching "the American way"—and then went after faculty members who disagreed. The faculty held their ground, however, and in 1959 asked the Union administration and trustees to stop making loans under the National Defense Education Act became of its loyalty oath requirement.

The Red Scare was as endemic an intrusion on private life as "national security" would be sixty years later, and a similar militaristic rhetoric toward America's enemies prevailed. Anglers in New York City's Hudson Valley reservoirs were required to take a loyalty oath to catch a fish there. Civilian Observer Corps stations on prominent *keekuten* ("overlooks") were revived and local volunteer observers began looking for Russian planes as fervently as they had searched the skies for the Luftwaffe a decade earlier. Public school teachers were regularly challenged over their politics. In Catholic elementary schools nuns railed violently against "the Devil" (in this case, Karl Marx), and local church leaders delivered sermons denouncing the friends of Stalin. Veteran organizations often led the hue and cry, sometimes with force. Even the art world seemed to conspire: abstract expressionism dismissed sympathies toward New Deal art because of its proletariat origins.

There were, to be sure, legitimate reactions to Soviet expansion in America's response to activities in Europe. Hungarians in Peekskill burst with pride in October 1956 when thousands of students occupied Joszef Bem square in defiance of their own army, and then shared in their homeland's desperation "at the sight of the Russian tanks running through the streets of Budapest," as George Pataki recalled from his childhood. A month later a new wave of immigrants arrived in the city, refugees of the defeated nation.

For Aaron Copland—whose Pulitzer Prize for *Appalachian Spring* was awarded on V-E Day, May 8, 1945—the world began unraveling in 1949 after his name was linked with Henry Wallace and he was associated with the "dupes and fellow travelers" of world peace advocacy—radicals like Albert Einstein, Langston Hughes, and Charles Chaplin. Copland had played into the Red Scare problem in 1948 by naively chastising Soviet composers Dmitri Shostakovich (1906–75) and Sergei Prokofiev (1891–1953) for failing to understand that the times had changed, instead of castigating them as Soviet dupes. Virgil Thompson (1896–1989) criticized Copland's Third Symphony—which Serge Koussevitzky (1874–1951) called America's "greatest" symphonic work—as too reminiscent of Wallace's 1942 "Century of the Common Man" speech, a paean to democracy now seen as pro-Soviet propaganda. Wallace (1888–1965), Vice President during the war years and Progressive Party candidate for President in 1948, repudiated his liberal sentiments in later years and supported Dwight D. Eisenhower's reelection in

1956. An expert agriculturalist (he had been hailed as "America's greatest" Secretary of Agriculture by Arthur M. Schlesinger in the 1930s), Wallace retired to his farm on Truesdale Lake in South Salem, where he developed the most prolific egg-bearing chickens in the world.

This was the end of niceness toward the whole New Deal world. An FBI file was started on Copland, and the scheduling of his *Lincoln Portrait* for one of the concerts for Eisenhower's first inauguration was withdrawn two weeks before the event when a right-wing congressman denounced Copland's work as Communist propaganda. Four months later he was called before HUAC, yet treated gently by Congressman Joseph McCarthy, who did not know who he was. Eventually, Copland's reputation was restored, although his response to it all in the *Connotations* score that opened the new Lincoln Center Philharmonic Hall in September 1962 breathed defiance.

Marc and Bela Chagall had been among the 1,500 refugees from Europe saved by Varian Fry and the Emergency Rescue Committee in 1941. Bela (1895–1944) succumbed to an apparent viral infection at Cranberry Lake in Westchester County. Chagall (Mark Zakharovich Shagal, born Moishe Shagal 1887–1985) published the first volume of his wife's touching childhood reminiscences in 1946. That year he purchased a home on Mohonk Road in High Falls and lived there until the summer of 1948 with his former assistant and now lover, Virginia Haggard (1915–2006); a son, David, was born in 1947. The FBI maintained a folder on Chagall over these years because of his outspoken political views. He sold the house in 1954, possibly because of trouble with the State Department over reentering the United States. He returned in 1963 to visit Union Church in Pocantico Hills on commissions that David Rockefeller had arranged for stained glass windows. Henri Matisse's window already paid homage to the Rockefellers' mother, Abby, and David and his brothers had decided to ask Chagall to design nine stained glass windows at the church.

The hills of Westchester within a few miles of the Hudson River were the setting for Jewish summer camps and colonies organized around leftist political views in the 1920s and 30s. The colonies—Mohegan, formed in 1924; Goldens Bridge (1927), Followers of the Trail (1929), Croton Point Colony (1930), the Three Arrows Cooperative Society (1936), and Shrub Oak Park (1938)—included entertainments involving the songs and stories of labor movements and unionism, cooperative-style ownership arrangements, and insularity from the outside world. Others of similar bent or persuasion nearby included the first of these colonies, Belle Terre; *Nitgedeiger* ("No Worry") in Beacon; the Circle Lodge, the Unser Camp of the Farbend in Highland Mills; and the Bundist Camp Eden in Cold Spring. After Belle Terre folded, an attempt to revive the camp took place at Mount Airy in Croton, and some of these "colonists" remained until the 1970s. Max Eastman, Elizabeth Moos, George Biddle, William Gropper, and Chaim Zhitlovsky, a Yiddishist, were among the occupants.

Sylvan Lake in Dutchess County had two children's camps facing each other across the lake, Kinder Ring (next to Circle Lodge), organized by the Workmen's Circle, and Kinderland, associated with the International Workers Organization. An emphasis on nature rambling and learning to live off the land went hand-in-hand with sloganeering, the wearing of special dress such as Russian blouses and peasant dresses for Saturday night socials, and songs of the Spanish Civil War, the Irish revolution, or against the Nazis. Americanization of the youth was also emphasized, since these families were immigrants grateful for the opportunities and challenges of the new world. Margaret Sanger owned one of the Mohegan Colony lots, but sold it in 1928 without having used it.

An anarchist educator, Harry Kelly, founded Mohegan Colony, the largest and longest-lasting of the camps, in February 1924 when he purchased 400 acres for $76,875 in Courtland and Yorktown on Lake Mohegan. Lewis Mumford, newly of Amenia, an "admirer of Kropotkin and student of historical utopias," set out a plan for the colony in one-acre lots in 1930. Kelly established a school that emphasized individual initiative, personal expression through art and writing, and a love of nature. When William Z. Foster (1881–1961), the head of the American Communist Party, visited Mohegan, clashes among Stalinists and Trotskyite youths resulted.

Goldens Bridge Cooperative Farms drew a hundred families to a colony in Lewisburg, near Katonah. The Camp Followers, a very radical group, settled in Buchanan, initially on only 23 acres. Fifty of this group, all associated with the International Fur Workers Union (which was under Communist Party control), became permanent residents. Camp Croton (Croton Park Colony after 1936) was organized by the Milliners Union two miles south of Mohegan Lake. The Shrub Oak Colony was established on the edge of Yorktown. American socialists were represented at Camp Three Arrows, which settled on a

125-acre dairy farm on a lake in Putnam County in 1937, the arrows representing the Austrian Social Democratic Party symbols against Capitalism, Fascism, and Reaction. The Socialist Party held its annual conventions at Three Arrows, and perennial Socialist Party presidential candidate Norman Thomas (1884–1968) was a frequent lecturer and resident; the meeting hall was named for him.

These colonies, despite their own efforts to remain aloof from the locals, were treated as pariahs and reviled by their neighbors for the rest of the century. A 1930 trolley brochure to Mohegan Lake warned: "No Hebrews." A sign near Lake Katonah was even more specific: "Restricted—No Jews or Negroes." Lewisboro residents tried unsuccessfully to stop Goldens Bridge from filing their plot map with the town in 1944. Federal agents also abounded, searching for communists and sharing in the local anti-Semitic prejudices. These came to a head in the late summer of 1949 when a radicals group, the People's Artists Inc., tried to raise funds for the Harlem chapter of the Civil Rights Congress, a Communist-front organization. They invited Paul Robeson (1898–1976) to come and sing "Ol' Man River." This was to be Robeson's fourth visit in the area, all under the same sponsors, but this time the concert would not be held.

Robeson, whose bass-baritone voice was revered and celebrated, had debuted the song on Broadway in *Showboat* in 1936. His run as the title character in *Othello* in New York, the first by a black actor in that role, made it the longest-running Shakespeare play in Broadway history. He was a charismatic and eloquent former Rhodes scholar whose passion was equality for the races in America and elsewhere. He was not a communist in 1946, and in fact had studied law under Harold Medina (1888–1990), the presiding judge at the trail of the communist leaders in Foley Square whom the Civil Rights Congress was supporting.

Robeson had incited the ire of the veteran community with a remark that African Americans should not fight in any American "imperialist war." A protest parade by the Joint Veterans Council of Westchester broke into a two-hour melee when they blocked the road, burned the sheet music, and attacked workers setting up chairs for the concert. When Helen Rosen, Robeson's friend, picked him up for the concert at the Peekskill train station, she quickly turned south for a return train to New York from Ossining. The concert was finally held, on Labor Day, at the defunct Hollow Bridge Golf

Course three miles from Peekskill, with as many as 20,000 attending. They had their own guard, members of the Fur and Leather Workers Union, but trouble broke out again at the end of the concert when cars left via a narrow country lane. They were pelted with rocks—again, as the local police looked on—with forty injured, the attack continuing to Route 9 and south as far as Ossining.

Governor Dewey ordered an investigation, but wound up accepting the report of the Westchester district attorney, George Fanelli, who exonerated everyone. The American Civil Liberties Union concluded that the rioting was provoked by anti-Semitism precisely because of the growing summer population of Jews. The anti-Semitism abated after this incident, as improved transportation allowed vacationers to range deeper into the Valley and the southern Catskills. The old social issues dissipated into the modern fabric of the times.

By 1949, when activists like folksinger Pete Seeger were drifting away from the communist influence—disillusioned by the news coming out of Stalinist Russia as well as America's growing concerns with Russian military power—anti-communist sentiment became strident. Seeger's family had an impeccable musical pedigree, although his father, the noted American musicologist Charles Louis Seeger (1886–1979), quietly served as music critic for the *Daily Worker* under the pseudonym Carl Sand in the 1920s. His son, an Army veteran, became a folk singer. He and Lee Hayes founded The Weavers, whose 1952 hit, "Good Night, Irene," made them famous and allowed Seeger and his wife Toshi to move to Beacon. Then—with the controversial Paul Robeson concert violence in 1949—"the blacklisters came out with a blast against us," Seeger told PBS in 2008. In 1961, Seeger was found guilty of not providing information to HUAC and sentenced to a year in jail (the case was overturned after seven years of appeals) which precipitated more and greater prejudicial actions against him locally. The American Legion vehemently protested a Vassar College Seeger concert in April 1962, which was held anyway with great success. On April 19, Sonia Malkine's popular "World of Folk Music" program on WKNY-CBS in Kingston was cancelled by the station because she chose to interview Seeger for a segment. As late as 1967, the prejudice toward Seeger continued. When he sang "Waist Deep in the Big Muddy" on the Smothers Brothers Comedy Hour—with its pointed criticism of President Johnson ("the big fool says to push on")—CBS would not allow it to be aired. The brothers held their ground, however, and he did appear in 1968, but the controversy ultimately led to their being dropped by the network in the following year. By then, Pete Seeger was a true folk hero and American icon.

Dashiell Hammett (1894–1961), the former Pinkerton detective and celebrated noir-fiction writer, was one of the intellectuals hounded by the FBI. His star had risen between the publication of *Red Harvest* and the last of his *Thin Man* series of novels, and by 1947 he was living with playwright Lillian Hellman (1905–84) at her farm in Pleasantville. Hammett was serving as president of the Civil Rights Congress. A team of FBI investigators came to the farm searching for evidence of his complicity with bail-jumping Communists convicted under the Smith Act. Hammett faced more serious charges in 1949, after eleven of the Congress leaders were convicted of criminal conspiracy in the celebrated Foley Square case—the cause for which the Robeson concert was organized. Hammett contributed to a $260,000 bail fund and was chair of the committee. Four of those convicted jumped bail after the US Supreme Court declined to hear the case. The writer was brought to court in 1951 and interrogated by the future Rosenberg prosecutor, US district attorney Irving Saypol (1905–77). Hammett gave no names and refused to answer any questions, received a six-month sentence for contempt (the sentiment was genuine), and served twenty-two weeks. He emerged, at 57, in poor health, moved into the gatekeeper's cottage near the old farm, and lived unmolested but ill, financially drained, and unable to work, with the FBI continuing to watch him. Hellman asserted in her memoir that he had acted out of conscience, and that she had to sell the farm to cover his $67,000 in legal expenses.

Hammett was called before Senator McCarthy's Permanent Senate Subcommittee in 1953, and invoked his rights before the senator and his aide, Roy Cohn (1927–86). He wryly suggested that the best way to fight communism was to ban books for people, and that was his fate as an author for a number of years. His novels were removed from America's libraries, the film version of *The Maltese Falcon* (1941) reviled by vigilantes when revived, and the IRS claimed he owed $10,000 in back taxes. Hammett still taught during these troubling times, and eventually obtained a veteran's pension. He was buried in Arlington National Cemetery, at his own request, in 1961.

Hammett and Seeger were not the only creative Hudson Valley individuals harmed by the scare. Howard E. Koch (1901–95), a Woodstock screenwriter and producer, and co-writer of *Casablanca*, was blacklisted by Hollywood for his screenplay for *Mission to Moscow* in 1943. This memoir of World War II by a pro-Stalinist had been serialized in *Reader's Digest* with no ill effect. Jack Warner even claimed that FDR had pressured his studio to make the film, yet it was Koch who suffered the consequences.

Senator Joseph McCarthy brought HUAC to the federal building in Albany for hearings in December 1953 and February 1954. His target was the General Electric plant at Schenectady and the United Electrical Workers Local 30. McCarthy became furious when all of the union officials called to testify invoked their rights against self-incrimination—which of course had the effect of incriminating them all on the spot. Eight months later, on October 20, 1954, his own star falling precipitously on the national stage, McCarthy (who was not present) was taken to task at a Schenectady Chamber of Commerce dinner attended by 1,100. The speaker, Ronald Reagan of California, railed against "super patriotism" and its use by demagogues to pursue suspected communists. Reagan was the former president of the Screen Actors Guild and the guest of General Electric for a tour and dinner that day. The city sponsored a rally and made him an honorary Schenectady Patroon. He expressed wonder at why Senator McCarthy should question the movie industry for not being forthcoming in answering his committee's questions when Hollywood already had thousands of lawsuits in the works against the government over his scare tactics. The senator from Wisconsin was censured by Congress on December 2 of that year, effectively ending his witch-hunting career.

37. Betty Friedan's Morning Coffee

> As a human being walks in safety with both his limbs, while with
> one only he hobbles and is in constant danger of failing; so has
> human government, forgetting that God has made two sexes,
> depended for its movements hitherto on one alone. The march
> of human improvement is scarce a proper term to express its past
> progress, since in order to march, both limbs are required.
>
> —EMMA WILLARD (1848)

Women's health issues and the right to abortion came to national attention, and considerable controversy, with the activities of the Planned Parenthood Federation of America after the war, and particularly after the appointment of Mary Steichen Calderone (1904–94) as medical director in 1953. Calderone, a 1925 Vassar College graduate, daughter of photographer Edward Steichen and niece of Carl Sandburg, was a physician who overturned an American Medical Association stricture against doctors disseminating birth control information in 1964, and then left Planned Parenthood to form SEICUS, the Sexuality and Education Information Council of the United States, whose message was the positive value of sex. An article of hers in the *Vassar Quarterly* in 1969 rebutted conservative assaults on sex education. Calderone lectured on the subject as the President's Distinguished Visitor at Vassar in 1983. She was considered the equal of Margaret Sanger on birth control, and was hailed by Jeffrey Moran as "the grandmother of sex education" in America in a 2000 article in the *Vassar Quarterly*.

But it was a suburban housewife who made the most lasting contribution. Betty Naomi Goldstein Friedan (1921–2006) and Carl Friedan (1919–2005) raised three children in the baby boom following the war, and Betty was a typical housewife and mother in the postwar expansion era, although she had an edge. Her Smith College *summa cum laude* education gave her the opportunity to pursue part-time work by writing articles for *Mademoiselle*, *Cosmopolitan*, *Reader's Digest*, and such. Betty's edge was more than her education and intelligence, however; her various editors often looked askance at some of the story angles she pursued. A *Redbook* article about Hickory Hill near Tappan examined several young couples who came up from the city, established a community, and raised their children "almost like one big family." People did not do those things, or think those ways, or act like that, her editors said.

Betty and Carl Friedan married in 1947. They lived in Parkway Village, an international community sponsored by the United Nations in Queens. Some of her neighbors formed a co-op and moved to land on the Ossining-Briarcliff Manor border, but the experiment failed when the local school refused to accept people of mixed race. The Friedans relocated to Rockland County in 1956, at first renting a cavernous stone barn in Snedens Landing.

"In some ways it was the most romantic place I've ever lived," Betty told an interviewer later in her life. "I would type with gloves on because every time you turned the heat up, you felt like dollar bills were being burned." One winter's $1,800 fuel bill led Betty in search of a new home, which she found six miles further north in Grand View-on-Hudson. The house was on River Road, a rambling Victorian in a sylvan acre they bought for $25,000 on a G.I. mortgage. For a while, Betty was almost content chauffeuring the children around, scraping paint off the fireplace, helping to lead the local PTA, and otherwise acting the dutiful housewife.

These were both difficult and glorious years for the Friedans. Their three children were growing in special ways, and an involved and dedicated community of families benefited from Betty's skills at organizing, yet their marriage was slowly crumbling amidst violent arguments. Carl was in the advertising business, which he despised even though he was successful at it. Betty continued to write small, harmless articles for the women's magazines, most of which were cut by editors who did not approve of her radical thinking about housewives and their lives. Friedan's experience was a casebook on a change in magazine thinking that began around 1949 and mirrored the retrogression of the times, from an emergent embrace of women moving into male professions into the notion of women role models as husband-supporters and child-rearers.

An article about Julie Harris's natural childbirth was rejected as too graphic for the tender readers of the day. Friedan's story about an innovative sculptor, Beverly Pepper (b. 1922), was turned down with scorn because market research had shown that women only wanted to read about motherhood and household matters. She came to the attention of an editor at W. W. Norton, George Brockway, with "The Coming Ice Age: A True Scientific Detective Story," a long and intelligent piece for *Harper's* in September 1958 about scientists at Lamont-Doherty Earth Observatory, but declined an offer of a book contract.

The Friedans were typical suburbanites in many ways. The precocity of their son Danny's interests in physics—he was accepted to Princeton at age fifteen—led his mother into organizing a program at the local Rockland Center for the Arts for talks and seminars by notable professionals from the city. C. Wright Mills came up from Columbia to talk about sociology; marine biologist Robert Menzies expounded on science; George Mathews, also from Columbia, lectured on Western civilization. Betty and the Rockland Foundation's director, James Fitch, created a Community Resources Pool that recruited seventy-five of these experts, partly through a $13,000 grant that also provided Betty with a small salary.

"She was brassy," Fitch said of Betty Friedan. "She was always very dramatic. She had a big house on the edge of the river, and she had outrageous taste in décor—orange, red, purple—and dressed like that, too. Betty is an authentic home-grown radical."

She placated local teachers whose egos were bruised by the attention paid to the experts, yet she also had a harsh side that led the Foundation into assigning their school district liaison, Joseph Kastner, to monitor her activities and "keep her out of trouble." As with her situation with Carl, Betty "had no problem getting personal in an argument," Kastner said. "Her language was genital and scatological. Women didn't speak that way in those days. The fear was that she would blow it. She didn't . . . She knew well when to be tactful." The teachers came around, helped with field trips, asked for seminars, and involved the speakers in other school districts through the English departments. Betty became locally famous—her parties were "county-wide salons, attended by distinguished people"—and a better school system, as well as some residual hostility, resulted.

Her awakening came in 1957 when she did a survey of fellow members of the Smith College class of '42 (she had graduated first in the class) and found that many of them covered over the doubts, frustrations, anxieties and resentments over the changes taking place since the war with a patina of sweet passivity; of the two hundred who responded to her survey, 121 expressed serious dissatisfaction with their lives. *McCall's* rejected a subsequent article as "unbelievable." It was badly rewritten by the *Ladies' Home Journal,* forcing Friedan to recall the story. *Redbook* said it applied to "only the most neurotic housewife," not the average mom ("Betty has gone off her rocker," the editor told her agent). In 1960, *Good Housekeeping* ran "a rather tame version, under the title, 'Women Are People, Too.'"

Betty Friedan changed her thinking after meeting Vance Packard (1914–96), who had turned his articles about subliminal influences in advertising into *The Hidden Persuaders* (1957) after its rejection by the magazines. The Norton editor whom she had earlier turned down was now delighted with her new book idea. Betty at first called the book *The Togetherness Woman*, and she promised a manuscript to George Brockway within a year; instead, it took five. She wrote while also raising her children, setting the manuscript aside when other housewives came for coffee, and confessed later that none of those around her, including her husband and editor, ever thought she would finish.

Although Betty never fit the mode, these were times when women's pursuit of intellectual interests were accepted with polite courtesy in traditional circles; "Wives Are Getting Brighter" was the title of a December 6, 1959, *New York News Colorato Magazine* article about New York University "Sunrise Semester" television courses that housewives took very early in the morning before turning to their household chores. When her book was finally published in 1963 (with a new title), the response to *The Feminine Mystique* slowly developed and then quickly became a phenomenon. More than three million copies were sold in the first three years. The book ultimately transformed modern thinking about women, feminism, and a whole set of antiquated attitudes that had survived the war, and turned Betty Friedan into a national figure.

In 1957, echoing what Theodore Roosevelt had told Dutchess County fairgoers fifty years earlier, Adlai Stevenson (1900–65) told the Smith College graduates that their futures would be in the home, but it was Stevenson who was becoming an anachronism. Betty Friedan was the trend-maker in these times, no longer an upstart with a brash idea, and although she brought in a revolution in feminist thinking she also defined the sickness of the times. Hers was not a working class audience, but her topic extended into all facets of postwar America—"the whole nation stopped growing up," she wrote:

> In this sense, what happened to women is part of what happened to all of us in the years after the war . . . Women went home again just as men shrugged off the bomb, forgot the concentration camps, condoned corruption, and fell into helpless conformity;

just as the thinkers avoided the complex larger problems of the postwar world. It was easier, safer, to think about love and sex than about communism, McCarthy, and the uncontrolled bomb . . . There was a kind of personal retreat, even on the part of the most far-sighted, the most spirited; we lowered our eyes from the horizon, and steadily contemplated our own navels.

Some women, like Irene Norman Betar, retained their jobs by training return-ing veterans—Irene taught thirty at a time how to thread machines at the Binch Lace factory on Warren Street in Glens Falls—but many were left by the wayside.

The malaise that Friedan traced spread across society and took different forms—a religious revival that mirrored the rise of psychotherapy as mutual searches for identity, creativity transformed into a modern art "that flaunted discipline and glorified the evasion of meaning," and a theater of anger and "the absurd." Self-realization for women, Friedan forecasted, lay in breaking the mental chains of "the problem with no name—which is simply the fact that American women are kept from growing to their full human capacities." In the complacency of a time in which success meant the number of cars in the family and the quality of a President was measured in his golf game, the same was true for men.

38. Arts, Culture and the Heritage Revolution

That's what [as a child] I thought people did.

—SARAH MECKLEM of Woodstock,
on becoming an artist

The Harlem Valley was emerging with the times in the postwar years, and rural as ever. Oliver Chester Potter had restored the Old Drovers Hill on the Great Road in South Dover, leaving the barn sign from the 1840s still hanging on the premises. Webutuck Craft Village spread across a former Ebenezer Preston family farm with three mills and a marble dam, but Ebenezer's kin still had farms, mills and quarries for several miles along Ten Mile River in Webutuck.

The Good Times Track at Goshen in Orange County—still going strong in Averell Harriman's later years—hosted the Hambletonian Stakes since its removal from Syracuse in 1930. In 1947, the favorite, *Hoot Mon*, beat a fast trotter named *Rodney* in two of three heats. *Rodney*'s driver was Bion Shively, then 69 years old. In 1952, he returned with *Sharp Note* and won two out of three, garnering $47,360 for the owner. The horse went on to become the first trotter to win $100,000, all the while ridden by Shiveley, who continued racing until age 82 in 1960.

After Clayton "Peg Leg" Bates (1907-98) appeared on the Ed Sullivan radio show twenty times, more than any other performer in the 1940s, he retired and moved to Kerhonkson in 1951. He remained as gregarious as ever, running a country club until the late 1980s, staying active in community service, talking with kids about drugs and staying in school, and performing benefits around the Valley. A friend of the disabled, Peg Leg performed in every local town that had an auditorium that featured variety shows for the community.

In northern Ulster County, Woodstock remained wonderfully eccentric as the zaniness of the Maverick days mellowed in the aging of its artists in the new era. "I thought everybody's family were artists," artist Sarah ("Sallie") Mecklem (b. 1946) recalled in a *Chronogram* interview:

> I would get home [from Montessori school] and break out the pencils—not just No. 2s but also the HB leads, the soft ones, and every other thing. So my earliest artistic sensations were about the quality of lines in pencil drawings. I remember loving sharp pencils. And my parents [Austin Mecklem and Marianne Appel] were in the studio, hanging out with friends like Reginald Wilson, or we'd go visit Ed and Jenny Chavez. I remember playing in Anton Refregier's studio, and posing for him as a child (which my sister did, too).

When Sallie was seven she was the "tattoo marquee" of the artist parties, artists like Julio de Diego pausing to decorate her with doodles to parade around in top hat, high heels, and bikini bottom "advertising" herself. In later years she returned to Woodstock and purchased the home that Ed Chavez built on Plochman Lane.

A new generation came to Woodstock in these times. J. C. van Rijn, a Dutch engineer, was a World War II exile who built a cooling device that led to the founding of Rotron Inc., which employed 750 by the late 1970s. William Pachner (b. 1915), a nationally known anti-fascist illustrator after emigrating from Prague in 1939, purchased Juliana Force's Woodstock home in 1945, and soon became a close friend of Wilna Hervey and Nan Mason. When Pachner learned that his entire family—eighty members—were exterminated in the Holocaust, he foreswore illustration and became a full-time artist instead. Painter Kurt Sluizer (1911–88) and his wife, weaver Esther Sluizer, moved into Bolton Brown's old house in Zena. Raoul Hague (1904–93), a veteran of the Woodstock scene, was a reclusive sculptor of fine wood carvings who arrayed his works on display in three sheds to which no one was invited for viewings. Frances Archipenko Gray, the sculptor's widow, managed a foundation in Archipenko's name at their home in Bearsville.

Father Francis (William Henry Francis Brothers, b. 1885) was an artist, in a way, except his medium was religion. "An eccentric Englishman," he left the Church of England and joined an obscure Roman Catholic sect called the Old Polish Church. In his lifetime, Father Francis supported the suffragettes, campaigned for birth control with Margaret Sanger, and advised Clarence Darrow during the Scopes evolution trial. He was asked to marry the Duke and Duchess of Windsor, and eventually became known as "the hippie priest" in presiding over the Church on the Mount as a miniscule "cathedral" halfway up Meads Mountain. The church quickly became an icon for the town and all things Woodstock.

Actor Lee Marvin (1924–87) came home from the war with a Purple Heart and became a plumber's assistant to Adolph Heckeroth in Woodstock. Edith Heckeroth recalled Marvin as "a humorous character who enjoyed acting out his exploits as a Marine during the war." He used the local people he met on his plumbing rounds to create character sketches. He was also a notorious regular at the Irvington Inn (and most other Woodstock bars he had not been thrown out of), not infrequently causing fights after having too much to drink. He bought a large estate near the Kingston-Rhinecliff bridge that had been built for Jack "Legs" Diamond.

When Joe Sinnott of Saugerties returned home after the war—he had lost an adored older brother early on—he finished high school, then moved to New York to attend cartoonists and illustrators school and work for Marvel Comics. Joe illustrated for Stan Lee for 64 years, 24 of them as the inker for "Spider-Man." He worked from a second floor studio on sedate, tree-lined

Spaulding Lane in the village of Saugerties, as if he were a disguised superhero himself. Every Friday, he and his wife drove to Manhattan with the latest exploits under arm, received his assignment from Stan Lee for the new week, had lunch at their favorite restaurant, and drove home. He also captured the local heroes (many of them his friends) in stylized cartoons for the American Legion Baseball Hall of Fame banquet every year, and was a familiar and well-liked local figure in town. Ironically, this mild-mannered magician in ink held a different cartoon character as his personal hero and role model: "The Timid Soul" from his childhood, Caspar Milquetoast.

Education, like art and culture generally, expanded by leaps and bounds in the postwar years. The one-room schoolhouses fell in flocks as the new wind of consolidation swept the state. An economy of resources was attained, better trained educators emerged, and education was much improved. Mrs. Wagert no longer needed to come over from Rhinebeck on the Kingston ferry and walk four miles to the Anderson School in Port Ewen every day, sometimes in below-zero temperatures and with snow so deep the boys could sink in it up to their chests. Teachers could now teach closer to home, the children brought to them at the new buildings the consolidated districts sprouted. Centralizing also allowed for a more consistent education pattern, yet the intimacy of the learning setting in the "old school" style was forever lost.

Each community had its battles, some over the loss of the traditional way, many over the location of the new schools and the costs involved. Queensbury managed to avoid serious disruption by consolidating at the site of a former airport. The Italian hamlet of Glasco in Ulster County lost its small, well-run district and was treated rudely by the town's WASPish majority, for whom ethnic resentments of earlier decades persevered. Louis Francello, their attorney and a respected bill-drafter in Albany, got an audience with the governor's representative, who told him to bring his committee and they would talk about. When he showed up with almost two hundred fellow residents, the state agent paled and said he meant his committee, not the whole community. "This is the committee," Francello replied. The interview was fruitless, however, as Glasco was ultimately denied its own district and was hard hit financially because they had to pay off a debt that had accrued for making a good, small district for themselves.

West Point survived a damaging cheating scandal in 1976 by revising the role of the Academic Board, whose conservative practices had long been considered inhibitors to progressive change. Lieutenant General Andrew J. Goodpaster shifted the center of administrative power to the superintendent. As its student body grew from 500 at the turn of the twentieth century to 4,417 by 2012, the academy retained its reputation as, in the words of Brigadier General (Ret.) Lance Betros (class of '77), "an elite undergraduate institution and one of the premier leader development institutions in the world." The general knew whereof he spoke, having established the Center for Oral History and the Center for Genocide and Holocaust Studies at the academy. Betros warned that the relatively short-term impacts of the superintendent (the service was usually for five years) threatened continuity in the prime directive of West Point, to develop men and women of character and intellect. He also criticized West Point's modern athletic focus on national football, even though he was recruited for the academy as a high school player himself.

Westchester Community College began as the White Plains Technical Institute in a former high school on the estate of the millionaire son of the founder of the A&P Corporation. Diplomas of proficiency in electrical and mechanical crafts, food administration, and building construction were awarded to 128 graduates in 1949. The institute became a formal community college in 1953, and accepted its first class of student nurses two years later. By 1957, the Westchester Board of Supervisors authorized an expenditure of $750,000 for an English Tudor manor home and estate in Valhalla. Thirty years later, more than forty associate degree programs were offered.

A recuperation center for tuberculosis patients since 1928 became the home of Dutchess Community College in 1958, with Dr. James F. Hall the first president. The first 250 full-time and 412 part-time students were educated by twelve faculty members. Dutchess was fully accredited by June 1964, more than 3,000 full- and part-time students enrolled in the following year. Orange County Community College opened in 1950 with 160 students on the estate of a benefactor, Christine Morrison. In 1952, Orange County became the first school in the country to offer an associate's degree in nursing. The Harriman family contributed a new hall in 1955, with eight more buildings added by 1975. The college developed a reputation as "the cradle of college presidents" with the appointment of nine former students or faculty members as presidents of community colleges in the United States.

Rockland Community College's origin traced to a doctoral dissertation that prompted fifty county leaders to organize in 1954. The first entering class typified the cross-section of the student body. Veterans, the disabled, homemakers, recent immigrants eager to make their mark in America, and former or failed four-year college students made up the class. Self-study at home became a hallmark of the Rockland experience, as did evening and weekend classes for working adults. By the 1980s, more than 6,000 students were enrolled.

Among private institutions, Siena College in Loudonville survived fitfully during the war and came alive when the GI Bill brought thousands of returning veterans to the college campuses. A Reserve Officer Training Corps unit operated out of Quonset huts tucked in a corner of the Siena campus. The college became famous for its basketball program under coach Dan Cunha, who compiled a 246–225 win-loss record (a 52% winning percentage) over 1941–65, including a 22–6 record in 1947–48. Siena won the National Catholic Invitational Tournament in the 1949–50 season, but at first withdrew from the tournament when its star player, 6' 2" African American Billy Harrell of Troy, was refused admittance into the same hotel with his team. The college weathered a scandal involving recruitment perquisites and returned to its winning ways in 1965, when center Jack Mulvey broke the school's rebounding record.

Hudson Valley Community College in Rensselaer County, the site of an Army Signal Corps training camp during the war, was turned into a veterans' vocational school, and then the Troy Technical Institute, with 88 students initially in 1953. A new 165-acre campus was created in 1959 for $3.26 million on the Troy–North Greenbush town line, following a landmark court case giving counties the right to fund community colleges even though students often came from adjoining areas. HVCC became so well regarded that its graduates were accepted with full credit as juniors at Rensselaer Polytechnic Institute.

The region was also home to the only level-1 trauma and academic medical center between New York and Montreal, Albany Medical College, one of the oldest medical schools in the nation. AMC awards 140 medical degrees each year. Vassar College, Bard, Union and the Rensselaer Polytechnic Institute remained the premier higher education bodies in the Valley, each advancing the noblest principles of pedagogy into real world—and often whole world—applications. With the fall of the USSR, Bard established an undergraduate honors college in collaboration with St. Petersburg State University in the 1990s; the college also partnered with the American University of central Asia in Kyrgyzstan and universities in South Africa and Palestinian East Jerusalem. At RPI, president Livingston W. Houston (1891–1977; RPI '13) guided the college through the phenomenal period of growth and change following the war. He created the modern administrative structure, established a graduate school and research division, and provided more non-technical subjects for students, changing the face of engineering studies in the process.

The Normal School at New Paltz continued through the decades despite an antipathy by the Board of Regents toward its becoming a full-fledged college. A state surplus allowed for the funding of a four-year college in 1942, with Lawrence van der Berg as the first president. The name was changed to the New Paltz State Teachers College, its development under B. H. Matteson and William J. Haggerty (b. 1908) leading to full-fledged acceptance as the State University College of Education at New Paltz in 1959. Haggerty led the college faculty into creating its own curriculum, instead of adopting a statewide one, which reflected the actual needs and situation of the students. New Paltz's initiative was followed by other colleges in the state system over time. A liberal arts degree program was approved by the Regents in 1960. After Edward Coykendall left his American art collection to the school in 1957—which included George Bellows' *The Romanian Girl*—the college transformed its small art gallery into the Samuel Dorsky Museum of Art in 1964, a $2.6 million public-private partnership project.

Governor Dewey signed into law the new State University of New York in 1948, consolidating the former New York State College for Teachers with dozens of other normal schools for teacher training. Albany's campus went through two name changes, becoming SUNY at Albany in 1962 and eventually growing into the University of Albany, one of four university centers in the 64-campus network of two-, four-year, and specialty colleges consolidated under Governor Nelson Rockefeller.

An expanded cultural footprint extended the interest in the Hudson Valley's aesthetic and heritage treasures for travelers. Indeed, one could trace the pattern of growth of the small community tourism centers by the improvements in automobiles and roads, whole neighborhoods and ethnic confluences relocating to however far the new transportation would take them in a day—to the Highlands for one generation and Leeds, Tannersville and Windham for later ones. Yet the impacts of growth were taking a toll and the Hudson Valley's poetic sense of place was fast becoming a romantic artifact. At a 1978 conference on Lewis Mumford at Bard College, Vassar professor Harvey K. Flad challenged the formerly picturesque rural identity of the Hudson Valley's "middle landscape," terming its modern manifestation a muddling of rural, urban and suburban elements displaying a continuum of decreasing intensity in land use from urban to "a rural-urban fringe" before finally yielding, too often imperfectly, to open rural lands.

The Valley as a refuge diminished, yet its beauty and historical importance were not completely built over, and instead received new impetuses in the postwar years. John D. Rockefeller, Jr.'s farsighted acquisition, at the behest of the Historical Society of the Tarrytowns, of the Upper Van Cortlandt Mills in 1940 gave the society a headquarters and a home for Sleepy Hollow Restorations, a nonprofit corporation created by Rockefeller to acquire and manage the site in 1951. A ten-year reconstruction program commenced in 1959. Nails to restore the old mill, wharf, and dam were made the old-fashioned way, on-site. Accessories from the 1750s-era added to the authenticity, and the newly restored Upper Mills were opened to the public on May 21, 1969. The interpretation extended to a full-scale reenactment of the mill's operations, including the growing and harvesting of crops the same way as 250 years earlier.

Art and literature on Hudson Valley subjects and themes moved hand-in-hand with a renewed sense of the past. Returning to Glenburn, the family estate, after the war, Olin Dows, the neighbor and young friend of Franklin Roosevelt, created a commemorative book on the president that hewed to the traditions he came from with nostalgic grace. Dows considered his river estate life as the source of his lifelong aesthetic sensibilities, and savored "the quiet passing of that way of life" and its romantic allure. Similar themes were echoed in literature. Anya Seton's *Dragonwyck* (1944), which revisited the manor world of Rensselaerswick, illuminated a particular sense of place about Hudson Valley life and culture. William B. Lemoney's *Mooney* (1950), John Beck's *Troubled Spring* (1950) and *Jubilee* (1951), Oriana Atkinson's *Twin Cousins* (1951) and *Golden Season* (1953), Cyril Harris' *Trouble of Hungerfords* (1953), Marjorie K. Rawlings' *The Sojourner* (1953), and Howard Breslin's *Shad Run* (1955) followed the heritage trail.

A sense of history imbued major federal and state advances. Mary Butler's attempt at systematizing Hudson Valley archaeological sites while working at Vassar College under a Works Progress Administration grant in 1939–40, albeit fledgling given the size of the subject, had an outsized impact on the scientific community. William Ritchie brought the science of archaeology to new levels, here and elsewhere around the state. Yet prehistoric sites were chewed apart in the rush to build; almost as if to compensate, federal laws, followed by state ones, set new standards and goals for saving and recording both the historic and prehistoric past. "Mission 66," the National Park Service's ten-year parks improvement program begun in 1957, led to an expansion and modernization of the Saratoga National Historic Site. A Cultural Resource Management (CRM) program begun with the federal Highway Salvage Act of 1958 established far-reaching protections for heritage resources. The National Historic Preservation and National Environmental Policy Acts of 1968–69 followed. Construction on the new Interstate 84 in Dutchess County had to stop and await an archaeological report on Donald K. Fisher's discovery of mastodon remains.

The salvage act also necessitated the excavation of the Fort Orange site in Albany in 1970–71, the first time that a major Dutch site in America was examined by modern professionals. Paul Huey and his hearty crew uncovered a veritable "time capsule" of seventeenth-century information. Those and other artifacts in time would become integral attractions for downtown Albany's tourism industry.

The Clean Waters Act programs created by the federal Environmental Protection Agency resulted in major data recovery efforts in lieu of actual preservation of sites, affecting at least eight upper Hudson Valley locations in ten years after 1977—in Schuylerville, Mechanicville, Waterford, Snake Hill, Pleasantdale, and Little Wood Creek. The state followed in 1979–80 with the Environmental Quality Review and Historic Preservation acts, and a dozen years later with Hudson Valley Greenway. Together these programs, despite efforts by private industry and even governments to avoid their requirements, transformed New York State into a more heritage-conscious society.

A celebration of the Hudson River's history received an impetus in 1980 with the creation of the Hudson River Maritime Museum along the Rondout Creek in Kingston. Steamboat and tug enthusiasts came together and developed a major interpretive site over time. The automation of lighthouses and buoy-tending operations by the US Coast Guard led to the closing of river beacons and disputes about the disposition of lighthouses centered on their historic value. Local nonprofit groups emerged to save the old nostalgic structures. Ruth Reynolds Glunt, a photographer of the Hudson-Fulton

Celebration of 1909 and wife of the last of the civilian buoy tenders, joined Governor Rockefeller's Hudson River Valley Commission specifically because of the lighthouses. She published two books on the subject and worked with Rhinebeck architect Elise Berry in 1978 to have the Saugerties Lighthouse placed on the National Register. In 1985, a local committee headed by Clifford Steen and including architect Alexander Wade and a coalition of craftsmen from both sides of the river came together as the Saugerties Lighthouse Conservancy. Legislation by then-state Assemblyman Maurice D. Hinchey led to the Coast Guard's gifting of the property for $1. Their work began in eerie earnest when, accompanied by a Coast Guard officer, the group entered the building for the first time, fearful that a complete rewiring would be needed. The officer turned and tried the switch, and the lights came on for the first time in twenty years.

The team built an ingenious scale model of an interior scaffold, cut the beams offsite and transported a full-scale scaffold by barge to the lighthouse, rebuilding it brick by brick into its original state. After the restoration, the light was reactivated and a popular bed-and-breakfast established. A wetlands leading to the structure was named the Ruth Reynolds Glunt Nature Conservancy by artist/columnist Jean Wrolsen.

The Hudson-Athens Lighthouse Preservation Society, formed in 1982, entered into a twenty-year lease with the Coast Guard; title of the lighthouse was finally transferred to the society in 2000. The last civilian keeper, Emil J. Brunner, lived there with his family from 1930 to 1946, and then rowed out alone to tend the light until it was automated in 1949. The Brunners were featured on a *Saturday Evening Post* cover on December 28, 1946, Emil arriving on the boat with a Christmas tree while the family (a few extra children added by the artist) waited with glee.

The Sleepy Hollow Lighthouse—often called the Tarrytown Lighthouse—was slated for disposal by the federal government just like Saugerties, in this case because the opening of the Tappan Zee Bridge in 1955 obviated the need for a light. The structure was built in 1882–83 a quarter of a mile off shore to avoid an expensive acquisition of vineyards on the mainland; that property eventually became Kingsland Point Park. The expansion of the General Motors automotive plant in 1923 resulted in river fill that reduced the distance to the lighthouse to about fifty yards. Demolition was avoided when the Westchester County Board of Supervisors accepted the structure from the

General Service Administration in 1969; it was opened to the public in 1983.

The "most beloved lighthouse in America" was one, like Sleepy Hollow, that was no longer needed because of a new bridge, in this case the George Washington. Activated in 1921, the Jeffrey Hook Lighthouse was slated for demolition by the federal government as well, but saved by an outcry from readers of the Hildegard H. Swift-Lynn Ward book, *The Little Red Lighthouse and the Great Grey Bridge* (1942), which taught children the importance of the small.

An ameliorating factor that tempered the intrusion of progress and became more important as time went on arose in the Hudson River Valley's interest in American history and the heritage that remained. The great upsurge in historical interest generated by the American Scenic and Preservation Society early in the century continued in the postwar years. The Huguenot Historical Society acquired the 245-year-old Hugo Freer homestead in "the oldest street in America" in the spring of 1955. The society was following the trend of the times. Artist Iver Ellis Evers, who died that year, had purchased and restored the Abraham Hasbrouck House on the same street in 1918 and enjoyed showing visitors the fireplace (large enough to roast a pig) and a cellar where cockfights were held centuries earlier. Evers' son Alf, the future Catskills historian, helped his father as a boy in renovating the house's unique staircase. More than five hundred attended the village's Stone House Inspection Day in 1956, the sixth year of the event.

The events at New Paltz signaled a new awareness of the extent, as well as the importance of the Valley's resources. In time, a revolution in thinking married a highly developed environmental acuity to the physical resources of the geography. "Heritage tourism" developed from the elements of these Valley characteristics—the beauty and richness of the past, a healthy, science-driven ecology, and a wealth of resources made available across the full spectrum of life—and defined a new sense of place for the Hudson River Valley.

VI. MODERN TIMES

DeWitt. [Still half-seen]
And welcome you are to the age, too, an age of witches
and sandwiches, an age of paper, an age of paper money
and paper men, so that a poor Dutch wraith's more
man than the thickest of you!
[He steps back and vanishes. It is now dawn.]
—MAXWELL ANDERSON, High Tor (1937)

39. The Prince of Pocantico

There was an invisible flypaper around the man.
People stuck to Nelson.   —AL MARSHALL

Politics, one might have surmised with some justification, would be the last refuge of any self-respecting Rockefeller, yet two grandsons of John D. excelled at the art. Nelson Rockefeller (1908–79) went further than his brother Winthrop, at least in the attempt, his ambitions rising to the highest office in the land. Born on his grandfather's birthday, the third child and second son of John D. Rockefeller, Jr. always had appropriately outsized ambitions, even for a Rockefeller.

After John D. Rockefeller (1839–1937) settled into his first mansion in Pocantico Hills in western Westchester County, he purchased the hamlet of East View and had it moved to improve the view from his estate. When the first home burned to the ground in 1902, his son "Junior" (1874–1960) started a new estate on a nearby hilltop appropriately named Kykuit for its panoramic views from West Point to Long Island. The new house would soon eclipse even Uncle William's nearby palatial mansion, Rockwood Hall, where rare birds from around the world—William's passion—cavorted among a lush thousand acres.

Their ruthless reputations in business notwithstanding, both brothers became world-class philanthropists. William Rockefeller (1841–1922), who frequently declined to take credit for his good works, financed the first road construction in Tarrytown, the Headless Horseman Bridge across the Pocantico Creek, a fountain tribute to a neighbor (John C. "The Pathfinder" Frémont), and the college educations of many local children whose families could not afford it. When he died in 1922, his mansion became a country club, which soon failed, and was then purchased by Nelson's brother Laurance.

John D.'s mansion, Kykuit, built of local stone on a solid rock terrace, was set amid elaborate gardens that featured fountains designed on classical themes. A circular Greek temple overlooking the Hudson River contained the Altovite Venus, a sculpture attributed to Praxiteles (c. 390–330 BCE). Junior took over the estate in 1922 and continued with his own tradition of grand giving. Just after World War II, when Philipsburg Manor was threatened by developments, he established Sleepy Hollow Restorations and saved the manor and the Upper Mills, which he then had restored to its eighteenth century look. Irving's Sunnyside and Van Cortlandt Manor were also in the Restorations portfolio.

Junior raised his children as his father had, as Baptists. Sunday meals were always formal, and all of the family was expected to be home for dinner on Father's Day. Nelson's childhood was marked by a dogged effort by his father to break the boy of his left-handedness. At the dinner table one night, Junior slipped a rubber band over Nelson's wrist, tied with a string that the father yanked every time the son reached for a utensil or dish with his left hand. Nelson cheerfully tried to conform and became ambidextrous in the process.

Abby (Abigail Aldrich Rockefeller, 1903–76), the oldest child, whom everyone called "Babs," rebelled in her youth, smoked cigarettes at fifteen, and spooned with her beau, David Milton (1900–76), in full view of the servants; Babs and David later married and moved west. John (1906–78) and David (b. 1915) eventually had homes that bordered the estate. Laurance's residences and Nelson's were close to its center. After his father died, Nelson lived at Kykuit, and eventually the whole estate was converted into a permanent park and preserve. The estate had seventy-one other homes, many of them in the village of Pocantico Hills for employees and others associated with the family. The Kykuit amenities included a "playhouse" with a bowling alley, billiards, squash court, indoor tennis and swimming, croquet, and a nine-hole golf course. Seventy miles of roadway were constructed within the family's holdings, many of the routes chosen by John D. himself for the dramatic views.

Nelson's son Steven (b. 1936) had a romance with a Kykuit maid in 1956, Anne-Marie Rasmussen of Norway, whom he married. Nelson liked Anne-Marie, but the marriage was destined to fail when she embraced her newfound wealth and lost her fairytale charm. Nelson's own relations with his brothers became strained in 1963 when he divorced his wife Mary ("Tod") and married Margaretta "Happy" Murphy (1926–2015), who had four children and went through a messy divorce herself in order to marry Rockefeller. Nelson was nearly twenty years her senior, yet they survived the age difference to enjoy life together. Although the breakup and marriage was highly publicized—Nelson was in his second term as governor—he survived the fallout and went on to run successfully for two more terms.

Nelson Rockefeller maintained thirty-seven running antique cars in mint condition at Kykuit and used a 1965 Mustang around the estate. He gave Happy a new Rolls-Royce that hardly ever left the grounds. In the early 1970s, Nelson brought in architect Junzo Yashimaro (1908–97) to design a new house at Kykuit. Eight Japanese carpenters imported for the project had to return to Japan because of improper papers; Nelson put his staff on the job and saw to their legal return so that the house could be completed, at a cost of $650,000. Happy lived there after her husband's death. Meanwhile, the house served as a guest residence for the world's notables, including Emperor Hirohito, Anwar Sadat, Lord Louis Mountbatten, King Hussein, and Empress Farah Diba, the wife of the deposed Shah of Iran.

Rockefeller paid tribute to his mother when she died by approaching Henri Matisse (1869–1954) about a stained glass window for the family chapel at Union Church of Pocantico. Matisse wrote to Nelson that he had attempted the design but was unsuccessful. The letter reached Rockefeller the day after Matisse died, and a few days later another letter arrived in which the artist related that he had worked out the design problem on the wall of his studio. Again, Nelson put staff on the job; the studio "scheme" was discovered and the window, the last work of art by Henri Matisse, became a reality.

Having served in the administrations of Roosevelt, Truman, and Eisenhower, Rockefeller was seasoned in bureaucratic service. He was part of a government reorganization committee within the first Republican administration after the Roosevelt-Truman years, and served Eisenhower as Under Secretary in the Department of Health, Education and Welfare (HEW) and Special Assistant to the President on Foreign Affairs. At HEW, a department recommended by the reorganization committee, Rockefeller helped to expand Social Security to ten million new Americans, finance schools in under-developed areas, and advance health care insurance in innovative ways. In 1955, when tapped by Governor Harriman to head a constitutional convention commission, Rockefeller, without Harriman's knowledge, had already privately decided that elective office was his logical next step.

The men were socially friendly, as were their families, although Harriman was the more gregarious and intelligent member of the Valley's aristocracy. A "dashing figure" in his youth, he had been FDR's personal emissary to Winston Churchill and ambassador to Russia and Joseph Stalin in the war years when Rockefeller, a much younger man, was championing the United States in South America for the President. Averill almost won the Democratic presidential nomination in 1952, and took the party nomination for governor two years later. Harriman brought new and energetic talents to Albany, including 28-year-old Daniel Patrick Moynihan (1927–2003), first as an assistant to executive secretary Jack Bingham and then as acting executive secretary when Bingham ran for the state senate.

Harriman's energies faltered when faced with empty coffers after Tom Dewey's departure, and he became "tightfisted" in spending. He saw no potential political damages from a Rockefeller appointment, even though warned by Milton Stewart that Nelson was "the very sonofabitch we are going to have to beat" in the next gubernatorial election. Harriman also forgot or ignored the last advice Dewey had given him: everything he did in Albany would be political and to lose sight of that would put him in peril. Rockefeller, meanwhile, used the commission to familiarize himself with state government and establish a network of influential political connections.

"Harriman had unwittingly given New York Republicans their own Eisenhower," his biographer, Rudy Abramson, contended. The constitutional referendum that had prompted Rockefeller's appointment was defeated by 100,000 votes, yet Harriman's attempt to place the blame on Rockefeller was ineffective. Republicans kept Nelson in the limelight by making him chairman of a special legislative commission on constitutional modernization—a think tank first proposed by Harriman! A month later, an office opened in Manhattan staffed by volunteers who wanted to draft Nelson Rockefeller for governor. Still, the incumbent was so convinced that he could beat any Republican, Rockefeller included, that he singled Nelson out for a bow at the 1958 Legislative Correspondents Association annual lampoon. They had a good laugh about that afterwards. Moynihan—a committed urbanist—attributed Harriman's defeat to "the radical/liberal contempt" emerging among state Democrats, whom he considered class-oriented compared with city Dems.

The incumbent might have read the writing on the wall when he kicked off his 1958 reelection campaign at the Dutchess County Fair in Rhinebeck. He was booed by the mostly Republican crowd—his dog Brum and two grandchildren beside him—and that after he had favorably responded to Fair manager Dick Murray's request that bingo be legalized by the state. The Harriman campaign eventually unraveled in bad feelings at the Buffalo Democratic Party convention, while Rockefeller took to the statewide stage like "a duck in water." In his first action after announcing his candidacy for governor in 1958, Nelson Rockefeller picked up his running mate, Assemblyman Malcolm Wilson (1914–2000), at his White Plains office, and continued on the Taconic State Parkway to meet with the five Columbia County delegates to the state Republican Party convention, who endorsed him the same night. (On the way, they passed a Bentley. "That was my father," Nelson told Malcolm, and had the limousine pull off to the side for a roadside chat.) He was the first New York politician to use his own wealth to get elected.

Rockefeller's youthful vitality stood in contrast to Harriman, seventeen years his senior, and he came on as a brash and flashy candidate admired for his charm. He had a bagful of political tricks, like his habit when riding from one speaking engagement to the next of changing into a fresh shirt and tie, so that he looked new as the day when he emerged into the next crowd. He also kept up a bruising schedule. On October 16, 1958, Rockefeller visited the West Virginia Pulp and Paper Company at Mechanicville, the Ballston-Stillwater Knitting Company, and stopped in Hudson Falls and Glens Falls, where he had lunch with the Kiwanis, Lions, Optimists Club and Rotary before viewing the Mrs. Louis F. Hyde collection of modern and Renaissance Art, which Rockefeller termed "superb." Then he flew by seaplane into Speculator in the Adirondacks, fulfilling a campaign promise to visit every county in the state. That night he gave a rousing speech at the Governor Clinton Hotel in Kingston on the need to streamline and reorganize state government.

Harry Truman joined Harriman in a campaign motor trip, through Yonkers, White Plains, Spring Valley, and Newburgh to Albany, rallying crowds with bullhorns along the way. The former President had to sharply rebuke the governor for continuing intra-party antagonisms during the trip. As Republican prospects dimmed nationally because of an economic depression, Rockefeller managed to maintain a distance from the Washington administration. *The New York Times* endorsed him on October 15, calling Harriman's last four years as "pedestrian," "disappointing," and "unpromising"—a serious personal blow to the governor from a newspaper he always felt he could count on. Finally, at Port Jervis at the end of October, Harriman criticized Rockefeller for favoring a retrenchment in America's support for Israel during the 1956

Suez crisis, a harsh judgment that at first went unnoticed but was repeated again a few days later. The second time, the reaction was stunning. On November 3, 1958, the day before the election, the *New York Post* issued a front-page editorial withdrawing its support for Harriman and lambasting his insinuation that Rockefeller was anti-Israel. Rockefeller workers distributed thousands of copies of the editorial outside polling places the next morning.

In a year when a Democratic resurgence was happening across the country, Rockefeller, a Republican running against an entrenched incumbent, won in a landslide of more than 500,000 votes. Four years later, he secured almost the same majority running against a popular New York district attorney, Robert Morgenthau (b. 1919).

The State of New York proved every bit the Rockefeller province, although it would take him some years to create an "empire" state suitable to his proportions. Sometimes he used the family PT boat (a full-time crew of five were always on hand at the Tarrytown dock), and at times he traveled by plane from Westchester to work in Albany on Mondays—his favorite was a Grumman Gulfstream II. He began barking orders to flustered staff as soon as he alighted, arriving at the capital in "a flying wedge," as speechwriter Joseph Persico (b. 1930) described it, a chevron of aides dutifully trotting behind. A recurring image held by staff was of the governor amidst his people at a meeting at Kykuit, absentmindedly using the arm of his eyeglasses to stir saccharin into a cup of coffee. The quality of the coffee did not matter, since his tastes were "astonishingly unsophisticated." Yet Rockefeller's brash style and politics resulted in a new political animal, appropriately called the Rockefeller Republican, whose conservative instincts were sublimated by liberal causes and programs and, in Rockefeller's case, a world-sized family philanthropy. Political scientists Robert H. Connery and Gerald Benjamin went further, characterizing "the context created by the domestic initiatives in the 1960s" as enabling Rockefeller, "through lobbying in the national executive and legislative branches" to dynamically impact "the enormous changes in federalism" that were occurring during Rockefeller's years as governor.

Since modern art was a Rockefeller priority, the new governor immediately created a state Council for the Arts, sublimely ignoring the cackles of the legislature. It was the first such council in the nation and a model that other states eventually emulated. The $50,000 initial appropriation grew to $20.5 million ten years later, the money dedicated to the performing arts and spreading culture statewide. Rockefeller also "persuaded" the state legislature to include money for the arts in the design of the South Mall, and handpicked the members of the committee that reviewed the works.

"Guv, how do these grab you?" his aide Al Marshall asked when the committee sent a binder of art pictures to Albany for consideration.

"Just fine, Al," Rockefeller responded without looking over the list. "I picked all of them myself."

Rockefeller's taste for modern art, albeit pedestrian, was comprehensive and in stark contrast to his interest in other cultural areas. He never was comfortable at a theater, hated opera, and thought that copies he had made of his own extensive art collection were just as good as the originals, some of which, like an expensive Miró that went to MOMA, he donated for tax write-offs.

Rockefeller achieved respect among Albany politicos—and nationally, given his exuberance—in his handling of the state government, although the way he manipulated the budget to finance capital projects were often questioned. Connery and Benjamin suggested that Rockefeller's "series of decisions on taxing and borrowing" were "perhaps his greatest error" as governor. He declared a "pay-as-you-go" policy in the 1959-60 executive budget (echoing Thomas Dewey), and then got around that policy by using public authority spending and ladling the budget in large, lump-sum "advance appropriations" that were routinely criticized by the Democratic state comptroller.

A public authority tactic that Rockefeller used to avoid voter approval of large expenditures—there were twenty-eight independent, stand-alone authorities in 1965—was a lease-purchase agreement using state retirement system money for new state buildings. Rockefeller rarely faced deadlocks or even problems with the legislature's leadership, since both houses were controlled by Republicans. He routinely arrived at meetings—which he usually called—with a full contingent of staff, all of whom were simply Nelson yes-men, to secure agreements with the Senate and Assembly leaders for Rockefeller program initiatives. Frequently the Democratic leaders were not present for these meetings, but in 1965 the Democrats took over both houses for a year, and retained the Assembly through 1968. Thereafter Rockefeller would meet on occasion only with the Democratic Speaker, Anthony J. Travia (1911–93), eschewing the principal seat at the head in deference to Travia.

The governor's biggest battle with the legislature came in 1971, when he recommended a billion-dollar budget increase largely driven by new taxes.

The stage was set to mollify legislator concerns over taxes during the mid-1960s, after Albert Abrams, then a staff aide to Republican Senate leader Walter J. Mahoney (1908–82), suggested that legislative staff also be included in the budget meetings. Rockefeller was not averse to the idea and thereafter routinely supported many of their ideas. When the need for a tax increase came up during a dinner meeting at the governor's mansion one year, Rockefeller suggested that they allow him to propose the increase, and take the heat over the public outcry. The leaders agreed, of course, but then crossed him a few years later when the heat of such expenditures became too intense. In 1971, fellow Republican Assembly Speaker Perry B. Duryea, Jr. (1921–2004) led the opposition over the governor's $8.45 billion budget, working with the Senate in crafting an independent budget for the first time, reducing the total appropriations to $7.7 billion. Since Travia's days, the legislature had been expanding its potential, and now the fruit of their labors were realized, at least this one time.

"I don't think he ever forgave me for the way we approached that budget," Duryea later said of Rockefeller. His success led Duryea into creating a central staff that could rival the governor's in research and analysis, the predecessor of the modern program and counsel oversight authority that legislative leaders exercised over all budgetary and legislative matters and that, because of this authority, contributed to the three-men-in-a-room budget discussion scenarios so distasteful to the media in the later modern period. Subsequent lawsuits brought by state employees and by Arthur Levitt challenged the governor that year on the huge lump-sum capital projects appropriations and authority to move the money around as needed to complete the Mall, but were not successful.

Rockefeller's most monumental creation was the State University system, which involved the transformation of 28 small, autonomous campuses with 38,000 students, into a system of 241,000 full-time students at 71 colleges, many of them built using architects whom Rockefeller had chosen. A total higher education enrollment of 380,000 statewide in 1958, 63% of it in private colleges, became 842,000 in 1972, 62% now enrolled in public institutions, and for most of them, the education was free. New York also became the first state to provide direct aid to private institutions.

A State University Construction Fund was created for the building program, another Rockefeller sleight-of-hand maneuver, an invention of a Wall Street lawyer named John N. Mitchell (1913–88), later to be Richard M.

Nixon's disgraced attorney general. "Moral obligation" financing allowed bonds to be sold on a promise, not as a legal obligation. "Back-door borrowing," as it was also termed, was another way of avoiding voter approval. The method had accounted for $175 million in borrowing in Averell Harriman's 1958 budget, and rose to $5.6 billion over 1962–72—yet Comptroller Arthur Levitt, who called the practice "a subterfuge," could not get the governor to state that the faith of the government was behind the bonds—since that would have kicked in the provisions of 1846 state constitutional changes that required voter approval.

The Empire State Plaza, also called the South Mall and eventually named for its creator, was a bright idea that Rockefeller conceived in the middle of an embarrassment. He was deeply chagrined that Princess Juliana (1910–2004) of the Netherlands, in Albany in 1960 on a state visit, had to pass a neighborhood of slums while in a parade with the governor and Mayor Erastus Corning II (1909–19). Rockefeller conceived of a plan for a government mall that afternoon, and soon named Lieutenant Governor Wilson to lead an eighteen-member commission. A site across State Street from the capital of 98 acres in an old Albany neighborhood—called "the Gut," a term that spread to some working class river towns as a result of the Albany reputation—was chosen, state and city officials surmising that it consisted of rundown housing, bars, brothels and marginal businesses, although several old and established neighborhoods were included. Rockefeller chose as architect his old friend, Wallace K. Harrison, the designer of Rockefeller Center and the United Nations, and initially projected a budget of $250 million. That number rose to $2 billion over the ten-year life of the project.

The slums were cleared and a wooden wall built around the project site. A steel frame was constructed, and Mohawk steelworkers brought in to erect a forty-four story tower backed by four twenty-three-story towers, a quarter-mile-long motor vehicle department building, offices for the attorney general and the legislature, and a performance and convention center ovoid that quickly became known as the Egg—all faced in white marble. Hugh Carey subsequently quipped that Rockefeller's mistake was adding the Legislative Office Building to the mall project, "because now they'll think they're important!" The governor had that finished first as a reward for their budgetary approvals. The entire mall frame housed an underground "concourse" that connected the agency buildings and became a showcase for the artwork that Rockefeller personally chose for the mall.

The governor secured the votes of the legislature, even though most Republican members paled at the size of the proposal, by wheeling and dealing with the individual members; Assemblyman Eugene Levy of Rockland County (d. 1990) got a new Thruway exit—14B at Suffern—in return for his vote. Financing the South Mall was a sticky-wicket for the state, which could not afford such a price tag at the time, yet Rockefeller was saved by the wily Mayor Corning, who saw an opportunity for Albany to revive its deteriorating downtown. Corning created a "sinuous" financing plan whereby the county owned the mall and sold the bonds to build it. The state paid for the costs in a lend-lease arrangement that both covered the financing and the city's lost taxes.

In his final State-of-the-State message on January 3, 1973, Rockefeller called the South Mall "the most beautiful state capital in America." He also joked that it was "the best thing since the pyramids"—and Senate secretary Albert Abrams considered the governor "a latter-day Cheops" in the monument that he left—but lofty opinions were not shared by architectural critics. *Washington Post* columnist Wolf Von Eckhardt (1918–95) called The Plaza "a battleship floating on a lily pond." Jane Jacobs (1916–2006), a feisty critic of neighborhood displacement, cited the "planning insanity" of the project—and over the years traffic impacts alone severely disrupted the surrounding residential-and-small-business neighborhoods. Paul Goldberger of *The New York Times* characterized the mall as "foolish, silly, and impractical," more suitable for "the planet Krypton" than earth. Another critic called it "totalitarian architecture." Historian David Stradling suggested that the structure fulfilled "the adage that power corrupts." Indeed, the Empire State Plaza, "the most controversial and costly state government complex in America" and one uniquely wedded to art (if not high culture), was monumentally modern, dunked in marble like a lollipop of white chocolate, an aloof presence on a hill separated organically from the city—yet its impact on Albany's economy was a saving grace because the county was guaranteed a $435,000 annual payment through 2004. And—except for the transportation mess—the mall also happened to work as a state capital, consolidating dozens of offices that had been spread around the city for years in rentals and imparting to its users a sense of purpose aligned with the gods of good governance. If anything, the South Mall was more than New York deserved—it was Rockefeller-sized.

During these years, the state debt rose from $900 million to more than

$6.7 billion, for which the governor exhibited little concern. State payments for debt rose by 1,633 percent over 1958–73. Back-door borrowing was an ethically suspect tool that Rockefeller did not hesitate to employ, yet he did so openly and with a smile, Rockefeller-style. Peter Slocum's claim that Rockefeller created "a pattern of government behavior that keeps creating debt" related to the modernization of government that Rockefeller brought in and that required greater capital to become fleshed out and work. A smaller yet comparable legacy was left by Franklin Roosevelt, and even by the "narcotic government" hater himself, Thomas E. Dewey, and was only validated by the habits of subsequent governors and legislatures. Had New York State government needed retrenchment, it would have happened; as it stood, the Rockefeller era had only just begun.

Governor Rockefeller's principal mistakes—if one can forgive him his spending—were the mishandling of the Attica prison riots and the drug laws he forced through in 1973. Harsh laws against cocaine and other drug possessions were proposed by Rockefeller after a visit to Japan, where he saw arcane methods of dealing with society's dregs. The concept of harsh and long imprisonments for nonviolent offenses was not in keeping with conventional Western trends. In a basement meeting at Kykuit in 1972, his counsel, Michael Whiteman, was instructed to draft legislation with these provisions, and later chastised when he produced a bill that strengthened programs for drug abusers but failed to include the draconian sentences Rockefeller wanted. The governor was also annoyed by Richard Wiebe's attempt to explain the illogic of such a law and its potential impact on a criminal justice system already overburdened with inmates. His adamancy reflected a condescending racism when Howard Jones, the chairman of the Narcotics Addiction Control Commission in Albany (which was not con-sulted on the bill), tried to reason against it and Rockefeller commented to a staffer that Jones, a black man, was "just worried about his people."

When the legislature received the bill on January 3, 1973, liberals who thought they could rely on this liberal Republican were shocked. The bill's passage was obstructed for a few weeks in the Assembly Codes committee, but by May it had become law. By the 1990s, as a result of the Rockefeller drug laws, drug crimes accounted for 47% of those incarcerated. The governors in those years, Mario Cuomo (1932–2015) and George Pataki (b. 1945), were busy building prisons.

Transportation, health care, and environmental policy were concerns for the state government for decades, but it was Nelson Rockefeller who brought each of these areas, as well as higher education and high culture, onto the front stage of state policy. His administration constructed 4.5 miles of new highways for every day he was in office. He was responsible for the creation of fifty-five new state parks and, in an affectionate nod to his brother Laurance, the protection from commercial uses of the Adirondack Park. His achievements as governor included the creation of 90,000 low- and moderate-income housing units; 23 new mental health facilities; 109 hospitals; and the Metropolitan Transit Authority.

Senator Robert F. Kennedy initiated efforts to expand health care insurance for the poor in New York; Nelson Rockefeller sought to out-do the nationals by expanding upon the new federal plan (Medicaid) and proposing health care for one in four New Yorkers. This was in keeping with his family's philanthropic traditions: "For the present needy aged and for the 'medically indigent' who cannot afford to pay for protection even under basic health prepayment plans, financing from general tax revenues—federal, state, or local, or a combination of the three—seems essential," the Rockefeller Brothers Fund had reported in 1955. The change was not adopted, however; Senator Jacob Javits (1904–1986), "frantic" about Rockefeller's health plan implications in the face of limited federal dollars, helped convince the governor to do something uncharacteristic—back down. Nelson then tried to have the state itself create a plan of universal health insurance—he spent five legislative sessions at it, at one point proposing coverage to 45% of all New Yorkers, but also to no avail.

"Access to good health care ought to be a basic human right," he said.

The State Department of Mental Hygiene had been established in 1925 in Governor Al Smith's reorganization of government; thirty years later the in-patient mental health population in the state had risen to 93,000. Medicaid and Medicare allowed the state to transfer elderly patients from hospitals to nursing homes, but that was not enough for the state to avoid being tainted in 1971, when Geraldo Rivera (b. 1943) won a Peabody Award for ABC News with "The Last Great Disgrace," an investigative journalism exposé of overcrowding conditions at Letchworth Village in Rockland County and Willowbrook State School on Staten Island. Residents of these facilities were placed in group homes, the last leaving Letchworth Village in 1997. In 1972, SSO and SSDI allowed many mentally ill to live independently, thereby further relieving the problem with overcrowding.

Rockefeller's political acumen was evident in the Medicaid gambit. He predicted that the federal government would enact the new plan, and set a standard for other states with his one-in-four initiative. A similar insight guided the proposal to float a $1 billion pure waters bond before the voters in 1965, which was overwhelmingly approved. New York State became first in line for the increased federal aid that followed because of Rockefeller's strategy. His pure waters initiative was part of a wider environmental strategy that the governor initiated because of pollution, mainly to the Hudson River and its tributaries. Henry Diamond called him "the improbable tree-hugger," although sanitation and clean water had long been the Rockefeller brothers' interests internationally. The localities, which had been dumping fecal wastes into watersheds for decades, received just what they needed to clean up their act (money), and the public appreciated the effort. DDT as an agricultural pesticide was banned first by New York. Corporate polluters were fined with a vengeance when they failed to toe the line. Rockefeller made his presence felt on the national level when it came to aid to localities. While attempted to reduce a 21% income tax, he called upon Congressman Hugh Carey to help bring in a federal revenue-sharing plan for the country. New York got $300 million as a result.

A new New York State Department of Environmental Conservation was signed into law on the first Earth Day, April 22, 1970, predating the United States Environmental Protection Agency and becoming a model for other states. The teach-in grassroots nature of Earth Day added a real context to the environmental work that organizations like Riverkeeper, Clearwater, and Scenic Hudson would be doing, giving impetus to real benefits to the environment. In New York City, where one of the largest observances were held, Clearwater members four hundred strong cleaned up Central Park's boating lake. Events took place in numerous communities, often featuring lectures, flyers and music to draw in young people. The White Plains rail station was addressed by Highlands Junior High students, and the Pearl River in Rockland County cleared of debris by local students there.

Rockefeller made three attempts at the presidency. At the annual governors' conference in May 1960, he sought the high ground on national defense by proposing a number of goals that would have placed America on high alert in the nuclear arms race. President Eisenhower suggested that the rationale that Rockefeller used was "based on flimsy evidence," and was surprised some weeks later when the governor and Republican presidential candidate Richard M. Nixon reached an agreement advocating the kind of expenditures that Rockefeller propounded. Rockefeller's national defense platform may have been a carrot offered to Nixon in return for the compromises that Rockefeller demanded which he and the Vice President developed in the July 1960 "Compact of Fifth Avenue," a meeting that conservatives later referred to as the "Munich of the Republican Party." Nelson's liberalism was in strident contrast to Barry Goldwater's conservatism four years later, when he had the best chance for the nomination and the election. "I thought of Rockefeller as a New Deal Republican," Goldwater later said. Rockefeller railed against the rise of the right at the San Francisco convention—"such hawkers of hate, such purveyors of prejudice, such fabricators of fear"—but he did not have a chance against Goldwater's grass roots support.

Rockefeller did not intend to seek high office again, but when Lyndon Johnson withdrew his reelection aspirations in the spring of 1968 and Martin Luther King was assassinated in the same week, Rockefeller again announced his candidacy. He turned over the reins of state government to the governor's secretary, Al Marshall, a career civil servant who first came to Rockefeller's attention as an analyst with the Division of the Budget and replaced William Ronan as secretary in late 1966. Again, Rockefeller was unsuccessful; yet, unperturbed, he went on to win election to his fourth term by a 730,000-vote plurality.

Ultimately the governor settled for second best when President Nixon's successor, Gerald Ford, offered the vice-presidency after Nixon resigned in August 1973. Rockefeller resigned his state position on December 11, 1973, having served in that office more than any other man since George Clinton, a total of 5,459 days.

Who was Nelson Rockefeller? Senate secretary Al Abrams saw in part "the storied 'Rocky'; garrulous, backslapping, eye-winking, offering a gravelly 'Hi ya, fella' to one and all," and also an "imperial" side that accounted for the "lusty septuagenarian" in him. To the 4-H kids at the Dutchess County Fair in 1974, he was the man who ended the Governor's Day tradition by invoking the taboo subject of politics and not having the time to walk the fairgrounds and meet the fairgoers. For provincial mid-Hudson area special interests disgruntled by land use restrictions in the river's historic mansions district, he was a tyrant whose local eagles on the scene, state troopers, were called "Rockefeller's cowboys." Conservatives saw in him a "reviled and discredited amalgam of tax-and-spend big government liberalism and avid internationalism," an opinion that remained fixed in those circles over the years. His friend and lawyer Oscar Ruebhausen (1912–2004) described Nelson as the fabled elephant on the Republican banner—some who viewed him saw one piece of the man, others saw another piece, but no one saw "the entire elephant." Joseph Persico considered him "the best governor in New York's history," even with the caveat that his "administrative style was often wasteful, not simply of money but of people and human energies." He cited the learned estimations of Neal Peirce, author of *The Megastates of America*, that Rockefeller created "the most complex, fascinating and socially advanced state government in US history," and of Robert H. Connery and Gerald Benjamin, who concluded that Rockefeller "tried to do too much too fast."

Connery and Benjamin's response to Nelson Rockefeller was much more complex than that, yet for every break in the silver lining of progress recorded in their summary chapter in *Rockefeller of New York*—the creation of the state university prompting a threat to the independent colleges, the investments in water pollution abatement failing to prevent the banning of commercial fishing, the mental hygiene policy improvements without proper post-release supervision that enabled a new nursing home industry populated "by greedy and unscrupulous operators," the major advances across a wide policy swath tainted by the long-term impacts of moral obligation bond financing—in these very areas New York and the nation were benefited more than harmed by Rockefeller's policies and style. Historically, Nelson Rockefeller's crime and drug abuse policies failed miserably—for America as well as New York—and his response to the Attica uprising was almost criminally uninformed. He had a mixed record in terms of anti-discrimination and the promotion of African-American issues, promising much and delivering little. He considered handgun regulations in New York "disgracefully inadequate and uneven," yet was unable to change them.

These negatives (and more) notwithstanding, to his credit, and whatever his motives, he was New York's first modern environmentalist governor in the cleanup of the Hudson and open space land acquisitions that he promoted. He could not have foreseen the commercial fishing ban of 1976, which followed a process that began with restrictions on upriver consumption due to sediment migrations of polychlorinated biphenals after the removal of the

Fort Edward Dam in 1974. His "edifice complex" (in Peter Siskind's term)—10,000 new nursing home and hospital beds, 100,000 low- and mixed-income housing units, $1 billion in state support for new sewer plants in addition to SUNY and the Empire State Plaza—was not so extraordinary considering the man and his family's traditions. The Empire State Plaza deserved all of the criticisms heaped upon it, yet achieved two important goals, protecting Albany's fractured economy and bringing the state government within a central location.

Rockefeller initiated and set a tone of acceptance for the taxation policies that made New York the most expensive state in the nation, yet an expansive state government was becoming necessary for an expansive baby boomer generation. That he hastened that process accrued to his legacy's benefit as well as his detriment in the institutions and improvements he created.

40. Deconstructing Indian Point

Al-vin the ad-a-mant at-om, / Long may his tribe in-crease, / From the mo-ment he saw, he was scheduled for war, / He got ra-di-o-ac-tive for peace.

— LEO COOPER, "Alvin the Adamant Adam" (c. 1953)

Goats grazed at Indian Point Park in the 1950s. Fifty years later a few small patches of grass remained on a level ground to the south of the plants and along a rocky slope to the north, where only a goat might walk. The rest was all the Indian Point Energy Center at Buchanan (IPEC): a dart, two domes, and a massive rectangular front of stone, the "tea kettle" of Robert Fulton's steamboat days returned with a vengeance in the harnessing of nuclear fission to boil water. Seen from a gritty little beach across the river at Jones Point a nautical mile away, the plant shimmered in a haze-clouded skyline on a sultry summer afternoon. Indian Point was not a point, actually, but a piece of the Verplanck protuberance, tucked between Charles Point to the north and Verplanck Point to the south.

The sense of the place was overwhelming: this might have been Agra, and the domes a Taj mirage, the enormity appearing as illusionary as a fantasy in the distance, all bulbous forms specked in grey. Penetrating the haze, two puny kayakers entered the river at Jones Point and made a run across the lightly choppy waters. The temperature was in the 80s, the humidity laying over the river like a towel. The plants were on the east side, 37.4 nautical or 43 statute miles north of the Battery; they gave off no sound, no movement, nothing to suggest what lay within, just a couple of channel buoys perched like lazy blemishes in a half mile of empty river. The river's ghostly eminence—invisible and awesome—appeared as a natural and benevolent doppelganger to the awful force inside the manmade testament to progress. Now and then a pleasure boat churned by, flopped the kayaks about on little waves, and was gone. The paddlers paddled on, like pesky invaders, bobbing and gurgling, on a mission to cross over and return, as if by penetrating the mirage they could make it disappear.

The nuclear reactors at Indian Point were the brainchild of Hudson "Roy" Searing (d. 1957), Consolidated Edison's visionary chairman who set about resolving the utility's massive postwar energy needs. Searing oversaw the purchase of the 380-acre Indian Point Park in Buchanan from a bankrupt Hudson River Day Line in 1954. The first of the pressurized water nuclear reactors took seven years and $142 million to build, and began producing 275 megawatts of energy on September 16, 1962. The plant soon experienced technical problems that required the addition of an oil-fired unit to help raise the steam temperature. Two additional reactors were added in 1974 and 1976, and an economical and practical transmission network substation built at nearby Buchanan. By then the complex was enmeshed in a firestorm of criticism over fish kills in the water intake screens, an estimated 1.1 million dead fish a year, which the state and the utility at first tried to hide.

Unit 1 was shut down in 1974. Unit 3, which was sold to the New York Power Authority before completion, generated 980 megawatts of power until 1976, when it was upgraded to 1080; its license was extended to December 12, 2015. Unit 2, 970 megawatts upgraded to 1080 as well, was licensed until September 28, 2013. The two plants produced enough megawatts to power two million homes a day (when fully operational)—almost all the public power needs of Westchester County and New York City met in a place where goats once grazed. Statewide, nuclear represented 5.3% of the total installed generating capacity, yet produced 10.1% of the electricity.

The plants grew in size as the kayaks approached. These waters harbored many river ghosts. The paddlers passed by World's End, the deepest part of the

Hudson and the setting for a T. C. Boyle novel about some of those ghosts. South of Jones Point the Navy had mothballed most of the World War II fleet before junking them for steel thirty years later. Behind the kayakers, only the towering bulk of Dunderberg Mountain intruded noticeably, the last of the Ramapos in New York and a scary place to the Dutch, who named it for the thunder of its storms. No ships now filled the void of Haverstraw Bay and the Tappan Zee, not even Maxwell Anderson's ghostly seventeenth-century *Onrust* ("tiny, with black, square sails; low and small") in his 1936 play, *High Tor*, about the mountain whose crest and most of its face were destroyed by quarrymen in the rush to build New York City a hundred years ago.

The afternoon light struggled through the thick air. There was no wind. A jet ski passed behind the kayaks in a faint howl. Another pleasure craft glided north. The paddlers bobbed and rowed, two men in their own age, their own dawn, the future before them measured for the moment in spent fuel rods and afflatus of uranium. Seven English warships lay here once, precisely here at the same afternoon hour in the same kind of sultry heat, in 1776. They captured forts on either side of the river, and a short while later, after the ships had gone, a band of American fighters emerged like ghosts from the woods of the Dunderberg and took one of the forts back without a shot.

Small white beaches associated with Verplanck Point harbored the residue grudges of a stone quarry that went out of business because of the nuclear plants. A quarry at Tomkins Cove on the west side of the river, behind the paddlers, still churned out tons of Highlands rubble for the construction industry in New York. Next to the stone works lay the five Lovett power plants, whose towers and power lines lolled in the distant heat like a pointillist illusion. Riverkeeper John Cronin came here with a *Time* magazine reporter in 1999 and counted off the existing polluting plants and the detritus left by others long gone. A bitterness remained among the river conservationists over the approval given an expansion of the utility's overhead lines from New City without public review by the Hudson River Valley Commission in 1967— aerial now, they said, underground later, but that did not happen. Congressmen John Dow (1905–2003) and Richard Ottinger (b. 1929) tried to intervene but were unsuccessful.

The kayaks drifted south. They came at slack tide, and the new tide had not yet started to arrive, yet the river insisted that the small craft move along, like a pair of lazy logs, tugged at, pulled. They turned easily to the east and faced the plants. As the kayaks neared the buoys that marked the eastern channel, the plant outlines became crisp and the small details along the shore began to emerge. The slow drone rose louder. The men were stunned at the size that now loomed before them. A guard boat was tucked among loading docks between the tower and the south dome. No men appeared, yet the kayakers sensed they were being watched. Perhaps they would burst from the mooring and sidle up to the tiny crafts and tip them; that was the best intruders at Indian Point could expect. A quarry operator once dumped a conveyor belt of rubble into a Riverkeeper boat, just for spite.

The water intake was also hidden, below the surface, and an impingement pit where young environmentalists worked in the 1960s, counting fish and whatever else got sucked in. Charles Point had a trash burning plant. Lent's Cove defined the northern curve on the other side of Peekskill, but one could not see Indian Point from there. The neighborhoods around Indian Point were variously Irish or Italian before the first plant was built, each ethnic group fiercely hating the other yet both loyally Catholic. There were few blacks in those days; one family had a cross burned on their lawn to chase them off. A few hotels for the businessmen and occasional traveler, a Seagram's plant a couple of miles north in Peekskill; beer gardens and bars and a pretty good roadside diner, this was the run of the trade in the 1950s.

The kayakers entered the east channel of the river and were coming closer to the plants when a rumble in the rear prompted them to look back. Dark clouds rose over the Dunderberg as thunder echoed forth in peals of anger. They would have to leave or face the mountain's rage, yet Indian Point seemed so close, its drone bidding them forward like the siren call of an alluring impingement pit—what to do? Another growl from the mountain fluttered in flecks of heat lightning as the darkened Dunderberg sky began moving quickly toward the river. They turned back, paddling quickly, racing the rage of the river waters that were gathering with the mountain's command. Yet something there was about the river that seemed to hold back the storm, the energies of nature as well as man collected and subsumed in the mighty waters. As the kayakers neared Jones Point, the mountain quieted again and all became calm, as if their mere withdrawal from the sacred waters were enough to calm nature's frustrations over man's intrusion. There would not be a storm after all; the threat was gone. The kayakers packed their craft in a few droplets of rain—not enough to wash away the haze—and as they drove over a hill above

Iona Island and a bit of the sun returned the plant seemed more distant and grainy, its masculine outline settled once again into an illusion of tranquility and peace.

Indian Point was built in the old style, before Storm King and the environmental awakening that eventually cast a regulatory pall over any major plant sites. The business assumption was that the new energy plants would all be nuclear ones; twenty of them were planned for the state as a whole. On September 10, 1968, a World War II torpedo bomber fitted with infrared mapping and piloted by state conservation officials flew down the Hudson and profiled the river's heat patterns on behalf of the New York State Atomic and Space Development Authority, which wanted to find the best sites for new nuclear plants to discharge heated water without too much damage to local ecosystems. This was the second run of the yellow and blue flyer, the first having mapped the upper Hudson region, where the Authority had its test station at Malta. If suitable sites were found, the Authority could acquire them and hold them for future power generating uses. Yet, even though the need for significant new power sources was evident to regulators and industrialists, it was also understood that the impacts of nuclear power plants were substantially greater than anything heretofore considered. In 1965, thirty-two large industries between New York City and Troy used Hudson River water for power—making their infrared fingerprints on the waters and the river life— yet none even approximated the 233 million gallons per day drawn for the nuclear plants' use.

Local fears about radiation poisoning were rising and the placement of these plants so near to the population hub of the Northeast increased attention to the region. The fears arose in the national memory of the Hiroshima and Nagasaki bombings, the threat of nuclear war between the United States and the USSR, and a popular culture infused with doomsday themes like the apocalyptic *Gojira* (*Godzilla*, 1954) and Nevil Shute's *On the Beach* (1959). Early in his tenure, Governor Nelson Rockefeller cheerfully urged that fallout shelters become a part of every home. To add to the pessimism, in May 1959 E. B. White began a column in *The New Yorker* on "Man's progress in making the planet uninhabitable," adding pesticides, smog, and waste dumping to the litany of mistakes.

Indian Point was producing 280 megawatts of power in 1968. Consolidated Edison had vowed in 1966 not to build any more conventional plants, and now proposed a nuclear power plant fourteen times that size for David's Island, an eighty-acre site off New Rochelle in Long Island Sound. The island was the former site of Fort Slocum, an Army post, and home to Nike intercontinental ballistic missiles silos. The mayors of New Rochelle and New York City were delighted with the 4,000-megawatt project, but a looming sense of threat and danger was growing around the nuclear issue. *The New York Times* ran a sobering editorial about fish kills by thermal pollution at nuclear plants, and endorsed a new proposal by Senator Edward M. Kennedy for a moratorium on new constructions and an independent two-year study for any proposed. A Long Island fishermen group's report claimed two million striped bass had been killed at Indian Point in 1966. The debate continued in New Rochelle as politicians and local neighborhood organizations favored the anticipated reduction in electrical rates, while scientists, conservation and fishing groups opposed the project on environmental and safety grounds. A sixteen-degree increase in the temperature of the waters around the island was forecasted. "You are not giving the utility just a piece of real estate," consulting biologist Dominick Pirone told the Council. "You are possibly surrendering your whole nine-mile shore line . . . and the waters of the Sound for miles around for a few quick dollars." Finally, the City Council withheld a decision about necessary zoning changes for the Con Ed proposal to allow the city to sell the island.

In the summer of 1968 a 125-acre site adjoining George's Island Park was proposed for two more nuclear plants. The land, which including the 50-acre former Frederick W. Seward estate (the home of William Seward's son, where Lincoln may have stopped on his secret 1863 visit to the Valley) was owned since 1953 by the 700-member Catholic Kolping Society, which opposed the idea. Bowline Point north of Haverstraw was also under consideration for nuclear power.

A 1,000-megawatt plant proposed by Central Hudson Gas & Electric, Consolidated Edison and Niagara Mohawk on the former Jova brickworks at Roseton that July was transformed into a coal-fired plant as the nuclear option faded. In August, pressures from conservationists, heritage proponents, the New York State Department of Health, and Governor Rockefeller's Hudson River Valley Commission led Niagara Mohawk Power Corporation to cancel plans for a $125 million nuclear power plant along the Hudson River in Easton, 140 miles north of Indian Point adjoining Malta in southwestern

Washington County. The plant would have been directly across the river from the Bemis Heights Revolutionary War battlefield, creating "infinite community cost in relation to the scenic view" impacts according to White Plains engineer Martin Goldstein (1925–2015) in a January 1968 report for the Hudson River Valley Commission. Goldstein's "system flow diagram" on Easton impacts depicted "critical" aquatic habitat problems, "critical" problems with evaporation and oxygen loss due to high water temperature discharges, and "critical" supply limit impacts on water for other industrial uses. The Health Department criticized the company's forecasted heat discharge rates into the Hudson River—Niagara Mohawk claimed only a five-to-nine degree change in water temperature in that narrow stretch of the river above the Troy dam—and in fact the industry generally was wrestling with difficulty over new high water temperature impact regulations coming out of the Clean Water Act of 1965. Any nuclear power facility in the Hudson River Valley "will consume major portions of the river flow" to dissipate the waste heat, Goldstein warned.

When the utility withdrew its plans, Niagara Mohawk contracts with General Electric for a nuclear reactor and other equipment were transferred to the Power Authority of the State of New York (PASNY), which was pursuing its first nuclear power project at Oswego on Lake Ontario. Governor Rockefeller had sought to limit nuclear to private companies, but PASNY was given the authority to produce electrical power through nuclear generation "under pressure from the late" Senator Robert F. Kennedy, according to *The New York Times*. Keeping it public meant keeping a sharper eye on the industry's progress. In the late 1970s, under the leadership of its feisty chairman, John S. Dyson, the agency undertook a nuclear plant project in the midst of the struggling cement industry at Alsen in southeastern Greene County, the last of the major nuclear siting attempts in the Hudson River Valley. The application prompted an antagonistic and noisy response from naysayers who included John Nickolich, a Cementon resident who put a new roof on his house with "Solar No Nukes" written in shingles, and John Hall, leader of the rock group Orleans and a future congressman. The organizational opposition included an unusual alliance of the state Department of Environmental Conservation, the grassroots group Citizens to Preserve the Hudson Valley, a young think tank for the region called the Catskill Center for Conservation and Development, and a dozen anti-nuclear groups with representatives from Albany to Poughkeepsie.

Dyson took the case to the people in a meeting in Athens, acknowledging that the state looked upriver because a coal plant in Staten Island was unthinkable. The project failed on the merits: the mobilization of the people by Hall and others, a report by the Hudson *Register-Star* that the Lehigh Portland Cement Company claimed the project was so large the company would have to close its cement works and move on, and an emerging look at the situation by cultural interests in Washington over the impact of cooling towers on the view from Olana, Frederic Church's Moorish castle five miles north in Greenport. The impact on heritage and aesthetic views was established as a newly legitimate environmental consideration in such reviews.

The nuclear option was erased in New York's long-term power need scenarios, yet Indian Point's thirst remained almost twice as great as all the drinking water needs for the city of New York—and here as in the Catskills no benevolent Manitou was on hand to prevent the killing of fish and larvae, despite the 2003 ruling. In 2013, faced with the likelihood of state regulations requiring that cooling towers be built to protect these creatures, the current owner, Entergy Corporation, remained confident that the units—by now 39 and 41 years old—would continue to operate. Yet Morgan Stanley analysts on Wall Street forecasted that the $2 billion tower cost was simply greater than the plants were worth.

The state continued to look upriver to resolve its metropolitan-area energy needs. A Con Ed proposal supported by Governor Mario Cuomo for a gas-fired plant in northwestern Dutchess County in the 1990s was shelved, with a mix of embarrassment, after Hudsonia Ltd. reported that the plant would be built partly on a wetlands. Scenic Hudson played a pivotal role in limiting the siting of a major power station in a sheltered area of Athens after the New York Department of State, preservationists at Olana, and an aroused citizenry complained of impacts on the Hudson River estuary settings. Clearwater—while continuing its hugely popular Pumpkin Sails, Hootenanny Sails, and dozens of seasonal visits to Hudson Valley ports—addressed sustainability as a threshold requirement for any new growth or development in the Hudson River Valley. One of the organization's targets was East Fishkill, where chemical pollution from an IBM semi-conductor plant, most of it airborne, more than doubled (to 186,188 pounds) over 1993–95.

Indian Point continued to operate, slumbering along Rip Van Winkle-style, while public interest groups danced to its demise. The defining issue concerned the impacts on fish kills from the 2.4 billion gallons of water drawn from Haverstraw Bay a day. Power plants and fish kills in the richest area of the Hudson River estuary took center stage when Consolidated Edison's proposed a pumped storage plant at Storm King, and here at Buchanan was the greatest consumer of water and greatest killer of fish of them all.

41. Woodstock Nation

Then America had its nervous breakdown, the 1970s.
—ALLEN GINSBERG, "Smoking Typewriters," 1981

After Albert Grossman (1926–86) settled in Woodstock in the early 1960s—Milton Glaser (b. 1929) had told him about some cheap land in the area—rock musicians whom Grossman represented such as Peter Yarrow (b. 1938) and Bob Dylan (b. 1941) followed suit. At first, Dylan stayed in Grossman's small farmhouse on the hill above Bearsville hamlet, the house where Albert and Sally married. That was Sally with Bob on her wedding day in the Elliot Landy photograph on the cover of *Bringing It All Back Home* (1965), sitting on the couch given to her and Albert by Peter, Paul and Mary.

In 1962 (or 1963), Dylan invited a friend and fellow harmonica player from Greenwich Village, John Sebastian (b. 1944), for a Halloween weekend visit. They played music, tooled around on Dylan's Triumph Daytona motorcycle, and attended an artists and models ball on Saturday night. At the time, Dylan was starting to think about a band for his road work, and likely had Sebastian in mind. John became acquainted with Grossman and visited again over the years, not as one of his stable of musicians but as a friend. Grossman confided in Sebastian and showed him his plans for the Bearsville complex of theater and restaurants that he created down the road from his farmhouse.

Other musicians who came to Woodstock included Paul Butterfield (1942–87), Van Morrison (b. 1945), and Jimi Hendrix (1942–70). Some were local or homegrown, as John Herald had become with years of summer visits from Greenwich Village to the Peter Pan Farm in Saugerties and Camp Woodland in Woodland Valley. Morrison's "Old Old Woodstock" captured the quiet thrill of "the cool night breeze" of the Taconic State Parkway as he sped north from the city to the fabled town.

As the decade wore on, it was not an uncommon weeknight for Butterfield or others to show up with a few friends at the Café Espresso, formerly The Nook, which grew hip with the clientele it attracted, and play a long set. Joyous Lake became a hot after-hours venue every summer, and neither paid the musicians nor charged a cover in the early days. The players might include Tim Hardin (1941–80), John Hall (b. 1948), Jackie Lomax (b. 1944), Dave Mason (b. 1946), Bonnie Raitt (b. 1949), Todd Rundgren (b. 1948), and Taj Mahal (Henry Saint Clair Fredericks, b. 1949).—Taj frequently returned to Woodstock in the years thereafter, and Hall lived under the shadow of Overlook in nearby Saugerties and continued with his advocacy and local politics. A local watering hole, the Elephant Emporium on Rock City Road, had Dylan singles on its jukebox in early 1962.

Bob Dylan toured the world in 1965-66 with a backup band, The Hawks, that included Canadians Rick Danko (1942–99), Richard Manuel (1943–86), Garth Hudson (b. 1937), Robbie Robertson (Jaime Robert Klegerman, b. 1943), and Levon Helm (1940–2012). Returning to Woodstock, Dylan resumed riding his Triumph Daytona motorcycle, at times with Joan Baez on the back, until he crashed on July 29, 1966, sustaining a mild concussion and several cracked vertebrae. During his recuperation, the group came to Woodstock (Helm had left The Hawks by this time) and began recording what came to be more than a hundred covers and original songs that redefined Dylan the artist and established the basis for the emergence of The Band. Danko rented a newly built farmhouse off Stoll Road in Saugerties that they called Big Pink; Robertson had a house nearby. By the spring of 1967, Dylan was recording with them at Hi-Lo-Ha, his rental at Byrdcliffe, and the whole group moved to Big Pink that summer, using equipment borrowed by Hudson and set up in the basement. Cowboy songs, Irish and Appalachian folk tunes, gospels, sea chanteys, covers of songs by Johnny Cash, Hank Snow and others, and dozens of throwaway ditties came pouring out.

The group spent several weeks performing songs by other artists before moving on to new material. When they lived away from Big Pink, Dylan and Robertson would show up at the house each morning. Dylan might have lyrics for a new tune, or type one up while the others waited or experimented with melodies. Among the thirty new songs that he wrote and recorded with the group were "I Shall Be Released," "This Wheel's On Fire," and "Tears of Rage." "That's really the way to do a recording—in a peaceful, relaxed setting —in somebody's basement," he told *Rolling Stone* publisher Jann Wenner, "with . . . a dog lying on the floor."

Critic Greil Marcus (b. 1945) considered the basement tape compositions—more than a hundred songs were recorded over these months— Bob Dylan's way of reinventing the folk music tradition of Harry Smith's *Anthology of American Folk Music* (1952). Some of the basement songs were circulated among fellow artists and musicians, and some covered with success by other artists, including "Too Much of Nothing" by Peter, Paul and Mary, "Tears of Rage" by Ian and Sylvia, and Manfred Mann's "Quinn the Eskimo (The Mighty Quinn)," which rose to number one on the United Kingdom charts.

Dylan later retreated to Big Pink with his growing family in search of the quiet life, so paranoid by now about hippies and hangers-on coming in search of their hero that he purchased a shotgun. He was also quietly contemplating the seriousness of the motorcycle incident and how it almost cost him his life. The backup group, rejoined by Helm and about to be known as The Band, produced *Music from Big Pink* (1968), an auspicious debut album that influenced Eric Clapton, George Harrison, and just about every hip young person in America. The songs were recorded in New York and California and produced by John Simon (b. 1941), who joined in some of the instrumental work. A collection of Dylan's earlier cuts and seven songs from the basement tracks was released in July 1969 as *The Great White Wonder*, considered the first "bootleg" or illegal rock album. Twenty-four songs—sixteen of the basement tracks and eight by The Hawks (including Helm) not recorded in Woodstock —became *The Basement Tapes* (1975), a landmark album in the history of rock 'n' roll.

One Tuesday evening in August 1969 a small party gathered at a long table in the Café Espresso, enjoying a quiet chatter after dinner. The door was locked, but a couple of burly young guys were allowed in and placed at a window table, looking like bodyguards for the group. After a while, the table quieted and a small man sitting in the middle arose and turned to the old upright piano on the landing near the bathrooms. Bob Dylan played his new piano music for half an hour, and the party ended in applause. Two weeks later the same piano riffs accompanied his new album, *Nashville Skyline*, this had been the closing dinner celebrating the release.

Dylan eschewed social or intellectual interpretations attributed to the lyrics of his music, at times with exasperation, yet could not stop such speculation. Critic Tor Egil Førland, in a *Journal of American Studies* article, viewed his foreign policy philosophy as expressed in his lyrics as virtually the same as the progressive isolationists of the Midwest at the turn of the twentieth century. Indeed, although Dylan was no William Jennings Bryan, he was at least, consciously or not, the pied piper of the Aquarian Age and very much the prophet of a time that was "a-changin'."

Neither hippie nor New Ager, Pete Seeger (1919–2014) was a World War II veteran who influenced the new sound through his example and his music. The son of a noted musicologist who eschewed folk music as "dead relics" before awakening to its strengths, Pete became part of that awakening while working for his father after high school for a summer in Washington, where he met Alan Lomax.

"Talk about ivory towers," Seeger later told David Dunaway. "I grew up in a woodland tower . . . I knew all about plants and could identify birds and snakes, but I didn't know that anti-Semitism existed or what a Jew was until I was fourteen years old. My contact with black people was literally nil." Seeger became disenchanted with Harvard University and left in 1938, later joking that his class boasted one of Harvard's most famous graduates (John F. Kennedy), as well as its "most famous dropout" (Seeger). He served in the Army during the war, emerging as a mature adult whose singing, picking, and social sense had become exceptional, and traveled across America with Woody Guthrie.

Pete's wife Toshi (d. 2013) spent part of her childhood on Boggs Hill Road in Woodstock. Seeger learned the Cuban patriotic song, "Guantanamera," from Cuban students at Camp Woodland in Ulster County in the late 1940s. Eila Kakkonen, later a Woodstock resident and archivist of the Alf Evers collection at the Woodstock Byrdcliffe Guild, was eighteen when she first heard him sing at a Henry Wallace rally in Chicago in 1948. His short, highly technical columns in *Sing Out!*, the small and influential music publication of the folk movement, gave musicians new and old tools for the times. Seeger wrote "Where Have All the Flowers Gone?" in 1961, having derived the idea from a Mikhail Sholokhov novel, and then, in typical Seeger style, encouraged other artists to add new verses of their own. The last line of the song, as popularized by The Kingston Trio and Joan Baez, ended with "armies" gone to "graveyards" in that manner; Seeger's original line was "They're all in uniform." His songs "If I Had a Hammer" (written with Lee Hayes of The Weavers) and "Turn, Turn, Turn!" were also covered in popular versions by artists of the 1960s. Seeger popularized "We Shall Overcome," changing the title from "We Will Overcome."

He was a huge influence on Dylan, as was Guthrie and Seeger's friend Hank Williams (1923–53), and Seeger always defended the young man in his changeover into rock. David Dunaway, whose Seeger biography *How Can I Keep from Singing?* was published in 1981, called him "the self-sufficient craftsman and a communalist, looking for his tribe." Dylan called him "a saint"; Carl Sandberg called Seeger "America's tuning fork," and Joan Baez said all of the folk artists of the 1960s owed a debt to him.

With most of his concert gigs at East Coast colleges, John Sebastian returned to the Woodstock scene around 1975 after living in Los Angeles. He and his wife Catherine kept a small flat in Greenwich Village, but John usually drove from Kennedy Airport directly to the Mill Stream Motel in Woodstock, as more convenient and closer to the schools where he appeared. They decided to stay one winter, with Albert Grossman and Dylan's help and the hospitality of several homes in the town. When John's song "Welcome Back" became a national hit, they were able to move to Woodstock permanently. He and Butterfield resumed a friendship from the Greenwich Village days and John played out locally, backing other musicians as he had done so many times in New York.

Happy and Artie Traum were musicians who settled in Woodstock in 1967 and went under contract to Albert Grossman three years later. They had extensive careers both together and independently, and were recognized as masters of the folk tradition. Happy (Harry Peter Traum, b. 1938) established Homespun Tapes in 1965, a mail-order music lesson business that featured a popular "Listen and Learn" series of packaged music and lesson material that involved friends like John Sebastian, Richard Thompson and Paul Butterfield. Traum's first appearance on vinyl was on a 1962 Folkways Record, *Broadside Ballads, Vol. 1*, that included Pete Seeger, Phil Ochs, and Bob Dylan. His group The New World Singers, with Bob Cohen and Gil Turner, were the first to record Dylan's "Don't Think Twice, It's All Right." Artie Traum (1943–2008) produced a more extensive discography than his brother, although the two were best known for their three records together; the first, *Happy & Artie Traum* (1969), was considered "one of the best in any field of pop music" by *The New York Times*. Artie's documentary film work included *Deep Water: Building the Catskill Water System*, with Tobe Carey and Robbie Dupree. Pete Seeger and his sister Peggy came to Woodstock for a concert with Happy in 2012.

Studios grew in Woodstock in response to the recording demand that emerged, and provided full sixteen-track performance settings where professional albums were cut. Alan Lomax's 1970 album for Warner Brothers, *Home Is In My Head*, was produced by John Simon in Woodstock, the producer stuffing the strings of the piano with Kleenex to achieve an acoustic effect on the "Lavender Dream" track. In time, Sebastian developed a close relationship with Chris Anderson's Nevessa Studio in Woodstock. He also resumed a close friendship with Paul A. Rothchild (1935–95), a legendary producer who had delivered The Doors' first five albums—Sebastian, using the pseudonym G. Pugliese (his father's name), was the harmonica player on the "Roadhouse Blues" track. Sebastian was also close with Jimmy Vivino (b. 1955), who became the bandleader for talk show host Conan O'Brien some years later. In 1996, the two joined jug band veterans Fritz Raymond and James Wormworth as the J-Band on Sebastian's *I Want My Roots* album.

Well known musicians like Bill Keith (1939–2015)—he developed the "fiddle style" of country banjo playing during a stint with Bill Monroe and his band—came to live in Woodstock, performing regularly with local friends. Small pick-up bands of high school friends or country cousins got together and played at local church fairs, taverns, nightclubs, and for family and other occasions. Some of these musicians, like Bruce Ackerman of Saugerties (b. 1935), were also multitalented craftsmen and artists; Ackerman joined the board of the Woodstock Artists Association and made fine guitars along with oils, watercolors, woodcuts, silkscreen prints, and other artwork on the side. His caricatures appeared regularly in the *Woodstock Times*. Mike Winfield was a homegrown bass player who fit in well with the noted players who came to town. Many lesser known artists, like James "Jimmy Jumper" Giampa (b. 1943)—he played conga on Looking Glass's "Brandi" in 1973—"played out" over the years in the loosely organized club scene.

NRBQ, a quirky and hugely popular rhythm and blues quartet led by Kentucky native Terry Adams (b. 1948), settled into a big old farmhouse off

Bulls Head Road in Dutchess County in the early 1970s. Their first show west of the Hudson was at Checkers, a short-lived youth club in the heart of mid-town Saugerties that drew the ire of the local police chief. Adams and bassist Joey Spampinato (b. 1950) started NRBQ in 1967. The band had an inauspicious appearance early in their career before dozens of record moguls at New York's Fillmore East that doomed their potential as the American Beatles, yet the music was so infectious it was impossible to dismiss. Their catchy beat—part rock, part jazz, part rockabilly, part blues, part sheer novel inventiveness—spread across small-venue America for almost fifty years, drawing a huge cult following in the process.

"I *love* those guys," John Sebastian said of NRBQ; he once bought a house from Terry Adams. Thanks to his friend Keith Richards, Spampinato was under consideration as the replacement bass player for Bill Wyman of the Rolling Stones in 1993.

Music was part of the fabric of the Hudson Valley even as the region enjoyed a burst of national attention because of Woodstock. Steven Victor Talarico (b. 1948) was a Bronx kid whose mother determined he would follow in the footsteps of his father, a Julliard trained pianist. He was enrolled in music classes when ten years old, and three years later became the drummer in his dad's band. The family moved to Yonkers, where they had a house (instead of an apartment), with woods in the back and a lake nearby.

"Getting moved. . .took a little adjusting to," he later wrote. "It was too white and Republican for a skinny-ass punk from the Bronx." Talarico entered Roosevelt High School in 1962, failed in his academic studies, became the front man in an aptly named Yonkers band, The Strangers, and was busted on a dozen counts of marijuana possession in June 1966, when 18 years old. Eventually he remade his image, changed his name to Steven Tyler, and became the front man for Aerosmith, which closed the 25th anniversary Woodstock concert at the Winston Farm in Saugerties for 150,000 spectators at 5 a.m. on a Sunday morning in 1994.

A rich local tradition involved men and women with day jobs who took on "gigs" on weekends, some of them colorful characters like Richard "Red" Praetorius, a junk car parts dealer caught up in roadhouse hijinks at times. Buswell, the Paul Luke Band, and dozens of other homegrown groups with niche fan bases filled the night hours with energetic playing and partying. Performers like Bobby Farris and Phil Paladino came out of the union hall tradition and played for local weddings and other engagements, their mastery of the craft belying the small scene venues that they plied.

The mid-Hudson music scene was adumbrated by comedy, theater, and universal good times. Mikhail Horowitz (b. 1950), a SUNY New Paltz dropout from Brooklyn, joined the art scene in New Paltz in a stand-up comedy duo with Francesco Patricolo called Null and Void until 1979, when Horowitz returned to Woodstock and began working with Gilles Malkine, the Paris-born son of Sonia and Georges Malkine and a talented musician and composer. Malkine had performed with Tim Hardin at the original Woodstock concert and Carnegie Hall and elsewhere, had done Off-Broadway theater, and played Mozart in Peter Schikele's hilarious *A Little Nightmare Music* for the Woodstock Lyric Opera Company. He and his mother released *Plaisir d'Amour; 16 French Love Songs* in 1994, and Sonia May Malkine (b. 1923) was loved and admired for her radio show on folk music and frequent performances in the area. She and the family mounted several seminal exhibitions of Georges Malkine's Dada and surrealist-based paintings in the area. Her son and Horowitz delighted audiences in more than 800 zany performances across the Northeast. Their records bore such titles as "So Whaddaya Want for Ten Bucks?" and "Live, Jive, and Over 45." Horowitz also served for a few years as the "Cultural Czar" (arts editor) of *Woodstock Times* and eventually settled into a distinguished public relations position with Bard College while continuing with a brisk performance schedule with Malkine. At a benefit for the Alf Evers Archives at Woodstock Byrdcliffe Guild in 2015, joined by other musicians they performed "Rip Van Hip," Horowitz's hilarious send-up about "a double-Dutch dude with just one quirk / He was highly allergic to any kind of work" who escaped to the mountains and returned with "a long white beard stretchin' down to me crotch!" only to find:

> Instead of that village of the Knickerbock,
> There was Cumberland Farms, a CVS,
> A Taco Bell—man, what a mess!
> And right at the spot where his cottage had been
> Was the cocktail lounge of a Ramada Inn.

Meanwhile, Pete Seeger hosted dozens of benefits for social and political causes, and seemed to be ubiquitous on the music scene. His annual parties at the Croton waterfront to benefit the Hudson River Sloop *Clearwater* continued to attract huge crowds. Numerous musicians in the folk tradition emerged in the Hudson Valley—many because of Seeger's influence—and made notable professional careers. Don McLean (b. 1945) graduated from a Catholic high school, Iona Preparatory Academy in New Rochelle, and won the top prize in Raphael's Talent Search in its first year at the Dutchess County Fair in Rhinebeck. McLean developed a close relationship with Raphael Mark, the popular WEOK radio personality who created the "big-time event" in the music tent at the fair. He arranged for McLean to perform at the new Dutchess Community College that year, where "American Pie" was heard locally for the first time. McLean skyrocketed to fame in 1971 with that tune, an impressionistic and nostalgic recollection of February 3, 1959—"the day the music died"—when a plane crash took the lives of Buddy Holly, Ritchie Valens, and J. P. Richardson (The Big Bopper). The boy was delivering newspapers in New Rochelle the next day when he heard the news. The popularity of the song inspired an interest in *Tapestry*, McLean's early album, and songs like "Vincent" and "Castles in the Air." In 2001, "American Pie" was rated the fifth most popular song in the twentieth century by Billboard's Easy Listening, although Frances Marks (d. 2002), Raphael's wife, did not think it had a chance back in 1964.

"This song is never going to make it," the *Poughkeepsie Journal* quoted her as saying. "It's too long."

Jay Ungar (b. 1946) and Molly Mason were the best of the performers to emerge in the Seeger tradition. Their concerts and outreach efforts supported a range of community and cultural efforts from the early 1970s, and made them noted American folk musicians and composers who popularized infectious fiddle-and-dance roots music drawn from nineteenth and twentieth century traditions in national venues like Garrison Keilor's "A Prairie Home Companion." Married in 1991, they often performed with Jay's daughter, Molly, and Michael Merenda as the Jay Ungar and Molly Mason Family Band. Ungar and Mason established the Ashokan Music and Dance Camps at Olivebridge in Ulster County in 1980. They were awarded the Hudson River Maritime Museum Roger W. Mabie Award in 2014.

"Ashokan Farewell," (1982), Ungar's haunting violin solo after a Scottish-style lament on the closing of the camps one summer—"written by a Jewish kid from the Bronx," the composer quipped—became a national anthem as the theme music for Ken Burns' eleven-hour documentary, *The Civil War* (1990), the most-watched program in PBS television history at the time. The song was reprised throughout the series for a total of fifty-nine minutes. Ungar later recalled with humor some of the offers he received for use of the theme, including one for a bizarre sci-fi porn film. The US Army offered $100,000 for the rights for a recruiting video at a time when he needed the money, but he declined after reading the script, which credited the Army with making the West safe for settlers by defeating the Native Americans in wars.

Natalie Merchant (b. 1963), the lead singer and principal lyricist for 10,000 Maniacs, settled into Ulster County after becoming a solo artist in 1993. An environmentalist and social activist, she supported local causes through benefit performances and other work. She directed a well-regarded documentary on homeless shelters that was shown at the Old Dutch Church in Kingston in February 2013 and continued to perform locally and nationally.

The rise of popular music that characterized the radical reenvisioning of America in the postwar period was not limited to "Woodstock Nation" or the mid-Hudson area. A student jazz band performed in staid old Memorial Chapel on the Union College campus in 1948, and a formal concert followed in 1952 featuring the Billy Taylor Trio that was termed "probably the first college-sponsored jazz concert" in the country. Union's denial of a student group's desire to hold a rock 'n' roll concert in 1965 was overruled by the Committee on Religious Life, and concerts held thereafter, including one by Chet Arthur and the Flaming Aces that featured a student driving a motorcycle down the center aisle. Schenectady "townies" routinely attended such events. Hard rock concerts were banned in the chapel by 1982, however.

Late twentieth century culture in the Hudson Valley extended to all forms of art and music, its catholic reach a characteristic of the Valley's special identity. Fine performance arenas and hundreds of small venues attracted crowds for everything from heavy metal to chamber music. An exceptional and unique classical entertainer associated with Woodstock and the mid-Hudson Valley was the gifted and versatile composer, (Johann) Peter Schickele (b. 1935), also known under his satirist *nom-de-plume*, "P. D. Q. Bach," whom he described as "the youngest and the oddest of the twenty-odd children" of Johann Sebastian. Schickele won the Best Comedy Album Grammy four years in a row and had a long career as a classical composer. He created a popular music education program, *Schickele Mix*, for local National Public Radio affiliate WAMC, produced albums for Joan Baez (among others), and was an accomplished bassoonist—the only one to come out of Fargo, North Dakota, he claimed. The Kennedy Center characterized him as "one of the great parodists of the twentieth century."

The first Woodstock festival was planned by Woodstock Ventures, a company formed in January 1969 by Michael Lang, John Roberts, Joel Rosenman, and Artie Korfeld to take advantage of well-known performers who frequented the Ulster County art and cultural community. The festival evolved from a series of small, underground-style concerts in a field off the Glasco Turnpike in Saugerties that were often harassed by the local constabulary. Lang initially planned the festival for the nearby Winston Farm, but the local town supervisor, A. Michael Schovel, quickly passed an assembly law to prevent it. The event, which drew 400,000 and thirty-two performers, took place later that year more than forty miles to the southeast in Bethel. The 25th anniversary concert was hosted at the Winston Farm in 1994 under permit from the same assembly law, drawing more than 150,000 to the beautiful 800-acre site. The town reaped a million dollar windfall in revenues, and the site, albeit trampled and abused and poorly maintained in terms of waste management during the three-day affair, was restored to its pristine state within days afterwards.

Meanwhile, the Maverick Festival continued every summer in Hervey White's old haunts in Hurley, also strongly identified with the Woodstock hamlet scene, growing in renown and prestige while the Bethel event became the iconic and seminal moment in the history of rock 'n' roll. Nestled between these two widely different yet strangely related music venues, a variety of sites developed in the Valley that included old vaudeville stages like the Last Chance Saloon in Poughkeepsie, classic settlings like the Tarrytown Music Hall, the Palace in Albany, the Bardavon in Poughkeepsie, and the Paramount in Peekskill; new and exotic showcases such as Caramoor in Katonah and the Fisher Center in Annandale-on-Hudson, and popular multi-showcases like the Saratoga Performing Arts Center and Ulster Performing Arts Center in Kingston. The Valley's connections with music, dance and performance were constantly reinvented for modern, youthful audiences as well as traditional and classical ones. Bard College's brilliant and eccentric president, Leon Botstein (b. 1946), embraced the premise of the American Symphony Orchestra when founded by Leopold Stokowski in 1962—to "Americanize" classical music by broadening its range for a wider audience.

Under his musical direction, the ASO succeeded in reviving interest in little-known composers, many of them American, and created a popular local venue in the Summerstage series at the college in Annandale-on-Hudson. Bard has also launched a new initiative in advanced music studies, the Longy School of Music, with a master's degree in music in curatorial, critical, and performance studies.

Botstein became the college president at age twenty-eight in 1975, having served for five years as the youngest college president in American history at Franconia College in New Hampshire. Under his tenure, the $62 million Richard B. Fisher Performing Arts Center was designed by architect Frank Gehry and opened in 2003—a stunning visual experience with a theater center exterior of undulating stainless steel sheeting that some Bard students dubbed "the mechanized turtle" for its shape set against a stand of firs in the northeast corner of the Annandale campus. The architectural wonder experienced an early challenge when the first choice for a location, on the southern edge of the campus along Fish Creek, was denounced for its intrusion on the views from Montgomery Place. In 2016, Bard also purchased that iconic estate.

The profusion of galleries attested to a voracious appetite for fine art, while also helping in the revivals and health of local downtowns. The Valley continued to serve as a second home for creative talents across a wide spectrum of the arts, from classical music and ballet to fine writing and rock 'n' roll. Again, the proximity to the metropolitan area made these migrations convenient, the Valley serving as a door to the city that swings both ways.

Edward Sanders (b. 1939) and his wife, writer and artist Miriam Sanders, came to Woodstock when Sanders was already well known as a transitional figure between the Beat and hippie generations because of his poetry, social activism, and the band he co-founded, *The Fugs*. He became well known for a poem written while in jail after a demonstration at a nuclear submarine facility in Rhode Island. While in the East Village, he was arrested for publishing "Cock-Man," a poem by George Montgomery about all the women he bedded from uptown to Hoboken—certainly a misogynistic piece for today but merely amusing then. The two men did not know each other, and met in jail.

Sanders was an admirer of Charles Olsen, friend of Allen Ginsberg and minor figure in Beatnik literature. The success of his book, *The Family:*

The Story of Charles Manson's Dune Buggy Attack Battalion (1971), a solid piece of scholarship and the first major critical study of the Manson murders, enabled the Sanders' to move out of the city. On Meads Mountain Road he became involved in local land use and zoning, and, perhaps as a nod to his degree in Greek studies from Columbia University, Sanders began a multivolume chronicle of America's history in verse. The Fugs, a satirical anti-war band formed by Sanders and Tuli Kupferberg in 1964, was revived by the two men in 1988 at the Byrdcliffe Barn in Woodstock. On another occasion, Ginsberg and Country Joe McDonald appeared in a Sanders send-up of the commercialization of Woodstock '94 in "The Real Woodstock Festival."

George Montgomery also relocated to Ulster County where he joined Billy Guldy and his band of pranksters in the 1970s in a wild and irreverent community of partying iconoclasts around Guldys' Main Street bars in Rosendale, The Well and the Astoria. Guldy had a habit of attending New York Yankee games in a king's ermine cloak and crown. Montgomery published a well-received local column in the *Daily Freeman* called "Van Gogh's Ear" and popularized the practice of poetry readings around the county.

The term "Woodstock Nation" was coined by Abbott Howard "Abbie" Hoffman (1936–89) in his account of the 1969 festival, and ill-fit the Ulster County community save for a brief period of a few years when hippies and countercultural visionaries populated the town, often in poverty, giving rise to Family of Woodstock, a grassroots social services organization established by Michael Berg that would in time become a model for the state. The community was much more diverse and cultural, yet alternative notions had long been a part of its character. An expostulation about Overlook Mountain as the "Mount Sinai of the aborigines," published as a tourist draw by the Overlook Mountain House in the late nineteenth century (before Radcliffe's arrival), was followed around 1902 by old-timer folk tales about Indians on the mountain and in time a full-blown elaboration of a local Indian cult concocted by hippies in the late 1960s. Studies continued into the new century over whether or not local rock piles were cairns dated to Celtic or other Old World origins.

"Here, we feel is the heart of the matter," a *Woodstock Aquarian* editorial (of the "Nation" phase) declared in 1971.

We have been asleep a long, long time . . . and now we have just begun to awaken. This awakening is none other than the remembrance of something that we long ago forgot. We forgot that we were one with a greater Self . . . We feel that it has reached the point where cosmic truth is out of the realm of super personal domain. This is the message of the Aquarian Age. Group Consciousness, Tribal Consciousness, Spaceship Earth.

An aboriginal provenance for the locally celebrated Lake Hill Stone in Woodstock—which appeared to be carved—was disproved in a visit by William Ritchie, the state archaeologist, who declared it a common piece of dolomite limestone pitted by magnesium carbonate. Although long piles of stones and other unusual accumulations of rocks in the California Quarry and Lewis Hollow areas of Woodstock were often theorized as of "a vast [aboriginal] funerary complex," a more logical explanation suggested farmers clearing land to work the soil. "Ranger" Dave Holden, the trails keeper at the Comeau town hall property for twenty-five years and a Woodstock naturalist of note, continued with others to explore the B. C. theories as Native American in origin with tours of the local geography over the years.

A latter-day manifestation of the effusive 1960s spirit came in the pronouncements of "archaeoastronomers" who linked stone shelters built into hillsides, mostly in Westchester and Putnam counties, with Celts, Carthaginians, or other supposed Stone Age visitors to America's shores. The "America B. C." movement was led by Enrique Noguera in the mid-Hudson Valley and achieved a sense of legitimacy in the study of these mysterious stone rooms, until the Putnam County Historical Society archives yielded a farmer's report of a nineteenth century "frolic" associated with the construction of one of them. They were all root cellars built before refrigeration.

In 1971, Russell Roefs (b. 1943) became Woodstock's perennial Santa Claus and plotted with the Christmas Eve Committee surprise arrivals of Old St. Nick on the village green each year. They were continuing a tradition begun in 1932 by Agnes Schleicher, owner of the Jack Horner Shoppe, in which Santa arrived by truck after a nativity scene was played out by locals dressed in costumes from Persia and Palestine at the Dutch Reformed Church. The inaugural event was poignantly recorded by Marion Bullard in her *Kingston Daily Freeman* column that year, and repeated each year thereafter without revealing beforehand the method by which Santa would be arriving. Roefs' predecessor for fourteen years was Joe Holdridge Sr., who once slid down the guide wire to the steeple of the Woodstock Reformed Church dressed as Santa. Another time, Joe appeared on the roof of the Longyear Building with a sleigh and live reindeer. Roefs came one year by traditional sleigh pulled by a pony; in another, in a hot air balloon. He arrived on magic carpets, by "rocketship," on an elephant, and also down from the steeple. The tradition was renewed each year as another uniquely Woodstock iconic expression of small-town America.

The "new age" and Morrison's "old, old Woodstock" were indeed something new and strange to the town's established art community. Woodstock's association with the 1969 rock festival did not sit well with the older crowd, some of whom still remembered the colorful Maverick festivals and Wilna Hervey and Nan Mason's parties. Manette Van Hamel, who grew up on the Maverick and returned to Woodstock in retirement around 1975, was disillusioned with the new generation's attraction to the town for what she considered to be shallow reasons. Her lifelong work as an artist of "sculpture-to-wear" led her to join the Guild of Craftsmen and help cultivate a fine art perspective for the gallery scene in the town. Van Hamel transformed the Kleinert Gallery with the first of its thematic shows, "SOUND," in February 1978, drawing upon her husband Dick's retirement pastime of making violins in a studio at their streamside home. Lectures and concerts among the art works at the gallery were other innovations she helped to bring to the Woodstock scene.

Gediminas E. ("Geddy") Sveikauskas (b. 1939) arrived from Boston-via-the West Village in 1972. The New England chess champion and Harvard graduate, he had had to decide if he wanted to go on to the grandmaster level or follow a different star, and opted to pursue his abiding passion in journalism. He established *Woodstock Times* by drawing on the design expertise of Milton Glaser in developing a new look in weeklies and tapping into the region in a hip, eclectic, and yet traditionally newsy style. The *Times* found an eager talent base of writers, artists and photographers, and reached a phenomenal circulation for a small-town newspaper. The letters to the editor, appropriately called "Feedback," offered a wild and often mad mix of opinions, announcements, declarations and exclamations that typified the town's energies. Its editors included talented individuals in their own right, among them Marguerite Culp, Perry Teasdale, and Brian Hollander. Sveikauskas eventually accumulated half a dozen local papers through his company, Ulster Publications, had a fling with a periodical, and played a behind-the-scenes role in economic growth and furthering progressive policies in Ulster County and the Catskills. He served for many years on the board of The Catskill Center for Conservation and Development.

Woodstock Times, like Family of Woodstock, proved that culture could survive its own excesses. A sense of the town's importance in the art world traditions prevailed in institutions like the Woodstock Guild (later the Kleinert Byrdcliffe Guild) and Woodstock Artists Association (later the Woodstock Artists Association Museum). The Arts Students League returned, though in the later years, as Raymond Steiner related, the League's "romance with the art colony waned" with a drop in enrollments and rise in the cost of living for artists in Woodstock. Yet the climate of the arts continued unabated. At least seventeen commercial galleries were established in the town, the Maverick Concert series continued an unbroken streak of seasons, the nightlife flourished in the quality of musical talent readily available, and Arnold Branch founded a series of Friday Town Forums that included speakers such as Joseph Morgenstern, the movie critic for *Newsweek*, and Happy Traum, editor of "Sing Out."

The Woodstock School of Art was formed in 1968 by Robert Angeloch (1922–2011), Franklin Alexander (1925–2007), Eduardo Chàvez (1917–95), Lon Clark, and Wallace O. ("Jerry") Jerominek. The school initially worked from studios on Millstream Road before purchasing the beautiful old setting of the WYA complex east of the hamlet from the city of Kingston. Angeloch was a noted landscape painter who had studied at the Art Students League over 1946–51 and reinstituted an ASL landscape course in the summer in 1964. His art was the subject of a retrospective at the Albany Institute of History and Art in 1965. Other ASL instructors associated with Woodstock included Chàvez, Bruce Dorfman, Karl Fortress, Philip Guston, Fletcher Martin, William Pachner, and John Pike. Of the initial eighteen instructors who signed on, twelve of them had been associated with the Art Students League at Woodstock. Paula Nelson Kleinhans, a League student in the 1960s and its local registrar, worked with Angeloch over the years and became a guiding influence in the new school's development.

Rolph Scarlett (1881–1984), Eduardo Chàvez, Marko Vukovic (1892–1993), Hannah Small (1903–92), Doris Lee (1905–83), Sally Michel Avery

(1902–2003), Milton Avery (1885–1965), Ethel Magafan (1916–93), Eugene Gershoy (1901–1983), Anton Otto Fischer (1882–1962), Eva van Rijn (b. 1936), Milton Glaser (b. 1929), and Sophie Fenton (1915–2005) were among numerous other "Woodstock" artists whose work became closely associated with the community. Jenne Magafan (1916–52) was a precocious and beautiful young artist married to Eduardo Chàvez whose premature passing was a poignant tragedy in the history of the art colony.

The spirit of the age was not limited to its flagship town. Many communities had their share of young, eager, energetic hipsters, some tuned into the intellectual babble of the Beats and *the beat*, some voicing the Aquarian Age themes of the new awareness, the new sensibilities, or simply the new pharmaceuticals, some just tooling along to the rhythms of their peers, and many just hanging on. A nondescript house in a rundown development might hold a group of teenagers sitting around a scratchy record player listening for the first time to "The Times They Are A-Changin'" and wondering what it was all about. Kids in a few towns close to Woodstock snuck off in the night to party at the beer joints after hours, regardless of their age, while the older, more serious crowd gathered at the Beatnik-inspired Espresso for poetry readings.

These were heady intellectual times for youth. A bright young freshman in high school might impress her friends by reciting most of Allen Ginsberg's *Howl*. Robert Heinlein's *Stranger in a Strange Land* (1961), Ayn Rand's *Atlas Shrugged* (1957), and, after the apocalyptic *Cat's Cradle* (1963), everything by Kurt Vonnegut, Jr. (1922–2007), were devoured by these generations of readers. Vonnegut's fourth novel was his hilarious variation on his brother Bernard's work as an atmospheric scientist at General Electric in Schenectady, where he developed a nucleating agent for seeding clouds with ice crystals— except that "ice nine," the substance that destroys the world in *Cat's Cradle*, does just the reverse by changing all water crystals to solid form when accidentally dropped into the Atlantic Ocean.

Marijuana was readily available in most Valley towns in the mid-1960s and was soon the "cool" substance to abuse. The attraction of new drugs like lysergic acid diethylamide (LSD) and mescaline and the growing availability of "speed" (methamphetamine) and cocaine glamorized the underculture and depleted their pocketbooks and, in the case of hard drugs like heroin, their lives. Timothy Leary (1920–96) became a pop icon when Dutchess County Sheriff Lawrence Quinlain, District Attorney John Heilman, and a cadre of deputies that included the future Watergate burglary mastermind went after him. For Leary, Millbrook was "a non-stop festival of life with ceremonies, seminars, music, fertility rites, star gazing, moon watching, forest glade revels."

G. Gordon Liddy (b. 1930), later the leader of the Watergate burglars but then an eager, pistol-toting assistant district attorney, Quinlan lieutenant Charlie Borchers, and "some twenty to thirty deputies" waited shivering in the bushes at the Hitchcock estate in Millbrook in March 1966 for the sheriff and DA to arrive and execute a warrant, all of them convinced that a wild drug-and-sex party was unfolding inside. Liddy's account of the raid read like a parody of real police work. The DA took a wrong turn and got lost on the 1,500-acre estate. The deputies were seriously disappointed when they discovered that the movies that Leary's guests were watching were not porno-graphic, not even any "broads jumpin' in and out of the water or something" as one of them hoped to find, but simply films of waterfalls. The police found, once the evidence was collected, "that we were long on scientific jour-nals" that Leary kept, "but short on the drugs themselves." Some pot was found; a second raid produced more serious drugs, but this was the spring of the Miranda decision and none of those arrested were properly told of their rights.

Liddy later campaigned for Congress on a law-and-order platform, pointedly wearing his jacket open at speaking events so the local church groups and civic associations could see his shoulder holster. He yielded to a more le-gitimate Republican candidate, Hamilton Fish Jr. (1926-96), and in return received an appointment to the Republican National Committee in Washing-ton, which led to his role as the leader of the Watergate burglars. In later years, he and Leary lectured together on the college circuit. Fish, the amiable, handsome son of the reactionary congressman of FDR's day, became the Republican leader of civil rights legislation in his tenure in Congress.

Meanwhile, real drugs killed young people in the Hudson Valley, destroying families, frustrating police and prosecutors, and leaving communities quietly devastated in their wake. Heroin came north in the early 1970s like a silent scourge, killing off a few in most places along the way; those who did not die then awoke thirty years later with hepatitis C, spending their last years worrying and sometimes dying over liver problem complications and related illnesses. The Rockefeller laws only succeeded in filling prisons; scientifically inaccurate as well as unequally applied, the laws were used by rabid district attorneys who found reelection heaven in every well-publicized bust. Pot was classified with heavier substances, and the mere possession of small amounts of cocaine was enough to send young men—almost always African-American or Hispanic—to jail for fifteen or more years. County prosecutors and the media unwittingly fueled the growth in the use of illicit substances by stoking the flames of public outrage, in effect strengthening the bonding of young people who found common cause in opposing Vietnam and the hypocrisies of the older generations.

Stoned, strung-out young men and women lived dazed and self-deluding lives of desperate longing in cold and drafty hovels on the edges in these sad days, places like Palmer House in Croton, once occupied by the reservoir superintendent yet gone to seed in its dislocation and become, as far as the locals were concerned, a squatters' lair for "draft dodgers" and "hippies" during the anti-war era. Some youths spent weeks living in the Croton dam tunnel system, which was eventually sealed because of the practice. Many went to Canada to avoid the draft, while most faced the music of their own dislocation as veterans returning to an America that had misrepresented and estranged them.

Family of Woodstock defined the model and became the most successful of the new social agencies dealing with the whole panoply of ills and eccentricities that arose with the Aquarian Age. A typical day at the crisis hotline in 1971 might involve helping a walk-in from the rain find dry clothes, offering an abortion referral, arranging for transportation to a hospital for a young girl bleeding from a uterine coil break, helping a guy broken down on the road ("Call to Sid. He'll take his jeep out there to see what he can do"), talking to an emancipated minor with nowhere to go, referring a Sufi teacher or kids looking for a campsite, or taking a call—every Monday afternoon this happened —from a person quietly crying on the other end of the line. The Vietnam War also gave rise, organically at least if not formally by the government, to support agencies that could help with drug abuse, post-traumatic stress disorder, and the psychological impacts of coming home to a country without heroes. Louise Ringe was a junior at the University at Albany in 1970 who created a crisis hotline for students with the help of the college's counseling center. Like Family, the program expanded, meeting the needs of the college community through the hotline, outreach, and, the latest program, peer career advising. Middle Earth, as the program was called, also ran a weekly support column in the *Albany Student Press.*

Even as it embraced the new times and pacifist sentiments, the Valley remained as patriotic as it had been in the past, with many scorning those who did not serve or expressed pro-Vietnam sentiments. Most of those who served were typical American youths from small towns and villages who rose to the call of duty and, in some instances, beyond it. The first Medal of Honor recipient in Vietnam (and first Special Forces soldier given the honor) was Captain Roger H. C. Donlon (b. 1934) of Saugerties, who led the repulsion of a two-battalion attack on the outpost of Nam Dong on July 6, 1964, sustaining several serious wounds. Donlon had two years at West Point, yet usually took for his role models his parents and other local hometown figures during his youth. In talks around the country, he preached teamwork and the core values of service as synonymous with citizenship, calling the family "the first team." Donlon was the first drum major of the Father Hardy Drum Corps of St. Mary of the Snow Church, a highly popular marching band that participated in parades around the Valley. Donlon and his wife Norma lived in Leavenworth, Kansas, yet always remained the hometown hero to the veterans of Saugerties, saluted and lionized whenever he returned.

Vietnam had a special aura for West Point cadets. According to one of them, the cadet in the war days considered the war "like the centerfold in *Playboy*. . . . The academy opened naturally to the page which sold the place," Lucian Truscott wrote. "War was the reason West Point existed. Everything else was filler." Companies of 160 cadets served under thirty-two tactical officers, all majors. Four regimental commanders, all colonels, had eight cadet companies, and commanding overall was a brigadier general, "a position which was traditionally a key step on the ladder of army success."

The FBI had expansive wiretapping authority that J. Edgar Hoover used in pursuing 1960s radicals with the same vigor as Nazi fifth-columnists. A July 5, 1968, counterintelligence memorandum sent by Hoover to the Albany office laid out a twelve-point master plan to undermine and disrupt anti-war efforts through subversive activities such as sending anonymous letters to university officials or alumni, leafleting campuses with "obnoxious" photos of SDS speakers, creating the impression that the radical leaders were government informants, confusing and disrupting through misinformation, and exploiting the local press and police to harass intellectuals with pot arrests and ridicule in the newspapers. Black nationalist "hate" groups were targeted as well. An August 23, 1967, memorandum ordered that a secret control file be created and "an experienced and imaginative Special Agent" be assigned to disrupt, discredit, misdirect or otherwise foil the black power movement. In addition to the FBI, the Internal Revenue Service had two agencies involved in collecting confidential information and using tax audits to spy on writers the government thought were dangerous.

The events at Nanuet and Nyack in Rockland County in October 1981—when an armed robbery of $1.6 million from a Brink's armored car carried out by Black Liberation Army and former Weather Underground veterans resulted in the killings of two Nyack police officers, Edward O'Grady and Waverly Brown, and a guard, Peter Paige—seemed to provide a chilling coda on the Aquarian Age. Paige was killed in the initial robbery, O'Grady and Brown at a Thruway entrance after spotting a U-Haul truck and yellow Honda identified as the getaway vehicles. Kathy Boudin (b. 1943), a former Weather Underground activist now associated with this so-called May 19 Communist Organization, was driving the truck, which momentarily relaxed the suspicion of the officers because their reports were that only black assailants were involved. Six men emerged from the van in body armor and began shooting, killing the two officers and wounding three others. Boudin was arrested after attempting to flee on foot. Three of those who escaped were held at gunpoint by Spring Valley Police Chief Alan Colsey after crashing their Honda. Two others were involved in a shootout with police two days later, killing one robber, and three others arrested several months later.

Boudin had effectively begun the robbery when she dropped her infant child at a babysitter's and rented the U-Haul van. She was the only defendant represented by counsel at the Goshen trial that ensued and received a twenty-year-to-life jail term, which she served at the Bedford Hills Correctional Facility for Women. In prison she helped create teen, parenting, AIDS and women's health, adult literacy and college programs. She wrote and published prolifically and was given an International Pen award for her poetry in 1999. Boudin was released in 2003 following her third parole hearing and subsequently worked in an HIV/AIDS clinic in Manhattan.

42. The Other Side

Dreams are just when you're starting off, that's the image, you have the dream to push the motivation. . . . People say I'm going to be a million-dollar fighter. . .well, I know what I am and that's what counts more than anything else, because the people don't know what I go through. They think I'm born this way. They don't know what it took to get this way.

—MIKE TYSON (1984)

Impacts of the Great Migration of African American families from southern to northern communities in the mid-twentieth century were mitigated in Poughkeepsie by the uniform origins of those who arrived and the family and personal connections that they brought with them. The same factors played a role in the eighteenth century migration of High Germans to the Hudson Valley after 1710. The Great Migration was a larger version of what happened in the 1920s and 30s, many coming to fill the new war industry jobs, and later to expand the urban workforce in the technological industries of the 1950s. Many of the twentieth-century newcomers hailed from Virginia and North Carolina, following earlier patterns of migration, arriving usually on Labor Day weekends with carloads of relatives and their belongings. The white population of Pough-keepsie diminished from 41,023 to 32,029 over this score of years.

Black professionals who came north to join IBM in this period reported a uniform pattern of "rigid residential segregation" in which the company itself participated by not providing relocation services as it did for whites. Some white homeowners who were feeling crowded out by the newcomers rented their houses and moved into other parts of the city or the country, but most were lucky to get a cold-water flat in "the Negro ghetto" along Lower Main Street. Many relocated to the new suburban areas that were close to the industries they served. Urban renewal attracted black families, as planned for Pough-keepsie, targeting a 55%-45% population ratio with whites in the new housing, and by 1973 the black share of the population became dominant. The 1952 W. W. Smith public housing project (built on the site of an old city landfill) increased to over 75% African American because of the Great Migration. With the new growth came new neighborhood arrangements, new churches, and new social patterns among Poughkeepsie's black community.

The migration of black families from Warrenton, Georgia, to Catskill, New York, began in the late 1890s, according to historian Ted Hilscher. Warrenton was one of the most racist communities in the South, and—particularly after 1930—many who did migrate were likely escaping for fear of their lives. The first to arrive may have been Jeremiah M. (Jerry) Walker (b. 1865) and his family; he was one of five African American heads of households in the village in 1900 who came from Georgia. They worked the brickyards with Italian immigrants, and were likely recruited by brickyard "agents" in the South. By mid-century the community was well established, and included several businessmen who set up shop in the village. Some found work at American Valve, which produced sand mold products for construction and industrial uses. In 1958, the federally funded Hop-O-Nose housing project, which resulted from a small urban renewal project, provided better housing for many of the families. Many of the children of the early migrants fared well—Eugene Wyman became manager of the village's largest retail store, and his brother Philip rose to become an assistant deputy commissioner of the state Department of Corrections. Vallie Ruff's son became a state trooper.

Edsall Walker (1910–97) was the "most prominent of the migration's second generation" in Catskill. Walker was a southpaw pitcher who started with the Albany Black Sox in 1929 and joined the Homestead Grays in the Negro Baseball League in 1933. He was a part of the nine-season championship wins of the Grays, an average hurler by major league standards but with a good sinking fastball. Walker out-dueled Satchell Paige in one memorable game in Washington. As a slugger he batted right and averaged .297 in the 1943 season.

In the period after World War II, as industrial patterns changed the nature of the urban areas suffered in the Hudson Valley. Rising crime rates, greater vacancies in storefronts and the old housing stock, the impacts of taxes on a steadily diminishing base, the proliferation of shopping centers and malls just beyond municipal limits, and changing patterns of upward mobility created neighborhoods that seemed desolated by a purge. Newburgh became the characteristic Hudson Valley city in that mold, "one of the worst cities in America" because of the prevalence of drugs, crime and homelessness.

"This street was beautiful up until the early 1980s," a resident of East

Parmenter Street observed in 2007. "My wife and I are one of the few families left here. The house next to me was a meth factory and the police closed that down." Successive waves of heroin and other hard drugs decimated the youth and imbued a sense of hopelessness among those who survived the addiction in other communities, including white ones in smaller numbers. A working class generation was devastated by the drug's consequences—some dying, some living miserable lives, some—especially among those returning from Vietnam carrying the monkey on their back—bereft of hope and struggling just to survive. And many of those who did survive and managed to clean up their act faced the shadow of hepatitis C twenty years later, the hopes and dreams that they had not thought possible shattered in lesions, bad blood tests, failed livers and other "symptoms" that took many lives.

Newburgh itself was also a city constantly seeking its own rebirth, and a mild success story for some years after 2000 when Habitat for Humanity of Greater Newburgh forged partnerships in the rehabilitation of the dilapidated stock of buildings. Thirty acres of prime waterfront property were revived under a partnership with Leyland Alliance of Tuxedo, whose architect, Andres Duany (b. 1949), was called "the father of new urbanism" for his innovative concepts nationwide.

In Peekskill in 1980, 35% of the residents survived on government assistance. Troy found its downtown declining in the loss of business to a new modern shopping mall across the river at Latham. Elsewhere small, neighborly, busy main streets that once provided everything a family might need became desolate. The bedroom communities of the new industries (particularly IBM) that had proliferated on their outskirts took their business to the big-box stores that grew around where they worked, leaving only the local newsstands for the aging population that remained, trapped in their own economic prisons.

Urban renewal plans that included low-income housing and the redistricting of black neighborhoods were resisted by black middle-class families in Yonkers, where a strong political profile existed. The Nepperhan-Runyon Heights community of 1,300 mostly black residents had benefited from redistricting in 1930, when most of the neighborhood came under the city's sixth election district in the tenth ward. In 1941, changes in the government structure led to greater district powers through the appointment of a city manager and reduction in the mayor's authority. The neighborhood lost its clout in the city's redistricting plan in the 1980s when it was included in a larger, mostly white Republican district. Regardless of the ward arrangements, Nepperhaners remained politically active and were largely issues-oriented and willing to cross party lines in support of a cause. These families also had ties to white neighborhood leaders and politicians through the schools their children attended, giving them greater sophistication in their interactions as well as greater access to city jobs.

Milton Holst, prominent in the Runyon Heights Improvement Association, was considered the "mayor" of the Heights. He began as a Republican district worker in the 1960s and became involved in city hall activities. Most Nepperhaners were Republican in the early years, more than 75% in 1930. The pattern changed in the 1940s, but then "Eisenhower Republicans" brought the neighborhood in for Nixon/Lodge with 51% of the 1960 presidential election vote. That pattern changed dramatically again because of Republican opposition to the 1964 Civil Rights Act nationally; by the 1980s, only 16% of the Nepperhaners were registered with the Grand Old Party. Lyndon Johnson and Hubert Humphrey carried the district with 92% of the vote, compared with a 62% share of the Yonkers citywide vote.

Republican support in Yonkers shifted generally from 58% to 42% from 1980 to 1992. In the Nepperhan neighborhood, the shift was driven in part by new patterns of racial discrimination that were emerging over the city's schools and housing policies. A desegregation lawsuit brought against Yonkers by the United States Justice Department and the NAACP led to a 1986 decision by District Court Judge Leonard B. Sand that the city had practiced intentional segregation. A strong white backlash to the decision—even as the local board of education worked to eliminate the problem—arose to prevent the city from distributing a thousand units of low- and moderate-income housing across the community. The white argument was class-based yet scarcely hid a deeply biased undercurrent of racism. The city began to comply with the desegregation order in 1993, after first submitting a plan that was rejected by Judge Sand. Yonkers was encouraged to move forward with the new housing policies after the judge ruled that New York State was partly responsible for the pattern that had developed. Yonkers secured $16.4 million in funds to finish the work, yet Nepperhaners successfully resisted sharing in the new low-income housing in their neighborhood. Voters also agreed to restore a strong-mayor form of government, abandoned in 1941, although that also did not solve the city's racial problems.

In some places, like Kingston, urban renewal was supported by local police and district attorneys interested in removing pawn shops and other marginal businesses that fueled local crime patterns. Troy turned to the new thinking to revive its business district. Building blight and deterioration and a lost sense of pride drove most renewal efforts in one way or another, and often with negative consequences as well as good ones. Kingston lost an entire culture in its downtown Rondout makeover—very ably evoked in Stephen Blauweiss and Lynn Woods' 2014 film *Lost Rondout*—as did Albany when the ambitions of Nelson Rockefeller and Erastus Corning razed a colorful old neighborhood to make way for the Empire State Plaza.

Urban renewal hit Nyack in Rockland County in the early 1960s, displacing the village's largest black population in the removal of three blocks of shops and homes. Many of those displaced moved to Spring Valley. The black population in the Nyacks (2,429 of 12,000 residents) remained in Nyack, South Nyack, and the hamlet of Central Nyack; all of Upper Nyack was white. The village police were nervous on the night of July 19, 1967, because of reports of disturbances by black youths in Newark and elsewhere in New Jersey and the urban troubles generally in that hot summer. Three false alarms had been rung that month, and two nights earlier the police had to break up a street fight. Yet when "a band of Negro youths" became boisterous in the parking lot across from his station, the police chief walked over and asked them to keep it down, as he usually did in such situations, and they complied. In a later incident that evening, kids broke the windows of a local school and pelted a night watchman with stones. The police saw it as a riot and called for additional help. Officers came in from nearby towns, and the sheriff contributed a posse. Within two hours fourteen black teenagers were arrested.

A community dialogue ensued over the next several days. A committee issued a report calling for better recreation, education, work and family opportunities, which the village then tried to pursue. But tension had developed in the community that was not so easily assuaged. The Congress of Racial Equality (CORE) was denied permission to hold a rally, and held it anyway for a small turnout with many of the police present. CORE wanted a commission to handle the complaints. The Orangetown Conservative Party wanted stronger enforcement measures.

Several fires and false alarms exacerbated matters in September. A petition said to represent the eight fire companies of the Nyacks (all white) called for state police support if a small group of troublemakers were not removed. Five hundred signed the petition, the leaders of the group calling for the mayor's resignation. On October 4, a hot and muggy Wednesday, a police car sent to investigate a crowd of fifteen young blacks was pelted with rocks. In the incident that followed, the chief and two officers were injured. Other police and the sheriff responded. Three small fires and some broken windows resulted. Among those arrested were a former paratrooper, three reporters, and the captain of the high school football team.

The Rockland County Human Rights Commission, created just four years earlier, called for greater dialogue and a survey of black sentiments. The Ethical Culture Society and South Nyack's Methodist church pointed to "social ills" as the root cause of the troubles. *The New York Times* and the *New York Post* were surprised at the notoriety of the place; the *Times* saw CORE's involvement as central to the unrest, and in a sense that was the case since its leader exhorted his followers to "make a stand here" against "a particularly reactionary, unmoving white establishment." CORE's message approved of Black Power but not "the hate line," and instead demonstrated against "the elements in this town that don't want black and white together."

Congressman John Dow set up a public hearing. One of the young speakers complained about police harassing blacks for gathering on the street but not the audiences breaking into the street for intermissions at the nearby summer stock theater. The chief agreed with the need for places for young people to congregate, pointed out that the violence happened just past the 9 p.m. curfew where there was a high occurrence of violence generally. Several remarked on the troubles nationwide, each side accusing the other of preparing for related violence locally. Both sides also blamed the media. Newark was on fire and it was all in the news, its proximity fueling the conflagration in the Nyacks. A new group, the Committee of Concern for the Nyacks, was formed to try and deal with the high rents, the dearth of housing and jobs, and problems with education and recreation. Village businessmen formed a similar group. As Carl Nordstrom reported, eventually the dialogue moved "from the concrete to the abstract," and a kind of calm returned to the community in the shared knowledge of their common American identity.

Indeed, a new identity was emerging. As European decolonization after World War II led to an uplifting of the African identity and the creation of independent African nations, the pre-war degraded identity of African Americans was transformed postwar in the United States into one of greater acceptance and even an embrace of black identity. A transformative shift in thinking was apparent, and some communities were proactive about it, albeit belatedly. Saugerties acted after the turn of the century to change the pejorative name for an abandoned shunpike where poor blacks had once huddled in makeshift shacks by asking State Comptroller H. Carl McCall (b. 1935) to deliver a keynote address naming Augusta Savage Road after the Harlem Renaissance sculptor and teacher (1892–1962) who relocated to the community after the war. The local historical society mounted an exhibition of a dozen new sculptures that Savage had created in her self-imposed exile and that were unknown to the wider art world; the exhibit drew national attention in the interest of Jacob Lawrence (1917–2000), a former student of Savage, and the Schomberg Center for Research in Black Culture.

Mary Lou Williams (1910–81), a great jazz pianist and composer, found peace upstate as Savage had done, but in another setting. Williams stopped at the Graymoor monastery and retreat in Garrison while on a casual drive with her manager in the summer of 1958. She struck up a friendship with a young black Franciscan, Brother Mario (born Grady Hancock), in the gift shop and returned a few months later and spent time in the Sisters of the Atonement retreat. Williams visited frequently over the next six years, and Brother Mario returned the compliment when he and other brothers were in New York. On one occasion, Williams came north with two friends, Lorraine Gillespy and Lillian Armstrong, who each purchased an expensive rosary in the gift shop. Williams also met some radical Catholics through the Thomas More Society in New York, including Dorothy Day, and later came to Day's Catholic Workers farm at Tivoli and performed a jazz mass, among other works.

A black youth from Brooklyn who would become prominent in another field entered Catskill Junior High School in 1980. Michael Gerard Tyson (b. 1966) was furiously ranting in the hall one day at three girls who taunted him about his mother. They ran into the girls' room; he followed, and punched the towel dispenser off the wall. Principal Lee A. Bordick took him outside in a cold and slow November rain and talked to him quietly, exhorting him to "learn control" despite the unfair treatment he was receiving. They were saying he hated black people, even his mother, because he lived at the white people's house three miles from the school. Mike Tyson had been taken in by the professional fighter manager Cus D'Amato (d. 1985), and roomed with eight other young would-be boxers at D'Amato's home.

The fight scene was in twilight in those days. Small communities near the river had athletic clubs and halls with gaming rooms and pool tables, and often a room where a makeshift ring could be fashioned. Local young men came and fought for the change thrown in the ring, often no more than $14 or $15 for the winner. D'Amato had risen to the top of the game in the 1950s when his young protégé, Floyd Patterson (1935–2006), won a 1956 competition to succeed Rocky Marciano (1923–69) as heavyweight champion of the world. Years later, D'Amato was hurt by a promotions scandal, and struggled for six years to make light heavyweight José Torres a champion. He acted paranoid about dubious characters in the fight trade shadowing him, and then became an obscure and shadowy figure himself.

D'Amato bought the Catskill house and had the title put in his companion Camille Ewald's name. When he moved there with Camille in 1968, he began training young boys and offered advice to rising professionals who called, including Cassius Clay (Muhammad Ali, 1942–2016). D'Amato had been in New Paltz for two years, training another heavyweight prospect, Buster Mathis (1943–95), who had defeated Joe Frazier in the US Olympic trials the year before. Frazier defeated Mathis in 1968 and went on to a famous victory over Ali in 1971, while Mathis's hopes declined. D'Amato, who was often suspicious about real and supposed enemies, thought that Mathis's backers were out to kill him while he was in New Paltz. He locked himself in a training camp room for two days.

"It was as if he [D'Amato] had decided to sleep for a while," Tyson's biographer Montieth M. Illingworth wrote of the trainer's removal to Catskill, "just as Rip Van Winkle had, according to the fable, in the nearby Catskill Mountains. Winkle logged a full twenty years. D'Amato did thirteen before being awakened by Mike Tyson."

It was the summer of 1980. Tyson's roommates were all brash, tough, and white. They lived under Camille's rules—she cooked the dinners, they cleaned up and made all their other meals themselves—a routine that the shy young Tyson adopted as well. He learned table manners from watching the other boys. He hardly understood the lectures that Cus constantly gave about boxing—

"Who is your best friend? . . . Fear is your best friend!"—and was baffled when the trainer handed him a book called *Zen and the Art of Archery* to read.

Tyson had grown up on the Brooklyn streets. He created small problems —swearing at Camille, stealing ice cream, walking away from Cus's lectures— yet gradually came around to D'Amato's ways. The trainer's agreement with the state Division of Youth was to train Tyson as a fighter on condition that the young man would remain in school. Mike was fourteen and had not been in a school in three years when he enrolled in Catskill junior high.

He was a big kid among the seventh graders with whom he was paired academically. Principal Bordick knew he was "special," so he worked with him by providing "constant reality checks for Mike to make sure he understood what was expected of him." Tyson walked out on some classroom sessions the first few months, but knew enough to maintain a thin connection to satisfy Cus and his social worker. D'Amato looked the other way as Mike ignored his homework. Meanwhile, Tyson trained like a boxer. He ran the three miles to school each morning until Bordick told him he smelled too bad from the sweat he generated, so he took the bus and instead ran the three miles home. Tyson was up at five each weekend morning, running the Catskill roads, at the gym every day after school at five and most of Saturday and Sunday, and stayed close to the other boys in the house. The racial tensions at the junior high that year worried Bordick that Tyson might get involved, but he stayed distant from this and other school affairs. Bordick could never convince him to join in the occasional trips to New York to the baseball games. Tyson was only interested in boxing.

His size, the lisp in his voice, his unrelenting interest in boxing, and his residence were provocations for the girls who harassed him in the halls. One of them kicked Mike when Bordick brought them all into the principal's office, but he maintained his composure. He knew how much he had to lose, and by the second semester he was using his old street con skills to charm his teachers and fellow students.

D'Amato trainer Teddy Atlas took Tyson through the boxing basics and taught him the D'Amato system. Since Patterson's decline, the boxing world had soured on Cus's approach, but that was after Patterson had changed the system on his own. With Tyson, the trainers had a clean slate with which to work. "He was a perfect piece of clay," Atlas said. Tyson's weaknesses were his height (5'9") and 71" reach, similar to only two other major champions,

Marciano and Frazier. D'Amato taught him to crouch and punch upward in combinations (Frazier-style), which maximized his power.

When Tyson won the Junior Olympic heavyweight title in Colorado in 1981, he became a Catskill celebrity. The local fame was a distraction at school, however, where the officials decided, over his caseworker's objections, to move him into high school without the necessary tests. The new principal, Richard Stickles, was less forgiving of his acting out in class than Bordick had been. The racial tensions had continued as well, and black students continued to taunt Mike about where he lived. A series of suspensions resulted, during which Tyson, without notifying anyone, would leave Catskill. D'Amato usually asked Torres to track him down in the Brownsville neighborhood of Brooklyn and bring him home. Atlas's response was to bar him from the gym, as he would with any of the boys, but D'Amato did not allow that punishment for Tyson. Ever since Patterson, D'Amato had decided to remain impersonal and objective about his fighters, and particularly Tyson, because of his championship potential.

Catskill expelled Mike Tyson from school in January 1982. Meanwhile, his power and brooding presence had created a "mystique" about him that was attracting national fight attention.

After his mother's death in September 1982, Tyson accepted the Catskill house as his home and earnestly began preparing to be heavyweight champion of the world. D'Amato, solely to ensure that his champion would stay with him, took steps to become Mike's legal guardian.

A schism developed between D'Amato and Atlas, who saw through his boss's duplicity. Atlas believed that D'Amato had been paying off local authorities to keep Tyson out of trouble; one case involved alleged sex with a twelve-year-old. When his own daughter, also twelve, told him that Tyson had fondled her, Atlas went into a rage and confronted Tyson with a gun at the Catskill gym. Tommy Atlas, whom Cus D'Amato had saved from prison just as he had with Tyson, was quickly fired. Kevin Rooney, Atlas's childhood friend, took over as trainer.

Greene county administrator Bill Hagan had secured a $25,000 federal grant for D'Amato's gym some years before. (Atlas later learned that he was supposed to be paid from those funds, but never was.) D'Amato told Hagan that other promoters were trying to steal Tyson from him. When D'Amato and his lawyers went into court with a set of fully-executed guardianship papers, the petition was quickly granted.

When Atlas attempted to continue as trainer for the other boys in Camille's home, D'Amato spread the rumor that he had ties with the mob. He elaborated with tales, some true and some not, about Atlas's troubled youth and suicide attempts. Atlas became a Catskill pariah and was subsequently unable to find training work in upstate New York.

"Maybe Cus was right," Atlas rationalized years later over his training arguments with D'Amato. "If we did it my way, Tyson might never have become champion."

The bond between Mike Tyson and Cus D'Amato grew and strengthened. They sat up nights together watching old fight films or reading boxing books, which Tyson would then question his mentor about. For all his lack of school smarts, Tyson had a perfect memory about aspects of a fighter's history, but relied on D'Amato to explain the significance of a career or aspect of the fight trade. In time he became one of the most well read fighters in the business. His training intensified as well; Tom Patti, who had the room below Tyson's, often heard him through the night "shadowboxing for hours. I could hear the thumping and grunting."

Tyson was developing into a great fighter, but the old problem about his security continued to haunt him. He lost the 1982 US National championship after being knocked down three times, and the 1983 National Golden Gloves Tournament. Each time, he just stopped fighting and allowed his opponents to pile up points. He forgot or ignored all of D'Amato's teaching. He acted out his frustrations in lies and cruelty to animals. He spit on D'Amato during screaming matches they had together. When he lost in his bid for the Olympics in 1983, D'Amato and his backers were stunned.

Tyson's first three professional bouts were in Albany, all in 1985, against Hector Mercedes, Trent Singleton, and Donald Halpin, two first-round technical knockouts and a fourth-round knockout. He knocked out Larry Sims in the third round in Poughkeepsie on July 19. He scored a technical knockout in the first round against Sterling Benjamin in Latham on November 1, three days before Cus D'Amato died. Tyson returned to Albany on November 22, knocking out Conroy Nelson in the second round, and forced Mark Young out in the first round in Colonie two days after Christmas.

Prior to his winning the WBC World Heavyweight Championship in Las Vegas on September 6, notable Tyson fights in the Hudson Valley in 1986 included two at Glens Falls, a ten-round decision (his first) against James

"Quick" Tillis on May 3 and a first-round knockout of Marvis Frazier on July 26; in Albany (first-round TKO of Dave Jaco on January 10), and Troy (Jesse Ferguson, TKO in the sixth on May 3, and William Hosea, first round knock-out on June 28). He never fought in the Hudson Valley again.

Tyson's rise and the demons he dealt with were a paradigm for the African American experience generally—great potential buffeted and harmed by outside forces. The Great Migration was a collective effort at improving lives in the face of intolerable prejudice and the backlash over having come from the South. Another highly pronounced "migration" of people of color into the Hudson Valley, and of a completely different sort, involved the state prisons and the Rockefeller drug laws. Crime was not limited to the poor, the downtrodden, or the minorities here or elsewhere, yet young blacks and Hispanics were incarcerated in much greater proportions than whites. A kind of cynical pattern developed with the arrest of (mostly) low-level drug dealers in the New York metropolitan area and their incarceration for years in prisons upstate. This was not an upstate-downstate issue because the country folk— or at least their assemblymen and senators—welcomed the jobs that came with all the new prisons that needed to be built. The city folk thought they were getting a safer city. The pattern translated to urban centers in the Valley as well, fueled by district attorneys for whom convictions meant votes and news-paper editors who loved the lurid details of high-profile cases.

The noble experiment of agricultural work for prisoners, begun at Wallkill in 1932 and expanded into individual programs at other correctional facilities, had fallen before a more hard-edged embrace of incarceration as the most appropriate prison model. The prison's relationship to the local community became more protective as a greater emphasis on medium-to-maximum incarceration became necessary.

When David Miller (b. 1942) came into the prison's education division as director of programs at Eastern and Green Haven, he had considerable experience working with juveniles. There were eighteen prisons or correctional facilities within an hour's drive of Miller's New Paltz home that delivered rehabilitation services for hundreds of young boys caught up in crime. He began at the Highland State Training School in the mid-1960s. Other schools for delinquents were located at Otisville in Orange County, Red Hook in Dutchess, and Hudson and Claverack in Columbia County. After serving as head of programs at Green Haven and Eastern, Miller was appointed first deputy superintendent at Shawangunk, superintendent at Wallkill and Eastern, and finally hub supervisor for eight institutions in the mid-Hudson area.

Women's services were focused on the Bedford Hills facility in Westchester County, where high-profile white inmates like Jean Harris and Kathy Bowdoin carried a kind of star power when they arrived, and time worked to provide opportunities like college study and nursery programs for African American inmates. Harris (b. 1923), convicted of murdering Scarsdale diet doctor Herbert Tarnover following a sensational trial in the fall of 1980, started GED and college programs at Bedford Hills, taught a parenting class, and developed a nursery for pregnant inmates. She was granted clemency by Governor Mario Cuomo while awaiting heart surgery, on December 29, 1992.

A national dialogue about prison conditions and practices was underway since the state's botched effort to end an inmate standoff at the Attica Correctional Facility in 1971. The changes that were emerging represented the cyclical process that prison reform had reflected over the course of the state's history, as well as the governor's simple need for either more beds or fewer prisoners. The state had few counseling or workshop programs at the time, and only a few Quaker worship groups within the system. Hutteran Brethren ministers focused on capital punishment in particular, patiently lobbying Albany every session in an attempt to influence state legislation. Attica prisoners were transferred to other facilities around the state, including the maximum facility at Green Haven near Stormville in Dutchess County, where new ideas were already being tried. Carl Berry, the deputy superintendent for programs and an African American, reached out to the men for their own thoughts and ideas, and found that college-level education opportunities and more calls home to the family were the priorities. The Community on the Move vocational program at Green Haven included Leroy Lewis, convicted of a 1955 murder-robbery, whose term was commuted after he saved the life of an officer experiencing a seizure in 1973.

Green Haven was similar to other prisons in its lack of adequate supervision and even protection for the men incarcerated there. Loan-sharking was common, drugs readily available, and gambling prevalent. The facility's senior chaplain, Ed Muller, had created a program called Think Tank in 1968 that involved the men themselves in developing programs and services. Roger Whitfield, Larry White and, after his arrival in 1972, Eddie ("Easy Eddie") Ellis were among the leaders. With Attica in their shadows now, Green Haven

Think Tank aligned with the Quaker Project on Community Conflict and Larry Apsey (1901?–1997), a Red Hook resident and Harvard lawyer who had turned to nonviolence work and civil rights after a career as a tough corporate counsel for Raytheon, a defense contractor, and Celanese, a chemical company. Apsey brought in Bernard Lafayette, an aide to the Rev. Martin Luther King, and Steve Stalones, for the first workshop in March 1975. The program concentrated on incarcerated youths and how they could respond nonviolently to the provocative conflicts and stresses of ordinary life.

Ellis called Apsey "a magnet and a ball of energy" who "made it all happen." The model project developed at Green Haven resulted in the Alternatives to Violence Program, a three-day intensive workshop, twelve hours each day, with some "unheard of" amenities for the participating prisoners, like being counted outside their cells and eating meals during the workshop sessions. The AVP approach sought to "re-humanize" these "inmates" into "incarcerated men" or "people in prison" utilizing a range of positive-reinforcement approaches that redefined their attitudes toward society, and to some extent how society viewed them.

AVP programs developed in most of the state prisons, including Otisville, Greene, Ellenville, Sing Sing, and Bedford Hills in the Hudson Valley, and expanded into more than thirty states and fifty countries worldwide. Similar programs were developed for at-risk schools and communities. The Community Justice Center was created by the AVP in Harlem in the 1990s. Medgar Evers College, a part of the City University of New York, developed the Center for NuLeadership on Urban Solutions, the only academic center at a major university run by formerly incarcerated men and women. Easy Eddie became an adjunct CUNY lecturer and executive director of the center.

Charles Piera (1940–2012), a young, dedicated professional, came to Eastern Correctional Facility to run a literacy program in the late 1970s. He went on to establish a college program, work with inmates in solitary, and become Eastern's Supervisor of Volunteer Services. His talents and facility with Spanish also made him the team leader of the prison district's Crisis Intervention Team. Eastern was modernized into a maximum security facility in the early 1980s, but continued with new programs. Piera pioneered one for tutoring inmates to obtain their high school equivalency diplomas, which led to the development of higher education programs with SUNY New Paltz and Ulster County Community College. He credited Dave Miller with leading the post-Attica reforms while superintendent at Eastern. "They produced a model that changed the idea of a maximum security prison," Piera said. The incidence of gangs, drug dealing and assaults diminished over these years.

A strike by prison guards across the state in April 1979 created an emergency situation for Governor Hugh Carey, who called out the National Guard and later employed state troopers at prisons. The 1,800 inmates at Green Haven in Stormville responded almost immediately in a positive fashion to the 210th Armored Division watching over them. At Coxsackie, which housed 700 young men between 16 and 21 years of age, complaints poured forth about the 239 correctional officers the 254 guardsmen replaced. The inmates had had extra long lock-up time, a lack of programs and recreation, and often missed a meal a day.

Piera's Crisis Intervention Unit was called to diffuse an uprising at the Greene Correctional Facility in Coxsackie in the summer of 1988. A four-day melee ensued when inmates, frustrated and pent up with overcrowding and a very hot summer, took over the solitary confinement unit and assaulted some of the guards. The CIU came in and calmed the situation, getting the inmates back to their cellblocks without further trouble. Similar incidents drew the team to Sing Sing and, in a predawn raid, to a state facility on the Arthur Kill in Staten Island.

Piera saw the dramatic rise in the prison populations of minorities and the evolution of what amounted to a prison industry as results of the punitive drug laws and a failed war on drugs in the 1970s. The population grew from 21,000 in 1979 to almost 67,000 in 1994, most of the new additions nonviolent, non-white offenders from the metropolitan area. As Assemblyman Daniel Feldman, chair of the corrections committee, pointed out, city voters ignored the racist underpinnings of New York's drug laws as necessary concessions to the protections they felt with the bad guys in jail, and upstate voters looked away because the new prisons meant jobs for many of their families. Other factors also influenced this growth, notably a rise in conservative values in political thinking among both Democrats and Republicans, and the public and media's continuing reaction to incidents of crime and violence.

Innovative programming such as higher education for inmates were seen in two lights, as progressive thinking in reengaging former inmates into civilian life and as unjust perquisites for dregs of society who did not deserve it. Yet Bard College's Prison Initiative for inmates at five upstate prisons to secure a higher degree—established in 2001—became the largest such program in the nation, with 300 prisoners participating and twenty-five bachelor's degrees awarded in 2014, a quarter of them in mathematics. The program received the early support of administrators like Deputy Superintendent Jean King at Woodbourne and turned out men more ready to face the real world when released. One of the Woodbourne benefits was a fresh vegetable garden to supplement the bland, pre-frozen and often undernourished food inmates were used to there.

Governor Rockefeller's Narcotics Addiction Control Commission was based on the principles and teachings of the Synanon and Daytop rehabilitation movements and included an education division within the prison system. The governor turned punitive toward the system with the introduction of new, harsher drug laws. Investments in rehabilitation and early release programs returned as Governor Cuomo's focus as the prison population expanded and the legislature, after the expensive maxis, refused funding for more prison cells. Some of the programs were developed using urban development bonds originally planned for low-income housing. With George Pataki's arrival as governor in 1995, the death penalty was restored by a largely jubilant legislature, two expensive "maxi-maxi" prisons were built, and a "three-strikes-you're-out" law requiring life sentences for a third felony conviction —harkening back to the punitive practices of the 1920s—was enacted. The maxis were designed to house "the worst of the state" in more secure institutions away from the general population. The Hudson Valley was graced with one of these 600-bed prisons (expanded to 900 in 2005) on the grounds of the Wallkill prison and named Shawangunk for the mountain ridge in which it nestled. Raymond Cunningham arrived there as a watch commander in 1985.

The prison population peaked at 72,500 in 2005, an increase of more than 50,000 over a mere twenty years due to convictions under the Rockefeller drug laws. The cost of the prison industry in New York rose from $250 million to $2.6 billion. The population consisted of 55% African Americans and 30% of various Hispanic origins. In time, "good leadership" (in David Miller's words) and innovative programs like Boot Camp and a ninety-day merit program for nonviolent parole violators contributed to a population reduction to 58,000 by 2010. Releases due to 2007 Rockefeller law revisions were initially "negligible" in influencing that number, Miller noted.

H. Rap Brown (Jamil Abdullah Al-Amin, b. 1943), one of the Attica inmates transferred downstate, was the quarterback for a football game between

Eastern inmates and New York City police officers. Brown was serving five years for a robbery in New York City. The team also played city firemen at Eastern. Competitive games were held from time to time with local teams—basketball at Coxsackie, baseball at Eastern among others—and sports figures at times visited the prisons in exhibition games. Babe Ruth was said to have hit his longest ball ever—620 feet over the wall, according to Dave Miller—in a game against inmates at Sing Sing.

Meanwhile, the Hutterian Brethren, a 350-member Christian community on a 190-acre Ulster County farm, lobbied against death penalty laws and visited inmates and helped the families of those facing the penalty. The community—another was established on Platte Clove at the former New York City Police Academy—practiced a life of simplicity and prayer that, unlike their cousins the Amish, accepted modern conveniences like electricity and automobiles. Jehovah's Witnesses, Seventh Day Adventists and other evangelical and Pentecostal faiths also became involved in prison programs.

One of the high-profile cases that influenced the state's approach to the courts and corrections involved Willie Bosket (b. 1962) and two vicious murders that he committed when fifteen years old. The crimes led to the enactment of the Juvenile Offender Act of 1978, which allowed children as young as thirteen to be tried and sentenced as adults for crimes such as murder. Bosket assaulted two guards while in prison, one a stabbing at Shawangunk in the early 1990s. The knifing incident was particularly egregious because his victim, as Raymond Cunningham described him, was a "very nice guy" who often worked to make life easier for his inmates.

District attorneys and city presses fed off each other's needs—voter attention for the politicians and sales of newspapers for editors—in daily incantations on the progress of the most violent cases. Rarely did a DA ever admit a mistake; someone always had to pay. Cases against high-profile (white) criminals like Gary McGivern (1944–2001) and mob hitman Harold "Kayo" Konigsberg (b. 1922) were similarly pursued across the front pages, often for months at a time. McGivern and Charles Culhane, who were serving long prison terms for an armed robbery in which two police officers were wounded, escaped from custody a few miles south of New Paltz on the New York State Thruway while being transferred to a court in White Plains in 1968. Deputy Sheriff William Fitzgerald was killed after his gun was wrestled from him, along with a third inmate, Robert Bowerman, whom McGivern and Culhane claimed did the killing. The other guard, Joseph Singer, said that all three were involved in the escape and McGivern killed Fitzgerald. After three trials, the pair was convicted of felony murder in 1982.

The case took on some unusual aspects. The Ulster County Legislature attempted unsuccessfully to recoup the trial costs by instituting a lawsuit against Westchester County for negligence in provided adequate security, but was unsuccessful. Harry Thayer used his WGHQ "Editorial of the Air" format to lambaste the juries for "Lace-Panty Justice" in failing to immediately convict the defendants. He called for the death penalty when they were convicted after the second trial, and they spent thirty-three months on death row in Green Haven Correctional Facility. A Court of Appeals ordered a new trial in 1973, citing among other things "substantial questions of credibility" in the prosecution's case. The third trial resulted in the convictions and a life sentence. In each of the trials, Bowerman's previous escape attempts were suppressed from the jury and no fingerprint evidence presented. McGivern passed two polygraph tests in his defense in 1979. The Green Haven chaplain recommended clemency, as did Lieutenant Governor Mario Cuomo. Meanwhile, Marguerite Culp, the editor of the *Woodstock Times,* led a highly publicized effort to secure McGivern's pardon that involved notables such as William F. Buckley, Jr., Allen Ginsberg, and Pete Seeger as sponsors of a defense fund. Clemency was granted by Governor Cuomo in a controversial New Year's Eve decision in 1985. The case went before a three-member panel of the Parole Board, which denied the request partly on the basis of strenuous Republican Party opposition to it, and then before the full board, which approved it. McGivern was paroled in March 1989. He and Culp married at Green Haven in 1978 and divorced in 1991. In 1994, he was arrested on a drug charge, a parole violation, and sent back to prison, where he died of cancer in 2001.

Organized crime touched the Valley in different ways over the years. The Senate Committee to Investigate Crime and Interstate Commerce, chaired by Senator Estes T. Kevaufer of Tennessee, conducted high-profile hearings in 1950–51 that were televised over WPIX in New York. Mobster Frank Costello (1891–1973) appeared at the Ballston Spa courthouse in August 1952 in response to a subpoena issued by a special grand jury investigating mob money in the nightclub business in Saratoga County.

Governor Harriman used the organized crime influence at harness racing tracks in running for governor, but did not pursue the issue further once elected.

This came back to haunt him in his race against Nelson Rockefeller when sixty-five Mafia figures, including three heads of families, were arrested in a raid in Apalachin in 1957. Harriman's failure to act was a factor in his defeat.

Some of the more successful "bad guys" in the criminal world identified with the Hudson River Valley, as had the robber barons of yore, as places to establish elaborate second homes and live quietly among the locals. Mount Kisco Police Chief William J. Nelligan once boasted to author Alex Shoumatoff that, except for Peekskill or Ossining, his town had the highest concentration of criminals in Westchester County, but they did their crimes elsewhere. Shady characters in Saugerties included Brooklyn longshoreman leader Anthony Scotto and the Persicos, Alphonse ("Alley Boy"), Teddy, and brother Carmine ("The Snake"). Scotto (b. 1934) was a noted labor figure in the 1970s, a contributor to Hugh Carey's gubernatorial campaign and Mario Cuomo's 1977 New York City mayor's race, and was under consideration as secretary of labor under President Jimmy Carter. The FBI eventually identified him as a made member of the Carlo Gambino crime family. His trial on racketeering charges in 1979 revealed his bribery of dockside businessmen, including one who built a swimming pool cabana for Scotto at his Highwoods estate for nothing. Local contractors routinely had their pick-up trucks searched by the FBI before entering the estate.

Kayo Konigsberg and Anthony ("Tony Pro") Provenzano (1917–1988) were convicted of murdering a Teamsters rival of Provenzano's in 1961. Provenzano, secretary-treasurer of Teamsters Local 550 and an occasional golfing partner of President Nixon, was identified as a captain of the Genovese crime family. Carmine Persico was reputedly the Colombo family crime boss for twenty-five years. The family's Blue Mountain "Mafia house," as it was called, became locally famous for the spectacular Christmas light displays each year. The estate also had a lost grave in its woods, but not from some unfriendly "hit"; this was the farm where Captain Jeremiah Snyder and his sons were abducted by Tories and Indians in 1778 and where Snyder was buried. Federal and state law enforcement converged on the upstate Persicos in May 1972 and arrested four family members, notably Alley Boy, in connection with the shooting of gangster "Crazy Joey" Gallo in New York City. A massive federal indictment in 1981 led Alphonse and Carmine into seclusion. Alphonse was captured in 1986, sentenced to forty-five years upon conviction, and died three years later of throat cancer. Carmine ran the family from prison for years, but stepped down in 1996 following a brutal mafia war with a rival family. Carmine's son Alfonse ("Little Alley Boy") became the family leader until convicted in 2007, with former crime underboss John ("Jackie") DeRoss, for arranging the murder of another mobster, William ("Billy Fingers") Cutulo, in 1999. One of the capos involved in the 1991–92 war, Joseph ("Joe T.") Tomesallo, went into hiding when the indictments came down and was captured in 1998 in Catskill.

An unusual case emerged in Poughkeepsie on November 28, 1987, when a sixteen-year-old girl was found in Wappingers Falls after four days of being absent, claiming to her family that she had been sexually assaulted by six white men over that time period. One of them, she said, had a police badge. The lurid details and her appearance when found turned the incident into a national sensation. She was found partly wrapped in a plastic bag, her hair chopped off and her body smeared with feces.

The allegation became a sensation when two black lawyers, C. Vernon Mason and Alton H. Maddox, Jr. (b. 1945), and an activist and confrontational minister, Alfred Charles "Al" Sharpton, Jr. (b. 1954), came to the defense of Brawley and began accusing local officials of racism in the case. "We beat this, we will be the biggest niggers in New York," Sharpton was quoted as having said by a former aide, Perry McKinnon, in testimony before a grand jury.

The case unfolded on three levels, the incendiary actions and statements of Brawley's handlers and their supporters and the reactions to them by local and state officials, a veritable storm of regional media attention emphasizing the racial aspects of the case, and the slow accumulation of facts that ultimately proved Brawley's undoing.

Tawana Brawley was a cheerleader and track team member in high school. Her mother, Glenda Brawley, had a common-law relationship with Ralph King, 40, a man with a violent past. He had killed his first wife in 1970 and was still on parole after serving a prison term for manslaughter. As the information developed, it became apparent that the young woman's claims were not holding up. She said she was taken into the woods and sodomized for four days, yet the temperatures were in the low 20s during that time and it rained "one entire night." She had also called a friend during those days. A similar case was discovered dating eighteen months prior that might have served as a model for her claims. King's van was seen outside the Wappingers

Falls apartment where she claimed to be held for three of the four days.

Mason, Maddox, and Sharpton at first focused their attack on the Dutchess County district attorney, William Grady, who withdrew from the case in January 1988. County Judge Judith A. Hillery named Poughkeepsie attorney David Saul as special prosecutor, but he soon resigned, along with his assistant, attorney William T. Burke. Rallies by 200 supporters of the Dutchess County Commission Against Racism in Poughkeepsie and 1,200 protestors in Newburgh called for a special prosecutor to be named by Governor Cuomo. The Rev. Louis Farrakhan (b. 1933), head of the Nation of Islam, spoke at the Newburgh rally.

Cuomo ordered a joint law enforcement task force to investigate the case. On January 26, he appointed the state attorney general, Robert Abrams (b. 1938), as special prosecutor. The appointment was termed "unacceptable" by Maddox, who wanted Charles Hynes (b. 1935), the special prosecutor in a 1986 racially motivated murder case in Howard Beach. Abrams named John Ryan, his best staff prosecutor and the head of the Crime Prosecution Unit, to lead the investigation. A dozen investigators from Abrams office began work on the case on February 3.

The governor met with ten black ministers who came up to Albany from the mid-Hudson with an appeal for assistance and a message from Brawley delivered by the Rev. Saul Williams of Newburgh. In a bizarre twist, Cuomo also talked with Maddox, Mason, and Sharpton on a Manhattan call-in radio show for more than twenty minutes, "a dramatic on-air exchange" according to *The New York Times*. Three hundred and fifty more rallied at Newburgh on January 31. Students in local colleges demonstrated. Representative John Conyers (b. 1929) weighed in, as did Congressman Hamilton Fish, Jr., who called for a national commission on racism.

As questions began to arise over Brawley's story, the media frenzy increased. The *Poughkeepsie Journal* published a sensational nine-page spread on February 14. Alan Chartock, publisher of the *Legislative Gazette* in Albany, called Farrakhan "one of the invisible 'elephants' on the table in this case." Chartock implied that Maddox and Mason did not want Abrams as prosecutor because he was Jewish. A dozen local, regional, and national media had reporters working the case. *The New York Times* assigned up to seven writers, led by Robert D. McFadden, and in the end produced a book provocatively entitled *Outrage: The Story behind the Tawana Brawley Hoax.*

Incidents of race hatred and racist crimes increased. On November 10, the Midchester Jewish Center in Yonkers was vandalized with swastikas and "Heil Hitler" slogans painted on walls. Temple Beth Ann in Yorktown Heights was similarly vandalized on January 18, 1988. On December 31, Daniel Pantola, a dark-skinned Hispanic, was attacked by a dozen white youths outside a hot dog emporium in Yonkers. An active KKK group accosted and hurled racial epithets at a black state senator in February 1988.

Actor Bill Cosby and *Essence* publisher Ed Lewis offered a $25,000 reward for the identity of Brawley's assailants. The Greater Newburgh NAACP offered $2,500 for information on Brawley's whereabouts from November 24-28, 1987. On February 16, a bit belated given the pace of events, former heavyweight champion Mike Tyson, his wife Robin Givens, and the flamboyant promoter Don King arrived in separate stretch black limousines in Wappingers Falls to meet Brawley. Tyson gave her $50,000 toward college, and King, who wore a full-length white mink coat, did the same.

Governor Cuomo and DA Abrams were exceptionally patient in handling the tinderbox of relations with Brawley's lawyers. Abrams had eight lawyers and twelve investigators on the case. A special hotline was established to take calls. The governor set aside $500,000 for a new civil rights unit in the attorney general's office and convened a meeting of district attorneys about the unit and penalties for bias-related crimes. Following a three-hour meeting with the governor on February 13, 1988, the lawyers agreed to Brawley's testifying before a grand jury, but the agreement fell apart four days later, despite twelve more hours of talks, because of conditions placed on trial tactics by Maddox, Mason, and Sharpton.

The pattern was beginning to play against the attorneys. On February 9, Abrams spoke with NAACP lawyer George Hairston, who had represented the family during the first few weeks before Maddox and Mason were brought in. Hairston called Maddox's position—by now hardlined against any cooperation—as "ludicrous." Governor Cuomo and Jesse Jackson had a long telephone conversation on March 1, after which Jackson refused to get involved. Assemblyman Roger Green (b. 1949), a respected black legislator from Brooklyn, criticized the tactics of Brawley's lawyers. Laura Blackbourne, an NAACP lawyer, accused them of exploiting the girl on the NBC television "News 4orum" show. Charles J. Hynes, the lawyer whom Maddox originally wanted on the case, harshly criticized them over their actions.

"I think they're only going to deny justice to this kid," he said. "I don't understand it." Conrad Lynn, 80, the black lawyer on the Scottsboro Boys case fifty years earlier who had worked with Maddox on the death of Jimmy Lee Bruce by an Ellenville guard in 1968, called the handlers' actions "devious maneuvering."

Suddenly, on March 14, 1988, Brawley's handlers switched tactics and abruptly called for the arrest of assistant Dutchess County district attorney Steven Pagones as the alleged "police" person involved in Brawley's assault. No evidence supported the allegation, which Governor Cuomo termed "an extremely ugly charge." The case eventually led to a $30 million defamation suit filed by Pagones in 1991, wherein State Supreme Court Judge Ralph Beisner of Poughkeepsie ruled that Brawley had inflicted emotional distress on him by her false claim. Of the $385,000 awarded Pagones in the case, only Sharpton's $38,000 share was paid.

By then, the case was over, Brawley having been proved to have fabricated the incident in testimony before a grand jury. The twenty-three-member jury issued a 170-page report that fall. The former Sharpton aide, Perry McKinnon, testified that the advocates had no evidence in support of Brawley's claims and instead determined to focus the case "about Mason, Maddox, and Sharpton taking over the town." McKinnon's statements were corroborated by another former aide, Simeon Kitt. The grand jury findings were leaked to the press—apparently by the FBI—further fueling the frenzy.

Information that came out over time only confirmed the findings. In April 1989, Brawley admitted to a boyfriend that she concocted the story out of fear of her stepfather, whom she said was "hitting on her." Tawana moved to Virginia Beach, changed her name to Maryann Muhammed, and briefly attended Howard University on the money that had been given to her.

Glenda Brawley was convicted of obstruction of justice and given a thirty-day jail sentence by a Poughkeepsie court. She fled the state. Maddox and Mason were brought up on charges, their cases proceeding through the courts until 1990, when Maddox's suspension as a lawyer was upheld and Mason was disbarred (for reasons unrelated to this case). As for Sharpton, who had accompanied Brawley to Howard University and remained closely in touch with her in the early years following the scandal, his prestige rose when he ran for mayor of New York City in a 1992 Democratic primary and garnered a respectable 166,665 votes. Yet as late as May 2011 he was still defending his actions in Poughkeepsie in a television interview.

"I have thought about that a million times," he told "60 Minutes Extra." "I just don't believe they treated this case fairly."

In his 1990 review of the *Times'* book *Outrage*, David J. Garrow cautioned his readers that "larger truths about American racism are in no way disproved simply because one accidentally designated symbol of black suffering became caught up in a huge falsehood." Anthropologist Stanley Diamond struck a similar note in an article by Jeff Jones of Albany in *The Nation* in 1988, stating that "it may be too much of the white community to excuse the Brawley deceit; but they misunderstand it at their peril."

43. Saving Storm King

We've got a fight on our hands."

—JAMES CAGNEY, *Sports Illustrated*,
February 22, 1965

Storm King Mountain, forty miles north of New York City and at 1,355 feet the tallest and northernmost of the Hudson Highlands west of the Hudson, exhibited such a brooding presence over the river in the nineteenth century that it inspired Nathaniel Parker Willis into changing its name from sedate "Butter Hill," a throwback to its pastoral eighteenth century aspect. In 1885, much of the mountain was purchased by James Stillman (1850–1918), the president of what would become Citibank, as a power move to rival snobbish Tuxedo Park, which Pierre Lorillard IV was creating to the southeast. Stillman's wealth had not attained the maturity that the Lorillards expected of their friends, and the banker's dream of a grand estate on the mountain terraces was never realized. Black Rock Forest, a part of his holdings, was gifted to Harvard University after Stillman's death, and some of the property dedicated to the Palisades Interstate Parkway Commission.

Stillman was, along with William Rockefeller, one of the organizers of the Consolidated Gas Company, the predecessor of Consolidated Edison of New York. In 1962, once Indian Point Unit #1 was operational at Buchanan, Con Ed set into motion a plan to use Storm King for hydroelectric pumped storage as a supplement during peak demand times in the summer. The Storm

King site was suggested by the chief engineer at Central Hudson Gas & Electric, which planned a smaller pumped-storage plant for Breakneck Ridge across the river. "No difficulties are anticipated," Con Ed chairman Harmland Forbes said in announcing the project on September 26, 1962, yet what ensued was one of the most difficult and protracted arguments in the Valley's history—whether or not Storm King Mountain should be used for industrial purposes or saved for recreation.

Modern environmentalism began with the Storm King fight, although an awareness of the importance of conserving the Hudson Valley environment was already established in pockets along the river, along with some adamant advocates, years before Storm King came on the horizon. Theodore Cornu, a noted Croton illustrator and canoe maker, kept a watchful eye on Croton Point and western Westchester County in the decades after 1920. As a conservationist, he hunted "the biggest offenders'"—the railroad, the landfill, the highway builders, and Consolidated Edison. Cornu organized Hudson Valley Echoes, a league of conservation-minded residents concerned with quality and the environment along the river.

Following the success of the PIPC in saving the Palisades, a Hudson River Conservation Society (originally called the Hudson River Society) was formed in 1936 by William Church Osborn (1862–1951) and others to save the Hudson Highlands from continued demolition by quarrying companies. Maxwell Anderson used the theme in his popular Broadway play, *High Tor* (1936), which raised consciousness about protecting the lower Valley's mountain landscapes. The new society—which included garden clubs, hikers, and historical groups—raised funds to purchase lands that were threatened; Laurance Rockefeller and Carl Carmer were among its leaders. Saving Boscobel was one of their projects. This stately neoclassical home built over 1804–08 and originally located in Montrose in Westchester County began as the country seat of Staats Morris Dyckman (1755–1806), a loyalist clerk in the quartermaster general's department with the English during the American Revolution. The effort resulted in its physical removal to a safer and highly scenic site north of Breakneck Ridge.

At a Hudson River Valley Conference called in 1946 to bring attention to the region's needs, historian Evarts B. Greene pointed out that the landscape of the Hudson Highlands was "a historical document," as David Stradling wrote in 2008, in that it held the geography of important aspects of American history. Greene also drew an early connection between conservation and heritage protection by noting the support that statewide historical societies expressed for protecting the Highlands.

Even Robert Moses weighed in, although not in a friendly way. In a 1947 talk before the National Conference of State Parks at Bear Mountain, he emphasized the need for recreation resources only. He criticized protecting "the mansion where Washington slept" as impractical when it came to delivering state recreational services, and opposed limiting recreational development in the Adirondack and Catskill Parks.

As the Storm King case began, other attempts to address protections for the Highlands were made. A Hudson River Valley Commission, created by Governor Rockefeller in 1966, called for "commercial, industrial and other economic development" to be "consistent with the preservation and rehabilitation of the natural, scenic, historical, and recreational resources of the Hudson Riverway." The Commission, which was based at Iona Island (now a part of the Palisades Interstate Park), was charged with reviewing any projects within a mile of the river or within view of the river and within two miles distant. Their approach remained narrowly scenic-based, however, not environmental. The staff included an ecologist and organic chemist but was made up mainly of architects, engineers, and public finance specialists. A Rockefeller Foundation study of the Hudson Basin in the 1970s—based on ecology instead of the HRCS's viewshed approach or Moses's recreational theme—pointed to a diverse list of environmental constraints that needed addressing, the first of which concerned controlling urban sprawl.

Con Ed applied to the Federal Power Commission in January 1963 for a license to construct a 2,000-megawatt pumped storage facility with an 800-foot-long power house at the base of Storm King Mountain, a reservoir a mile wide in a depression behind the mountain, fifteen miles of transmission lines across Putnam and Westchester counties, and appurtenant structures. The proposal included a tunnel from the river to the top of the mountain—forty inches in diameter and two miles long—to pump six million gallons of river water a day to the reservoir and discharge it back into the river through electric generating turbines in the tunnel. The power would come into play when overloads threatened brownouts or worse in the metropolitan area, usually during the hottest summer days. The 240-acre reservoir would sit in a (modified) natural basin between White Horse Mountain and Mount Misery—part of it in the Black Rock Forest. The project was expected to take five years and cost $162 million.

Cornwall-on-Hudson Mayor Michael "Doc" Donahue had become an advocate after a briefing in the summer of 1962 at Central Hudson's Newburgh office. His village would have to sacrifice its reservoir, but Con Ed would pay for a new one and the village would receive at least $1 million a year in new tax revenues, more than half the annual budget needs. Donahue met with Buchanan Mayor William Burke, where the nuclear complex accounted for $34 million of the village's $38 million in assessed value, and learned that a host of new amenities had come to Buchanan as a result of the complex. Other local politicians also saw economic benefits for their communities in the Storm King project.

Problems arose with the PIPC chairman, Laurance Rockefeller, who objected to having the riverside facilities on the park's side of Storm King, and with General William Westmoreland (1914–2005), the superintendent at West Point, whose concerns focused on the transmission lines' interjection into the normal helicopter route to the academy and potential effect on approach lanes to Stewart Air Force Base. William Osborn, president of the Hudson River Conservation Society and a brother of PIPC commissioner Frederick Osborn and, more fortuitously, a neighbor directly across the way in Garrison, opted to support the project if the transmission lines were removed. That was consistent, he reasoned, with the Society's interest in promoting the economic health as well as the conservation of the region, yet it would redound to his detriment as playing into the hands of the utility in the future. Relocating the lines added $6 million to the cost for a submarine cable. Con Ed agreed to all the terms and these potential major opponents were eliminated, including in Rockefeller a nationally known conservationist.

Part of Black Rock Forest would have to be submerged by the new reservoir, but Harvard did not offer substantial objections. The university had not pursued any programs for the property after receiving Stillman's gift, since it was too far from the Boston campus to be of much use. New York City's Bureau of Water Supply notified the utility that a construction permit would be needed to enter into the Catskill Aqueduct right-of-way. This would prove a difficult snafu later on but seemed harmless at the time.

Cornwall was promised $3 million in new water facilities, including a tap-in to the Catskill Aqueduct supply (twenty-three other towns already did that), plus a mile-long new waterfront with a park and visitor center for the facility. A requirement that any transferal of public reservoir lands be subject to local referendum was overcome by an obliging state legislature, which exempted Cornwall from the need. Con Ed also paid for their attorney, a total of $138,000 overall that represented a serious conflict of interest for the village at the time and only became public because of the dogged insistence of the *Times-Herald-Record.* The utility purchased the land and demolished most of the buildings at Cornwall Landing before applying for the permit.

The first visual rendition of the project appeared at a Con Ed stockholders meeting in May 1963, two months after the FPC issued notice of the license application. The public received some information about the plan at a March 7 meeting of a Citizens Committee for the Hudson Riverway in Nyack. Immediately, Cold Spring and Garrison property owners were annoyed that the transmission lines surfaced on their side of the river and ran for thirteen miles across Putnam County to a Niagara-Mohawk Power Company transmission link. The sheer size of the plan as visualized prompted the interest of Nature Conservancy director Walter Boardman and New York-New Jersey Trail Conference president Leo Rothschild, each of whom had been concerned that scenic sites in the Highlands were becoming threatened by industrial and commercial interests. Rothschild had cut his environmental teeth in working to save the scenic quality of the Palisades when the George Washington Bridge was built. The two men set about securing support among residents and local hiking, gardening, environmental and outdoor groups.

Hudson River historian Carl Carmer, hiker Robert Burnap, Boscobel restoration director Benjamin Frazier of Garrison, antiques dealer Virginia Guthrie, and advertising executive Harry Nees met with Boardman and Rothschild at Carmer's Irvington home on November 8, 1963, and created the Scenic Hudson Preservation Conference. Also joining early on were *Sports Illustrated* writer Robert H. Boyle and Frances "Franny" Reese of Dutchess County, who served at the helm of the organization through the 1970s and 80s.

Nelsonville manufacturer Alexander Saunders also joined the effort. Cornwall's "mountain people"—about twenty-five wealthy families with homes above the village—remained aloof because of the "euphoric" support below them for the project, except for Beatrice "Smokey" Duggan, whose mother had donated the reservoir to the village. Her husband Stephen (d. 1998), a Wall Street lawyer, became involved in the spring of 1964 when a neighbor asked him for help in Con Ed's interest in the well rights to his meadow.

In January, three weeks before the FPC examiner's hearings, Boardman secured a Washington lawyer, Dale C. Doty, a former FPC commissioner, to represent the Conference in requesting intervenor status. The utility had dismissed the group as "a few local dreamers" interested in their own "self-centered complaints" about recreation and aesthetics, but Doty's reputation and the interest of *The New York Times*, among other reasons, led the FPC examiner into granting status. Over the next few months, Doty and his few sponsors squared off in hearings against a phalanx of utility lawyers and the village of Cornwall backed by dozens of enthusiastic Orange County construction workers. The license was approved by the hearing examiner in June, setting the stage for a full review by the FPC commissioners in November.

Meanwhile, sympathy for the small band of opponents grew as a David-versus-Goliath scenario emerged. A month after the examiner's decision, members of the Hudson River Conservation Society, charging that the group had been "infiltrated" by the utility, reversed William Osborn's support and came out strongly against the proposal. The Conference received support from activists including Robert F. Kennedy and Pete Seeger, artists like Aaron Copland and James Cagney, and the Sierra Club and National Audubon Society. The effort took on national overtones when James Cope and a dogged researcher, William ("Mike") Kitzmiller, of Selvage, Lee and Howard uncovered flaws in Con Ed's plans, placed a sympathetic article in *Reader's Digest*, and had a flotilla of boats "surround" Storm King in September 1964, drawing the interest and cheers of the New York press corps. A *Newsweek* article on the flotilla led Stephan Currier of the Taconic Foundation to involve attorney Lloyd Garrison in the case.

A growing consciousness about how utilities kill fish and the consequences to commercial and recreational fishing made progress even more difficult for the utility. The issue was first raised in June 1963 when pilot and *Outdoor Life* writer Art Glowka and Dominick Pirone, a biologist for a sportsmen's organization, rowed to the Indian Point nuclear reactor and saw more than 10,000 dead fish in the water. Fish were drawn into the intake screens by powerful pumps, and scalded in the hot water returning to the river. The utility had been using two trucks to haul them to a dumpsite every day.

Con Ed and the state Department of Environmental Conservation denied the fish kills and remained insulated from criticism until Robert Boyle tracked down George Yellot, a Peekskill banker who had worked for the DEC and taken Polaroid photographs. Boyle, an experienced researcher and writer for *Sports Illustrated* since its fourth issue in 1954, had moved to Croton in 1960 to take up striper fishing, and got to know fishermen Charlie White and Ace Lent and his cousin Spitz Lent at Verplanck. The Lents were the Everett Nacks of Haverstraw Bay, colorful local seine fishermen whose knowledge of the river was legendary.

At his home at Finney Farm Boyle kept an aquarium with a striped bass, eel and other river fish in an aquarium that mimicked the bottom of the bay. In following the Indian Point lead, he quizzed Yellot about the fish kills. As the conversation ensued, Yellot reached into a drawer and produced a set of photographs. "You know," he said, referring to the agency's demand that he turn in the "duplicates" of the pictures, "they never asked me for triplicates."

Boyle set about determining where the fish spawned in the lower river. In the 1964 review that led to FPC approval, Con Ed relied on Alfred Perlmutter, a utility ichthyologist and New York University professor who testified that the last inquiry, in 1938, showed no striped bass spawning areas that far downstream. After the examiner recommended approval of the license, a colleague of Boyle's at the magazine handed him a seven-year-old *New York Fish and Game Journal* article that painted a completely different picture about the striped bass footprint in the Hudson River. The article was by two young biologists, Warren Rathjen and Lewis Miller, who had investigated the estuary in 1955 and found "the principal spawning area" (88.8% of all the eggs) lying over a seven-and-a-half mile stretch between Highland Falls and Denning's Point, with Storm King exactly in the middle. Boyle also learned that Rathjen and Miller had worked under Perlmutter, who signed their report. John Clark demonstrated that the information failed to consider the impact of tides on the kills, which accounted for another 35 percent in mortalities.

A Joint Legislative Committee on Natural Resources chaired by local Republican Assemblyman R. Watson Pomeroy began hearings two days after the FPC review, in November 1964, and heard that pumped storage was not the best way to achieve greater power at peak demand. Alexander Lurkis, a former chief engineer of the city's Bureau of Gas and Electricity, projected a savings of $132.5 million over fifteen years if the utility used gas turbines instead. Boyle announced his findings during the hearing and John Clark, a federal biologist, testified that Perlmutter's figures were in error, but the FPC issued the license anyway in early 1965. *The New York Times* then came out against the Con Ed plan.

Boyle's article, "A Stink of Dead Stripers," appeared in *Sports Illustrated* on March 26, 1965. By July, Scenic Hudson had filed suit in the federal Circuit Court of Appeals, working with Lloyd Garrison's bright young assistant, Albert Butzel. Kitzmiller created a cogent analysis of the Pomeroy hearings record, and Scenic Hudson used information from congressional subcommittee hearings on the fisheries issue in Yonkers in support of its argument. Garrison developed an argument that the scenery of the Hudson Highlands warranted greater attention under the provisions of the Federal Power Act, a novel idea at the time. On December 29, 1965, after more than 1,900 pages of testimony, the three-man panel reached a landmark decision that gave the citizen organization full standing in the proceedings and ordered new hearings. The "Storm King Doctrine" held that "injury to aesthetic or recreational values was sufficient to provide an aggrieved party with constitutional 'standing,'" an abrupt and historic blow to Con Ed's plans. The decision—some of it said to have been written by candlelight during the Northeast blackout on November 9—began with an evocation of Karl Baedeker's comparison of the Hudson River with the Rhine. The court chastised the FPC for not having examined the "need for preserving the area's unique beauty and historical significance, which the Federal Power Act required." The FPC also would have to consider the fisheries question since it had over-relied on Perlmutter's disputed testimony. Most devastating of all for the FPC, the court challenged its claim as the sole "representative of the public interest" and asserted that the commission was required to provide "active and affirmative protection" of that interest for all parties.

After the landmark Court of Appeals victory, Robert Boyle continued to go after polluters on the Hudson River. He discovered that two old federal laws—the New York Rivers and Harbors Act of 1888 and the Federal Refuse Act of 1899—prohibited dumping in the river and provided for half of any fines resulting to be given to those who reported violators. Boyle reported on these laws to a packed audience in Crotonville that had joined together to form the Hudson River Fishermen's Association. He was a damned good journalist and dogged researcher, yet his genius lay in his connection with the common man in pulling together the new organization. The standing-room-only meeting in the American Legion hall was packed with local fishermen, factory workers, carpenters, masons, and a lone individual who was astonished at what he saw: Westchester Congressman Richard Ottinger (b. 1929).

Ottinger canceled his appointments and immediately joined in the cause. The first target was New York Central Railroad, which had been dumping diesel and other oils into the river at least since 1929. The fishermen received their share of a $4,000 fine, printed up "Bag a Polluter" cards calling on ordinary people to let them know about pollution of the river, and grew in membership to more than 300.

Out of this effort came Hudson Riverkeeper, Inc., a potent new citizen police force that focused in particular on the relationship between the state regulating agency, the department of environmental conservation, and Indian Point fish kills. ("After you read this, destroy it so Riverkeeper doesn't get it," one internal DEC memorandum advised.) Boyle was the founding president of the organization and the pugnacious guardian spirit behind it.

"His was a bare-knuckled advocacy that used science and law as weapons and pitted people directly against polluters," John Cronin and Robert Kennedy Jr. wrote in the seminal history of the organization. "The organization reflects his philosophy and personality, and he was mentor to both of us."

Thomas Whyatt was appointed the first Riverkeeper in 1973 and established a people's monitoring program of river industries. Riverkeeper was funded initially by the association, as well as the Hudson River Conservation Society, Cortlandt Conservation Association, Hudson River Sloop Clearwater, and Scenic Hudson. Clearwater brought on Cronin and Karen Limburg of Vassar College as "River Rats" to track down polluters, and Cronin became Riverkeeper in 1983. Kennedy joined as prosecuting attorney a year later, and the two men established a clinic at Pace University Law School that used student interns to prosecute as many as forty lawsuits at a time. Their work was so successful that Westchester County Executive Andrew O'Rourke promised to use law clinic alumnae as advisors after the clinic forced the county to clean up a notorious storm sewer discharge problem at Croton.

Cronin made national headlines in catching an Exxon oil tanker dumping its bilge water in the Hudson. The exposure led to a new state law and a $3 million fine against the oil company. The advocate also kept the pressure on Indian Point, which was drawing up to 2.5 million gallons of Hudson River water a day to cool its two reactors, despite a study that showed that 1.2 billion eggs, larvae and fish were killed annually in the practice. Consolidated Edison plants also experienced serious fish kills—up to 40%—in their cooling processes. Riverkeeper attacked these practices throughout the 1990s, yet it was not until 2013 that the DEC required that Indian Point replace the "once-through cooling" process with a closed cycle system. Ninety-five percent of the kills were expected to be eliminated in this change, which included an order prohibiting any water draws during the spawning season.

In May 1966, the US Supreme Court refused to hear a challenge to the Storm King Doctrine decision. This was the first time a federal agency was required by a court to undertake a complete environmental review. The action led to the enactment of the National Environmental Policy Act (NEPA) by Congress in 1969, which required any federal agency to conduct a review on actions the agency funded or influenced. The Clean Air Act and Clean Water Act were also direct consequences of the Scenic Hudson decision.

Enter Nelson Rockefeller. The governor favored the utility's plan and had initially responded carefully to the objections that began to accumulate on his desk. In September 1964, his executive assistant, Alexander Aldrich, attempted to reassure Carmer and Rothschild that the project was not "basically objectionable." Aldrich cited the PIPC's successfully lobbying for an underwater river crossing of the power lines and orienting the plant, the reservoir and the retention structure in a less conspicuous fashion. The governor raised the potential jobs benefit, but Carmer and Rothschild replied that prob-ably no more than three hundred new jobs would be created, and most of those would have to be filled by out-of-state specialists. (In time, Con Ed itself awarded the contract to a California firm and hired skilled workers from outside New York State.) Nelson and Laurance's support never wavered, however, even though Nelson's second son, Steven, aligned himself against the project.

Storm King became intertwined with the general management question of the lower Hudson River corridor—and with Rockefeller holdings in Pocantico Hills—after Congressman Ottinger, whose district included Kykuit, entered the picture in Washington in 1965, the first year of "arguably the most productive [Congress] in American history." This was Ottinger's first year in the legislature, yet the Mamaroneck attorney had distinguished himself already as a founder and director of the Peace Corps. Ottinger, who had brought Mike Kitzmiller onto his staff, proposed legislation to create a Hudson Highlands National Scenic Riverway, which Rockefeller immediately termed "a federal power grab." The governor created his own Hudson River Valley Commission—with brother Laurance as chair—that included an array of regional notables, including the former governor, Averell Harriman, Vassar president Alan Simpson, Lowell

Thomas and IBM chairman Thomas J. Watson, Jr. As support for the Ottinger idea grew among regional congressmen, including Leo O'Brien (1900–82) of Albany, the governor responded with a commission plan for protecting the entire Hudson River corridor from the Adirondack Park to the Verrazano Narrows. His intention was quickly perceived, however; the day after the filing of the Senate bill on June 7, 1965, *Newsday* called the plan "an attempt . . . to forestall creation of a federal park along the lower Hudson from Newburgh to Nyack."

With Robert F. Kennedy sponsoring the legislation in the Senate, Ottinger's Hudson River Compact law was enacted in 1966 and subsequently used by US Secretary of the Interior Morris Udall to stop a Niagara Mohawk Power Company transmission line plan for across the river and an industrial development proposal for Veteran Administration property at Castleton. President Johnson had already called for a study on the feasibility of underground lines in this area; an unnamed high administration official termed the huge new transmission lines "raping the Hudson." In a 1968 report to the President, Udall proposed a tripartite commission (New York, New Jersey and the federal government) to decide upon sensitive Hudson River issues. Although Alexander Aldrich, now the executive director of the Hudson River Valley Commission, quickly welcomed Udall's recommendation, Governor Rockefeller, in addition to claiming that the plan "invites paralysis of development instead," objected because almost all of the Hudson and Mohawk rivers were in New York. Congress mandated that any major transportation department work avoid deleterious environmental impacts. Federal agencies were required to ensure coordination in any actions that might affect fish and wildlife, and Hudson River sturgeon were among the species protected in the Endangered Species Act.

The question of federal or state hegemony over Hudson River waters was compounded by the enforcement issue. US Attorney General John Mitchell criticized his New York office for using 1888–89 federal laws against industrial polluters Standard Brands of Peekskill and General Motors in Tarrytown. Two federal institutions—West Point and the Watervliet Arsenal—were among the major river polluters; who would police them?

The Rockefellers convinced Central Hudson to drop its Breakneck Ridge pumped storage plan, and had the 670-acre mountain purchased at the same $861,638 price Con Ed had paid for the property in 1963 by Jackson Hole Preserve (a Rockefeller interest)—which gave it to the state for the Hudson Highlands State Park. The issue became clouded by a 1965 governor's plan, long kept secret, to build a 47-mile-long six-lane expressway from Beacon to the city. The enabling legislation was pushed through the Senate and Assembly without a memorandum of support (a violation of the state constitution). The road would have bifurcated Tarrytown, North Tarrytown and Ossining—requiring the relocation of more than two hundred African American families—while avoiding Pocantico Hills. Four miles of the project required filling in part of the river; the entire 10.4-mile shoreline between Tarrytown and Crotonville would have been affected. A companion bill approved at the same time created a new Route 117 connection with Route 9A that relocated traffic away from the family estate, a pet project of Rockefeller's father since 1932. (This road was actually built.)

The US Department of the Interior, Hudson River fishermen, a new Citizens Committee of the Hudson Valley, the New York City Conservation Department, and 75 conservation organizations came out in opposition to the expressway, arguing among other points that its construction would seriously damage important breeding grounds for shellfish in the Hudson River. The newly organized state Department of Transportation—on the governor's team—approved the plan, following public hearings attended by 1,500 angry people. Conservationist furor over the Hudson River Valley Commission arose in its approval of the plan after taking testimony in which forty-one of forty-three speakers expressed opposition; *The New York Times* called the commission "the Hudson despoilers." One of the two who spoke in favor, Will Osborn, resigned a month later when 97% of the Conservation Society voted against the expressway. A Bureau of Outdoor Recreation report revealed that the Rockefellers would benefit from the expressway even though they were donating 165 acres of riverfront property; another 75 acres planned for commercial development was owned by the family.

Then a new twist developed. On May 3, 1968, as a result of a conference Rockefeller held with the federal staff, Secretary Udall quietly reversed his position and supported the expressway before reports were filed by his own task force and the US Army Corps of Engineers. He did not make his decision public at the time. "The whole thing was a matter of Laurance laying all his influence on the line," Udall later said of the pressure put upon him by the Rockefellers. When Udall's decision was made known in November (a month before he was to leave office), the Citizens Committee, the Sierra Club, and the village of Tarrytown went to federal district court and obtained an order preventing the engineers and state DOT from building dykes in the Hudson River to shore up the route. The Court of Appeals relied on an 1899 law forbidding dykes in navigable waters without congressional approval. New York attorney David Sive, who had also become involved in the FPC hearings on Storm King, successfully argued the case for the Sierra Club.

An attempt by state Attorney General Louis Lefkowitz to discredit the Citizens Committee in a subsequent appeal backfired in a ruling that emphasized the public's right to participate. Again, the US Supreme Court refused to hear an appeal of a Storm King order. By November 1971, after voters rejected a $2.5 billion transportation bond issue that included expressway monies, the governor declared the project "a dead issue."

In addition to his support for Storm King and a state takeover of Stewart Air Force Base, the governor created a power plant siting board that could overrule local zoning and jurisdictional matters. He pushed for a new bridge connecting Rye in Westchester County with Oyster Bay on Long Island. However, the studies done for the Rye bridge and other pro-growth initiatives supported by the governor were only marginally factual, relied on dated data and information, and projected costs that were either unrealistic or did not take all expenses into account. The governor attempted to mollify conservationists over a Metropolitan Transit Authority takeover of Stewart Airport by proposing an 8,000-acre preserve as a noise buffer for nearby communities. The MTA plan called for a footprint to accommodate 60 million passengers a year—three times as many as Kennedy International Airport—on five runways with parking for 88,000 cars and a high-speed rail connection to the city. The plan remained secret until accidentally revealed in 1972.

Meanwhile, the power commission resumed hearings in 1966 following the landmark Court of Appeals decision, and went ahead with the approval of the Storm King construction by a 2-to-1 vote. This time their action was upheld by the Court of Appeals. The supervisors of Cornwall, Highland Falls, Highland; Newburgh Mayor George F. McKneally; and Assemblyman Gordon K. Cameron were "enthusiastic" about the project going forward, but numerous obstacles remained. The cost had risen to over $183.5 million and the project had been in litigation since January 1963. Far from being exhausted, the Scenic Hudson Preservation Conference stepped up its advocacy into the "broadest aspects of conservation" by setting forth an agenda for acquiring and saving land, cleaning and restoring the Cornwall and Newburgh waterfronts, promoting tourism and conservation planning, and even suggesting that the West Point Foundry be saved and restored.

"I think Scenic Hudson should be the permanent watchdog of the Hudson," Robert Boyle wrote at the time. The organization had more than 15,000 contributors from fifty states and more than twenty countries by April 1968.

New York City came out against the project and moved for intervener status on October 25, 1968, because of its proximity to the Catskill Aqueduct crossing at the Moodna Tunnel—Con Ed precipitated the decision by offering to bury its powerhouse as a concession to the scenic Highlands argument. The FPC reopened the case on November 19; Con Ed moved to mollify the city by moving the power plant into the Palisades Interstate Park lands, prompting the PIPC to intervene in opposition. A year later, in December 1969, the hearing officer again recommended licensing and the FPC again issued one. The DEC issued water quality certification for the project in September 1971; the state Supreme Court revoked the certification the following March, and two months later the Appellate Division reinstated it. In time, the state Attorney General joined the case, the DEC, the Public Service Commission, the US Department of the Interior, and even the FPC staff, all for reopening hearings. Meanwhile, Stephen and Smokey Duggan, along with John Adams and a number of legal colleagues, established the Natural Resources Defense Council, with Stephen as chair and Adams as executive director. Over the next ten years the new think tank was turned into an national force for the environment.

The tide had turned in favor of the fish and the band of dedicated intervenors. In May 1974, the Court of Appeals ordered the FPC to conduct additional hearings on the fishing issue. Assemblyman Maurice D. Hinchey of Ulster County sponsored a key Hudson River Study Act in 1978 and new Hudson River Fisheries Management Program Act a year later, and on October 28, 1979, Boyle presented Hinchey and state wildlife pathologist Dr. Ward Stone with Clearwater's Environmental Quality Award—Stone for having brought new pesticide contamination to light. Stone and Hinchey would continue to work together—often frustrating Stone's own state agency—in exposing government acquiescence in industrial pollution, each becoming legendary among environmentalists, Native Americans and progressives in the process.

In 1979, Russell Train (1920–2012), a former EPA administrator and president of the World Wildlife Fund, volunteered to mediate the Storm King case. The case had now been joined by four other utilities, four public agencies, and dozens of environmental and recreational groups. Boyle was a key figure in developing the concessions that Train engineered in what came to be called the "Hudson River Peace Treaty." Frances Reese signed the document for Scenic Hudson on December 19, 1980. Consolidated Edison dropped the licensing effort, donated five hundred acres of Storm King for a park (in return for concessions at other power plants), and established a long-term $12 million fund to support Highlands and Hudson River fishing interests. By mid-2000, Hudson River Foundation for Science and Environmental Research-sponsored research had developed a library of hundreds of articles, reports and graduate school publications on education, public policy, history, and hard science on the resources and nature of the Hudson River.

The seventeen-year controversy did not end with Consolidated Edison's concessions at the river shore, since the case remained a hot one in the village. Con Ed turned its Cornwall Landing properties into a park and gave it to the village, which named it in September 1992 after Michael J. Donahue, the mayor whose support never wavered. An inscription in his memory was carved into a large black rock. In 2009, the other shoe dropped when the administration of Mayor Joseph Gross retrieved the other half of the rock from nearby Black Rock Forest and placed it near the first rock—but this one facing Storm King—with an inscription celebrating the defeat of Con Ed in the Storm King case. Arguments ensued all around.

44. "1-800-323-9262"

Let it ride!

—ERASTUS CORNING II to
Alan Chartock (1979)

The radio broadcast from Union College, on October 14, 1920, was heard as far away as Hartford, Connecticut. Wendell W. King, the engineer, was an experienced Army Signal Corps soldier and president of the Troy Amateur

Radio Club. King served in the Signal Corps during the war, returned to Union in January 1919, and remained until 1921. A youth from Troy who enrolled in Union in 1916, he was the first black student attending the college "for a significant length of time." King unwittingly provoked a wildcat strike involving 3,000 machinists when the college sent him to a summer job at General Electric. Machinists mistakenly believed that the young 09man was part of the new black migration from the South that Northern white workers deeply resented. The strike was not supported by the union, a mediator was brought in to settle the dispute, and GE insisted on keeping King, but the company moved him from the drill press operator's job he had and agreed to refrain from hiring newly migrated blacks.

King's broadcast initiated a regular weekly radio program at Union, nineteen days before KDKA of Pittsburgh broadcast the returns of the presidential race; a Detroit station was operating before either of these. The first portable receiver—"the progenitor, as it were, of the 'ghetto blaster'"—consisted of a "wireless baby carriage" powered by batteries and rigged with an early receiver. A newsreel company film of the contraption on the Union campus, with "a real baby, Marion D. Smith" (a Union graduate twenty-three years later), was seen across America and Europe. Union received a broadcast license for the call letters WRL in March 1922, but the license lapsed. The Union Broadcasting System was begun in 1941 and WRUC, the college's station, in 1947.

General Electric's WGY—which was heavily promoted by Martin Rice—went on the air on February 20, 1922, and within three years radio was assuming the venue for which it best survived into the new century, as a vehicle for local communities to air their interests. General Electric in time also owned WGFM, and created its own television station, WRGB, in 1939, although it had "broadcast" the first demonstration of television on January 13, 1928, into Ernst F. W. Alexanderson's home in Schenectady. The initials stood for Dr. W. R. G. Bates, a General Electric vice-president; the station's permanent home on Balltown Road in Niskayuna opened in 1957.

A Woodstock Show was conducted at Kingston's WDG2 radio station on January 8, 1925. The event was run by Boy Scouts at city hall and included piano pieces, English and Scottish ballads, and a rendition of Clarence Bolton's "The Overlook Blues." The performers enjoyed themselves immensely, but the show did not catch on with the network and was not repeated.

The inventor of frequency modulation was a Yonkers man, Edwin

Howard Armstrong (1890–1954), who built a makeshift antenna tower in his backyard while a youth, helped the US Signal Corps during World War I (he was awarded the French Legion of Honor in 1919), and was a millionaire by 1920. His difficulties with the RCA Corporation's preference for AM frequency broadcasting delayed the approval of FM by more than twenty years, and Armstrong committed suicide over the problem in 1954. A twelve-year lawsuit that he initiated ended when the US Supreme Court, apparently misreading the technical information, sided with RCA, although the company later paid for the patents in negotiations with Armstrong's widow. His Yonkers home was placed on the National Register of Historic Places in 1986, and then demolished.

AM radio caught up with the new youthful exuberance of the postwar times in stations like WABC in New York City, where the signals were directed north from the Empire State Building, filling the airwaves for more than a hundred miles into the Hudson Valley. "Cousin Brucie" Morrow (b. 1937) arrived in 1961 with the explosion in the new sounds of rock 'n' roll. Previously, as 45 rpm singles became available to teenagers, rhythm and blues, rockabilly, and early rock had supplanted the crooners of the 1940s. With the onset of the Baby Boom came a generation of young Americans with income to spare—$7 billion among 13 million teenagers in 1956, *Scholastic* magazine reported, 26% more than only three years earlier. The transition from 45s to 33 format, creating the album concept, arrived in the early 1960s and initiated another huge spurt in modern popular music.

Radio changed with General Electric's development of stereophonic broadcasting in 1961, prompting the Federal Communications Commission's approval of commercial stations. A 1966 FCC ruling requiring broadcasters in large cities to offer separate AM and FM programming gave rise to greater options and a wider array of music, ranging from country to rock and jazz and classical. WDST-FM in Woodstock went on the air on April 29, 1980, just as FM began eclipsing AM as the principal broadcasting milieu. WRRV in Middletown and WCZX in Hyde Park were among a group of similar, albeit more youth-oriented stations that Bruce Morrow and entrepreneur Robert F. X. Sillerman created during the same period.

In the late 1970s, GE looked toward a merger of its on-air interests with Cox Broadcasting Corps of Atlanta, but needed to divest of three television and eight radio stations that it owned in order to do so. WRGB, Channel 6 on the television dial, was one of them. A $24 million agreement was announced in

April 1979 whereby a group of managers led by James Delmonico ("Basically me and my staff," he said) purchased the station and ran it on an independent basis.

Meanwhile, National Public Radio had begun in 1969 and accumulated 220 affiliated stations along the way, including WAMC in Albany, an FM station run by the Albany Medical College. The college was facing severe budget constraints in 1979 and decided to close the radio station. AMC was a small operation at the time, broadcasting under a 10,000-watt license, and used mainly as a service to doctors who might listen in on operations, lectures, and other hospital events. Yet the station had also developed a serious if small audience of aficionados because of its music and news programming. Alan Seth Chartock (b. 1941), a SUNY New Paltz graduate and professor of political science and communications at SUNY Albany, expanded public interest by introducing a half-hour news program, *The Legislative Gazette*, based on the newspaper he created for his student interns in the state capital. He offered to help with a fundraising program—a novel idea for the staid managers of the station at the time—and made radio history in the state as a result.

Chartock was into the second day of the fund drive, and not very successful at it, when Mayor Erastus Corning came on as a guest. Chartock made his pitch—always an exuberant one—for donations, but the two lonely telephones for taking pledges remained silent.

"Professor, maybe I can try it," the mayor said. He announced that he had $800 "in my pocket" and would match any donations received. In reminiscing about the day on a later fund drive, Chartock attributed the response to the mayor's political sway over Albany city employees. Corning was also a leader of the O'Connell political machine, so his voice on the radio attracted the interest of businesses and families across the city as well.

"The phones took off," Chartock recalled, and within a short time the $800 was matched. "Let it ride," Corning said, and the donations continued to pour in. Chartock invited Pete Seeger and Arlo Guthrie to come and perform, but they were abruptly cancelled by the station director because (he told Chartock) "they are communists." By Thursday—three days later—$129,000 had been promised. The money was quickly appropriated by the medical college and Chartock rather summarily dismissed as no longer needed, despite the tremendous enthusiasm that the event had generated. He was also denied a seat on the radio station's board of directors. Yet he found himself congratulated wherever he went.

In time Chartock led an effort to acquire the station after a chance meeting on the Amtrak rail with Allan Miller, the state commissioner of mental hygiene under Governor Rockefeller who also happened to be associate dean of the Albany Medical College. The intrigues continued as the effort gained steam. Political pressure was applied through Governor Carey's office against Chartock, and a local Catholic college interested in joining in the effort set stringent requirements that Chartock could not abide. One was that "certain words"— "abortion" being one of them—were never to be used on the air. When Chartock firmly rejected such restrictions, a Republican state senator who was attending the meeting of the two boards told Chartock he would never receive a charter from the state for the radio.

The plucky promoter would not be denied. Chartock used his *Legislative Gazette* forum and his growing power on the radio to challenge the establishment by making the new station independent of the medical college. He secured a contract to utilize broadcasting towers on Mount Greylock in North Adams, Massachusetts, increasing the radio's reach from 10,000 to over 200,000 watts. WAMC/Northeast Public Radio was born in 1981 and over time became a major NPR affiliate, eventually covering eastern New York State, most of the Mohawk Valley, a large swath of the North Country, and western New England. Twenty-two stations, all broadcasting the same content, were created; the daily recitations of their call letters under FCC regulations taking on an almost comical challenge in itself because the rule required that all be included within only a thirty-second format. Chartock also continued to challenge the political establishment through his *Capitol Connection* talk show, a personal blog and weekly syndicated column, and in pointed commentaries as the station's political expert. A frequent guest in the early years was Governor Mario Cuomo, one of the most articulate statesmen in America, who even appeared after his defeat by George Pataki in 1994, creating permanent enmities between Chartock and the new governor at the time.

Chartock was indefatigable in leading the semi-annual million-dollar fund drives, often ending weeklong performances in exhaustion. His persistent interjection of the 800-call number for making a pledge became such a characteristic of the show that it was translated into song by AMC enthusiasts and committed to a CD. 1-800-323-9262 became the mantra for thousands of supporters of this eccentric and brilliant public radio promoter and the station he created.

45. The Silence in the Stones

My predecessor as governor owned one political party and leased
the other. —HUGH CAREY

Poor Hugh. I drank the champagne and Hugh Carey got the
hangover. —NELSON ROCKEFELLER

Remember, New York is to the nation as the church spire is to
the village—the symbol of aspiration and faith, the white plume
saying the way is up, not down. Excelsior! Let's keep going up.

—From MARIO CUOMO's concession speech (November 1994)

In the halls of the New York State capitol in Albany the men and women
come and go, never talking of Michelangelo. A grand staircase elaborately
carved with stone faces by Italian masons peers down on their movements,
but no one looks up in admiration. They glance to the imaginary stars in frustration, yes; at times in jubilation, and in weariness—more frequently as the
night wears on—but rarely in appreciation of the magnificent surroundings,
and never to admire the fine stone carvings.

Every spring the lobbyists congregate in this side hall on the second floor
of the capitol in Albany, where the "Million Dollar" sandstone staircase rises
like a massive Italian sculpture through the west side of the building. They
come to make laws (or to kill them), or at least to abide their making as a supportive chorus. The legislative session winds to a late-night close in this hall,
eighty to a hundred lobbyists and their kind strewn around like tchotchkes,
chatting in small talk among themselves, awaiting the fate of their bills. Some
sit uncomfortably on the sandstone stairs—this one starch-perfect with satin
hankie in breast pocket, that one a ceramic figurine in green dress and teased
hair, another in black specs and pushed-back hair tensely bent over a bill's
wording, another and another leaning and lost in thought.

The hall between the library and the Assembly's rear entrance passes by
the entrances to the minority leader's office and a small conference room where
aides can gather with a member for a final rundown on a bill or a debate. Whenever the elevators open all eyes turn to see who emerges—usually a harried staff

member entering the chamber with an armful of files. A cell phone is raised to this ear or that, an occasional notepad fumbles into use, and somewhere forever a brow is furrowing—the fate of someone's bill is hanging by a nail—while a casual smile hides the serenity and security that a sure winner feels.

The Assembly members come, too, with an aide or two usually beside them engaged in the busy work of arranging files, pulling out bills, jotting notes, or talking on cell phones. The members look to their left and right and firmly ahead, acknowledging this or that favored friend, pointedly ignoring the ones they dislike, smiling, nodding, at times pausing for a word or two before moving on. As they enter the chamber they both relax and become more formal, for they have arrived at the place where they serve best their constituents, the State of New York, and their own agendas.

The halls around the stairway bridge the entrance to the Senate side of the capital, short, narrow, ill lit passages where quiet conversations transpire. A rear entrance to the Speaker's office was once at the end of one of these short corridors, but that was closed off soon after the Sulzer impeachment in 1913, the night that Charles L. Boothby may or may not have discovered Speaker Alfred E. Smith with piles of money on his desk that may or may not have been used to pay off the eight assembly members who changed their votes and sealed Sulzer's fate.

A small group of scientists following the progress of a professions bill exits the elevator, chatting quietly and quickly with their lobbyist. Now that we have the bill filed and ready to go, they are saying, what are the chances of it becoming law? "Oh," the lobbyist deadpans, "We are doing very well in that regard. I would say we have a 14 percent chance of getting the bill passed this session." The innocents are crestfallen at the news, until he smiles and explains the rule about it being illegal for a lobbyist to predict the outcome of a bill.

"I cannot tell you how our bill will do," he says, "but I can say that of all the bills filed in the last couple of sessions, about 14 percent became law, and that is exactly the chance we have." The scientists get the joke and laugh. They like this guy; he was the only honest one they interviewed.

A prominent assemblyman pauses to spend a few minutes in jovial talk with a lobbyist or former aide. A visit by a senator prompts a flurry of interest, since he likely comes to finalize talks with a colleague in the other house or report on passage of a bill of particular interest to a committee chair. The senators are always noticed when they appear on this side of the hall; they are better dressed than most of the assemblymen and always look cleanly shaven. Governors never come here, and they enter the chambers only on formal occasions, for an inaugural or a state of the state.

The real news passes by in snippets and is missed by none who come and go in the shadows of the grand stone staircase—a casual remark of a senior staffer (or just her appearance), a nod from someone behind a glass wall, the breathless acknowledgement of an aide rushing by,

"They'll be here tomorrow, damn it!"

"The ways and means agenda is coming."

"If the governor vetoes it, there'll be all hell to pay!"

"The sonofabitch laughed when I said it was stalled. And he's the bill sponsor!"

Someone peels an orange. Several lounge on the stone stairs, biding time, catching a nod or two, checking their notes. Most stand around in pairs or trios, their heads bobbing in pantomime as they talk. Some are discouraged, even disgusted with the slow pace, and all are relieved as the session ends; and the carved stone faces of the modern Michelangelos look down upon them and never nod.

Session watchers say the sessions "wind down" as spring approaches summer, but in fact they ratchet up. The tension grows as time elapses. A staffer entering the plaza on the street level below might find a cool and rainy late May evening, but on the third floor the temperature is rising. People who wait in the halls late at night perspire. The place does not get dank and smelly, but some of the younger staff begin to look bedraggled, their shirt tails hanging, collars open, ties askew; it is easy to tell that the ones with the premature beer bellies will not be around next year. The veteran staffers will be back, carrying a new set of files for a new set of laws; the perennial lobbyists, too, will return, wearing their new portfolios like boutonnieres, some junior staff still with them and still looking tired and shiftless as the hours wane on; and always returning are the plodding and deliberative program staff who work directly under the Speaker, the resident experts in their fields, fiercely possessive of the expertise they have learned over the years—many are women, who are paid less than the men—and of course the members and their senior staff, for in these years few are ousted in disgrace or facing felonies that have driven them from the scene. The 1992 crop is still largely peopled with the progressive members of "the class of '74," who came in riding high on principle and honesty in the wake of Richard Nixon's fall from grace.

It is 11 p.m. Someone comes out of nowhere and tells someone that Codes Committee has just reported his member's bill. This is real news, since it was only a few years earlier—an immensely negligible span of time in these well-worn halls—that Codes was known as the black hole of the Assembly; nothing that went into that committee ever came out. The lobbyist thanks the aide and puts a cell phone to his ear. Someone in Syracuse, Rochester, or Babylon is smiling. Somewhere someone's wife, or secretary, or illicit other decides to book that Bahamas cruise after all.

The legislature came into its own as an independent arm of government in the post-Rockefeller years, largely in response to Nelson's iron grip on how legislative matters were handled and the ballooning costs of his pet plaza project. In 1971, the Citizens Conference on State Legislatures ranked New York's as one of the top four in the nation. In the Hugh Carey years, both senate and assembly beefed up their ways and means and program staff to the point that each house could present its own state budget every year, and better argue the governor's budget as a result. Under Stanley Fink's tenure as Assembly Speaker, as Assemblyman Daniel L. Feldman reported,

> . . . the majority conference discussions were uninhibited, free-wheeling, honest and ferocious exercises in intellectual combat, resulting in policy decisions that had survived that form of trial by fire.

But things changed once Fink retired, and Speakers Saul Weprin and Sheldon Silver increasingly became "less responsive" and used appointments and perquisites to control the members and keep them in line. This shift equalized the playing field with the governor yet also isolated the process, leading to the three-men-in-a-room budget development scenarios much criticized (correctly) in later years by the press and public as undemocratic and secretive.

Partisan bickering remained just as strong—stronger as the members became more knowledgeable—yet when times were halcyon the changes also produced a cordiality that enabled the art of compromise to come into its own and a slate of new laws to be enacted. Members would fiercely criticize their colleagues of the other persuasion in the other house with whom they shared district territory during the biannual political seasons when they faced reelection, but otherwise and often quietly worked hand-in-hand once reelected in developing legislation that was beneficial to both districts.

The strengthening of the legislative branch was abetted by a pattern of severe gerrymandering that the two houses—many of them the supposed idealists of the post-Nixon years—used beginning in 1981, when Democrats took control of the Assembly for the first time since 1894. Sheldon Silver was the architect of the Assembly's iron grip on the process. A state constitutional change in 1930 had required a decennial reapportionment, but left the process in the hands of the very parties and people who would benefit. The pattern remained intact despite frequent expressions of public criticisms and attempts by well-meaning elected officials to change it—including Mario Cuomo's son, Governor Andrew Cuomo, in 2010. Changes in the financing of political campaigns, often trumpeted as necessary by candidates, also remained stillborn each year, demonstrating that true reform in New York went just so far.

An erosion of confidence in the state legislature in the post-2000 years accelerated beyond the usual pattern of public grumpiness over anything political for two reasons: the breakdown of the two-party structure in the state senate caused by wheelings and dealings on the leadership level, and the rise in prosecutions for criminal activities. Candidate recruitments shifted from the old hierarchy run by county political committees to campaign committees driven by money and special interest groups. The class of '74 had aged out and the new crop of legislators that succeeded them lacked a unifying sense of idealism to carry them through the tempting times of a fast new era. Assemblyman Dan Feldman recalled, almost with nostalgia, the so-called "Bear Mountain Compact," an unstated agreement that "shenanigans in Albany, generally assumed to be sexual, were not talked about south of Bear Mountain" in the late twentieth century. From time to time a senator or assemblyman would be caught with a hand in the campaign till and drummed out accordingly, usually with prison time as recompense. Yet, not since the days of Boss Tweed did "shenanigans" of all sorts run as rampant as it did in these later years, when a governor and the leaders of both houses were among those toppled in the consequences of their actions. The carved stone faces looking over the session lobbyists, staff and members in the late spring evenings on the third floor of the capitol in these new, uncomfortable times remained unfazed, even as the characters in the hall below continued to wait, more impatiently than ever, for their times to come.

46. A New Consciousness

As for garbage, the usual dumping or burning of this
valuable agricultural compost remains one of the persistent sins of unscientific municipal housecleaning.

—LEWIS MUMFORD (1961)

The Storm King fight and the national and state legislation that resulted
made environmentalism a signature theme of the late twentieth century.
The rise of Scenic Hudson occurred as Robert Boyle had predicted—its birth
termed "the miracle of the century" by Mrs. Carl Rowe of the Scarsdale
Audubon Society in 1965—from a handful of concerned property owners to one
of the most important advocacy groups for the Hudson River. This happened
independently of the work of Pete Seeger's Hudson River Sloop Clearwater,
an iconic presence and gentle persuader of good science and environmental
stewardship on the river. Riverkeeper and Robert Kennedy, Jr. pursued similar
causes using the courts as the persuaders, and continued to patrol the river as
a predatory fish when it came to polluters. The federal government made the
Hudson a national estuarine sanctuary; the state created a popular new Hudson
River Estuary grant program and established Greenway, an innovative new
structure for state and local governments to work together in benefiting the
region. The Hudson Valley National Heritage Area, signed into law by President Bill Clinton, brought federal agency support in protecting these resources.

One of the fertile new areas of interest used land conservation as a
permanent tool to fend off development and government intrusion. Conservation already had a history in the Valley in land acquisition components of
Governor Rockefeller's 1962 bond issue and the 15,500 acres of prime farmland saved by the American Stewardship Association (ASA) in Washington
and Rensselaer counties. The Open Space Institute had been quietly saving
land for decades as well. Within thirty-five years Scenic Hudson saved more
than 35,000 acres of pristine Hudson River Valley landscape and improved
or established sixty-five parks.

Land conservation entered the modern era when William R. Ginsberg

(1930–2006), a former commissioner of parks and recreation under the Lindsay administration in New York City, successfully litigated Mohonk v. Town of Gardiner (1979), which established tax exemption rights for nature preserves protected by easements. Ginsberg was one of the state's leading environmental lawyers and a co-author with Philip Weinberg of the best environmental law text in the state. He lived on Happy Valley Road in Woodstock and helped the Woodstock Land Conservancy acquire its first conservation easement, a field donated by Aileen Cramer under Guardian Mountain. Ginsberg's deep involvement with the Open Space Institute (OSI) and presidency of the Catskill Center for Conservation and Development from 1981 to 1996 established methods for land preservation among nonprofits that enabled the protection of thousands of acres in the Hudson Valley and the Catskills, including 600 acres in the Woodstock organization's Campaign to Save Overlook and the creation of Esopus Bend Nature Preserve in Saugerties. The Center also extended its influence into historic preservation by playing a key role in the acquisition of the Thomas Cole home site in Catskill as a National Historic Site.

Woodstock became the setting for a protracted land use controversy in the 1980s over an interest in protecting Overlook Mountain from "landscape skimming," a new threat to conservation involving the purchase of lands with spectacular views by developers interested in creating homes that "blighted" the appearance of the mountain from afar. Zoning changes increased minimum acreage for buildings based on location and aesthetic significance, and the town adopted a scenic overlay district for areas more than 1,200 feet above sea level to protect the higher climes of 3,150-foot Overlook Mountain. The argument was a fierce one involving old- versus new-guard Woodstock interests. The zoning amendment was approved by the Woodstock Town Board in 1989, and subsequent efforts to prevent the installation of light towers on the mountain (to warn approaching aircraft) helped to temper, if not eliminate, the intrusion of that visual annoyance as well.

During these years Saugerties fought off a strenuous Ulster County attempt to site a countywide landfill at the Winston Farm, an 800-acre former livestock farm. Local struggles against government intrusions, increasingly ones involving land takings, had become frequent in the new environmental era, and the siting of a regional landfill only became of special interest because a new direction had been taken in state legislative thinking on disposal. The waste burn option, which was already adopted in several counties, was discarded as environmentally unsound, and resource recovery agencies were created to find other solutions.

In 1988, when the Ulster County Legislature undertook a multimillion dollar, three years effort to site a landfill at the farm site that J. O. Winston had created, the community rose up almost in unison, playing a confident David to Goliath, and established a baseline for grassroots success on the local level. The property was located just across the Thruway from the largest waste-paper producer in the county, a company owned by the county's Resource Recovery Agency chairman; the chairman resigned after attention was called to his conflict at a large rally at the high school in August 1989. The county's environmental consultant, Malcolm Pirnie of Westchester County, produced a map with a topography that partially whited-out the sloped lands where the percentage grades were contrary to proper landfill siting; neither the RRA board, the county legislature, nor the county press took issue with the deceit.

The mobilization of the people included the creation of an active new organization, the Winston Farm Alliance, and a "Paint Out" in which artists took to the Winston Farm and created almost two hundred works of art that were quickly sold. A mural of Saugerties entitled "Not Here Never" was created by artists Kate Boyer and F. Tor Godmundson in a prominent village location. John Hall, the future congressman and leader of the rock group Orleans—and coincidentally president of the local school board—composed a song that was taken up by the community. Vernon Benjamin (b. 1945), the newly elected town supervisor (and humble author of this book), led the town's and, as the principal staff member, Assemblyman Hinchey's opposition. At one point Benjamin asked Mario Cuomo's "commerce czar" to relocate the Catskill Park boundary in exchange for a pet Cuomo project, the siting of an innovative brick-making plant south of the Winston Farm. The state agreed to make the effort, but Benjamin's all-Democratic town board would not agree and the brickyard was never built. The county finally pulled out in 1991.

Numerous fights like this around the Valley were successful largely because of a new consciousness and new tools to support the thinking. The environmental arena had shifted to Albany and the state legislature with the election of the spirited group of new members in the wake of Richard Nixon's disgrace and downfall. The energy of change rushed the environmental agenda forward. Citizen lawsuits and environmental quality review were brought together in the state legislature in 1975 under the leadership of Assemblyman Herbert Posner and Senator Bernard Smith, each chair of their respective environmental committee. The members were at loggerheads over what to do when Paul M. Bray, the bill drafter assigned to Posner, suggested using a new model law that drew upon the National Environmental Policy Act (NEPA). Out of this came the State Environmental Quality Review Act (SEQRA), which Bray drafted and Posner took up in the Assembly while Smith focused on citizen suits. Governor Hugh Carey sought to limit environmental quality reviews to mere information and reportage of the facts, but Posner insisted on the need for alternatives and ways to mitigate any harm that an action might create. SEQRA became one of the most important tools in local governance, frustrating compliant state regulators as well as developers while enabling advocacy groups and citizens to ensure protections of the environment. The transition was untidy, long-term, and never fully achieved, but eventually developers began to realize it was cheaper and easier to achieve their growth goals by complying with SEQRA, even if it meant working with environmentalists. Towns that had resisted challenging what they saw as the beneficial tax impacts of runaway growth eventually understood that intelligent land use policies enabled even greater economic gains.

The state had responded favorably in the past to environmental topics when its economic vitality was threatened. As early as the 1920s, when all the shellfish acreage north to Tarrytown was condemned, the state made efforts to reverse the trend. Authoritative information about the river's ecology appeared in 1936 with a New York State Conservation Department-sponsored summer study of fish and rooted plants. New York University's Institute of Environmental Medicine conducted its first ecological survey of the lower river in 1963, involving both the state Department of Health and the US Public Health Service.

A commercial fish catch of 2.6 million pounds in 1887 had fallen to only 163,000 pounds by 1967. Striped bass had an oiled or "tainted" flavor when taken from the river. Anaconda Wire and Cable had been dumping oil wastes directly into the river at Hastings-on-Hudson until caught by Robert Kennedy Jr. and John Cronin of Riverkeeper in 1969–71. The state initiated cleanup enforcement actions against six municipalities and five industries in 1965, but that was not enough. Only four full-time commercial fishing operations remained on the river in 1968, along with 69 part-time operations. The potential for sport fishing was also demolished—35,000 acres between Yonkers and Poughkeepsie were completely useless. Penn Central at Harmon, which dumped large amounts of diesel fuel at the mouth of the Croton River, was a major polluter. The Croton was severely impacted with turbidity and silting caused by a large gravel mining works that operated without a permit—that is, until one was promptly granted in 1969 by the Conservation Department after a freshet washed away the evidence. The Theodore Gordon Flyfishers vigorously protested the action.

US Senator Robert F. Kennedy, spurred by conservation and fishermen's groups and his own family's interests in the Hudson River, was instrumental in convening conferences on the pollution in these years. In 1965, at the first of these get-togethers, he described the river as "an open sewer." At the same conference, Governor Rockefeller, having secured a $1.6 billion bond issue, said the state should achieve its environmental goals by 1972. By 1967, $357 million from the state bond was at work in 176 projects, a $21 million contribution alone helping Albany County clean up its river act. Industrial waste cleanup efforts were undertaken in the late 1960s for the Continental Can Company and General Aniline & Film Corporation's plant in Rockland County; the DMF Company in Dutchess County; and the Humble, Metropolitan, and Mobil oil companies and General Electric in Albany. American Felt in New Windsor and General Motors in Tarrytown made local arrangements for the treatment of their wastes, contributing revenues to the municipal systems as a result.

Apart from these efforts, however, the dumping of sewage and industrial waste was so commonplace that health department action was required. Fifty orders for remedial work were issued by Commissioner Hollis J. Ingraham in 1972, and a volunteer schedule developed for 101 other waste dischargers. New York funded 34 studies at $2,824,099, twenty of which were underway by that year. Forty-four additional proposals were reviewed or already approved, and 37 municipal cleanup projects along the Hudson either begun or completed. In all, during these environmentally conscious years New York contributed $220 million in support above and beyond the bond issue.

A $3 million federal project for long-needed secondary waste treatment at West Point was begun but then diverted to other uses, "a step backward and a disconcerting precedent," Department of Health Assistant Commissioner Paul W. Eastman told a New York City audience in June 1969. At least the United States was taking some steps to clean up its act. The toilets at the Troy lock and dam were electrified and the wastes incinerated in an innovative effort to avoid river dumping. A complex treatment facility for handling cyanide wastes was developed at the Watervliet Arsenal. Stewart Air Force Base near Newburgh got a new $188,900 sewer plant.

The pollution problem was compounded by the need to dredge the river to accommodate large vessels. The channel was deepened from 27 feet to 32 in 1965. Waste materials disposal areas were designated—some creating actual islands in the river—in a 1967 Army Corps of Engineers report, and soils removed from the channels and harbors north of Hastings-on-Hudson, but not without public opposition in some cases.

Under the Clean Water Act in 1972, a US Environmental Protection Agency program to abate pollution by municipalities provided New York State with more than $149 million in federal aid, but this was hardly sufficient to address the problem. The Hudson River was receiving 190 million gallons per day of sewage and nine million tons a year of pollutants from the transportation industry. Raw effluent was discharged in huge amounts from the Mohawk Paper Mill in Cohoes and Cluett-Peabody upriver. Republic Steel Company in Troy dumped "solids, phenols and cyanides" regularly into the river. Dyes routinely colored the Hudson at General Aniline in Rensselaer and the Esopus Creek below the Cantine paper-coating plant in Saugerties. Green Island's papermaking plant dumped 7.4 million gallons of waste a day into the river. Metal finishing and plating wastes entered the waters from numerous large and small manufacturing plants. In addition to these industrial wastes, raw sewage entered the Hudson River at Waterford, Troy, Rensselaer, North Greenbush, Castleton, Cohoes, Coeymans, Selkirk, Catskill, Athens, Coxsackie, Cold Spring, and Newburgh. Some sites—Newburgh, Cornwall, Catskill, and Rensselaer County among them—had new plants underway, yet even those with treatment plants dumped raw sewage regularly because of capacity flow, mismanagement, avoidance of regulations and other reasons. Major efforts at separating storm water runoff from sewage did not begin for another twenty years.

Albany brought two new sewer plants online in 1973 at a cost of almost $729 million; more than 54 million gallons were treated on a daily basis. The 1965 bond act ($1.6 billion) was followed by $1.5 billion in 1971, of which $650 million was designated for municipal sewer plants. A Troy plant that treated 24 million gallons a day was on line by January 1976. Yonkers had begun a $93 million 9.2 million-gallons-per-day plant that would also serve Irvington and Tarrytown. An $18 million plant at Ossining also consolidated local towns starting in 1978. The need was stupendous, especially in light of the population growth. The eight mid-Hudson Valley counties were expected to swell to more than 2.6 million in population by 1985, a 75% rise since 1960.

More than 1,200 commercial ships used the Hudson River in 1973. Molasses, bananas, wood pulp, hemp, and motorcycles were among the products hauled. More than a million bushels of wheat were sent to Russia, scrap iron to Japan, corn to Bangladesh. The 29 million short tons of freight shipped by water in 1972 were 35% more than the tonnage in 1963. When United Fruit moved its unloading operations from New York City to Albany, 1,200 feet of dock space was built at a $4.5 million cost. Seventeen major oil companies had operations at Albany involving 400 tankers and 800 barges. In the spring of 1972, when 10.3 million tons of goods were processed at the Albany port, 8,500 new Volkswagens arrived.

Commercial uses were heavy downriver as well. The A. C. Dutton Lumber Company in Poughkeepsie handled large ships. Atlantic Cement near Hudson constructed a mammoth silo complex on the river to fill large barges for shipment overseas as well as through the Northeast. The cement industry involved four major producers along the Greene County waterfront plus a new challenger, St. Lawrence Cement from Canada, which came in and undercut prices so severely for two years that two plants were forced to fold.

Compounding the pollution problem was the growing prevalence of foreign or "invasive" species crowding out the natural flora in the estuary. These included purple loosestrife (*Lythrum salicaria*), which arrived in wool waste delivered to a Newburgh factory, and Japanese lady's thumb (*Persicaria caespitosa*), carried in rice straw used as packing for china. A smut (*Ustilago commelinae*), "hitherto known only from the Yalu River in Korea," also appeared at the Albany port. Water chestnuts (*Trapa natans*) became the most difficult to eradicate, the spiny shells causing dangers for beach users as well as other flora.

Cultural, aesthetic and heritage factors as aspects of concern were implicit in the origins of conservationism and its history, from the PIPC's assertion of landscape appreciation "as a core value" in 1899 to the creation of Hudson River Valley Greenway in 1989. Vassar professor Harvey K. Flad emphasized the importance of Hudson River Valley aesthetics in opposing a proposed nuclear power facility in the town of Lloyd during a meeting of the New York State Geological Association in 1976. "Environmental impacts are both physical and social," he wrote, "and may include qualitative as well as quantitative assessment . . . Aesthetic impacts are those that change the cultural landscape in ways that are visible, experiential and psychologically meaningful." When the decision ending the siting of a proposed nuclear plant at Cementon in 1979 affirmed that aesthetic values were valid factors for such proceedings, the Storm King victory was in effect confirmed.

A visual impacts analysis was added to environmental impact requirements by New York State soon after the Cementon decision, and by the end of the century had become so important as to factor strongly in defeating a St. Lawrence Cement proposal for a huge works on the Hudson River at Hudson. The development of the Local Waterfront Revitalization Program (LWRP) under the state Department of State was another factor in protecting the character and aesthetics of local waterfront communities. A Catskill Hudson Cultural Cluster was created on the theme of visual resources around Olana. A new ecological consciousness was emerging, one that forged common ground between those who wanted to protect high-wealth river zones like the Highlands with the fisherman's world and that of tourist, traveler, naturalist, and commoner.

The Hudson River Conservation Society's budding interest in historic preservation in the 1940s and 1950s was echoed thirty years later when the state legislature, through funding sponsored by Assemblymen Maurice Hinchey and Robert Connor and Senator Jay Rolison, created a Heritage Task Force for the Hudson River Valley. The Task Force, which encompassed a ten-county region adjoining the estuary, was charged with protecting and enhancing the region's natural, cultural, historic, scenic and recreational resources. Programs that developed included lighthouse preservation—a great success over several years—the environmental compatibility of major development projects, land acquisitions, scenic districts, and a grant awards program to assist nonprofits and small communities. The Task Force also, under contract with the Department of Environmental Conservation, initially managed the four National Estuarine Research Reserve sites in the estuary.

The Task Force's *Lower Hudson Basin Tributary Study* (1990) set recommendations on protecting and managing the tributaries of the Hudson, which were described as forming "a vital aquatic system" with clear and specific management needs. At the time, DEC estimated that the area's tributary systems contributed 14% of the total Hudson River flow, or 290 million gallons a day. Tributaries were placed within the context of complex regional ecosystems with specific impacts and characteristics, yet the *Study's* attention was focused mainly on the shoreline and river corridor.

The Hudson River Estuary Management Act of 1987 involved nine state agencies, as well as the support of seven federal agencies and an advisory committee of nonprofit community and environmental organizations with stakes in the estuary's health. The estuary focus was expanded to include tributary streams and watersheds even when blocked by manmade structures (such as dams)—in effect including most of the Valley below the Mohawk River. A rise in regional easement conservation organizations to protect the lands around the streams and a growing consciousness about the economic advantages of protecting natural habitats everywhere were added to the mix. In time, the Hudson River Estuary Program under Frances Dunwell redirected the thrust into a whole estuary approach that included the tributaries as well as the river itself and its shorelines.

Hudson Valley Greenway was developed by the New York State Legislature as a vehicle for conceptualizing the entire estuary as a biological region important for its cultural, heritage, and recreational resources. Greenway used a theme of linkages to connect twelve counties and eighty-two towns and villages in a "compact" of mutual interests. A small, reactionary opposition emerged in Saugerties, Maurice Hinchey's hometown, because of supposed similarities to the Adirondack Park restrictions imposed during Governor Rockefeller's administration. In time, however, the town discarded its negativity and became a Greenway Compact community.

One of the most visible of the Greenway themes, albeit not originating with the agency, was the "linkage" that the transformation of the Poughkeepsie railroad bridge into a "walkway" tourist draw made with communities on both sides of the Hudson River and with the spirit of the new heritage tourism. The new thinking was catching on. A theme of bioregionalism emerged that encompassed the elements of estuary protection and enhancement, species protection, visual resources, and enlightened growth as a way to explore cultural heritage values and ecological resources in an integrated model that transcended jurisdictional boundaries.

The arrival of the Hudson River Valley National Heritage Area (NHA) by act of Congress in 1996—the brainchild of Bill Clinton and local Congress-man Maurice Hinchey—united the Valley's rich history, government, educa-tional resources, parks and historic sites, science studies, and its cultural life in a celebration that spurred tourism growth, estuary protection, and economic expansion. At President Clinton's request, Hinchey used his legislation to create a generic law for more than thirty other NHAs established around the country. Congressman John Sweeney, a Hudson Valley conservative Republican who op-posed most Democratic program efforts in the 1990s, could not avoid allowing his district's Saratoga National Battlefield to be considered within the Hudson Valley NHA, but would not countenance sacrificing other areas of his congres-sional district, including most of Dutchess, Columbia, and Greene counties, to such liberal thinking. The heritage area was extended after Sweeney left office.

Most congressmen addressed river issues as they arose in their districts, some negatively if more closely tied with industry interests, yet only US Senator Robert F. Kennedy consistently brought the Hudson River's health to the table in his house. Senator Daniel Patrick Moynihan was an urbanist, not an environmentalist. He considered such issues class-based and called acid rain "a gentleman's issue, a trout fisherman's issue."

The National Heritage Area extended from Yonkers to Troy, with a nod toward Saratoga and special emphases on the military history and the Valley's importance in the rise of American art and culture in the nineteenth century. Congress also recognized the iron, textile, and collar and cuff industries, and the early growth of men's and women's cooperative labor organizations. The state of New York assisted the NHA program with the Greenway Conservancy and Hudson River Greenway Communities Council. The Hudson River Valley Institute (HRVI) was established at Marist College in Poughkeepsie, its purpose to disseminate and celebrate the region's rich heritage and provide a training ground for public education professionals. Under the spirited leader-ship of HRVI chair Thomas Wermuth and executive director Colonel James Johnson, HRVI partnered with other heritage organizations in programs such as Revolutionary War reenactments. Marist furthered its imprint on regional history, as well as its tradition of academic scholarship, by adopting the *Hudson Valley Regional Review*, which Bard College had created in the late 1980s; the journal was renamed *The Hudson River Valley Review*.

The estuary and its tributaries hosted more than 200 species of fish at the end of the twentieth century. The resource included the only substantial acreage of tidal wetlands in New York, as well as large areas of submerged vegetation essential to species health. More than 16,500 acres of river habitat were designated "significant coastal fish and wildlife habitat" by the DEC and New York Department of State. DOS managed the Waterfront Revitalization Program, an important new tool to help localities clean up their Hudson River shorelines, create more public access, and enact appropriate land use standards for protecting the estuary.

A Natural Heritage Program was developed to identify areas where rare plants and animals, as well as special natural communities were found. The estuary was considered especially important for its turtle habitats; at Arlington High School in Dutchess County, Hudsonia Ltd. designed and helped establish a new habitat for the rare Blanding's turtle to allow for the high school's expansion into an existing habitat—one of the celebrated instances of success in adapting natural resources and human needs.

The return of the bald eagle was an important part of this revitalization effort. As the river pollution abated and the natural environment stabilized again, DEC instituted a successful return-to-the-wild program for eagles in the 1980s. A juvenile eagle (less than two years old) released at Bristol Beach in Malden in 1990 built a nest in the woods along the old, abandoned beach and raised a family that still resided there twenty-five years later. The Palisades Interstate Parks Commission refrained from developing Bristol Beach, partly because of the eagle's presence, but did clean out an abandoned oil tank that threatened the environment. Below the Highlands, Iona Island, now protected as an important estuarial wetlands, became an eagle feasting grounds, viewed by distant tourists at the overlooks on the east side of the river every morning. Kayakers in the Stockport flats area of Columbia County routinely saw a dozen or more eagles in a morning by century's end. Osprey was an important migratory species that also used the upper estuary productively —Stockport Creek providing a fine feeding area during the anadromous fish migrations in the spring.

Barriers along tributary streams inhibited the movement of the river species into the tributaries to spawn, and these manmade dams, locks, and other obstacles were often no longer needed for their original economic purposes. In May 1996, Robert E. Schmidt and Susan Cooper's *A Catalog of Barriers to Upstream Movement of Migratory Fishes in Hudson River Tributaries* delineated these obstacles and the prospect for fish passages around them. The

Hudsonia Ltd. report was done for the Hudson River Foundation in response to the enormous decline in the Atlantic river herring stocks. Commercial hauls in 1980 were 30% fewer than those in the late 1960s, even as the water quality improvements of those intervening years helped stabilize the population and generate increases. Removing barriers to spawning areas would promote greater population growth, the scientists reasoned.

Schmidt and Cooper examined sixty-two tributaries and found only one, the Vlockie Kill in Rensselaer County, without barriers. Thirty-one of the rest of the tributaries had natural barriers, and thirty had artificial dams, culverts, and other impediments. The naturalists identified ten highest-priority tributaries for enhancement of the migratory fish runs, in a descending order of priority: the Rondout (Ulster), Pocantico (Westchester), Coxsackie Creek (Greene), Stockport Creek (Columbia), Sparkill Creek (Rockland), Muitzes Kill (Rensselaer), Poesten Kill (Rensselaer), Wappingers Creek (Dutchess), Quassaick Creek (Orange), and Black Creek (Ulster). Most of these streams were healthy with moderate-to-large spring runs.

The Catskill Creek was one of the few tributaries where rainbow smelt (*Osmerus mordax*), so plentiful in the 1940s and 50s, were reported. The Rondout also supported smelt in some years, and had no barriers for the first four miles to the Eddyville Dam, which was already partially broken open. The Crum Elbow, Wappingers and Fishkill Creeks to the south, and Saw Kill to the north also had good herring runs and water quality. Striped bass (*Morone saxatilis*) followed the herring into the Croton River in Westchester County. The Esopus at Saugerties still had the 36-foot Cantine Dam, inactive since the 1960s, as a terminal barrier, and the tributary, Schmidt reported, never had a spring fish migration past the rocks below the dam. This stretch of the river was a prolific striped bass area that yielded several state-record catches.

Despite the Schmidt-Cooper report, no fish ladders were built and the topic lay fallow for another twenty years, until revived under new DEC grant programs. Governor Andrew Cuomo's New York Rising initiative had the effect, in some cases, of also aiding the restoration of fish corridors by upgrading undersized culverts that contributed to severe storm flooding events.

Ecological science from environmental think tanks like the Cary Institute for Ecosystem Study in Millbrook and Hudsonia Ltd. in Red Hook provided the scientific underpinning for a budding new consciousness about habitat and ecological protections. The Cary Institute, founded in 1983 by

Dr. Gene E. Likens, used science to expand an understanding and awareness of man's relationship to his ecology in ways that benefited a wide range of environmental concerns from freshwater resources to forest management. Hudsonia, founded in 1981, operated with a smaller budget and staff and worked with local communities and state and federal agencies in developing scientific reports and programs to help communities protect estuarial ecosystems and the flora and fauna of the Valley. Its illustrated *News from Hudsonia* became an attractive, science-based periodical in wide dissemination. Both institutions eschewed any political involvements while quietly working to support legislative and other governmental initiatives.

Hudsonia spurred a local embrace of environmental protection with the development of a *Biodiversity Assessment Manual for the Hudson River Corridor* (2001), designed to train community planners and zoning officials in mapping habitats and using that knowledge to make better land use decisions. The *Manual* grew in popularity over the ensuing years partly because it demonstrated that a proactive approach to local land use practices saved time and money and resulted in better growth.

By 1990, when Hudsonia was beginning to develop this tool, the mid-Hudson region had benefited from two decades of serious pollution prevention and mitigation efforts by the state. The rise of SEQRA in challenging potentially deleterious private development had battered local governments trying to help the growth interests, and now they were beginning to understand the wisdom of environmental stewardship as a significant and, indeed, essential economic development tool. Erik Kiviat and Gretchen Stevens provided the knowledge to employ that wisdom, and save time, frustration, and local taxpayer costs in the process. Teams from local communities experienced eleven-month in-depth training in using the biodiversity tools to determine if a particular local geography was suitable for any development schemes.

New York spent $256 million on protecting the Hudson River during the first five years of the Governor George Pataki administration, an unusual legacy for a Republican administration. The Waterfront Esplanade Park in Yonkers was one of the projects supported by state funds over these years. The governor, a Peekskill resident, helped to save three times as much Hudson River land as his predecessor, while also retaining and taking some credit for the success of established environmental initiatives like the Hudson River Estuary Program. Pataki eventually proposed "a Woods Hole on the Hudson" estuarial research institute that developed in Beacon following a highly public site search effort; John Cronin became the first director.

The governor also played a pivotal role in forging an agreement between New York City and the Catskill Mountains communities when the federal EPA threatened New York with the need to build a $5 billion filtration plant to keep clean water flowing to customers in the city. The result was an infusion of $300 million in city dollars in developing infrastructure, Main Street revitalization, and other programs to make the Catskills healthy and green again.

Pataki endorsed these initiatives even as he faced opposition from his traditional support areas, like the Business Council of New York, for ideas like tax credits for green building projects, seen by the Council as one step away from state mandates on all its new buildings. His history reflected his years in the New York State Assembly, when he was an involved minority member of the environmental conservation committee. In other ways, the governor failed the environment, however, by underfunding DEC regional staff so that proper diligence was abrogated in the state's environmental stewardship responsibilities.

After Storm King, the Valley's loudest and most significant environmental fight—and the only one with full regional implications—concerned the disposition of thousands of tons of polychlorinated biphenals (PCBs) that had been used by General Electric in mill operations at Fort Edward, Hudson Falls and elsewhere from 1947 to 1974. The chemical was used in the making of capacitators, some as large as metal barrels, that were submerged in the substance. PCBs were more expensive than mineral oils, but not flammable. GE had permits to create their industrial wastes dating to the 1920s, when New York began to regulate water pollution. The dregs of the cleanup operations at these plants were dumped with the wastewater in the river. Most of the sediment accumulated behind a downstream dam that was torn down in 1973, spreading more than a million cubic yards of PCB wastes downstream. Two years later, incidents of contaminated fish were reported to the DEC.

The chemical structure of PCBs was similar to dichloro-diphenyl-trichloroethane, known as DDT and exposed as a major health threat by Rachel Carson (1907–64) in *Silent Spring* (1962). The first of the independent PCB studies was done by Dr. Renate Kimbrough of the Center for Disease Control in 1975. The study showed that heavy doses of the chemical caused liver tumors in rodents, which led to a congressional ban on the use of the substance and the enactment of a toxic waste cleanup law in 1980. The science was not that clear-cut, however. Kimbrough went on to do an epidemiological survey of employees who had worked with the chemical for General Electric in 1990 that showed no unusual incidence of cancer. EPA scientists, who considered the study well designed, eventually concluded that exposure to PCBs, including consumption in drinking river water, was below levels of concern. EPA administrator Carol Browner told a New York Assembly Environmental Conservation Committee in July 1998 that when she and EPA director Christine Whitman called for dredging of the substance from the river, they omitted the EPA's opinion that drinking the river water was safe and only eating fish in defiance of the state ban was dangerous.

Initially, the EPA decided to leave the PCBs in the river, believing that the heavy substance remained on the bottom embedded in siltation, but the work of geochemist James Simpson (1943–2015) and his graduate student Richard Bopp at the Lamont Dougherty Earth Observatory in Palisades led the agency to reevaluate that determination and order GE to remove 2.9 million yards of the sediments by dredging. "Simpson's work on Hudson sediments also provided the first accurate accounting of radionuclides in the river stemming from nuclear-bomb testing" and of "significant releases of radioactivity" from Indian Point, a Lamont-Dougherty tribute to Simpson reported.

The company steadfastly denied both responsibility for a cleanup (based on an old agreement with the state of New York) and the danger of the substance. EPA was seen as playing politics in pursuing the dredging, even though the call for dredging spanned the presidencies of both Bill Clinton and George H. W. Bush. (A Clinton official, Interior Department deputy assistant secretary for policy Lisa Guide, concluded that the Bush administration pursued GE "to stop the bloodletting" over how environmental issues were harming the administration.) Some allegedly "flawed reporting" of *The New York Times* and other press was scored by critic David Schoenbrod, who claimed that none of the *Times'* 150 articles and editorials since 1975 had reported the EPA's risk assessment findings regarding the safety of the water for human consumption. The argument became a nasty one involving conflicting upstate and downstate interests fueled by the abrasive personality of GE's bullish and confrontational CEO, John Welch, Jr. (b. 1935), and his annual compensation, which was $39.8 million in 1996. His ally in skillfully playing the upper Hudson Valley interests against the Mid-Hudson region was Congressman Gerald Solomon (1930–2001), who later became an industry lobbyist.

Schoenbrod, as if measuring the PCB case by its popularity, stated that a Zogby International poll of 809 voters in 14 counties along the Hudson River reported 59% favored GE's limited cleanup strategy, with 27% against it and 14% unsure. Presumably most of those surveyed were from the upriver counties most supportive of GE. As "Blame GE" bumper stickers appeared throughout the mid-Hudson region and the intensity of the argument fueled more extensive scientific studies of the movement of PCBs and other pollutants in the lower river, some took their umbrage to their pocketbooks. The city of Beacon affirmed its support for the cleanup by denying a municipal insurance contract with a company owned by a General Electric holding company.

The PCB "hot spots" around Fort Edward were the largest and most notorious, but not the only areas polluted with polychlorinated biphenyls. Less than five weeks after receiving Clearwater's Environmental Quality Award in 1979, wildlife pathologist Ward Stone (b. 1938) uncovered high levels of PCBs created by GE's Waterford silicon plant and dumped in the former Palmer Dump in Stillwater. The Caputo landfill in Moreau was an even larger site, prompting DEC Commissioner Robert Flacke to express confidence that the federal government would help in a cleanup effort. A significant GE PCB problem was discovered in Pittsfield, Massachusetts, just across the state line, and smaller ones emerged at repair sites for electric motors and transformers, like the Vatrano Road Service Center in Columbia County, which was under an order on consent to clean up the site in 1990. At another polluted site, an internal Central Hudson Gas & Electric memorandum identified drums of oil and pyranol at the former Bouchard Junkyard along Route 20 in New Lebanon in October 1980. The junkyard, which became a state superfund site, was operated by Henry Bouchard and Edward Weisberg between 1959 and 1971, but the cleanup waited until April 2008 to begin.

A Napanoch PCB pollution case involved the celebrated and eccentric Stone, who was already legendary among Akwesasne Indians for identifying and forcing a cleanup of PCB pollution by Alcoa Aluminum on the St. Lawrence River at Massena. At Assemblyman Hinchey's initiative, Stone identified serious PCB contamination at the former paper mill site in Napanoch. Old printing operations were considered suspect because the color dyes used in comics and other newspaper sections contained the contaminant. Ruins of the abandoned paper works dotted a highly picturesque section of the Rondout Creek just before the stream entered the long plain of the Rondout Valley and turned north toward Kingston. The Ulster County location was sensitive because it had been a popular and beautiful swimming hole and was still used by the local fire department to refill tankers after fires. The exclusive Yama Farms Inn, which was closed by 1940, was just above the mill site near Honk Lake.

"I can smell it," Stone said as he walked onto the Napanoch field in 1991, adding that PCBs had a distinctive aroma for those who had worked with the substance or been around it. His educated hunch was borne out by subsequent tests. The abandoned mill property was declared a superfund site by the regional DEC after Hinchey's exposure of the agency's failings, yet when the assemblyman went on to Congress in 1993 the final cleanup at Napanoch lapsed for want of funds and was never completed.

The GE PCB cleanup continued into 2015, but did not extend to other "hot spots" identified in the river. A campaign spearheaded by Clearwater involved dozens of localities and environmental groups in urging the company to complete the cleanup and the EPA joined in the effort as well. If the new consciousness was waning and had aged with the state legislature's "class of '74" that promoted it, the dedication and intensity of advocates like Clearwater, Riverkeeper, and Scenic Hudson, and the new consciousness of local towns and communities suggested otherwise. All rallied against the proposal of a new oil pipeline carrying crude oil from Albany to refineries in New Jersey and returning with fuel oil, gasoline and other refined products. A promoter for Pilgrim Pipeline termed the opposition to its project "a NIMBY reaction" —"not in my backyard"—to which a local official replied, "Yes, but you need to keep in mind that this was the birthplace of environmentalism in America. The whole Valley is NIMBY to projects like yours."

Epilogue: Escarpment Sunset

"The Mountain House died hard," Annabar Jensis wrote in a *Catskill Daily Mail* editorial a few days after the New York State Department of Conservation torched the many-columned ruins of the first and most famous of the grand mountain houses at 6 a.m. on Friday, January 25, 1963:

> She was too lovely, and too proud to fall into decay. She was weathered and tumbled and ravaged by fire, but still she stood, defying the elements of the windswept mountaintop. She had to die because her rotted beams endangered the thousands who came to pay homage . . . Let us remember her as she was: as a white-pillared elegance looking over the mountain and valley; as a weathered crone clinging to life as long as she was permitted to live; and, lastly, as a fast sheet of flame bringing wonder and fear to all who saw it.

A man standing in Catskill saw the blaze burst from atop the northeast face of the Catskills and thought "for one awful moment" that the sun now rose in the west.

In its day, the Catskill Mountain House represented the epitome of the Romantic era in America, a magnet for artists, writers, heads of state, wealthy travelers, and tens of thousands of tourists drawn to the dramatic setting that Erastus Beach created on the Catskills escarpment. Resentment over the structure's unceremonious demise—resentment and, for many, a nostalgic sense of loss—accompanied the wonder of the scene. Few accepted the state's reasoning—safety for visitors who came snooping—and many concluded that the act was senseless, committed at that time of day in a cowardly fashion because of the cries any announced intention would have provoked. The sense of dilapidated old mansions of a bygone era as romantic ruins worth saving had not yet settled into the consciousness of the times, yet the end of the mountain house coincided with the birth of a new era in land use and conservation thinking in the state. Even though the setting was now dramatically different, the romantic retreat the building evoked for a previous era continued as a mecca for heritage and cultural visitors and the new breed of weekend campers and day-hikers to the region. The old names—the Mountain House, the Pine Orchard—fell into disuse and in time were forgotten, and even the twin lakes that the Native American envisioned as the eyes of the giant monster that Manitou had laid low in the formation of the mountains also disappeared when the Department of Environmental Conservation merged the two lakes into one. North Lake became the most popular camping venue in the state of New York.

In terms of the Hudson Valley's history, the end of the mountain house heralded, as a metaphorical coda, the final fiery moments of the "creation" theme that Natty Bumppo, James Fenimore Cooper's fictional Leatherstocking, considered as the defining characteristic of the region that he saw in his youth in the eighteenth century. After creation came the coming-of-age of the Hudson Valley setting, and in a way the time and history that continued to unfold for fifty years after this conflagration were a denouement for the entire modern era. A phoenix of a new era in environmental stewardship rose from the ashes.

The theme appeared in the visual excesses—something new and beautiful around each turn, across each panoramic viewshed, in the minutiae of the Valley's rich ecology, and in the small and intimate epiphanies in the vast anecdotage in the Valley's story— but the American world entered into a completely new historical context on the fateful morning of September 11, 2001, when two airplanes violated the Hudson Valley's airspace and destroyed the World Trade Center in New York City. The Hudson Valley landscape defined what America was and what it could be, and in the violation of its airspace by the WTC planes ominously what it would become in the attack's aftermath.

Surprise and wonder, and a certain contradiction lay at the core of this history. Just as the region was defined almost immediately as upriver and downriver when the Dutch established a fur trading post 150 miles into the interior, the history remained rudely dichotomous in succeeding waves—

harming upriver commercial interests to the point of revolutionary action, creating a political structure dominated by the larger population in the emerging metropolitan area, taking the region's water by fiat for pittances in compensation, despoiling the environment in the name of progress and commerce, harming mid-Valley consumers in everything from hospital reimbursements to car insurance, using legislative majorities to favor school aid formulas that benefited wealthy school districts to the detriment of the poor ones—an uncomplimentary history in many ways, yet one also rich with the progress that defined America. National population trends, changing economic patterns, a more complex political and cultural environment, and the measure of society's values were altering David Maldwyn Ellis's traditional view of the Northeast as the "microcosm" of wider America, yet the region still represented "the America that is to be" in the democratic idealism it displayed.

In January 1981, the Highland Falls mayor insisted that the buses to the Hotel Thayer at West Point carrying the Iran hostages on their return from 444 days of captivity follow the route into the academy through the village's main street, instead of an alternate route that avoided any populated areas. The bus had come over from Stewart Airport on a route lined with cheering Americans, and now the streets of Highland Falls were filled as well—people standing in the cold, cheering, waving yellow ribbons, bringing the hostages to tears as they passed. This could have been a scene anywhere in small-town America, yet its unfolding here at the onset of the Highlands, where Washington once rode, where the Hudson River school artists painted, where romanticism in America flowered, where the upriver and downriver interests met despite their differences, all of it reflected the theme of the Hudson Valley as "the landscape that defined America."

The population of the ten Hudson River counties rose by 15% from 1980 to 2006, or 50% more than the state as a whole, with most of the increase occurring in the lower river counties. Yonkers alone added more than 7,000 units of housing. A large, mixed-use development of the former General Motors 95-acre site in Tarrytown, including residences, a hotel and commercial area, was approved. Haverstraw added more than 850 residential units, along with restaurants and shops, on another former industrial site along the river. The consequences of the 9/11 terrorist attack on the World Trade Center affected the Valley in a greater population shift northward, yet the effects of this shift, because of the state's increased vigilance, local efforts, and a greater awareness by the general public, were not as dramatic as development pressures had been in the past. An "ecosystem-based approach" particularly suitable to the Hudson River estuary expanded beyond the beaches and shores of the tidal river to include tributaries and inland communities in a "multi-objective, multi-stakeholder" approach. The work of Riverkeeper and the popularity of the DEC's Hudson River Estuary Program drew attention nationally in the creation of similarly styled river system management efforts. The successful return of the bald eagle—carefully cultivated through thoughtful, habitat-based planning—seemed to open the possibilities of recovering the past. The National Heritage Area pioneered a partnership approach involving the state government and local institutions like the Hudson River Maritime Museum. Hudson Valley Greenway's emphasis on linkages with its "compact" communities promoted environmental and Main Street improvements with the best of the region's heritage.

The changes were in a way a throwback to Lewis Mumford and the tenets of the Regional Planning Association of America. Mumford chafed at the obfuscation of his principles in the placement of the New York State Thruway—for good reason, given the dislocations that project created—and now state agencies were downplaying their overbearing roles of governance and management and yielding to smaller, more local solutions to managing growth and change. By conceptualizing the region as a whole, as Greenway and the Estuary Program did, linkages like the highly popular Poughkeepsie railroad bridge walkway became practical means for connecting the public with its urban and rural landscapes. Even energy generation itself would be decentralized into "community cogeneration" models for the future, the emphasis falling on the small and intimate as the preferred model for the future.

Sunsets at the Pine Orchard escarpment were as dramatic as the sunrises that Natty Bumppo might have seen, a recessional parade of bright illuminations breaking through the clouds on patches of the Valley quilt. Off to the south, sheltered by the northeast range, a coral sky lingered over the Skunnemunks. The view, for all its grandness, remained only a partial one of the Hudson River Valley, its extent reaching a hundred miles in either direction to the rising of the Adirondacks in the north and the hills of the Highlands in the south. The shade draws now on our history, its seamless web "from wilderness to modern times" enclosing behind us as we leave, the future and all its promises and possibilities beckoning in the dawning to come.

Sources

ABBREVIATIONS

(p) prime document or material

(s) scientific document or publication

(g) government document or publication

(r) reference work

(c) creative (art, fiction, poetry, theater, dance, music)

(m) music

(n) newspaper, journalism publication; radio or television

(br) book review

(th) thesis or dissertation

LTC   Lowell Thomas Collection (Marist College)
STC   Storm King Collection (Marist College)
OSC   Office of the State Comptroller

PRIME SOURCES

Adams, Arthur G. *The Hudson: A Guidebook to the River*. Albany, 1981.

"The African Voice in Albany, New York: Harriettee Bowie Lewis Van Vranken Remembers," in Williams-Myers, ed., *On the Morning Tide*, 120-139.

"The African Voice in Ossining, New York: Henry Gourdine and the Challenge of the River," in Williams-Myers, ed., *On the Morning Tide*, 110-117.

Alderfer, Henry F. "The Flora Catalogued on a Nature Trail Made from the Knoll House to the Gun Club at Quaker Lake." June 1939. (LTC)

Aldrich, Margaret Chanler. *Family Vista: The Memoirs of Margaret Chanler Aldrich*. Collections of the Dutchess County Historical Society, VIII: New York, 1958.

Anderson, Maxwell. "Kurt Weill." Liner notes to "Tryout: A Series of Private Rehearsal Recordings—including Actual Performances by Kurt Weill and Ira Gershwin." New York, 1979 (1953).

Aptheker, Herbert, ed. *A Documentary History of the Negro People in the United States*. 4 Vols. New York, 1951.

Atkinson, J. Brooks. *East of the Hudson*. New York, 1931.

Barrus, Clara. *Whitman and Burroughs: Comrades*. Port Washington, 1968 (Boston and New York,1931).

Bennet, William S. "The Reminiscences of William S. Bennet." Oral History Research Office, Columbia University (New York, 1950?), 115-136.

Benton, Charles E. *Troutbeck: A Dutchess County Homestead*. New York (Dutchess County Historical Society Monographs No. 1), 1916.

Bigelow, John, ed. *Letters and Literary Memorials of Samuel J. Tilden.* 2 Vols. Port Washington, 1971 (1908).

_____. *Retrospections of an Active Life.* 5 Vols. New York, 1909-13.

Bigelow, Poultney. *Seventy Summers.* 2 Vols. London, 1925.

Boller, Paul F. Jr., and Ronald Story, eds. *A More Perfect Union: Documents in U. S. History (Volume II: Since 1865).* Third Edition. Boston, 1992.

Burroughs, John. *Notes on Walt Whitman as Poet and Person.* New York, 1867.

_____. *Wake-Robin* (New York, 1871). Project Gutenberg (*www.gutenberg.org*).

_____. "Our River," in *Scribner's Monthly*, XX:4 (August, 1880), 481-493.

_____. *A River View and Other Hudson Valley Essays,* Croton-on-Hudson 1981; 1886.

_____. *A Sharp Lookout: Selected Nature Essays of John Burroughs.* Ed. Frank Bergon. Washington, 1987.

_____. *Ways of Nature.* New York, 1995.

Child, Hamilton, comp. *Gazetteer and Business Directory of Ulster County, N. Y., for 1871-2.* Syracuse, 1871.

Copland, Aaron, and Vivian Perlis. *Copland: 1900 through 1942.* New York, 1984.

Cronin, John, and Robert F. Kennedy Jr. *The Riverkeepers: Two Activists Fight to Reclaim Our Environment as a Basic Human Right.* New York, 1999 (1997).

Davis, John P. "What Price National Recovery?' in Aptheker, ed., IV, 49-55.

_____. "A Black Inventory of the New Deal," in Aptheker, ed., IV, 167-174.

Depew, Chauncey M. *My Memories of Eighty Years.* New York, 1924.

Dewey, Thomas E. *Public Papers of Thomas E. Dewey: 1943.* Albany, 1944. (g)

Farley, James A. *Behind the Ballots: The Personal History of a Politician.* New York, 1938.

Feldman, Daniel L., and Gerald Benjamin. *Tales from the Sausage Factory: Making Laws in New York State.* Albany, 2010.

Fish, Hamilton. *FDR The Other Side of the Coin: How We Were Tricked into World War II.* Torrance, Calif., 1976.

Flower, Roswell P. *Public Papers of Roswell P. Flower: Governor, 1893.* Albany, 1894. (g)

Foner, Dr. Philip S., ed. *W. E. B. Du Bois Speaks: Speeches and Addresses 1920-1963.* New York, 1970.

Glynn, Martin, Comptroller. *Annual Report of the Comptroller of the State of New York.* Albany, 1909. (g)

Grant, Ulysses S. *Personal Memoirs of U. S. Grant.* 2 Vols. New York, 1885-86.

Gunnison, Herbert Foster. *Seventy Years on a Motorcycle: An Up-to-the-Hilt Reminiscence by a College Literature Professor.* N. p., 2002.

Hammer, Armand, with Neil Lyndon. *Hammer: Witness to History.* N.p., 1987.

Hansen, Judith. "National Youth Administration: Woodstock Resident Work Center." Registration, U. S. Department of the Interior, National Park Service, National Register of Historic Places. March 26, 1992. (g)

Harriman, W. Averell. *Public Papers of Averell Harriman: Fifty-Second Governor of the State of New York.* Albany, 1955. (g)

The Hudson Highlands: William Thompson Howell Memorial. N.p., 1982 (January 23, 1923; 1934).

Hull, Cordell. *The Memoirs of Cordell Hull.* 2 Vols. New York, 1948.

Joseph, Richard. *Growing Up on the Hudson: Memories of a Shad Fisherman.* N.p. (Esopus), 1997.

King, Charles. "Cadet Life at West Point," in *Harper's New Monthly Magazine*, LXXV (New York, 1887), 196-219.

Kelley, Elizabeth Burroughs. *A West Parker Remembers When.* N. p., 1987.

Leary, Timothy. *Flashbacks: An Autobiography.* Los Angeles, 1983.

Levitt, Arthur. *Proceedings of Conference on Town and Village Government in Westchester County*

. . . *Held at White Plains, New York, April 21,* 1958. Albany, 1958. (OSC) (g)

_____. *Watchdog for the People: A History of the Comptrollership of New York State.* Albany: October 1967. (OSC) (g)

Liddy, G. Gordon. *Will: The Autobiography of G. Gordon Liddy.* New York, 1980.

Long, Frances G., ed. "Coast to Coast by Railroad: The Journey of Niels Sears—May, 1869," in *New York History,* L:3 (July 1969), 302-315.

Lourie, Peter. *River of Mountains: A Canoe Journey down the Hudson.* Syracuse, 1995.

Lowell, Robert (Saskia Hamilton, ed.). *The Letters of Robert Lowell.* New York, 2005.

MacArthur, Douglas. *Reminiscences.* New York, 1964.

MacKaye, Benton. "An Appalachian Trail: A Project in Regional Planning," in *Journal of the American Institute of Architects,* 9 (October 1921), 325-330.

Malcolm Pirnie. *Draft Generic Environmental Impact Statement: Ulster County Solid Waste Management Program.* 2 Vols. Kingston, n.d. (1989). (g)

Marranca, Bonnie, ed. *Hudson Valley Lives.* Woodstock, 1991.

Marsh, Luther R., *et al. Report to the New York Legislature of the Commission to Select and Locate Lands for Public Parks in the Twenty-third and Twenty-four Wards of the City of New York, and in the Vicinity Thereof.* New York, 1884. (g)

Matthiessen, Alex. "20 Years of Stewardship: Riverkeeper Interview with Robert F. Kennedy, Jr.," in *Riverkeeper* (Spring 2004), 8-11.

Morris, Fordham, Pres. *Report of the Bronx Valley Sewer Commission,* New York 1896. (g)

Mumford, Lewis. *My Work and Days: A Personal Chronicle.* New York, 1979 (1929).

_____. *The Conduct of Life.* New York, 1951.

_____. *In the Name of Sanity.* New York, 1954.

New York State Comptroller's Office. *Competitive Bidding and Conflict of Interest Violations as Shown in the Audits of Local Units of Government.* Albany, 1962. (OSC) (g)

New York State Department of Audit & Control—Division of Audits and Accounts. *Audit Report on the South Mall Project.* Albany, March 31, 1971. (OSC) (g)

New York State Division of Audits and Accounts. *Construction and Financing Costs, South Mall Project.* Albany, November 30, 1978. (OSC) (g)

Nixon, Edgar B., comp. and ed. *Franklin D. Roosevelt & Conservation: 1911-1945.* Vol. One. Hyde Park, 1957. (g)

Pataki, George, with Daniel Paisner. *Pataki: An Autobiography.* New York, 1998.

Proceedings of the Court for the Trial of Impeachments: The People of the State of New York by the Assembly thereof Against William Sulzer, as Governor. Albany, 1913. (g)

Pulling, Edward. *The Early Years of Millbrook School: As Recalled on a Tour of the Campus.* Oyster Bay, 1980.

Raymond, John A. *Vassar College. A College for Women in Poughkeepsie, N. Y.: A Sketch.* New York, May 1873.

"Report of the Committee on Legislation of the Citizen's Union." New York, 1913.

Robbins, Russell W., Plan Project Manager (Alan N. Bloom, Chair, Plan Technical Committee. NYSDOT Region 8). *21st Century Mobility: The Transportation Plan for the Hudson Valley.* N.p., June 1992. (g)

Roberts, James A., Comptroller. *1797 to 1897: A Century in the Comptroller's Office.* Albany, 1897. (OSC) (g)

Rockefeller, Governor Nelson A. *Public Papers of Nelson A. Rockefeller: Fifty-Third Governor of the State of New York.* New York, 1973. (g)

Roosevelt, Eleanor. "Franklin D. Roosevelt and Hyde Park: Personal Recollections of Eleanor Roosevelt." U. S. Department of the Interior, National Park Service. Washington, n.d. (1974). (g)

_____. *The Autobiography of Eleanor Roosevelt.* N. p. (New York, 1992 (1961).

Roosevelt, Franklin D. *Public Papers of Franklin D. Roosevelt, Forty-Eighth Governor of the State of New York, Second Term 1931.* Albany, 1937. (g)

———. (Elliott Roosevelt, ed.). *The Roosevelt Letters, Being the Personal Correspondence of Franklin Delano Roosevelt: Early Years (1887-1904).* London, 1949.

Roosevelt, Mrs. James (Sara). *My Boy Franklin.* New York, 1933.

Schoonmaker, Ella Joyce Oliver. *Short Stories of My Family.* Third Edition, n.p., 1998.

Secony Map of New York (1932).

Sohmer, William, Comptroller. *Annual Report of the Comptroller: Fiscal Year Ending September 30, 1912.* Albany, January 6, 1913. (g)

Starer, Robert. "Kaaterskill Quartet" (Hudson Valley Philharmonic Chamber Players, 1989). Text by Washington Irving, James Fenimore Cooper, Robert Steuding. (m)

Stimson, Henry L., and McGeorge Bundy. *On Active Service in Peace and War.* New York, 1948.

Sulzer, William. *Life and Speeches.* Albany, 1916.

Thomas, Lowell. *Good Evening Everybody: From Cripple Creek to Samarkand.* New York, 1976 (LTC)

Tilden, Samuel J. "Report on the Difficulties Existing between the Proprietors of Certain Lease-hold Estates and Their Tenants" [1848], in Bigelow, ed., *Letters and Memorials,* 186 *ff.* (g)

Tremaine, Morris S., Comptroller. *Annual Report of the Department of Audit and Control: Fiscal Yar Ending June 30, 1933.* Albany, 1934. (g)

Tully, Grace. *F.D.R.: My Boss.* New York, 1949.

Tyler, Steven, with David Dalton. *Does the Noise in My Head Bother You? A Rock 'n' Roll Memoir.* New York, 2011.

Van Hamil, Manette. *The Flamboyant Tree: Memoirs of Manette van Hamel.* Woodstock, 2000.

Van Santvoord, C. *One Hundred and Twentieth Regiment New York State Volunteers. . . .* Rondout, 1894.

Van Santvoord, Seymour. *Random Addresses.* New York, 1930.

Vassar College: Its Foundation, Aims, Resources, and Course of Study. New York, May 1873.

Vidal, Gore. *Homage to Daniel Shays: Collected Essays 1952-1972.* New York, 1973.

———. *United States: Essays 1952-1992.* New York, 1993.

———. *Palimpsest: A Memoir.* New York, 1995.

———. *Imperial America: Reflections on the United States of Amnesia.* New York, 2004.

"The Waterways of New York: A Portrait of Life Aboard a Hudson River and Erie Canal Barge," in Hudson River Maritime Museum *Pilot Log* (2014-15), 26 *ff.*

Ward, Geoffrey, ed. *Closest Companion: The Unknown Story of the Intimate Friendship between Franklin Roosevelt and Margaret Suckley.* New York, 1999.

Ward, Seely E. "Recollections of the Sloatsburg Area," in *Orange County Historical Society,* 2 (1972-73), 7-22.

Watson, Thomas J. Jr., and Peter Petre. *Father Son & Co.: My Life at IBM and Beyond.* New York, 1990.

Weaver, Robert C. "The New Deal and the Negro: A Look at the Facts," in Aptheker, ed., IV, 174-180.

Williams-Myers, A. J., ed. *On the Morning Tide: African Americans, History and Methodology in the Historical Ebb and Flow of the Hudson River Society.* Trenton, N. J., 2003.

SECONDARY SOURCES

Abramson, Randy. *Spanning the Century: The Life of W. Averell Harriman.* New York, 1992.

Adams, Jeff. "Meeting the Future on Purpose: The Regional Approach," in *Meeting the Future on Purpose,* n.p.

Alexander, Edward Porter. "Scenic and Historic Possessions," in Flick, ed., *History of the State of New York: Volume X. The Empire State* (New York, 1937), 257-290.

Allen, Frederick Lewis, "The Coming—and Disciplining—of Industrialism, 1850-1950," in Knowles, ed., 105-127.

Alvarez, Luis A. *Alfred E. Loomis 1887-1975: A Biographical Memoir*. National Academy of Sciences. Washington, 1980 (1950). (g)

"The Amenia Conference of 1916," in Aptheker, ed., III, 130-135.

Amory, Cleveland. *The Last Resorts*. New York, 1952 (1948).

Andrews, John. "The Struggle for the Republican Party in 1960," in *The Historian*, 59:3 (Spring 1997), 613-631.

Anonymous (Raymond Beecher). *The Quarterly Journal* (Greene County Historical Society), 1 (Spring 1977).

_____. (Robert Kerker?). *The Executive Budget in New York State: A Half-Century Perspective*. Albany, 1981. (g)

Antliff, Allan. *Anarchist Modernism: Art, Politics, and the First American Avant-Garde*. Chicago, 2001.

Antos, Bethany J. "The Legend of Sleepy Hollow Restorations," in Rockefeller Archive Center *Newsletter* (2008), 16-18.

Armstead, Myra B. Young, ed. *Mighty Change, Tall Within: Black Identity in the Hudson Valley*. Albany, 2003.

Armstrong, William H. *Barefoot in the Grass: The Story of Grandma Moses*. Garden City, 1970 (1948).

Arnold, Harry. "Ice Harvesting on the Hudson River." Undated, 16-pp. typed ms.

Ashbery, John. "Foreword," in Fone, *Historic Hudson*, 6-7.

Atkinson, Brooks. *The Catskill Mountain House* (Roland Van Zandt), in *New York History*, XLVIII:4 (October 1967), 388-390. (br)

Atlas, James. *Bellow: A Biography*. New York, 2000.

Auchincloss, Louis. *The Vanderbilt Era*. New York, 1989.

"Awards and Competitions," in *Music Educator's Journal*, 65:6 (February 1979), 11*ff.*

Bacon, Edgar Mayhew. *Chronicles of Tarrytown and Sleepy Hollow*. New York, 1902.

Bailey, Frankie and Alice P. Green. *Wicked Albany: Lawlessness & Liquor in the Prohibition Era*. Charleston, S. C., 2009.

Baker, Norman R. *The Way It Was in North Rockland*. Orangeburg, 1973.

Barker, Elmer Eugene. "The Story of Arbor Hill and the Ten Broeck Mansion at Albany, New York," in *New York History*, XXXIV:4 (October 1953), 417-429.

Barker, Virgil. *A Critical Introduction to American Painting*. New York, 1931.

Barry, Elise M. "National Register of Historic Places Registration: Stonihurst." New York State Office of Parks, Recreation and Historic Preservation (April 1982). (g)

Bass, Herbert J. "David B. Hill and the 'Steal of the Senate,' 1891," in *New York History*, XLI:3 (July 1960), 299-311.

Bayles, Richard M. "Modern Catskill," in Beers, J. B., *History of Greene County*, 118-146.

Bayne, Martha Collins. *County at Large*. Poughkeepsie, 1973.

Bedell, Cornelia F. *Now and Then and Long Ago in Rockland County, New York*. Rockland County, 1941.

Beecher, Raymond. "A Winter's Ice Harvest: 1900-1901," in *The Quarterly Journal* (Greene County Historical Society), 3:4 (Winter 1979), 1 *ff.*

_____. *Kaaterskill Clove: Where Nature Met Art*. Hensonville, 2004.

Benjamin, Gerald, and Robert T. Nakamura, eds. *The Modern New York State Legislature: Redressing the Balance*. Albany, 1991.

Benjamin, Vernon. "The Saugerties Lighthouse: Current Status and Restoration Potential." Village of Saugerties (January 1982), 34 pp. (g)

_____. *Yama Farms: A Most Unusual Catskills Resort* (Harold Harris, Wendy E. Harris, and Dianne Wiebe), in *The Hudson River Valley Review*, 25:1 (Autumn 2008), 113-116. (br)

Bent, Flora E., prep. "Obituaries," in *New York History*, XXV: 2 (April 1944), 282-288.

Benton, Helen Hemingway, pub. *The Annals of America Volume 17, 1950-1960: Cold War in the Nuclear Age*. Chicago, 1968.

_____, ed. *Greeley on Lincoln; with Mr. Greeley's Letters to Charles A. Dana and a Lady Friend to which are added Reminiscences of Horace Greeley*. New York, 1893.

Berg, S. Carol. "Arthur C. Parker and the Society of the American Indian, 1911-1916," in *New York History*, 81:2 (April 2000), 237-246.

Bergon, Frank, ed. "Introduction," in Burroughs, John, *A Sharp Lookout*, 9-64.

Bigelow, John. *The Life of Samuel J. Tilden*. 2 Vols. New York, 1895.

Bigelow, Poultney. *The German Emperor and His Eastern Neighbors*. New York, 1892.

_____. "Byrdcliffe Colony of Arts and Crafts," in *American Homes and Gardens*, VI (October 1901), 389-393.

Bindas, Kenneth J., and Craig Houston. "'Takin' Care of Business': Rock Music, Vietnam and the Protest Myth," in *The Historian*, LII:1 (November 1969), 1-23.

Bliss, Edward Jr. "Lowell Thomas," in *The Quill*, 62:8 (August 1974), 14-18. (LTC)

Bliven, Rachel (original draft by John Bond). "Harmony Mills." National Register of Historic Places Registration Form, National Park Service, U. S. Department of the Interior (June 20, 1998), 36 pp. (g)

Bloodgood, Josephine. "The Spirit of the Maverick: Introduction & Acknowledgements," in Wolf, Rhoads, *et al.*, 7-10.

Bowers, Claude G. *The Tragic Era: The Revolution after Lincoln*. Cambridge, Mass., 1957 (1929).

Boyd, Joseph H. Jr., and Charles R. Holcomb. *Oreos & Dubonnet: Remembering Governor Nelson A. Rockefeller*. Albany, 2012.

Boyle, Robert H. *The Hudson River: A Natural and Unnatural History*. New York, 1969.

Bradley, Hugh. *Such Was Saratoga*. New York, 1940.

Britten, Evelyn Barrett. *Chronicles of Saratoga*. Saratoga Springs, 1959.

Bronx Board of Trade. *Parks and Parkways in the Borough of the Bronx, New York City*. Bronx, 1914. (g)

Brooks, Van Wyck. *The Ordeal of Mark Twain*. New York, 1920.

_____. *The Confident Years: 1885-1915*. New York, 1952.

Bruno, Maryann and Elizabeth A. Daniels. *Vassar College*. Charleston, S. C., 2001.

Burmeister, Walter F. *Appalachian Waters 2: The Hudson River and Its Tributaries*. Oakton, Va., 1974 (1962).

Burt, Mary E. *Little Nature Studies for Little People from the Essays of John Burroughs*. Boston, 1895.

Butterfield, Roy L. "On the American Migrations," in *New York History*, XXXVIII:4 (October 1957), 368-386.

Cady, Edwin Harrison. *The Gentleman in America*. Syracuse, 1949.

"Calm After Storm: Grandmother of Environmental Lawsuits Settled by Mediation," in *Environmental Law Reporter*, 11 (1981), 10074-10077.

Carlson, Elof Axel. *Unfit: A History of a Bad Idea*. Cold Spring Harbor, 2001.

Carmer, Carl. *The Hudson*. New York, 1968 (1939).

_____. *Dark Trees to the Wind: A Cycle of York State Years*. New York, 1949.

_____. *My Kind of Country: Favorite Writings about New York*. New York, 1966.

Carr, Virginia Spencer. *The Lonely Hunter: A Biography of Carson McCullers*. New York, 1975.

Carso, Kerry Dean. "Ruins on the Hudson and Beyond: The Nineteenth-Century Delight in Decay," in *The Hudson River Valley Review*, 31:1 (Autumn 2014), 38-49.

Cashman, Sean Dennis. *America in the Age of the Titans: The Progressive Era and World War I.* New York, 1988.

_____. *America in the Twenties and Thirties: The Olympian Age of Franklin Delano Roosevelt.* New York, 1989.

Chafe, William H. *The Unfinished Journey: America since World War II.* New York, 1986.

Chandler, Alfred D. Jr. "The American Businessman: Industrial Statesman or Robber Baron?" in Grob and Billias, eds., 103-126.

Cheli, Guy. *Images of America: Putnam County.* Portsmouth, N. H., 2004.

Chappaqua Kiwanis Club. "Chappaqua 200th Anniversary Celebration and Formal Opening of the Grade Crossing Elimination Bridge." Chappaqua, September 6, 1930.

Cherry, Robin. "Laurence Apsey, an Appreciation," in *Egbert Benson Historical Society of Red Hook* (Spring 2010).

Chessman, G. Wallace. *Governor Theodore Roosevelt: The Albany Apprenticeship, 1898-1900.* Cambridge, 1965.

Christman, Henry. "Iona Island and the Fruit Growers Convention of 1864," in *New York History*, XLVIII:4 (October 1967), 332-351.

"City of Glens Falls," in Warren County Bicentennial Citizens' Advisory Committee, 23-26.

Clapp, Margaret. *Forgotten First Citizen: John Bigelow.* Boston, 1947.

Claridge, Laura. *Emily Post: Daughter of the Gilded Age, Mistress of American Manners.* New York, 2008. New York, 2008.

Clark, Robert C. "The Bridge That Came to Be: Descendant of the Bridge that Never Was," in *Orange County Historical Society,* 9 (1979-80), 19-23.

Clarke, Gerald. *Capote: A Biography.* New York, 1988.

Coffee, Ronnie Clark. *Images of America: Bear Mountain.* Portsmouth, N. H., 2008.

Coffin, Margaret. "The Fabulous Butlers of Brandy Hill," in *New York History* XXXIV:3 (July 1953) 351-358.

Collier, Peter, with David Horowitz. *The Roosevelts: An American Saga.* New York, 1994.

Commager, Henry Steele. "Who Is Loyal to America" in Knowles, ed., *Gentlemen, Scholars and Scoundrels, 95-105.*

Comstock, Anita Inman. "Rural Westchester to the Turn of the Century: Farmers, Squires and Just Plain Folk," in Weigold, ed., 21-48.

Conant, Jennet. *Tuxedo Park: A Wall Street Tycoon and the Secret Palace of Science that Changed the Course of World War II.* New York, 2002.

Connery, Robert H., and Gerald Benjamin. *Rockefeller of New York: Executive Power in the Statehouse.* Ithaca, 1979.

Cook, Blanche Wiesen. *Eleanor Roosevelt.* Vol. I: 1884-1933 & Vol. II: 1933-1938. New York, 1992, 1999.

Cooper, Leo. "Alvin the Adamant Atom," in *Sing-Out,* 3:7 (March 1953), 6-7. (m)

Cowley, Robert, and Thomas Guinzburg, eds. *West Point: Two Centuries of Honor and Tradition.* New York, 2002.

Crane, Fred. "Lewis Mumford and the Celebration of the Region," in *Meeting the Future on Purpose,* n.p.

Crawford, John W. "Maxwell Anderson," in Magill, ed., *Critical Survey of Drama,* I, 35-41.

Crichton, Judy. *America 1900: The Turning Point.* New York, 1998.

Crissey, "Story of the Carleton Hudson Scoop," in *The Quill,* 3:3 (April 1915), 5 *ff.* (LTC)

Crofut, Doris. "Who Was Augusta?" in *Orange County Historical Society,* 10 (1981-82), 3-9.

Cronin, R. David. "Assistant Secretary of the Navy," in Graham and Wander, eds., 7-9.

Croog, Charles F. "FBI Political Surveillance and the Isolationist-Interventionist Debate, 1939-1941," in *The Historian,* 54:3 (Spring 1992), 441-458.

Cull, Nicholas J. *Selling War: The British Propaganda Campaign Against American Neutrality in World War II.* Cary, S. C., 1996.

Curtis, Edgar. "Bittleman, Arnold Irwin," in Somers, ed., *Encyclopedia,* 107-108.

Cuscuna, Michael. "Woodstock: A Music Community," in *Words & Music,* 2:8 (November 1972), 51-53.

Dahl, Linda. *Morning Glory: A Biography of Mary Lou Williams.* Westminster, Md., 2000.

Dahlberg, Jane S. *The New York Bureau of Municipal Research.* New York, 1966.

Daniels, Elizabeth A. *Bridges to the World: Henry Noble MacCracken and Vassar College.* Clinton Corners, 1994.

————. and Clyde Griffen. *"Full Steam Ahead in Poughkeepsie": The Story of Coeducation at Vassar 1966-1974.* Poughkeepsie, 2000.

Davis, Kenneth S. *Eisenhower: American Hero; The Historical Record of His Life.* N.p. (New York), 1969.

Davis, Kevin S. "Education," in Graham and Wander, eds., 108-111.

Delafield, John Ross. "Montgomery Place," in *Year Book: Dutchess County Historical Society,* 14 (1929), 26-31.

De Lisser, R. Lionel. *Picturesque Catskills Greene County.* Cornwallville, 1971 (1894).

Dempsey, Janet. *Cornwall Revisited: A Hudson River Community.* Monroe: 1997.

De Witt, William C. *People's History of Kingston, Rondout and Vicinity.* New Haven, Conn.: 1943.

Diachisin, Alex N. *Drainage Basins of Streams: Entering the Hudson River in Albany, Columbia , Greene and Rensselaer Counties.* Albany, 1962. (g)

"The Diary of Annie McElhone DuBois," in *Newsletter (*Historical Society of Shawangunk & Gardiner), 7:2 (Spring 2010), 1 *ff.*

Dominy, Michèle. "A Place for Bioregionalism in the Hudson Valley? A Report," in *Hudson Valley Regional Review,* 11:2 (September 1994), 81-92.

Douglas, Ann. *Terrible Honesty: Mongrel Manhattan in the 1920s.* New York, 1995.

Dows, Olin. *Franklin Roosevelt at Hyde Park.* N.p., 1949.

"Dr. James G. Graham: A Strong Man in Shawangunk's Early History," in *Newsletter* (Historical Society of Shawangunk & Gardiner), 7:1 (Winter 2010), 1 *ff.*

Dumond, C. Chester (Commissioner of Agriculture). "New York State's Battle on the Food Front.," in *New York History,* XXV (1944), 532-539.

Du Mond, Frank L. *Walking through Yesterday in Old West Hurley.* Kalamazoo, 1990.

Dunn, Violet B., Editor-in-Chief. *Saratoga County Heritage.* N. p. (Saratoga Springs), 1974.

Dunwell, Frances F. *The Hudson River Highlands.* New York, 1991.

DuPont, M. Jill. "Chester A. Arthur (1829-1886)," in Schechter and Bernstein, eds., 564-575.

Dyson, Lowell K. "The Milk Strike of 1939 and the Destruction of the Dairy Farmers Union," in *New York History,* LI:5 (October 1970), 523-543.

Eckel, Edwin C. "Early History of the Portland Cement Industry in New York State," Appendix A in *Bulletin of the New York State Museum,* 44:8 (November 1901), 849-859.

Eckhardt, Joseph P. *Living Large: Wilna Hervey and Nan Mason.* Woodstock, 2015.

Edwards, Rebecca. *New Spirits: Americans in the Gilded Age, 1865-1905.* New York, 2006.

Eisenstadt, Peter, ed. *The Encyclopaedia of New York State.* Syracuse, 2005.

Ellis, Mark. *Race, War, and Surveillance: African Americans and the United States Government during World War I.* Bloomington, Ind., 2001.

Emsley, Joseph W. "Dr. Henry Noble MacCracken 1880-1970," in *Year Book: Dutchess County Historical Society,* 55 (1970), 24-31.

Engeman, Jack. *West Point: The Life of a Cadet.* New York, 1956.

Erdman, David and Susan. "Summering in Palenville," *The Quarterly Journal* (Greene County Historical Society), 1 (Spring 1777), 2-3.

Evers, Alf. *The Catskills: From Wilderness to Woodstock.* Garden City, 1972.

————. *Woodstock: History of an American Town.* Woodstock, 1987.

————. *Kingston: City on the Hudson.* Woodstock, 2005.

Ewan, William H. Jr. *Steamboats on the Hudson River.* Charleston, South Carolina, 2011.

Fein, Michael R. *Paving the Way: New York Road Building and the American State, 1880-1956.* Lawrence, Kan., 2008.

Ferber, Linda S. "'The Geography of the Ideal': The Hudson River and the Hudson River School," in *The Hudson River Valley Review,* 31:1 (Autumn 2014), 2-15.

Findlay, Stuart. "Linkages between People and Ecosystems: How Did We Get from Separate to Equal?" in Henshaw, ed., *Environmental History,* 7-12.

Flad, Harvey K. "Visual Pollution of the Proposed Nuclear Reactor Site in the Town of Lloyd, Ulster County, New York," in John H. Johnson, ed., B-9-12-51 B-9-50.

————. "The Country and the City," in *Meeting the Future on Purpose,* n.p.

————. "Scenes 'most impressive and delightful': Nineteenth-Century Artists in the Shawan-gunks," in *The Hudson River Valley Review,* 31:1 (Autumn 2014), 95-120.

————. and Clyde Griffen. *Main Street to Mainframes: Landscape and Social Change in Pough-keepsie.* Albany, 2009.

Flad, Mary. "Eleanor Roosevelt, Val-Kill, and the American Crafts Movement," in *Dutchess County Historical Society Yearbook,* 81 (1997-1998), 58-65.

Fletcher Gallery. Anton Refregier Exhibition "Programme". Woodstock, August 23-October 5, 1977.

Flick, Alexander Clarence. *Samuel J. Tilden: A Study in Political Sagacity.* New York, 1939.

Fogel, Nan. "Changes in Dutchess County's Art Scene," in *Dutchess County Historical Society Yearbook,* 80 (1995-1996), 34-39.

————, Joyce Ghee, and Stephanie Mauri. "Do-It-Yourself 'Arttours' of Dutchess County," in *Dutchess County Historical Society Yearbook,* 80 (1995-1996), 48-74.

Fogel, Nancy, ed. *FDR at Home.* Poughkeepsie, 2005.

Foner, Dr. Philip S., ed. *The New American History.* Philadelphia, 1990.

Førland, Tor Egil. "Bringing it All Back Home *or* Another Side of Bob Dylan: Midwestern Iso-lationist," in *Journal of American Studies,* 26:3 (December 1992), 337-356.

Forty-Second Annual Report of the Trustees of the State Museum of Natural History, for the Year 1888. Albany, 1889. (s, g)

Foster, Amy. "Digging in the Garden: Historical Excavations at Mills Mansion State Historic Site in Staatsburg, New York—Second Season," in *The Hudson Valley Regional Review,* XVI:1 (March 1999), 63-74.

Fox, Dixon Ryan. "A Retrospect for Yorkers," in *New York History,* XVIII:1 (January 1937), 30-40.

Fried, Marc B. *The Huckleberry Pickers: A Raucous History of the Shawangunk Mountains.* Hen-sonville, 1995.

Friedan, Betty. "The Coming Ice Age: A True Scientific Detective Story," in Knowles, ed., 573-586.

————. *The Feminine Mystique.* New York, 1963.

Friedman, Stephen J. "Industrialization, Immigration and Transportation to 1900," in Weigold, ed., 49-89.

Furman, Bess. *White House Profile: A Social History of the White House, its Occupants and its Fes-tivities.* New York, 1951.

Gaede, Jean Lasher, Ed. *Woodstock Recollection by Recipe.* Woodstock, 1967.

Galusha, Diane. *Liquid Assets: A History of New York City's Water System.* Fleischmanns, 2002 (1999).

Gates, John D. *The Astor Family.* New York, 1981.

Gates, Paul W. "Agricultural Change in New York State, 1850-1890," in *New York History,* L:2 (April 1969), 115-142.

Ghee, Joyce, and Burnstine, Lyn. "Folk Songs of the Region," in *Meeting the Future on* Purpose, n. p.

Ghee, Joyce, and Joan Spence. *Harlem Valley Pathways: Through Pawling, Dover, Amenia, North East, and Pine Plains.* Charleston, S. C., 1998.

Ghee, Joyce C., and Stephanie Mauri, "Do-It Yourself Women's History Tour of Dutchess County," in Dutchess County Historical Society *Yearbook,* 82 (1999-2000), 93-107.

Glunt, Ruth Reynolds. *Lighthouses and Legends of the Hudson.* Monroe, 1975.

Goderre, Frank. *Images of America: New York State Police Troop K.* Portsmouth, N. H., 2007.

Gody, Lou, editor-in-chief. *The WPA Guide to New York City: The Federal Writers Project Guide to 1930s New York.* New York, 1982 (1939).

Goeke, Joseph F. "T. S. Arthur (1809-1885)," in Ljundquist, 16-28.

Goewey, David. *Crash-Out: The True Tale of a Hell's Kitchen Kid and the Bloodiest Escape in Sing Sing History.* New York, 2005.

Goodwin, Doris Kearns. *No Ordinary Time. Franklin and Eleanor Roosevelt: The Home Front in World War II.* New York, 1994.

Gordon, Allen, ed. *The Woodstock Aquarian: Good Medicine from Woodstock,* II:1 (1971).

Gordon, Jim. "Trading Green for Gold: Kingston's Rush to Approve Industrial Park Endangers Pristine City Forest," in *Woodstock Times,* February 15, 1996.

_____. Katie Cahill and Steve Hopkins. "DEC to the Rescue? St. Lawrence Proposal Dealt Administrative Judicial Blow," in *Saugerties Times,* June 26, 2003.

Gorkin, Michael. "At 86 Lowell Thomas Looks for New Worlds to Conquer," in *50 Plus,* 19:1 (January 1979), 10-15. (LTC)

Gottlieb, Robert. *Forcing the Spring: The Transformation of the American Environmental Movement.* Washington, 2005.

Graham, Otis L. Jr., and Meghan Robinson Wander, eds. *Franklin D. Roosevelt His Life and Times: An Encyclopedic View.* Boston, 1985.

Grant, Madison, Chair; James G. Cannon & Dave H. Morris, Commissioners. *Report of the Bronx Parkway Commission.* Ch. 669 of the Laws of 1906. Albany, 1907. (g)

Greene, Nelson, ed. *History of the Valley of the Hudson: River of Destiny 1609-1930.* 5 Vols. Chicago, 1931.

Green, Nancy E., ed. *Byrdcliffe: An American Arts and Crafts Colony.* Ithaca, 2004.

Grob, Gerald N., and George A. Bilias, eds. *Interpretations of American History: Patterns and Perspectives, Vol. 2, Since 1865.* New York, 1967.

Grondahl, Paul. *I Rose Like a Rocket: The Political Education of Theodore Roosevelt.* New York, 2004.

Hacker, Louis M., and Benjamin B. Kendrick, with the collaboration of Helene S. Zahler. *The United States Since 1865.* Fourth Edition. New York, 1949 (1932).

Hacker, Louis M. *The Triumph of Capitalism: The Development of Forces in American History to the Beginning of the Twentieth Century.* New York, 1965 (1940).

Halberstam, David. *The Fifties.* New York, 1993.

Hale, William Harlan. *Horace Greeley: Voice of the People.* N.p. (Scranton, Pa.), 1950.

"The Half-Moon of the Hudson-Fulton Celebration," in *De Halve Maen,* I:1 (October 1922), 1.

Hall, Edward Hagaman, prep. *The Hudson-Fulton Celebration 1909: The Fourth Annual Report.* . . . 2 Vols. Albany, 1910. (g)

_____. "The New York Commercial Tercentenary, 1614-1914," in *Nineteenth Annual Report, 1914.* (g)

Hammond, John Winthrop (Arthur Pound, ed.). *Men and Volts: The Story of General Electric.* Schenectady, 1941.

Hansen, Harry. *North of Manhattan: Persons and Places of Old Westchester.* New York, 1950.

_____. *Scarsdale: From Colonial Manor to Modern Community.* New York, 1954.

Harris, Harold; Wendy E. Harris and Dianne Wiebe. *Yama Farms: A Most Unusual Catskills Resort.* Cragsmoor Historical Society, 2006.

Hart, Larry. *Schenectady's Golden Era (between 1890 and 1930).* Scotia, 1974.

_____. *Steinmetz in Schenectady: A Picture Story of Three Memorable Decades.* Scotia, 1978.

Havey, Paul. "Woodstock Family Is," in Allen Gordon, ed., 13-14.

"'Hawkers of Hate': Nelson A. Rockefeller's 1964 Warning on Extremism," in Rockefeller Archive Center *Newsletter* (2008), 13-14.

Hayden, Dolores. *Building Suburbia: Green Fields and Urban Growth, 1820-2000.* New York, 2003.

Haynes, Bruce D. "Race and Class Politics in a Black Middle-Class Suburb," in Armstead, ed., 175-189.

Hearn, Donna P. *Images of America: Dover.* Portsmouth, N. H., 2008.

Heiman, Michael K. *The Quiet Evolution: Power, Planning, and Profits in New York State.* New York, 1988.

Hendrickson, Kenneth E. Jr. "George R. Lunn and the Socialist Era in Schenectady, New York. 1909-1916," in *New York History,* XLVII:1 (January 1966), 22-40.

Hennessee, Judith. *Betty Friedan: Her Life.* New York, 1999.

Henshaw, Robert E., ed. *Environmental History of the Hudson River: Human Uses that Changed the Ecology, Ecology that Changes Human Uses.* Albany, 2011.

Heimer, Mel. *Fabulous Bawd: The Story of Saratoga.* New York, 1952.

Heppner, Richard. *Women of the Catskills: Stories of Struggle, Sacrifice & Hope.* Charleston, S. C.: 2011.

_____. and Janine Fallon-Mower. *Legendary Locals of Woodstock, New York.* Charleston, S.C.: 2013.

Heritage Task Force for the Hudson River Valley, Inc. (David Church, Study Director). *The Lower Hudson Basin Tributary Study: Recommendations on Protection and Best Management of Tributaries to the Tidal Hudson River.* N. p. (New Paltz), December 1990. (g)

Hinchman, Hannah. "Character Studies," in *Sierra,* 79 (March/April 1994), 30-31.

Hill, C. P. "American Radicalism: Jackson, Bryan and Wilson," in Allen and Hill, eds., 225-243.

Hilscher, Ted. "Warrenton to Catskill: A Story of the Great Migration," in *The Hudson River Valley Review,* 32:1 (Autumn 2015)34-49.

Hinchey, Office of Assemblyman Maurice D. (Vernon Benjamin). *Staff Report: Town of Saugerties Sewers Project.* Albany (September 1988), 111 pp. (g)

Hirsch, E. D. Jr. *Cultural Literacy: What Every American Needs to Know.* New York, 1987.

Historical Records Survey, Division of Women's & Professional Project, Works Projects Administration (prep.). *Inventory of the County Archives of New York State: No. 1 Albany County (Albany).* Albany, October 1937. (g)

Hodgson, Geoffrey. *The Gentleman from New York: Daniel Patrick Moynihan: A Biography.* New York, 2000.

Hoffer, Peter Charles, ed. *Commerce and Community: Selected Articles on the Middle Atlantic Colonies.* New York, 1988.

Hoffman, Andrew J., and Ventresca, Marc J. *Organizations, Policy and the Natural Environment: Institutional and Strategic Perspectives.* Stanford, Calif., 2004.

Hoffman, Elizabeth. "Cultural Landscape Management at Three Historic Sites in the Hudson Valley: Vanderbilt Mansion National Historic Site, Clermont State Historic Site, and Montgomery Place," in *The Hudson Valley Regional Review,* 13:2 (September 1996), 23-54.

Holmes, John. "Sarah Gibson Blanding (1898-1985), An Appreciation," in *Vassar Quarterly,* LXXXI:3, 28-31.

Hoogenboom, Ari. "Spoilsmen and Reformers: Civil Service Reform and Public Morality," in Morgan, H. Wayne, ed., 69-90.

Horne, Field. "Life on a Rocky Farm 1862-1902," in *The Hudson Valley Regional Review*, 7:1 (March 1990), 30-41.

_____. *Saratoga Springs: The Complete Visitor's Guide*. N.p. (Saratoga Springs), 2014.

Hudson *Gazette. Columbia County at the End of the Century.* 2 Vols. Hudson, 1900.

"Hudson River Damage and GE: Do the Math," in *Clearwater Navigator*, XXVIII:4 (September/October 1997), 16.

Hudson River Estuary Program, Hudson River Environmental Society, Center for Biodiversity and Conservation (American Museum of Natural History). "Biographies and Abstracts for Conserving Biodiversity in Hudson River Habitats: New York Harbor to Troy," New York, 2000.

Hudson River Sloop Restoration, Inc. "Hudson River Sloops: A Brief History and Technical Description, together with Excerpts from a Nineteenth Century Travel Journal." Hastings-on-Hudson, 1970.

Hughes, Thomas P., and Agatha C. Hughes, eds. *Lewis Mumford: Public Intellectual.* New York, 1990.

Huntington, David C. "Olana: 'The Center of the World,'" in *The Magazine Antiques*, 88 (November 1965), 656-663.

Huston, John W. "Arnold, Henry Harley ('Hap')," in Graham and Wander, eds., 7-8.

Hutton, George V. "The Zenith and Sudden Decline of the Great Hudson River Brick Industry," in *The Hudson Valley Regional Review*, 19:1 (March 2002), 16-29.

Ilingworth, Montieth. M. *Mike Tyson: Money, Myth, and Betrayal.* New York, 1991.

Institute on Man and Science. "Changing Human Relations: An Account of the Summer Institute" (July 1968), Rensselaerville, 1968.

Johnson, Denise Love. "Black Neighborhood Formation in Poughkeepsie during the Great Migration, 1950-1970," in Armstead, ed., 163-174.

Johnson, Colonel (Ret.) James M. (Hudson River Valley Institute). *Carved from Granite: West Point Since 1902* (Lance Betros), in *The Hudson River Valley Review*, 29:1 (Autumn 2012), 118-120. (br)

Johnson, Paul. *Intellectuals.* New York, 1988.

_____. *The Birth of the Modern: World Society 1815-1830.* New York, 1991.

Jones, Landon Y. *Great Expectations: America and the Baby Boom Generation.* New York, 1980.

Jones, Peter. "Historic Context," in *Marianne Appel & Austin Mecklem*, 4-8.

Josephson, Robi. *Images of America: Mohonk Mountain House and Preserve.* Portsmouth, N. H., 2002.

Kadt, Maarten de. *The Bronx River: An Environmental & Social History.* Charleston, S. C.: 2011.

Kallir, Otto. *Grandma Moses.* New York, 1984 (1973).

Kammen, Michael. "The Quest for Tradition and the Role of Preservation in Upstate New York," in *New York History*, 58:2 (April, 1977), 157-172.

Kane, Joseph Nathan. *Famous First Facts: A Record of First Happenings, Discoveries, and Inventions in American History.* 4th Edition. New York, 1981.

Kapp, Friedrich. *Immigration and the Commissioners of Emigration of the State of New York.* New York, 1870.

Keith, Claire. "The Lowell Thomas Papers. Part II: 1918-1923," in *The Journal of the T. E. Lawrence Society*, 8:2 (1998), 44-96. (LTC)

Kennan, George. *E. H. Harriman: A Biography.* 2 Vols. Boston, 1922.

Kennedy, William. *O Albany! Improbable City of Political Wizards, Fearless Ethnics, Spectacular Aristocrats, Splendid Nobodies, and Underrated Scoundrels.* New York, 1983.

Kilgannon, Corey. "New Film, 'Out of the Furnace,' Accused of Stereotyping Ramapough Indians," in *The New York Times*, December 12, 2013.

Kimball, Warren F. "Churchill, Winston Leonard Spencer," in Graham and Wander, eds., 58-62.

Klein, Aaron E. *New York Central.* New York, 1985.

Klein, Maury. *The Flowering of the Third America: The Making of an Organizational Society, 1850-1920.* Chicago, 1993.

Kline, Polly. "Biographical Note," in *Marianne Appel & Austin Mecklem,* 9-11.

Kline, Reamer. *Education for the Common Good: A History of Bard College—The First 100 Years (1860-1960).* Annandale-on-Hudson, 1982.

Knowles, Horace, ed. *Gentlemen, Scholars and Scoundrel: A Treasury of the Best of Harper's Magazine from 1850 to the Present.* New York, 1959.

Koeppel, Gerard T. *Water for Gotham: A History.* Princeton, N. J., 2001.

Korda, Michael. *Ike: An American Hero.* New York, 2007.

Koszarsk, Richard. *Hollywood on the Hudson: Film and Television in New York from Griffith to Sarnoff.* New Brunswick, N. J., 2008.

Koziol, Mark J. "Riding to the Rescue: How Theodore Roosevelt Saved the Erie Canal," in *The Hudson Valley Regional Review,* 18:2 (September 2001), 17-28.

Krout, John A. "Sports and Recreation," in Flick, ed., *The History of the State of New York, X: The Empire State* (New York, 1937), 217-254.

Kutz, Myer. *Rockefeller Power: America's Chosen Family.* New York, 1974.

Lankler, Rev. Dr. Ralph Conover. *Lowell Thomas of Quaker Hill.* Pawling, 1990. (LTC)

Larkin, F. Daniel. *Pioneer American Railroads: The Mohawk and Hudson & the Saratoga and Schenectady.* Fleischmanns, 1995.

Lears, T. J. Jackson. *No Place of Grace: Antimodernism and the Transformation of American Culture, 1880-1920.* New York, 1981.

Leckie, Robert. *The Wars of America.* New York, 1992 (1968).

Legislative Commission on Expenditure Review. *State Historic Preservation Programs.* Albany: November 1, 1974. (g)

"Letchworth Village Name Changed to Hudson Valley DDSO," in *OMRDD Reports,* 11:1 (July 1999). (www.omr.state.ny.us/reports)

Levine, Lawrence W., and Cornelia R. Levine. *The People and the President: America's Conversation with FDR.* Boston, 2002.

Lifset, Robert D. *Power on the Hudson: Storm King Mountain and the Emergency of Modern American Environmentalism.* Pittsburgh, 2004.

Linner, Edward R. (Elizabeth A. Daniels, ed.). *Vassar: The Remarkable Growth of a Man and His College 1855-1865.* Poughkeepsie, 1984.

Livney, Lee. "Let Us Now Praise Self-Made Men: A Reexamination of the Hilton-Seligman Affair," in *New York History,* LXXV:1 (January 1994), 67-115.

Loeks, D. David, Project Director (Rockefeller Foundation). *Anatomy of an Environment: Final Report of the Hudson Basin Project.* N.p. (June 1976), 82.

Love, Richard H. *Carl W. Peters: American Scene Painter from Rochester to Rockport.* Rochester, 1999.

Lubick, George M. (Northern Arizona University). *From Coastal Wilderness to Fruited Plain: A History of Environmental Change in Temperate North America, 1500 to the Present* (Gordon G. Whitney), in *American Historical Review,* 101:5 (December 1996), 1618. (br)

Luccarilli, Mark. "Planning and Regionalism in the Early Thought of Lewis Mumford," in *The Hudson Valley Regional Review,* 7:1 (March 1990), 1-19.

_____. *Lewis Mumford and the Ecological Region: The Politics of Planning.* New York, 1995.

Lynes, Russell. *The Tastemakers.* New York, 1949-54.

_____. *The Lively Audience: A Social History of the Visual and Performing Arts in America, 1890-1950.* New York, 1985.

Lyons, Eugene. *Herbert Hoover: A Biography.* Garden City, 1964.

Mabie, Carlton. *Promised Land: Father Divine's Interracial Communities in Ulster County, New York.* Fleischmanns, 2008.

_____. "Gardiner's Aqueducts," in *Newsletter* (Historical Society of Shawangunk & Gardiner), 5:3 (Fall 2008), 1 *ff*.

MacDonald, Charles B. *The Mighty Endeavor: American Armed Forces in the European Theater in World War II*. New York, 1969.

Maddox, Kenneth W. "'His Nooks and Hiding Places': Asher B. Durand's Retreats in the Hudson Highlands," in *The Hudson River Valley Review*, 31:1 (Autumn 2014), 81-94.

Magill, Frank N., ed. *Critical Survey of Drama*. Englewood Cliffs, N. J., 1994.

Majovski, Barbara Deyo. "Sifting for Reflections: Research Preliminary to Excavation of the Mills Mansion Greenhouse Complex," in *The Hudson Valley Regional Review*, XVI:1 (March 1999), 50-55.

Mamiya, Lawrence H. "Bessie Harden Payne (1895-1991)," in Dutchess County Historical Society *Yearbook*, 82 (1999-2000), 24-28.

Manchester, William. *American Caesar: Douglas MacArthur 1880-1964*. Boston, Boston, 1978.

Maney, Patrick J. *The Roosevelt Presence: A Biography of Franklin Delano Roosevelt*. New York, 1992.

Marcus, Greil. *Invisible Republic: Bob Dylan's Basement Tapes*. New York, 1997.

Marianne Appel & Austin Mecklem: Remembering Two Artists from the Maverick Years. Woodstock Artists Association, October 23, 1999-January 10, 2000.

Marshall, Donald W. "Bedford Yesterday," in League of Women Voters, *This is Bedford* (Katonah, 1976), 5-8.

Martin, Neil S. "Westchester as an Evolving Suburb," in Weigold, ed.

Matthiessen, Alex, with Lisa Rainwater van Suntum and Kyle Rabin. "The Real Deal: Energy Reliability in a Post-Indian Point World," in *Riverkeeper* (spring 2004), 11-14.

Mayer, Bob. "The Asylum Base Ball Club: Middletown's Crack Semi-Pro Team, 1888–1894." 12 pp. (John Thorn Collection).

McCauley, Hugh J. "Visions of Kykuit: John D. Rockefeller's House at Pocantico Hills, Tarrytown, New York," in *The Hudson Valley Regional Review*, 10:2 (September 1993), 1-49.

McConnell, Curt. *The Record-Setting Trips: By Auto from Coast to Coast, 1909-1916*. Stanford, California, 2003.

McCormick, Richard L. *From Realignment to Reform: Political Change in New York State, 1893-1910*. Ithaca, 1981.

_____. "Public Life in Industrial America, 1877-1917," in Foner, ed., 93-117.

McFarland, Gerald W. *Inside Greenwich Village: A New York City Neighborhood, 1898-1918*. Amherst, 2005.

McGlinchey, Gain Susan Lvy, "Why Teach?," in *Vassar Quarterly*, LXXXI:3 (Summer 1985), 14-15.

McGloughlin, Kate. "An Angeloch Sky," in *Woodstock Times* (March 24, 2011), 1 *ff*.

McIlvaine, Robert S. *Technology as Freedom: The New Deal and the Electrical Modernization of the American Home* (Ronald C. Tobey, Berkeley, 1996), in *American Historical Review*, 4:103 (October 98), 1342-1343. (br)

McKay, Charles. "'There Goes God!' The Story of Father Divine and His Angels," in Aptheker, ed., IV, 156-163.

McMahon, Jane. "Westchester from the Roaring Twenties to V-J Day," in Weigold, ed., 109-146.

Meacham, Jon. *Franklin and Winston: An Intimate Portrait of an Epic Friendship*. New York, 2003.

Meeting the Future on Purpose: Papers in Honor of Lewis Mumford. Proceedings, "A Sense of the Region" Conference. Bard College, Annandale-on-Hudson, 1978.

Meiselbach-Dankert, I. Carolyn. *The Best of DayHops. . .and Then Some! In and about the Beautiful Mid Hudson Valley: An Annual Book*. New York, 1987.

Mele, Andy. "Dealing with Development: Clearwater's Challenge for the Coming Decades," *Clearwater Navigator*, XXVIII:4 (September/October 1997), 6 ff.

Menand, Louis. "Young Saul," in *The New Yorker* (May 11, 2015), 71-77.

Mercier, Stephen M. "John Burroughs and the Hudson River Valley in Environmental History," in *The Hudson River Valley Review*, 25:1 (Autumn 2008), 56-77.

Merrill, Arch. "Covered Bridges in New York State," in *New York History*, XXXIII:1 (January 1952), 84-93.

Merwin, John. *The Battenkill: An Intimate Portrait of a Great Trout River—Its History, People, and Fishing Possibilities.* New York, 1993.

Meyer, Adolphy E. *An Educational History of the American People.* New York, 1957.

Meyer, David K. *Networked Machinists: High-Technology Industries in Antebellum America.* Baltimore, 2006.

Michaels, Joanne, and Mary Barile. *Famous Woodstock Cooks and Their Favorite Recipes.* N.p. (Woodstock), 1987.

Mid-Hudson Pattern for Progress Inc. *An Economic Resources Inventory: Volume I: The Mid-Hudson: New York's Natural Growth Area.* Poughkeepsie, September 1983.

Milford, Nancy. *Savage Beauty: The Life of Edna St. Vincent Millay.* New York, 2001.

Miller, Donald L. *Supreme City: How Jazz Age Manhattan Gave Birth to Modern America.* New York, 2014.

Miller, Nathan. *The Roosevelt Chronicles.* Garden City, 1979.

Miller, Paul. *Organized Crime's Involvement in the Waste Hauling Industry: A Report from Chairman Maurice D. Hinchey to the New York State Assembly on Environmental Conservation.* Albany, July 24, 1986. (g)

Mills, C. Wright. "Introduction to the Mentor Edition," in Thorstein Veblen, *Theory of the Leisure Class* (New York, 1953), vi-xix.

———. *The Power Elite.* New York, 1970 (1956).

Mires, Charlene. "The Search for the 'Capital of the World'," in *Research Reports from the Rockefeller Archive Center* (Fall 2005), 1-3.

Moffett, Glendon L. *Down to the River by Trolley: The History of the New Paltz-Highland Trolley Line.* Fleischmanns, 1993.

———. *Uptown-Downtown Horsecars-Trolley Cars: Urban Transportation in Kingston, New York 1866-1930.* Fleischmans, 1997.

Morgan, H. Wayne, ed. *The Gilded Age: A Reappraisal.* Syracuse, 1963.

———. "An Age in Need of Reassessment: A View Beforehand," in Morgan, H. Wayne, ed., 1-13.

Morgan, Ted. *FDR: A Biography.* London, 1986.

Morris, Edmund. *The Rise of Theodore Roosevelt.* New York, 1979.

Morris, Elizabeth Woodbridge, ed. *Miss Wylie of Vassar.* New Haven, Conn., 1934.

Morrison, Van. "Old Old Woodstock," in *Words & Music*, 2:8 (November 1972), 42-43. (m)

Mugridge, Donald H., and Blanche P. Crum, comp. *A Guide to the Study of the United States of America: Representative Books Reflecting the Development of American Life and Thought.* Washington, 1960. (g)

Mumford, Lewis. *The Golden Day: A Study in American Literature and Culture.* New York, 1968 (1926).

———. "The Story of Troutbeck," 7 pp unpublished manuscript, n.d. (Adriance Memorial Library).

———. *The Brown Decades: A Study of the Arts in America 1865-1895.* New York, 1931.

———. *The City In History: Its Origins, Its Transformations, and Its Prospects.* New York, 1961.

Munson, Gorham. *The Awakening Twenties: A Memoir History of a Literary Period.* Baton Rouge, La., 1985.

Munson-Williams-Proctor Institute. *1913 Armory Show 50th Anniversary Exhibition 1963*. New York, 1963.

Murlin, Edgar L. *The New York Red Book*. Albany, 1908 (g)

Murray, Stuart. *Thomas Cornell and the Cornell Steamboat Company*. Fleischmanns, 2001.

Mylod, John. *Biography of a River: The People and Legends of the Hudson Valley*. New York, 1969.

Naier, Aryeh. "Surveillance as Censorship," in Rips, 9-18.

National Research Council Committee on Alternatives to Indian Point for Meeting Energy Needs (National Academy of Sciences). *Alternatives to the Indian Point Energy Center for Meeting New York Electric Power Needs*. Washington, 2006. (g)

Nein, Charles M. *Albany Molding Sands of the Hudson Valley*. N.Y.S. Museum Bulletin No. 4 (February 1901). (g)

Nesbit, Robert. *The Present Age: Progress and Anarchy in Modern America*. New York, 1988.

Nevins, Allan. *Grover Cleveland: A Study in Courage*. New York, 1932.

Nordstrom, Carl. *Nyack in Black and White: Race Relations over Three Centuries*. Albany, 2005.

Nutting, Wallace. *New York Beautiful*. Garden City, 1936 (1927).

Obrien, Raymond J. *American Sublime: Landscape and Scenery in the Lower Hudson Valley*. New York, 1981.

O'Donnell, Patricia (Landscapes Inc.), and Cynthia Zaitzevsky (Zaitsevsky and Associates, Inc.). *Cultural Landscape Report for Vanderbilt Mansion National Historic Site*. National Park Service, North Atlantic Region. Boston, 1992. (g)

Owens, William A. *Pocantico Hills: 1609-1959*. Tarrytown, 1960.

Parks, Lillian Rogers, and Frances Spatz Leighton. *The Roosevelts: A Family in Turmoil*. Englewood Cliffs, N. J.: 1981.

Patkus, Ronald D., and Elizabeth A. Daniels, eds., and Karolyn B. Strickland and Marian Thomas, writers. *An Administrative History of Vassar College*. Poughkeepsie, 2004.

Patrick, James B., ed. (text by Franklin D. Mares; photographs by Richard Cheek). *Springwood*. Hyde Park, 1993.

Paxson, Frederick Logan. "The Highway Movement, 1916-1935," in *American Historical Review*, 51 (January 1946), 236-253.

Pealle, Elizabeth. *Socioeconomic Impact Assessment and Nuclear Power Plant Licensing: Greene County, New York*. Oak Ridge, Tenn., 1980. (g)

Pearl, Kenneth. "New York State and the Hudson-Fulton Celebrations of 1909," in *The Hudson River Valley Review*, 25:2 (Spring 2009), 3-11.

Perry, Mark. *Grant and Twain: The Story of an American Friendship*. New York, 2005.

Persico, Joseph E. *The Imperial Rockefeller: A Biography of Nelson A. Rockefeller*. New York, 1982.

Philip, Cynthia Owen. "Olin Dows, Painter," in *The Hudson Valley Regional Review*, XVI:1 (March 1999), 34-45.

Piera, Charles (1940-2012). "Charlie Piera: Excerpt from How I Can Help" (state prison inmates). 4 pp. ms.

Pilcher, V. E., "Jackson, Isaac Willow," in Somers, ed., *Encyclopedia*, 410-411.

Platt, Frances Marion. *A History of Binnewater in the Cement Mining Times*. Rosendale, 2003.

Plum, Dorothy A., and George B. Dowell, comps. *The Magnificent Enterprise: A Chronicle of Vassar College*. Poughkeepsie, 1961.

Plungis, Jeff. "Mario Cuomo, Excelsior," in *Empire Sate Report* (December 1994), 62.

Polito, Robert. *Invisible Republic: Bob Dylan's Basement Tapes* (Greil Marcus), in *The New York Times Book Review* (May 4, 1997), 12. (br)

Pottker, Jan. *Sara and Eleanor: The Story of Sara Delano Roosevelt and Her Daughter-in-Law, Eleanor Roosevelt*. New York, 2004.

Poughkeepsie Board of Education. *Fifty-fifth Annual Report*. Poughkeepsie, 1888. (g)

Powys, Llewellyn. *Henry Hudson*. New York, 1928.

"Preface," in *Collections of the New-York Historical Society for the Year 1917* (New York, 1918), i-x.

Proceedings at the Unveiling of a Memorial to Horace Greeley at Chappaqua, N. Y.: February 3, 1914. Albany, 1915 (g)

Proceedings of the New York State Historical Association: The Thirty-First Annual Meeting, Newburgh, 1930, XXIX (n. p., 1931). (*Quarterly Journal,* Vol. XII.)

Proceedings of the New York State Historical Association: The Twenty-Third Annual Meeting, with a List of Members, XXI (n.p., 1931), 123, 194, 199, 260.

Proceedings of the New York State Historical Association, XLII (Cooperstown, 1944), 4-17. Also cited as *New York History,* XXV (1944).

Pryslopski, Christopher. "Cultivating the Greenhouse Complex at Mills Mansion," in *The Hudson Valley Regional Review,* XVI:1 (March 1999), 57-62.

Rampersad, Arnold. *The Life of Langston Hughes: Volume I: 1902-1941 I, Too, Sing America.* New York, 1986.

Randall, Marti. "Counterpoint Rebuttal" (Winston Farm). Town of Saugerties Historic Review Commission. Unpub 78 pp ms, Saugerties, April 29, 2007. (g)

Randall, Monica. *Phantoms of the Hudson Valley: The Glorious Estates of a Lost Era.* Woodstock, 1995.

Regan, James. "An Asylum for Poughkeepsie," in *The Hudson River Valley Review,* 27:2, 99-108.

Reich, Cary. *The Life of Nelson A. Rockefeller: Worlds to Conquer, 1908-1958.* New York, 1996.

Reid, Brian. "Two Centuries of Ice Yachting on the Hudson," in Dutchess County Historical Society *Year Book* (2001-2002), 76-83.

Renehan, Edward J. Jr. *John Burroughs: An American Naturalist.* Post Mills, Vt., 1992.

_____. *Dark Genius of Wall Street: The Misunderstood Life of Jay Gould, King of the Robber Barons.* New York, 2005.

"Rescue of the Half Moon," in *De Halve Maen,* I:2 (January 1923), 4.

Rhinevault, Carney (and Helen Myers). *The Home Front at Roosevelt's Hometown: Small Town American during World War II.* Hyde Park, 2010.

Rhoads, William B. "Olin Dows: Art, History, and a Usable Past," in Wiles and Zimmerman, eds., 427-440.

_____. "Franklin D. Roosevelt and Dutch Colonial Architecture," in *New York History,* LIX:4 (October 1978), 430-464.

Richardson, Robert Charlwood Jr. *West Point: An Intimate Picture of the National Military Academy and of the Life of the Cadet.* New York, 1917.

Rips, Geoffrey. *The Campaign Against the Underground Press.* San Francisco, 1981.

Robinson, Frank S. *Albany's O'Connell Machine: An American Political Relic.* Albany, 1973.

Roberts, Sam. *Brother: The Untold Story of the Rosenberg Case.* New York, 2003.

Robertson, Cheryl. "Nature and Artifice in the Architecture of Byrdcliffe," in Green, Nancy E., ed., 120-158.

Rollins, Alfred B. Jr. "Young F.D.R. and the Moral Crusaders," in *New York History,* XXXVII:1 (January 1956), 3-16.

Rose, Peter G. *Foods of the Hudson: A Seasonal Sampling of the Region's Bounty.* Woodstock, 1993.

Rosen, Elliot A. "Brains Trust," in Graham and Wander, eds., 40-41.

Rosen, Hy, and Peter Slocum. *From Rocky to Pataki: Character and Caricatures in New York Politics.* Syracuse, 1998.

Rosen, Robyn. "The Shifting Battleground for Birth Control: Lessons from New York's Hudson Valley in the Interwar Years," in *New York History,* 90:3 (Summer 2009), 187-215.

Rosenberg, Nathan. "America's Rise to Woodworking Leadership," in Hindle, ed., *America's Wooden Age,* 37-62.

Ross, Alex. *The Rest Is Noise: Listening to the Twentieth Century.* New York, 2007.

Salmon, Lucy Maynard. "Research for Women," in Vassar Quarterly, LXXXII: 3 (Summer 1986), 18-24 (reprint of December 1926 "Women's Work" article).

Sanchis, Frank E. *Westchester County, New York: Colonial to Contemporary.* Bicentennial Committee of Westchester Inc.: 1977.

Sanders, Edward. "Salute to Maurice Hinchey." Unpub. mss. (July 19, 2015).

Sauer, Carl O. *Selected Essays 1963-1975.* Berkeley, Calif., 1981.

_____. "European Backgrounds of American Agricultural Settlement," in Sauer, *Selected Essays,* 16-44.

_____. "The Settlement of the Humid East," in Sauer, 3-15.

Saunders, Lorna. "Surviving Apprenticeship in the Seventies," in *Vassar Quarterly,* LXXXI:3 (Summr 1985), 18-19.

Savelle, Isabelle K. *Wine and Bitters.* New York, 1975.

_____. *The Tonetti Years at Snedens Landing.* Second Edition. New City, 1981.

Scenic Hudson. *Revitalizing Hudson Riverfronts: Illustrated Conservation & Development Strategies for Creating Healthy, Prosperous Communities.* Poughkeepsie, 2010.

Schlesinger, Arthur M. Jr. *The Rise of the City 1878-1898.* New York, 1913.

_____. *The Crisis of the Old Order: 1919-1933.* Boston, 1957.

_____. *The Coming of the New Deal.* Boston, 1959.

_____. *The Politics of Upheaval.* Cambridge, 1960.

Schoenbrod, David. *Saving Our Environment from Washington: How Congress Grabs Power, Shirks Responsibility, and Shortchanges the People.* New Haven, 2005

Schwartz, Joel. "Morrisania's Volunteer Firemen, 1848-1874: The Limits of Local Institutions in a Metropolitan Age," in *New York History,* LV: 2 (April, 1974), 159-178.

Scott, Anne Firor. *Making the Invisible Woman Visible.* Urbana, Ill., 1984.

"Serendipity at the Rockefeller Center Archive," in Rockefeller Archive Center *Newsletter* (Spring 2002), 7.

Shargel, Baila Round. "Leftist Summer Colonies of Northern Westchester County, New York," in *American Jewish History,* 83:3 (September 1995), 337-358.

Shattuck, George Burbank. *Some Geological Rambles Near Vassar College.* Poughkeepsie, 1907.

Shearer, Augustus H. "The Church, the School, and the Press," in Flick, ed., *History of the State of New York,* III, 45-90.

Sherwin, Martin J. "Atomic Bomb," in Graham and Wander, eds., 13-16.

"The Ship Half Moon," in *De Halve Maen,* II:3 (April 1924), 4.

Skinner, Willa. "The Beacon-Fishkill Connection," in Nancy Fogel, ed., 40-45.

Shivers, Alfred S. *The Life of Maxwell Anderson.* New York, 1983.

Shlaes, Amity. *The Forgotten Man: A New History of the Great Depression.* New York, 2007.

Shultis, Neva. *From Sunset to Cock's Crow.* Woodstock, 1957.

Silverman, Miriam D. *Stopping the Plant: The St. Lawrence Cement Controversy and the Battle for Quality of Life in the Hudson Valley.* Albany, 2006.

Siskind, Peter. "Shades of Black and Green: The Making of Racial and Environmental Liberalism in Nelson Rockefeller's New York," in *Journal of Urban History,* 34:2 (January 2008), 243-265.

"Sixteen-Mile Riverfront Historic District," in *Year Book: Dutchess County Historical Society* (1979), 38-44.

Smiley, A. Keith. *An Anecdotal History of Mohonk.* Rev. & ed. Pril Smiley & Keith LaBudde. N.p.; 27 pp.

Smiley, Ruth H. *Reflections of Mohonk: An Essay in Color of Mohonk and Surrounding Nature.* N.p., 1984.

Smith, Marion C. *Hudson Valley Sketchbook.* Hudson, n.d.

Smith, Richard Norton. "Dewey, Thomas E.," in Graham and Wander, eds., 101-102.

"Snead, Sarazen Break Par on Thomas' Golf Course," in *Pawling-Paterson News-Chronicle*, June 17, 1954. (n, LTC)

Somers, Wayne, comp. & ed. *Encyclopedia of Union College History*. Schenectady, 2003.

Spain, Daphne. "What Gladys Did" (Sheila Rowbotham, *Dreamers of a New Day*), in *TLS*, 5599 (July 23, 2010, 5. (br)

Sparling, Reed. "More than the Wright Stuff: Glenn Curtiss' 1910 Hudson Flight," in *The Hudson River Valley Review*, 26:2 (Spring 1910), 1-4.

Starr, Paul. *The Social Transformation of American Medicine*. New York, 1982.

State University of New York, Office of University Affairs and Development. *Sixty-four Campuses: The State University of New York to 1985*. Albany, 1985. (g)

Steuding, Bob. *The Last of the Handmade Dams: The Story of the Ashokan Reservoir*. Fleischmanns, 1983.

_____. *Rondout: A Hudson River Port*. Fleischmans, 1995.

Stiles, Lela. *The Man behind Roosevelt: The Story of Louis McHenry Howe*. Cleveland-New York, 1954.

Story, Mrs. William Cumming. "Proceedings at the Dedication of the Fort Tryon Tablet," in *Fifteenth Annual Report*, Appendix C, p. 359-361.

Stowell, David O. "Albany's Great Strike of 1877," in *New York History*, LXXVI:1 (January 1995), 31-56.

Struble, Mildred E. (Mrs. Amos). "Pleasantville in Retrospect," in *The Westchester Historian*, 29:3 (July 1953), 60-69.

Sullivan, Patrician. *Lift Every Voice: The NAACP and the Making of the Civil Rights Movement*. New York, 2009.

Swanner, Grace Maguire. *Saratoga: Queen of Spas*. Utica, 1988.

"Take a Powder," in *The Speaker* (Newsletter of Friends of the Senate House), Spring 2003, 1 *ff*.

Talbot, Alan R. *Power Along the Hudson: The Storm King Case and the Birth of Environmentalism*. New York, 1972.

Tartaro, John. *The Mission: A Story of Pawling and the Bygone Days*. N.P. (Pawling), 1966. (LTC)

Teasdale, Parry D. *Videofreex: America's First Pirate TV Station & the Catskills Collective that Turned it On*. Hensonville, 1999.

Thomas, Lately. *The Astor Orphans: A Pride of Lions*. 2nd Edition. Albany, 1999 (1971).

Tilden, Freeman. *The State Parks: Their Meaning in American Life*. New York, 1962.

Tipple, John. "The Robber Baron in the Gilded Age: Entrepreneur or Iconoclast?" in Morgan, H. Wayne, ed., 749-758.

Titus, Robert. "The Quartz Sea" (*from* 1996 Slabsides Nature Talk), in *Wake-Robin*, 30:3 (Autumn 1997), 8.

Tomasi, Katherine. *The Village of Salem 1761-1994*. Glens Falls, 1995.

Tompkins, Christopher R. *Images of America: The Croton Dams and Aqueduct*. Portsmouth, N. H., 2000.

Tompkins, Louise. "Hell's Acres," in *Year Book: Dutchess County Historical Society* (1979), 48-49.

Town of Rhinebeck Comprehensive Plan Committee (Mary Myerson, ed.). Town of Rhinebeck Comprehensive Plan (Draft for Public Review). Rhinebeck, June 13, 2008. (g)

"Town of Queensbury," in Warren County Bicentennial Citizens' Advisory Committee, 59-62.

Trebilcock, Evelyn, and Valerie Balint. "Glories of the Hudson: Frederic Church's Views from Olana," in *The Hudson River Valley Review*, 31:1 (Autumn 2014), 62-81.

Tripp, Wendell, comp. *Coming and Becoming: Pluralism in New York State History*. Cooperstown, 1991.

Turbin, Carole. *Working Women of Collar City: Gender, Class, and Community in Troy, 1864-1886*. Champaign, Ill., 1992.

Ultan, Lloyd (Historian for Storch Associates). "A History of Van Cortlandt Park Borough of the Bronx." City of New York Department of Parks and Recreation, May 1984. (g)

Urofsky, Melvin I. "A Note on the Expulsion of the Five Socialists," in *New York History*, XLVII:1 (January 1966), 41-49.

Vale, Lawrence J. "Designing Global Harmony: Lewis Mumford and the United Nations Headquarters," in Hughes and Hughes, eds., 256-282.

Van Orden, Elsie and Barbara. "Smith's Landing—Now Cementon," in *The Quarterly Journal* (Greene County Historical Society), 3:1 (Spring 1979), 1 *ff.*

Vitz, Robert C. "Struggle and Response: American Artists and the Great Depression," in *New York History*, LVII:1 (January 1976), 81-98.

Vollmer Associates *et al. Final Report for Long-Term Needs Assessment and Alternative Analysis I-287 Tappan Zee Bridge Corridor.* N.p., April 2000. (www.tbzsite.com) (g)

Wadlin, Beatrice Hasbrouck. *Times and Tales of Town of Lloyd.* N. p., 1974.

Wagner, Stephen T. "The Decline of the Republican Left, 1952-1964," in *Research Reports from the Rockefeller Archive Center* (Spring 1998), 14-16.

Waldman, John. *Running Silver: Restoring Atlantic Rivers and Their Great Fish Migrations.* Guilford, Ct., 2013.

Walker, Jeff. "'Our River': The Essay Art of John Burroughs," in *The Hudson River Valley Review*, 25:1 (Autumn 2008), 41-55.

Walker, Martin. *America Reborn: A Twentieth-Century Narrative in Twenty-six Lives.* New York, 2000.

Ward, Geoffrey. *Before the Trumpet: Young Franklin Roosevelt 1882-1905.* New York, 1985.

Warren County Bicentennial Citizens' Advisory Committee. 1813-2013: Warren County, New York, a commemorative bicentennial magazine (2013).

Warren, James Perrin. "John Burroughs' Writing Retreats," in *The Hudson River Valley Review*, 25:1 (Autumn 2008), 12-40.

Watson, Denton L. "The NAACP and the Civil Rights Movement," in *The Historian*, 55:3 (Spring 1993), 453-468.

Weidner, Charles H. *Water for a City: A History of New York City's Problem from the Beginning to the Delaware River System.* New Brunswick, N. J.: 1974.

Weigold, Mailyn E., editor-in-chief. *Westchester County: The Past Hundred Years 1883-1983.* Valhalla, 1984.

_____. "Introduction: The Way We Were—Westchester in 1883," in Weigold, ed., 1-20.

Weimer, David R. "Anxiety in the Golden Day," in *The New England Quarterly*, 36:2 (June 1963), 172-191.

Werlah, Elizabeth. *Images of America: Plattekill.* Charlestown, S. C., *et al:* 2008.

Wermuth, Thomas S. "Painters, Writers, and Tourists in the Nineteenth Century," in *The Hudson River Valley Review*, 31:1 (Autumn 2014), ix-xiv.

Wesser, Robert F. "Election of 1910," in Graham and Wander, eds., 112-113.

West, Patricia. "Irish Immigrant Workers in Antebellum New York: The Experience of Domestic Servants at Van Buren's Lindenwald," in *Hudson Valley Regional Review*, 9:2 (September 1992), 112-126.

White, Theodore H. *The Making of the President 1960.* New York, 1961.

Whitfield, Stephen J. *The Culture of the Cold War.* 2nd Edition. Baltimore, 1996 (1991).

Wicks, Arthur H. (comp. by George B. Snell, Charles H. Valmer, Norman S. Weiss). "A Decade of Achievement: 1943-1952. A factual summary of the epochal accomplishments of a Republican Administration and a Republican Legislature working together during a period of national stress." N.p. [Albany], n.d. [1953]. (g)

Wiebe, Robert H. *The Search for Order 1877-1920.* New York, 1967.

Williams-Myers, A. J. *Long Hammering: Essays on the Forging of an African American Presence in the Hudson River Valley to the Early Twentieth Century.* Trenton, 1994.

Wilson, William ("WW"). "Jones's Mountain Railroad: 'Pluck and Perseverance,'" in *The Hudson Valley Regional Review*, 19:1 (March 2002), 31-36.

Wisbey, Herbert A. Jr. "Bolton Brown: Dresden's Other Famous Son," *The Crooked Lake Review* (November 1995). (www.crookedlakereview.com/articles)

Wolf, Tom, and William B. Rhoads, essayists; Josephine Bloodgood and Tom Wolf, co-curators. *The Maverick: Hervey White's Colony of the Arts, 1905-1944.* Woodstock, 2006.

Woodsruff, Marcia. "Woodstock and Hyde Park Intersect." Unpub. ms. frag., Woodstock School of Art, n.d.

Woodward, C. Vann. "Clio with Soul," in *The Journal of American History*, LVI:1 (June 1969), 5-20.

Zimring, Carl A. *Cash for Your Trash: Scrap Recycling in America.* New Brunswick, N. J., 2005.

Zinn, Howard. *A People's History of the United States: 1492-Present.* New York, 1995 (1980).

SCIENTIFIC SOURCES

Anonymous (Alan McKnight). "'Cool, Clear Water': A Saugerties Resource," in *Toodlum Tales*, 1:6 (September 1979), n.p.

Berger, J. D., D. R. Styers, and M. R. Landis. *Radiological Survey of the Nuclear Lake Site, Pawling, New York: Final Report.* Oak Ridge, Tenn., 1988. (g)

Daniels, Robert A., Robert E. Schmidt, and Karin E. Limburg. "Hudson River Fisheries: Once Robust, Now Reduced," in Henshaw, ed., *Environmental History. . . ,* 27-40.

Giese, G. L., and J. W. Barr. *The Hudson River Estuary: A Preliminary Investigation of Flow and Water-Quality Characteristics.* N.Y. Conservation Department Water Resources Commission Bulletin 61 (1967). (g)

Goldestein, Martin, P.E. *Study of the Impact of Nuclear Power Plants on the Hudson River and Adjacent Lands.* Hudson River Valley Commission (January 31,1968 draft). (g)

Hartgen Archeological Associates. *From Bank to Barge: A Cultural Resource Study of the Washburn Brothers Company Brick Yard, Hamlet of Glasco, Town of Saugerties, Ulster County, New York.* 2 Vols. Troy, August 1985. (g)

Heath, R. C., F. K. Mack and J. A. Tannenbaum. *Ground-Water Studies in Saratoga County, New York.* Albany, 1963 [U. S. Geological Survey]. (g)

Henshaw, Robert E., ed. *Environmental History of the Hudson River: Human Uses that Changed the Ecology, Ecology that Changed Human Uses.* Albany, 2011.

Hetling, Leo J. "An Analysis of Past, Present and Future Hudson River Wastewater Loadings," in Hudson River Environmental Society, *Hudson River Ecology: Proceedings of a Symposium* (Poughkeepsie, 1976), irr. p. (1-35).

Hudson River Environmental Society. *Hudson River Ecology: Proceedings of a Symposium.* Poughkeepsie, 1976. (4th Symposium on Hudson River Ecology, Bear Mountain, March 28-30, 1976.)

"Hudson River: Wappinger Creek to Hudson" (Chart 12347). United States Department of Commerce. National Oceanic and Atmospheric Administration, Coast and Geodetic Survey. (g)

Kieran, John. *A Natural History of New York City.* New York, 1982 (1959).

Kiviat, Erik. *The Northern Shawangunks: An Ecological Survey.* New Paltz, 1988.

_____ and Gretchen Stevens. *Biodiversity Assessment Manual for the Hudson River Estuary Corridor.* N. p. (Red Hook), 2001.

Lintner, J. A. "Report of the State Entomologist," in *Forty-Second Annual Report. . .* (Albany, 1889), 145-326. (g)

Mack, Frederick K. "Geology and Groundwater Resources of the West Milton Area," in Heath, Mack and Tannenbaum, *Ground-Water Studies in Saratoga County.* (g)

Ries, Heinrich. "Lime and Cement Industries of New York," in *Bulletin of the New York State Museum*, 44:8 (November 1901), 639-848. (g)

Schmidt, Robert E., and Susan Cooper. *A Catalog of Barriers to Upstream Movement of Migratory Fishes in Hudson River Tributaries.* Annandale: May 1996.

Smith, C. Lavett. "The Hudson River Fish Fauna," Paper 35, Hudson River Environmental Society, *Hudson River Ecology,* irr. p.

Worzel, J. L. and C. L. Drake. "Structure Section Across the Hudson River at Nyack, N. Y., from Seismic Observations," in *Annals of the New York Academy of Science,* 80 (1959), 1092-1105.

CREATIVE WORKS

Anderson, Maxwell. *High Tor: A Play in Three Acts.* Washington, D. C.: 1937.

Boyle, T. Corraghesan. *World's End.* New York, 1987.

_____. *The Road to Wellville.* New York, 1994.

Breslin, Howard. *Shad Run.* New York, 1955.

Casey, Jack. *The Trial of Bat Shea.* Troy, 1994.

Frederic, Harold. *In the Valley.* New York, 1890.

Gordon, Mary. *Men and Angels.* New York, 1985.

Hoffman, Malcolm. "A Trip to Glen Island" (1887) (m). *https://www.youtube.com/watch?v=xZDE1o1snO8* Feb. 19, 2015.

Kennedy, William. *Legs.* New York, 1975.

_____. *Billy Phelan's Greatest Game.* New York, 1978.

_____. *Ironweed.* New York, 1983.

Kerbert, John H. (1854-1941). *Poems and Songs.* Unpub. mss.

Myer, Anton. *Once an Eagle.* New York, 1968.

Powers, Horatio Nelson. *Poems, Early and Late.* Chicago, 1876.

Promised Gifts '77: An Exhibition. . . . Vassar College, Poughkeepsie, 1977.

Ribikoff, Belle Krasne, *et al.* (Exhibition Committee). *Centennial Loan Exhibition: Drawings & Watercolors from Alumnae and Their Families—Vassar College—Poughkeepsie, New York.* Poughkeepsie, 1961.

Roe, Rev. C. P. *A Day of Fate.* New York, 1880.

Sanders, Edward. *Thirsting For Peace in a Raging Century: Selected Poems 1961-1985.* Minneapolis, 1987.

Truscott, Lucian K. IV. *Dress Grey.* Garden City, 1978.

Untermeyer, Louis, ed. *Modern American Poetry: A Critical Anthology.* 5th Ed. New York, 1936 (1919).

Wharton, Edith. *The House of Mirth.* New York, 2000 (1905).

_____. *Hudson River Bracketed.* New York, 1962 (1929).

_____. *The Buccaneers.* New York, 1938.

REFERENCE WORKS

Anderson, Beatrice, and Maurice North. *Cassell's Colloquial German: A Handbook of Idiomatic Usage.* New York, 1980 (1968).

Applegate. E. C. *American Naturalistic and Realistic Novelists: A Biographical Dictionary.* Westport, Conn., 2001.

Bard College: Alumni/ae Directory 2001. White Plains, 2001.

Fuller, Elizabeth Green. *Index of Personal Names in J. Thomas Scharf's History of Westchester County New York.* Westchester County Historical Society, 1988.

Mencken, H. L. *The American Language: An Inquiry into the Development of English in the United States.* New York, 1937.

Menke, Frank G. *The Encyclopedia of Sports: New and Revised Edition.* New York, 1953.

Murray, James A. H., ed. *A New English Dictionary on Historical Principles.* Oxford, 1897.

Oxford English Dictionary. 1971 Edition.

Reports and Publications from Hudson River Foundation-Sponsored Research. Hudson River Foundation for Science and Environmental Research, "through" June 30, 2000. 55 pp.

Supplement to Encyclopaedia Britannica (Ninth Edition): A Dictionary of Arts, Sciences and General Literature. New York, 1888.

The World Book Encyclopedia. Chicago, 1937.

THESES AND DISSERTATIONS

Benjamin, Bob. "The Artists Arrive in Woodstock, 1902-1915." Vassar College, 1977.

Glazier, Philip. *Yellow Journalism and the* USS Maine *Explosion.* . . . University of North Carolina at Asheville (B.A.), 2004.

Josephson, Roberta. "In the 'Silent Sweet Woods': John Burroughs In and Around the Shawangunks." SUNY New Paltz (M.A.), June 1990.

LaValle, Amanda. "Watershed Bridges and Watershed Divides: An Examination of the Watershed Based Approach in Water Resource Management." SUNY: Empire State College (M.A.), 2012.

Mooney, Donald J., O.F.M. *A History of Siena College from the Beginning to July 1943.* Siena College (M.A.), 1956.

Staley, Allen. "Byrdcliffe and the Maverick: A Discursion in the Arts and Crafts." Yale University (M.A.), 1960.

Wingo, Patricia Wesson. "Clayton R. Lusk: A Study of Patriotism in New York Politics, 1919-1923." University of Georgia: Athens, Georgia (Ph.D.). 1966.

NEWSPAPERS AND NEWS JOURNALS

Amenia Historical Society. "Amy Spingarn—Last Mistress of Troutbeck," in *The Millerton News,* July 24, 2003.

"Annual 'At Home' at Bigelow Homestead," in *Saugerties Telegraph,* October 11, 1929.

Anonymous. "Atom-Power Plan Dropped Upstate," in *The New York Times,* August 9, 1968.

_____. "Aldrich Hails Udall's Plea for New Hudson Commission," in *The New York Times,* September 23, 1968.

_____. "Conservationists Fight Plan to Sell Ft. Slocum for 'A' Plant," in *The Reporter Dispatch* (White Plains), September 1968.

"A Plum in Pawling," *The New York Times,* February 27, 1983. (LTC)

Associated Press. "Treasury Plans Silver Vaults at West Point; Huge Strongbox Will Hold 70 Tons of Metal," in *The New York Times,* March 27, 1937, 1.

"Attempt at Suicide," in *Saugerties Daily Telegraph,* August 10, 1898.

Beemer, James. "Black Bear Sightings on the Rise," in *Pointer View* (54:22), June 12, 1997.

Bender, Marilyn. "Quaker Hill, Where Lowell Thomas is Patriarch of the Quiet Celebrities," in *The New York Times,* November 10, 1968. (LTC)

Benjamin, Vernon. "My Lunch With Ed Sanders," in *Ulster: A Regional Magazine,* 4:3 (Summer 1989), 70-77.

_____. "The Winston Farm," in *The Woodstocker's Journal,* (June-July 1994), 1ff.

_____. "New Life for Old Documents," in *The Herald* (New Paltz), October 9, 1997.

_____. "Long Night's Journey: Agony and Ecstasy among the Lobbyists at Session End," in *Woodstock Times,* June 26, 2003.

"Bigelow's Tribute to Birge Harrison, Noted Artist," in *Saugerties Telegraph,* May 24, 1929.

Boyle, Robert H. "Uncrowned King of Caviar," in *Sports Illustrated,* November 3, 1969.

_____. "Step in and Enjoy the Turmoil: So Says Chanler Chapman, 76. . . ," in *Sports Illustrated,* June 13, 1977.

Cronin, John, and Robert Kennedy. "It's Our River, Let Us Get to It," Op-Ed, *The New York Times*, July 26, 1997.

DePalma, Anthony. "Weather History Offers Insight into Global Warming," *The New York Times*, September 16, 2008.

"Dewey's Pawling," in *Life*, 17:11 (September 11, 1944). (LTC)

Dicker, Frederick U. "Coxsackie: Troops yes, guards no," in the Albany *Times-Union*, April 27, 1979.

Dunleavy, Dan. "Thomas Home, Aura Offered for $1 Million," *The News-Times*, December 26, 1982. (LTC)

"Explosion at Grenade Plant," in *Saugerties Telegraph*, November 15, 1918.

Fiess, Mary (Associated Press). "Guardsmen Popular Inside Green Haven," in the Albany *Times-Union*, April 26, 1979.

"Filming 'Brickdust Row' on the South Side," *Saugerties Telegraph*, August 16, 1918.

Gehman, Richard. "Jackie's Round House," in *The American Weekly*, December 6, 1959, 7-9.

Goldberger, Paul. "Robert Moses, Master Builder, Is Dead at 92," *The New York Times*, July 30, 1981.

Grutzner, Charles. "State Legislators Get a Look at What's Despoiling Hudson River," in *The New York Times*, September 12, 1968.

Harper's Weekly (July 30, 1870).

Hernandez, Raymond. "Hyde Park Ponders Symbol of its Most Famous Smoker," in *The New York Times*, July 29, 1995, 1*ff.*

Hinchey, Maurice D. "Playing Politics with a Prisoner," *The New York Times*, February 11, 1986.

"Highway Commissioner Greene," in *The New York Times*, November 26, 1920.

High, Stanley. "The Case for Dewey," in *Life*, March 22, 1948.

"Hudson River Ice Crop a Failure," in *Saugerties Telegraph*, March 4, 1919.

"Ice Houses in This Vicinity Well Filled," Albany *Evening Journal*, February 20, 1915.

Jacob, Klaus. "Standing on Shaky Ground: Eastern U. S. Is Vulnerable to Quakes," *LDEO News* (Spring 1996), 1 *ff.*

Kahn, Kathy. "Long-down Newburgh Looks Up," in *Hudson Valley Business* (I:40), October 8, 2007, 1 *ff.*

Kaplan, Thomas. "For Albany, Yet Another Corruption Case," in *The New York Times*, April 2, 2013.

Keller, Helen. "How I Became a Socialist," in the New York *Call*, November 3, 1912.

Kolbe, Carla. "Dam Continues to Hold its Own," in *Amsterdam Recorder*, June 9, 2011.

Lardine, Bob. "Wives Are Getting Brighter," in *New York Daily News Colorato Magazine*, December 6, 1995, 20 *ff.*

Larson, Kay. "Cage was Not Only All Ears, He Was All Eyes, Too," in *The New York Times*, February 4, 2001.

LeFever, John. "The Swans of Olivebridge," in *The Olive Press*, February 13, 2003.

"Letters," in *Life*, January 26, 1948.

"Levitt Denounced Rockefeller 'Joke' as a Poor Policy," in *The New York Times*, February 5, 1964. *http://www.nytimes.com/1964/02/05/levitt-denounces-rockefeller-joke-as-a-poor-policy.html?_r=0*, August 23, 2015.

Madden, Richard L. "Unified Approach to Hudson Urged," in *The New York Times*, September 21, 1968.

Martin, Douglas. "Petra Cabot, Designer of the 1950s-Era Skotch Kooler, Dies at 99," in *The New York Times*, October 29, 2006.

Marzulli, John. "How Colombo Crime Family Boss Bill Cutulo's Son Paid Back His Killers," *New York Daily News*, October 19, 2008.

"Mill Awards All Not Allowed," in *Saugerties Telegraph*, September 27, 1918.

Neville, Ron. "Health Dept. Disagrees with Utility on A-Plant," in *Albany Times-Union*, May 17, 1968.

"Obituaries," in *New York History*, XIX:2 (April 1938), 173-186.

O'Neil, Paul. "Flags on the Front Yard," in *Sports Illustrated*, 7:7 (August 12, 1957), 60-63. (LTC)

Parisi, Kassie. "Middle Earth—44 Years of Service to Students," in *Albany Student Press* (23: May 6, 2014), 1.

"Plan for Training Young Americans," in *Pawling-Patterson News-Chronicle*, Thursday, October 17, 1940. (LTC)

"Pollution of Hudson and Other Waters of State, Major Problem," in *Catskill Mountain Star*, January 28, 1949.

"Public Hearing Monday in Teacher Dismissal," in *Catskill Mountain Star*, September 30, 1949.

Quinn, Charles N. "Rockefeller Makes Tour in Seaplane," in *New York Herald Tribune*, October 17, 1958.

Richards, Tad. "Prohibition Days," in *Saugerties Times*, September 10, 2015.

"Rockefeller Buys Van Cortlandt Manor House," *The New York Times*, June 4, 1983, 27.

Sanford, Ben (Chair of Civilian Defense). "Civilian Defense Program Here Planned to Care for New York Refugees Should Bombs Strike," in *Saugerties Daily Post*, December 5, 1950.

"State Senate Kills Bill for Anti-Pollution Suits," in *Schenectady Gazette*, July 3, 1975.

Stevens, William K. "An Infrared Device is Mapping Water Temperatures," in *The New York Times*, September 11, 1968.

Sveikauskas, Geddy. "Beyond IBM," in *Saugerties Times*, August 7, 2014.

Toodlum Tales. Saugerties, 1978-80.

"Thruway Alignment Virtually Established at Route 28 Crossing," in *Catskill Mountain Star*, October 28, 1949.

"Thruway Chairman Defends Plan to Span Hudson at Widest Point," in *Saugerties Daily Post*, December 22, 1950.

"Treasury Plans Silver Vaults," in *The New York Times*, March 27, 1937.

Updegraf, Allan. "Music Goes Back to Nature," in *The New York Times*, July 30, 1916.

Wise, Mike. "Partners, Horse and Man, in Prison Pasture," in *The New York Times*, August 10, 2003, 1 *ff.*

Woods, Lynn. "Midtown Treasure: A Tour of Kingston's Beautifully Restored Old City Hall," in *Almanac Weekly* (Ulster Publishing), February 26, 2015.

FILMS AND DOCUMENTARIES

Blauweiss, Stephen, and Lynn Woods. *Lost Rondout: A Story of Urban Removal*. Kingston, 2014-15. (*www.lostrondout.com*)

"Eels." *Nature*, PBS, January 14, 2014.

France, Dani, dir. "How to Survive a Plague." *Independent Lens*, PBS, December 30, 2013.

Hollywood on the Hudson Mixer. Woodstock Film Festival, 2009.

Traum, Artie, Tobe Carey and Robbie Dupree. "Deep Water: Building the Catskill Water System." Glenford, 2005. (DVD based on Bob Steuding's *Last of the Homemade Dams*.)

BROCHURES, POSTERS & EPHEMERA

"Discover Historic Kinderhook: A Walking Tour."

John Burroughs Association. "Trail Guide."

Millbrook Historical Society. "Walking Map: The Museum in the Streets"; "Walking Tour of Historic Millbrook."

Smiley, A. Keith ((rev. & ed. Pril Smiley and Keith LaBudde). "An Anecdotal History of Mohonk."

COLLECTIONS & ORGANIZATIONS

(The principal large reference collections used were those of the New York State Library and New York State Archives in Albany and the James A. Cannivino Library and Hudson River Valley Institute at Marist College in Poughkeepsie. Listings for whole collections do not necessarily mean that whole collections were perused, nor were materials consulted usually limited to the listed collections; some items consulted in archives are listed elsewhere in these Sources.)

Alf Evers Archive, Woodstock Byrdcliffe Guild (Eila Kokkinen, archivist; Edward Sanders). Art Students League file; Nilsen Laurvik, "The Art Students' League Summer School," May 1911; First Biennial Exhibition of Contemporary American Painting. . ., Whitney Museum of American Art (1932); C. A. Winchell, "The Story of David Bishop," *Ulster County Press*, December 7, 1937; "Old House Bought by State Society," *The New York* Times, April 25, 1955; Charles Grutzner, "Saving a Colonial New Paltz House," *The New York* Times, September 9, 1956; Edwin McDowell, "Corporations as the New Medicis," *Saturday Review* (December 1980), 45-60; David Dunaway, typed mss. fragment of Dunaway's 1981 biography of Pete Seeger, *How Can I Keep from Singing?*; Blue Dome file; Henry L. Diamond, et al, *Greenways in the Hudson River Valley: A New Strategy for Preserving an American Treasure* (Tarrytown, 1988); Frederick Steuding, "Overlook Mountain Conservation," M.A. thesis, University of Massachusetts at Amherst, December 18, 1992. .

Amenia Public Library. Miriam Divine, Librarian. Local History Collection (Lewis Mumford).

Catskill Public Library. *The Quarterly Journal* (Greene County Historical Society).

Esopus Creek Conservancy (Saugerties).

Filson Historical Society (Louisville, Kentucky). Beatty-Quisenberry Family Papers. (p)

Hudson River Museum, Yonkers. (Ruth Reynolds Glunt Collection).

Marist College Archives & Special Collections. James A. Cannavino Library (John Ainsley, Director; Nancy Decker). Lowell Thomas Collection (LTC), Angelo Galeazzi, prep.; Poughkeepsie, 2009; Jonah Sherman Collection; Scenic Hudson Collection: Records Relating to the Storm King Case 1963-81: Meetings 1965-1968; "Governor Names 37 to Study River," *The New York Times*, June 12, 1965; "A-Plant Land Grab May Explode," *Sunday News*, July 14, 1968 (SHC). (p, r)

Marist College. Hudson River Valley Institute (Thomas Wermuth, James Johnson, Christopher Pryslopski).

New-York Historical Society. William Sulzer Papers; Joseph Reed Papers. (p)

New York State Archives (nysl.nysed.gov). Paul Mercer, Bill Gorman. Richard G. Dorr Letters (1848-52) (p) New York "State Council of Defense: Correspondence Files, 1917-18" (p); Mrs. James C. Harding, ed. *History of the Westchester County Defense and War Councils. Condensed Versions: 1940-1945.* 4 Vols. (p); Attorney General Robert Abrams, "Brawley Clips" folders (three boxes; a fourth was lost in a New Scotland Avenue warehouse fire) 1987-88 *ff.* (n); Drainage Basin Subject Files c. 1904-77 (g); "St. Stephen's College" (p);."Saratoga Baths," "Saratoga Development," and "Saratoga Commission" (g); "Sing Sing Prison"; "Westchester County Investigation" (p); "Wickersham Report" (g); "Women's Committee for Repeal of the 18th Amendment".

New York State Comptroller. Rosemary DelVecchio, Librarian.

New York State Department of Environmental Conservation. Albany: Constance R. Alesse (Associate Librarian, Division of Information Services), Charles St. Lucia, Pat Connery, Dam Safety Bureau ("Cantine Dam Files"). Amsterdam: FOIL Coordinator Toni Galluzzo.

New York State Department of Environmental Conservation. Hudson River Estuary Program (New Paltz). Frances Dunwell (Director), Scott Cuppett, Kevin Grieser (Riparian Buffer Coordinator).

New York State Legislative Library. Albany. (p)

Pawling Free Library. Local History Collection.

Saugerties Historical Society. Karlyn Knaust Elia, Collections Committee Chair (1999-2000). "E. R. McCormick Notebooks" (p); Jean Wrolsen Collection (Donation of Paula Nelson). Exhibits: "The Artist's Touch," Fall 2000 (c).

Saugerties Public Library. Local History Room. Nathan Aaron; Jean Wrolsen; Audrey Klinkenberg; Betty Pietrek; Frank Rees.

Siena College Archives, Loudonville. Rene LeRoux, "Siena College Basketball: A Winning Tradition."

Town of Saugerties Historic Preservation Commission.

Ulster County Hall of Records; Ian Kier (Kingston) (www.co.ulster.ny.us/countyclerk/recordshall.html). Roswell Randall Hoes Collection summaries; New York State Historical Records Survey; District Attorney records (1909-13).

Westchester County Archives (Elmsford) (westchesterarchives.com). John R. Fairchild, "Report to the Bronx Valley Sewer Commission," January 29, 1896; Bronx River Parkway Commission (Series 103 Minutes of the Commissioners of Appraisal; Series 104 Appeals); Westchester County Park Commission; Series 14—Historic Building Inventory Forms; Series 215 and 216—Board of Supervisors 1853-1913 and Minutes; Series 248—Airport Scrapbook; Series 270—Commissioner of Public Works Subject Files; Series 84—Site Search Records 1937-1946; Series 164—Commission on Government Records 1921-56; Series 161 Westchester County Association Records 1950-52; Series 41—Horseshoers Register 1899-1904; County Executive Herbert C. Gerlach Annual Message for the Year 1951 to Board of Supervisors.

Woodstock Land Conservancy. "Vernal Fling," Saturday, May 9, 2015.

Woodstock School of Art. Nancy Campbell, Executive Director. "A New Deal for Youth: Eleanor Roosevelt, Val-Kill Industries and the Woodstock Resident Work Center," organized by Eleanor Roosevelt National Historic Site (National Park Service) and the Woodstock School of Art. Woodstock, July 9-November 5, 2011.

CONFERENCES, PRESENTATIONS & EVENTS

Adams, Annon. Kingston Architectural Conference, SUNY New Paltz, April 24, 2003.

Benjamin, Vernon. "A Walk *to* the Woods: What Made John Burroughs Possible in the World?" Slabsides Day, John Burroughs Association, October 3, 2015. (*www.johnburroughsassociation.org*)

Berman, Avis. "Distilling the American Flavor: Juliana Force, the Whitney Museum, and the Woodstock Connection." Woodstock Artists Association Museum, September 26, 2015.

Cramer, Eileen. Woodstock School of Art, July 19, 1997.

Dwyer-McNulty, Sally. "The Sisters of Charity: Navigating Politics and Gender Along the Hudson." Marist College Catholic Studies Program. Poughkeepsie, February 13, 2009.

Fasoldt, Staats. Art Students League (Woodstock).

Flad, Harvey K. "The Art of Protecting Scenic Views: The Olana Viewshed and the Development of Visual Impact Assessment in New York State." The Olana Symposium: Franking the Viewshed: The Transformative Power of Art and Landscape in the Hudson Valley. Olana (Greenport), April 16, 2011.

Hambleton, Else. University of Massachusetts. Commentator, New York State Conference on History, SUNY New Paltz, June 6, 1996.

James Cox Gallery at Woodstock. "Wilna Hervey & Nan Mason: Two Woodstock Originals." Willow, July 10-August 2, 2015.

Rodenhausen, George A., Esq. Hudson River Watershed Alliance, *Sustainable Tributary Strategies: Workshop on Water Resources Laws, Policies and Local Options for Watershed Protection.* SUNY Orange, Newburgh, May 13, 2015.

Jacobs, John. "Growing Up on a Clintondale Farm." Ulster County Historical Society, August 10, 1996.

Jacobson, Vivian *et al.* "Marc Chagall in High Falls." SUNY New Paltz, March 28, 2011.

Johnson, Kathleen Eagen. Curator of Collections, Historic Hudson Valley. "The Hudson-Fulton Celebration: New York's River Festival of 1909 and the Making of a Metropolis." Great Estates Consortium, *400 Years: Life on the Hudson River.* Henry A. Wallace Center, FDR National Historic Site. Hyde Park, March 28, 2009.

Jones, Robert F. (Fordham University). State University at New Paltz, June 8, 1996.

Kolakowski, Christopher. "The Capitol Fire of 1911," New York State Library, May 8, 2003.

Kowsky, Francis. "Kingston Architecture" Conference, SUNY New Paltz, April 24, 2003.

Lake, Tom. "Hudson Valley Heritage" Conference. SUNY New Paltz, September 27, 1997.

Lowry, Glenn C. (MOMA). Symposium on Rockefeller Art Collection, Empire State Plaza, October 26, 2002.

Mabry, James C. (Columbia University). "Becoming an Industrial City: Yonkers, 1840-60." SUNY New Paltz History Conference, June 7, 1996.

Meany, Dr. Joseph F. (Acting State Historian). "A Century of Preserving Local History." Ulster County Historians. Kiersted House, Saugerties, October 16, 1999

Walker, Jeffrey (Vassar College). "The Long Road: John Burroughs and Charles Darwin 1862-1922," Vassar College (Poughkeepsie), March 29, 2008.

Wheeler, Walter. Kingston Architectural Conference, SUNY New Paltz, March 24, 2003.

Wiles, Richard (Bard College). Commentator and Moderator ("Economics of Community Founding"), New York State Conference on History, SUNY New Paltz, June 6, 1996.

PROFESSIONAL

Ash, Herman, M.D. (Saugerties). (p)

Barbour, J. G. (Spider). Naturalist-Author (Saugerties). (s)

Buff, Jimmy, WDST-FM (Woodstock).

Burroughs, Joan. John Burroughs Association (West Park).

Campbell, Nancy. Executive Director, Woodstock School of Art.

Cox, James. James Cox Gallery (Woodstock).

Cunningham, Raymond. Department of Correctional Services (Ret.) (Wallkill).

Deyo, Gabriel. Office of the New York State Comptroller (Albany).

Doyle, Dennis. Director of Planning. Ulster County.

Francello, Louis P., Esq. (d. 2004) May 15, 1996. Saugerties. (p)

Fuoto, Lydia. Registrar, Hudson River Museum (Yonkers).

Funk, Robert. State Archaeologist.

Hinchey, Maurice D. N. Y. S. Assemblyman (1975-92); U. S. Congressman (1993-2013) (Saugerties-Stone Ridge). Hudson River Study Act, 1978; Hudson River Fisheries Management Program Act, 1979; Temporary Legislative Commission of Inquiry into the Impeachment and Removal from Office of Governor William Sulzer in 1913 (1982-84); Waste Solvent Burning, Northeast Solite Corporation, Saugerties, 1987-88; PCB Discovery & Removal Project, Kerhonkson, 1988-89; Hudson River Valley Greenway Act, 1991 (with Senator Steven Saland); Clayton "Peg Leg" Bates Resolution, U. S. House of Representatives, July 10, 1995. *(See also Miller, Paul.)* (p, g)

Hollander, Brian. Editor, *Woodstock Times.*

Horowitz, Mikhail. Writer-Artist. Saugerties. (p)

Hudsonia, Ltd. (Red Hook). Erik Kiviat, Executive Director; Gretchen Stevens, Biodiversity Resource Center Director. (s)

Kier, Ian. Ulster County Hall of Records (Kingston).

Kleinhans, Paula Nelson. Past President, Woodstock School of Art (Woodstock).

Klinkenberg, Audrey. Genealogist and Saugerties town historian.

Madej, Henry. Assembly Research Service (Albany).

McKnight, Alan. Artist-Cartographer (Willow).

McNamara, Mary. Water Resources Specialist (Woodstock and Saugerties).

Mecklem, Sarah. Artist (Woodstock).

Mercier, Stephen. Marist College (Poughkeepsie).

Miller, David. Department of Correctional Services (ret.) (New Paltz).

Munch, Janet Butler. Archives Library, Herbert Lehman College (Bronx).

Ness, Susan. Bedford Historical Society.

Payne, Bill. American Legion Museum (Saugerties).

Philippon, Patti; Beatrice Fox Auerbach (Chief Curator). The Mark Twain House and Museum (Hartford, Connecticut).

Piera, Charles. Department of Correctional Services (Ret.) (Sundown).

Richards, Tad. Opus 40, Highwoods. (p)

Rinehart, Bill (Winston Farm Alliance). Archaeological Survey of Winston Farm and Vicinity (Saugerties, 1989-90); Bill Rinehart to Vernon Benjamin (November 24, 1989); Robert Funk, State Archaeologist, to William Rinehart (December 5, 1989);

Sebastian, John B. Musician & Songwriter. Woodstock.

Sidamon-Eristoff, Constantine. Malden-on-Hudson and Highland Falls.

Sinnott, Joe. Artist (Marvel Comics). Saugerties.

Sysak, Roger. Agricultural Agent. Ulster County-Cornell Cooperative Extension (Kingston). (g)

Sveikauskas, Geddy. Ulster Publishing Company (Kingston).

Tetor, Dave. Cornell Cooperative Extension Field Crops Specialist (Poughkeepsie).

Thaler, Dr. Jerome S. Hudson Valley Climate Service (Yorktown Heights).

Thorn, John. Official Historian, National Baseball League. "When Baseball was Big in Kingston"; "Finding Frank Pidgeon"; "Hoops, Hebrews, and the Hudson River League."

Traum, Happy (Woodstock).

Wiles, Richard C. (Bard College Hudson River Studies Program). *Hudson River Valley Review*.

Wilson, William (Bard College). *Hudson River Valley Review*.

Woolston-Smith, A. J. Investigator, New York State Assembly (Albany). (g)

Zaloom, Carole. Artist. Saugerties (p)

INDIVIDUALS

Benjamin, Alice M. (1909-90). (Saugerties).

Benjamin, Richard M. (1943-2013); IBM history (Saugerties).

Bub, John (1908-2005). January 10, 1905. Veteran (Saugerties). (p)

Curtiss, William (1921-2004). West Saugerties. (p)

Finger, Foster (March 6, 1996). Katsbaan. (p)

Furboter, Henry (b. 1926). Echo Hill (Saugerties). (p)

Gage, James V. Saugerties. (p)

Glunt, Chester B. Saugerties. (p)

Hackett, Wesley. Saugerties.

Higgins, Patrick J. Milan (Dutchess County).

Keefe, Joan Waters. Saugerties. (p)

Kick, Peter. Saugerties.

Kirk, Tom. Elka Park. (p)

Knaust, Herman. Stroomzeit (Saugerties) (p)

Ledwith, James (d. 2010). Saugerties.

Lafavre, John. Rhinebeck..
Lynch, Connie. Connie Lynch Papers (Saugerties). (p)
Randel, Walter. New York City.
Rose, Marian. Bedford.
Russell, Robert Snyder (d. 1996) (Saugerties).
Saporito, Michael. Photographer (Saugerties).
Shults, Ed. Saugerties.
Shults, John. Kingston.
Smith, Michael Sullivan. Artist-Local Historian (Saugerties).
Snyder, Clifford (b. 1926). High Woods.
Steier, Aline Gilbert (b. 1925?). Katsbaan. (p)
Taylor, Susan. Frankfort, Kentucky. (p)
Trumpbour, William and Eliner. Trumpbour's Corners (Saugerties).
Unbersadt, John. Town Historian (Wawarsing). (g)
Van der Poel, Andy. Van der Poel's Hudson River Brick Collection. (Kingston).
Winchell, Foster. West Camp. (p)
Winchell, Rosetta Josephine O'Banks (1902-97), December 7, 1996. West Camp. (p)
Wolven, Francis C. (1913-2005). Highwoods. (p)
Wrolsen, Jean Anderson. Artist-Writer. Highwoods. (p)

LEGAL SOURCES

Chapter 1021 of 1895 (Bronx River Sewer Commission)
Chapter 170 of 1900 (Palisades Interstate Park Commission)
Chapter 146 of 1913 (Railroad Full Crew).
Chapter 195 of 1929. (Reforestation Constitutional Amendment) (OSC)
Chapter 143 of 1950 (Thruway Authority).
Chapter 593 of 1952 (Billboards Prohibition, New York State Thruway).
Title IX: Public Law 104-333 (October 1996) Hudson River Valley National Heritage Area
    Act
Hudson River Fishermen's Association v. Federal Power Commission, 498, F.2nd 827 (2nd Cir. 1974)
    (Fish Kills).
Hidley v. Rockefeller, 28 N.Y.2d 439 (1971) (State Budget Appropriations) http://www.leagle
    .com/decision/197146728NY2d439_1411/HIDLEY%20v.%20ROCKEFELLER
Levitt v. Rockefeller, 69 Misc.2d 337 (1972) (State Budget Appropriations) *http://www.leagle
    .com/decision/197240669Misc2d337_1320.xml/LEVITT%20v.%20ROCKEFELLER*

WEBSITES & MEDIA

(Note: A number of these cites, and particularly Wikipedia, were used as corroborative reference sources principally. Wikipedia matured considerably over the course of this research, but when used for factual information the sources given were vented for veracity as well.)

About.com (boxing.about.com). "Mike Tyson Fight-by-Fight Career Record."
A&E Biography. "The Vanderbilts: An American Dynasty." New York, 1996.
Albany (albanyny.org).
Albany Rural Cemetery (albanyruralcemetery.org).
Albany Times-Union (timesunion.com; blog.timsunion.com). Dr. Peter A. Myers, "Kelton Court
    Memories," March 9, 2010.
Alternatives to Violence Project—New York (avpny.org). Easy Eddie Ellis, ""AVP's Beginnings
    at Green Haven."

American Craft Magazine (americancraftmag.org). Caroline Hannah, "Crow House Rising," *American Craft* (June/July, 2008).

American Memory (memory.loc.gov). *The Stars and Stripes*. 1918-19.

Appleton's Encyclopedia (http://famousamericans.net).

Arlington National Cemetery (arlingtoncemetery.net). Henry Lincoln Johnson; Joe Louis; Lee Marvin.

The Art Students League, "Founded by Artists, for Artists." September 16, 2015. (*www.theartstudentleague.org*.)

Art Times (Saugerties) (*arttimesjournal.com*). "Profiles by Raymond J. Steiner." *www.askart.com* (A. A. Champanier).

Associated Press. "Report on Sing Sing is Laid on the Table," in *The Cornell Daily Sun*, XXXVI:57 (December 2, 1915). *http://cdsun.library.cornell.edu/cgi-bin/cornell?a=d&d =CDS19151202.2.48&st=0*; August 6, 2015.

The Atlantic. Digital Edition (theatlantic.com). Cleveland Rodgers, "Robert Moses: An Atlantic Portrait," February 1939.

Bancroft Library (Salem). (p) (slibrary.org)

Bard College (*www.bard.edu*). Emily Friedman, "Carlos Rosado Earn's Bachelor's Degree, Plants Garden while Serving Time" (May 18, 2010); Elizabeth Redden, "Laying a Liberal Arts Foundation, On Shaky Ground" (September 1, 2010); "WATCH: Colbert Grills Bard President Leon Botstein" (October 4, 2011);

The Barrett Art Center (Poughkeepsie). *http://www.barrettartcenter.org/about/about-thomas-w -barrett*; August 8, 2015.

Bartleby.com (*http://bartleby.net*).

Baseball Reference.Com: "Edsall Walker." (*www.baseball-reference.com*)

Bell, Trudy E. "The Great Easter 'Midwest' Flood of 1913 in New York State." (*www.trudyebell .com*) (Ms. Bell delivered this paper at the 2009 New York State History Conference)

Biographical Directory of the United States Congress (http://bioguide.congress.gov). Richard L. Ottinger; Maurice D. Hinchey; Bella Absug; John Hall; John Dow; Joseph Y. Resnick.

Botstein, Leon. "Echoes of the Armory Show: Modern Music in New York" (October 3, 2013); "John Cage at 100" (December 13, 2012); "An American Biography: The Music of Henry Cowell" (January 29, 2011). (http://leonbotsteinmusicroom.com)

Bray, Paul Marshall (braypapers.com). Paul Bray, "Twenty Fifth Anniversary of SEQRA," May 2000.

Brickmaking. (*www.brickcollecting.com*).

John Burroughs Association. Nancy Macknechnie (Special Collections Librarian, Vassar College), "Personal Name Index" (john-burroughs.org)

Alexander Calder home, Croton-on-Hudson. (http://www.phillymag.com/property/2013)

Cardinal McCloskey Services (cardinalmccloskeyservices.org). "John Cardinal McCloskey."

Castro, Nash; Klara Sauer, Frances Dunwell and Tom Lake. "A Fond Farewell," in *Hudson Valley Magazine*, December 2004. *http://www.hvmag.com/Hudson-Valley-Magazine/ December-2004/A-Fond-Farewell*; August 15, 2015.

Cat Rock (osborncastle.com).

CDex Information Group. "The Presidential Papers: Franklin D. Roosevelt." N.p., 1997 (p); "Influenza 1918." June 16, 2008.

The Century House Historical Society. "Stories: Samuel Coykendall." (www.centuryhouse.org)

The Chance (Poughkeepsie) (*www.thechancetheater.com*; August 30, 2015).

Cho, Renee. "H. James Simpson; Tracked Pollutants in Hudson and Far Beyond." Obituary, Columbia University Lamont Doherty Earth Observatory, May 26, 2015. *https://www .ldeo.columbia.edu/news-events/h-james-simpson-tracked-pollutants-hudson-and-far-beyond* (June 28, 2015).

Chronogram (chronogram.com). "Portfolio: Sarah Mecklem."

Collections at the Chapman Historical Museum (Glens Falls); "The Corners"; "Out to Work: The Transformation of Women's Labor"; Kim Harvish, "The Story is in the Archives." (*chapmanmuseum.org*)

Columbia University Rare Books and Manuscripts Library (library.columbia.edu). "Life and Legacy of Herbert H. Lehman." (Duane Tanenbaum)

Copland House (Tarrytown) (coplandhouse.org).

Cornell University Library Windows on the Past (http://digital.library.cornell.edu). Benton, Joel. "John Burroughs," in *Scribner's Monthly*, 13:3 (January 1877), 336-342; Anonymous. "The Late John L. Stephens," in *Putnam's Monthly Magazine of American Literature, Science and Art*, I:1 (January 1853), 64-68.

Crandall Public Library (Glens Falls). (p) (www.crandalllibrary.org)

Croton Friends of History (crotonfriendsofhistory.org). Postcard Tour.

Crow House (New City) (henryvarnumpoor.com).

The Cyber Boxing Zone Encyclopedia (http://cyberboxingzone.com). Frank Baillargeon, "I Am the Man! The Honorable John Morrissey (1831-1878)"; "'Iron' Mike Tyson (Michael Gerard Tyson)."

Disavino, Scott. "Entergy May Have to Shut NY Indian Point Reactors by 2018" (September 13,2013).(*www.reuters.com/article/2013/09/13/*; October 20, 2015)

Earlyamerica.com. Edison Company. "Films of Naturalist John Burroughs." West Park, 1914. (p)

Encyclopedia Americana (magnumArchive.com). "Inland Waterways" (1918).

"Ethics Matter: A Conversation with Leon Botstein, President of Bard College and Champion of Liberal Arts," Carnegie Council for Ethics in International Affairs (February 9, 2015). (*www.carnegiecouncil.org*)

Feron, James. "If You're Thinking of Living In: Bronxville," *The New York Times*, January 29, 1984   (*http://www.nytimes.com/1984/01/29/realestate/if-you-re-thinking-of-living-in-bronxville.html*).

Ferncliff Forest (Rhinebeck) (*http://fernclifforest.org*). "Come Climb the Tower!"

Findagrave.com. Gabrielle Rosamond Greeley Clendenin.

First Principles (Intercollegiate Studies Institute, Wilmington, Delaware) (firstprinciplesjournal.com). Bruce Cicero, "Bell, Bernard Iddings."

"Fish Criticizes Diedling," in *The Cornell Daily Sun*, XXXVI:134 (March 29, 1916). *http://cdsun.library.cornell.edu/cgi-bin/*; August 6, 2015.

Fordham University: Archives & Special Collections (library.fordham.edu).

Fort Edward Free Library (fortedwardlibrary.sals.edu)

Franklin D. Roosevelt Presidential Library. (g, p)

General Electric (ge.com). "Five Generations, One GE Family."

Greenwich Free Library. (p) (greenwichfreelibrary.com)

Hall of Governors (*www.hallofgovernors.ny.gov*). William P. McDermot, "Levi P. Morton"; Laura Eve-Moss, "Benjamin F. O'Dell Jr."; Charles S. Whitman.

Hanson, David J. "Alcohol Problems and Solutions: William H. Anderson." *www.potsdam.edu* Feb. 20, 2015.

Historic Hudson Valley (hudsonvalley.org). Union Church of Pocantico Hills.

Historic Pelham (historicpelham.com). "A Chronology of the History of Pelham."

Hoffman, Malcolm. "A Trip to Glen Island" (1887) (m). (*https://www.youtube.com/watch?v=xZDE1o1snO8* Feb. 19, 2015.)

Hudson-Athens Lighthouse (hudsonathenslighthouse.org).

Hudson Falls Free Library (hudsonfallslibrary.sals.edu)

Hudson River Maritime Museum (hrmm.org).

James Cox Gallery (jamescoxgallery.com). "Represented Artists."

Jay Ungar and Molly Mason (jayandmolly.com; ashokan.org).

John Thorn (http://hudsonriverbracketed.blogspot.com). "When Baseball Was Big in Kingston"; Mark Thorn and John Thorn, "Let Freedom Sting: The Wasp, The Bee, and the Valley; Part II."

The Kennedy Center (*www.kennedy-center.org*). "Peter Schickele."

Kreisberg, Glenn, with David Holden and Norm Muller. "The California Quarry & Nearby Stone Cairns of Woodstock, NY." (www.ashnews.org/Documents/NEARA_Sub-mission_022007_MSWord...); October 31, 2015.

Lake Minnewaska Mountain Houses (minnewaska.org). "Minnewaska History."

Lake, Tom, comp. *Hudson River Almanac,* August 4-August 10, 2004. *http://www.dec.ny.gov.*

Lakewood Public Library (Lakewood, Ohio) (lkwdpl.org). Women in History.

Lamont-Doherty Earth Observatory (ldeo.columbia.edu). "In Upstate New York, 42,225 Daily Temperature Readings, and Counting" (May 6, 2010); "Hudson River Estuary Enters Middle Age" (February 5, 2004).

Lehigh University Digital Library (digital.lib.lehigh.edu). "The Vault at Pfaff's."

Library of Congress (Washington. D. C.) *Biographical Director of the United States Congress; New-York Daily Tribune* (1908). (http://congress.gov/scripts; http://chroniclingamerica .loc.gov).

The Literature Network (online-literature.com). L. Frank Baum.

Malkine, Gilles; "Local Program Goes Off Air," April 19, 1962 (www.gillesmalkine.com).

Marist College (Poughkeepsie) (www.marist.edu). "Largest Gift in Marist History Establishes Leadership Institute."

Marist Environmental History Project: "The Scenic Hudson Decision" (*http://library.marist .edu/archives/mehp/scenicdecision.html*)

Mark Twain Papers (http://bancroft.berkeley.edu).

Mark Twain Project Online (http://marktwainproject.org).

Marshall, Natalie J. "The Early History of a Dutchess County Law Firm." McCabe & Mack LLP (1996). *http://www.mccm.com/history/.* (accessed Dec. 18, 2014)

Maverick Concerts (maverickconcerts.org). Cornelia Hartmann Rosenblum, "The Maverick Horse" (1979); Leon Barzin, "Leon Barzin Recalls the Early Years."

Mayone, Cathy and Michael, "The Gentleman from Ulster" (Joseph Mayone) (*www.brickcollecting .com/mayone*).

McKnight, Dale. "Scenic Hudson's 50th Anniversary: A History and the 17-Year Battle to Preserve Storm King," in *Hudson Valley Magazine* (October 2013). May 14, 2015: *http://www .hvmag.com/Hudson-Valley-Magazine/October-2013/Scenic-Hudsons-50th-Anniversary-A -History-and-the-17-Year-Battle-to-Preserve-Storm-King-Mountain/*

Michener Museum (michenermuseum.com). "Bucks County Artists: Charles Rosen."

Mohonk Mountain House (mohonk.com).

National Archives Docs Teach. "Famous New York [African American] soldiers return home. Henry Johnson. . . ."; "Two American Negroes Win Croix de Guerre" [Henry Johnson]; "Act of October 28, 1919 [The Volstead Act]"; "Franklin D. Roosevelt's First Inaugural Address" (March 4, 1933); "Franklin D. Roosevelt Letter to Robert Kennedy and Reply" (July 12, 1935); "Fireside Chat on Reorganization of the Judiciary" (March 9, 1937); "Civil Rights Act of 1964";

National Parks Service (nps.gov). "Emergency Rescue Committee."

National Public Radio (npr.org). "Morris Kantor's *Baseball at Night*: A Russian immigrant's homage to small-town America" (July 14, 2001).

New York State Education Department. James Folts, *History of the University of the State of New York and the State Education Department 1784 – 1996* (1996, nysl.nysed.gov/edocs/education /sedhist).

New Paltz: State University of New York (newpaltz.edu). "Hervey White and the Maverick Art Colony."

"Sisters Protest Con Ed Memorial," in *News from Cornwall and Cornwall-on-Hudson*, May 14, 2015 (Storm King Memorial controversy). May 14, 2015: *http://www.cornwall-on-hudson .com/business.cfm?page=4081.*

New York State Military Museum and Veterans Research Center (http://dmna.state.ny.us) (g) *The New York Times* (nytimes.com).

Open Space Institute (*http://www.osiny.org/site/-PageServer?pagename=Project-_list_Shawangunks*; May 10, 2015).

Poughkeepsie Journal (pooughkeepsiejournal.com).

The Poultney Bigelow Page (poultneybigelow.org). "A Visit to the Bigelow Homestead: The Birthplace of the Late President of Our Public Library," *Valentine's Manual of the City of New York 1917-1918.*

Pound Ridge Historical Society (poundridgehistorical.org).

Public Broadcasting Service. (pbs.org). *The American Experience*. Robert Stone, dir. "The Civilian Conservation Corps," New York, 2009.

Raoul Hague (http://raoulhaguefoundation.org). "Interview: Paula Giannini and Raoul Hague" Woodstock, 1981 (1979).

Rensselaer Polytechnic Institute (rpi.edu; http://rpiarchives.wordpress.com). Rensselaer Alumni Hall of Fame; "The Approach." "RPI History Revealed" (Amythe Archivist).

Riverkeeper (riverkeeper.org). Anonymous (Robert F. Kennedy Jr.), "A Brief History."

Rockefeller Archives Center; Rockefeller Family Archives Collections (http://archive.rockefeller.edu; rockarch.org). Research Reports; David Stradling, "The Hudson River and the Boundaries of Environmentalism" (2008)

Rockland County Arts & Leisure (co.rockland.ny.us/Arts). Anonymous (Peter Schiebner), "Toward the End of the Light," in *It's About Time: Archival Newsletter*, Rockland County, II (October 1990).

Rough Rider Archive, City of Las Vegas (Mexico) Museum and Rough Rider Memorial Collection. Fick, Alvin S. "Last of the Rough Riders."

Saugerties Lighthouse Conservancy (lighthousefriends.com).

Schwartz, John. "Stephen Crohn, Who Furthered AIDS Study, Dies at 66," *The New York Times*, September 14, 2013. (http://www.nytimes.com/2013/09/15/health/stephen-crohn -who-furthered-aids-study-dies-at-66.html).

"Shad Fishing on the Hudson," in *Voices: The Journal of New York Folklore*, 29 (Spring-Summer 2003). *http://www.nyfolklore.org/pubs/voic29-1-2/onair.html*; August 15, 2015.

Smithsonian Institution Archives; Archives of American Art (http://siarchives.si.edu; *aaa.si.edu*). Edgar Alexander Mearns Papers; *Joseph Trovato, "Oral History Interview with Anton Refregier," November 5, 1964; Konrad and Florence Ballin Cramer Papers, 1897-1968.*

Southeastern New York Library Resources Council (senylrc.org; hrvh.org). Hudson River Valley Heritage.

Spartacus Educational (spartacus.schoolnet.co.uk). Max Eastman, Floyd Dell, Dorothy Day, Doris Stevens.

Sports Illustrated (sportsillustrated.cnn.com).

Steve Anderson (nycroads.com). "Tappan Zee Bridge: Historic Overview"; "Cross County Parkway: Historic Overview."

Stone Ridge Library (stoneridgelibrary.org). Library eNewsletter.

SummitPost.org (summitpost.org). Schunnemunck Mountain.

Third World Traveler (thirdworldtraveler.com). Howard Zinn, "Discovering John Reed" (2010).

Thirteen New York (thirteen.org). American Masters Series: "Pete Seeger," February 27, 2008; "American Experience: Influenza 1918," June 16, 2008; "Pete Seeger: The Power of Song," September 5, 2008.

Time Magazine (time.com). "Books: World's End, Hudson Division" (Robert Boyle: *The Hudson River* [*sic*]), April 27, 1970 (br); "Crime: The Mobs Maneuver," May 8, 1972; "Scotto: Out of the Dock," November 26, 1979;

The Times-Herald-Record (*http://archive.recordonline.com*).

Trinity Episcopal Church. (*www.trinitychurchsaugerties.org*)

University at Albany; University Libraries: University at Albany (albany.edu; http://library.albany.ed). Kendall Burr, "Back to the Future: An Illustrated History of the University at Albany" (Albany, 1996); M. E. Grenander Department of Special Collections and Archives; Alden Hall.

U. S. Department of Defense (defense.gov; globalsecurity.org). Knolls Atomic Power Laboratory—Kesselring; SSN 575—Seawolf; Staff Sgt. Marcia Twiggs, "Black WWI Hero Received Due Honors."

United States Environmental Protection Agency (*http://www3.epa.gov/hudson/actions.htm*). Hudson River PCBs Superfund Site: "Actions Prior to EPA's February 2002 Record of Decision (ROD)" (retrieved November 20, 2015).

U. S. House of Representatives. Women in Congress (http://womenincongress.house.gov). Katherine St. George.

University at Albany. M. E. Grenander Department of Special Collections and Archives: "New York State Modern Political Archive." (*http://library.albany.edu/speccoll/nysmpa.htm*); retrieved November 4, 2014.

University of Texas (*www.utexas.edu*). Horace Britt.

Vassar College; Vassar Encyclopedia; Special Collections (Vassar.edu; http://vcencyclopedia .vassar.edu). "Vassar Myths & Legends" (JLD, 2006); "Vassar Visitors" (SL, 2004); "Alumnae/i of Distinction"; "Athletics: 1865-1945" (CBC, 2005); Guide to the Vassar Family Papers, 1804-1891.

Village of Croton-on-Hudson, New York (http://village.croton-on-hudson.ny.us). "About Croton-on-Hudson."

Village of Tarrytown, New York. (*www.tarrytowngov.com*). Richard Miller, Village Historian, "A Brief History of Tarrytown" (2005).

Vladimir Kagan (http://vladimirkagan.typepad.com/vladimir-kagans-blog). "A Nostalgic Visit to Woodstock," May 2010.

WAMC Northeast Public Radio (Albany Public Radio) (WAMC.org). "The Best of the Fund Drive" (2008); "Latest Headlines" (January 3, 2015).

Wave Hill (wavehill.org). Wave Hill; Glyndor House.

Wawarsing.Net Magazine. Marion M. Dumond, "Cragsmoor's Stone Church," (October 2003), 24 *ff.*

Westchester County (westchestergov.com). Virtual Archives: *Serving the Public: The History of Westchester County Government*; White Plains War Mothers (1918).

White Mountain Art & Artists (http://whitemountainart.com)

"Whitman's Endorsement Given Osborne's Methods," in *The Cornell Daily Sun*, 36:35 (November 5, 1915). *http://cdsun.library.cornell.edu/cgi-bin/cornell?a=d&d=CDS19151105.2.62 &srpos =3&e=———en-20—1—txt-txIN-Diedling+———*; August 6, 2015.

Wikipedia (Wikipedia.org). Adirondack Northway; Warren Hamilton Anderson; Edwin Howard Armstrong; John Kendrick Bangs; *The Basement Tapes* (1975); Henry Billings; Willie Bosket; Briarcliff Farms; Brink's Robbery (1981); Bronxville; Jennie Augusta Brownscombe; John Burroughs; Alexander Calder; Camp Shanks; Capital Cities Communications; Carnegie Libraries in New York State; Civilian Conservation Corps; 89th United States Congress; *Cat's Cradle*; cement; George M. Cohan; George Armstrong Custer; David's Island; Jack Dempsey; Mel Colm-Cille Gerard Gibson; William Ginsberg; George Henry Hall; Hiram Halle; Helen Hayes; Harmon Trophy; Ben Hecht; DeWolf Hopper; Mikhail Horowitz; John Houseman; Joseph Howland; Dard Hunter; Interstate 87; Henry

Lincoln Johnson; Thaddeus Kosciusko Bridge; William Van Duzer Lawrence; Lawrence Park Historic District; Charles MacArthur; Dudley Field Malone; Glenmere Mansion; Maverick Concert Hall; Gary McGivern; Natalie Merchant; Mary and John Mowbray-Clarke; *Music from Big Pink* (1968); 1978 in Organized Crime; "Nature fakers controversy"; Pace University; Norman Vincent Peale; *Personal Memoirs of Ulysses S. Grant*; Henry Varnum Pool; Anton Refregier; Riverkeeper; William H. Robertson; William Rockefeller; Archibald Rogers Estate; Julius and Ethel Rosenberg; Edward Sanders; Ted Shane; Peter Schickele; Semi Automatic Ground Environment (SAGE); Alexander Smith Carpet Mills Historic District; John H. Starin; Norman Thomas; Three Arrows Cooperative Society; Toonerville Folks; Artie Traum; Happy Traum; William A. Welch; Nathaniel Parker Willis.

Woodstock Artists Association & Museum (woodstockart.org).

Woodstock Music & Art Fair, informally called the Woodstock Festival (woodstock69.com).

Woodstock School of Art. Angela Gaffney-Smith, "Louise Kamp (1867-1959): August 14 – October 2, 2010." (*www.woodstockschoolofart.org*)

WTZA (Kingston). "On The River" [Seeger, Pete]. September 17, 1994.

Yosemite Online (yosemite.ca.us). "Edward Henry Harriman" by John Muir (1912). (p)

Index